IFIP Advances in Information and Communication Technology 324

T0180956

IFIP – The International Federation for Information Processing

IFIP was founded in 1960 under the auspices of UNESCO, following the First World Computer Congress held in Paris the previous year. An umbrella organization for societies working in information processing, IFIP's aim is two-fold: to support information processing within its member countries and to encourage technology transfer to developing nations. As its mission statement clearly states,

> IFIP's mission is to be the leading, truly international, apolitical organization which encourages and assists in the development, exploitation and application of information technology for the benefit of all people.

IFIP is a non-profitmaking organization, run almost solely by 2500 volunteers. It operates through a number of technical committees, which organize events and publications. IFIP's events range from an international congress to local seminars, but the most important are:

- The IFIP World Computer Congress, held every second year;
- Open conferences;
- Working conferences.

The flagship event is the IFIP World Computer Congress, at which both invited and contributed papers are presented. Contributed papers are rigorously refereed and the rejection rate is high.

As with the Congress, participation in the open conferences is open to all and papers may be invited or submitted. Again, submitted papers are stringently refereed.

The working conferences are structured differently. They are usually run by a working group and attendance is small and by invitation only. Their purpose is to create an atmosphere conducive to innovation and development. Refereeing is less rigorous and papers are subjected to extensive group discussion.

Publications arising from IFIP events vary. The papers presented at the IFIP World Computer Congress and at open conferences are published as conference proceedings, while the results of the working conferences are often published as collections of selected and edited papers.

Any national society whose primary activity is in information may apply to become a full member of IFIP, although full membership is restricted to one society per country. Full members are entitled to vote at the annual General Assembly, National societies preferring a less committed involvement may apply for associate or corresponding membership. Associate members enjoy the same benefits as full members, but without voting rights. Corresponding members are not represented in IFIP bodies. Affiliated membership is open to non-national societies, and individual and honorary membership schemes are also offered.

Nicholas Reynolds
Márta Turcsányi-Szabó (Eds.)

Key Competencies in the Knowledge Society

IFIP TC 3 International Conference, KCKS 2010
Held as Part of WCC 2010
Brisbane, Australia, September 20-23, 2010
Proceedings

 Springer

Volume Editors

Nicholas Reynolds
The University of Melbourne, Melbourne Graduate School of Education
Melbourne, VIC 3010, Australia
E-mail: nreyn@unimelb.edu.au

Márta Turcsányi-Szabó
Eötvös Loránd University
Faculty of Informatics, Informatics Methodology Group
Pázmány Péter Sétány 1/C, 1117 Budapest, Hungary
E-mail: turcsanyine@ludens.elte.hu

CR Subject Classification (1998): I.2.6, H.5, H.4, H.3, J.1, K.4

ISSN   1868-4238
ISBN-10   3-642-42294-2 Springer Berlin Heidelberg New York
ISBN-13   978-3-642-42294-2 Springer Berlin Heidelberg New York

springer.com

© International Federation for Information Processing 2010
Softcover re-print of the Hardcover 1st edition 2010

Typesetting: Camera-ready by author, data conversion by Scientific Publishing Services, Chennai, India
Printed on acid-free paper   06/3180

IFIP World Computer Congress 2010 (WCC 2010)

Message from the Chairs

Every two years, the International Federation for Information Processing (IFIP) hosts a major event which showcases the scientific endeavors of its over one hundred technical committees and working groups. On the occasion of IFIP's 50th anniversary, 2010 saw the 21st IFIP World Computer Congress (WCC 2010) take place in Australia for the third time, at the Brisbane Convention and Exhibition Centre, Brisbane, Queensland, September 20–23, 2010.

The congress was hosted by the Australian Computer Society, ACS. It was run as a federation of co-located conferences offered by the different IFIP technical committees, working groups and special interest groups, under the coordination of the International Program Committee.

The event was larger than ever before, consisting of 17 parallel conferences, focusing on topics ranging from artificial intelligence to entertainment computing, human choice and computers, security, networks of the future and theoretical computer science. The conference History of Computing was a valuable contribution to IFIPs 50th anniversary, as it specifically addressed IT developments during those years. The conference e-Health was organized jointly with the International Medical Informatics Association (IMIA), which evolved from IFIP Technical Committee TC-4 "Medical Informatics".

Some of these were established conferences that run at regular intervals, e.g., annually, and some represented new, groundbreaking areas of computing. Each conference had a call for papers, an International Program Committee of experts and a thorough peer reviewing process of full papers. The congress received 642 papers for the 17 conferences, and selected 319 from those, representing an acceptance rate of 49.69% (averaged over all conferences). To support interoperation between events, conferences were grouped into 8 areas: Deliver IT, Govern IT, Learn IT, Play IT, Sustain IT, Treat IT, Trust IT, and Value IT.

This volume is one of 13 volumes associated with the 17 scientific conferences. Each volume covers a specific topic and separately or together they form a valuable record of the state of computing research in the world in 2010. Each volume was prepared for publication in the Springer IFIP Advances in Information and Communication Technology series by the conference's volume editors. The overall Publications Chair for all volumes published for this congress is Mike Hinchey.

For full details of the World Computer Congress, please refer to the webpage at http://www.ifip.org.

June 2010
Augusto Casaca, Portugal, Chair, International Program Committee
Phillip Nyssen, Australia, Co-chair, International Program Committee
Nick Tate, Australia, Chair, Organizing Committee
Mike Hinchey, Ireland, Publications Chair
Klaus Brunnstein, Germany, General Congress Chair

Preface

It is fitting that there was a World Computer Congress in the 50th anniversary year of IFIP. Within the Learn IT Stream of WCC2010, the conference, Key Competencies in the Knowledge Society (KCKS), brought together some 43 papers from around the world covering many areas of ICT and its role in education.

Of the papers presented here, three were selected as key theme papers for the KCKS conference. These papers' by Adams and Tatnall, Tarragó and Wilson, Diethelm and Dörge, are included in these proceedings. We congratulate these authors for the quality of their work that led to selection.

The range of issues covered within this volume is too broad to set out here but covers, amongst other things, e-examination, Twitter, teacher education, school-based learning, methodological frameworks and human development theories.

It has been an exciting and rewarding task to put these papers together. They represent a coming together of great minds and cutting-edge research. We thank our contributors and our reviewers for producing such an impressive body of work.

Nicholas Reynolds
Márta Turcsányi-Szabó

Organization

Program Chairs

M. Turcsanyi-Szabo	Eotvos Lorand University, Hungary
N.J. Reynolds	University of Melbourne, Australia

Program Committee

R.M. Bottino	Istituto Tecnologie Didattiche Consiglio Nazionale Ricerche, Italy
A. Breiter	University of Bremen, Germany
B. Cornu	CNED, France
V. Dagiene	Institute of Mathematics and Informatics, Lithuania
B. Davey	RMIT University, Australia
M. Kendall	East Midlands Broadband Community, UK
U. Kortenkamp	University of Education Karlsruhe, Germany
D. Kumar	Bryn Mawr College, USA
K.-W. Lai	University of Otago, New Zealand
J. Magenheim	University of Paderborn, Germany
J. Moonen	Moonen & Collis Learning Technology Consultants
W. Mueller	University of Education Weingarten, Germany
C. Quinn	Quinnovation, USA
C. Redman	University of Melbourne, Australia
S. Rosvik	Giske Municipality, Norway
E. Stacey	Deakin University, Australia
L. Stergioulas	Brunel University, UK
A. Tatnall	Victoria University, Australia
B. Thompson	University of Sunderland, UK
S. Wheeler	University of Plymouth, UK
J. Zhang	University at Albany, USA

... ...

Table of Contents

Use of ICT to Assist Students with Learning Difficulties: An Actor-Network Analysis

Tas Adam and Arthur Tatnall

School of Management and Information Systems, Victoria University, Australia
{Tas.Adam,Arthur.Tatnall}@vu.edu.au

Abstract. This paper reports on an investigation of the use of Information and Communications Technologies (ICT) to aid in the teaching of students with learning disabilities. The term 'learning difficulties' is used in reference to a heterogeneous group of students who are seen to have significant difficulties in the acquisition of literacy and numeracy skills. Other terms sometimes used in this context are 'learning disabilities' and 'special needs'. The study involved participant observation of the use of ICT in two outer suburban Melbourne Special Schools, and an investigation of the role and impact of Education Department policies on these school environments. Research at the two Special Schools revealed that use of ICT can have a very beneficial impact on these students by improving their self esteem and facilitating their acquisition of useful life skills. The study was framed by the use of actor-network theory.

Keywords: Information and Communications Technologies, Actor-Network Theory, Learning Difficulties, Special Schools, Students with Special Needs.

1 Students with Learning Difficulties

A significant number of students with learning disabilities, or special needs, require assistance and support in their learning. The introduction of Information and Communications Technologies (ICT) and use of the Internet have played a major part in shaping the knowledge and skills of these students. Assistive technology has introduced awareness for both educators and students and for the past decade there has been a growing effort in the design and development of ICT-based platforms to enhance the learning outcomes of these students [1, 2].

The study described in this paper involved participant observation in two outer suburban special schools in Melbourne, and in addition examined the role and impact of Education Department policies on these school environments [3]. The study also identified different categories of students with special needs, ranging from physical disabilities to mainstream students who have the need to maintain some continuity with their studies while temporarily placed in a hospital.

One of the problems in working in this area is terminology, with the terms: Learning Difficulties, Children at Risk, Special Needs and Learning Disabilities all being used in different countries and different contexts to describe these children. In this paper the term Learning Difficulties (LD) will be used to cover all of these other

N. Reynolds and M. Turcsányi-Szabó (Eds.): KCKS 2010, IFIP AICT 324, pp. 1–11, 2010.

terms [4]. The definition for the term Learning Difficulties that is used in Australia is similar to that used in the USA:

> *A generic term that refers to a heterogeneous group of students who have significant difficulties in the acquisition of literacy and numeracy and who are not covered in the Commonwealth's definition of a student/child with a disability... Learning disability is believed to be a difficulty that is intrinsic to the individual and not a direct result of other conditions or influences [5].*

Given the complexity of the definition of learning difficulties, one way to represent the differences is with the following Venn diagram where the term Learning Difficulties is used to refer to a large group of children who need extra assistance with schooling and Learning Disabilities refers to students who constitute a small sub-group that exhibit severe and unexplained problems.

Fig. 1. Learning Difficulties and Learning Disabilities

Although policies have existed for some time in many countries to integrate students with learning difficulties into the mainstream classroom, this has not always provided the best learning environment for these students [6]; hence the need for some Special Schools. Bulgren [7] and Agran [8], support the view that some students with LD required an alternative approach to their learning and numerous 'integration' or 'remedial' programs have proved inefficient towards the total learning of this group of students. The literature also shows that in some selected fields, for example in mathematics and social studies, specialist instruction has been applied to this group of individuals with little success.

2   A Case Studies of Two Melbourne Special Schools

2.1   Special School-A

School-A is a purpose built 'Specialist School' providing a range of educational programs for students with special learning needs including global development delay, autism spectrum disorder, physical, social and emotional disabilities. It is located in

Melbourne's north-west and is one of over 80 Government funded Specialist School Facilities in Victoria.

In addition to delivering the key learning areas as part of the curriculum the school provides a broad range of programs that are designed to further enhance the independence of its students. Some of the programs include Augmentative Communication, Work Education, Outdoor Education, Bike and Road Safety Education, Music Therapy, Swimming and Hydrotherapy Programs, Riding for the Disabled, Home crafts, Recreation and Leisure and Health and Human Relations Programs. The school has around 90 students, 8 full-time and 3 part-time teaching staff, 15 part-time school support officers and 2 part-time administration staff. The students are quite diverse in their special needs, both physical and intellectual. In the early 2000s the school had limited ICT resources for their learning with several Acorn machines, but very few PCs. The majority of the software was based on the DOS operating system platform where graphics and sound quality were limited. The library had a PC that was used to allow the students' access to the Internet, and PCs were used predominantly to reinforce language and numeracy skills. By 2010 the Acorn computers had been replaced by PCs.

The list of computer skills as was evidenced by a student survey indicated some key programs were used to assist the students in their learning. The teaching staff were quite happy with these programs as they felt these were adequate for their students' needs. An examination of the school's technology policy and curriculum showed that the use of ICT was an integral part of the classroom teaching and learning. The school heavily relied on ICT policies and support from the Department of Education, both for network access and software supplies. The administration systems were also provided and supported by the Department.

A research project over several years investigated the infrastructure to set up links between different classes at the local level. Given the limited support and availability for video-conferencing by the Education Department's resources, the attempt was welcomed by relevant school staff. The students showed a tremendous level of enthusiasm and immediate engagement when they began to communicate via the webcams. The main issue was, as expected, the limited bandwidth from the Local Area Network. Another significant issue was the security constraints and filters that are imposed on the Education Department's VicOne Network. This matter was further investigated in the following year of the research, and it was discovered that the Education Department had found that video-conferencing was not very much in demand for Victorian schools, and hence its support was downgraded considerably.

2.2 Special School-B

The vision of this school community encompasses a commitment to achieving excellence in education for students with additional learning needs through a curriculum which integrates learning technologies with best practice in teaching and learning. The values embraced by the school community are: Respect, Personal Best, Happiness, Cooperation, and Honesty. These values are imbedded in the Student Code of Conduct and the Staff, Principal and School Council Codes of Practice.

Located on two campuses in the northern suburbs of Melbourne, School-B is a day specialist school which caters for students with mild to moderate intellectual disability between the ages of 5 and 18 years. Students come from a wide geographical area and diverse socio-economic backgrounds. The school's junior annexe (on another site) provides three classrooms for students aged between 5 and 9 years of age. The school itself is situated in attractive, well maintained grounds with excellent facilities which include: a Technology Centre, fully equipped gymnasium, Healthy Living Centre, Art and Craft room, well-resourced library, modern playground equipment, four school excursion buses, computer networking across the school, multi-purpose room and shaded outdoor playing areas.

The school, with 71 teaching and ancillary staff, has an enrolment of approximately 250 students. Enrolment is dependent on eligibility criteria as determined by the Department of Education and Training. A significant number of teachers at the school have post-graduate qualifications in special education. School-B supports integration into and from mainstream schools. Support services available to parent/carers and students include social workers, guidance officers, speech therapists and visiting teacher services.

The implementation of the Early Years Literacy and Numeracy Program at Junior and Middle school levels has increased opportunities for improved student skills in literacy and numeracy. The Secondary School has a focus on the enhancement of student engagement through Middle Years strategies based on improved Literacy and Numeracy, and the introduction of a 'Thinking Curriculum'. The Transition Centre caters for students sixteen to eighteen years of age with the focus on the development of dual pathways to cater for the diverse needs of the students. The school has a high level of commitment to a curriculum which integrates learning technologies with best practice in teaching and learning in order to enhance educational outcomes for its students. The Technology Centre has facilitated important opportunities for the school's students, its staff and for staff from neighbouring schools [9].

In 2006 School-B introduced a number of social and networked learning activities and practices, with software such as Lumil, WordPressMU, ccHost, Urdit, Gregarius and Scuttle. This paper reports on some of the activities undertaken, technologies used and the progress made during this period. For the purposes of this research the individual items of social software used at School-B have been appraised separately, yet in practice these tools and technologies are complimentary and have been used concurrently. In fact, much of the power of social software is its interoperability. By using these tools the school expects its students to create and publish content and respond to the content creation of others. Created content can be aggregated to show progress and richness and depth of learning. Students can respond to the work of others, provide feedback and learn through their interactions with others online. Not only are the students learning, but they are also learning how to be independent learners [1].

Collaborative Web 2.0 technologies and practices strongly support effective knowledge management practices. By using open web-based standards, such as RSS and XML and open API web services, complimentary software can share data in rich and unique ways. In future years, interoperability may well be the key criteria for introducing new technologies and systems as teachers and administrators become more familiar with working in networked environments. In introducing the social software it was attempted to integrate with existing practices, using web-based tools and technologies to construct richer tasks for the students. For example, using web-based photo sharing, students and teachers tagged photos which were then used in student digital portfolios. By using this approach not only did they introduce the required skills and practices but the school also reduced the workload for teachers who had previously organised the resources for use in the previous student digital portfolios [1, 9].

By looking at their existing curriculum they identified opportunities to use web collaboration. For example, they found that they could use the social media sharing website ccHost within their loop-based music creation topic. Having traditionally used the audio samples that came with the software, they discovered they could easily integrate online networked learning to increase learning outcomes. Now students can find audio samples based on tags, use these samples in their composition and then share their composition online, highlighting the samples that they used. Other students could then make derivative works by taking samples from the composition of others. The school has attempted to provide all of the social networking web services on their Intranet to ensure that the students' privacy and security can be carefully monitored.

3 Actors and Networks: Actor-Network Theory

Special Schools are complex socio-technical entities and research into their curriculum needs to take account of this complexity. A significant difficulty arises in framing research in a situation like this that involves both technological and human actors. When dealing with the related contributions of both human and non-human actors, actor-network theory [10-12] provides a useful framework. Actor-network theory (ANT) reacts against the idea that characteristics of humans and social organisations exist which distinguish actions from the inanimate behaviour of technological and natural objects, instead offering a socio-technical approach in which neither social nor technical positions are privileged.

The actors involved in the adoption of this technology to assist students with special needs include: students, parents, teachers, school principals, school ICT specialist teachers, the School Council, the Web, computers, Education Department policies, learning technology policy, the school environment, classroom environments, learning approaches and paradigms, delivery methods of instruction, engagement methods, thinking processes, technology infrastructure-bandwidth, curriculum, Internet resources, digital libraries and other schools.

In an ANT framework, actors are seen to contest and negotiate with each other in an attempt to influence the final outcome in a direction to their own liking. The Education Department, for example, might want ensure that all schools offer a similar level of service to students and to ensure their accountability. The parents of a student with LD, on the other hand, would want the best for their own child regardless of what was going on in other schools. The technology (both hardware and software) itself acts in the way it was designed, both intentionally and unintentionally, to act.

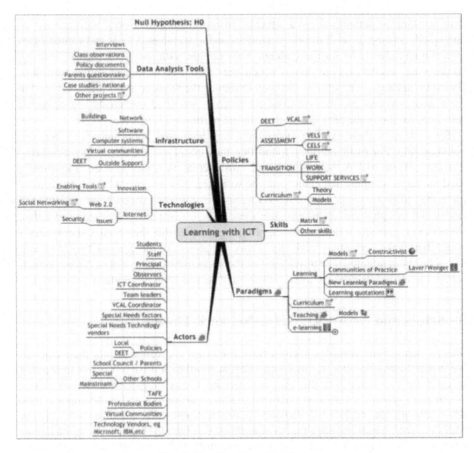

Fig. 2. Identification of the Actors

A major challenge to schools of this type is to get all these actors to form a common problematisation [10] of their task – to all see the problem in the same way. If this can be achieved then all the actors can work together to achieve a common goal, and ANT offers some ideas on how this might be achieved. ANT considers associations and interactions between human and non-human actors but its proponents make no claim that this approach can do any more than shed a little light on how a given approach is taken or technology is adopted. Despite this, we believe that if a researcher understands how the factors involved in the adoption of a new technology interact then it is possible to affect the outcome by assisting favourable interactions and doing one's best to reduce unfavourable interactions.

The concept of an actor underlies ANT, where an actor is the term used to represent any physical entity that has an effect on the phenomenon under investigation [10, 13]. An actor is considered as any entity able to associate texts, humans, non-humans and money [14]: "Accordingly, it is any entity which more or less successfully defines and builds a world filled by other entities with histories, identities, and interrelationships of their own" [14]. An actor is an abstraction which enables the analysis of situations where heterogeneous entities are encountered [13]. The purely social or technological approaches are essentialist and deterministic in nature, whereas ANT is designed to be anti-essentialist and non-deterministic. The concept of an actor allows sociologists to write about the situatedness of innovation and technology without the need to use demarcations separating the social from the natural; or sociological conventions from technological ones. The abstraction frees the analysis from the boundaries of disciplines, thereby allowing the observer to resist the need to reduce complex phenomena to a few well-defined political, social or technological categories [15].

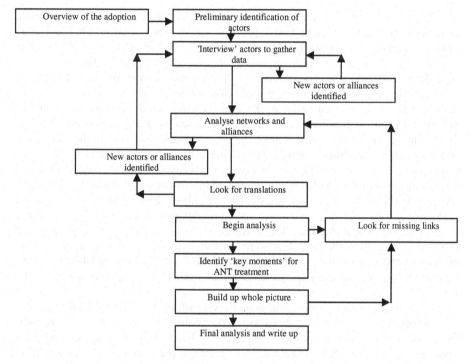

Fig. 3. The ANT Research Process [16]

The main method advice offered by Latour in conducting an ANT research project is to "Follow the Actors" [11], but this is just a beginning. When using ANT the research process that is followed is far from linear and not just simply a matter of collecting data, analysing the data then writing it up. The process could better be seen as an iterative one, something more like that shown in Fig 3 above [16, 17]. After the actors have been identified and 'interviewed' and networks of interactions between actors have been examined, the process continues to look for new actors and for how the technology may have been translated in the process of adoption. This figure attempts to illustrate something of the complexity and iterative nature of this process.

A good deal has been written on how ANT can be employed for socio-technical analysis. For example, Bigum [18] provides one interesting application of ANT, while

Gilding [19] and Tatnall [20] also provide studies applying ANT to Education and Technology. Other examples include the studies of Hull [21], Law [22] and Walsham and Sahay [23]. More recently, the Queensland education department used ANT to investigate the impact of ICT in education [24, 25]. There are also recent examples of how ANT was used to analyse ICT infrastructure [26], financial institutions [27], call-centres [28] and on-line communities [29].

4   Data Collection and Analysis

For this research data was collected by attending and observing specific classes at these two schools on a regular basis. The first school was visited in 2003 and 2004 while the second was approached in 2005 and 2006. At School-B a specific project was set up by the school community, and the researcher was asked to take part in this through the assistance and co-operation of the Principal, as well as several key staff members. He became a team member and worked very closely with a class of senior students who were referred to as the Transition Group which showed varied ability and special needs or handicap. The project was called the 1-2-1 project and it was a significant step to providing the state of the art 'hands-on' resources to the group. For example, each student was provided with a Laptop to use and carry in class or to take home. The research was conducted in a very supportive manner. It should be noted that funding was also provided by the school of Information Systems at Victoria University and this allowed an analysis of the ICT infrastructure and provided several PDAs along with Dragon digital voice recording equipment. The school gave access to all available data at the time. The students were assessed in the main domains of knowledge and, in particular, data were provided to the research that showed an analysis of the key indicators for each class in ICT for teaching and learning. The 1-2-1 project was later extended to include many other groups in the middle of the school.

The original concept by now had gone beyond what anyone could have imagined with the introduction of Social Networking programs. The main observations high-lighted the strong self-esteem and engagement by the groups of students. Other data were collected by the ICT coordinator to determine the background of teachers in ICT. In fact at this time, the Victorian Government introduced the 'ICT Potential Project' with the aim to diagnose the various ICT skills of teachers in schools and how these were applied in the curriculum. The researcher became an actor himself in this process whilst endeavouring to discover the impact and existence of other actors and actor-networks or ensembles. Using participant observation the researcher be-came an observer and participant at school meetings and regular class sessions that involved technology and computer programs through the Web. In addition to observa-tions he interviewed these actors and collected relevant documents in order to identify further actors and their networks.

The research found that there are several actors whose work is particularly impor-tant to the achievement of a good outcome in the school. Firstly, the ICT system, social software and networked learning activities must be appropriate and also they must be induced to co-operate with the students and teachers. This co-operation can be facilitated by another important actor: the ICT specialist teacher who should have both a good idea of what is required educationally, and also of the capabilities of students and teachers to understand and use the software and hardware. It does not take much observation to see that the students are readily willing to work with ICT and enjoy using it: they do not need much convincing. Hopefully the other teachers can also see the benefits of using ICT, even if they do not use it themselves, but this is not always the case and this is where another important actor comes in. The School Principal is crucial to the success of this program as without the Principal's support, many things will not be possible. One area where the Principal can be of considerable use is in influencing, or perhaps coercing other teachers to support the program. Another is with the provision on funds for hardware and software purchases and the provision of time for the ICT coordinator to find out about new products and services. One thing to come out very clearly from our research is the importance of the school Principal and without an actively supportive Principal, there is little chance that the project of using ICT with these children will succeed.

5 Conclusion

Our research shows that there is no doubt that the use of ICT can have a beneficial impact on the education of children with learning difficulties. It can do this both by improving their self esteem by providing the means by which they can achieve something they consider worthwhile and also by facilitating the acquisition of useful life skills. To achieve this result however, the actors involved, both human and non-human must be induced to work together to produce the desired result. In this, the role of one particular actor is crucial: the School Principal. This actor has the power to provide appropriate funds when required, to coerce his colleagues into working towards a common goal, to encourage the school ICT specialist to make good use of the software and make it easy to use and to reassure the parents that the school is doing its job well. The use of actor-network theory as a research framework facilitates the holistic analysis of schools such as these and how they operate.

References

1. Adam, T., Tatnall, A.: Using ICT to Improve the Education of Students with Learning Disabilities. In: Kendall, M., Samways, B. (eds.) Learning to Live in the Knowledge Society, pp. 63–70. Springer, New York (2008)
2. Adam, T., Tatnall, A.: Building a Virtual Knowledge Community of Schools for Children with Special Needs. In: Abbott, C., Lustigova, Z. (eds.) Information Technologies for Education and Training (iTET), pp. 185–193, ETIC Prague. Charles University, Prague (2007)
3. Adam, T.: Determining an e-learning Model for Students with Learning Disabilities: An Analysis of Web-based Technologies and Curriculum. In: Management and Information Systems, Doctor of Philosophy. Victoria University, Melbourne (2010)
4. Commonwealth of Australia: Literacy for All: The Challenge for Australian Schools. Commonwealth Literacy Policies for Australian Schools. Australian Schooling Monograph Series No. 1/1998, vol. 2010. Commonwealth of Australia, Canberra (1998)
5. Rivalland, J.: Definitions & identification: Who are the children with learning difficulties? Australian Journal of Learning Difficulties 5, 12–16 (2000)

6. Shaw, S., Grimes, D., Bulman, J.: Educating Slow Learners: Are Charter Schools the Last, Best Hope for Their Educational Success? The Charter Schools Resource Journal 1 (2005)
7. Bulgren, J.: Effectiveness of a concept teaching routine in enhancing the performance of LD students in secondary-level mainstream classes. Learning Disability Quarterly 11 (1998)
8. Agran, M.: Teaching Self-Instructional Skills to Persons with Mental Retardation: A Descriptive and Experimental Analysis. Education and Training of the Mentally Retarded 21, 273–281 (1997)
9. Adam, T., Tatnall, A.: ICT and Inclusion: Students with Special Needs. In: Lloyd-Walker, B., Burgess, S., Manning, K., Tatnall, A. (eds.) The New 21st Century Workplace, pp. 75–85. Heidelberg Press, Melbourne (2008)
10. Callon, M.: Some Elements of a Sociology of Translation: Domestication of the Scallops and the Fishermen of St. Brieuc Bay. In: Law, J. (ed.) Power, Action & Belief. A New Sociology of Knowledge?, pp. 196–229. Routledge & Kegan Paul, London (1986)
11. Latour, B.: Aramis or the Love of Technology. Harvard University Press, Cambridge (1996)
12. Law, J., Callon, M.: The Life and Death of an Aircraft: A Network Analysis of Technical Change. In: Bijker, W., Law, J. (eds.) Shaping Technology/Building Society: Studies in Sociological Change, pp. 21–52. MIT Press, Cambridge (1992)
13. Law, J.: Notes on the Theory of the Actor-Network: Ordering, Strategy and Heterogeneity. Systems Practice 5, 379–393 (1992)
14. Callon, M.: Techno-Economic Networks and Irreversibility. In: Law, J. (ed.) A Sociology of Monsters. Essays on Power, Technology and Domination, pp. 132–164. Routledge, London (1991)
15. Callon, M.: The Sociology of an Actor-Network: The Case of the Electric Vehicle. In: Callon, M., Law, J., Rip, A. (eds.) Mapping the Dynamics of Science and Technology, pp. 19–34. Macmillan Press, London (1986)
16. Tatnall, A.: Innovation Translation in a University Curriculum. Heidelberg Press, Melbourne (2007)
17. Tatnall, A.: Researching the Adoption and Implementation of Innovative Enterprise Information Systems. In: Cruz-Cunha, M.M., Varajao, J.E.Q., do Amaral, L.A.M. (eds.) Conference on ENTERprise Information Systems (CENTRIS), pp. 245–254. Universidade de Tras-os-Montes e Alto Douro, Ofir (2009)
18. Bigum, C.: Solutions in Search of Educational Problems: Speaking for Computers in Schools. Educational Policy 12, 586–596 (1998)
19. Gilding, T.: Student Construction of a Knowledge-based System as an Actor Network, School of Education, p. 198. Deakin University, Geelong (1997)
20. Tatnall, A.: Innovation and Change in the Information Systems Curriculum of an Australian University: a Socio-Technical Perspective, Doctor of Philosophy. Central Queensland University, Rockhampton (2000)
21. Hull, R.: Actor network and conduct: The discipline and practices of knowledge management. Organization 6, 405–428 (1999)
22. Law, J., Hassard, J.: Actor Network Theory and After. Blackwell Publishers, Oxford (1999)
23. Walsham, G., Sahay, S.: GIS for District-level Administration in India: Problems and Opportunities. MIS Quarterly 23, 39–65 (1999)
24. Simpson, N.: Studying Innovation in Education: the Case of the ConnectEd Project. In: Jeffery, P.L. (ed.) Australian Association for Research in Education (AARE 2000), Sydney (2000)

25. Australian Government Department of Education, E.a.W.R.: Project to Improve the Learning Outcomes of Students with Disabilities in the Early, Middle and Post Compulsory Years of Schooling. Part 1: Research Objectives, Methodology, Analyses, Outcomes and Findings, and Implications for Classroom Practice Canberra (2007)
26. Cordella, A.: Information Infrastructure: An Actor-Network Perspective. International Journal of Actor-Network Theory and Technological Innovation 2, 27 (2010)
27. Iyamu, T., Roode, D.: The Use of Structuration Theory and Actor Network Theory for Analysis Case Study of a Financial Institution in South Africa. International Journal of Actor-Network Theory and Technological Innovation 2, 1–26 (2010)
28. Naidoo, T.R.: A Socio-Technical Account of an Internet-Based Self-Service Technology Implementation: Why Call-Centres Sometimes 'Prevail' in a Multi-Channel Context? International Journal of Actor-Network Theory and Technological Innovation 2, 15–34 (2010)
29. Zammar, N.: Social Network Services: the Science of Building and Maintaining Online Communities, a perspective from Actor-Network Theory. International Journal of Actor-Network Theory and Technological Innovation 2, 49 (2010)

Use of Graph2Go in M-Learning: A View from the Pedagogical Model

Silvia Batista[1], Patricia Behar[2], and Liliana Passerino[2]

[1] Instituto Federal Fluminense Campus Campos-Centro, Rio de Janeiro, Brazil
[2] Postgraduate Program in Computer Science in Education - Universidade Federal do Rio Grande do Sul, Brazil
{silviac@iff.edu.br, patricia.behar@ufrgs.br,
liliana@cinted.ufrgs.br}

Abstract. Characteristics such as interactivity, mobility, reaching a higher number of people, learning in real contexts, among others, are considered advantages of using mobile devices in education. M-learning (mobile learning) can favor learning, not only in distance learning, but also in face to face and blended learning. This paper particularly focuses on mathematical learning, considering it can benefit from m-learning potential in several educational modalities. However, this requires structured actions and, in this sense, development of pedagogical models is important. Such models serve as base for the knowledge building process through organized actions, with defined objectives and established strategies to reach them. Within this context, this paper presents a pedagogical model that was built and applied in a pilot study for mathematical learning using Graph2Go in college students.

Keywords: M-learning, Mathematics, Pedagogical Models, Graph2Go.

1 Introduction

Popularization of mobile devices and wireless Internet access networks has contributed to changes in social practices and to how information is produced and accessed. In this society, which can be understood as the Mobile Communication Society, time and space are the aspects more directly expressing such social change [1].

Within this context, wireless mobile technologies have also raised interest in educational terms. M-learning (mobile learning) is a field that comprehends wireless technologies and mobile computing to enable learning to occur at any time and place, maximizing the student's freedom [2]. M-learning is not only a matter of learning or mobility, but a totally different concept, which is part of a new conception of mobility of a connected society [3].

Several studies have been published on m-learning, such as those related to learning environments for mobile devices [4, 5, 6] and those aiming at the development of didactical materials [7, 8, 9].

In particular, studies have tried to analyze how m-learning can be useful to the teaching and learning process of Mathematics [10, 11, 12]. In general, the studies above indicate several advantages of using mobile devices in mathematical learning,

N. Reynolds and M. Turcsányi-Szabó (Eds.): KCKS 2010, IFIP AICT 324, pp. 12–22, 2010.

such as: i) dynamic visualization and investigation of mathematical facts; ii) different forms of approaching concepts (for example, through videos, working on visual approaches); iii) autonomy in the study of mathematical themes; iv) learning in real situations. Applications for mobile devices have been developed, specifically for Mathematics, such as those designed by the Math4Mobile project.[1] Among these applications is Graph2Go, which allows establishing connections between graphic and algebraic representation for a given set of functions through dynamic changes.

Development of such applications is essential, but it is also necessary to organize forms of applying them in varied educational modalities (face to face, blended and distance learning). In this sense, development and analysis of pedagogical models for this purpose are important. Such models allow organizing pedagogical practices, making them more objective. Based on a pedagogical model, actions can be structured with defined objectives and established strategies to reach them.

Thus, this paper presents a pedagogical model built and applied in a face to face pilot study, using Graph2Go in an m-learning experiment with college students. Section 2 defines what is understood here as pedagogical model, stressing its importance. Section 3 discusses the field of m-learning application in several educational modalities, particularly focusing on mathematical learning. Section 4 describes the pilot study and the pedagogical model applied in its development. Section 5 presents analysis of the pilot study using data obtained from observation and a questionnaire. Finally, section 6 brings some considerations on the present paper.

2   Pedagogical Models

A model is a shared mental representation of a set of relations defining a phenomenon, aiming at a better understanding of it [13]. The concept of model is the foundation for scientific activity, enabling comparison, simulation and understanding of phenomena. In education, such concept has been wrongly considered a synonym for learning theory or teaching methodology. Although a pedagogical model can be based on one or more learning theories, they are generally "reinterpretations" of such theories, based on individual conceptions by teachers [13]. A pedagogical model is "a system of theoretical premises that represent, explain and guide the way the curriculum is approached and that is consolidated in the pedagogical practices and in the interactions professor-student-object of knowledge" [13], p. 4. According to Dabbagh [14], pedagogical models are cognitive models or theoretical constructions derived from models of knowledge acquisition or conception about cognition and knowledge, which in turn are the base for learning theories.

Figure 1 shows the structure of a pedagogical model, based by one (or possibly more than one) learning theory [15]. According to Behar [15], p. 25, a model is composed by a pedagogical architecture (PA) and strategies for its application. PA is the main structure of a model, in which organizational aspects, study content or object, methodological and technological aspects are included.

---

[1]   Math4Mobile is a project of the Institute for Alternatives in Education that operates within the Faculty of Education at the University of Haifa, Israel (http://www.math4mobile.com/).

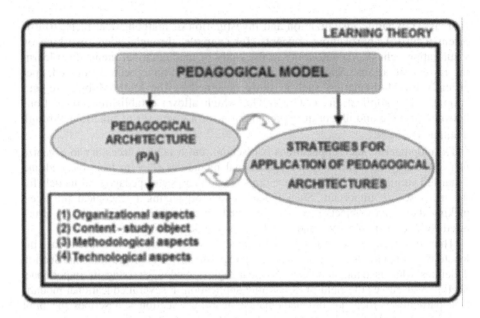

Fig. 1. Structure of a pedagogical model. Source: Behar [15] - p. 25 - adapted with permission from the author.

Putting a PA into practice requires strategies. They are dependant on the real application context and are influenced by several variables that permeate the educational process. Strategies for PA application are the dynamics of a pedagogical model [15]. They are didactical actions focused on articulation and adaptation of a PA into a given context.

Therefore, an application strategy is how the teacher will put PA into practice, already adapted to its reality according to the adopted learning theory [15].

Although the focus discussed by Behar [15] is distance learning, and the model elements are explained from the model itself, it is possible to widen the focus, analyzing them in general terms. In the present study, PA elements were adapted to meet all educational modalities:

- Organizational aspects: comprehend the basis of a pedagogical planning/proposal and include the purposes of the teaching and learning process, organization of time and space and expectations relative to the participant's interaction;
- Aspects regarding study content or object: include didactical materials to be used (texts, booklets, didactical resources, either digital or not);
- Methodological aspects: include activities, interaction/communication forms, evaluation procedures and organization of such elements into a didactical sequence that favors learning;
- Technological aspects: refer to the technological support structure to be used in activities (for example, selection of virtual learning environments, communication tools, inclusion of mobile devices, among others).

Such aspects should not be considered separately, since they form a whole in which a decision about an aspect influences the others. In addition, it is important to consider that the same PA can be applied differently, depending on the strategies used. Application strategies make PA individualized, as they depend on the actors' personal variables.

Development of pedagogical models allows confluence of aspects related to content and organizational, methodological and technological elements, in favor of pedagogical actions with more defined purposes. Pedagogical actions with a better foundation, clear objectives and organized means of achieving them can enable a more adequate use of resources, more coherence with the real context and reduction in unpredictable situations.

This study defends the idea that mobile devices can favor not only distance learning, but also face to face and blended learning. In this sense, pedagogical models including use of these devices can be important in the structuring of activities to be promoted in several modalities. Sections 3 and 4 deal with these respective issues.

3   M-Learning and Mathematics: Educational Modalities

Several studies associated m-learning with e-learning. Quinn [16] states that m-learning is e-learning[2] developed by mobile devices. In agreement with that, Georgiev et al. [17] claim that m-learning can be understood as a new stage in distance learning and e-learning. Wains and Mahmood [3] also state that m-learning aims at meeting some aspects that still impair e-learning, such as lack of infrastructure of Internet access in developing countries and the issue of student mobility.

However, some studies have associated m-learning with face to face and blended learning as well [11, 12, 18, 19]. According to Khaddage and Lattemann [18], it is possible to use mobile devices within the classroom context, favoring aspects such as accessibility, collaboration and flexibility. To Zeiller [19], blended learning can use both Web resources and mobile devices in the communication between students and teachers and in collaborative work.

Thus, association of m-learning with e-learning no longer reproduces the real context. Considering that research has indicated that m-learning potentiality can also collaborate in face to face and blended learning, this study proposes a wider mapping (Figure 2). In that figure, two-way arrows between m-learning and educational modalities indicate there is benefit in both senses. Studies involving m-learning collaborate to the development of this area, either by identification of new application forms, limitations and advantages, or by increase and enhancement of resources.

Within the context of Figure 2, educational modalities are defined as: i) *Face to Face Learning* - modality in which teacher and students are physically present at the same place, at a preestablished time, to perform pedagogical activities; ii) *Distance Learning* - modality "[...] in which didactical-pedagogical mediation in teaching and learning processes takes place with use of information and communication means and technologies, with students and teachers developing educational activities at varied places or times" [20], p.1; iii) *Blended Learning* - modality that aims at combining two educational modalities – face to face and blended learning – into one, supported by digital technologies.

---

[2] Form of distance learning based on computer and the Internet.

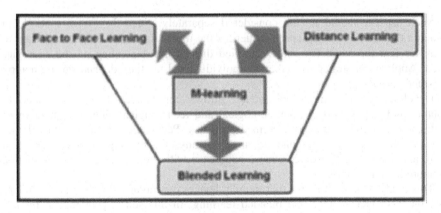

Fig. 2. M-learning: educational modalities

In particular, the teaching and learning process of Mathematics requires forms of making it more accessible to students. Mathematics taught at schools often plays an excluding role, labeling and classifying people as able or unable to participate in society's decision-making processes [21]. In this sense, taking into account the justifications for Figure 2, which point out that m-learning has a potential to contribute to learning in several educational modalities, this study proposes the mapping presented in Figure 3. It is an adaptation of that proposed in Figure 2 to the context of Mathematics.

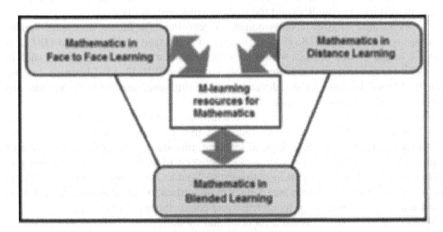

Fig. 3. M-learning in mathematical learning: educational modalities

It is important that further studies include all three modalities (Figure 3), aiming to analyze the importance of m-learning for the teaching and learning process of Mathematics. In this sense, stress should be given to the need of developing peda-gogical models on which to base the knowledge building process in Mathematics through m-learning. Such models, as discussed in section 2, aim at structuring peda-gogical practices, defining and outlining several aspects involved in the process.

4   Pilot Study Using Graph2Go: Building a Pedagogical Model

A pilot study using the Graph2Go[3] application was performed with the aim of developing and analyzing a pedagogical model involving use of mobile devices at a face to face experiment. This application works as a graphic calculator for a set of functions, allowing to establish connections between graphic and algebraic representation through dynamic changes.

The pilot study using Graph2Go was held in November 2009 and it lasted 4 hours. It was performed as part of a research project,[4] and the target audience was college students at Instituto Federal Fluminense Campus Campos-Centro (RJ, Brazil): eight students of Control and Industrial Automation Engineering (1st semester), and four undergraduate students in Mathematics (2nd semester).

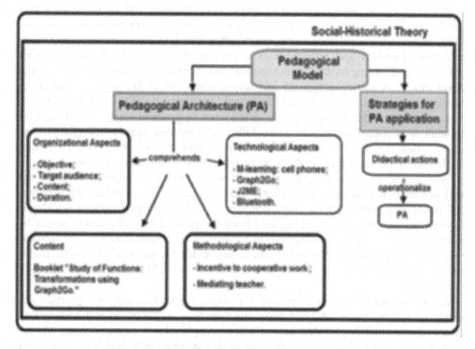

Fig. 4. Pedagogical model – pilot study using Graph2Go

The pedagogical model (Figure 4) aimed at setting the foundation for elements that would be included in the experiment, making it more structured and better defined. Answering questions in several aspects of the pedagogical model implies analyzing

---

[3] Free application (for non-commercial purposes), specific for cell phones, developed by Michal Yerushalmy and Arik Weizman - project Math4Mobile
(http://www.math4mobile.com/).

[4] Project "Information Technologies and Communication in the Teaching and Learning Process of Mathematics" (http://www.es.cefetcampos.br/softmat/projeto_TIC/portal.html).

and making decisions that would not often be considered in advance. Such procedures might reflect into safer actions and a lower number of unexpected situations.

As shown in Figure 4, the social-historical theory was adopted as theoretical background, providing the basis for the entire model. In this theory, mediation includes use of instruments and signs within the social context, and the combination of use for such resources allows development of superior psychological processes [22]. In addition to instruments and signs, the role of a human mediator, encouraging reflections through assistance, is also essential for student autonomy and knowledge appropriation [23].

The pilot study, defined in organizational aspects, aimed at providing the study of graphic changes of functions using Graph2Go. The target audience, as mentioned earlier, was composed by college students. The booklet[5] of activities, mentioned in the content aspect, is divided into three sections: the first has general information on Graph2Go and instructions of use; the second brings activities to study changes in graphs of quadratic functions through changes in coefficients; and the third provides a similar study to that performed with quadratic functions, but involving the sine function.

To encourage cooperative work, teacher-mediated pair activities were proposed, providing questions and reflections (methodological aspects). Interaction between individuals, according to the social-historical theory, plays an essential role in human development. A particular type of interaction stands out in this paper – mediation. Mediation takes place in the Zone of Proximal Development (ZPD - distance between real and potential development levels, determined by problem solving supervised by an adult or in collaboration with more skilled partners) and includes use of tools and signs within the social context [22]. Digital technologies are mediating tools that might contribute to creation of ZPDs, in which context Graph2Go is inserted.

With regard to technological aspects, mobile devices (cell phones) were chosen with pedagogical purposes (m-learning). Transfer of the application into the students' cell phone was performed via Bluetooth using a laptop equipped with such technology. Direct transfer of the application, from the Internet to cell phones, would be more practical, but it was avoided due to connection and download costs (the application itself is free). When the participants were selected for the study, they were told it was necessary to have cell phones with Bluetooth and J2ME platform (required by Graph2Go).

As mentioned in section 2, putting a pedagogical architecture into practice demands certain strategies. A brief description on how the proposed architecture was effectively applied is provided here. First, the application was transferred. At that time, there were a few problems: one participant who thought he had J2ME in his cell phone did not actually have it, which prevented execution of the application. Furthermore, although all cell phones had Bluetooth, some transfers were only possible through memory card. Thus, two other participants whose cell phones had the necessary requirements, but no memory card, could not have the application due to transfer problems.

After the initial stage, nine out of 12 students had the application in their cell phones. However, since the work was performed in pairs, development of activities was not impaired by this problem. The first section of the booklet, which explained Graph2Go features, was then discussed with the students. They had no difficulty

---

[5] Available at: < http://www.es.cefetcampos.br/softmat/projeto_TIC/atividades.html>.

understanding the application resources, nor using the keys. Next, activities related to graphic changes were performed, after the importance of such theme to learn integral calculus had been highlighted. Having analyzed the graphic influence of changing coefficients in quadratic functions, students performed a similar analysis relative to the sine function. Both analyses were then commented and, based on the perception of association between them, some generalizations were discussed.

The following section brings an analysis of the experiment using data obtained from observation of the students' actions and from a questionnaire.

5   Pilot Study: Analysis of Results

In general, the students actively participated in proposed activities. Questions to the teacher – the process mediator – and exchanges with classmates showed their interest in what was being studied. There were no comments or actions that showed difficulties in using the application, and understanding of the issue was achieved.

To ensure a deeper qualitative analysis of the experiment, a seven-item questionnaire was organized, with six semi-open questions (including request of comments) and one open question. The questionnaire aimed at collecting data on the application's learning facility, advantages and disadvantages, importance for learning the theme and the role of classmate's and teacher's mediation. In general, data were collected on several aspects of the proposed pedagogical model.

None of the participants had used an application for cell phone in the study of an educational theme (not restricted to Mathematics). Even so, 75% of the participants reported being "easy" to learn the Graph2Go resources, and the remaining considered it as "very easy." Comments generally stressed the fact that the application is well organized, user-friendly, with intuitive, simple and objective resources. The percentage confirms what was mentioned about not having any evidence of difficulty by the participants when using the application.

They all considered that the booklet activities, developed with the aid of Graph2Go, collaborated to the understanding of the theme under study. The possibility of visualizing the variation of function graphic behavior by changing coefficients was the most stressed aspect by the participants. Such data reinforces the importance of using tools in the individual's development, as supported by the social-historical theory.

One of the questions was about the advantages and disadvantages of using Graph2Go. In general, advantages included visualization and movement, easy to understand and use, practicability, mobility, being free, graphs for the derivative and integral function (with possibility of changing the integration constant). Disadvantages were limitation of options of functions; impossibility to draw graphs of different functions on the same screen; language (the application is in English, with which not all students were familiar); size of graphs. It is important to analyze the potential and limitations of a didactical resource. As proposed by Cabero [24], thought should be given to adequacy of a given didactical resource to planned objectives, students' characteristics and adopted pedagogical proposal.

With regard to use of applications for cell phones for mathematical learning, 67% of the participants considered it "very important" and the remaining classified it as "important." It was stressed that, with cell phone popularization, such device is a resource that can be useful for learning. In addition, in terms of face to face learning, use of these applications would eliminate the need of going to computer laboratories. The rates are in agreement with studies on m-learning in the process of Mathematics teaching and learning [10, 11, 12].

Classmates' collaboration during activities using Graph2Go was considered as "very important" by 58% of the participants, while the others considered it as "important." In general, interaction between students was stressed as being significant to discuss proposed concepts and to better understand them. The participants' view is coherent with what is proposed by Vygotsky [22]. According to that author, shared activity is important for cognitive development, as it enables living in the external level what will be further internalized. Moysés [25] reinforces that by claiming that learning of Mathematics should always include such interpersonal action.

Teacher's role as a mediator during activities using Graph2Go was classified as "very important" by 75% of the participants; for 17%, it was "important," and for one participant (8%) it was "little important." The participants stressed that, although the application was easy to understand and use and activities were clear, the teacher's work of making students think about the concepts was essential. The justification of the student who classified it as "little important" is as follows:

> Little important because it is possible to understand the application without the teacher's help, although extremely important to help with the mathematical thought (Participant 4).

Therefore, even the participant who considered it as "little important" stressed the teacher's role as a mediator, as supported by the social-historical theory. Mediated learning goes through an active participation of a more experienced partner that selects, modifies and interprets context conditions present in the learning process of another subject that is less experienced [26].

It should be stressed that, although short, the experiment was significant. In this sense, it was possible to notice the importance of developing a pedagogical model to enable more efficient actions. The pilot study showed that: i) the difference between available devices and resources in cell phones is a setback for their use with educational purposes; ii) Internet-related costs are another factor making use of mobile devices difficult; iii) the participants' skill to deal with cell phone keys is quite favorable; iv) practicability of cell phone use (very similar to how a calculator is used, being available when needed) is a very interesting aspect in educational terms; v) it is important that pedagogical models take into account the role of teacher and classmate mediation in the learning process.

6 Final Considerations

In Mathematics, digital technologies create possibilities, allowing simulations, visualizations, experiments, hypothesis generation, among other actions. M-learning adds extra possibilities, such as practicability, mobility, reaching a higher number of people, learning in real contexts, among others. In this sense, use of mobile devices, specific applications or even general resources, such as text messages, photographs, videos, among others, can favor the process of Mathematics teaching and learning, making it more accessible and closer to the student's reality.

Studies indicate that m-learning has potentialities that might enrich the teaching and learning in several educational modalities, going beyond the initial focus on distance learning. In this sense, studies on m-learning and Mathematics should deal with distance, face to face, and blended learning. Such studies can favor not only mathematical learning, but also the very evolution of m-learning through developed resources, identification of forms of use and feedback.

Pedagogical models considering use of mobile devices in varied educational modalities can favor more structured practices of m-learning. Development of these models can allow a more consistent foundation and organization of pedagogical practices and a better use of resources, in this case, mobile devices. Analysis of the pedagogical model in the pilot study pointed to a profitable use by the students, taking into account their actions and comments and the data collected by the questionnaire. The model allowed identification of difficulties and stressed potentialities in the use of cell phones with educational purposes.

References

1. Castells, M., Fernandes-Ardevol, M., Qiu, J.L., Sey, A.: The Mobile Communication Society: a across-cultural analysis of available evidence on the social uses of wireless communication technology. In: International Workshop on Wireless Communication Policies and Prospects: a Global Perspective (2004),
   http://arnic.info/workshop04/MCS.pdf
2. Wains, S.I., Mahmood, W.: Integrating m-learning with e-learning. In: 9th Conference on Information Technology Education, pp. 31–38. ACM, New York (2008)
3. Traxler, J.: Current State of Mobile Learning. In: Ally, M. (ed.) Mobile Learning: transforming the Delivery of Education and Training. AU Press, Canada (2009)
4. Meisenberger, M.: MLE - Mobile Learning Engine. FH Joanneum - University of Applied Sciences, Graz, Austria, Diploma Thesis (2004)
5. Brown, R., Ryu, H., Parsons, D.: Mobile helper for university students: a design for a mobile learning environment. In: 18th Conference on Computer-Human Interaction-Design: Activities, Artefacts and Environments, pp. 297–300. ACM, New York (2006)
6. Tesoriero, R., Fardoun, H., Gallud, J., Lozano, M., Penichet, V.: Interactive learning panels. In: Jacko, J.A. (ed.) HCI 2009. LNCS, vol. 5613, pp. 236–245. Springer, Heidelberg (2009)
7. Costello, F.: The use of Flash Lite and Web authoring tools in mobile learning course design. In: Keegan, D. (org.) Mobile learning: a practical guide, pp. 79–91 (2007),
   http://www.ericsson.com/ericsson/corpinfo/programs/
   incorporating_mobile_learning_into_mainstream_education/
8. Costabile, M.F., De Angeli, A., Lanzilotti, R., Ardito, C., Buono, P., Pederson, T.: Explore! Possibilities and Challenges of Mobile Learning. In: 26th Conference on Human Factors in Computing Systems, pp. 145–154. ACM, New York (2008)
9. Sá, M., Carriço, L.: Supporting End-User Development of Personalized Mobile Learning Tools. In: Jacko, J.A. (ed.) HCI 2009. LNCS, vol. 5613, pp. 217–225. Springer, Heidelberg (2009)
10. Botzer, G., Yerushalmy, M.: Mobile application for mobile learning. In: International Conference on Cognition and Exploratory Learning in Digital Age (2007),
    http://www.iadis.net/dl/final_uploads/200714C043.pdf

11. Franklin, T., Peng, L.-W.: Mobile math: math educators and students engage in mobile learning. Journal of Computing in Higher Education 20(2), 69–80 (2008)
12. Nokia: Mobile learning for Mathematics (2009), http://www.nokia.com/corporate-responsibility/society/mobile-technology-for-development/mobile-learning-for-mathematics
13. Behar, P.A., Passerino, L.M., Bernardi, M.: Modelos Pedagógicos para Educação a Distância: pressupostos teóricos para a construção de objetos de aprendizagem (Pedagogical Models for Distance Learning: theoretical background for the construction of learning objects). Revista Novas Tecnologias na Educação 5, 1–12 (2007)
14. Dabbagh, N.: Pedagogical models for E-Learning: a theory-based design framework. International Journal of Technology in Teaching and Learning 1(1), 25–44 (2005)
15. Behar, P.A. (org.): Modelos Pedagógicos em Educação a Distância, Pedagogical Models for Distance Learning. ArtMed, Porto Alegre (2009)
16. Quinn, C.: mLearning: mobile, wireless, in-your-pocket learning (2000), http://www.linezine.com/2.1/features/cqmmwiyp.htm
17. Georgiev, T., Georgieva, E., Smrikarov, A.: M-learning - a new stage of e-learning. In: 5th International Conference Computer Systems and Technologies, pp. 1–5. ACM, New York (2004)
18. Khaddage, F., Lattemann, C.: Towards an ad-hoc mobile social learning network using mobile phones. In: 12th Interactive Computer Aided Learning, pp. 374–380. Fachhochschule Kärnten, Villach (2009)
19. Zeiller, M.: Podcasting-based mobile learning in blended learning courses. In: 12th Interactive Computer Aided Learning, pp. 518–527. Fachhochschule Kärnten, Villach (2009)
20. Brasil.: Decreto n° 5.622 (Decree n° 5.622) (2005), http://portal.mec.gov.br/seed/arquivos/pdf/dec_5622.pdf
21. Matos, J.F.L.: Matemática, educação e desenvolvimento social – questionando mitos que sustentam opções atuais em desenvolvimento curricular em Matemática, Mathematics, education and social development - challenging myths that sustain current options in curriculum development in Mathematics (2005), http://www.educ.fc.ul.pt/docentes/jfmatos/comunicacoes.html
22. Vygotsky, L.S.: Mind in Society: The Development of Higher Psychological Process. President and Fellows of Harvard College, USA (1978)
23. Passerino, L.M., Santarosa, L.M.C.: Autism and Digital Learning Environments: Processes of interaction and mediation. Computers & Education 51, 385–402 (2008)
24. Cabero, J.: Avaliar para melhorar: meios e materiais de ensino, Evaluation for improvement: methods and teaching materials. In: Sancho, J.M. (Org.) Para uma Tecnologia Educacional, pp. 257–284. ArtMed, Porto Alegre (1998)
25. Moysés, L.: Aplicações de Vygotsky à Educação Matemática, Application of Vygotsky to Mathematics Education, 8th edn., Papirus, Campinas-SP, Brasil (2007)
26. Gindis, B.: Remediation through Education: Sociocultural Theory and Children with Special Needs. In: Kozulin, A., Gindis, B., Ageyev, V.S., Miller, S.M. (eds.) Vygotsky's Educational Theory in Cultural Context, pp. 200–221. Cambridge University Press, New York (2003)

ICT in Teacher Education: Developing Key Competencies in Face-to-Face and Distance Learning

Ana A. Carvalho

University of Minho, Campus de Gualtar,
4710-057 Braga, Portugal
aac@ie.uminho.pt

Abstract. This paper reports the training of 56 Teachers in ICT and Education Course. This course included one week face-to-face and seven weeks in distance learning. Students developed several ICT competencies during theses weeks, reporting its use in their classes. A characterization of the subjects' digital literacy is presented, as well as their participation in chat sessions and in the forum, which were not mandatory but highly recommended. The majority of students did not participate in the synchronous and asynchronous communication facilities. However, those that participated in the chat sessions and forum debates completed all tasks and assignments. The students recognized the importance of learning about ICT and how it changed their teaching methods.

Keywords: ICT, Key Competencies, WebQuest, Treasure Hunt, Concept maps, Podcast.

1 Introduction

This paper presents the challenge of motivating teachers to use and reflect about ICT, particularly Web 2.0 tools in teaching and learning, during a face to face week and seven weeks of online learning. The key competencies emphasized within this course are particularly related to ICT but also to the three broad categories identified by the DeSeCo Project's conceptual framework for key competencies: use tools interactively, interact in heterogeneous groups, and act autonomously [1]. The UNESCO's project "ICT Competency Standards for Teachers" stressed that schools and classrooms "must have teachers who are equipped with technology resources and skills and who can effectively teach the necessary subject matter content while incorporating technology concepts and skills" (p. 1) [2].

The ICT and Education Course belongs to a training program -"Online Teaching and Learning & Professional Development of Teachers in the Republic of the Maldives" - supported by UNICEF Maldives and developed by the University of Minho, in Portugal, during the 2008 and 2009 academic years. It included four compulsory courses and three optional courses (Table 1). The compulsory courses lasted 80 hours, during eight weeks and the optional courses 36 hours during three weeks. All courses used the LMS (Learning Management System) Blackboard and were distance learning courses, but Teaching/ Teacher Education, Supervision and Monitoring, and ICT

N. Reynolds and M. Turcsányi-Szabó (Eds.): KCKS 2010, IFIP AICT 324, pp. 23–34, 2010.

and Education courses had a face to face week in Male, Maldives, in May and seven weeks online. The face to face week was a requirement of UNICEF Maldives. The full program lasted 408 hours.

Eighteen Portuguese lecturers participated in this training program along with fifty-six Maldivian' teachers, who needed to update their knowledge about teaching and ICT. The language of the program was English, a foreign language for both lecturers and students.

Table 1. Training Program Structure

Compulsory and Optional Course Units	Course Units	
Compulsory Course Units Duration: 80 hours each at 10hrs/week		-Teaching/ Teacher Education -Supervision and Monitoring -ICT and Education -Online and Distance Education
Optional Course Units Duration: 36 hours each at 12hrs/week	A	-School Administration -School Management
	B	-Change Management in Education -Educational Management and Leadership
	C	-Behaviour Management -Special Educational Needs

During the five face to face sessions in Male, students attended three two-hour lectures daily. The first went, from 8am to 10am, the second from 10.30am to 12.30pm, and the third from 2pm to 4pm.

At the University of Minho we suggested dividing the students into three groups thus giving them more personalized feedback and orientation during the activities. When in Male, we realized that this purpose was fundamental, not only to ICT as each student had access to a computer, but also to the other two courses as most students lack technical and scientific knowledge.

2 ICT and Education Course

The ICT and Education Course had four learning outcomes: assess website quality, use Web tools (blogs, podcasts, and Google pages), distinguish collaboration from cooperation and the implications for students' group work, and select and use Web-Quests and Treasure Hunts with students. The syllabus attempted to familiarize students with technical words, tools, and pedagogical uses of resources available online. Concepts such as the Internet, the Web, Web 2.0 tools, social networking, connectivism, synchronous and asynchronous communication, collaboration and cooperation, searching the Web, criteria for evaluating websites, quoting and plagiarism, editing online, concept maps, WebQuest, and Treasure Hunt were approached and their pedagogical benefits discussed.

The main focus of this course unit was to motivate students to use and integrate ICT appropriately in the classes they teach. Theoretical aspects were discussed in the forum but the main purpose of all discussions was a reflection about its use in teaching contexts. We intended that our students applied the tools (blogs, podcasts, concept maps, etc.) and activities (WebQuest, Treasure Hunt) with their own students reporting their difficulties, enjoyments and reflections regarding its use.

We also intended that students work in groups in their own school to experience collaborative and cooperative activities.

2.1 Course Structure

As mentioned previously, this course had a face to face week in May 2008, 2 hours per day with each group of students (Table 2). This option proved to be appropriate for students as each one had computer access; however it was somewhat tiring for the tutor. She had six hours per day every day during the week, from Sunday to Thursday.

The other 7 weeks online only took place in March and April of the following year. Every week possessed the same structure: a new topic was introduced with readings and activities, there were two chat sessions at 8pm for students (and at 4pm for the tutor). They also had one or two threads in the forum helping them to reflect about the readings and activities of the week.

Table 2. ICT and Education Course Structure

Course duration	Course structure
Face to face week [May 2008]	-Participants characterization -Introduction to ICT -Introduction to Blackboard facilities -Create a blog and post comments to their colleagues -Create a podcast (audio) -New literacies.

7 weeks online LMS: Blackboard [March-April 2009]	Each week:
	  -A new topic was introduced
	  -2 chat sessions (1 hour each)
	  -Forum (1 or 2 threads)

Not all of the Maldivian teachers had Internet access at home therefore; they had to go to school at night if they wished to participate in the chat sessions. The time of the chat sessions was based on students' preference.

3 Students' ICT Characterization

During the first face to face session, students filled out a questionnaire regarding digital literacy. It included information about their gender and age, followed by eight questions: (1) their knowledge about online tools or resources , (2) if they had a blog, podcast or website; (3) if they used some of the tools or resources listed in item 1; (4)

if their school had a website; (5) frequency of access to Internet resources with their students; (6) if the teachers publish their students' work online; and finally if they have a computer at home with Internet connection.

The questionnaire was filled in by 56 students, 32 male and 24 female. Most of the students (39) were aged between 31 to 40 years old, 12 between 20 and 30, and 5 were older than 41. They were very interested in participating in this training program and were selected by the Maldivian Education Department. They were from different atolls, but a small group of two to five students belonged to the same atoll to support each other and to work collaboratively.

All of them knew Google, 48% YouTube, 34% blog, 27% Movie Maker, 20% Wiki and Flickr, 16% hi5, 9% Podcast, 7% WebQuest, 5% Treasure Hunt, and one individual knew Second Life and Delicious (Table 3). These results showed that the students required an ICT update.

Table 3. ICT tools or resources known by students (n=56)

ICT tools or Resources	f	%
Google	56	100
Blog	19	34
Podcast	5	9
Wiki	11	20
YouTube	27	48
Flickr	11	20
Delicious	1	2
Hi5	9	16
Movie Maker	15	27
WebQuest	4	7
Treasure Hunt	3	5
Second Life	1	2

When inquired if they had blog, podcast or website, only a few answered positively (Table 4). Only 11% had a blog, 9% a website, and 5% a podcast.

Table 4. Students' presence online (n=56)

Web 2.0 tools and website	f	%
Blog	6	11
Podcast	3	5
Website	5	9

When asked if they used the tools or resources presented in table 3 with their students, only 30 participants answered affirmatively (Table 5). From those (30), almost all of them (29) use Google, 4 students WebQuests, 2 blogs, and one YouTube and Treasure Hunt. These results evidenced the need to update these teachers. This need to update teachers to ICT competencies is supported by UNESCO [2] and by authors such as Richardson [3] or Siemens [4].

Table 5. Tools and resources used in classes (n=30)

Tools and resources used in class	f	%
Google	29	97
WebQuest	4	13
Blog	2	7
Treasure Hunt	1	3
YouTube	1	3

With regard to a school website, 22 of the participants indicated that their school had one. A large group of teachers (46%) rarely used the Internet with their students, and 11 never did (Table 6). Only 7 used the Internet daily, 8 weekly, and 4 monthly. Later on they explained that some schools had a computer lab but most of them only contained one or two computers for staff use. The government was sensitive to this problem and was making an effort to update the Internet connection and buy computers for the schools. This situation occurred in other countries such as Malaysia reported by Kader [5] and Bhutan by Won [6].

Table 6. Using Internet resources with students (n=56)

Frequency of Internet use with students	f	%
Daily	7	13
Weekly	8	14
Monthly	4	7
Rarely	26	46
Never	11	20

Only 5 participants published their students' work online. Finally, we asked them if they had a computer at home with an Internet connection (Table 7) because this was a prerequisite for the courses online.

As we may verify in Table 7, 93% of the participants had a computer at home, but only 71% had an Internet connection. Some of them had to use school facilities during the course, particularly for the chat sessions at late evening.

Table 7. Computer and Internet connection at home (n=56)

Computer and Internet connection at home	f	%
Computer	52	93
Internet connection	40	71

4   The Face to Face Week

The students completed a questionnaire regarding Digital Literacy. They were introduced to the ICT and Education course and its learning outcomes. Particular emphasis had been placed on the weekly goals that intended to create a new framework about learning methods and Web 2.0 tools, such as blogs and podcast. Students had to distinguish Internet and World Wide Web, create their own blog and podcast, and reflect about the implications of new literacies for learning (Table 8). Simultaneously, it was very important that they felt comfortable and familiar with the LMS Blackboard thus, every day they had something to do to remember its functionalities. The technical preparation for distance learning as well as the comprehension of the role of a distance learner is very important. Mason [7] states:

> "Those who have poor study habits, lack self-discipline or motivation, have been educationally disadvantaged, or are driven almost solely by extrinsic reasons for wanting a degree, tend to find the student-centred pedagogy bewildering, too demanding, or too much hard work. (…) Students do need a gradual process of learning to be self-directed. They need training and practice in ICT skills such as research, analysis and management of web-based resources; they need a student-friendly online environment that encourages and rewards interaction. They also need supportive tutoring to help them adapt their study patterns from linear working through textbooks and lecture notes to interactive engagement with ideas, resources and other students" (p. 65-66).

Table 8. Contents of the first week

Session	First week contents
1	Internet and World Wide Web. Blackboard: an introduction.
2	Blog: features, and learning implications. Create a blog. Blackboard: Chat.
3	Podcast: characteristics, and implications in learning. Create a podcast. Blackboard: Discussion board (forum).
4	Record a text in Audacity and save it as mp3. Post it in Podomatic. Insert a picture.
5	New literacies and its effect in learning. Blackboard: upload a file to Discussion Board, Digital Dropbox, and Group Pages.

The students were very interested. For some, everything was new and a few were unable to distinguish an e-mail address from a URL. One of the problems that occurred when they created a blog was to remember its URL and password. They were able to upload a picture, embed a video, and incorporate a link into blog posts. I used Richardson´s [3] and Siemens' [8] ideas about the use of blogs in educational contexts. "Blogging is a genre that engages students and adults in a process of thinking in words, not simply an accounting of the day's events and feelings" (p. 20) [3]. It is important that blogs be used as places of critical thinking and analytical writing and reflection. They can be used as class portals, e-portfolios, collaborative space, etc. Richardson [3] also considered that there is no better way to understand the impact of the Read/Write Web than by becoming a part of it. This was one of the main purposes of the week.

The podcasts were introduced, mentioning several ways to use them in education. For example, to record local stories or historical events, to challenge students to do a group project, to invite students to report their group work, to summarize content, and so on. The podcasts created by the teacher or the students have a good impact on listeners, as reported by studies conducted by Carvalho et al. [9], [10], Salmon et al. [11] and Frydenberg [12]. Students like hearing their teachers' voice as stated by Durbridge [13], Richardson [3] and Carvalho et al. [14]. All students created their first podcast using Podomatic. In the following session, the software Audacity was introduced and students recorded their episode. Next, they uploaded it to Podomatic. In the class, it was referred again "that's what the Read/Write Web is all about: being able to share what you create with others" (p. 118) [3].

During the last face to face session, we approached the new literacies as a concluding session of the topics focused. We stressed that for more than a hundred years we have defined being literate as being able to read and to write, although those core abilities are central to learning, they are no longer sufficient to ensure understanding [3]. Writing is no longer limited to text, we can use words, audio, video, and photography. It is difficult to deny that more and more we have become a multimedia society. We can combine many forms of writing into a process of "rip, mix, and learn", taking a piece of content here and another there, combining it to produce powerful text and nontext messages and interpretations [15]. Readers of the Web content must learn to be active consumers instead of just passively accepting it as legitimate. The classroom of the Read/Write Web is one seamless transfer of information, of collaborative, individualized learning, of active participation by all class members. It is marked by the continuous process of creating and sharing content with wide audiences. Our students are learning that their voices matter, that people are reading and responding, and that their ideas count. Moreover, when writing, for example in the blog, "ideas are presented as the starting point for a dialogue, not the ending point" [8]. By inviting students to become active participants in their own learning, we teach them how to be active participants in their lives and future careers. Teachers will have to see themselves as connectors, of content and of people. To use Web 2.0 tools effectively, educators must learn to use them effectively. They need to become bloggers and podcasters, to use other social tools effectively with their students. Teachers need to think of themselves as coaches who model the skills that students need to be successful and motivate them to strive for excellence.

Students were invited to keep their blogs and podcasts updated, until the next distance learning sessions of this course.

5 Learning ICT Online

The second week of the course started in March 2009. Every Saturday an announcement regarding the weekly activities was posted on the LMS and was sent by email to students via Blackboard. It included the topic that would be learned, the readings, the chat sessions timetable, the deadline for answering the forum questions, and students were reminded to read the week's guidelines in Course Documents. If they preferred, they could listen to a podcast with the announcements of the week. As they were familiar with the tutor, listening to her voice could have a motivational effect on them, as mentioned previously [3], [13], [14], [16]. A slide presentation and the readings were also available in the Course Documents.

The second week was devoted to reviewing the concepts approached during the first week and to debate Prensky's paper about Digital Wisdom [17].

The third week focused on WebQuest which was also the topic of the first assignment. Students had to select a WebQuest and analyse it, based on a grid developed by the tutor. Then, they invited their students to solve it in class and they had to report their reactions – if they liked it, if they solved it autonomously, if they learned the topic addressed in the WebQuest, and finally what were the advantages of using the WebQuest in learning. As during the chat some students mentioned that they did not have Internet connection in the school or computers in class, they only responded to the last item.

In her assignment one student wrote:

"It was really a great experience. They [the students] were very much involved in the activity. Even the two groups had a competition. Each group wanted to complete the task before the other. I found that the students enjoyed the webquest very much and they wanted to do more tasks. Also, I found that they were solving problems eagerly. I believe that if we could use such activities and facilities in our classrooms more often, the pupils would be more motivated".

Another student said:

"Solving WebQuests has many advantages for students because it includes higher level thinking, questions to be answered or solved and problems which are related to real life. To solve a WebQuest, students have to work in pairs or group, which promotes their social skills. In my opinion solving a WebQuest has the following advantages: WQ encourages critical thinking and cooperative learning, active learning, students have to make sense of what they are reading, it motivates students, and it improves students' synthesis, analysis, and evaluation skills".

The fourth week was about Treasure Hunt and students had to compare its structure with that of WebQuest. They were invited to create a Treasure Hunt in their own blog. They could send the tutor their Treasure Hunt before editing it online. After publishing it on the Web they invited their students to solve it.

During the fifth week they had to evaluate website quality, based on Alexander and Tate's criteria [18],Web Site Evaluation [19], 23 Quality Criteria [20], the Ten C's for Evaluating Internet Resources [21].

The sixth week focused on meaningful learning and modelling with technology according to David Jonassen [22]. Some audio podcasts containing excerpts from the book were available on the Blackboard, particularly for students that did not have access to the book. A native speaker was invited to read the book excerpts.

In the following week, the topic was concept maps and students had to read the chapters related to it in Jonassen's book [22] or listen to the podcasts. Students had to install Cmap tools and create a concept map; afterwards they should use it with their students. A tutorial about Cmap Tools was available for them. The second assignment was a report about the use of concepts maps by teachers or by their students in the classroom.

During the last week, the connectivism purposed by George Siemens [23], [24] and Stephen Downes [25] was introduced. Two important concepts in the digital age were distinguished: quoting and plagiarism, showing how one cites references. Finally, the collaborative and cooperative learning and its implications in group work was stressed.

The students had a final exam in October in Male.

5.1 Students' Participation in the Chat Sessions and Forums

Students' participation in the two weekly sessions and in the forum threads was not mandatory but highly recommended. Only a small group of students participated in the forums. In all fourteen chat sessions the number of participants ranged from 4 to 15. We realized that the students that participated in the chat sessions could clarify their doubts. Most of the time, they asked for questions about the topic under discussion. Some were checking what they knew regarding the subject at hand while others were learning it as they did not read the proposed d reading material.

The seven forums included nine threads. The number of respondents ranged from 12 to 14. They had time to think about their answer, and for each reply the tutor wrote a constructive comment.

At the end of the course, after submitting their assignments, the students were invited to complete a course unit evaluation questionnaire, but only six did so. Half of them participated in the forum threads and chat sessions. Those that did not participate provided different reasons. One reported technical problems in accessing the Blackboard platform and he did not have Internet access at home. The student wrote: "During the ICT course I had a dial up connection at School, its speed is 21kbs. I travelled to nearest TRC [Teacher Resource Centre] but uploading and downloading materials is expensive and only during the daytime. Night travelling is not possible and the next day cannot report to school if I do so". Another student did not participate in the forums or in the chat sessions, because "I was too busy with my job due to certain unavoidable reasons. I wanted to participate in the forums and chat but I could not. But I read the chat recordings". The third one answered the forums threads but she could not participate in the chat sessions, she said: "I completed all the forum work but it was very difficult for me to participate in the chat sessions as I was in Australia at the time. The time for the chat session for us was 2 o' clock in the morning. Anyway, I participated in many chat sessions too".

A student commented the following strategy: "you [the tutor] had listed the list of participants for the chat sessions and forums. That was one of the best things you did to get the participants to pay attention to the course unit".

6 Final Remarks

Some particular situations arose during the course due to the students' lack of ICT key competencies and the failure to read the recommended texts. Sometimes in the chat sessions some students were writing in Dhivehi to help each other, particularly in the first sessions. Some of them did not read the papers before the chat and most of the time the tutor was explaining the subject rather than clarifying their doubts. Due to this fact, one student wrote: "the chat session was not much useful as many of the participants were out of the topic".

When Cmap Tools were introduced, they mentioned having some difficulties in installing it. So, during the chat session I was explaining what they should do. Then, the download time generated a sort of race. It became fun because some of them downloaded faster than others, and they were providing details about the download percentage.

During this course unit some students were in Australia taking another course and there was a 6 hour difference, so at 8pm (chat session) it was 2am in Australia. Some of those were complaining about the time of the chat sessions.

The University sent to Maldives twenty books per course. Some students did not get the Jonassen's book, but "we managed to get the copy of the units that u recommended for us to read from another school". The podcasts about the book were intended to help those that had difficulties in getting it. A student that listened to podcasts indicated that he listened to the podcasts about the book, "because I did not get the book, I love reading rather than listening". One student that read the book also listened to the podcasts. She commented "I preferred listening to the podcasts about the book". This student is the only one that indicated that in other distance learning courses she would like to hear the teacher's voice giving advice or guidelines, all other respondents preferred reading the guidelines. All others preferred to get written feedback instead of audio. In a study conducted in Portugal [10] the students liked receiving audio feedback. The different reaction of the Maldivian students may be justified by the fact that the tutor and the students were not native speakers therefore, reading a text would probably be easier to understand.

On a five points scale ranging from poor to excellent, students considered very good or excellent: the relevance of the course unit contents, the organization of the course in modules (one per week), the guidelines for the week, the adequacy of the assignments compared to the aims of the course unit, and the support from the teacher. They mentioned that the course unit contents were useful for their job.

The students were asked to give a free comment about the ICT in Education course. Their comments were positive and showed the impact of this training in their professional life: "The course unit was very interesting and we learned a lot which can be used in our educational system". Another student wrote: "I have learnt how to use WebQuests and Blogs for the teaching purposes and in the capacity of a teachers' educator as well. ICT is something without which we teachers cannot just teach these days". One student recognized not only the importance of the course but also the need to update the equipment and the Internet access in schools: "ICT course is a very useful one. I learned a lot from this course. I introduced some of the components to my colleagues and they also found them very useful. For me, the main difficulty is that most of our students do not have Internet access. We are unable to use (in the class) what we have learned from this course but gradually parents are also becoming aware of the importance of the Internet and we can use this in the class very soon. It is also important to note that our classrooms are not ICT friendly classrooms. However, we are using the Teacher Resource Centre to teach some lessons using the smart board. Anyway, I found that this course is very useful to me". This initiative of training teachers first and updating the system after is much better than the other way around. Finally, one last comment to synthesize everything: "The ICT course unit was the most useful unit for my personal and professional development during this course. As you can understand, during the face to face week, many of us were not able to explain much about podcasts, blogs, WebQuest, Treasure Hunt, concept maps, web tools etc. But after completing this unit, now we are the first batch of people who can explain to many of the Maldivian teachers and students these useful things for the teaching and learning process of our students and teachers".

We may conclude with John's and Wheeler's [26] words, now these "teachers hold the key to future developments" (p. 15) and with their commitment to ICT use, many of the opportunities to innovate and transform education and learning will be seized.

References

1. OECD: The Definition and Selection of Key Competencies. Executive Summary (2005), http://www.oecd.org/dataoecd/47/61/35070367.pdf
2. UNESCO: ICT Competency Standards for Teachers. UNESCO, Paris (2008)
3. Richardson, W.: Blogs, Wikis, Podcasts, and Other Powerful Web Tools for Classrooms. Corwin Press, Thousand Oaks (2006)
4. Siemens, G.: Knowing Knowledge (2006), http://www.knowingknowledge.com
5. Kader, B.: Malaysia's Experience in Training Teachers to Use ICT. In: ICT in Teacher Education: Case Studies from the Asia-Pacific Region, pp. 10–22. UNESCO, Bangkok (2008)
6. Won, P.: Bhutan "Support for Teacher Education" Project. In: ICT in Teacher Education: Case Studies from the Asia-Pacific Region, pp. 3–9. UNESCO, Bangkok (2008)
7. Mason, R.: The university: current challenges and opportunities. In: D'Antoni, S. (ed.) The Virtual University, pp. 49–69. UNESCO, Paris (2006)
8. Siemens, G.: The art of blogging. Elearnspace: Everything elearning (2002), http://www.connecivism.ca/about
9. Carvalho, A.A., Aguiar, C., Carvalho, C.J., Cabecinhas, R.: Influence of Podcasts Characteristics on Higher Students' Acceptance. In: Bonk, C.J., Lee, M.M., Reynolds, T.H. (eds.) Proceedings of E-Learn, pp. 3625–3633. AACE, Chesapeake (2008)
10. Carvalho, A.A., Aguiar, C., Maciel, R.: A Taxonomy of Podcasts and its Application to Higher Education. In: Damis, H., Creanor, L. (eds.) ALT-C – Conference Proceedings, pp. 132–140. ALT (2009)
11. Salmon, G., Nie, M., Edirisingha, P.: Informal Mobile Podcasting And Learning Adaptation (IMPALA). e-Learning Research Project Report 06/07, University of Leicester (2007)
12. Frydenberg, M.: Principles and Pedagogy: The Two P's of Podcasting in the Information Technology Classroom. ISECON – EDSIG, vol. 23, pp. 1–10 (2006)
13. Durbridge, N.: Audio cassettes. In: Bates, A.W. (ed.) The Role of Technology in Distance Education, pp. 99–107. Croom Helm, Kent (1984)
14. Carvalho, A.A., Aguiar, C., Santos, H., Oliveira, L., Marques, A., Maciel, R.: Podcasts in Higher Education: Students and Teachers Perspectives. In: Tatnall, A., Jones, A. (eds.) Education and Technology for a Better World, pp. 417–426. Springer, Berlin (2009)
15. Levine, A.: Rip. Mix. Learn...The digital generation, social technologies, and learning. A presentation for the Training Expo Partners Conference, September 23 (2004), http://graphite.mcli.dist.maricopa.edu/emerging/wiki?RipMixLearn
16. Carvalho, A.A., Lustigova, Z., Lustig, F.: Integrating new technologies into blended learning environments. In: Stacey, E., Gerbic, P. (eds.) Effective Blended Learning Practices: Evidence-Based in Perspectives in ICT-Facilitated Education, pp. 79–104. IGI Global, Hershey (2009)

17. Prensky, M.: H. Sapiens Digital: From Digital Immigrants and Digital Natives to Digital Wisdom. Innovate 5(3) (2009), http://www.innovateonline.info/index.php?view=article&id=705
18. Alexander, J.E., Tate, M.A.: Web Wisdom: How to evaluate and create information quality on the Web. Erlbaum, Mahwah (1999)
19. Schrock, K.: Web site evaluation & Internet lesson plan guide (2002), http://kathyschrock.net/abceval/teacherwebeval.pdf
20. Treadwell, M.: 23 Quality Criteria. Teacher@work: internet tools for teachers (2006), http://teachers.work.co.nz/23_criteria.htm
21. Richmond, B.: Ten C's for Evaluating Internet Resources. University of Wiscounsin – Eau Claire, McIntyre Library (2003), http://www.uwec.edu/Library/guides/tencs.html
22. Jonassen, D.: Modeling with technology: mindtools for conceptual change. Pearson Education, Upper Saddle River (2006)
23. Siemens, G.: Connectivism: A learning theory for the digital age. International Journal of Instructional Technology & Distance Learning 2 (2005), http://www.itdl.org/Journal/Jan_05/article01.htm
24. Siemens, G.: New structures and spaces of learning: The systematic Impact of Connectivism, and Networked Learning. In: Carvalho, A.A. (ed.) Actas do Encontro sobre Web 2.0, pp. 7–23, CIEd, Braga (2008)
25. Downes, S.: Seven habits of highly connected people. Elearn Magazine (2008), http://www.elearnmag.org/subpage.cfm?section=opinion&article=97-1
26. John, P.D., Wheeler, S.: Teachers and technology. In: The Digital Classroom: Harnessing Technology for the Future, pp. 15–24. Routldge, London (2008)

Recommendation of Learning Objects Applying Collaborative Filtering and Competencies

Sílvio César Cazella[1], Eliseo Berni Reategui[2], and Patrícia Behar[2]

[1] Universidade do Vale do Rio dos Sinos (UNISINOS)
Av. Unisinos, 950, CEP 93022-001, São Leopoldo, RS - Brasil
cazella@unisinos.br
[2] Universidade Federal do Rio Grande do Sul
Av. Paulo Gama 110, prédio 12105, Porto Alegre, RS, Brazil
eliseoreategui@gmail.com, pbehar@terra.com.br

Abstract. This paper presents a recommender system for learning objects which uses a collaborative filtering mechanism based on competencies. The model enables students to receive recommendations of learning objects automatically, according to students' interests but also according to competencies that have to be developed. The prototype implemented was able to recommend relevant contents to students, aiming at helping them in the development of competencies. The paper also presents a couple of experiments showing that the recommender system has a good level of accuracy for the suggestions made.

Keywords: Recommender Systems, Collaborative Filtering, Competencies.

1 Introduction

One of the biggest challenges educators face nowadays is the organization of content and activities to develop certain competencies. This challenge is even bigger when one tries to identify and recommend different material to different students, based on individual needs, interests and skills.

This paper presents a recommender system for learning objects which can suggest learning materials according to students' interests as well as to skills that have to be developed. Learning objects are understood here as digital learning material constructed in a modular way so that they can be used together or separately [1]. In this sense, a scientific paper, a web page, a simulator, a question and answer software, all may be considered learning objects.

The recommendation of learning objects focusing on competencies requires a change in traditional educational paradigms where pedagogical models follow rigid curricula and favor transmissive methodologies. The focus on competencies requires that social characteristics, interests, needs and limitations of each individual also be considered. The concept of competence can be understood as "practical intelligence for situations that rely on knowledge and mobilizes, transforms them according to the complexity of the situations" [2]. In this sense, knowledge and skills (know-how) are part of the concept of competence [3]. Although the recommendation of personalized

N. Reynolds and M. Turcsányi-Szabó (Eds.): KCKS 2010, IFIP AICT 324, pp. 35–43, 2010.

learning objects is a desirable feature for any area of knowledge, our focal point has been the curricula of undergraduate programs in Information Technology (Computer Science, Computer Engineering and Information Systems). These programs have courses distributed throughout eight or nine semesters according to a set of prerequisites. The documents that describe these courses usually list a series of competencies which students should develop. For example, the databases course may require the student to develop competencies in "multidimensional modeling". The artificial intelligence course may require the development of competencies in "multiagent systems design", and so on.

The research presented here is based on this organization and notion of competencies. Our project aims to facilitate the access to learning objetcs that seem to be more appropriate at certain times, according to students' features as well as to competencies that need to be developed and distributed accross the planningof a course.

Among the computational techniques to assist in the search for relevant information, Recommender Systems [4] are able to automatically identify contents that are appropriate for each individual based on their characteristics or "tastes." This paper describes a model for recommender systems that is able to suggest learning objects relevant to undergraduate students, focusing on competencies to be developed. This paper is structured as follows: Section 2 extends the discussion on the concept of competence, emphasizing its implications in the development of the recommender system. Section 3 presents the technique of Collaborative Filtering, while section 4 describes in detail the proposed model, as well as its prototype and a set of experiments carried out to validate the model. Section 5 presents conclusions and proposals for future work.

2   The Concept of Competence

It is possible to find in the literature several definitions for the concept of competency. The Cambridge English dictionary defines it as: "an important skill that is needed to do a job". This definition, however, does not explicit relationships between important concepts such as: skills, issues, knowledge. Other authors enhance the definition: competence can be defined as the set of knowledge, skills and attitudes necessary for a person to develop their roles and responsibilities [5]. Perrenoud [6] defines competence as the ability to mobilize a set of cognitive resources (knowledge, skills, information, etc) to address the appropriateness and effectiveness of a variety of situations. In this way the skills are linked to cultural, professional and social conditions.

In all definitions, we can easily see the relationship between the concept of competence and skills (know-how), knowledge and attitudes. Therefore, the question arises as to when and how we can make a recommendation of a learning object which may enable students to build knowledge related to specific issues, to develop particular skills related to given contents, to develop a critical awareness about the importance of competence to to understand how to use it.

Thus, our goal in this research has been to use a recommender system to filter relevant information to students, and to select learning objects that are most appropriate in accordance with the competencies to be developed. The next section introduces the concept of recommender systems.

3   Recommender Systems

Several content retrieval applications try to assist users in identifying items of interest. However, it is common that these applications return irrelevant contents as a result [4]. Trying to minimize this problem, recommender systems have emerged, focusing on the search for relevant information according to users' features, as well as to certain requirements of the items sought. Different techniques may be used in recommender systems to find the most appropriate contents for users. In Sarwar et al. [7], for example, different algorithms are compared according to accuracy and performance. Here, our focus is the technique of Collaborative Filtering (CF) [8], a technique that is based on information collected about the entire community of users and has already proved suitable for several applications [9].

3.1   Collaborative Filtering

Collaborative Filtering is based on one of the most popular techniques for recommendation and is used in many systems on the Internet [10]. The technique is based on the analysis of preferences in a group of people who have common interests and have a "taste" for similar items. According to this approach, contents that may be recommended are filtered based on the evaluation of users about the items. For each user, a set of "neighbors" with similar behavior is sought [4]. The following subsection presents computational details about how to compute the coefficient of similarity between two users, one of the first steps in the collaborative filtering process. Then, the method to select subsets of users with a high similarity degree is described. In this last step, we present how to compute predictions in order to indicate how appropriate an item is for a particular user.

3.1.1   Computation of the Similarity and Prediction Coefficients

To compute the similarity between students, the model proposed in this paper applies the Pearson's coefficient, which is an approach widely used in Recommender Systems based on Collaborative Filtering [8]. This coefficient measures the degree of correlation between two variables, resulting in values between -1 and +1, where the value -1 represents complete lack of correlation between variables, and the value +1 represents a strong correlation between them.

Once you get the correlation between the opinions of students on certain learning objects, it is possible to compute the prediction of how much students would appreciate receiving a specific recommendation (prediction refers to the evaluation the student would give the object if he/she had access to it). This is done independently of the coefficient used for computing the similarity degree, since the predictions are computed according to a weighted average of the ratings given by students identified as closest neighbors (individuals who obtained a similarity coefficient less than a predetermined threshold). Through equation 1 one may determine how suitable object i would be for student a (p_{ai}), where r_a is the average of grades given by student a; n is the number of students; r_{bi} is the grade each student b gave to object i, r_b is the average of grades given by student b; and $corr_{ab}$ is the correlation of the target student a with a particular student b.

$$p_{ai} = \overline{r_a} + \frac{\sum_{b=1}^{n}(r_{bi} - \overline{r_b}) * corr_{ab})}{\sum_{b=1}^{n}|corr_{ab}|} \qquad (1)$$

3.1.2 The Recommendation Process Applying Competencies

After the prediction value of an object has been computed, indicating how a particular student would rate that item, the rules of competencies have to be applied. These are designed to filter out learning objects according to competencies that need to be developed. Through this procedure, the system is able to identify learning objects with a high predictive factor that are likely contribuite to the development of competencies noted as important at certain times.

After applying the rules of competencies, the system checks the database for recommendations whenever a student logs in.

4 Proposed Model

The recommender model proposed here has been designed as a service to be made available in an application server. The model proposes the following sequence of steps for its operation:

1) Teachers plan their classes based on the competencies detailed in the course description. In their plans, learning objects for the development of those competencies are suggested. For example, in the fifth meeting of a database course, students should develop the competence of "*developing projections through the use of relational algebra*". Learning objects that can be used in the development of this competence should also be listed by the teacher;
2) At the first time the system is run, the similarity degree (Pearson's coefficient) between all users registered in the database has to be computed. Then, the system calculates the prediction value for all registered contents in the database. Afterwards, only new users, new contents or new objects that were rated are processed;
3) After the computation of the similarity and prediction coefficients (subsection 3.1.1), the system employs the rules of competencies to filter out the content for a particular user. For example, the learning object for "*developing projections through the use of relational algebra*" may recommended to a student as a consequence of his/her similarities with other students that rated the object positively, and because the student is starting to study topics that demand the development of this competence.

4.1 Prototype and Experiments

A prototype of the model was developed in order to evaluate its efficiency in making appropriate predictions. Initially, some students were invited to participate in an experiment for the evaluation of learning objects (in this case scientific papers) that were recommended by the system. The scale used to evaluate learning objects was a

Likert scale of 5 points. A tool for the evaluation of learning objects was developed as a web page that could be accessed by any device with a browser and an Internet connection. Figure 1 shows the interfaces of the prototype running in a PDA (Personal Digital Assistant).

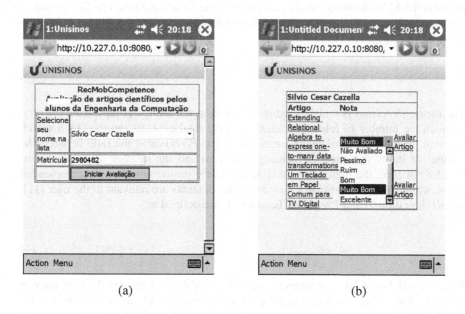

(a)   (b)

Fig. 1. (a) Prototype interface for mobile devices (b) Interface for the evaluation of papers

The prototype was developed in Java, and the persistence layer was developed using the JDBC API. The database was implemented using MySQL5.

4.1.1 Research Method
The prototype was evaluated in two experiments with convenience samples of 10 students that were at the end of the undergraduate course of Computer Engineering. A number of papers in the area of databases were selected by a teacher, and were classified according to the competencies that had to be developed. The experiments had the following goals:

1) To evaluate whether the prediction rate calculated by the prototype matched students' rates, using the evaluation metric *MAE* (Mean Absolute Error) [11];
2) To evaluate the accuracy of the recommendations made by the system through the metrics *Recall* (coverage) and *Precision*.

In the context of recommender systems, it is said that accuracy is the relationship between the rating given by the user to an item and the rating computed by the prediction system. To evaluate the prototype, the metrics described below have been applied.

4.1.2 Evaluation Metrics

The *MAE* metric was used to compute the mean absolute deviation between the predictions of the recommender system and the actual rate given by students. The difference obtained was taken as the prediction error [9]. With this metric in hand, it was possible to evaluate how accurate were the recommendations made. Equation (2) presents the MAE formula, where p_i represents the values predicted by the system, r_i are users' ratings to items recommended, and n represents the number of items considered.

$$|E| = \frac{\sum_{i=1}^{n} |p_i - r_i|}{n} \tag{2}$$

The metric *Precision* is widely used in information retrieval, and represents the ratio between the number of relevant contents and the total contents returned by a search function. In the context of recommender systems, *Precision* is the ratio between the number of items that the user considers relevant and the number of items recommended. In turn, the metric *Recall* is based solely on the number of recommended items, while *Precision* estimates how much the contents are relevant to the user [11]. *Recall* (Equation 3) and *Precision* (Equation 4) are defined as:

$$Recall = \frac{|RA|}{R} \tag{3}$$

$$Precision = \frac{|RA|}{A} \tag{4}$$

RA is the number of relevant items recommended by the system, *R* is the total number of items that should be recommended, *A* is the number of items actually recommended by the system, taking into account positive results and false positives.

4.2 Experiments and Results

The first experiment was set in order to select an initial base of learning objects for the databases course, considering the competencies that had to be developed. Thirty papers were selected and catalogued by the teacher, relating them to the competencies that had to be developed. Thus a database with a 1:N cardinality was built, where each competence had N papers cataloged to be used during the course. The competencies were distributed according to the class plan, and the learning objects were organized according to the competencies they represented. These papers were then reviewed and rated by students, which is a way to minimize a collaborative filtering limitation known as *cold start* [9].

Students were then requested to evaluate papers that had been allocated randomly. These papers were distributed to students, thereby generating an array of initial assessments "Paper x User", totalling 103 ratings. On the average, 10.3 items were assigned to be evaluated by each student, and these initial assessments were meant to identify the preferences/profile of each student. Based on the assessments provided, the system could compute the coefficient of similarity between the students (Pearson coefficient, ranging from -1 for a weak correlation, to 1 for a strong correlation). For example, the correlation value between students U4 and U6 was 1, showing a strong correlation according to Pearson's. For students U2 and U4, a correlation value of -1 was computed, meaning a total lack of similarity between them. As a result, it was found that 27.59% of the correlations computed between students were considered strong (these students had "tastes" that were similar to the objects evaluated), 20.69% were considered weak (these students had "tastes" different from the objects evaluated). For 51.72% of the correlations computed, nothing could be said.

In a second experiment, students evaluated a number of scientific papers recommended to them based on the rates provided in the first experiment. The system recommended only items with prediction rates higher than 3, for a Likert scale of 5 points. After computing the correlation values and the similarity prediction values, the rules of competencies were applied to select the most appropriate papers. As reported earlier, the papers were cataloged by competencies and were distributed in the class plan for each meeting. For instance, the lesson about "developing projections through the use of relational algebra" was assigned for the period starting in the eighth meeting and ending in the tenth meeting. Students during this period should receive recommendations of learning objects suitable for the development of this competence.

Table 2 shows the *MAE* and *Precision* values computed for the second experiment. The *MAE* metric showed an average difference between the predictions made by the prototype and the assessments made by students (1). The accuracy achieved by the prototype's predictions was 76%, which was considered satisfactory. Table 1 shows that the integration of collaborative filtering with the filter of competencies produced 16 recommendations, the same as the number of meetings planned for the classes. All of these recommendations were tailored to the development of competencies. It should be noted that the student U4 does not appear in Table 1 as he/she did not evaluate the papers recommended by the system.

Table 1. Results of the experiment concerning *Precision*

User	Recommended Article	Prediction	User evaluation	MAE	Precision
U1	19	4.54	5	0.46	90.80%
U1	22	3.35	4	0.65	83.75%
U1	23	3.62	4	0.38	90.50%
U2	20	4.04	5	0.96	80.80%
U3	20	3.29	4	0.71	82.25%
U3	22	3.92	4	0.08	98.00%
U3	23	4.37	5	0.63	87.40%
U5	19	4.53	3	1.53	66.23%
U5	22	3.67	3	0.67	81.74%
U6	19	5	2	3	40.00%
U7	19	3	1	2	33.33%
U7	22	3	2	1	66.67%
U8	20	5	4	1	80.00%
U9	19	5	3	2	60.00%
U10	20	3.5	3	0.5	85.71%
U10	23	4.5	4	0.5	88.89%
Media:				1.00	76.00%

Table 2 presents the experimental results concerning the relevance of the recommendations for the students.

Table 2. Results of the experiments concerning the relevance of the recommendations

User	Number of articles recommended by the CF algorithm	Number of articles recommended by CF and competency	Number of relevant art. recommended by CF and competency	Recall	Precision
U1	7	3	3	0.75	1.00
U2	7	1	1	0.25	1.00
U3	7	3	3	0.75	1.00
U5	4	2	2	0.50	1.00
U6	5	1	0	-	-
U7	3	2	0	-	-
U8	8	1	1	0.25	1.00
U9	7	1	1	0.25	1.00
U10	5	2	2	0.50	1.00
Total:	**53**	**16**	**13**		

For 7 out of the 10 students, we can say that the system succeeded to recommend appropriate items that were relevant for the users to develop competencies in the period of time established, as the *Precision* factor reached 1, and the *Recall* factor was below this value. Students U6 and U7 received, respectively, one and two recommendations each, recommendations based on collaborative filtering and competencies. However, the ratings that these users gave to the recommendations were not satisfactory for the computation of the prediction values, which had to be at least 3. Therefore, it was not possible to say anything about these students in particular. Again, additional assessment would be necessary to reach any conclusion regarding these students.

5 Conclusion

The main goal of this research has been to integrage collaborative filtering with a mechanism based on competencies in order to (a) help students find educational materials related to the development of specific competencies, (b) give some flexibility to the suggestion of materials to be consulted or used by students, to the extent that the interests of each are considered in the process of recommendation. By supporting students in their learning process, the system proposed here also gives support to the work of teachers, by organizing materials and learning situations, and by providing better links between knowledge and competencies.

In this sense, the proposed model tries to be aligned with these principles, recommending learning objects that best suit the interests of the student, but in accordance with competencies that need to be developed at any given time. Through empirical experimentation with a group of undergraduate students in Computer Engineering, it was found that the degree of precision achieved by the recommender system was satisfactory. The accuracy level of 76% showed that the system was able to recommend learning objects that satisfied the students for their studies, without neglecting the competencies required in the summary of the courses they were taking. As for the evaluation metrics *Precision* and *Recall*, it can be said that the prototype succeeded to get the students to have access to those materials that were relevant to the competencies to be developed in that moment, considering the set of learning resources available.

As future work, we intend to test the system with other types of learning objects to verify if its performance remains satisfactory. Using information from learning objects' metadata is another future goal. Such feature should allow us to select objects according to specific requirements also related to competence development (e.g. level of difficulty, level of interaction, etc.). We are also working on the forming of virtual communities with users with a similarity coefficient within a certain range.

References

1. Wiley, D.A.: Learning object design and sequencing theory. Doctoral thesis, Brigham Young University (2000)
2. Zarifian, P.: La politique de la compétence et l'appel aux connaissances à partir de la stratégie d'entreprise post-fordiste. Contribuition to the Coloque of Nantes (December 13, 2002), http://www.scoplepave.org/ledico/auteurs/zarifian%20 competence%201.htm (2002)
3. Fleury, A.C.C., Fleury, M.T.L.: Estratégias empresariais e formação de competências. Atlas, São Paulo (2000)
4. Adomavicius, G., Tuzhilin, A.: Toward the Next Generation of Recommender Systems: A Survey of the State-of-the-Art and Possible Extensions. IEEE Transactions on Knowledge and Data Engineering 17(6), 734–749 (2005)
5. Dutra, J.S.: Gestão por Competências. Editora Gente, São Paulo (2001)
6. Perrenoud, P.: Construir as competências desde a escola. Porto Alegre, Porto Alegre (1999)
7. Sarwar, B.G., Karypis, G., Konstan, J., Riedl, J.: Analysis of recommender algorithms for ecommerce. In: ACM E-Commerce Conference, Minneapolis, MN, pp. 158–167. ACM Press, New York (2000)
8. Shardanand, U., Maes, P.: Social information filtering: Algorithms for automating "word of mouth". In: Human Factors in Computing Systems, Denver, Colorado, USA (1995)
9. Herlocker, J., Konstan, J., Terveen, L., Riedl, J.: Evaluating Collaborative Filtering Recommender Systems. ACM Transactions on Information Systems 22(1), 5–53 (2004)
10. Schafer, J.B., Konstan, J., Riedl, J.: E-Commerce Recommendation Applications. Data Mining and Knowledge Discovery 5(5) (2001)
11. Cazella, S.C., Corrêa, I., Reategui, E.: Um modelo para recomendação de conteúdos baseado em filtragem Colaborativa para dispositivos móveis. Revista Novas Tecnologias na Educação 7, 12–22 (2008)

Teaching Practice from the Perspective of ICT Student Teachers at the Faculty of Education, Charles University in Prague

Miroslava Černochová

Charles University in Prague, Faculty of Education, Dpt. of Information Technology and Technical Education, M.Rettigové 4, 116 39 Praha 1, Czech Republic
miroslava.cernochova@pedf.cuni.cz

Abstract. The author worked for some years as a coordinator, methodology consultant and supervisor of teaching practice of ICT student teachers at the Faculty of Education in Prague. In her paper she summarizes experiences and data collected by questionnaires during years 2004-2008 by student teachers within their teaching practice on subjects related to Computer Science, Informatics and ICT Education in Czech Basic and Secondary Schools. The results came out of evaluative questionnaires and comments published in on-line support. A video-record will form a part of the paper presentation.

Keywords: Teaching practice, ICT teacher, information education, Informatics, computer technology, teacher education, lesson plan, Primary/Secondary school, Moodle.

1 Introduction

The paper is dedicated to a teaching practice of student teachers implemented into a study program of a Master's Degree study of Information and Technical Education at the Faculty of Education in Prague.

During five years of their study ICT student teachers have to successfully get through two periods of teaching practice in basic or secondary schools in subjects dedicated to ICT, Informatics or Computer Science.

After graduation they are fully qualified basic or secondary school teachers. They would work as primary or secondary school teachers of ICT, Informatics or Computer Science. They would work at schools also as a computer nets supervisor and they might be employed as ICT coordinators and consultants. They would provide advice how to apply ICT in school practice to teachers or head teachers.

1.1 Teaching Practice of ICT Student Teachers in Primary or Secondary Schools

Generally, the teaching practice of student teachers of the Faculty of Education in Prague is organized in the Year 4 and Year 5. Each of them takes four weeks.

N. Reynolds and M. Turcsányi-Szabó (Eds.): KCKS 2010, IFIP AICT 324, pp. 44–55, 2010.

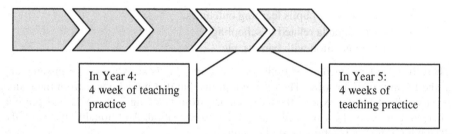

Fig. 1. A position of teaching practice in a study program of student teachers at the Faculty of Education

Within each of four weeks of an obligatory teaching practice the ICT student teachers assist or stand-by teachers in classrooms. During this period they design their own lesson plans and teach a minimum of 12 lessons in the classroom environment. (I.e. during the university study, students teach at least 24 lessons in Basic or Secondary schools). They analyze and evaluate their teaching experience together with their mentors who work in a close collaboration with a didactic consultant from the Faculty of Education.

For each lesson ICT student teachers design their lesson plans while using an identical template (see Appendix 1). They can ask a mentor for advice to tailor lesson plans or they can consult with a didactics consultant or their peers from the Faculty of Education on-line. Via the on-line support organized in Moodle, ICT student teachers deliver a set of lesson plans, a questionnaire, reports and news about their teaching practice. Together they can discuss some technological problems or pedagogical situations in forums then.

ICT teacher students can complete their four-week teaching practice in Basic or Secondary schools not only in Prague, but also whenever in the Czech Republic. Some students prefer conducting their teaching practice at schools they attended as a child. Their former teachers can become their mentors and colleagues and can monitor their first professional achievements. In such cases ICT student teachers find good relationships with their mentors as very important for their teaching practice.

In 2002 we introduced in Moodle on-line support in order to improve coordination and management of teaching practice for our ICT student teachers. The on-line support is very useful and helpful for all, student teachers and mentors, who should visit, monitor and supervise each student teacher in their schools.

From 2007 onwards we also started recording our student teachers by a digital camera in schools. After teaching practice in schools all video-recordings are analyzed in a seminar together with all ICT student teachers. Video-records allow them to see the real situation in the classroom of various schools, the equipment of their computer-labs, the interactions between ICT students and pupils etc.

Some ICT student teachers, during their university study, are employed in basic or secondary schools as non-qualified teachers of informatics or computer science subjects. In such cases their work is validated as teaching practice; it means they complete their teaching practice in the schools where they work. The ICT students who work as non-qualified teachers, unlike their student colleagues who are not employed in schools, have been prepared not only to teach children, but also in other fields and responsibilities of the teacher profession, primarily in:

- assessment of pupils learning outcomes,
- a legal agenda related to schooling,
- communication with parents, etc.

These ICT student teachers who already work in schools are very active in seminars at the Faculty of Education. They ask questions that distinguish them from their university school-mates, exploit their experience from teaching in schools and present interesting ideas on how to implement ICT into education. Additionally, they usually design high-quality teaching or study materials.

1.2 How ICT Student Teachers Develop Lesson Plans

During a teaching practice in schools ICT student teachers must develop lesson plans in identical templates (see Appendix 1).

The items of the template don't correspond with a structure of lesson plans that (teachers) students usually prepare. The template serves not only to describe a scenario of their teaching lesson, but also as a didactic exercise to develop some of student teachers' skills and to support their own thinking about teaching and learning from different perspectives: most of the student teachers have a problem formulating clever questions or suggesting an interesting problem to be solved. Most of student teachers don't consider a terminology and lexis of their subjects. And it is difficult for them to develop a concept structure of ICT subjects in minds of their pupils.

Most of the ICT student teachers (66%) design their teaching without any help of their mentors. The question of how to design a lesson is more complicated. The reason is that in most schools[1] ICT teachers do not use any textbook. Most of teachers (about 79%) develop their own study materials for pupils. For making lesson plans ICT students mainly use the Internet (90% of students – see Fig.2).

In the lesson planning process the ICT student teachers pay great attention to these aspects:

- Time table of teachers and pupils activities and a structure of lesson
- Educational content of lesson
- Proposal of activities and assignments for pupils.

The ICT students found out that designing timetables for lessons and motivating pupils to take active participation (see Fig. 3) are the biggest problems. Sometimes activities they prepare for pupils are either too easy or not stimulating tasks without any respect to personal priorities, interests or preferences of their students. Another problem that ICT student teachers met with was how to motivate children for ICT activities.

Among Czech schools there are a lot of differences in approaches to teaching ICT subjects. Most of them concentrate on development of fundamental ICT skills of pupils. They mainly focus on training in MS Office software. In some schools children produce animations or multimedia applications using digital cameras and special SW. Rarely the Czech Basic or Secondary schools implement basis of programming into compulsory ICT subjects (see Fig. 4). Some Czech schools organize for children

---

[1] In 2004 - 2007 only 13% ICT teachers in Primary or Secondary schools used text-books in their teaching with children.

facultative courses in programming. ICT student teachers found out that in basic schools some teachers[2] are dedicated to programming in Karel and in secondary schools mainly in HTML or Pascal. Most of ICT student teachers would prefer to teach programming than to train fundamental ICT skills with editors or spreadsheets.

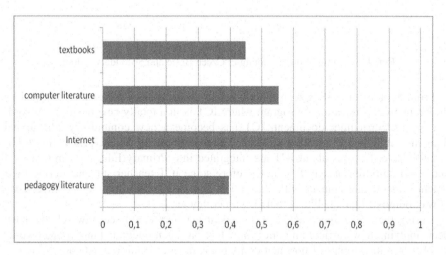

Fig. 2. Types of resources used by ICT student teachers for lesson plan development

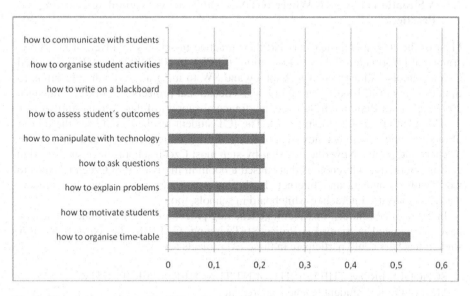

Fig. 3. The main problems the ICT student teachers have met during their teaching practice (% student teachers)

---

[2] Imagine and Baltik have become a favorite SW for pupils' development of programming thinking and algorithm skills in Czech primary schools.

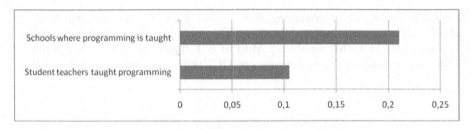

Fig. 4. Teaching of programming in Czech Basic and Secondary schools

From September 2007 Czech schools apply a new curriculum concept defined by the Framework Educational Program where ICT is in a totally new position. According to this curriculum document, ICT has become a new compulsory educational domain with a similar position as Math, Languages, Art or Science Education traditionally have. Lessons about ICT are integrated into Primary Education in Grades 4 and 5 (for children of age 9- 11). Therefore some ICT teacher students during their practice also taught courses with children of age 11-12. There they could experience how children of that age like activities with computers.

During their teaching practice ICT student teachers could see how schools have been applying new curriculum policy, how ICT has been integrated into project works at schools, which topics of Informatics are being taught to children in Grade 4, etc.

1.3 A Situation in Schools Where ICT Student Teachers Complete Teaching Practice

Most of the ICT student teachers did their practice in schools involved in the "Governmental Information Policy in Education" (GIPE). In 2002-2006 the GIPE equipped Czech schools with computer technology and SW to integrate ICT into education, to train teachers in ICT skills and to organize educational projects within ICT. But since 2007 the Czech Republic hasn't had any financial support of that sort and further ICT development at schools doesn't exist. The ICT student teachers could see the impact of this fact and experience how schools differ in ICT equipment, SW and services for teachers and pupils. Nevertheless, step-by-step most Czech schools have succeeded in getting interactive whiteboards that caused a boom in motivation of Czech teachers to work with computers and Internet. In the last two years most of the ICT student teachers could use interactive whiteboard in schools, too.

In 2006 some schools, that facilitate teaching practice to our ICT student teachers, have participated in many EU Projects (eTwinning, CALIBRATE, etc.). Some ICT student teachers could participate in these EU projects activities.

SCHOOLS FROM THE ICT STUDENT TEACHERS' PERSPECTIVE
Most of the ICT student teachers appreciate:
a) **high-tech equipment at schools** (data-projector, interactive whiteboard, wireless mouse and keyboards, etc.). Computer labs in schools are arranged as multifunctional classrooms with very modern furniture, where they could be given not only Informatics lessons, but also lessons of Music or Art Education.

In the last two years student teachers had the opportunity to use an interactive whiteboard in most schools.

"I really liked the computer labs; there are three computer labs in the school that are all arranged in non-traditional ways. A teacher in my school designed the furniture. I also liked the Internet cafe and library in the school."

b) **a good "climate" and partnership among teachers** in schools. Their open approaches to pupils enable them to find more flexible solutions for unknown problems. Teachers teach pupils skills of teamwork. From ICT student teachers' point of view there are a lot of kind people at schools.

c) **teachers' effort to upgrade HW and SW** in schools. ICT student teachers were surprised by how much effort teachers had to make if they wanted to upgrade the equipment and SW applications at the schools. During their university study, the ICT student teachers had no reason to think about it because the Faculty offered them the use of professional SW and high-quality HW. However, at schools today ICT teachers can't only teach their subjects, but they also have to take care of SW and HW. In many schools there is also a lot of "old fashion" technology; schools don't have enough money to buy new technology. For maintaining old computers it is necessary to have enough spares and components. ICT student teachers were surprised by *"teachers' active attempts to get needed components and spare parts for old fashioned computers and hardware"*. ICT student teachers could get experience with some SW that has not been applied at the Faculty of Education – for example Master Eye that helps teachers to organize work on PC with children and that could be very useful in computer labs without data-projects.

d) **a chance to use an interactive whiteboard.** Till 2007 ICT student teachers haven't been able to use an interactive whiteboard at the Faculty of Education. However, most of the schools where they do teaching practice are equipped with them. ICT student teachers appreciated the possibility to work with this new type of whiteboard.

e) **ways how in some primary schools** children from age 7 to 10 are being encouraged to work with ICT. These schools decided to find a space in their school timetable to allow teachers to work with young children in computer labs.

"I was surprised by a strong-willed effort by my supervisor teacher who was not only an ICT and Art Education teacher, but also a principal of the school. His pupils master graphic techniques and Art thinking – you can see the pupils' pictures and presentations in school halls, classrooms and teachers rooms – the school looks like a Gallery of Art."

f) the high interest of children in computers

g) a fact that in few schools all teachers could use ICT in all classrooms.

In some schools ICT student teachers could see how schools utilize Moodle.

Some ICT student teachers had some critical comments to:

a) conditions for ICT Education

"In my school there were limited technical conditions for ICT education. It is a pity that children couldn't learn more about WWW."... *"In the computer lab there was clutter and very often some teachers came in to speak with my supervisor teacher. I expected that it would be possible to use a data projector for my teaching as I was accustomed at the Faculty of Education, but the school didn't have it. It threw me into confusion. Therefore I decided to create my Web pages where I could publish all study and teaching materials and instructions for my pupils (www.vyukarudna.wz.cz)."*

b)   and to approaches to teaching of ICT subjects:

"In my school, children prefer to play computer games what isn't so difficult and boring according them therefore they regard ICT lessons as not very important. ...Teachers didn't give special professional attention to gifted pupils who knew a lot about technology and more than their teachers. In the school there dominates a practical orientation of ICT education to develop only fundamental user's skills and to achieve a general "computer literacy".... "I don't agree children cannot learn programming and haven't any textbooks."

TECHNOLOGICAL CONDITIONS IN SCHOOLS

Teaching practice in schools is a good opportunity for ICT student teachers to see a real situation in schools with all problems that schools have with ICT services and ICT in education:

"In my school where I did teaching practice there were three supervisors for administration of computer labs. But I know some schools without any qualified supervisors where supervision of the computer lab is done by a teacher without any qualification in ICT." ... "My supervisor- ICT teacher was very busy; he is the only specialist for ICT subjects in the school and also a supervisor of computer classrooms. He also helps his colleagues with their computers to solve their user problems – this hectic schedule sometimes influences the quality of his teaching."

According to comments by ICT student teachers in 2005, student teachers were faced with teachers who had very low computer literacy. Therefore teachers who mastered work with ICT were very busy and overloaded by activities with ICT. *"In my school some teachers even rejected installing computers in their working room."*

Some ICT student teachers struggled with a lot of technical problems. In 2007 some of them had to use very old computer machines without any data projectors and with low speed connectivity to the Internet. For instance, in 2007 one basic school didn't have a computer-net, there were only 10 isolated computers in a classroom.

Generally, some schools have no data projector or have very low speed connectivity to the Internet. Other problems that influenced the teaching practice of ICT student teachers were a lack of scanners, printers or multimedia workstations. Some problems originated in a bad conception of network administration and in setting users´ rights.

"In my school non suitable user data security could protect against abuse or their complete discarding by other pupils." ... "For teachers who don't teach ICT subjects it was very difficult to use a computer lab. The lab could be used only for ICT lessons." ... "I didn't like the school had two computer labs, but only one of them was connected to the Internet." ... "Computers were situated in the computer lab in a manner that pupils were sitting with their backs to a teacher and to a data-projector."

WHAT SHOULD BE IMPROVED AND CHANGED IN SCHOOLS?

ICT student teachers were asked to propose what could be improved in a school where they did their teaching practice. Most of their recommendations on how to change a situation in their school related to a technological improvement of schools:

"I recommend to install a bigger monitor for teachers (in labs for Biology Education and Foreign Language Education) and for students, too." ... "I would reduce a path to a common directory on a server where children can save their work. It was a problem for children."   "I would install Total Commander that could be for children more practical and understandable." ... "I would move the teacher workstation to another place in the computer lab." ... "I would change how the computers are arranged in a net; I would change the administration of user's profile."

"I would support more the Internet activities of students, but it would be necessary also to have better security for the computer network." ... "I would like to recommend to a computer-net administrator to equip schools with advanced technology" ... "and to upgrade SW."

"It would be very useful for teachers to install dataprojectors in all classrooms with computers."

"I would prefer to install in all computer labs of school the same operating system (for example Windows XP)."

"I would like to install more educational SW."

"In my school in a computer lab where I had lessons with children there wasn't a dataprojector, so I always had to borrow it from another classroom and after my lesson I had to put it back. It was not very practical. The security setting did not allow me to open an e-mail account on a public portal and children didn't have any e-mail accounts in the school server either. No existing e-mail accounts forced the school to break collaboration with other schools."

In 2005 the ICT student teachers recommended
to school ICT administrators and ICT coordinators:

To get rid of blackboard and to install a new one in a better place in the classroom. To re-arrange workstations in a classroom. To buy a dataprojector or to install Master Eye. To have computer labs accessible to all teachers and students. To integrate Moodle into school work. To buy more computers. To install other e-mail system (not GroupWise). To use also another graphic editor that could be used also at home by students. To employ more ICT administrators and ICT coordinators.

to ICT teachers:

To introduce textbooks for students. To teach programming.

to head teachers:

To recruit qualified ICT teachers for ICT subjects.

In 2006 ICT student teachers recommended
to school ICT administrators and ICT coordinators:

To allow pupils to work in computer labs after their school activities and during breaks. To darken computer labs. To install another computer lab. To buy another SW – also for a teaching basis of database and programming. To change arrangement of computers and furniture in computer labs.

to teachers:

To extend ICT courses to others grades. To involve pupils (school) into an international or national project activity. To motivate pupils to apply ICT in practice and in life.

In 2007 ICT student teachers advised to school ICT coordinators:

To use Vision studio or similar SW for monitoring student's individual activities. To install a camera-control system (to protect technology equipment against losses). To install dataprojectors in all computer labs. To allow teachers to conncet a notebook. To install an interactive whiteboard

1.4 Student Teacher Professional Development from a Student Teacher Perspective

After teaching practice ICT student teachers have to fill evaluative questionnaires where they have to answer some questions related to conditions for information education in schools and to the approach of teachers and school management to a new curriculum concept of ICT education. All lesson plans, video-recordings and documents developed by ICT students in their teaching practice form a part of a student portfolio that is applied in some courses oriented on methodology and didactic aspects of information and ICT education.

QUESTION: WHAT HAVE ICT STUDENT TEACHERS LEARNT IN SCHOOLS DURING THEIR TEACHING PRACTICE?

In 2004:

"I have learned very much. As a teacher I met so many problems (SW, computer net, HW, connectivity) that I didn't expect that I had to think about how to solve them." ... *"It was my first experience with young students as my pupils."* ... *"Teaching practice was super. You could see that theory and practice are two totally different things! It seems a lot of my teachers at the Faculty of Education forgot this fact!"* ... *"I was surprised how easy it was for me to teach!"* ... *"At first I was slightly afraid to teach children a subject that I couldn't learn personally in my basic school. But at the end it was a fantastic experience for me!"* ... *"I was teaching at a basic school – it was nice practice for me. I am curious about how it would be to teach at a secondary school."*

"I completed my practice at a secondary school. I was curious about how my female colleagues would be able to teach teenagers like I had to teach." ... *"I designed learning activities for children by my own concept to be interesting also for me personally. I exploited my personal experiences with ICT."* ... *"I was kindly surprised how teachers, school management and my supervisor-teacher accepted me. I was very happy to be and to teach there. It influenced me to become a teacher!"*

In 2006:

"The teaching practice is very short, but for student teachers it is very exacting. During four weeks we have to get experience with teaching in two specializations. Fortunately my practice was successful – I am employed in this schools and my teaching practice was realized with my pupils. There was only one problem – my supervisor-teacher is a student of the Technical University, who is an expert in ICT and Computer Science, but he has no pedagogical background like me. He could be more convenient as a supervisor-teacher for ICT subjects with talented children."

In 2007:

"I liked my teaching practice. It was my first experience with being a teacher. At first I was afraid but after my first lesson I discovered that it is a fantastic and creative job to be a teacher. I was glad to see how my pupils collaborate and work. Step by step I have managed to motivate all pupils to do given assignments. Maybe I will succeed in it because I was a new "non-hackneyed element" in a classroom and my pupils did not know what they could expect from me."

QUESTION: WHO HAS INFLUENCE ON TEACHING STYLES OF ICT STUDENT TEACHERS?

In Fig 5 you can see who has the greatest impact on the teaching style of the ICT student teachers. Their own basic or secondary school and university teachers have had the most important influence on their approaches to pupils and teaching strategies. Some ICT students are not thinking about professional patterns and they try to tread their own path without any models or patterns.

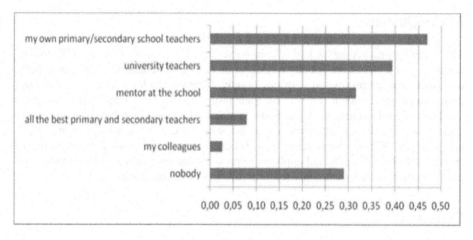

Fig. 5. Professional patterns of who has an influence on ICT student teachers

THE BIGGEST PROBLEMS FOR ICT STUDENT TEACHERS IN TEACHING PRACTICE

For most of ICT student teachers there is a problem organizing their teaching into 45 minute lessons. Another problem that they had relates to a motivation of pupils to be active. ICT student teachers did not see any problem in communication with their pupils (Fig. 3). Some ICT student teachers were faced with teaching both ICT beginners and ICT experienced pupils. They didn't know how to design lesson in class with a big differences in ICT knowledge and skills of teenager students and whom should they dedicate their teaching to in their 45 minute lessons.

"I was not ready to teach students with such big differences in ICT skills and knowledge: I hadn't time and space to develop the advanced ICT users and at the same time I couldn't teach beginners in ICT."

2 A Role of Moodle in Teaching Practice of ICT Student Teachers

A few years ago we decided to use Moodle for coordinating and managing teaching practice of ICT student teachers. In Moodle we publish instructions for students on what to do and documents (lesson plan template, templates for time-table, etc.). In Moodle ICT student teachers can ask colleagues and didactics specialists and inform them about the situation in their schools. We endeavor to answer students immediately.

"I would like to appreciate a clear structure and function of Moodle support. Thanks to very clear instructions I could see how teaching practice proceeds in other schools of my colleagues, what I have to do. Our teachers from the Faculty of Education answered us immediately. Each important question was answered." ... "I would appreciate the Moodle support which helped me very quickly understand a system on how teaching practice is organized. It is a pity, that other departments of the faculty do not use similar support."

3 Conclusions

The teaching practice has a key role in university teacher education of ICT student teachers. It is a pity at the Faculty of Education in Prague student teachers can experience their teacher profession with pupils only during 8 weeks. It is a too short time period to prepare student teachers for their profession and to demonstrate mastering key professional competences [6]. Some students who study in a full-time study program at the Faculty of Education and at the same time work at schools as part-time non-qualified ICT teachers, achieve in didactic courses and in their diploma thesis significantly better results and apply more professional approaches to given tasks and problems than students who only study in full-time study programs.

References

1. Moodle, http://moodle.pedf.cuni.cz
2. Van der Linde D., van der Hoeff A., van Hans, P: AST Michel ICT Knowledge base. Version 1.0. (2009)
3. JOMITE Group SpriTE Teaching Practice Assessment Checklist (2009)
4. Vlastní hodnocení škol. ČŠI, Praha
5. Janík, Tomáš Didaktické znalosti obsahu a jejich význam pro oborové didaktiky, tvorbu kurikula a učitelské vzdělávání. Brno (2009)
6. Hodnocení studentů studijních programů učitelství při plnění souvislé pedagogické praxe z oboru it (IKT) KITTV, PedF UK, Praha (2010)

Appendix 1 Lesson Plan

Subject: Grade: School: Topic:
Lesson plan author:
Educational program (curriculum document) applied by the school:
1. Preliminary requirements for pupil's knowledge: *Give a list of pupil's knowledge and skills to be able to understand a topic for a lesson. For example*
   - Pupils are able to..., Pupils understand..., Pupils master in ...)
2. Main aim of the lesson:
   - Particular goals:
   - ICT competencies (related to the document of the Framework Educational Program) *Give a list of competencies that you will contribute to develop in your lesson.*
3. Text-books, study materials that would be used by pupils for your lesson.
4. Aids, tools that would be used in a lesson.
5. A list of technology equipment and HW that would be used in your lesson by a teacher and by pupils. For each tool explain for which activity it will be used.
6. A list of SW that would be used in your lesson and to prepare for your lesson.
7. Draw a scheme of classroom arrangement.)
8. Teaching methods and strategies with the explanation how you will apply teaching methods and which teaching strategies you will prefer for your teaching.

9. Procedure: *Describe instructions on how to order lesson procedures. Your description ought to be formulated as a manual on how to realize your lesson plan.*
10. Questions that pupils should be able to answer at the end of the lesson.
11. Assignments and problems to be solved by students. Give also their solution and numeral account).
12. Homework. Formulate problems and activities for homework.
13. Evaluation: Explain criteria how student outcomes will be evaluated.
14. Addition and extra topics, assignments for talented pupils: Propose how you will organize a lesson with a classroom where you have found some talented pupils.
15. WWW: Give a list of WWW pages used in your teaching.
16. Learning objects: Give a list of learning objects that you will use.
17. Vocabulary of terms from ICT and Informatics related to the topic: Give a list of terms with explanations understandable and dedicated to your pupils.
18. Term and its explanation: .....

===

TEACHER SELF-EVALUATION AND AUTO-REFLECTION
1. How did you succeed your lesson?
2. What didn't you manage?

Intentions to Pursue a Career in Information Systems and Technology: An Empirical Study of South African Students

Jason F. Cohen and Poonam Parsotam

School of Economic and Business Sciences, University of the Witwatersrand,
2050 Johannesburg, South Africa
jason.cohen@wits.ac.za

Abstract. This paper reports on a study of the IT career interests of 263 South African university students. Drawing primarily on social cognitive career theory, a number of variables were selected and their effects on student intentions to pursue an IT career and choice of major were examined. Results revealed very low IT career intentions amongst students. Occupational self-efficacy, computing experience, computer anxiety, computer self-efficacy, and perceived career rewards were found to be important factors. Student perceptions of the core introductory IS course are also strongly linked to their intentions. Demography (gender and race) had mostly indirect effects.

Keywords: Careers, choice of major, self-efficacy, computer anxiety, computer attitude, experience, outcome expectations.

1 Introduction

A strong information technology (IT) workforce is considered part of the core human capital needs of a knowledge society. However, high school and university students are expressing little interest in pursuing information systems (IS) or IT careers, and enrolment figures in IT related majors has declined globally since the Dot-com failures of 2001 [1], [2]. Although there are some reports that enrolments may soon increase, there remains concern over impending IT workforce and skills shortages [3]. To better predict enrolment trends, IT educators are calling for an improved understanding of factors associated with students' IT career intentions and choice of major.

Initial contributions describe changing enrollment patterns and the outlook for IT graduate demand e.g. [4], and point to external market factors, including the general economy and the outsourcing phenomenon, as driving students away from IT [5]. Some researchers have chosen to direct attention inward at IS/IT faculty. They recommend changes to course design and the use of leading edge technology as ways to attract and retain students [6], [7], [8].

Yet, others consider student backgrounds, attitudes and their perceptions of IT as the primary determinants of their career and study choices. To this end, some exploratory studies are uncovering student awareness and expectations of an IT career [9], the factors important to them in the selection of a major [10], [11], as well as the

N. Reynolds and M. Turcsányi-Szabó (Eds.): KCKS 2010, IFIP AICT 324, pp. 56–66, 2010.

stereotypes they may have of IS/IT professionals [2]. The role of gender and ethnicity in influencing attitudes and IT career intentions has also been explored [12] along with perceptions of job availability, interests in IS, perceptions of the curriculum, and views of family and professors [13]. Recently, social cognitive career theory has been drawn upon to successfully test a model of students' intentions to select a computing major. This theory models student intentions as a function of their interests, self-efficacy beliefs and outcome expectations [14].

The aim of this study is to contribute to such explanations of student interest in IT oriented careers. We draw on social cognitive career theory (SCCT), and prior work in the IT career literature, to examine a set of factors for their influence on South African students' interests and intentions in relation to IT careers.

The success of the knowledge society will require a committed and dedicated IS/IT workforce and being able to influence, impact and predict the career choices of our students is important to preventing potential labor shortages [10]. Therefore, by identifying the factors that influence student intentions, we can prevent missed opportunities for attracting students into the field, we can define interventions to address those factors within our full or partial control, and we can understand the nature and extent of the impact of those factors outside of our immediate control.

2 Background to the Study

This study focuses on both 'choice of major' and 'career intention' as reflections of student interest in IT. This allows us to make a distinction between the educational aspirations of students and their career aspirations. IT career intention is a career aspiration and is defined as the subjective probability of the student choosing to pursue a career in the IT field [12]. Choice of major, on the other hand, is considered an educational aspiration and thus part of the preparation for a career choice [15] but not a precise determinant [16], [17]. Although a number of degree programs exist to serve the educational aspirations of students interested in IT [18], we focused on the study of Commerce students and their intentions to major in Information Systems.

2.1 Research Variables

SCCT describes the career development process by explaining through Bandura's social cognitive theory how people will develop goals for future activity involvement, such as the intention to select a college major or to pursue a career path, consistent with their interests, self-efficacy assessments and positive outcome expectations [15]. For this reason, this study explores student self-efficacy beliefs, attitudes and interest in IT, and outcome expectations (rewards) of an IT career.

SCCT also accounts for perceived barriers to career development that might influence career choices [17]. Even if an individual possesses high levels of self-efficacy and interest, perceived barriers to career entry or advancement may still inhibit the translation of interests into career choice [19]. Perceived barriers may arise from differential opportunities for development (e.g. education), or perceptions of gender or ethnic discrimination in the associated career. For this reason, this study also explores students' differential experiences and backgrounds in computing as well as their demography in an effort to better understand their career intentions.

Demography: There is concern that the under-representation of certain demographic groups in the IT field is limiting the human capital potential of the knowledge society [20]. Specifically, participation of females and certain ethnic/racial groups in the IT field has received attention and efforts to understand their perceptions and motivations to study and work in IT have been underway for the past decade e.g. [21]. Our study therefore seeks to provide additional empirical evidence on gender differences and the effects of racial demography on IT career intention and choice to major in IS.

Computer experience: Past research considers prior computer education (in high school), personal computer (PC) ownership, computer usage, and years since first contact with computers as key indicators of computing experience [22], [23]. Computer experience and past success may reduce career bias and inspire career choice [9], [24]. We therefore expect student computer experience to associate with IT career intention and the choice to major in IS.

Occupational self-efficacy is considered in SCCT to have a direct effect on career choice [16], and is defined as an individual's belief in their ability to succeed in a given career. Lent et al. [14] consider self-efficacy to influence choice of major directly and indirectly through effects on interest and outcome expectations. Johnson et al. [12] found that students' perceptions of their ability to work in the IT field correlated with attitude toward IT jobs, and Walstrom et al. [10] identify "I'm not suited for IT type work" amongst the reasons for students not wanting to pursue IT studies or an IT career. We thus expect student occupational self-efficacy to correlate with IT career intention and choice to major in IS.

Computer self-efficacy is an individual's confidence in their computer-related abilities. Research suggests that individuals who have high computer self-efficacy are more likely to be interested in IT studies [8]. We thus expect student computer self-efficacy beliefs to correlate with IT career intention and choice to major in IS.

Computer anxiety is the affective response of individuals when they use (or consider the possibility of using) computers and will manifest as worries, apprehensions, tensions and fear [25]. Computer anxious individuals are more reluctant to use computers [23], will generally avoid them [26], and may perform more poorly on computer-based tasks [27]. We consider that a student's computer anxiety may become a career and educational barrier, which will be inversely associated with IT career intention and choice to major in IS.

Attitude toward computers is an individual's feelings about the usefulness and impacts of computers for society and for their own daily lives [25], [28]. Negative attitudes and lack of interest are frequently cited reasons for why students do not select an IT major [9], [10]. We expect attitude toward computers and their usefulness to correlate with IT career intention and choice of major.

Perception of IT career rewards: SCCT suggests that individuals develop interest in activities which they believe will lead to positive outcomes – including anticipated tangible, social and self-evaluative outcomes [15]. Outcome expectations rank amongst the most important considerations in student selection of a major [9], [10], while perceptions of poor career prospects and lack of enjoyable work rank among the reasons cited for not selecting an IS major [29], [30]. We examine student perceptions of both tangible IT career outcomes (e.g. earning an attractive salary, job security) and perceptions of social and self-evaluative outcomes (e.g. doing satisfying work, doing good for society, and having a good home life), and expect them to influence IT career intention and choice of major.

Through the *introductory IS course*, IS/IT Faculty can positively influence student attitude, increase perceptions of career rewards [8] and enhance IT interest [6], [7]. Given that the introductory IS course is a core degree requirement for all students participating in this study, we examine whether the introductory course is stimulating student interest in IT.

3 Methods

The study was conducted at the authors' institution - the University of the Witwatersrand, Johannesburg[1]. The sampling frame consisted of 536 first year Bachelor of Commerce (BCom) students enrolled in a core introductory information systems course. Each of the students would subsequently have the option to abandon further IS studies or continue with the subject as a major. Students were invited to participate. Participation was completely voluntary and neither penalty nor benefit was attached to their participation[2].

3.1 Instrument

The survey instrument was a structured questionnaire. It was made available to students during their class session and clearance was obtained from the University's ethics committee.

The questionnaire asked demographic questions about age, gender and race. The questionnaire also asked students about their computer experience including a) whether they had taken an IT subject in high-school, b) whether they owned a personal computer (PC), c) the number of years they had been using computers, and d) the average amount of time spent on the computer per day (1=less than one hour to 4=more than 6 hours). Computer self-efficacy was measured using 10 items from Murphy et al. [31] on a 5-point scale. However, after principal components analysis (PCA), five items were removed as they seemed to capture more basic levels of self-efficacy, the remaining five items tapped into a more advanced computing self-efficacy factor and included items measuring student confidence in ability to troubleshoot computer problems, write simple programs, and understand issues related to hardware and software compatibility and the stages of data processing ($\alpha = 0.75$). General computer anxiety was measured using six items adapted from Nickell and Pinto [28] and Heinssen et al. [25] on a 5-point scale. Items asked about fear and intimidation in relation to computer usage in a work related context ($\alpha = 0.87$). Computer attitude was measured by asking students the extent to which they agreed with eight statements reflecting positive attitudes toward computers. The scale was adapted from Nickell and Pinto [28]. Following PCA, one item was eliminated and

---

[1] The University of the Witwatersrand, Johannesburg is divided into 5 Faculties comprising 34 Schools. It is a research focused university and, as one of only 5 universities in Africa (universities of Cape Town, Cairo, Natal and Pretoria being the other four) that are listed in the Shanghai Jaio Tong Top 500 rankings, it has an important role to play in Africa's hopes to become a knowledge society.

[2] Over the last decade, enrollments for further study in IS have fallen roughly 70% from their peak at the beginning of the millennium. The largest drop occurred in 2003 where enrollment fell by almost 50%, and in 2004 enrollments toward the major fell below 100 for the first time.

the remaining seven items captured student attitudes toward the impacts of computers on individuals, business and society ($\alpha = 0.83$). Perceived IT career rewards were captured through seven items [32] measured on a 5-point scale. Principal components analysis confirmed these items loaded onto two factors with five items reflecting perceived personal and social rewards ($\alpha = 0.70$) and two items reflecting perceived tangible rewards ($\alpha = 0.66$). Perceptions of the introductory IS course was measured using three items measured on a 5-point scale to assess the extent to which the various components of the course were stimulating the student's interest in IT ($\alpha = 0.82$). Occupational self-efficacy was measured using a single item asking students if they believed they possessed the skills and abilities needed to pursue an IT career. Intention to pursue a career in IT was measured using four items ($\alpha = 0.93$), which were adapted from Brinkley and Scholar [32]. These items captured student interest and intention to pursue an IT related career. Students were also asked to identify their most likely choice of major, and were provided an opportunity to select from across the options for a BCom major at the university e.g. Accounting, Finance, Economics, Human Resources, Information Systems, Management, and Marketing among others.

To facilitate subsequent analysis composite scores were created for the multi-item scales as the arithmetic average of the scale items weighted equally.

4   Findings

Roughly half the students (n=263) consented to participate by completing the survey instrument. The proportion of females/males and race groups returning the questionnaire was quite consistent with the overall demographic of the registered students and the sample is considered representative.

Approximately 15% of students (n=41) identified themselves as intending to major in IS. This is consistent with the proportion of IS/non-IS majors reported in a recent article [6] but also more promising than others [10]. Students who indicated their intentions were not to major in IS identified their most likely choice of major as Accounting/Finance (n=110) or Business Sciences/Economics (n=100), with very few undecided.

4.1   Demography and Computer Experience

Roughly 75% of the students report owning a personal computer (PC). Unfortunately, amongst South African students, PC ownership is not independent of race ($\chi^2 = 40.15$, $p<0.001$). Black students account for 96% of the students reporting no computer ownership. There is also a statistically significant difference ($\chi^2=33.65$, $p<0.01$) between race groups in years of computer experience. While most White and Indian students have been using computers for more than 6 years, about 40% of Black students had less than 2 years experience.

About half the students use computers for 2-3 hours per day, only 10% report that they spend more than 4 hours per day on the computer. There was no statistically significant difference across race or gender in usage.

Table 1 examines student intention to major in IS and finds, using χ^2 tests, that intention to major in IS is independent of age, race, gender, and all computer experience indicators except for past high school IT education. Students that take IT/computer studies in high school are more likely to major in IS at university level. It is pleasing to note that the taking of an IT subject in high school is independent of both race and gender, however only 20% of the students had taken an IT subject in high school and only 30.8% of those were intending to major in IS. This suggests that educational aspirations in high school do not necessarily translate into educational aspirations at university level and confirms students will "branch out" from high school experiences when considering career prospects [9].

Table 1. Comparison on Demographics and Computer Experience (Intention to Major)

Student Demographics and Computing Experience		No Intention to Major in IS (n=222)	Intention to Major in IS (n=41)	p-value
Age	< 20	199(84.3%)	37 (15.7%)	0.910
	> 20	21(84%)	4 (16%)	
Gender	Male	95(84.1%)	18 (15.9%)	0.895
	Female	127(84.7%)	23 (15.3%)	
Race	Black	142(84.5%)	26 (15.5%)	
	White	34 (82.9%)	7 (17.1%)	
	Indian	38 (92.7%)	3 (7.3%)	0.108
	Asian	4 (57.1%)	3 (42.9%)	
	Other	4 (66.7%)	2 (33.3%)	
IT subject taken in high school	Yes	36 (69.2%)	16 (30.8%)	0.001
	No	185 (88.1%)	25 (11.9%)	
PC ownership	Yes	165 (85.5%)	28 (14.5%)	0.344
	No	54 (80.6%)	13(19.4%)	
Hours of computer use (p/day)	0-1 hours	85(87.6%)	12(12.4%)	
	2-3 hours	115(82.7%)	24(17.3%)	0.729
	4-5 hours	15(78.9%)	4(21.1%)	
	> 6 hours	5(100%)	0(0%)	
Years of computer use	< 1 year	44(83%)	9(17%)	
	1-2 years	24(85.7%)	4(14.3%)	
	2-4 years	33(91.7%)	3(8.3%)	0.746
	4-6 years	26(81.3%)	6(18.7%)	
	> 6 years	93(83%)	19(17%)	

* sum of numbers differs from total n due to missing data in some cases.

Table 2 reveals that intentions to pursue an IT career are generally very low, and in all cases below the scale mid-point of 3 except for those intending to major in IS. Those students that took IT courses in high school are also significantly more interested in pursuing an IT related career. These findings confirm a significant relationship between career intention and educational aspiration.

Hours of computer use per day is also associated with intention, with Tukey post-hoc analysis confirming a significant difference between the group of students using computers for less than 1 hour per day and the group using computers for between 2 to 3 hours. Similar to Seymour et al. [33], it is interesting to note slightly higher interest amongst students that do not own computers.

While SCCT suggests that perceived gender or ethnic discrimination could act as a barrier to career choice, neither gender nor race were directly related to career choice.

Table 2. Comparison on Demographics and Computer Experience (Intention to Pursue IT Career)

Student Demographics and Experience	Computing	Mean Career Intention Score ± SD.	t-value (sig.) / F-value (sig.)
Age	< 20	2.40 ± 1.1	t=0.027 (p=0.979)
	> 20	2.39 ± 1.2	
Gender	Male	2.49 ± 1.1	t=1.184 (p=0.238)
	Female	2.32 ± 1.1	
Race	Black	2.42 ± 1.2	
	White	2.26 ± 1.1	
	Indian	2.40 ± 1.1	F=0.237 (p=0.917)
	Asian	2.60 ± 0.9	
	Other	2.55 ± 1.5	
IT subject taken in high school	Yes	2.75 ± 1.3	t=2.522 (p=0.012)
	No	2.31 ± 1.1	
PC ownership	Yes	2.36 ± 1.1	t=-0.924 (p=0.356)
	No	2.51 ± 1.9	
Hours of computer use (p/day)	0-1 hours	2.12 ± 1.0	
	2-3 hours	2.56 ± 1.2	F=3.473 (p=0.017)
	4-5 hours	2.68 ± 1.3	
	> 6 hours	2.10 ± 1.1	
Years of computer use	< 1 year	2.60 ± 1.2	
	1-2 years	2.13 ± 0.9	
	2-4 years	2.43 ± 1.1	F=1.219 (p=0.303)
	4-6 years	2.59 ± 1.3	
	> 6 years	2.30 ± 1.2	
Intention to major in IS	Yes	4.08 ± 0.7	t=13.188 (p<0.001)
	No	2.08 ± 0.9	

4.2 Self Efficacy, Anxiety, Attitudes and Perceptions

Table 3 shows that the male students have higher levels of computer self-efficacy (t= 3.5, p<0.001) and lower levels of computer anxiety (t=2.6, p<0.05) than their female counterparts. This is consistent with prior literature [12], [26]. Race also tends to be associated with computer anxiety, with Black and Indian students demonstrating the highest anxiety levels (F=2.54, p< 0.05). Prior education in computing appears important to increasing self-efficacy (t=5.83, p<0.001) and reducing anxiety (t=5.0, p<0.001). We also found PC ownership reduces anxiety (t=2.1, p<0.05), that students using computers between 4-5 hours per day have the highest self-efficacy levels (F=5.26, p< 0.01), and that students with fewer years of experience have the highest anxiety levels (F=10.77, p< 0.001). This confirms prior analyses in other contexts and suggests that computer anxiety is a 'state anxiety' that can be manipulated by training and exposure [23], [26], [34].

We find students with higher computer self-efficacy (t=5.1, p<0.001) and lower anxiety (t=4.7, p<0.001) are more likely to major in IS. All students seemed to share a positive attitude towards computers independent of gender, race, computing experience or choice of major. This supports the view that students not majoring in IS do not necessarily have negative perceptions of the field [2], but frequent users do have the highest positive attitudes toward computers (F=4.07, p< 0.01).

An independent sample t-test (t=3.08, p<0.01) confirms that females have lower IT occupational self-efficacy than males. We did not find differences by race. Occupational self-efficacy is highest for PC owners (t=2.14, p<0.05), those who took IT in high school (t=5.23, p<0.001), those intending to major in IS (t=6.22, p<0.001), those who've been using computers for longer (F=2.710, p<0.05) and are more frequent users (F=6.270, p<0.001).

Table 4 presents results of correlation analyses between student intention to pursue an IT career and the various computing attitudes and career perceptions. All variables are significantly associated with career intention except computer attitude.

We also confirm that students intending to major in IS differ significantly from those with no intentions on the perceived tangible rewards of an IT career (t=3.78, p<0.001) and the perceived personal and social rewards of an IT career (t=7.26, p<0.001). The mean ± SD for perceived tangible rewards of total sample, intended IS majors and non-IS majors was 3.38± 0.82; 3.82± 0.70; and 3.30± 0.81 respectively. The mean ± SD for perceived personal and social rewards for the total sample, intended IS majors and non-IS majors was 3.24± 0.69; 3.89± 0.54; and 3.11± 0.64 respectively. Thus changing student perceptions of IT careers is an important intervention needed to secure increased enrolment.

Table 3. Student Self Efficacy, Anxiety and Attitude

Student Demographics and Computing Experience		Occupational Self Efficacy	Computer Self Efficacy	Computer Attitude	Computer Anxiety
Age	< 20	2.92	3.17	4.21	1.97
	> 20	2.60	3.27	4.29	1.99
Gender	Male	3.13**	3.36 ***	4.18	1.82**
	Female	2.69	3.04	4.25	2.10
Race	Black	2.85	3.26	4.23	2.02*
	White	3.07	3.20	4.22	1.70
	Indian	2.85	2.90	4.17	2.22
	Asian	3.00	2.97	4.14	1.62
	Other	2.65	3.06	4.30	1.58
IT subject taken in high school	Yes	3.60***	3.68***	4.26	1.54***
	No	2.70	3.05	4.20	2.09
PC ownership	Yes	2.98*	3.19	4.22	1.90*
	No	2.63	3.18	4.22	2.17
Hours of computer use (p/day)	0-1 hours	2.53**	2.97	4.10	2.03
	2-3 hours	3.05	3.29	4.24	2.00
	4-5 hours	3.53	3.50**	4.59**	1.78
	> 6 hours	2.80	3.04	4.26	1.87
Years of computer use	< 1 year	2.59	3.06	4.29	2.52***
	1-2 years	2.57	2.99	4.10	2.16
	2-4 years	2.78	3.20	4.18	2.11
	4-6 years	3.22*	3.24	4.27	1.98
	> 6 years	3.04	3.26	4.20	1.65
Intention to major in IS	Yes	3.85***	3.69***	4.28	1.61***
	No	2.70	3.08	4.20	2.05

* p<0.05   ** p<0.01   ***p<0.001.

Table 4. Correlates of Student IT Career Intention

	IT Career Intention
Computer Self-Efficacy	0.386***
Computer Anxiety	-0.141*
Computer Attitude	0.082
Perception of Introductory Course	0.549***
Perception of Tangible Career Rewards	0.266***
Perception of Personal/Social Career Rewards	0.608***
Occupational Self-Efficacy	0.805***

* p<0.05   ** p<0.01   ***p<0.001

In evaluating perceptions of the introductory IS course, we found a statistically significant difference (t=5.29, p<0.001) between those students intending to major in IS (3.85± 0.86) and those reporting no interest (2.95± 1.02). However, it was sobering to observe that interest in IT was not being peaked very high for either group of students (less than 4 on the 5-point measurement scale).

Logistic regression indicated that set of variables (from Table 4) was 96% accurate in predicting the decision of students not to major in IS, but only 39% accurate in predicting the decision of students to major in IS. This suggests that while we are able to explain what leads to lack of interest, we are not as successful in predicting which students will be drawn to the IS major.

5   Conclusion

Declining student numbers in IT related disciplines is a cause for concern and a problem that has implications for the human capital potential of the knowledge society. We therefore sought to uncover the factors associated with students' intentions to major in Information Systems and pursue an IT career.

Results based on an analysis of 263 first year students unfortunately reveals very low IT career intentions amongst students, and only 15% of students indicated an intention to major in IS. This study has contributed to our understanding of these intentions by showing that the determinants of career choice, as predicted by social cognitive career theory, have deep psychological roots. We found that career and study choices reflect perceptions and expectations of reward (outcomes) and are driven by interests, anxieties, and self-efficacy beliefs. Importantly, we have also found that career aspirations tend to start much earlier than University level. Years of computing experience, early computer education, and PC ownership appear to have direct and indirect impacts on study and career choices.

Demography (gender and race) was also found to exert indirect effects on IT career intention and choice of major. Improving both occupational and computer self-efficacy and reducing computer anxiety amongst females may be critical to increasing their interest in an IT career. We also find that increasing the computer experience amongst Black students and reducing their anxiety may be important factors in raising their IT career interests.

Future research may wish to extend our examination to include variables such as subjective-norm and perceptions of job availability and the skills gap. Future research may want to account for the misperceptions that students may have of IT careers, for example that there are only technical career options. Repeat measures studies should be designed to explore how student attitudes, anxieties, self-efficacy, career perceptions and intentions to major change over the duration of the introductory course as certain interventions are made to curriculum design and course structure.

References

1. Becker, J., Hassan, N., Naumann, J.D.: Combating the Enrollment Downturn in IS/IT Programs. In: Proceedings of the Twelfth AMCIS, Acapulco, Mexico (2006)
2. Akbulut-Bailey, A.Y.: A Measurement Instrument for Understanding Student Perspectives on Stereotypes of IS Professionals. Commun. AIS 25, 321–338 (2009)
3. Beise, C.M., Robbins, J., Kaiser, K., Niederman, F.P.: The Information Systems Enrollment Crisis: Status and Strategies. In: SIGMS-CPR, Limerick, pp. 215–216 (2009)
4. George, J.F., Valacich, J.S., Valor, J.: Does Information Systems Still Matter? Lessons for a Maturing Discipline. In: Proceedings ICIS, Washington, pp. 1039–1048 (2004)
5. Baskerville, R., Adam, A., Krcmar, H., Peppard, J., Venable, J.: Panel: IT Employment and Shifting Enrolment Patterns in Information Systems. In: Proceedings of the Thirteenth ECIS, Regensburg, Germany, pp. 26–28 (2005)
6. Firth, D., Lawrence, C., Looney, C.A.: Addressing the IS Enrollment Crisis: a 12-step Program to Bring about Change through the Introductory IS Course. Commun. AIS 23, 17–36 (2008)
7. Street, C., Wade, M.: Reversing the Downward Trend: Innovative Approaches to IS/IT Course Development and Delivery. In: Proceedings ICIS, Montreal, pp. 1–5 (2007)
8. Akbulut, A.Y., Looney, C.A.: Improving IS Student Enrollments: Understanding the Effects of IT Sophistication in Introductory IS Courses. J. Information Technology Education 8, 87–100 (2009)
9. McInerney, C.R., DiDonato, N.C., Giagnacova, R., O'Donnell, A.M.: Students' Choice of Information Technology Majors and Careers: a Qualitative Study. Information Technology, Learning, and Performance Journal 24(2), 35–53 (2006)
10. Walstrom, K.A., Jones, K.T., Crampton, W.J.: Why are Students Not Majoring in Information Systems? J. Information Systems Education 19(1), 43–52 (2008)
11. Ferratt, T.W., Hall, S.R., Prasad, J., Wynn, D.E.: Why Students Choose MIS: What Makes a Major-Job-Career in Management Information Systems Interesting? In: ACM SIGMIS-CPR, Limerick, pp. 57–61 (2009)
12. Johnson, R.D., Stone, D.L., Phillips, T.N.: Relations Among Ethnicity, Gender, Beliefs, Attitudes, and Intention to Pursue a Career in Information Technology. J. Appl. Soc. Psychol. 38(4), 999–1022 (2008)
13. Zhang, W.: Why IS: Understanding Undergraduate Students' Intentions to Choose an Information Systems Major. J. Information Systems Education 18(4), 447–458 (2007)
14. Lent, R.W., Lopez, A.M., Lopez, F.G., Sheu, H.: Social Cognitive Career Theory and the Prediction of Interests and Choice in the Computing Disciplines. J. Vocat. Behav. 73, 52–62 (2008)
15. Lent, R.W., Brown, S.D., Hackett, G.: Toward a Unifying Social Cognitive Theory of Career and Academic Interest, Choice, and Performance. J. Vocat. Behav. 45, 79–122 (1994)
16. Rottinghaus, P.J., Lindley, L.D., Green, M.A., Borgen, F.H.: Educational Aspirations: The Contribution of Personality, Self-efficacy, and Interest. J. Vocat. Behav. 61, 1–19 (2002)

17. Lindley, L.D.: Perceived Barriers to Career Development in the Context of Social Cognitive Career Theory. J. Career Assessment 13(3), 271–287 (2005)
18. Computing Curricula 2005, Report of the Joint ACM and IEEE Curriculum Taskforce (2005), http://www.acm.org/education/curric_vols/CC2005-March06Final.pdf
19. Albert, K.A., Luzzo, D.A.: The Role of Perceived Barriers in Career Development: a Social Cognitive Perspective. J. Couns. Dev. 77(4), 431–436 (1999)
20. Trauth, E.M., Quesenberry, J.L., Huang, H.: A Multicultural Analysis of Factors Influecing Career Choice for Women in the Information Technology Workforce. J. Global Information Management 16(4), 1–23 (2008)
21. Nielsen, S.H., von Hellers, L.A., Greenhill, A., Pringle, R.: Conceptualising the Influence of Cultural and Gender Factors on Students' Perceptions of IT Studies and Careers. In: ACM SIGCPR Conference on Computer Personnel Research, Boston (1998)
22. Korobili, S., Togia, A., Malliari, A.: Computer Anxiety and Attitudes Among Undergraduate Students in Greece. Comput. Hum. Behav. (in Press), http://dx.doi.org/10.1016/j.chb.2009.11.011
23. Bozionelos, N.: Socio-Economic Background and Computer Use: the Role of Computer Anxiety and Computer Experience in Their Relationship. Int. J. Hum-Comput. St. 61, 725–746 (2004)
24. Adya, M., Kaiser, K.M.: Early Determinants of Women in the IT Workforce: a Model of Girls' Career Choices. Inform. Technol. and People 18(3), 230–259 (2005)
25. Heinssen, R.K., Glass, C.R., Knight, L.A.: Assessing Computer Anxiety: Development and Validation of the Computer Anxiety Rating Scale. Comput. Hum. Behav. 3(1), 49–59 (1987)
26. Chua, S.L., Chen, D., Wong, A.F.L.: Computer Anxiety and its Correlates: a Meta-Analysis. Comput. Hum. Behav. 15, 609–623 (1999)
27. Mahar, D., Henderson, R., Deane, F.: The Effects of Computer Anxiety, State Anxiety, and Computer Experience on Users' Performance of Computer Based Tasks. Pers. Indiv. Differ. 22(5), 683–692 (1997)
28. Nickell, G.S., Pinto, J.N.: The Computer Attitude Scale. Comput. Hum. Behav. 2(4), 301–306 (1986)
29. Lomerson, W.L., Pollacia, L.: CIS Enrollment Decline: Examining Pre-College Factors. In: Proceedings Southern AIS Conference, Jacksonville, pp. 93–103 (2006)
30. Granger, M.J., Dick, G., Jacobson, C.M., Van Slyke, C.: Information Systems Enrollments: Challenges and Strategies. J. Information Systems Education 18(3), 303–311 (2007)
31. Murphy, C.A., Coover, D., Owen, S.V.: Development and Validity of the Computer Self-efficacy Scale. Educ. Psychol. Meas. 49(4), 893–899 (1989)
32. Brinkley, T., Scholar, M.: Women in Information Technology: Examining the Role of Attitudes, Social Norms, and Behavioral Control in Information Technology Career Choices. WSU McNair Journal 3, 24–40 (2005)
33. Seymour, L., Hart, M., Haralamous, P., Natha, T., Wend, C.: Inclination of Scholars to Major in Information Systems or Computer Science. In: Proceedings of SAICSIT, Stellenbosch, pp. 97–106 (2004)
34. Tekinarslan, E.: Computer Anxiety: a Cross-Cultural Comparative Study of Dutch and Turkish University Students. Comput. Hum. Behav. 24, 1572–1584 (2008)

From Context to Competencies

Ira Diethelm and Christina Dörge

University of Oldenburg, Computer Science Education,
26111 Oldenburg, Germany
{Ira.Diethelm,Christina.Doerge}@informatik.uni-oldenburg.de

Abstract. For classes in informatics[1] it gets more and more important to develop a sustainable curriculum because computer technology and its related items are subject to frequent changes. This leads to the problem that the content of informatics courses suffers from fast decay time. And to make things worse: What we are teaching our pupils and students is far from sustainable knowledge. The scientific community has reacted on that by developing concepts like "key skills" and "competencies". But what does this mean for a teacher or lecturer? How can those skills be acquired by courses? In which way has the course to be constructed to meet these means? This paper discusses the relationship between educational standards in informatics and the development of teaching units to meet them. The concept of "context" will be introduced and used to show a way to plan courses by a context related approach on the one hand and to give an idea on how to find a different way to develop educational standards, how to improve and how to evaluate them on the other hand.

Keywords: Educational standards, Informatics in Context, competencies, key skills, Informatics education.

1 Introduction

Due to the changing situation in society, it became important to be familiar with some fundamental facts of informatics: Information technology and computers are a concept which is connected to every part of our life. Therefore, a general education of these topics is an important goal for schools and universities. But computer technology is a fast changing subject: New machines, programs and ideas pop up nearly every day. So it becomes hard for teachers and lecturers to develop a concept which helps them to educate their pupils and students for the demands of their future lives. "Life long learning" is the new buzz word for this problematic and the ideas of "key skills" and "competencies" were developed. But what does this mean? Do teachers have to get away from content-based curricula? How can we arrange teaching units to equip our students with the required "competencies", which enable them to adapt to the rapid changes specific for informatics?

The important questions for the development of a suitable curriculum are:
- What are the "important competencies" and which ones are more and which one are less important?

---

[1] Used in this paper as a summary for computer science, IT, ICT, etc., like in [8].

N. Reynolds and M. Turcsányi-Szabó (Eds.): KCKS 2010, IFIP AICT 324, pp. 67–77, 2010.

- How can be assured to cover all important "competencies"?
- What kind of content could be used to teach "competencies"?
- How can a system for the development of teaching units related to certain competencies be created?
- How can competencies be achieved in a motivating way?

In this paper, we will first give a short insight in the competency debate, the concept of educational standards, and how educational standards are created. In addition, we will present a different idea to develop educational standards in informatics which mostly orients on teaching practice - which is a context oriented approach. The context oriented approach for teaching informatics competencies will also be introduced in this paper. The conclusion will give a summarized overview.

2 Brief Overview on the Competency Debate

The debate on "key qualifications" and competencies was raised in Germany in 1974 by Dieter Mertens. His paper was a reaction to a change of the job market: Students were not well prepared for the needs of their job. Additionally, the students' education was not covering the demands to do a specific job for a whole life. "Life long learning" became a request due to the constantly changing job descriptions (see Mertens, [7]). He called his concept "key qualifications".

A lot of papers about competencies and key qualifications were published in the ongoing years after the "PISA-shock". The results especially of German students were, against all national expectations, below the international average in all three domains of the PISA test in 2001 (see [11], p. 147). By the end of the 1990s, in these publications the terms "qualification" and "competencies" were used so often, that it became nearly impossible to distinct between the different definitions and concepts: Some scientists used the same terms but different concepts and others the same concept with different terms. Some others were not giving a concept or definition at all. The whole discussion about "key qualifications" and "competencies" became a new updraft in Europe when the Bologna-Process started.

At that point a lot of scientists have discussed on what competencies are and if they are measurable or not. At the end - if it can be described in that way - the OECD (in co-operation with the UNESCO) gave a definition on what key competencies are in their report in 2005. They offered a concept of competencies, which included measurability. This was important, if competencies should be a concept of use for educational standards where the results of learning should be able to be evaluated (see [9], p. 8 and p. 10ff). A more detailed overview on that topic can be found in (see Dörge, [3]).

3 The Development of Educational Standards

Often the concepts of competencies are connected to educational standards. An educational standard itself can consist of many different types: There are content standards / curriculum standards, opportunity-to-learn-standards, performance standards and output-oriented standards. Performance standards are divided in three categories or levels, which are separated by the expected results: The first level is a minimal standard which means, that at very student of a certain age should have the required knowledge as a minimal level. Another level is the "norm" and means that the average student has the described knowledge (not necessarily every student). The last level means, that only the best students have the described knowledge. The output-oriented standards are based on competencies: Competencies are the "product" which will be measured at a certain age.

3.1   The Regular Way to Create Educational Standards

Usually, educational standards are created in a normative way by a group of some professionals which are working for a higher commission like the ACM, NCTM (National Council of Teachers of Mathematics), the German Kultusminister-Konferenz (KMK, Conference of the Ministers of Education) or other communities. Then, the outcome of this commission is somehow presented to the public. After some cycles of discussion, where input from the basis is followed to a certain degree, the educational standard is passed through some administration levels. Only some countries involve empirical evaluation in this process (e.g. in Switzerland, see [11], p. 277ff). In most countries research on this topic is postponed after publishing them and only used to evaluate if the educational standards are suitable. But it takes a lot of time until the results of this research is reflected and integrated in new versions of the standards.

Due to the fact that current educational standards focus on competencies, instead of teaching content, the lists of competencies are published in a context free way. Although professionals in these commissions[2] mostly think of possible teaching context

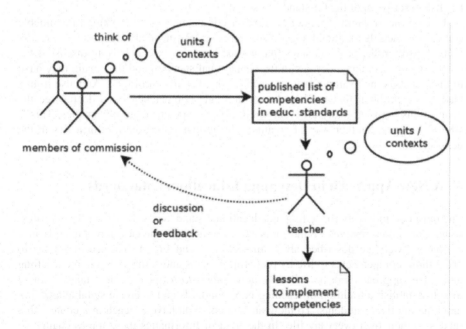

Fig. 1. The top-down process of creating lessons from educational standards

---

[2] Note: One of the authors of this paper has been part of such commissions.

for these competencies, it is common not to record them. This comes with some obstacles: Teachers have to develop didactical concepts and plan how to arrange teaching units to achieve these competencies. They need to decide what the right contents are, see Fig. 1. It would probably be more efficient if they knew the contexts the commissions thought about. These thoughts could support the teachers developing their lessons.

As an example we'll have a closer look at the educational standards for informatics next.

3.2 The Educational Standards for Informatics Lessons in Germany

Which competencies should be taught in informatics lessons? The "Gesellschaft für Informatik (GI, German Association for Informatics)" answered this question by developing educational standards (see GI, [4]) published in 2008. These GI-standards were meant as a recommendation for the German Government. The main difference between these standards and those of the German ministries of education is that the GI-standards are minimal standards instead of average ones.

The competencies of the minimal GI-standards are divided into two sections: The "Content sections", which are "content-related", and the "Process sections", where the competencies are "process-related". Both sections are not separated but interlocked with each other: Process-related competencies are gained with content. Without content it would not be specifically informatics (see GI, [4] p. 45). The structure of the GI-standard was derived from the US-standard NCTM from 2000 (p.2). For an English description of the GI-standards see [1].

To ease the problems creating lessons for competencies and thinking of a suitable context to reach them, the GI added some more or less detailed examples for teaching units. But often the problem stays like it was: First the experts have to discuss if the one or the other competency fits in the educational standard and then again they have to discuss about an example how to teach it, like displayed in Fig. 1. And also it may lead to the problem that teachers focus on single competencies and do not see the connections between many different sections of competencies in informatics. This is why we suggest another way of creating educational standards in informatics in the next section.

4   A New Approach in Designing Educational Standards

The most common way for setting up educational standards is done by a set of professionals or representatives of the ministry of education who develop standards in a normative way like described above in section 3 and Fig. 1. The teachers have to bring those competencies to life by preparing lessons and setting up suitable teaching units. This approach can be called *"competencies-to-lessons"*. But it takes a lot of time to establish a tradition of teaching new standards and to create suitable teaching units that motivate students. To motivate students you have to teach in a context that relates to their own everyday life. In the field of informatics these topics change so fast that there is not enough time for creating a tradition.

If we would use topics from the last decade we would annoy our students or would support the misjudgment that informatics at school has nothing to do with their life and future. This happens in classes where students are still forced to program tiny functions or games that their mobile phones do better. Other ways of creating standards and lessons for informatics are needed. One of this other ways could be called *"context-to-competencies"*, and will be described as follows and in Fig. 2.

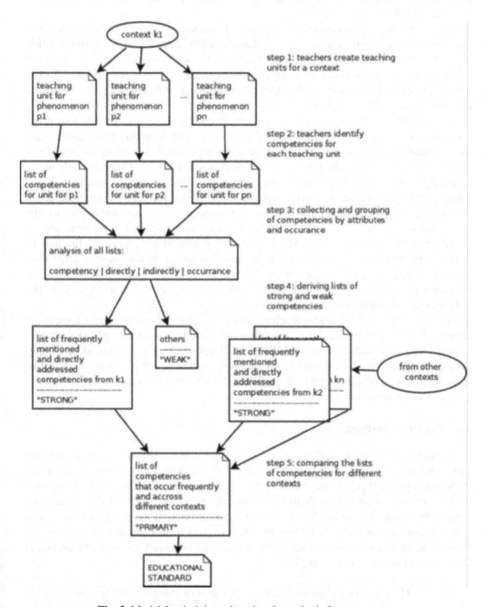

Fig. 2. Model for deriving educational standards from contexts

4.1 From Context to Competencies

For this approach a set of important contexts is derived from literature, observation of every day life and empirical research about the most important phenomena and contexts that relate to informatics. For example we name them $k_1,...,k_m$ and $p_1,..., p_n$, where many phenomena belong to one context k and define this context. It is also possible that a few phenomena belong to more than one context. The contexts are not disjoint regarding their phenomena.

In the first step of this approach, teachers create teaching units for these phenomena and nominate competencies $c_1,...,c_p$ that should be gained with these units within a given context in the second step. As a result we get a set of competencies c for each teaching unit for a context k as a suggestion from the teachers, see also Fig 2. The competencies will also have to be marked according to whether they are addressed directly or indirectly by that unit.

In the third step of this process we collect all competencies that belong to a given context k. Then all those competencies that may be gained by this given context are merged and classified if they are addressing the mentioned competencies directly or indirectly and how often they occur in different teaching units. Comparing them the following result will be expected: Some competencies are mentioned more often than others, some are addressed directly and some are gained indirectly during the set of lessons for a context. And some are context related and some are not. With this, the competencies can be divided in "strong" and "weak" competencies in the next step.

This process has to be repeated for every other context k. Comparing the lists of strong competencies there will be some that occur across different contexts and therefore are named "primary competencies". These competencies can now be listed in an educational standard together with the teaching units mentioned as a suggestion. We will illustrate this with an example unit in section 5.1.

Over the course of time new teaching units for changing contexts will have to be created. But we assume that after the analysis of these new units the "primary competencies" will be found there as well. So we will get teaching units that address long-lasting competencies which will fit in our fast changing world. To emphasize this idea, we will now discuss a time-independent context which is representative and not only related to informatics.

4.2 Example: Writing Text

Let's take a closer look at three ways of writing a text. The first way is the old-fashioned way - writing with a pen on paper. The second way is done with a type-writer on a piece of paper and the third one with a computer using a word processing system. Even though the medium has changed, the competencies for writing texts remain the same: The writer has to have the competency of designing a text, with a structure and the skill to use the words correctly and to give the text a meaning. In addition to these basic skills, other competencies are necessary to use and understand the medium correctly. For example:

1.   How is a pen used on paper – without scratching the paper without dropping ink on the paper, without smudging the already written letters?

2. How is a typewriter used? Included are competencies on how to type (e.g. 10-fingers-system) and to push down the types in that way, that all letters have the same density and the text is typed with an acceptable speed.
3. How is the computer used with its specific applications (the operating system, the word-processing system) to get the text ready and how is it printed out?

Due to the fact that software and hardware is fast-changing it is not appropriate to teach only competencies how to use a specific medium, it is necessary to prepare students for life-long-learning and to teach long-lasting competencies. The focus of informatics lessons is to make students *understand* the basic functions make them able to reflect and to cope with occurring phenomena during the use of information processing.

One thought behind all this might be tempting: Maybe, the context special competency has been gained with is changing during time. But this is not affecting the competencies required: If the idea is to write a letter we still have to teach our students the concept of a letter and what the structure of a letter is and how it can be written, to be official or romantic (this might be part of e.g. English lessons) - even so the program has changed, we are working with.

For informatics lessons this could mean: Even when the word-processing programs change during time - maybe from an older version of Mircosoft Word to the current one: The text still has to be formatted, saved, printed etc. And the word processing system won't have changed on the conceptual level. If we teach the concepts behind the programs and connect them to their phenomena of an actual context, we give our students something they could rely on for a lifetime.

Therefore, a better approach for designing educational standards could be to collect big amounts of contexts and competencies gained from these contexts like described above. This could lead to a set of *tools* which teachers could really use: competencies and the combination of contexts, from which they could learn from. To give a closer insight an overview on the context based approach and its roots will be provided in the next section.

5   What Is Informatics in Context?

The definition of competency given by Franz E. Weinert is not only based on cognitive understandings and abilities, but also on motivation and willingness to apply these to different problems and on interaction with other people (see [12]). As a result of this, students' motivation and the application of knowledge are not something that begins after the development of competency; they are parts of competencies and have to be considered already in the learning process (see [10]).

Context-oriented approaches for schools have been established in Germany, the UK, and other countries after the PISA-shock to achieve a higher motivation for natural sciences and to support the vocational decisions of students. The largest project, "Chemistry in Context – ChiK", has been implemented in schools since 2002. *ChiK* aims at the change of teaching practice for more "authentic science" in classes and thus make it more interesting for students (see e.g. Parchmann, [10]). Therefore, teaching units have to be based on relevant contexts. These contexts should not only be used as a motivation at the beginning but also be present in all following parts of the teaching unit. *ChiK*-units aim to raise the variation of teaching methods and to point out basic concepts (like the relationship between behavior and structure). *ChiK* provides a pattern with four phases per unit (see [10] or [2]):

1. Phase of contact (e.g. a question or debate): personal relevance, interest;
2. Phase of curiosity and planning (e.g. a mind map): identify important questions;
3. Phase of elaboration: inquiry, results, presentation;
4. Phase of deepening and connecting: reflection, understanding, personal relevance.

Koubek et al. suggested an approach of *Informatics in Context* which is called *IniK*, abbreviated from the German title *Informatik im Kontext*, which is derived from the other context projects (see [6]). *IniK* has three aims:

1. orientation on relevant contexts;
2. variety of teaching methods and
3. principles and standards.

Several quite usable teaching units for this approach can already be found in [5]. One of them covers the context of "file sharing". In the following part we show how this unit can be analyzed to identify competencies in the way described above.

5.1   Example for Informatics in Context: File Sharing

"File sharing" is a topic every student nowadays already came or will come across. Therefore this fits the requirement to choose a context which relates to the world of the students. Strongly connected to "file sharing" is the concept of copyright. "File sharing" is part of computer network technology but also a legal and moral problem in the Internet. There are several ways to make the topic "file sharing" interesting. For our approach we are going to describe four phases separately:

1. The Entry Phase
2. The Working Phase
3. The Immersion and Linking Phase
4. The Knowledge Assessment Phase

5.1.1   The Entry Phase
There are many different possible ways to enter this context. A first impulse could be given by writing the words "pirate copy" at the black board. Another way could be done by starting a discussion with a sentence like "I have heard that a student of a different (or this) school has been questioned by the police for sharing music files online". There are also many current articles from newspapers, journals, TV shows etc. which can be used. These are the phenomena p belonging to this context.

After this impulse the students have to discuss their perspective and their experiences with this topic. They state questions on pieces of paper for the lessons and sort them (Note: These questions will be the guide for the lessons). And now, goals have to be set about the outcome (possible outcomes: poster for the school, presentation for the class or parents) and working groups have to be formed.

Questions that students would state and answer later on could be as follows:

- How differs a pirate copy from a normal copy and how can they be distinguished?
- What is copyright, copyleft, freeware, shareware, GPL etc.?
- When is copying (a CD, DVD, file, program) legal or illegal?
- What does a file sharing program do?
- How comes that the police knows my address if they only had my IP?
- What kind of hints to my identity do I leave in the Internet while surfing?
- ...

5.1.2 The Working Phase
In working groups the students discuss their questions. The main aspect of the teachers work is to advise and NOT TO GUIDE. He / She can help to clear questions about the correctness and rightness of the answers they are looking for and he / she is preparing / providing the needed materials. The students make notes for their presentation and create their posters.

5.1.3 Immersion and Linking Phase
The students present their results in class and discuss these together. A lawyer could review the results of the class, if there is the possibility. The students discuss how to present the results to the whole school (e.g. in the format of an information event) and / or their parents and plan it.

5.1.4 The Knowledge Assessment Phase
Possible questions to control and assess the gained competencies about the topic could be like the following examples:

a. Explicate the way of data from the Net to your own PC when starting a download. (Draw a sketch from starting point of the data until the point of saving it on your hard drive)
b. Sort the necessary steps and technical parts of (a) by using the three-layer-model
c. Read the comic / the story (provided by the teacher). Describe the content of the comic / story with your own words
d. Explicate how the law was violated in (c) by the main character and by the other persons of this particular comic / story. Also explain what should have been different to assure that no law was broken.

A last possible step to conclude the experiences made above could be "decontextualization" (adopting the concept to other content), e.g. comparing the concept of file sharing with the streaming technology used by web-TV sites.

5.2 Possibly Gained Competencies

With a description of a teaching unit for "informatics in context" like the one above or even more detailed it is possible to discuss the competencies that may be gained using it. According to the fact that especially the process related competencies differ according to the teaching methodology the teacher uses and every class behaves a bit different, the list of competencies that are gained with a teaching unit differs also. It would be an important advancement in research if we had an approach to reliably derive the most important competencies from a teaching unit. Until then we have to work with examples like the one from section 5.1.

Let's assume that a big enough set of teachers thought about this unit for the context "file sharing" (k) and gave a list of possibly gained competencies each, (the direct and the indirect ones as introduced in section 4). These lists could be analyzed for the competencies mentioned most frequently for this context. These are the competencies c directly addressed.

The following list shows some example competencies, which could have been mentioned. The students are able to...

- c_1; characterize hardware and software components
- c_2: illustrate the function of P2P-systems with graphical models
- c_3: distinguish different license models like GPL or shareware
- c_4: plan group work
- c_5: cooperate during group work
- c_6: present their results and therefore choose suitable technical supplies
- c_7: work safely with download services of the Internet
- c_8: explain the function of the Internet
- c_9: discuss copyright issues for different scenarios
- c_x: ...

The indirectly addressed and the less often mentioned competencies are left out. Not all of the competencies listed are primary competencies. Some of them are strongly related to the context, like c_2 and c_3. Others have a better chance to be found in a similar list for a different context, like c_1, c_4 to c_6 or c_8. And some may even last if time and important contexts are changing, like c_1 or c_5. The latter are the primary competencies of the context "file sharing" and should be part of an educational standard for informatics.

We know that every step of this simulated analysis opens a wider field for further research. But this approach can be an opportunity not only to generate but also to evaluate existing educational standards if they are suitable for today and the future.

6 Conclusion

In this paper, we gave a brief overview on reasons why the debate on competencies and skills has been raised. Also an insight to the development of educational standards has been given. After this we showed a new approach for designing educational standards by using the idea of "Informatics in Context". We also opened the discussion if this way could offer a better and more reliable solution for the daily work of teachers.

A first sketch on how competencies can be gained by analyzing contexts was shown. Of course, a lot of work will still be necessary to gather a set of interesting contexts which can be useful as blueprints for teachers to develop their own contexts. On the other hand, we will have to identify the important ones from which to generate competencies from the wealth of available contexts. Also, this approach may be used to review existing educational standards for informatics, to decide if and which parts of them are suitable and also to help with their improvement.

References

1. Brinda, T., Puhlmann, H., Schulte, C.: Bridging ICT and CS - Educational Standards for Computer Science in Lower Secondary Education. In: ITiCSE 2009, Paris, France (2009)
2. Diethelm, I., Hildebrandt, C., Krekeler, L.: Implementation of Computer Science in Context - a research perspective regarding teacher-training. In: 9th Baltic Sea Conference on Computing Education Research, Koli Calling, Koli, Finland (2009)
3. Dörge, C.: Competencies and Skills: Filling old Skins with New Wine. In: Reynolds, N., Turcsányi-Szabó, M. (eds.) KCKS 2010. IFIP AICT, vol. 324, pp. 78–89. Springer, Heidelberg (2010)
4. Gesellschaft für Informatik (GI): Grundsätze und Standards für die Informatik in der Schule (Educational Standards for Informatics in secondary schools). LogIn, No. 150/151 (2008)
5. The IniK Project Group: Informatik im Kontext (Informatics in context) (2009), http://www.informatik-im-kontext.de
6. Koubek, J., Schulte, C., Schulze, P., Witten, H.: Informatik im Kontext (IniK) - Ein integratives Unterrichtskonzept für den Informatikunterricht (Informatics in Context - an integrated teaching concept for informatics lessons). Informatik und Schule, Berlin (2009)
7. Mertens, D.: Schlüsselqualifikationen – Thesen zur Schulung für eine moderne Gesellschaft (Key competencies - statements for education for a modern society). Mitteilungen aus der Arbeitsmarkt- und Berufsforschung 7, 36–43 (1974)
8. Mulder, F., van Weert, T.: IFIP/UNESCO's Informatics Curriculum Framework 2000 for Higher Education. SIGCSE Bulletin 33(4) (2001)
9. OECD: The Definition and Selection of Key Competencies – Executive Summary (2005), http://www.deseco.admin.ch/bfs/deseco/en/index/03.html
10. Parchmann, I., Gräsel, C., Baer, A., Nentwig, P., Demuth, R., Ralle, B., the ChiK Projekt Group: "Chemie im Kontext": A symbiotic implementation of a context-based teaching and learning approach. International Journal of Science Education 28(9), 1041–1062 (2006)
11. Waddington, D., Nentwig, P., Schanze, S. (eds.): Making it Comparable: Standards in Science Education, Münster, Waxmann (2007)
12. Weinert, F.E.: Leistungsmessung in Schulen (Assessments in schools). Beltz, Weinheim, Basel, Switzerland (2001)

Competencies and Skills:
Filling Old Skins with New Wine

Christina Dörge

University of Oldenburg, Computer Science Education,
26111 Oldenburg, Germany
`Christina.Doerge@informatik.uni-oldenburg.de`

Abstract. "Key competencies", "key skills" and "key qualifications" are buzzwords so prominently featured in contemporary scientific treatises that discussions have been prompted about an inflationary use of the terms and what they really should be taken to mean. A similar situation exists in the field of ICT and CS education: What meaning should we ascribe to terms such as "skill", "competency" and "qualification" and what should be taught as "basic information technology"? These questions merit a closer look, especially since the idea of teaching competencies received a new updraft in Europe by the Bologna-Declaration, and the teaching of basic ICT and / or CS skills is still a difficult issue in the educational sciences. This paper wants to provide insight into the discussion on skills in Anglo-American and German scientific research and wants to act as a call for more clarity in definitions and concepts regarding IT skills.

Keywords: Key competencies, key skills, IT, ICT and CS education, Bologna-Declaration.

1 Introduction

Today, computer technology can be found nearly everywhere. Most of us are in some way affected by developments in the field of Information Technology (IT), Information and Communication Technology (ICT) and Computer Science (CS). In 1985, Klafki stated that a basic education in computer science-related fields is important to equip young people with the knowledge they need to play a valuable part in the future of society (see [18], p. 60). There are several reasons why ICT knowledge is important: Computers now touch nearly every aspect of our working lives, even in jobs not immediately associated with computer science. The Computer Science and Telecommunication Board (CSTB) stated that the broad category of knowledge-workers make use – in one sense or the other – of information technology. The library science community of the US has compiled a list of skills which are important for finding, evaluating and using data (see [7], p. vii). The information flood we face every day affects us not only in our professional lives. In addition, the increasing impact on the economy is another important reason to learn how to use information technology efficiently. Hence it can be argued that a basic education in information technology is important for everyone.

N. Reynolds and M. Turcsányi-Szabó (Eds.): KCKS 2010, IFIP AICT 324, pp. 78–89, 2010.

One of the biggest obstacles arising for those who develop basic IT education courses or curricula is that IT / ICT / CS knowledge often has a rather short lifetime: Jaeger cites Charlier et al. and Staebler[1], who both give a half-life period of approximately 6 to 12 months for IT / ICT / CS knowledge (see [17], p. 148f; [6], p. 120; [29], p.148ff).

This leads over to another issue, the Bologna-Declaration, which was signed in 1998 by the four secretaries of education of France, Italy, Great Britain and Germany. One of the declaration's primary goals is to bring change to teaching styles at universities, a transition from the traditional idea of "content based"-learning towards "teaching key competencies".

With this, the discussion about "life long learning" was rekindled. Teaching key competencies appears to provide an answer to an important problem: Pupils and students are not equipped with the skills currently required by the job market. Even if they were, their knowledge would not last due to the rapidly changing nature of computer technology. Thus the education process bypasses pupils and students by not teaching them persistent knowledge and skills. What they need are ideas and patterns to acquire skills for life long learning. The notions of "competencies" and "key skills" seem to offer a way out of this dilemma. However, the most often practiced approach in IT / ICT / CS courses is to teach "user knowledge" (as a superficial product training might do) instead of the underlying concepts. This is not a good way to enable people to use or access new technologies or interest them in IT- / ICT- or CS-related jobs.

The dissertations of Doerig, Orth, and Jaeger address the concept of competencies (in general) and their possible implementation strategies (see [11], [25], and [17]). The more specific question what "key competencies" might mean in the field of computer technology has not been answered yet.

In the following chapters a brief chronological overview of the concepts of "key qualifications" and "key competencies" will be given – from the perspective of German (section 2) as well as from Anglo-American research (section 3). In addition, some insights in the development of ICT / CS standards will be presented in section 2.

2   The German Discussion on Competencies and Qualifications

Before it is possible to work on questions such as "How can I include the teaching of skills in my courses?" or "How can I teach competencies?", a few words are in order about what constitutes a competency and what makes a qualification. There are several problems: Some authors use the terms synonymously, others don't. With a closer look it also becomes obvious that not all authors talk about the same group of concepts. The reverse phenomenon, i.e. authors using different terms for what are essentially the same ideas and concepts, can also be found (see [17], p. 65ff).

However, there is evidence that a difference exists between "competency" and "qualification", as the researchers of the work group "Hochschul-Informations-System (HIS)" wrote in [28], p.1[2]: *"The terms „competency", „key competency" and*

---

[1] They speak about "EDV-Wissen" (EDV = electronical data processing, Wissen = knowledge), which describes more or less the usage of informatics systems and has its roots in the 50s, as established by IBM.

[2] Translated from German by C. Dörge.

„key qualification" pose a challenge. With changing theoretical background and usage the terms are defined differently. Their description is marked by vagueness and a deficiency in applicability. "

2.1 Mertens's Concept of Key Qualifications

Mertens, coming from the field of "Vocational Education", is often mentioned as the first who raised the term "key qualification"[3] in 1974. His aim was to initiate a discussion about the changing situation for people in the job market: He knew that some of the market's fundamentals had changed and that it was therefore necessary to adapt education to the new requirements. Mertens breaks "key qualification" (KQ) down into four subjects (see [21], p. 36)[2]:

1. **Basic qualifications** (e.g. structured and logical thinking),
2. **Horizontal qualifications** (e.g. transfer of knowledge about one foreign language to another),
3. **Ubiquitous elements** (cross-educational requirements such as basic arithmetic), and
4. **Vintage factors** (e.g. expiration of applicability of knowledge acquired at educational institutions).

The term "key qualification" was very frequently used in scientific publications and discussions. More and more it was felt that an "uncontrolled growth" with regard to the variety of meanings of the term had taken place. Therefore, the "Bundesinstitut für Berufsbildung (BIBB)" commissioned a survey: In 1999, Didi et al. discovered more than 600 KQ terms in use in the field of vocational education (see [8], Appendix part one pp. 1- 11 and appendix part two pp. 1-4, also cited in [17], p. 65 and [25], p. 2). They compiled a list with the terms most often used in the literature. These are[2]:

1. Ability to communicate
2. Ability to cooperate
3. Flexibility
4. Creativity
5. Associative thinking
6. Autonomy
7. Capacity to solve problems
8. Transferability
9. Willingness to learn
10. Ability to assert oneself

2.2 Key Qualifications for the Acquisition of Competencies

In 1999, Helen Orth, coming from the field of "Didactics in Higher Education", wrote her dissertation about several concepts used in the KQ discussion. Orth conducted a review of the field of KQ and gave a definition of "key qualifications" based on the

---

[3] In Germany, the idea was not new at that point: In the 19th century, the first steps in this direction had been taken by the discussion of "formale Bildung", "materiale Bildung", and competencies.

term "competency" ([25], p. 107)[4]: *"**Key qualifications** are acquirable common skills, attitudes, strategies and elements of knowledge which are useful in solving problems and in acquiring new **competencies** within as many scopes of content as possible. The goal is to gain an action ability which satisfies individual and society-related requirements."*

This definition raises the question in which way key qualifications are related to competencies. It is important to note that what was generally termed KQ in 1999 is often called KC today.

2.3 The "Action-Enabling Competency" as a Conceptual Focus

Two years later, in 2001, Jaeger employed a different approach, giving definitions of the terms "qualification" and "competency" with an emphasis on their distinction (see [17], p. 70).

Jaeger, a pedagogue, gives a number of ideas on how competencies could be applied in schools. He rejects the term "key qualification" in favor of the idea of "key competencies" (KC), giving a detailed list of what competencies and qualifications are. As a resume, he offers a grouping concept for KCs: Four "specialized" competencies (professional, social, methodical and personal) are combined into one super-competency, the **"action-enabling competency"** (see [17], p. 78 for a detailed mind-map)[4].

1. **Professional competency:** *Competency in a profession, such as knowledge, skill, quality of work, working technique, endurance...*
2. **Social competency:** *Ability to work in a team, ability to accept criticism, openness...*
3. **Methodical competency:** *Structured thinking, to act creatively, to act in innovative ways, analytical investigation...*
4. **Personal competency:** *Creativity, self-confidence, flexibility, autonomy...*

A concept of competencies in which the action-enabling competency is seen as a super-competency can now be found in many papers (see as examples: [27]; [2], p. 58).

A more general change has occurred as well: More and more scientific researchers have started to talk about "key competencies" instead of "key qualifications".

2.4 The OCED-Report as World Wide Standard

With the OECD-report "The Definition and Selection of Key Competencies" of 2005, we received a "standard definition" telling us what key competencies are. The paper was translated into several languages (English, German, Spanish, French, Italian and Japanese) and was created in close cooperation with the UNESCO (see [24], p. 8). It characterizes "key competency" as follows: *"Key competencies involve a mobilisation of cognitive and practical skills, creative abilities and other psychosocial resources such as attitudes, motivation and values."*

In a more detailed approach, key competencies are described by the OECD-report using "competency categories" (see [24], p. 10ff):

---

[4] Translated from German by C. Dörge.

1) Using Tools Interactively (1A – The ability to use language, symbols and text interactively; 1B – The ability to use knowledge and information technology; 1C – The ability to use technology interactively)

2) Interacting in Heterogeneous Groups (2A – The ability to relate well to others; 2B – The ability to cooperate; 2C – The ability to manage and resolve conflicts)

*3) Acting Autonomously (3A – The ability to act within the big picture; 3B – The ability to form and conduct life plans and personal pro*jects; *3C – The ability to assert rights, interests, limits and needs)*

The OECD's concept is not entirely new: Group 1) can be seen as "methodical competency", group 2) as "social competency" and group 3) as "personal competency" (compare with subsection 2.3). What may justifiably be described as "new" is the embedded aspect of IT (see category 1B and 1C). This aspect may be a starting point for further discussion: Its description is similar to the definitions found for "media competency", where critical and reflective use of media is the main focus. Hence the question arises whether it can cover the demand for a general CS-related education, which is our focus.

The definition used in the OECD-report is based on the competency definition of F.E. Weinert (see [31], p. 27f), a psychologist, and with this the discussion takes a new turn: The main factor of this competency definition is "measurability". The leading question for this approach might be: What is the value of an educational concept if we cannot evaluate its consequences? Here we must keep in mind that any measurement needs knowledge of the boundaries of the thing to be measured. If competencies "overlap across sections", their boundaries are not clearly defined and serious unsolved problems may arise from this in the future.

2.5 From Input- to Output-Oriented Educational Standards

There is a worldwide agreement that the purpose of a general education should be to enable learners to use their knowledge throughout the whole of their lives – not just on the job. Today it is believed that to achieve this, special competencies are needed.

In Germany, the traditional way to develop educational standards has been to describe the content to be taught. This changed with the discussion about competencies from an input-oriented approach to an output-oriented approach – competencies as the outcome of a successful education. But so far, output-oriented educational standards only exist for a few traditional subjects (e.g. mathematics, biology). In 2008, minimum standards for computer science and informatics courses for schools were developed and published by the "Gesellschaft für Informatik (GI)". These standards give a list of competencies which pupils should possess in the field of informatics by the end of the 10th grade (approx. age 16) of the German school system.

The GI educational standard is composed of two main sections, each of which contains several subsections (see [13], p. 11ff of the original report in German, and [5], p. 289f for an English article about this standard):

The "Content Standards":

- **Information and data** (e.g. connection between information and data, different types of data representation)
- **Algorithms** (e.g. knowledge of algorithms to execute tasks and solve problems from various fields of application)

- **Languages and automata** (e.g. use of formal languages for interaction with informatics systems)
- **Informatics systems** (e.g. understanding of the basic concept of how an informatics system is built)
- **Informatics, man, and society** (e.g. knowledge of interchanges between informatics systems and society)

The "Process Standards":

- **Model and implement** (e.g. implementation of informatics models for given situations; reflection on models and their implementation)
- **Reason and evaluate** (e.g. use of criteria for the evaluation of informatics contexts)
- **Structure and interrelate** (e.g. the structuring of a given content by appropriate dissection and ordering of the problem; recognizing and using relations within and without the scope of computer science / informatics)
- **Communicate and cooperate** (e.g. communicating professionally about computer scientific subjects, co-operating to solve problems in informatics)
- **Represent and interpret** (e.g. interpretation of different representations of contents)

The aspects of the *Content Standards* must be seen as parts of a whole: Competencies may be gained by working within complex and interlocked contexts. Tasks assigned to pupils must respect this as a guiding principle (see [13], p. 23).

The *Process Standards* contains ideas about how to deal with the content, i.e. the operational methods used in the fields of computer science and informatics, e.g. the implementation of a model or the illustration of some given content. Learners acquire process competencies through their interaction with the content (see [13], p. 45).

With this, the group of experts of the GI provides standards to work with. How these can be transferred into a "competency model" can be found in the dissertation of Kohl (see [19]). But what is missing in these standards is a definition of the term "competency".

2.6 Summary of This Section

Many scientists have used the first approach of Mertens. Unfortunately, this has resulted in a proliferation of KQ concepts rather than in unification and more clarity. Some scientists, like Orth and Jaeger, became aware of this and tried to streamline existing concepts and definitions. After some time, the "action-enabling-competency" was used as a focal point for concepts of competency. In 2005, the OECD-report set a landmark by defining their concept of key qualifications, which includes personal-, methodical- and social competencies, as well as an embedded aspect of IT. The educational standards described in subsection 2.5 were a first approach to describe those kinds of competencies which might cover the demands for a general CS-related education. What is missing in all those standards is a definition of what the term "competency" should be taken to mean. Several German scientific researchers in ICT and CS use the definition of competency by F.E. Weinert (for an example see [30], p. 13; [20], p. 1). This definition seems to be very handy since it offers "measurability". But we have to keep in mind that not all definitions of "competency" include that aspect: Some researchers maintain that competencies are not output oriented and therefore not measurable (see e.g. [17], p. 146).

3 The English Discussion on Competencies and Skills

In the English competency discussion, several critical terms are construed differently: It does not focus on a "competencies" versus "qualifications" distinction but on different forms of "skills" and "competencies". The term "qualification" as used in Anglo-American research usually refers to "a formal degree" while in Germany "qualification" also means "ability". The German term for "ability" ("Fähigkeit") on the other hand is often translated as "competency" (see also [26], Annotation).

However, the terms in the English discussion are prone to cause confusions as well.

3.1 Different Types of Skills

Taking a look at the English discussion shows that many scientific works use the terms "skill" and "competency". Especially the terms "generic skills" and "core skills" show up quite often.

Bennet, Dunne and Carré wrote (see [3], p. 74): *"The conceptualisation of core skills is problematic for several reasons. The term has several synonyms, including personal transferable, key, generic, common, and work or employment related skills. To add to this semantic confusion, these skills are often referred to as competences, capabilities, attributes, elements or learning outcomes, sometimes incorporating levels and sometimes not. Similarly, the various lists of skills elicited from employers, and contained in government reports, are diverse in both extent and purpose, reflecting differences in definitions and interpretations of their significance."*

This citation gives some insight into the situation of the English discussion and suggests that it is similar to the German one described in section 2. It is reasonable to assume that the quest for useful terms and concepts is a world wide problem.

Bennet, Dunne and Carré try to give a definition of different types of skills, e.g. "generic skills", by presenting a picture in their paper (see [3], p. 77), which contains four management skills *"of self, others, information and tas*k. *These skills are generic in that they can potentially be applied to any discipline, to any course in higher education, to the workplace or indeed to any other context."*

However, it may not always be possible to establish concepts of discipline-spanning competencies like this. E.g. a proper definition of "generic skill", "core skill" etc. may well depend on the discipline at which you choose to look (see [3], p. 80f).

3.2 Questioning the Skills Agenda

In 2000, Len Holmes wrote about *"questioning the skills agenda"* (the paper's title). His attempt is to bring more clarity to the discussion. For support of his views he refers to Hirsh and Bevan. These authors wrote about the situation of the job market and the *"requirements of the skills and competencies of managers"*. They found that *"there was a high level of agreement over the terms used,"* but *"there was not agreement at the level of meaning"* (see [16], p. 203 and [14]).

Similarly to the German situation with many different terms used as synonyms for "key qualification" (see Didi et al., section 2.1), there was a need to find and order all the terms in use for skills and competencies in the English speaking community. Holmes mentions Allen as a researcher who took a closer look at how many terms for skills other researchers had used (see [15], online document): Allen was part of a research project at Sheffield University which identified 108 "skills" (see [15]).

One of the main points of critique by Holmes is that *"in many cases it seems that lists [of skills] have been drawn up by select groups of staff engaging in nothing more rigorous than a form of brainstorming"*. He continues: *"Whilst such groups may gain a sense of achievement, the conceptual validity of their products must be surely be rated as low"* (see [16], p. 205).

Holmes is not the only one who criticizes the conceptual work of his fellow researchers. In 2000, Bridges describes the situation of the skills discussion as a *"conceptual mud"* (see [5], p. 44).

As a positive example, Bridges refers to the "National Committee of Inquiry into Higher Education Report (NCIHE)" in the UK, which is often named as "The Dearing Report", and which *"has given some authority both to the language of 'key skills' and the identity of these 'skills'"* (see [4], p. 44). The DEARING REPORT gives four key skills, which are (see [23], paragraph 9.17):

- *communication skills;*
- *numeracy;*
- *the use of information technology;*
- *learning how to learn*

In paragraph 9.18 they add: *"These are referred to as key skills throughout the remainder of our report. We believe that these key skills are relevant throughout life, not simply in employment."*

However "the use of information technology" does not imply knowledge in the field of CS. Therefore, further work may be necessary to ensure a successful basic education in CS.

3.3 Skills in CS

In 1997, in the US, the Computer Science and Telecommunication Board (CSTB) of the National Research Council initiated a study to address the subject of information technology literacy. The committee chose a broad definition of IT (see [7], p.viii): *"Information technology was defined to include the more traditional components of information technology (such as general-purpose computational devices, associated peripherals, operating environments, applications software, and information), as well as embedded computing devices, communications, and the science underlying the technology."* The aim of this study was to make people "fluent with information technology (FIT)", where the term "fluency" was used because it *"connotes the ability to formulate knowledge, to express oneself creatively and appropriately, and to produce and generate information (rather than simply to comprehend it)"* (see [7], p. viii and p.14). At the end, the term "FITness" was coined. While the above-mentioned defini-tion does not mention competencies, it appears rather close conceptually. The CSTB gives a list of the ten highest-priority items for the three types of knowledge they have found, which are (see [7], p. 4): Intellectual Capabilities, Information Technology Concepts and Information Technology Skills. This report is meant for the higher-education community (colleges or universities), but it also offers comments on FIT-ness for K-12 education (see [7], p. 51)[5].

Another Informatics Curriculum Framework for Higher Education comes from the International Federation for Information Processing (IFIP), from 2000. It contains twelve core curriculum themes, including "concepts" and "skills" (see [22], p. 31ff):

1. Representation of Information
2. Formalism in Information Processing
3. Information Modeling
4. Algorithmics
5. System Design
6. Software Development
7. Potentials and Limitations of Computing and Related Technologies
8. Computer Systems and Architectures
9. Computer-Based Communication
10. Social and Ethical Implications
11. Personal and Interpersonal Skills
12. Broader Perspectives and Context (includes links with other disciplines)

This Curriculum offers a complete coverage of the informatics field and clarifies the relationship of informatics with other disciplines – which is a much broader approach then the one by the GI (see section 2.5).

3.4 Summary for This Section

The discussion about skills in the English speaking community has created several interesting ideas on curricula and standards as well as in the CS related field. What it has not produced is a definition of what skills are (besides simply listing examples). The terms "competency" and "key competency" are entirely absent.

4   Conclusion

In Germany, the discussion about competencies vs qualification ended with the (preliminary) result that competencies constitute the basis for the newly developed ICT / CS standards by the GI. The notion of competency used is one which includes measurability.

The Anglo-American discussion does not focus on competencies or qualifications, but on skills. They are the basis for UK and US standards, and the IFIP's as well. It

---

[5] In 2000, the International Society for Technology in Education (ISTE) of the US published three standards called NETS, which address the skills students / teachers / administrators should have, including CS related topics.
(http://www.iste.org/AM/Template.cfm?Section=NETS, last checked on 30th of January 2010).

can be assumed that the notion of skill they use includes measurability. However, differently from the German GI-Standard, the US-version focuses on knowledge instead of skills and competencies, while the UK-version focuses on key skills. The IFIP-version centers on skills.

No definitions have been offered concerning what precisely the terms "skills", "key skills" or "competencies" should be taken to mean. Some researchers have given "definitions" by listing examples of competencies. It is a commonly accepted practice for scientists to use terms taken from colloquial language. However, an important part of scientific work is the clarification of those terms in order to avoid confusions and misunderstanding.

We have seen in this paper that there is a lot of groundwork still to be accomplished in order to achieve more clarity regarding the terms "skills", "competencies" and "qualification" – also in combination with the prefix "key". It would be instructive to see why a certain specific term was used in a research paper and not another one. This would make papers more comparable.

Finally, I would like to mention another aspect, one which goes beyond the scope of this paper. Should we transfer concepts of other areas of science into the competencies discussion of ICT and CS or should we try to develop our own concepts? There is no question that concepts from other scientific communities are applicable: Several papers, some of them mentioned in this one, have shown how to do it. It can also be shown that by teaching IT content, competencies can be gained – competencies such as those mentioned in the hit list in chapter 2 (see [10]). Competencies are not specific to ICT/CS or other scientific fields. Hence, a competency in "problem solving" (the ability to break down complex problems into smaller, more manageable parts) may refer to different concrete capabilities in different fields. Therefore, the aim should be not only to teach competencies, but *"IT competencies"*. The competency of "problem solving" should be narrowed down to "problem solving in IT". This would constitute a new conception of competency which has not been covered by scientific research yet.

References

1. Allen, M.G.: A conceptual Model of transferable personal skills. Employment Department, Sheffield (1993), cited by [15] and [16]
2. Arnold, R., Arnold-Haecky, B.: Der Eid des Sisyphos - Einführung in die systemische Pädagogik. In: Arnold, R. (ed.) systhemia - Systemische Pädagogik, Band 1. Schneider Verlag Hohengehren GmbH, Baltmannsweiler (2009)
3. Bennett, N., Dunne, E., Carré, C.: Patterns of core and generic skill provision in higher education. Higher Education 37, 71–93 (1999), http://www.springerlink.com/content/u6p58h83m8867827/ (05.10.09)
4. Bridges, D.: Back to the Future: the higher education curriculum in the 21st century. Cambridge Journal of Education 30(1), 37–55 (2000)
5. Brinda, T., Puhlmann, H., Schulte, C.: Bridging ICT and CS – Educational Standards for Computer Science in Lower Secondary Education. In: ITiCSE 2009, Paris, France, pp. 288–292 (2009)
6. Charlier, M., Henke, R., Rother, F.: Medien für die Weiterbildung: Scheibe statt Flug. In: Wirtschaftswoche, vol. 48 (1994), cited in [17]

7. Computer Science and Telecommunications Board (CSTB), National Research Council: Being Fluent with Information Technology. National Academy Press, Washington, DC (2000)

8. Didi, H.J., Fay, E., Kloft, C., Vogt, H.: Einschätzungen von Schlüsselqualifikationen aus psychologischer Perspektive, Bonn (1993)

9. Dörge, C., Schulte, C.: What are Information Technology's Key Qualifications? In: ITiCSE Conference Proceedings, Madrid, Spain, ACM Online Library (2008)

10. Dörge, C.: IT Key Qualifications For Students in Education. In: SITE Conference Proceedings, San Antonio, USA (2007)

11. Dörig, R.: Das Konzept der Schlüsselqualifikationen – Ansätze, Kritik und konstruktivistische Neuorientierung auf der Basis der Erkenntnosse der Wissenspsychologie. Dissertation, Hochschule St. Galen (1994)

12. Gesellschaft für Informatik (GI) e.V.: Grundsätze und Standards für die Informatik in der Schule – Bildungsstandards Informatik für die Sekundarstufe I. Beilage zu LOG IN, 28. Jg., Heft Nr. 150/151 (2008)

13. Hirsh, W., Bevan, S.: What Makes a Manager? In search of a language for management skills. In: Institute of Manpower Studies Report, No. 44, Institute of Manpower Studies, Brighton (1988), cited in [16]

14. Holmes, L.: The capability curriculum, conventions of assessment and the construction of graduate employability. Online-Document. Presented at Conference on 'Understanding the Social World', July 17-19. University of Huddersfield (1995),
http://www.graduate-employability.org.uk/publications/
cc_ca_gi.htm (verified: December 11, 2009)

15. Holmes, L.: Questioning the Skills Agenda. In: Fallows, S., Steven, C. (eds.) Integrating Key Skills in Higher Education – Employability, Transferable Skills and Learning for Life, pp. 201–214. Kogan Page Limited, London (2000)

16. Jäger, P.: Der Erwerb von Kompetenzen als Konkretisierung der Schlüsselqualifikationen: eine Herausforderung an Schule und Unterricht. Dissertation, Universität Passau (2001)

17. Klafki, W.: Neue Studien zur Bildungstheorie und Didaktik. Beltz Verlag, Weinheim (1985)

18. Kohl, L.: Kompetenzorientierter Informatikunterricht in der Sekundarstufe I unter Verwendung der visuellen Programmiersprache Puck. Dissertation, University of Jena (2009)

19. Kollee, C., Magenheim, J., Nelles, W., Rhode, T., Schaper, N., Schubert, S., Stechert, P.: Computer Science Education and Key Competencies. In: WCCE 2009, Brasilien (2009)

20. Mertens, D.: Schlüsselqualifikationen. In: Mitteilungen aus der Arbeitsmarkt- und Berufsforschung. Jg. 07, H.1, pp. 36–43 (1974)

21. Mulder, F., van Weert, T.: IFIP/UNESCO's Informatics Curriculum Framework 2000 for Higher Education. SIGCSE Bulletin 33(4) (2001)

22. NCIHE (National Committee of Inquiry into Higher Education): Higher Education in the Learning Society, The Stationery Office, London, Paragraphs 9.14-9.25 (1997)

23. OCED-Report: The Definition and Selection of Key Competencies - Executive Summary/ Definition und Auswahl von Schlüsselkompetenzen - Zusammenfassung/ La Définition et la Sélection des Compétences Clés - Résumé/ La definición y selección de competencias clave – Resumen (2005), http://www.deseco.admin.ch/bfs/deseco/en/
index/03.html (23.10.2009)

24. Orth, H.: Schlüsselqualifikationen an deutschen Hochschulen – Konzepte, Standpunkte und Perspektiven. Dissertation, Luchterhand Verlag, Neuwied (1999)

25. Reetz, L.: Schlüsselqualifikationen – Kommentar. Auszug aus "Duales System zwischen Tradition und Innovation". In: Twardy, M. (ed.) Wirtschafts-, Berufs- und Sozialpädagogische Texte (WBST), Sonderband 4, pp. 27–46. Müller Botermann Verlag, Köln (1991), `http://www-user.uni-bremen.de/~sept/current/deutsch/Pdf/Ma-A/Ma-A-II.pdf` (verified October 15, 2009)

26. Reetz, L.: Zum Zusammenhang von Schlüsselqualifikationen – Kompetenzen – Bildung (2003), `http://www.sowi-online.de/reader/berufsorientierung/reetz.htm` (verified September 17, 2009)

27. Schaeper, H., Briedis, K.: Kompetenzen von Hochschulabsolventinnen und Hochschulabsolventen, berufliche Anforderungen und Folgerungen für die Hochschulreform. Hochschul-Informations-System (HIS) – Kurzinformation, A6 / 2004, Hannover (2004)

28. Stäbler, S.: Die Personalentwicklung der, Lernenden Organisation, Berlin (1999), cited in [17]

29. Stechert, P.: Fachdidaktische Diskussion von Informatiksystemen und der Kompetenzentwicklung im Informatikunterricht. Dissertation, Uni Siegen (2009)

30. Weinert, F.E.: Vergleichende Leistungsmessung in Schulen – eine umstrittene Selbstverständlichkeit. In: Weinert, F.E. (ed.) Leistungsmessungen in Schulen, pp. 17–31 (2002)

Coping with Complex Real-World Problems: Strategies for Developing the Competency of Transdisciplinary Collaboration

Gitta Domik[1] and Gerhard Fischer[2]

[1] University of Paderborn, Warburgerstrasse 100, D-33098 Paderborn, Germany
domik@uni-paderborn.de
[2] University of Colorado at Boulder, Boulder, CO. 80301-0430, USA
gerhard@colorado.edu

Abstract. Real world problems are complex and therefore between and beyond disciplines. To solve them requires expertise across several disciplines. This paper argues that we need to teach students transdisciplinary collaboration as a competency demanded in future work places. We describe two learning strategies, "breadth-first" and "Long Tail", to help develop these competencies in graduate students. An implementation of these strategies in a computer science course with 48 graduate students from various disciplines is described. Finally, implications and future opportunities of our approach are discussed.

Keywords: Transdisciplinary Collaboration, Lifelong Learning, 21st century competencies.

1 Transdisciplinary Collaboration: A Necessity, Not a Luxury

Education in Computer Science (CS) is experiencing a period of profound transformation. Phenomena such as globalization [1], increasing trends to outsource high-level cognitive tasks [2], and the need to participate effectively in addressing complex real world problems cutting across disciplines are creating fundamentally new challenges. Requirements increase for students to enter work environments requiring collaboration with experts from multiple fields, pursue several career paths addressing different problems, and to interact and work with people of diverse backgrounds including those from outside academe. Such changes create new educational demands: students need to be educated for a diverse, technical, problem-oriented world that does not yet exist, which makes it imperative that they become self-directed, lifelong learners who can thrive and participate in collaborative environments with ever-changing disciplinary boundaries.

Real world problems are complex, they cannot be framed and solved by any single person, and they often cut across different established disciplines requiring expertise in a wide range of areas. In preparing students to live and work in the "knowledge age", one cannot predict or learn in school what one may need to know during a lifetime of work [3]. Coverage is impossible and obsolescence is guaranteed. These

N. Reynolds and M. Turcsányi-Szabó (Eds.): KCKS 2010, IFIP AICT 324, pp. 90–101, 2010.

requirements have led us to articulate our credo for a lifelong learning perspective on education [4]:

"If the world of working and living relies on collaboration, creativity, definition and framing of complex problems and if it requires dealing with uncertainty, change, and intelligence that is distributed across cultures, disciplines, and tools – then education should foster transdisciplinary competencies and mindsets that prepare students for having meaningful and productive lives in such a world."

Nevertheless, contemporary higher education is primarily characterized by receiving knowledge out of one single department (usually synonymous with one single discipline), therefore forming specialists with depth in unidisciplinary knowledge and discipline-dependent characteristics ("stereotypes"). We support "tribal behaviour" in our departments, creating "artists" and "computer scientists" and "geologists", each group harmonizing in knowledge, preferred color schemes and language. How can we continuously support quality and depth in education but additionally coach collaboration with other "tribes"? The objective of this paper is to present solutions for this problem that are aimed at having students practice meaningful collaboration with other disciplines.

In order to do so, we define and differentiate between multi-, inter- and transdisciplinary approaches to science and education and describe transdisciplinary collaboration as the soft skill, or competency, that is necessary to participate in inter- and transdisciplinary activities. Derived from a lifelong learning perspective, we postulate that being prepared for engaging in transdisciplinary collaboration at the work place, learners need to have opportunities to engage and experience transdisciplinary collaboration during education. Not to do so would postulate that graduates will undergo the "big switch" in professional life, transforming from being mostly consumers of educational material within their own discipline to become self-directed, responsible and socially competent learners in collaborative and diverse environments. We assess the pros and cons of collaborative education and postulate two strategies, breadth-first and Long Tail, that aid in the learning process. An implementation of theses strategies in a standard CS course with 48 graduate students is described. Furthermore, we discuss implications and future opportunities of our approach.

2 Transdisciplinarity and Transdisciplinary Collaboration

Transdisciplinary collaboration is a group process between individuals trained in different disciplines, e.g. astrophysicists, computer scientists, biologists, designers. Educators variously use the terms multidisciplinarity, interdisciplinarity, and transdisciplinarity to describe collaborations, often without clearly distinguishing among them, though these terms are well defined and distinguished by e.g. Klein [5], Rosenfield [6] and Nicolescu [7]. In short,

multidisciplinarity means that several disciplines are being involved either in a sequential or juxtaposed mode;

interdisciplinarity implies integration or blending of knowledge from different disciplines,

transdisciplinarity places the highest demand, namely forming new knowledge from available unidisciplinary awareness.

In a practical view of multi/inter/transdisciplinarity in education we use the example of teaching "Color" (standard lecture in a computer graphics course) to a group of students from multiple disciplines (e.g. students of physics, biology, computer science, and design). An educator from each of the four involved departments may give a talk on "Color" from their perspective. It is easy to visualize the different approaches each educator will take: a physicist might start with Newton's experiments; a biologist with the structure of the human eye; the computer scientist with the RGB color model; and the design expert maybe with the notion of "color and aesthetics". In a *multidisciplinary* approach, students are left with this input, and it is up to them to find the overlap and "in between" in these approaches on their own. In an *interdisciplinary* approach, each educator will overlap with content of other talks, and interdisciplinary student teams might form to work on an appropriate assignment together. Most probably these teams will split up the tasks according to their abilities but present a final, common solution for the assignment. In a *transdisciplinary* course, the interdisciplinary approach will be expanded by discussing the commonalities and differences of approaches. Educators together with students will attempt to create additional perspectives on the theme that were not inherent in each of the approaches. In transdisciplinary processes participants will learn from each other, and a collaborative knowledge construction can take place that will be expressed in entirely new chapters expressing the thus gained knowledge [8].

The step from multidisciplinarity (separate knowledge) to interdisciplinarity and transdisciplinarity (overlapping knowledge and knowledge beyond disciplines) is powerful. But at what educational level will students be mature enough to blend knowledge or to form new knowledge? Derry and Fischer [4] specifically argue for a transdisciplinary education at graduate level. Rosenfield [6] also places transdisciplinary training at the early graduate level, because a solid grounding in their own discipline, respect for the contributions that other disciplines can make, and the sensitivity to cooperative endeavour is a prerequisite to perform transdisciplinary research.

2.1 Transdisciplinary Collaboration

How can a team of scientists achieve a collaboration qualified to support transdisciplinarity? Stokols [9] observes in his scientific collaborations the following factors supporting transdisciplinary collaboration:

- members` strong commitment to achieving transdisciplinary goals and outcomes
- interpersonal skills of team leaders
- history of prior collaboration among team members
- spatial proximity of team members` offices and laboratories
- schedule frequent face-to-face meetings for brain-storming of ideas
- establish electronic linkages among participants
- foster institutional supports for transdisciplinary collaboration

And the following factors constraining transdisciplinary collaboration:

- substantial time required to establish common conceptual ground and informal social ties

- unrealistic expectations and ambiguity about shared goals and products
- conflicts among alternative disciplinary views of science
- bureaucratic impediments to cross-departmental collaboration.

While Stokols' research is on *scientific* collaboration (to improve understanding of nicotine addiction), these indicators now need to be understood in an educational setting. Table 1 transfers educational relevant indicators to a constructive condition in education.

Table 1. Demands for Transdisciplinary Collaboration in Science Transferred to Education

Demand by Stokols [9]	How educators can be of support:
support members' strong commitment to achieving transdisciplinary goals and outcomes	support students in ■ finding unique topics they feel passionate about; ■ team building process
reduce time required to establish common conceptual ground and informal social ties	establish common language and help establish social ties
schedule frequent face-to-face meetings for brain-storming of ideas	encourage and enforce face-to-face meetings; give help with structure of these meetings
establish electronic linkages among participants	encourage the use of free electronic linkages, e,g, Wikis, Skype, or ICQ additionally to Email
constrain unrealistic expectations and ambiguity about shared goals and products; constrain conflicts among alternative disciplinary views of science	participate in selected face-to-face meetings to constrain "tribal behav-iour" through own interpersonal and interdisciplinary skills

From Table 1 we can derive two issues that are paramount:

- students need to find a common ground for their communication;
- students need projects that they feel committed to out of personal interest.

Once these concerns are solved, the other issues (e.g. enforcing meaningful group meetings and electronic linkage) will be easier to solve. Solutions are proposed in the next chapters through breadth-first and Long Tail strategies.

3   Developing the Competency of Transdisciplinary Collaboration

"The CS curriculum is no interdisciplinary playground": Nowhere in the CS comput-ing curricula [10] do we define "soft skills" as a core or optional topic. Nevertheless, computer science students must and will learn essential soft skills during their years at the university: e.g. communication skills (in speech, in writing, visual), or working in teams. "[Soft] skills should not be seen as separate but should instead be fully in-corporated into the computer science curriculum and its requirements" as requested in [10]: Educators teach communication skills while giving a seminar or advising a

bachelor or master thesis; or use software projects to teach team work in software engineering.

We have to aim at teaching transdiciplinary collaboration in a similar way: focusing on the content of our CS curriculum but at the same time preparing students for that important competency. While a seminar is better than a lecture course in teaching the competency of oral presentation, we can identify in [10] areas of knowledge that will hold that promise for TD collaboration, e.g. the area of Graphics and Visual Computing, where courses on visualization, augmented reality, animation, or (more recently) game development, deepen the knowledge of graphics architecture or rendering algorithms. These knowledge units are already multidisciplinary by nature and gain by admitting students from other disciplines.

"Will we attract students from other disciplines?" Technical competency is ranked high in the job market, so students of other disciplines are showing sufficient interest in joining computer science courses if the prerequisites are manageable [11]. While an electrical engineering student might be interested in rendering and OpenGL programming to better utilize her knowledge on signal processing, a media design student might have interest in Flash scripting or a student of journalism to set up a Wiki.

"But it will take forever to teach programming skills to non-technical students": Acquiring skills in a successful course of mixed disciplines (at the graduate level) will be a suitable balancing of breadth and depth of participating students. In a visualization project for computer science and physics students using air flow data, computer science students will gain depth in developing and implementing real-time flow visualization algorithms, physics student will only acquire breadth knowledge in that area. With a joint lecturer of the physics department involved, computer science students can acquire breadth knowledge of modelling air flows while physics students can deepen their previous theoretical knowledge in fluid dynamics. There should be no need to take Physics 101 for CS students, or for Physics students to take the CS introductory course to C++, to work jointly on projects.

Sometimes CS educators complain about how long it takes to teach non-technical students the skills of programming before "real" work on joint projects can start, when they should concentrate on developing a *common ground* for *all* students so they could work together on a solution, each grounded in the skills of their own discipline and extending into the other discipline only to build necessary overlaps.

3.1 Breadth-First: Finding a Common Language between Disciplines

The breadth-first approach was suggested as one of three possible approaches to teach computer science by the CS computing curricula 2001 [10]. It can also be used to teach individual courses or topics. The idea of breadth-first is to start with a holistic view of each topic to teach (breadth) and undermine it with an application; then use depth to the level the students are ready for. The first part (breadth) provides overall understanding of the topic on an entry level. The application should give extra motivation to learn more about this topic. The second part (depth) will built up through sophisticated layers and is designed for a specific discipline. If a topic is prepared breadth-first, then the breadth part of the course can be simultaneously taught to students of various disciplines. Advantages for a breadth-first approach are:

- CS students get a holistic view of a topic before they learn about more complicated details;
- CS students can then move on to any depth-level;
- students of other disciplines learn of the importance of a topic through the goal of the application;
- students of different backgrounds can be taught together at the breadth-level;
- all students are being taught the same "language" to describe a topic;
- application oriented approaches are motivational to both men and women.

"SIMBA – Computer Pictures" is an educational tool to teach *computer generated color* and *computer generated visualization* via the breadth-first method [12]. Topics at the first level are comprehensible to students of all disciplines; each further level increases the difficulty in acquiring revealed knowledge. Thus found depth is appropriate for computer science students.

The result of this approach is that breadth-first leaves students of different disciplines with a common language that they can use to discuss goals and strategies for joint visualization projects. This common language is essentially the most important ingredient for transdisciplinary collaboration, because without it the door stays open for misunderstandings, unrealistic expectations and ambiguity about shared goals.

3.2 Long Tail: Passion-Based and Self-motivated Learning

The concept of the Long Tail (as developed in business environments) [13] postulates that our culture and economy are increasingly shifting away from a focus on a relatively small number of products and markets at the head of the popularity curve toward a huge number of niches in the tail. Research at the Center for LifeLong Learning & Design (L3D) reinterprets and explores the Long Tail business environments for transforming learning and education [14, 15] as seen in Table 2.

Table 2. Long Tail Concepts in Business and in Learning and Education

Web-Based Businesses	Learning and Education
unlimited shelf-space	unlimited knowledge
megahits (head)	core curriculum (head)
niche markets (tail)	passion for unique topics (tail)
hybrid model of distribution [16]	hybrid model of learning and discovery
many interesting books, movies, songs will not enter the traditional marketplace	many interesting topics and ideas will not be taught in traditional learning environments

Assessing passion-based, self-motivated learning based on Web 2.0/Long Tail requires fundamentally different assessment approaches compared to what standard educational testing can offer [17]. L3D is currently researching to understand the benefits to the kinds of education that this approach can afford, such as the ability of learners to pursue those topics of interest to them and to take responsibility for their

own education (examples of courses can be found at http://l3d.cs.colorado.edu/~
gerhard/courses/). By focusing on the tail of the Long Tail, we will not ignore the
head but we will create a *synergy* between the two. Interest driven activities are
boundary crossing: they move across settings of home, school, work, community, and
online. In the context to enhance the competency of transdisciplinary collaboration
and education this means that the Long Tail approach will be grounded in the following assumptions [18]:

- The activities of the head are the course topics that computer science students will improve their depth in, and students of other disciplines will
  learn to understand on a breadth level. The motivation for participation is
  mostly determined by extrinsic motivation (e.g. for credits; to improve job
  market value).

- The activities of the tail (the major contribution of Long Tail learning)
  should be focused on interest and passion allowing learners of all disciplines to pursue personally meaningful problems. The motivation for
  participation is mostly determined by intrinsic motivation. Learning and
  discovery are facilitated by passion-based participation on niche topics.

In the following chapter we will show the use of breadth-first and Long Tail in a one
semester graduate computer science course with 48 participating students representing
three different groups of disciplines: computer science, business information systems
and non-technical students (e.g. from media science or German language department).

4 Using Long Tail and Breadth-First Strategies in Graduate
Computer Science Course

Setting of the course: The University of Paderborn has 14.000 students and is divided
into five faculties. The course "Data and Information Visualization" is offered in the
CS graduate program as part of a computer graphics module. For the Summer Term
2009 it was opened to graduate students of all disciplines and thus gained 48 participants from three different faculties: 29 CS students (Faculty of Computer Science,
Mathematics and Electrical Engineering), 14 business information systems students
(Faculty of Business Administration and Economics), 5 non-technical students (media
science students and literature students – all from the Faculty of Arts and Humani-
ties). The visualization course included 90 minutes of lecture and 45 minutes of lab
time per week over a period of 15 weeks. Students received 4 ECTS[1] for the course,
which translates to an expected effort of 100-120 hours of work on the student's side.
In the lectures students learn methods and techniques to visualize information and
data in an expressive and effective way. Lab time is being used to practice concepts
and techniques. Starting in week 4, students worked on interdisciplinary projects of
their choice in teams of their choice (with the restriction that each team had to hold a
sufficient disciplinary mix).

Helping students to find a Common Ground: Computer-generated visualization
(including visualization of data derived from scientific measurements or scientific
computing, or collected by humans or machines) holds multitudes of examples useful

---

[1] European Credit Transfer and Accumulation System.

for teaching. Most of these are multidisciplinary, owing the context to an application outside CS, while the interactive graphics is clearly of interest to our CS students. Additionally, perception, design, and other areas of disciplines outside CS, play an important role in computer-generated visualization. The core topics to teach computer-generated visualization are [19]: definitions; data; user and tasks; mapping from data parameters to visual attributes; representation techniques; interaction issues; concepts of the visualization process; and systems and tools. These eight core topics constitute the *head of the knowledge* to be conveyed in a visualization course. Using the educational tool "SIMBA – Computer Pictures" (section 3.2) these core topics were taught with a breadth-first strategy during lectures. Of the typically four levels for each core topic (increasing level means increasing depth for computer science students) level one and two were presented in class, suitable for all disciplines. This strategy helps both to teach the content of visualization to *all* students, but also to remove misunderstandings in the communication by providing a common language: e.g. while an "effective" animation might mean "real-time" for a computer scientist it might mean "aesthetic" to a student of the arts department. However, "effectiveness" for visualization has been well defined by [20] to mean that one visualization is more effective than another visualization if the information conveyed by one visualization is more readily perceived than the information in the other visualization.

One major obstacle in interdisciplinary courses is that of building project teams over the first weeks of a course, while students of different disciplines are still unfamiliar with each other. So additionally to providing a common language, the goal was to also facilitate social ties to help in the team building process. While the use of social networks to get to know each other seems a good idea, the practical side of it makes it useless for a one semester course: Once each of the 48 students have become "friends" on a social network, they will slowly get to know each other. This process develops slowly for large groups and is hard to hurry. Alternatively, the solution in this course was an early lab assignment, requesting to fill out a "private profile". If a question appeared too private, students were allowed to skip it. It was also made clear that not handing in this assignment would not lead to a lesser grade. The form contained information such as "my abilities for the project group", "degree program of student", "former high school", "memberships in clubs or associations", or " favourite films/books". Students were also asked for 1-2 personal pictures and their first name. The resulting document was made available on the web (password secured). Every one of 48 students submitted this "private profile".

Helping Students in finding topics they feel passionate about: Starting in the first lecture, each core topic and concept was enforced by visualization examples in application contexts. This aided both the breath-first approach in teaching as well as the later search for unique project topics for students. Examples given included: visualization of large, multivariate environmental data; software visualization (e.g. algorithm animation, visualization of large code parts), augmented reality to support surgery; visualization of large information spaces, such as demographic data, etc. In each of these cases visualizations aid in the interpretation of complex data for a specific context (often outside CS), but are only possible through special visualization techniques: e.g. animation, flow visualization, GPU-based volume rendering, etc. These visualizations constituted the *tail of visualization knowledge* and offered context for other disciplines but also depth knowledge in visualization for computer science students.

In week 3 (out of 15 course weeks), students had each to submit a complex data set they desired to visualize as their semester project. They were asked to describe the data in a conceptual form (something they learned to do in the previous lecture), set visualization goals, suggest visualization techniques, and describe possible users. This, we hoped, would bring out the topics that the students personally cared about. The received project proposition brought to light many individual interests (e.g. visualization of 20.000 auctions from the on-line game World-of-Warcraft; visualization of web search results or of traffic analyses) but also of some "hot spots", e.g. visualization of medical, weather or ecological data. In a group effort between all tutors, 7 projects that seemed representative (and interesting) of the 48 data sets were selected: visualizing orthopaedic data on human striding styles utilizing a game engine; visualizing indicators of the very large OECD education data base; visualizing data of the European pollutant emission register; visualizing data of over 70 runs of one student in preparation for a marathon; network performance visualization; flow visualization of a hurricane; and medical volume visualization.

Supporting the team building process: The lecture time of 1.5 hours in week 4 was fully devoted to the team building process around these 7 projects. It was a requirement that students built teams by selecting team members from all three faculties. This ensured a distribution of similar core curriculum knowledge in each team. Students who had submitted the selected 7 projects where allowed to start the team building process. Support for the selection process was also provided through the "private profiles" collected from all students. Students sometimes declined their selection, if they wanted to be picked by another group. Such a declination was accepted, as the goal was to form groups that liked to work together and found interest in the niche topic at hand.

To help students in starting up the communication process in their group, the assignment for the first group meeting included a brainstorming session on the group project. This brainstorming session was a guided role play that made sure that each of the students had a communicative role in the discussion process. This assignment intended to dampen unrealistic expectations of team members, let everyone voice their understanding of the joint project and "break the ice" in their communication. After the first meeting, each team had to meet at least once a week and keep meeting notes using a strict protocol. Meeting notes were also sent to tutors and instructor. Team members present, action items for the week to come, and the date of the next meetings were obligatory items in the notes. Instructor or tutors would show up at the meetings without notice – both to help on the content of the project and with interpersonal problems, should any arise.

Qualitative and quantitative assessment of course: Admittedly, not everyone of the 48 students found the topic with their personal strongest passion because, in order to build teams with different disciplines involved, we reduced the amount of projects from 48 to 7. However, there were always several team members on each team that did feel passionate about the project goals. In all cases but one the team members became personal friends, sometimes even to the point that they would alter personal characteristics as in the case of the "Jogging Group": One runner had suggested providing data tracking over 70 of his runs via cell phone and tracker software, including running length, speed, altitude, temperature, etc. All members of the project group became runners (and very good friends) by the time the project ended. Only in one project (out of seven) the group worked incoherently, splitting into two groups, separating not disciplines but cultures.

A voluntary assessment of students reveals more about the course. Of 48 students, 30 students returned the survey: 18 computer science students; 9 business information systems students; and 3 non-technical students (two media science students and one literature student).

The survey revealed that only 33% of the students had previously participated in interdisciplinary (or transdisciplinary) courses at their university, 67% had not. The percentage of computer science students with experience in interdisciplinarity was lower than the average experience in this group. The desire of all students to later work in interdisciplinary teams was up at 90%.

Students were also asked what they would like to know about each other before teaming up in a project group: they showed a strong preference (53%) for "the abilities this person brings to the project" rather than "private information" (10%) or "project interest" (4%).

The number of actual face-to-face meetings for each team was one per week during the first weeks (the obligatory group meeting they had to report about) and 2, 3, or more meetings per week between week 9 and 15. Students used cell phones, Email, ICQ, SVN (a version control system), Wiki, and Skype to communicate between meetings.

The "private profiles" were used by 67% of the students to look up private information of course mates. Business information system and non-technical students used it to a higher percentage than computer science students.

After the project presentations, each student was asked to fill out an additional survey. In one of those questions the percentage of contribution to the project of each individual team member was requested. The closer knit the group had become, the closer these numbers matched. We found perfect matches in all numbers for the "jogging group", closely matching numbers in five other groups, but widely differing numbers in the culturally split group described earlier in this section.

5 Implications and Future Opportunities

Our educational objectives are grounded in the need for competencies in transdisciplinary collaboration to cope with the complexity of real-world problems. Our credo for transdisciplinary collaboration and lifelong learning argues that we must provide students with educational experiences to prepare them for this world. Many educational programs in computer science are still dominated by curriculum-driven learning (where the teachers set the goals and determine the content) rather than providing students with the opportunity to become reflective professionals allowing them to acquire the capacity for life-long learning and respect and ability to work with the perspectives of many, formerly separate disciplines. For the 21st century, educational experiences need to be focused on how to improvise, innovate, and learn when the answer is not known, and how to make all voices heard. This is especially important at a time where many high level objectives in education are focused on a climate for test taking, bookkeeping, and cutting expenses—the wrong strategies as economic competition heats up around the globe and societies are exploring new ways to make their individual members more creative, imaginative, and innovative. The authors are convinced that the competency of transdisciplinary collaboration and self-directed learning, awakened in our students, will support a new climate of problem solving in this century.

Acknowledgement

Both authors thank the members of the Center for LifeLong Learning & Design (L3D) at the University of Colorado at Boulder for providing background information and inspiring debates about the content of this paper. Gerhard Fischer's ideas and understanding about transdisciplinary collaboration and education have greatly bene-fited from collaboration with Sharon Derry (University of Wisconsin) and David Redmiles (University of California at Irvine). Gitta Domik thanks Ingrid and Stefanie Fischer for providing loving support to her son during her sabbatical at L3D.

References

1. Friedman, T.L.: The World is Flat: A brief history of the twenty-first century. Farrar, Straus and Giroux, New York (2005)
2. Aspray, W., Mayadas, F., Vardi, M.Y.: Globalization and Offshoring of Software - A Report of the ACM Job Migration Task Force (2006), http://www1.acm.org/globalizationreport/
3. Drucker, P.F.: The Age of Social Transformation. The Atlantic Monthly, 53–80 (November 1994)
4. Derry, S., Fischer, G.: Toward a Model and Theory for Transdisciplinary Graduate Education. Paper Presented at 2005 AERA Annual Meeting, Symposium, Sociotechnical Design for Lifelong Learning: A Crucial Role for Graduate Education, Montreal (April 2005), http://l3d.cs.colorado.edu/gerhard/papers/aera-montreal.pdf (2005)
5. Klein, J.T.: A Platform for a Shared Discourse of Interdisciplinary Education. Journal of Social Science Education 5(2), 10–18 (2006), http://www.jsse.org
6. Rosenfield, P.L.: The potential of transdisciplinary research for sustaining and extending likages between the health and social sciences. Social Sciences and Medicine 35, 1343–1357 (1992)
7. Nicolescu, B.: The transdisciplinary evolution of learning (1999), http://www.unesco.org/education/educprog/lwf/dl/nicolescu_f.pdf
8. Norman, D.A.: In defense of cheating (Electronic Version). From: Ubiquity 6(11) (2005), http://www.acm.org/ubiquity/views/v6i11_norman.html
9. Stokols, D.: Towards a Science of Transdisciplinary Action Research. American Journal of Community Psychology 38, 63–77 (2006)
10. Computing Curricula (2001), http://www.computer-org-portal-cms_docs_ieeecs-ieeecs-education-cc2001-cc2001.pdf
11. Rushmeier, H.: IEEE Workshop on Visualization Education for Non-Technical Majors: Post Workshop Materials (2006), http://graphics.cs.yale.edu/holly/vis2006/vis-non-tech.html

12. Domik, G., Goetz, F.: A Breadth-First Approach for Teaching Computer Graphics. Education Papers. In: Proceedings of Eurographics 2006, Vienna, Austria, September 4-8, pp. 1–5 (2006)
13. Anderson, C.: The Long Tail: Why the Future of Business is Selling Less of More. Publisher Hyperion 2006 (2006), ISBN 1401302378
14. Brown, J.S., Adler, R.P.: Minds on Fire: Open Education, the Long Tail, and Learning 2.0 (2008), http://www.educause.edu/ir/library/pdf/ERM0811.pdf
15. Fischer, G.: Cultures of Participation and Social Computing: Rethinking and Reinventing Learning and Education. In: Proceedings of the International Conference on Advanced Learning Technologies (ICALT), pp. 1–5. IEEE Press, Riga (2009)
16. Benkler, Y.: The Wealth of Networks: How Social Production Transforms Markets and Freedom. Yale University Press, New Haven (2006)
17. National-Research-Council: Beyond Productivity: Information Technology, Innovation, and Creativity. National Academy Press, Washington (2003)
18. Collins, A., Fischer, G., Barron, B., Liu, C., Spada, H.: Long-Tail Learning: A Unique Opportunity for CSCL? In: Proceedings of CSCL 2009: 8th International Conference on Computer Supported Collaborative Learning, vol. 2, pp. 22–24. University of the Aegean, Rhodes (2009)
19. Domik, G.: Do We Need Formal Education in Visualization? Visualization Viewpoint. IEEE Computer Graphics and Applications 20(4) (2000)
20. Mackinlay, J.: Automating the Design of Graphical Presentations of Relational Information. ACM Trans. on Graphics 5(2), 110–141 (1986)

Getting Granular on Twitter:
Tweets from a Conference and Their
Limited Usefulness for Non-participants

Martin Ebner[1], Herbert Mühlburger[1], Sandra Schaffert[2], Mandy Schiefner[3],
Wolfgang Reinhardt[4], and Steve Wheeler[5]

[1] Social Learning, Computer and Information Services,
Graz University of Technology, Graz, Austria
{martin.ebner,muehlburger}@tugraz.at
[2] Salzburg Research Forschungsgesellschaft, Salzburg, Austria
sandra.schaffert@salzburgresearch.at
[3] Center for University Teaching and Learning, University of Zurich,
Zurich, Switzerland
mandy.schiefner@access.uzh.ch
[4] Computer Science Education Group, University of Paderborn
Paderborn, Germany
wolle@upb.de
[5] University of Plymouth, Plymouth, United Kingdom
s.wheeler@plymouth.ac.uk

Abstract. The use of microblogging applications (especially Twitter) is becoming increasingly commonplace in a variety of settings. Today, active conference participants can post messages on microblogging platforms to exchange information quickly and in real-time. Recent research work was based on quantitative analyses in terms of the number of tweets or active Twitter users within a specific time period. In this paper, we examine the content of the contributions and aim to analyze how useful posts are for the "listening" Internet auditorium. It can be shown that only a few microblogs are of interest for non-participants of the specific event and that meaningful usage of a microblogging application requires greater care than previously anticipated.

Keywords: Twitter, microblogging, conference, analysis.

1 Introduction: Usage of Twitter at Conferences

Twitter is the most popular public microblogging system. After a period of testing this form of communication and interaction in science [1] and e-learning [2,3,4], microblogging has finally caught up with the scientific community: Some early adopters use it to share short notices about their work or to comment on the work of others, they use it to communicate and last but not least, they use it at conferences. In fact, there is growing body of research literature dealing with the use of Twitter for scientific purposes [5,6].

N. Reynolds and M. Turcsányi-Szabó (Eds.): KCKS 2010, IFIP AICT 324, pp. 102–113, 2010.
© IFIP International Federation for Information Processing 2010

Although the features of Twitter are widely known, we will describe them briefly: Twitter allows registered users to share short posts of up to 140 characters to anybody else registered on Twitter. Such posts are called "tweets" and they can be seen as publicly accessible SMS. On 22nd of February 2010 Twitter hit 50 millions tweets per day[1] and now surpassed 10 billion tweets altogether[2]. This overwhelming number of individual tweets evokes the need for the organization and selection of relevant tweets: Although Twitter was designed to be a one-way information sharing channel, community-driven approaches soon emerged to enhance the service with mark-ups that enabled more flexible communication within Twitter (see Java et al. [7]).

Therefore Twitter is equipped with a number of features:

(a) one can "follow" - that is, select the streams of interesting Twitter users;
(b) one can search for terms or tags (marked with "#"; known as hashtags) used within tweets;
(c) one can directly address other users by a public reply (marked with "@" before the name of the other user; e.g. @mebner) or via a private direct message (marked with "d" or "dm"; e.g. d wollepb);
(d) one can cite and copy interesting tweets by "retweeting" them (marked with "RT"; see Boyd et al. [8] for more information on retweeting messages in Twitter).

The growing success of Twitter has attracted the attention of other web services. Popular social networking platforms such as Facebook or LinkedIn allow the integration of tweets via a provided API and therefore make the application even more attractive. Twitter is not merely an additional communication channel; it appears that it has also been instrumental in changing the way people exchange information, links and their engagement with social media in general. The limited message size of 140 characters is often argued to be both strength and weakness of the microblogging service. In essence, the application offers fast, real-time and easy exchange but conversely, communication is mostly superficial, not sustainable over a long time period and rarely extends beyond single responses.

Twitter's initiating question *"What are you doing?"* to motivate people to talk about their private lives has already been advanced to *"What is happening?"* to encourage comments from those participating in events, especially within the context of media and e-learning. The special Twitter syntax (see (a) to (d)) suggests an obvious application for scientific conferences. In order to join a community's discussion about a topic or the participate within whole conference it is sufficient to tag one's messages with the official hashtag of the conference – a certain word following the number sign (#) – or other existing tags. Without knowing other people at the conference, it is simple to aggregate their tweets. It becomes easier to share ideas, impressions, comments and additional materials about the conference on such a filtered #channel. Furthermore, there is no setup required for the service - it is an online accessible application. Those who are interested in actively using Twitter need to be registered with the service and post their messages via the Twitter website or via one of the numerous clients using the provided API. Conference delegates and non-attendees can

---

[1] http://mashable.com/2010/02/22/twitter-50-million-tweets/ (last visited April 2010).
[2] http://mashable.com/2010/03/04/twitter-10-billion-tweets-2/ (last visited April 2010).

search for tweets within the conference hashtag and are therefore able to follow the ongoing microblogging stream from the conference.

Twitter emerged as a conference communication tool firstly as a result of the experimentation of early adopters. Initially Twitter usage was officially unannounced or unsupported by conference organizations and therefore this communication use of Twitter could be described as essentially a hidden backchannel as Ebner explains in [9]. "Hidden" in this sense does not mean that it was not available for everyone, but that it had been undiscovered by the majority of participants. Ebner and Reinhardt show that at tech and media conferences in particular, the public announcement of a hashtag and a short explanation of Twitter as a conference backchannel eventually became a common feature [10].

In addition to this unofficial usage of Twitter at conferences, several other conceivably intentional scenarios that had already been used:

- Make the Twitter communication visible to all participants: To do so a public extra screen with a Twitter wall, listening to all current tweets was placed at the front of the conference hall beside the normal whiteboard. For example, a twitter wall was used at the ED-MEDIA conference 2008 [9]. Reinhardt et al. pointed out how people are using Twitter at conferences [11], showing that different stakeholders use Twitter before, during, and after a conference with differing purposes in mind. The analysis of the usage of the wall shows a surprisingly high participation of the conference attendees at the wall. Nevertheless, to the best to our knowledge, no content analysis about the communication and information flow at the wall was done.

- As for the presumption that a Twitter wall without concrete ideas about its functionality tends to distract the public and the presenters; the usage of the Twitter wall seemed to be too low-key or leads to be a non-constructive murmuring in the background as Danah Boyd experienced [12]. Therefore, conference organizers tried to build on the positive aspects of the tool to try to focus the communication. For example, there have been requests to use Twitter as an additional channel to ask questions during panel discussions (see Campus Innovation 2009 in Hamburg[3]). Additionally Ebner elaborates that presenters sometimes ask directly for feedback, open questions or comments via Twitter [9]. This is used to make presentations more interactive, especially in large audiences where a microphone would normally have been required for interaction between delegates and presenters.

- Besides traditional scientific conferences, barcamps attract researchers too, at least within the tech and media related disciplines. Barcamps are a kind of "unconference" [13] that function without prepared scheduled presentations and presenters to encourage more spontaneous, interactive communications and knowledge exchange in ad hoc installed stand-up presentations, workshops and discussion groups. Barcamps build upon the use of Web 2.0 technologies, open formats and tools. For example, they typically use wikis for registrations and social networking platforms to send out invitations and promote the event. Even more interestingly, the usage of Twitter seems more

---

[3] http://www.campus-innovation.de/node/580 (last visited April 2010).

or less a matter of course for the participants. For example the announcement of workshops are typically amplified via Twitter; tweets are normally presented on screens in the lobby of the conference.

- Additionally, as Ebner and Reinhardt report, the conference organizers can actively use Twitter before and after the event: to promote the call for papers and event itself, to alert the full program, the registration possibilities, and afterwards the publication of the proceedings [10].

Nevertheless, these intended and "officially" announced and supported uses of Twitter at conferences are currently not widely used in every discipline and community of researchers. As Twitter is not limited to conference participants, it may encourage external participation. Additionally, Twitter is sometimes actively used to report conference activities to external participants.

To sum up, there are several clear ways Twitter can be used in the context of conferences:

(a) for communication amongst participants,
(b) for communication amongst organizers/presenters and audience,
(c) for reporting to non-participants about the conference.

Recent research work has focused mainly upon simple quantitative analysis, dealing questions such as how many tweets have been contributed from how many users in a specific time frame. This kind of measurement is used to gauge the success levels of Twitter use. In this publication we answer the main research question: "*Is Twitter proper to report from a conference in order to share the event with the scientific community from outside the conference?*" To do so we analyzed the Twitter stream of EduCamp 2010 in Hamburg, Germany.

2 Study

The Twitter API not only ensures there are numerous clients for sending and displaying tweets, but it also facilitates a systematic analysis of the content people publish on the platform. Reinhardt introduced an application that performed a basic analysis of tweets from communities of interest and visualized the main structural statistics about those communities, including a dynamic representation of the community's communication topics [14].

For this study we chose the EduCamp 2010 in Hamburg, because many participants are active Twitter users. Furthermore, the organization committee promoted the use of the microblogging platform by providing an appropriate hashtag (#ec10hh) and actively encouraged exchange and communication via Twitter. As the EduCamp is organized as a "barcamp" or "un-conference", no scheduled program with concrete talks or workshops was available before it starts.

We monitored the output of the Twitter usage between the 5th of February to the 4th of March 2010. The EduCamp itself took place on 5th and 6th of February 2010. So in our study tweets from after the event are also counted and analyzed. In summary 2.110 single tweets containing the mentioned hashtag constitute the data in this study. We therefore examined twice – the core conference output as well as the post conference phase for about one month. Due to the fact that Twitter is used for communication issues post-event microblog postings are collected until appearances of the official hashtag begin to tail off.

Furthermore it must be noted that the 5 of 6 authors did not participate within the conference to ensure a neutral view to each single tweet.

Focusing on our main research question, we took a closer look at the content of each single tweet. Would a non-participant be able to follow the conference by watching the live-stream or would he/she simply become lost in information overload? Is the information provided on Twitter useful for the followers on the World Wide Web without them being physically present at the (un-)conference?

In this study a two-stage analysis was chosen – first an automatic one by analyzing main keywords, a so-called Formal Concept Analysis (FCA) (a detailed description follows later on). Secondly, tweets were analyzed manually and categorized into the following four categories, which we describe more precisely:

- irrelevant tweets,
- administrative tweets,
- topical discussions,
- topical tweets.

Irrelevant Tweets

This category contains all tweets that are not relevant to the topic of the conference. This means there is no hint towards learning, educational technology and so on. These tweets are comparable to usual small talk on conferences and the Web. Typical tweets in this category are the following:

- "Who found my drinking cup? #ec10hh"
- "was online #ec10hh"

Administrative Tweets

This category consists of all tweets with an administrative meaning. Examples of such content might be about the room in which a session is going to take place, or any technical information such as wireless LAN or hotspot issues, video/audio streaming issues etc. Typical tweets belonging to this category include the following:

- "Wifi is not available #ec10hh"
- "Session: new music interfaces at 5:00 pm in room Durkheim #ec10hh"
- "#ec10hh streaming in room Humboldt not working?"

Topical Discussions

This category counts all tweets that are relevant in the context of learning and additionally are part of discussions on certain topics or replies to other participants. Typical tweets of this category are tweets include:

- "@mccab99 tell me about the relationship between technology and education? #ec10hh"
- "nice idea of @estudyskills Aggregation of all student weblogs at Tumblelog - gives overview. #ec10hh"

- "dito! rt @lisarosa dance education: @mons7 shows, what we need: creativity + passion + engagement. #ec10hh"

Topical Tweets

This category consists of all tweets relevant in the context of e-learning and that carry some valuable information with a strong focus on a conference topic. For example, in this category tweets consist of a little description and an additional link to another more detailed resource on the Web or simply describe / announce conference outcomes. Typical tweets of this category might be:

- "open-learning: initiative on OER usage for informal education: http://u.nu/4a7y4 #ec10hh"
- "session on exploring teaching and learning. Make a look to this article of Gabi Reinmann: http://u.nu/3g8y4 #ec10hh"
- "portal of TU Braunschweig integrates numerous services such as StudIP, library, plus community: http://bit.ly/atxvaR #ec10hh"

The first two categories can be summed up in order to represent all the tweets of no relevance in the context of e-learning or to the discussed conference topics, while the latter two categories can be summed up as representative of the relevant tweets that might enhance the knowledge of external followers.

3 Results

General Output

Before analyzing each single tweet, a short overview about the participant sample and their tweets is given. Overall in the mentioned time period 272 users posted at least one single tweet using the hashtag #ec10hh. Fig. 1 and Fig. 2 show that an average user posted about 8 posts and that there were some few users who contributed by using the application very extensively (one user posted 100 messages). At the other end of the spectrum, more than 108 users made just a single tweet. A detailed analysis showed that 272 users made an average of about 8 tweets (mean: 7.84; minimum: 1; maximum: 100; median: 3).

Automated Analysis – Formal Concept Analysis (FCA)

Our first approach uses Formal Concept Analysis (FCA) in order to categorize twitter users who write tweets about the same topics. A formal context is defined as set structure $K := (G, M, I)$, where G represents objects (in German "Gegenstände"), M refers to attributes (in German "Merkmale") and I describes a binary relation between G and M. It can be represented as a matrix where rows contain objects and columns contain attributes. If there were a binary relation between a certain row and a certain column, this would be expressed by the identified cell having the value of 1. If there is no relation the identified cell is assigned the value 0.

A formal concept of a formal context $K := (G, M, I)$ is defined as a pair (A, B) where A is a subset of G, B is a subset of M (A = B' and B = A'). A is called the extent and B is called the intent of the formal concept (A, B) [15]. The extent holds all objects belonging to a certain concept. The intent contains all attributes (e.g. properties, meanings) that apply to all those objects. As an entry point for further details on Formal Concept Analysis we refer to Wille and Ganter [15,16].

In this study we focus on categorizing different Twitter users depending on the tweets they wrote. The formal context $K := (G, M, I)$ is defined as follows: All the keywords used within the tweets represent the attributes (M) and the users who wrote these tweets represent the objects (G). A concept (A, B) is represented by a set A of keywords, which represents the intent and a set of twitter users (B) which represents the extent of this concept (e.g. all the Twitter users who used the keyword "e-learning" in their tweets).

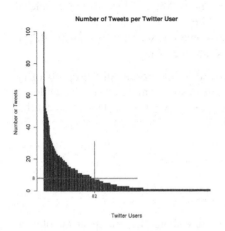

Fig. 1. Number of tweets per user   **Fig. 2.** Average of posts per user

In order to extract the keywords of the tweets we used the Yahoo Term Extraction Web Service[4]. The web service delivers a list of keywords for given tweets. For every Twitter user tweeting in the #ec10hh Twitter stream the keywords were extracted and as a result a formal context was created. Analyzing the formal context was done with ConExp[5]. ConExp allows users to explore, analyze and visualize formal concepts of a formal context.

In order to focus only on the conference context irrelevant keywords were manually deactivated from relevant ones. The result was a sparse matrix that means that the extracted keywords did not overlap in a significant manner. It can be interpreted in such a way that monitored twitter users wrote about many different topics (e.g. using a lot of different keywords in their tweets). The categorization of twitter users based on their tweets using FCA did not result in valuable categories. It can be stated that the tweets analyzed have high diversity and nearly no overlapping keywords. The result is that the tweets are required to be manually analyzed.

---

[4] http://developer.yahoo.com/search/content/V1/termExtraction.html (last visited April 2010).
[5] http://conexp.sourceforge.net/ (last visited April 2010).

Manual Analysis

In total 57% of 2.110 analyzed tweets could generally be categorized as irrelevant in the context of the (un-) conference outcome. As illustrated in Table 1, 13% of the tweets were categorized as administrative tweets, 9% were marked as discussions and 20% were categorized as relevant tweets.

Table 1. Categorization of tweets

	Topical Tweets	Topical Discussions	Administrative Tweets	Irrelevant Tweets	Total Number of Tweets
Number of Tweets including Retweets	456	201	278	1.175	2.110
	22%	10%	13%	56%	100%
Number of Tweets not containing "RT @" or "via @" - Clean Tweets	346	157	227	996	1.726
	20%	9%	13%	58%	100%

In the following section we offer a more detailed analysis of the categories relevant tweets and relevant discussions. Table 2 displays all categorized tweets over the monitored time period. Furthermore, the table also highlights all tweets sent during the conference time (February 5th to February 6th 2010) in parentheses.

Table 2. Detailed analysis of Tweets

	Topical Tweets	Topical Discussions	Administrative Tweets	Irrelevant Tweets	Total Number of Tweets
Number of Tweets including Retweets	456 (349)	201 (162)	278 (193)	1.175 (939)	2.110 (1.643)
Number of Tweets containing at least one link	249 (164)	37 (19)	123 (85)	207 (138)	616 (406)
Number of Replies	40 (32)	70 (61)	34 (26)	228 (179)	372 (298)
Number of Tweets containing "RT @"	101 (72)	42 (33)	50 (34)	172 (131)	365 (270)
Number of Tweets containing "via @"	10 (7)	2 (2)	1 (1)	8 (8)	21 (18)

Table 2. (*Continued*)

	Topical Tweets	Topical Discussions	Administrative Tweets	Irrelevant Tweets	Total Number of Tweets
Number of Tweets containing "RT @" and containing "via @"	1 (1)	0 (0)	0 (0)	1 (1)	2 (2)
Number of Tweets containing "RT @" or containing "via @" but not both	110 (78)	44 (35)	51 (35)	179 (138)	**384** (286)
Number of Tweets not containing "RT @" or "via @" - Clean Tweets	346 (271)	157 (127)	227 (158)	996 (801)	1.726 (1.357)
Number of Tweets not containing "RT @" or "via @" and containing at least one link	**175** (**120**)	28 (15)	84 (57)	148 (102)	435 (294)

4 Discussion

In the analysis of categories of interest the following crucial facts should be high-lighted:

- In the timeslot of the conference (5th to 6th February 2010) 1.643 tweets from 2.110 were tweeted by 272 users in total. It can thus be stated that on average each user posted an average 6 tweets during the conference period.
- During the analysis it was also attempted to separate participating active Twitter user from non-participating ones, but because many use their accounts anonymously more than 100 users could not be identified.
- Monitoring the conference: For a non-participant of a conference who wishes to monitor the event by checking the Twitter live stream this proves to be problematic. Based on the assumption that even relevant tweets containing simple statements are senseless without any distinct context of the occurrence, only messages containing additional material (such as pictures, videos, or similar) may be of interest. In other words, if a link to such an attachment occurs, it might be possible to understand the current conference situation. Only 175 out of 2.110 tweets offered such a possibility. 8% or only one out of twelve is maybe of interest. To follow the conference stream seems to be a challenge. If we reduce the tweets to those occurring during the conference

period (5th and 6th February) (Table 2) only 120 posts are of interest at all, which relates to about 6%.

- Retweets: Table 2 shows the high number of retweets (RT) in conference twittering. In summary 384 RTs occurred which is an overall percentage of 18%, but if the "relevant" category is analyzed towards RTs we see that 24% of all tweets are simply a copy of previous ones. On one hand the retweet seems to be a relevant message, otherwise it would not been multiplied by another user. But, on the other hand, it may hold no sense for people who are not at this conference because they need the context of the proposed tweet to understand the content.

- Bearing in mind that RTs are a good instrument for pointing out the importance of a tweet or helping to reach more Twitter user in order to spread the world with announcements, they are not helpful if someone is interested on the content/output of the conference.

- Subsequent to the keyword extraction and calculation, the FCA revealed that there is no direct correlation amongst the conference participants. In other words, with this method it was not possible to gain an overview about the conference topics, the main assumptions or statements.

5 Conclusion

Our analysis showed that the use of Twitter to distribute or explain (un-) conference topics, discussions or results to a broader public seems to be limited.

To interpret the data correctly, further comparative data and analysis are required. Our approach of analyzing tweets at a conference was merely the first foray into what has become a complex research field.

Our analysis demonstrated that the Twitter stream has a limited usefulness at his particular conference for external participants that wanted to follow the event from outside, and we conclude that our own ideas and implicit theories about the Twitter usage should be perhaps be reassessed. In this paper the content of tweets was analyzed for the first time and a first trend was carried out to give an overview of Twitter usage. As has been previously mentioned, further examination will be necessary to confirm these outcomes, even though Ross et al. [17] reports similar results: "[The analyzed data] raises the question of whether a Twitter enabled backchannel promotes more of an opportunity for users to establish an online presence and enhance their digital identity rather than encouraging a participatory conference culture."

Possible interpretations of the results could be that the Twitter usage follows other logic, e.g.:

- usage as a backchannel for conference participants or even a subgroup at the conference as a means to comment silently with limited comprehension potential for outsiders;

- usage of self promotion and profiling that means for example citations of people at the conference with a possible high retweet rate are posted to generate attention for the own profile;

- to document and illustrate connections, for example friendship, acquaintanceship, social ties to others ("I know ... and like her/his idea") in the same way as making new connections and friendship;

- usage as a public notepad to collect relevant ideas, quotes or links;
- usage as an evaluation tool, for example to collect quotes about the conference and the satisfaction of participants for use by the organizing committee.

Further research activities should combine the quantitative, semi-automatic analysis as we have achieved within this contribution with additional questioning and involvement about the aims and goals of the Twitter user at a conference. One weakness of the presented data is that there is no determining if a RT was sent by a conference participant or by external participants. The authors attempted to categorize each Twitter user but because of missing data this should be done beforehand in future studies.

Nevertheless, Twitter is a "new" tool and therefore adaptations of new forms of communications, e.g. etiquette for documentation of conference for outsiders or a more focused usage of tweets by the presenters or conference organizers could positively influence future usage.

Practically, the obviously limited usefulness of the tweets of the EduCamp participants for interested external participants evokes new ideas for practical and effective alternative usage of the tweets as well as the need for appropriate tools. For example, an individual's micro postings might be seen as personal notes, as they are obviously easier interpreted and meaningful for the writers themselves. Therefore, future tools could develop and support the self-archiving functionalities of Twitter (e.g. search functions about the own tags).

Acknowledgments. The authors would like to thank Michael Rowe and Alexandre Passant for their comprehensive, valuable reviews of an earlier version of this paper.

References

1. Ebner, M., Schiefner, M.: Microblogging - more than fun? In: Proceedings of IADIS Mobile Learning Conference, Portugal, pp. 155–159 (2008)
2. Ebner, M., Lienhardt, C., Rohs, M., Meyer, I.: Microblogs in higher education – a chance to facilitate informal and process oriented learning? Computers & Education 55(1), 92–100 (2010)
3. Costa, C., Beham, G., Reinhardt, W., Sillaots, M.: Microblogging in Technology Enhanced Learning: A Use-Case Inspection of PPE Summer School 2008. In: Proceedings of the 2nd SIRTEL Workshop on Social Information Retrieval for Technology Enhanced Learning (2008)
4. Grosseck, G., Holotescu, C.: Can we use twitter for educational activities? In: Proceedings of the 4th International Scientific Conference eLSE "eLearning and Software for Education" (2008)
5. Letierce, J., Passant, A., Decker, S., Breslin, J.: Understanding how Twitter is used to spread scientific messages. In: Web Science Conference, Raleigh, NC, USA (2010), http://journal.webscience.org/314/ (last visited April 2010)
6. Haewoon, K., Changhyun, L., Hosung, P., Moon, S.: What is Twitter a Social Network or a News Media? In: Proceedings of the 19th International World Wide Web (WWW) Conference, Raleigh, NC (USA), April 26-30 (2010), http://an.kaist.ac.kr/traces/WWW2010.html (last visited April 2010)

7. Java, A., Song, X., Finin, T., Tseng, B.: Why we twitter: understanding microblogging usage and communities. In: Proceedings of the 9th WebKDD and 1st SNA-KDD 2007 Workshop on Web Mining and Social Network Analysis, pp. 56–65. ACM, New York (2007)
8. boyd, d., Golder, S., Lotan, G.: Tweet, tweet, retweet: Conversational aspects of retweeting on twitter. In: Proceedings of the HICSS-43 Conference (2010)
9. Ebner, M.: Introducing Live Microblogging: How Single Presentations Can Be Enhanced by the Mass. Journal of Research in Innovative Teaching (JRIT) 2(1), 91–100 (2009)
10. Ebner, M., Reinhardt, W.: Social networking in scientific conferences – Twitter as tool for strengthen a scientific community. In: Proceedings of the 1st International Workshop on Science 2.0 for TEL (2009)
11. Reinhardt, W., Ebner, M., Beham, G., Costa, C.: How people are using Twitter during Conferences. In: Hornung-Prähauser, V., Luckmann, M. (eds.) Creativity and Innovation Competencies on the Web. Proceedings of the 5th EduMedia 2009, Salzburg, pp. 145–156 (2009)
12. boyd, d.: Spectacle of Web 2.0 Expo ... from my perspective (2009), http://www.zephoria.org/thoughts/archives/2009/11/24/spectac le_at_we.html (last visited April 2010)
13. Bernhardt, T., Kirchner, M.: Web 2.0 meets conference – the EduCamp as a new format of participation and exchange in the world of education. In: Ebner, M., Schiefner, M. (eds.) Looking Toward the Future of Technology-Enhanced Education: Ubiquitous Learning and the Digital Native, pp. 192–204. IGI Global, Hershey (2010)
14. Reinhardt, W.: Visualizing the dynamics of communication of Communities of Practice on Twitter. In: Proceedings of the 3rd International Workshop on Building Technology Enhanced Learning solutions for Communities of Practice (2009)
15. Wille, R.: Formal Concept Analysis as Mathematical Theory of Concepts and Concept Hierarchies. In: Ganter, B., Stumme, G., Wille, R. (eds.) Formal Concept Analysis. LNCS (LNAI), vol. 3626, pp. 1–33. Springer, Heidelberg (2005)
16. Ganter, B., Wille, R.: Formal concept analysis: Mathematical foundations. Springer, Heidelberg (1999)
17. Ross, C., Terras, M., Warwick, C., Welsh, A.: Enabled Backchannel: Conference Twitter Use by Digital Humanists, Department of Information Studies, draft version (2009), http://www.ucl.ac.uk/infostudies/claire-ross/Digitally _Enabled_Backchannel.pdf (last visited April 2010)

Beyond Pedagogical Content Knowledge:
The Importance of TPACK for Informing Preservice
Teacher Education in Australia

Glenn Finger[1], Romina Jamieson-Proctor[2], and Peter Albion[2]

[1] Griffith University, Gold Coast campus, Queensland, Australia
G.Finger@griffith.edu.au
[2] University of Southern Queensland, Queensland, Australia
Romina.Jamieson-Proctor@usq.edu.au,
Peter.Albion@usq.edu.au

Abstract. Since the emergence of computers in schools during the 1980's, there have been considerable developments by education systems and schools to develop policies and expectations for the use of information and communication technologies (ICT) to enhance learning and teaching. These have not always translated into practice, which has resulted in a focus on the need for improvements in preservice teacher education programs and professional development of practising teachers. This paper starts from the premise that most teacher education have been constrained by using Pedagogical Content Knowledge (PCK) developed by Shulman [1] [2] prior to the dynamic technological changes enabled by the Internet. The authors present the case for the importance of Technological Pedagogical Content Knowledge (TPACK) [3] [4]. Subsequently, the paper provides guidance for auditing the TPACK capabilities of teacher education students through the presentation of an instrument developed, and provides a summary of some of the findings of a study undertaken using that instrument.

Keywords: Technological Pedagogical Content Knowledge, TPACK, Preservice Teacher Education, Professional Standards, Information and Communication Technologies.

1 Introduction – Moving beyond PCK to TPACK to Design Teacher Education Programs

Preservice teacher education programs have the responsibility for preparing future teachers who are likely to be teaching their students in a world characterised by ongoing technological changes. How well are we designing our preservice teacher education students for present and future technological contexts? How are they currently designed? What guidance can be provided for improving their design?

Most teacher education programs in Australia have been designed using Shulman's Pedagogical Content Knowledge (PCK) [1] [2]. This paper argues that this is inadequate in building the professional capabilities of future teachers to use ICT to enhance

N. Reynolds and M. Turcsányi-Szabó (Eds.): KCKS 2010, IFIP AICT 324, pp. 114–125, 2010.
© IFIP International Federation for Information Processing 2010

learning and teaching in the 21st Century. The paper, in providing advice to move beyond PCK, draws upon the more contemporary conceptualization of Technological Pedagogical Content Knowledge (TPCK), now known as TPACK [3] [4] [5] [6]. Our position aligns with that of Koehler, Mishra and Yahya [5] who appropriately indicate that:

> ...intelligent pedagogical uses of technology require the development of a complex, situated form of knowledge we call Technological Pedagogical Content Knowledge (TPCK). At the heart of TPCK is the dynamic, transactional relationship between content, pedagogy and technology. (p. 741)

Throughout this paper, we use TPACK which has the connotation of Technological Pedagogical Content Knowledge being 'the total package' for teaching in the 21st Century. This paper provides guidance for undertaking an audit of the TPACK capabilities of teacher education students through a summary of the instrument developed by the authors. It provides some insights into the findings of a study undertaken by the authors using that instrument. Finally, we encourage others involved in teacher education to take up this approach, and design teacher education programs needed to develop future teachers' TPACK capabilities.

2 Expectations, Conceptualising TPACK and Stages of Preservice Teacher Education Programs

The following sections provide a discussion of the expectations for teachers, and identifies that the importance of TPACK is not yet well understood.

2.1 Expectations

Most teacher education programs in Australia have been designed by taking into account PCK, which Shulman [2] described as "the special amalgam of content and pedagogy that is uniquely the province of teachers, their own special form of professional understanding" (p. 8). Shulman's work [1] is reflected in many of the current conversations which the authors, all teacher educators in Universities in Queensland, a State in Australia have been engaged in relating to Government and public perceptions of literacy, numeracy and science teaching in primary schools in that State. The review, A Shared Challenge: Improving Literacy, Numeracy and Science Learning in Queensland Primary Schools [9], resulted in five recommendations, with the first recommendation being the preregistration testing of primary teacher graduates. Masters [9], in his report, articulated concerns about how well prepared teachers were in terms of their PCK.

A search throughout the report by Masters [9] reveals numerous references to 'content knowledge', 'pedagogical knowledge', and 'pedagogical content knowledge'. There were no references made to TPACK, though some mention is made in relation to the Queensland College of Teachers Professional Standards [7] for teachers requiring that teachers need to know and understand "ways of identifying, evaluating and selecting teaching, learning and assessment strategies, resources and technology" (p. 67) and that:

...the challenge of ensuring that every student completes primary school with the knowledge, skills and attitudes required for success in secondary school suggests that entirely new solutions will be required to some longstanding problems. Technology is likely to play a part in some of these solutions (p. 93).

While it is not the purpose of this paper to critique the report by Masters [9], we note that his report makes no contribution to the task of the Assessment and Teaching of 21st Century Skills (ATC21S) project [10] which aims to measure skills needed in the 21st Century, such as cross disciplinary, creative, adaptive and problem-solving skills as well as the ability to work cooperatively [10]. Involving Australia, Finland, Portugal, Singapore and Britain, the approach by ATC21S is further supported by McGaw [11] who stated that, "change on a global scale is required to equip students of today with the skills they need to succeed in the workforce of tomorrow" (p. 1). McGaw highlights that this has been elusive to date, as "We hoped to add information and communications technology (ICT) competence in PISA 2006 but did not succeed...We all need now to work together to advance assessment practice" (p. 1).

Furthermore, Finger [12] notes that, while there has been a growing focus on TPACK, particularly in the United States of America, TPACK is only emerging in Australia in conversations about teacher education program design. This paper attempts to play a role in adding to these early conversations to inform teacher education program design.

2.2 Conceptualising TPACK Knowledge and Preservice Teacher Education Programs

Mishra and Koehler [13] explain how TPACK enables teacher education students to develop understanding about how the selection of technologies can lead to good teaching with technology as one of "three core components – content, pedagogy and technology, and the relationships between them" (pp. 11-12). Moreover, TPACK incorporates the importance of context, and "solutions require nuanced understanding that goes beyond the general principles of content, technology and pedagogy" (p. 23). We suggest that where ICT initiatives have failed, there has not been any TPACK conceptualization informing the thinking, design and implementation. In many instances, teachers tend to find the professional development focused on technological knowledge through introducing them to new hardware or software applications, without considerations of context, pedagogy and content.

We agree with the assertion by Lee and Gaffney [14] that we need to move from a paper-based Industrial Age model of schooling to a digitally based paradigm more appropriate for an Information Age model of schooling. In attempting to explain teacher adoption of digital technologies, stages of teacher development have been proposed by Newhouse et al. [15] who suggest that teachers might move through stages of inaction, investigation, application, integration and transformation. Table 1 presents a synthesis of Lee and Gaffney's [14] characteristics of traditional paper-based and digitally-based paradigms, and Newhouse et al.'s [15] stages of teacher development, and teacher education programs.

Table 1. Stages of teacher development, stages of school development and TPACK (adapted from [16], pp. 220-221)

Stages of Teacher Development (adapted from [15])	Stages of School Development (adapted from [14])	Preservice Teacher Education Programs (adapted from [7])
Inaction	Traditional Industrial Age model of school organisation	Focus on content Directed instruction Teacher-centred
Investigation	Early stages of understanding of the Information Age	Focus on pedagogy and content Some interest in using ICT
Application	Exploration of digital technologies to enhance learning within existing curriculum and school organisation	Focus on pedagogy and content Courses included in programs with focus on learning about ICT
Critical Use Border		
Integration	Schools becoming digital schools – digital take-off; e.g. whole adoption of IWBs, classroom Internet connectivity, interoperability	Focus on technology, pedagogy and content Courses included in programs which focus on learning with ICT
Transformation	Networked school communities, incorporating learning within and beyond the place called school – including home-school nexus and school connecting with communities	TPACK framework is fully embraced throughout the entire program design and implementation Graduates demonstrate TPACK capabilities

3 Summary of a Study to Audit the TPACK Capabilities of Preservice Teacher Education Programs

The authors have conducted various studies to inform program and teacher development [17] [18] [19]. The study summarized in the following sections aimed to undertake an audit of final year students at the two Universities within which they work.

3.1 Aim and Significance of the Study

The central question which this audit sought to answer was – How well are our teacher education programs preparing graduates to have TPACK capabilities? The significance of the study relates to the need for future teachers to have the TPACK capabilities which enable them to enhance and transform learning and teaching by having the necessary technological, pedagogical and content knowledge. This begs the questions – how can we know they have these TPACK capabilities? How can we measure these?

These continue to be early days of research using TPACK as a framework. Recent studies include those by Sahin, Akturk and Schmidt [20] and Terpstra [21]. Sahin et al. [20] found that TPACK positively affected preservice teacher education students' vocational self-efficacy. Terpstra [21], among her findings, reported that the preservice teachers whom she studied demonstrated more Technological Knowledge than Technological Pedagogical Knowledge and Technological Pedagogical Content Knowledge. Interestingly, Terpstra [21] found that, while the preservice teacher education students used digital technologies in their daily lives, they did not connect this Technological Knowledge with their own teaching. While there is a growing list of TPACK research occurring, a thorough search revealed only one Australian study published by Holmes [22] which investigated the lesson activities developed by a 13 final year undergraduate secondary mathematics pre-service teachers. The study reported that the pre-service teachers were able to plan effectively to integrate IWB features within their mathematical lessons and demonstrated developing TPCK as a result.

Drawing upon the TPACK conceptualisation proposed by Mishra and Koehler [13] as the theoretical framework to guide this audit, this study is significant as being thirst Australian study of its kind, in relation to adding to our knowledge about TPACK capabilities of future teachers. The findings can be used as the basis for informing the design of teacher education programs.

3.2   Research Methodology and Demographic Information of Participants

The development of this TPACK Confidence Survey included aspects from previously validated instruments including the ICT Audit Survey [23] and the Learning with ICT: Measuring ICT Use in the Curriculum instrument [25]. The instrument was effectively administered online using Lime Survey. Demographic information was sought, and indicators were included which reflected those expected by the Department of Education and Training in Queensland in their ICT Certificate level of the Smart Classrooms Professional Development Framework [24].

Ethics approvals were obtained from both Universities involved in the study. Responses were obtained from 345 final year preservice teacher education students from two Queensland universities – one being a Metropolitan University and the other being a Regional University. Table 2 displays the demographic information of those studied.

Table 2. Demographic information of final year students – Gender, University Attended, and Age (N=345)

	Number	%
Gender:		
Female	273	79
Male	72	21
Total	**345**	**100**
University Attended:		
The Metropolitan University	199	57.7
The Regional University	146	42.3
Total	**345**	**100**
Age of Pre-service Teachers:		
Less than 20 years	4	1.2
20-29 years	177	51.3
30-39 years	90	26.1
40-49 years	61	17.7
50 + years	13	3.8
Total	**345**	**100**

Table 3 below displays the student teachers' level of confidence which they reported in relation to the use of ICT with school students for teaching and learning.

Table 3. Confidence to use ICT with students

Confidence to use ICT with school students for teaching and learning	Number	%
No confidence	14	4.1
Some confidence	113	32.8
Confident	151	43.8
Very confident	67	19.4
Total	**345**	**100**

For students who are about to graduate, there are almost 2 out of every 5 students who reported that they had either no confidence or some confidence. This is a disturbing finding, as confidence might be expected to reflect the students' perceptions of their capabilities. The following findings reported in this paper explore this further.

4   Summary of the Major Findings

The following summary provides data and analysis relating to TK and TPACK obtained through administration of the instrument developed.

4.1   Student Teacher Access to and Interest in Using ICT Resources

Students were found to have very high levels of personal ownership of computers (99.4%), regular access to broadband Internet (96.5%), and surprisingly only 41.2 % reported that they had access to mobile computing devices. The level of ownership of a personal computer and access to broadband Internet were similar to the 2003 student audit results [23]. For statements about interest in and perceived attitudes towards using ICT, means were calculated using a 4-point Likert scale where a mean of 1 = Not at all; 2 = Some extent; 3 = Great extent; and 4 = Very great extent. The pre-service teacher education students surveyed in this study expressed strong interest in using ICT for personal purposes (M = 3.06); strong interest in using ICT for teaching and learning purposes (M = 3.25); extensive use of ICT for personal purposes (M = 3.01); a moderate level of use of ICT for teaching and learning purposes (M = 2.68); and a strong belief that computers can improve student-learning outcomes (M = 3.19). A Pearson Chi-square test of significance indicated no significant difference between the two universities in this study. Interestingly, a lower mean was obtained for the extent that the pre-service teachers actually use ICT for teaching and learning purposes in comparison to their belief in the value of ICT to improve student learning outcomes. The lower mean for use of ICT for teaching and learning purposes might be explained either by limited opportunities to integrate ICT when students are at practicum, or the fact that these respondents are pre-service teachers and have had limited opportunities to use ICT for teaching and learning with students. For both inferences, it appears that, for these teacher education students, there is limited evidence of TPACK capabilities.

4.2 Technological Knowledge (TK)

To measure students' perception of their Technological Knowledge (TK) six items were framed as Koehler and Mishra [6] indicate that TK enables teachers to understand information technology, apply it properly, identify useful technologies, and continually adapt to changes in technology. Unlike the findings reported by Terpstra [21] that the students she studied had sound levels of TK, none of the items resulted in a high level (mean >3) of perceived competence from the pre-service teachers and, disturbingly, more than 10% of them responded that they had no competence at all with keeping informed about new digital technologies or about being able to solve their own technical problems (Items 3 and 4).

Table 4. Technological Knowledge (TK) - Perceived competence with digital technologies (N=345)

Technology Knowledge (TK) – Digital Technologies	Mean (SD)	% No Competence
1 I am comfortable using digital technologies.	2.76 (.96)	2.9
2 I learn about new digital technologies easily.	2.64 (.98)	5.2
3 I keep informed about new digital technologies.	2.28 (.99)	14.8
4 I know how to solve my own technical problems.	2.18 (.95)	16.2
5 I have the technological skills I need to use digital technologies to achieve personal goals.	2.61 (.98)	7.2
6 I have the technological skills I need to use digital technologies to achieve professional (teaching and learning) goals.	2.48 (.95)	7.0

Further items asked respondents to indicate their perceived competence in using various ICT applications. Comparisons with the 2003 audit data were able to be made for Items 1 to 14 inclusive, but additional items were added to reflect new applications available since 2003. These included Web 2.0 and social networking technologies, online learning, online publishing, accessing learning objects, and creating learning objects. Despite the assumption that social networking (e.g. Facebook), online learning (all students are expected to use Blackboard in their studies), and online publishing (e.g. blogging) might be used frequently by these students, the findings did not support these assumptions.

The low perceptions of competence in using learning objects was also concerning, and this suggests that for many of these students they will not be taking advantage of the significant resources available. The applications which the students perceived that they were most competent in using were word processing, presentation software, email, web browsers, and web searching, though these were not significantly stronger than the levels of perceived competence reported by students in the 2003 audit. These findings suggest that the teacher education programs might have tended to assume that students now had higher levels of TK through more pervasive access to digital technologies and applications. However, that assumption is not supported beyond a limited range of applications. The implications for TPACK are profound, as insufficient TK is likely to mean limited TPK, TCK, and TPACK.

Table 5. Technological Knowledge (TK) - Perceived competence with ICT applications

	Technology Knowledge ICT Software Applications (*Examples of Software*)	**2009 (N=345)**		**2003 (N=285)**	
		Mean (SD)	**% No Competence**	**Mean (SD)**	**% No Competence**
1	Word Processing (e.g. *Microsoft Word*)	3.51 (.89)	.6	3.61 (.56)	.4
2	Desktop Publishing (e.g. *Microsoft Publisher*)	2.47 (1.11)	16.8	2.70 (.99)	10.9
3	Presentation Software (e.g. *Microsoft Power Point*)	3.22 (.94)	1.2	3.01 (.92)	6.3
4	Spreadsheets (e.g. *Microsoft Excel*)	2.66 (1.05)	8.7	2.56 (.88)	9.5
5	Databases (e.g. *Microsoft Access, Filemaker*)	1.85 (.97)	37.1	2.06 (.89)	27.4
6	Graphics creation and/or editing (e.g. *Paint Shop Pro, Adobe Photoshop*)	2.03 (.97)	26.7	2.19 (1.00)	27.4
7	Digital image capture *(e.g. by Digital camera, scanning)*	2.92 (1.07)	5.8	2.35 (1.04)	23.9
8	Multimedia Development and Authoring (e.g. *Macromedia Director, Flash*)	1.59 (.89)	52.8	1.82 (.89)	42.1
9	Visual Thinking Software (e.g. *Inspiration, Kidspiration, CMap*)	1.50 (.89)	61.2	1.52 (.87)	65.3
10	Digital Video Editing (e.g. *iMovie, Adobe Premiere, MovieMaker*)	1.86 (1.06)	42.3	1.48 (.87)	65.6
11	Email (e.g. *Microsoft Outlook, Gmail, Lotus*)	3.36 (.97)	2.0	3.33 (.90)	4.2
12	Web Browsers (e.g. *Internet Explorer, Netscape, Safari, Firefox*)	3.38 (.94)	1.2	3.42 (.88)	2.8
13	Web Searching (e.g. *Google*)	3.50 (.89)	.3	3.45 (.78)	1.1
14	Web Page Development (e.g. *Macromedia Dreamweaver*)	1.73 (1.01)	49.6	1.92 (1.00)	38.9
15	Web 2.0 and Social Networking (e.g. *Facebook, MySpace, Flickr, Twitter, YouTube, Nings*)	2.90 (1.12)	9.6	NA	NA
16	Online learning (e.g. *Blackboard*)	2.24 (1.14)	27.8	NA	NA
17	Online publishing (e.g. *Blogging, Podcasts, YouTube*)	2.27 (1.06)	20	NA	NA
18	Access repositories of reusable learning objects	1.88 (1.0)	36.8	NA	NA
19	Create reusable learning objects	1.87 (1.02)	38.6	NA	NA

NB. NA = Not Available in the 2003 Audit Instrument.

4.3   Technological Pedagogical Content Knowledge (TPACK)

TPACK, as conceptualised by Koehler and Mishra [6], refers to the knowledge that emerges from the interaction of a teacher's content, pedagogy, and technology knowledge bases. They [6] note that Professional standards for teachers now have increased expectations for teachers to demonstrate an understanding of the complex interplay between these three key knowledge bases and how they are interpreted in specific

Table 6. TPACK - Perceived confidence to integrate ICT into student learning

In my class, I could support *students'* use of ICT to:	Mean (SD)	% No / Limited Confidence
1.1 acquire the knowledge, skills, abilities, and attitudes to deal with ongoing technological change.	2.48 (.99)	38.8
1.2 develop functional competencies in a specified curriculum area.	2.57 (.97)	34.8
1.3 synthesize their knowledge.	2.58 (.98)	32.2
1.4 actively construct their own knowledge in collaboration with their peers and others.	2.61 (1.00)	30.8
1.5 actively construct knowledge that integrates curriculum areas.	2.58 (.99)	35.4
1.6 develop deep understanding about a topic of interest relevant to the curriculum area(s) being studied.	2.68 (.99)	27.8
1.7 develop a scientific understanding of the world.	2.50 (.99)	35.9
1.8 provide motivation for curriculum tasks.	2.74 (.97)	23.2
1.9 plan and/or manage curriculum projects.	2.59 (.99)	31.3
1.10 integrate different media to create appropriate products.	2.47 (1.05)	39.1
1.11 engage in sustained involvement with curriculum activities.	2.53 (.98)	35
1.12 support elements of the learning process.	2.70 (.97)	25.2
1.13 demonstrate what they have learned.	2.75 (.99)	22.3
1.14 undertake formative and/or summative assessment.	2.68 (.99)	28.4
2.1 acquire awareness of the global implications of ICT-based technologies on society.	2.43 (1.02)	41.7
2.2 gain intercultural understanding.	2.55 (1.00)	33.6
2.3 critically evaluate their own and society's values.	2.50 (.99)	38.2
2.4 communicate with others locally and globally.	2.84 (1.04)	20.8
2.5 engage in independent learning through access to education at a time, place, and pace of their own choosing.	2.65 (.95)	30.4
2.6 understand and participate in the changing knowledge economy.	2.42 (.96)	41.8

teaching and learning contexts. In developing the instrument to measure the preservice teachers' TPACK in this study, the statistically robust, validated 20 item Learning with ICT: Measuring ICT Use in the Curriculum instrument [18] [25], was incorporated into this survey. That instrument has been shown to contain two strong factors. The first factor is comprised of 14 items that define student use of ICT as a tool for the development of ICT-related skills and the enhancement of curriculum learning outcomes ($\alpha = 0.94$). The second factor comprised 6 items that define ICT use as an integral component of reforms that transform what students learn and how school is structured and organised ($\alpha = 0.86$). This instrument utilises the theoretical constructs described in Good Practice and Leadership in the Use of ICT in Schools [26] and The Queensland School Reform Longitudinal Study [27] when defining ICT curriculum integration. Each of the items asks teachers to rate how their students use ICT for learning rather than how they use ICT. Because the instrument describes how students use ICT for learning as a consequence of how teachers integrate ICT into the curriculum, we contend that the 20 items measure teachers' TPACK as described by its underpinning theoretical constructs.

Overall, as shown in Table 6, the means and the percentage of preservice teacher education students reporting little or no confidence to integrate ICT into student learning in relation to the statements do not convincingly portray a story of strong TPACK capabilities. With little or confidence reported by 38.8% of the students to "acquire the knowledge, skills, abilities, and attitudes to deal with ongoing technological change" does not reflect personal and professional confidence in dealing with the technological changes one might reasonably expect will occur throughout the next 30-50 years of their careers. Similarly, 2 out of every 5 students surveyed indicated that they had little or no confidence in being able to "understand and participate in the changing knowledge economy".

When the generally low levels of TK confidence, with the exception of a limited range of applications, is also taken into account, it appears that those low levels of TK might be influential in these low levels of TPACK confidence.

5 Conclusion and Implications for Preservice Teacher Education Programs

The key implication and key message which has emerged from this study is that we need to urgently develop a greater understanding and strengthen the use of TPACK as a shared language among teacher educators and their preservice teacher education students. The findings reported here strongly suggest that assumptions that preservice teacher education students have strong TK needs to be made problematic. We need to audit these students early and develop students' TK confidence and competence throughout their teacher education programs as an essential set of knowledges needed upon which TPACK capabilities can be built.

This paper has highlighted the potential role which the TPACK conceptualisation can make to informing preservice teacher education programs which have tended to be largely informed by PCK. We have argued that PCK is no longer adequate for learning and teaching in the 21st Century. The paper also made a significant contribution through the development of an instrument which proved to be effective in measuring aspects of TPACK capabilities. The data reported illustrated that, apart from a limited range of ICT applications, the students studied have inadequate levels of TK confidence. Those limited levels of TK confidence were found to translate into limited TPACK capabilities to integrate ICT for curriculum applications.

We need to encourage the implementation of strategies to better prepare future teachers for learning and teaching in the 21st Century. To achieve this, we believe that we need a better, shared understanding of TPACK to inform teacher education courses and programs, to measure preservice teacher education students' TPACK capabilities throughout their program of study. To enable this, TPACK instruments, such as the instrument referred to in this study, need to be developed which draw upon research and evidence-based approaches.

References

1. Shulman, L.S.: Those who understand: Knowledge growth in teaching. In: Educational Researcher, AERA Presidential Address, pp. 4–14 (February 1986)
2. Shulman, L.S.: Knowledge and teaching: Foundations of the new reform. Harvard Educational Review 57, 1–22 (1987)
3. Mishra, P., Koehler, M.: Technological pedagogical Content Knowledge: A framework for teacher knowledge. Teachers College Record 108(6), 1017–1054 (2006)
4. AACTE Committee on Innovation and Technology. Handbook of Pedagogical Content Knowledge (TPCK) for Educators. Routledge/Taylor & Francis Group, New York (2008)
5. Koehler, M.J., Mishra, P., Yahya, K.: Tracing the development of teacher knowledge in a design seminar: Integrating content, pedagogy and technology. Computers & Education 49, 740–762 (2007)
6. Koehler, M., Mishra, P.: Introducing TPCK. In AACTE Committee on Innovation and Technology. In: Handbook of Pedagogical Content Knowledge (TPCK) for Educators. Routledge/Taylor & Francis Group, New York (2008)
7. Queensland College of Teachers. Professional Standards for Queensland Teachers, Graduate level (2009), http://www.qct.edu.au/standards/documents/PSQT_GradLevel_v3_Web.pdf
8. Jamieson-Proctor, R., Finger, G., Albion, P.: Auditing the TPACK Capabilities of Final Year Teacher Education Students: Are They Ready for the 21st Century? Paper presented at the Australian Computers in Education Digital Diversity Conference 2010, Melbourne, Australia, April 6-9 (2010)
9. Masters, G.N.: A Shared Challenge: Improving Literacy, Numeracy and Science Learning in Queensland Primary Schools. ACER Press, Camberwell (2009)
10. Australian Labor Party. Assessment and teaching of 21st century skills, Media Statement, Australian Labor Party (2009), http://www.alp.org.au/media/0609/msed090.php
11. McGaw, B.: Cited in News Release: Cisco, Intel and Microsoft collaborate to improve education assessments (2009), http://www.atc21s.org/Assets?Files/de10c023-ead5-4ccf-8a08-cbb273bb14fb,pdf
12. Finger, G.: Education Under the Microscope How competitive is Australia? Educational Technology Solutions (33), 44–48 (2009)
13. Mishra, P., Koehler, M.: Introducing TPCK. In: AACTE Committee on Innovation and Technology (ed.). Handbook of Technological Pedagogical Content Knowledge (TPCK) for Educators. Routledge/Taylor & Francis Group, New York (2008)

14. Lee, M., Gaffney, M.: Leading a Digital School, Camberwell, Victoria
15. Newhouse, P., Clarkson, B., Trinidad, S.: A framework for leading school change in using ICT'. In: Trinidad, S., Pearson, J. (eds.) Using ICT in education: Leadership, Change and Models of Best Practice, pp. 148–164. Pearson Education Asia, Singapore (2005)
16. Finger, G., Jamieson-Proctor, R.: Teacher Readiness: TPACK capabilities and redesigning working conditions. In: Lee, M., Finger, G. (eds.) Developing a Networked School Community: A Guide to Realising the Vision. ACER Press, Camberwell (2010)
17. Albion, P.: Graduating Teachers' Dispositions for Integrating Information and Communications Technologies into their Teaching. In: Crawford, C., et al. (eds.) Proceedings of the Society for Information Technology and Teacher Education International Conference 2003, pp. 1592–1599. Association for the Advancement for Computing in Education (AACE), Chesapeake (2003)
18. Jamieson-Proctor, R.M., Watson, G., Finger, G., Grimbeek, P., Burnett, P.C.: Measuring the Use of Information and Communication Technologies (ICTs) in the Classroom. Computers in the Schools 24(1/2), 167–184 (2007)
19. Jamieson-Proctor, R., Finger, G.: ACT to Improve IcT Use for Learning: A synthesis of studies of Teacher Confidence in Using ICT in two Queensland schooling systems. In: Australian Computers in Education Conference (ACEC): ACT on IcT, Canberra, September 29-October 2 (2008)
20. Sahin, I., Akturk, A.O., Schmidt, D.A.: Relationship of preservice teachers' technological pedagogical content knowledge with their vocational self-efficacy beliefs. In: Research Highlights in Technology and Teacher Education, pp. 293–301 (2009)
21. Terpstra, M.J.: Developing Technological Pedagogical Content Knowledge: Preservice Teachers' Perceptions of How They Learn to Use Educational Technology in their Teaching. Unpublished Doctor of Philosophy Dissertation, Michigan State University (2009)
22. Holmes, K.: Planning to teach with digital tools: Introducing the interactive whiteboard to pre-service secondary mathematics teachers. Australian Journal of Educational Technology 25(3), 351–365 (2009)
23. Watson, G., Jamieson-Proctor, R., Finger, G., Lang, W.T.: Auditing the ICT experiences of teacher education undergraduates. Australian Educational Computing 19, 3–10 (2004)
24. Department of Education and Training (DET). Smart Classrooms Professional Development Framework (2010),
    http://education.qld.gov.au/smartclassrooms/pdframework/
25. Jamieson-Proctor, R., Watson, G., Finger, G., Grimbeek, P.M.: An external evaluation of Education Queensland's ICT Curriculum Integration Performance Measurement Instrument. Griffith University, Brisbane (2005)
26. Department of Education Training and Youth Affairs (DETYA). Good Practice and Leadership in the Use of ICT in School, edNA Online, Adelaide (2000),
    http://www.edna.edu.au/sibling/leadingpractice
27. Lingard, B., Ladwig, J., Mills, M., Bahr, M., Chant, D., Warry, M., et al.: The Queensland school reform longitudinal study. Education Queensland, Brisbane (2001)

eExaminations Development and Acceptance

Andrew E. Fluck

University of Tasmania
Locked Bag 1307, Launceston, Tasmania, 7250, Australia
Andrew.Fluck@utas.edu.au

Abstract. Over three years students at the University of Tasmania have participated in eExaminations where they have responded to examination questions
using computers. Over these three years they have made the transition from
using institutional computers in laboratories to using personally owned laptops
in a traditional examination hall. This innovation and transition have been par-
alleled and enabled by the development of a modified live operating system
which preserves the fairness of the assessment process. The technical developments depended upon social innovation engineering efforts necessitated by the
range of adopters amongst students and faculty. National recognition was
achieved for this method which is being adopted more widely worldwide. The
technical materials are available for download from www.eExams.org. .

Keywords: computer based examination, innovation engineering, Ubuntu, USB
drive.

1 Introduction

With the explosion of eLearning over the last decade, there has been a corresponding
surge of interest in computer mediated assessment [1]. Computers can facilitate a
broader range of assessment techniques such as ePortfolios, blogs, discussion board
responses and a range of digital recording techniques such as podcasting or video
production.

These new techniques are themselves a smorgasbord of digital skills which add
rich variety to a blend of assessment within any one course. Good assessment of student learning uses a combination of diagnostic, formative and summative evaluations.
Summative assessment in particular needs to be valid, reliable and fair. The latter can
be interpreted as meaning some part of the total assessment for a course should be
done in such a way as to provide a reasonable level of assurance the submitted work
is entirely that of the candidate who will receive an award. In some cases where students take home their coursework assessments, they are required to sign disclaimers
such as "I hereby declare that I am the sole author of this paper and everything presented in this paper is my own" [2]. This does not enable the institution to be certain
the work is in fact entirely due to the individual – some may have friendship and
professional networks which help them develop ideas more than other candidates.

For assessments where self-certification is inappropriate, more formal examinations are conducted. As digital computers become more widely available to pupils in

N. Reynolds and M. Turcsányi-Szabó (Eds.): KCKS 2010, IFIP AICT 324, pp. 126–135, 2010.

schools [3] and students in universities, quality assurance organizations are looking at electronic assessment methods more closely. In Norway *The Knowledge Promotion* reforms have led to the acceptance of protocols of computer-based examinations in high schools and senior secondary colleges [4].

Leister, Fretland and Solheim [5] described how the 19 counties of Norway have adopted strategies to incorporate computer based examinations. A common assumption is that candidate identity will be checked and activity supervised during the examination by non-technical staff, often retired teachers.

When considering computer-based examinations there are a range of technological implementation aspects. These include ways in which questions should be delivered and answers collected (reticulation). The technology chosen will reflect a policy balance between security, convenience and reliability. This kind of policy response and those to other problems associated with computer-based examinations are described in Table 1.

Table 1. Areas of policy concern for computer-based examinations in schools

Area of concern	*Opposing policy stances*		
Reticulation of questions and answer responses	Networked	←→	Standalone
Computer ownership	Institutional	←→	Personal
Computer functionality	Kiosk (locked) mode	←→	Wide range of software (sometimes using virtualization or a compatibility layer)
Candidate communication	Function blocking	←→	Logging/monitoring
Candidate familiarity	Common learning environment	←→	Test environment requires familiarization/training
Licencing costs	Commercial	←→	Free, open source software

Each of the issues in Table 1 is now addressed in more detail.

The whole area of question and answer reticulation requires a fault tolerant approach to reliability of the examination system. Operational communication facilities during the examination allow answers to be progressively backed up, providing a measure of redundancy if a single candidate's equipment should fail. However, any operational communication link could be exploited by a mischievous candidate for the purposes of cheating, and this creates a potential security loophole. Furthermore, equipment failure at the level of a school wireless access point or router, or at the systemic server centre, or any point in between, could interrupt examinations for a very large number of candidates.

As more students and pupils acquire their own computers (laptops or netbooks) and are permitted to connect them to school networks, there is less pressure to provide information technology equipment within the institution. However, these machines may be prepared with special software to interdict examination protocols. Their use may be the only economic way of overcoming the logistical problems of supplying a large number of workstations required for examination purposes.

Generally, running an examination within a web-browser window (kiosk mode) requires the questions to be programmed using *Shockwave Flash* or a similar programming language. This may be very suitable for providing question tracking to each student during the examination, but is only viable for very large scale assessments with a long time-frame for preparation. Giving candidates access to the full operating system can allow the use of specialist software within the assessment process.

For the examination to be fair, it is generally accepted that candidates should not be able to communicate with one another or any other person. Additionally, digital communication beyond the location of the exam could be used to access pre-prepared answers or other helpful information which may not be equally accessible to all candidates. Function blocking works on the candidate's equipment or in a local router to make sure only permitted communications occur such as with a question server or answer backup database. The alternative approach is to allow all communications, but to log them and alert local supervisors if there is an exceptional message.

Candidate familiarity with the selected system appears to be a common request from awarding bodies, but is rarely well defined. In some case this has been interpreted as meaning Microsoft Windows (without actually specifying a commercial product) since many pupils use this operating system for their learning. There is certainly a good case for students being able to undertake standard operations such as launching software, entering text etc. without cognitive hurdles.

Whichever system is used by candidates for their exams, it must be within legal guidelines. If an operating system requires a licence fee for each installation, then this fee must to be paid. Such an economic argument is a strong one for basing a system on whatever software is already installed upon the machine each candidate uses.

In the Norwegian county of *Møre og Romsdal* the system adopted for trials was a networked, personal, wide range with function blocking in a novel test environment using FOSS (free, open source software). It has been argued that if learners conventionally use Microsoft Windows and Office, then the latter two areas of concern are in tension. It could equally well be argued that a FOSS environment for which the candidate has received familiarisation training can eliminate this tension.

2 Method

Our objective in this project was to determine the viability of a new approach to computer-based examinations in tertiary education. We commissioned the construction of a special version of the Ubuntu operating system and application software for the purpose. This eExam System was run on target computers by inserting a CD-ROM (or later, a USB drive) and holding down the 'one-time boot menu' key on power-up. This action generates a menu of bootable sources and the candidate selects the eExam disk or USB drive.

The investigation is described by a participant observer using a stepwise improvement method. In the context of rapidly evolving technology, any constant comparison approach would rapidly become unviable. In this sense the eExamination system has been updated by our support staff at Open Technology solutions[1] in Hobart as new versions of Ubuntu have been released, retaining core functionality at each stage.

The initial trials of the eExamination system have used only some of the potential that moving to computer-based assessment entails. Using computers can support complex, authentic, real-life contexts and activities in which candidates can demonstrate multiple learning perspectives. However, there are few examples of such digital assessment practices [6].

Speculation about intelligent computer-aided assessment [7] has not been considered in this research. This area is one which shows much promise, but would require an autonomous agent running between the operating system and candidate-initiated applications.

Additionally the method can be viewed as action research presented as a case study.

2.1 The Three Trials

2.1.1 First Trial

Trials began in 2007 at the University of Tasmania using a modified version of Ubuntu 7.04 and university lab-based computers. The unit of study was in the third year of a Bachelor of Education degree, and was intended to equip pre-service teachers to use ICT in their classroom practice. As with all the following trials, every student was issued with a CD-ROM and an example eExamination very early in the unit of study. The IT support staff agreed to waive normal operating conditions to allow one laboratory of computers to boot from this external operating system source, and students were shown how to activate the boot-menu of any personal computer at home. In this case Open Office and other software (such as The GIMP for creating diagrams) were on the CD-ROM together with the question file.

Our modified version of Ubuntu did not contain the IP stack, preventing internet connectivity using any kind of networking. To ensure the system was correctly loaded, a unique photograph was displayed on the desktop background of each candidate's computer. This could be quickly checked by the supervisors without technical knowledge. The software also prevented any access to the local hard disk drive, so digitally based system modification or access to previously prepared answers was prevented.

During the eExamination, students accessed videos and other materials for each question from the CD-ROM, but saved their answer files to the computer desktop. At the end of the assessment, a USB stick was passed from student to student to capture the finished answer files. The files were burned onto a CD-ROM before passing to various markers. Post-exam surveys showed students were divided between those that liked the new ICT-based format with 56% preferring to have formal tests conducted using computers instead of using handwriting on paper.

2.1.2 Second Trial

In the 2008 trial the eExamination was modified to be presented in two files. The first was a PDF document (therefore difficult for candidates to modify) and the second a

---

[1] http://www.opentechnologysolutions.com.au

mostly blank text document file with spaces for each answer response. Post-exam focus groups showed that the multiplicity of windows (some questions involved video or other files of pupil work) was very confusing. The process was altered slightly to allow students with their own laptops to bring those into the eExamination and use them in the same room as candidates using institutional desktop computers [8].

Only 35% of students in the post-exam survey preferred computers, and this was attributed to the greater complexity of handling multiple windows. A focus group identified dichotomous responses amongst the candidate cohort. Touch-typists considered themselves advantaged in the new situation, whilst those whose handwriting was considered faster, felt discriminated against.

2.1.3 Third Trial

An important change was made in the third trial by gaining agreement from the University Exams Office that the eExamination would take place in the same hall as all the other exams. There were two conditions – that the eExamination would be scheduled after all the other exams, and would be the only exam at the time. An inspection showed the hall had 21 mains electricity power points. Surge suppression devices were provided with outlets for up to six laptop mains adapters on each power point. Most students would use their own laptop computers, with the institution providing loan machines for the residue (about 10% of the cohort).

3   Results

These results relate to the third trial, where most students provided their own personal computer. When learning about the eExamination near the beginning of the teaching unit, students accepted the idea. As the time for the assessment drew closer however, some started to express apprehension. One of the lectures focussed on theories of innovation adoption, and they could see various levels of preparedness within the group, ranging from early adopters to laggards.

Students used the anonymous discussion board in the learning management system to sound out their worries:

> Having talked to a number of people, it's obvious a lot of us have concerns about using our own laptops in the exam. It would be excellent if everyone could let their opinions be known here... I think it puts some of us at a disadvantage. To begin with not everyone HAS a laptop, what about them? Also, batteries and charging are an issue depending on the type of laptop being used. Not to mention that some computers take longer to load than others...

These difficulties had already been solved by the arrangements above. However, the laggard section [9] of the cohort was quite strident in identifying objections:

> I have heard that there are differences in the running speed between the CD version and the USB version. I don't recall ever being in an exam where the type of booklet given determines the speed you can complete the exam. I think the real issue is that the Faculty wants to be the first to have an exam using laptops.

The students were experiencing a halo effect, and were becoming aware that this was a novel practice. This added to their concerns, and forced them to enquire deeply into the new system. Since it had not (to our knowledge) been used before, it was impossible to prove all their concerns would be addressed. Also, what were the metrics for comparison? This tension was expressed in this exchange between an anonymous student and the unit coordinator:

> I am totally for using a laptop for the exam, absolutely. But only if it can be proved that the conditions will be as equitable as those during hand writing exams.

> The speed question is an interesting one. You can look at it two ways. Firstly, the time required to boot up and get going. This can vary according to how fast your computer is (whether you are using USB or CD for instance), but won't affect the time you have because no-one will be allowed to start writing until everyone is booted up. The second is the speed you can enter your answers. Most of this is typing, and I doubt ANYONE can type faster than the slowest computer can accept text. So once again, you are on a level playing field.

This student uncertainty was communicated to the university administration, and several questions were asked by the head of school about the process. Fortunately the Faculty was supportive, and continued to permit the eExamination to proceed. Some students wrote strongly in favour of the course and the exam mode:

> I also do not feel that our concerns were going to change requiring a laptop to sit the exam, given much of Dr Fluck's research involves investigating electronic testing and examination. At the same time, I also feel that if certain people had accepted this earlier, then the valuable lecture and tutorial time could have been used discussing the content instead of answering tedious laptop preparation questions that had already been asked over and over. Complaining about and discussing this seemingly non-negotiable point has added to the perceived stressful occasion of sitting an exam, having inspired panic, fear and anxiety. Generally this has affected people whose ICT skills are lagging, those who need the most confidence leading up to the exam. I hope they do not regret not expending their energies in a more constructive way. I trust everyone involved, both staff and students, will look back on this experience subjectively as a first hand understanding of some of the realistic difficulties involved in implementing IT. In this life, sometimes you just have to do the best with the limitations placed upon you. Best of luck everyone.

The examination materials were presented in a new fashion to reflect the concerns of the second trial cohort. A single document file was provided which contained both the questions and spaces for answers. The questions were converted into images and the file placed in a read-only section of the USB stick issued to every candidate. This had two effects. Firstly, students could not type in answers until they had re-saved the file in the answers partition of the USB stick. Secondly, although a question might be inadvertently deleted, it would disappear in its entirety – thus preventing the subtle one-word alteration which might detract from the problem! If such an event took place inadvertently, the original file remained for reference.

The eExamination took place with only minor hitches. All students were provided with a USB stick containing the bootable modified version of Ubuntu, the questions and security desktop picture, and a blank partition for answers. Some had previously arranged to get CD-ROM versions of the bootable operating system. A few student laptops had USB (universal serial bus) sockets which were so indented the eExamination stick would not enter. These two students completed the exam using paper backups. One student had a complete computer malfunction close to the end and was required to re-sit the examination. This event has forced a re-think of the procedure for recording answers to ensure a backup remains on the USB stick. Student answer scripts were copied from the USB sticks and were then burned to CD before distribution to markers. Markers chose to assess on screen, annotating the scripts with marks awarded, and collated totals into a spreadsheet.

A week after the eExamination had been successfully completed, a national newspaper flew a photographer to Tasmania and a story was printed on page two of the higher education supplement [10]. It described how 124 students on three University of Tasmania campuses took their laptops into their exam rooms to sit what was thought to be the first tertiary eExam in Australia. It not only changed the way we assessed students, but also paves the way for changing what we teach.

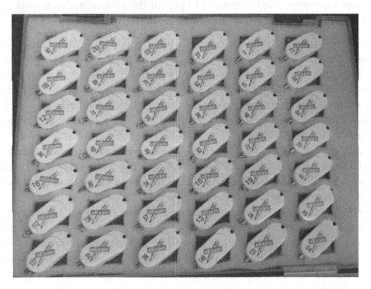

Fig. 1. A set of USB sticks each containing the eExamination system, question paper and answer partition

4 Discussion and Conclusion

This use of a live operating system for providing a fair environment for examinations is not unique. The DigEks software is based on Kubuntu, and works in a similar way.

It is more flexible than the current eExam System, in that both stand alone and restricted networked environments are catered for [5].

What are the lessons that can be learned from this case study?

Firstly, the impact of ICT on learning, even at the tertiary level, is not well understood by participants. In this case the participants were a 'cusp' generation, moving from the classroom practices they experienced as children, to creating new practices in their future roles as teachers. They are therefore a vital ingredient in transforming learning to a digital curriculum.

The first two trials and their impacts have been discussed in fuller length [8]. The move to personal laptops was seen by some candidates as the final straw – this was an exam (unusual in their course); it was computer-based (a unique situation); and furthermore they were expected to provide the computer themselves (costly and unheard of throughout the country). These appeared to be the main reasons for their apprehension.

The high noise levels reported by students in the first trial were quite absent from the third trial. Whereas institutional desktops in confined laboratories echoed to the noisy keyboards, the softer laptop keyboards in a large gymnasium space in the third trial were as quiet as pens on paper.

A critical question is the use of stand-alone computers compared to networked equipment. In the Norwegian case study [11] a systemic requirement to have restricted or monitored internet access required networking to be retained for the reticulation of questions and backup of answers.

Arguments for keeping active networking during the examination focus upon the ease of distributing questions and collecting answers. However, this comes with a penalty. Firstly, as discussed in the introduction, this ease of use increases the risk of unreliability because many infrastructure components must operate flawlessly throughout the assessment. A single point failure can affect many, if not all, the candidates. Also, active networking can also be exploited by cheats, or cause inadvertent exception alerts through the operation of software (such as operating system updates) without action by the candidate.

The trials at the University of Tasmania have used stand-alone computers for eExaminations with no networking at all. This has eliminated many causes of unreliability but has transferred the reticulation system to USB sticks. Hitherto a single person has formatted each stick in preparation, and transferred the answer files to CD-ROM before marking. Future trials will use a USB duplicator with a capacity to download all answer files into a controlling computer. With large batches of 20 sticks dealt with in minutes using this system, local reticulation becomes tolerant of time delays or intermittent electricity supply. On a larger scale the encrypted distribution of questions to the local venue some time before the eExamination could be mixed with the local programming of USB sticks.

Because the operating system is run from the examination CD or USB stick, this system is agnostic with respect to the ownership of the computing equipment. Institutional computers can be used just as easily as candidate-owned laptops.

The functionality of a kiosk-based system is highly restricted, and therefore full access to the operating system has greater potential to foster a digital curriculum. For example, if candidates were asked to prepare an analysis of economic trends using a spreadsheet, this would be difficult to do within a web-browser window without sophisticated software support. Ubuntu releases contain Open Office, which contains this kind of general purpose tool, together with the GIMP, a package for creating and manipulating pictures. If a more specialist piece of software (for computer-aided design for instance, or modelling chemical reactions) this could be included in the eExamination system. Linux-based software would be easy to include, and Windows-based software can often run under WINE[2].

As discussed above, the eExaminations system omits all computer-based communication, and therefore peer to peer messages are not possible, preventing collusion.

Some jurisdictions require candidates to have access to a 'familiar environment' when using computers for examinations. It could be argued that habitual users of Apple Macintosh computers would be disadvantaged if required to use a Microsoft Windows PC just for their exam – and vice versa. The process adopted at the University of Tasmania has been to briefly demonstrate the Ubuntu system to prospective candidates, and make a copy available for familiarisation over a month before the eExamination. This would not be permitted under the commercial licencing arrangements of the other two systems. Students have the chance to try it on their own computer (perhaps the one they will use for the exam) or on an institutional computer to undertake a previous year's questions.

Another advantage of the open source nature of the eExamination system based on Ubuntu, is that teaching staff can also be given copies for preparation of new examinations. These advantages have been embraced for further trials in the Faculties of Law, Arts (for History examinations), Science (for Architecture responses to detailed photographs of buildings) and potentially Human Life Science where movies of items in the pathology museum can be seen on screen with magnification.

These advantages for eExaminations can help make current exams better. However, in the longer term, this new medium for assessment holds promise which is far more significant. When the culminating summative assessment is conducted using a computer, candidates can be required to use sophisticated software analogous to that used by a practicing professional. For instance, engineers may be required to assess structures using a complex set of integral calculus equations. Software such as Maxima, Maple or Mathematica could be made available during the assessment to make such a complex problem soluble. In changing the way assessment is conducted, teachers can choose to alter course content to deal with topics in more authentic ways or at significantly higher levels of complexity. This is what is meant by the emergence of a digital curriculum.

In conclusion, the emergence of a digital curriculum appears to depend upon the availability of a digital assessment environment which is flexible, fair and scalable. Several systems can be expected to emerge in school education and tertiary learning institutions. The nature of the digital curriculum, its core content and the breadth of learning it embraces will all depend upon the characteristics of the eExamination system that becomes prevalent.

---

[2] WINE is a translation layer (a program loader) capable of running Windows applications on Linux or other operating systems.

References

1. Backroad Connections Pty Ltd: Assessment and Online Teaching (Version 1.01): Australian Flexible Learning Framework Quick Guides series. Australian National Training Authority (2004), `http://pre2005.flexiblelearning.net.au/guides/assessment.pdf`
2. Moos, D.: EDHD 420 Cognitive Development and Learning. University of Maryland (2006), `http://www.education.umd.edu/EDHD/course/syllabi/fall06/edhd420.pdf`
3. Trucano, M.: Uruguay's Plan Ceibal: The world's most ambitious roll-out of educational technologies? EduTech, World Bank (2009), `http://blogs.worldbank.org/edutech/videos/uruguays-plan-ceibal-the-worlds-most-ambitious-roll-out-of-educational-technologies` (January 30, 2010)
4. Norwegian Directorate of Education and Training: Hjelpemidler til eksamen I Kunnskapsløftet (September 2, 2009) (in Norwegian), `http://www.udir.no/upload/Eksamen/Hjelpemidler_til_eksamen_i_kunnskapsloftet.pdf` (last accessed January 30, 2010) (2008)
5. Leister, W., Fretland, T.: How to Perform ICT-based Exams in Compulsory Schools. Norwegian Computing Center. Presentation at NUUG mote, Oslo/Stavanger, November 10 (2009)
6. Cook, D.: Views of learning, assessment and the potential place of IT. In: McDougall, A., Murnane, J., Jones, A., Reynolds, N. (eds.) Researching IT in Education: Theory, Practice and Future Directions. Routledge, London (2010)
7. Bescherer, C., Spannagel, C., Kortenkamp, U., Muller, W.: Research in the field of intelligent computer-aided assessment. In: McDougall, A., Murnane, J., Jones, A., Reynolds, N. (eds.) Researching IT in Education: Theory, Practice and Future Directions. Routledge, London (2010)
8. Fluck, A., Pullen, D., Harper, C.: Case study of a computer based examination system. Australasian Journal of Educational Technology 25(4), 509–523 (2009), `http://www.ascilite.org.au/ajet/ajet25/fluck.html`
9. Rogers, E.M.: Diffusion of innovations, 5th edn. Simon and Schuster, New York (2003)
10. Lane, B.: Laptops pass the big exam. The Australian (newspaper), Sydney, November 18, p. 24 (2009)
11. Leister, W., Fretland, T., Solheim, I.: Preventing unwanted communication in ICT-based exams by using free software. Norwegian Computing Centre (2009), `http://publications.nr.no/nokobit2009_finalise_2.pdf`

Grundtvig Partnership Case Study 2009-2011 LifeLong Learning for Active Citizenship and Capacity Building LLLab

Anna Grabowska

PRO-MED sp. z o.o., Dolne Migowo 16 C,
80-952 Gdańsk, Poland

Abstract. Lifelong Learning (LLL) is the key concept of European Union (EU) and European Commission (EC) recommends Promoting Access and Participation in Lifelong Learning for All starting with 1996 European year of LLL and continuing with Feira (2000) and Lisbon (2000) European Council proceedings. With these principles in mind, the project Lifelong Learning for Active Citizenship and Capacity Building (LLLab) sets out to make the knowledge triangle (education, research and innovation) accessible to employed people to promote the concept to wider audiences and to build capacity of the employed in order for them to better respond to the new challenges of the EU standards in a developing intercultural knowledge-based society. LLLab is aimed to develop a culture of learning in the partner organizations to obtain a rise in skills levels, better employability, social inclusion, active citizenship and personal development which in the end will inevitably mean sustainable development of the European society.

Keywords: Lifelong Learning, e-learning, blended learning, U3A Online.

1 Introducing Lifelong Learning Program Grundtvig

The Grundtvig programme [1] focuses on the teaching and study needs of those in adult education and alternative education streams, as well as the institutions and organisations delivering these services. Supporting lifelong learning and mobility in this way also tackles Europe's ageing population problem.

Launched in 2000 and now part of the overarching Lifelong Learning Programme, Grundtvig aims to provide adults with ways to improve their knowledge and skills, keeping them mentally fit and potentially more employable.

It not only covers learners in adult education, but also the teachers, trainers, education staff and facilities that provide these services. These include relevant associations, counseling organisations, information services, policy-making bodies and others involved in lifelong learning and adult education at local, regional and national levels, such as NGOs, enterprises, voluntary groups and research centres.

At least 55% of the total funding for Grundtvig should go towards mobility and partnership activities.

N. Reynolds and M. Turcsányi-Szabó (Eds.): KCKS 2010, IFIP AICT 324, pp. 136–143, 2010.

Specific aims of the Grundtvig program are the following:

- Increase the number of people in adult education to 25 000 by 2013 , and improve the quality of their experience, whether at home or abroad
- Improve conditions for mobility so that at least 7 000 people per year by 2013 can benefit from adult education abroad
- Improve the quality and amount of co-operation between adult education organisations
- Develop innovative adult education and management practices, and encourage widespread application
- Ensure that people on the margins of society have access to adult education, especially older people and those who left education without basic qualifications
- Support innovative ICT-based educational content, services and practices

2   Introducing LifeLong Learning for Active Citizenship and Capacity Building – LLLab Project

LLLab project supports the better access and better implementation of LLL program in the organizations involved, empowers them and builds their social capital as well. LLLab incorporates the concepts of creativity and innovation in its activities since capacity for these concepts have their roots in cultural and interpersonal skills, values and the competencies in the European reference framework that can be gained only through education.

The objectives of the project partnership are the following:

- to promote the vision for LLL in partner countries, to educate the staff about its aims, outcomes and the background;
- to promote access and increase participation in LLL for the staff and clients of the partner organizations;
- to broaden access to LLL opportunities and innovative expressions;
- to promote flexible education and training methods and approaches to create a culture of learning;
- to create learning opportunities, seminars, workshops for the employees/members of partner organizations by the help of the identified practises and activities derived from these;
- to improve the quality and accessibility of mobility in adult education by increasing the volume of cooperation and to significantly improve the degree of involvement within the learning process and also the evaluation criteria;
- to visibly increase the investment in human resources in order to turn to good account most of the human potential; to make sure that everyone gets easy and permanent access to quality information and advice about what they want to learn in the country and in Europe;
- to develop capacity and institution building by developing LLL skills in general, basic competencies and critical thinking derived from knowledge based society to adjust them to the continuous change in the society and in their work;
- to support innovative and creative expressions at work and in the community;
- to facilitate personal growth and as result of it the social cohesion;

- to create a multinational and intercultural environment and promote intercultural dialogue;
- to provide motivation and foster language learning;
- to increase productivity at work and personal fulfillment both at work and in the community by developing skills, competencies and knowledge within personal, civic, social and employment perspectives.

3 Introducing Project Partnership

The project Partnership consists of 5 institution from 5 different European countries:

Coordinator: Bolu Valiliği, İzzet Baysal Cad. Merkez 14100 Bolu-Türkiye, Turkey
URL: http://www.bolu.gov.tr/
e-mail: boluvalilikpb@gmail.com

Governorship of Bolu is the centre of provincial administration and the representative of the government and each ministry including the Ministry of Education. Being in the pre-accession period, Turkey is expected to follow up with the EU standards in its institutions and capacity and institution building are essential for the government staff. For better social cohesion, the organization should take part in intercultural activities that will strengthen the internalization of EU decisions and cross-border cooperation. For a changing world, they want to prepare their staff and their clients by making lifelong learning a reality in the EU context.

Partner 1: Avalon, Initiatives per a les associations, Ronda Universitat 31, 5-2, 08007, Barcelona, Spain
URL: http://www.avalon.cat/
e-mail: avalon@avalon.catis

The Avalon association was born in 2001 in order to give support and strengthen little, middle and new born organizations in the Catalan associative net. Avalon's tasks are the following: advising and guiding organizations through their evolution and growth, educating, through associative management courses such as Fundraising, Project Management, Internal Communication and Team Work, New channels of Communication (ICT), etc., informing, through articles, documentation, publications, bibliography, links, etc, hanging from a webpage; and exchanging information through a forum created specifically to exchange information about all these subjects. Avalon target is the overall people involved in the non-profit sector. However, they have some programs and courses specifically addressed to the following communities: Immigrant Organizations, People with Special Needs Organizations, and Development and Cooperation Organizations.

Partner 2: Karpatská nadácia Slovensko- Carpathian Foundation Slovakia, Letná 27, 040 01, Košice, Eastern Slovakia, Slovakia
URL: http://www.karpatskanadacia.sk/, http://www.carpathianfoundation.org/,
e-mail: cfsk@cfoundation.org

The Carpathian Foundation was founded in 1994 by the East – West Institute, with generous financial support of the Charles Stewart Mott Foundation. The Foundation was created to serve as an active and unique cross - border grant maker in the

Carpathian region. The core activities are grant programs and scholarship programs. The Foundation makes grants to support nonprofit organizations, individuals and local governments in a variety of areas. To its grantees, the Foundation provides financial support, expert advisory services, training and technical assistance to local communities in order to facilitate development of networks, partnerships and collaboration in the region. The Foundation focuses on supporting multi-cultural and inter-ethnic communities, building cross-sector partnerships and public engagement. Within several of its programs, the Foundation has provided series of trainings for different target groups, such as nonprofit organizations, Roma etc. Also, the Foundation promotes the topics of corporate social responsibility and inter-cultural relations in a multicultural society. The Foundation is an active member of a high quality international network, and has an access to extensive international know - how and experience.

Partner 3: Inova Consultancy ltd/WiTEC UK, 45A Crescent Road S7 1HL Sheffield South Yorkshire, United Kinkdom
URL: http://www.inovaconsult.com, http://www.witec-eu.net/
e-mail: office@inovaconsult.com

The Inova Consultancy provides a flexible consultancy service that responds to the needs of organizations and individuals internationally in the area of diversity, equal opportunities and entrepreneurship. Inova's team has specialist experience and a proven track record in bid writing and the management of European and national funded projects in these fields. Inova has specialist experience in the development and delivery of programs in the UK and on an international level for women entrepreneurs and women in management. Inova represents WITEC, the European association for Women in SET (Science, Engineering and Technology). Inova has benefited from the knowledge and expertise of more than 20 years of experience in the delivery of gender programs across Europe. Inova's employees and associates combine experience and qualifications in organizational development, psychology, mentoring and coaching in addition to bringing in best practice from across Europe to assist organizations and individuals in the field of personal and business development.
Inova is also a member of the BME Business Forum in Sheffield.

Partner 4: PRO-MED Spolka z ograniczona odpowiedzialnością, Migowo Dolne 16 C, 80 952 Gdansk, Poland
URL: http://pro-med.org.pl/ http://blanka.moodle.pl/, http://utw.moodle.pl/
e-mail: anka.grabowska@gmail.com

PRO-MED sp. z o.o. activities on the Polish and international markets have been dated since 1989. PRO-MED sp. z o.o. main services are the following: installation and maintenance of medical equipment, translations and verifications of technical and medical literature and documentation, adaptation and localization of Web pages, developing and delivery of e-learning, blended learning courses, translation and localization of Polish Language Pack for Learning Management System (BSCW, WebCT, Moodle), taking part in EU projects: Phare (1998-2000), Leonardo da Vinci (1998 - 2008), Socrates (1998 - 2007), EQUAL (2005-2008), Interreg (2005-2006), Lifelong Learning Programs Grundtvig Partnership and Multilateral (2008-2011).

4 Introducing the Best Practice and "Share and Valorize" Approach (UTA Online, e-senior.eu in Action, MindWellness)

The author of the article is employed in PRO-MED sp. z o. o. as an e-learning expert. PRO-MED will offer at least 6 different e-workshops in the framework of LLLab project. The proposal is based on the idea "Share and Valorize" described in [3]. First of all the concept of virtual university will be used [4]. In order not "re-inventing the wheel" the best practice example from previous EU projects (e-senior.eu in action [5], Mindwellness [6]) will be offered. Fig. 1 presents the idea "Share and Valorize".

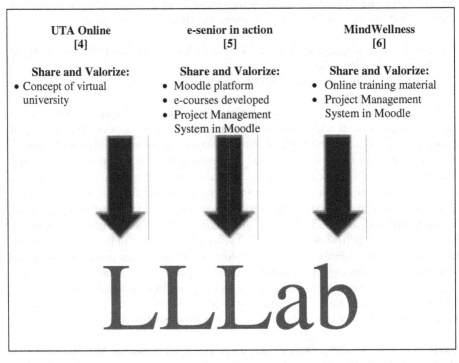

Fig. 1. The concept of "Share and Valorize"

The first good practice is U3A Online [4]. U3A Online is a world-first virtual University of the Third Age delivering online learning via the Internet. Their courses are open to all older people anywhere in the world. They are especially suited to older members of the community who are isolated either geographically, or through physical or social circumstances. All that is needed to study online is access to a computer with an Internet connection - and some basic computing skills. Before enrolling in a U3A Online (U3AOL) course, the user should become a member of U3A Online and receive a free username and password. UTA Online is based on Blackboard Learning Management System which is a commercial solution.

The second good practice is "e-senior in action" project (September 2009- April 2010) [5]. It has an aim to integrate and activate the members of the Seniors' Club at

Gdansk University of Technology (GUT). In "e-senior in action" computers workshops with elements of e-learning and open-air meetings, where their knowledge and skills gained during e-courses is verified (e.g. Nordic Walking) were offered.

Table 1. "e-senior.eu in action" work plan

Month	Activities done
September 2009	Open-air meetings in Czarlina GUT summer camp, meetings at the Senior's Club – the presentation of ideas and project tasks, additional recruitment of participants; *IMPROGE* - Grundtvig Partnership Programme meeting in Rome - presenting the idea of *e-senior.eu in action* project;
October 2009	Design and the implementation of the web site e-senior.eu; The choice and start up the Learning Management System (LMS); Workshops at Technical University of Gdansk- registration of LMS users; *Connecting +55, EuBiA* - Grundtvig Partnership Programs meetings in Gdansk - presenting the idea of *e-senior.eu in action* project;
November 2009	Preparation and implementation of e-courses; Workshops at Gdansk University of Technology;
December 2009	Preparation and implementation of e-courses; Workshops at Gdansk University of Technology;
January 2010	Testing and using of e-courses; Workshops at Gdansk University of Technology;
February 2010	Testing and using of e-courses; Workshops Gdansk University of Technology;
March 2010	Open air meetings and verification of knowledge obtained during e-learning training ; Workshops at Gdansk University of Technology; *IMPROGE* - Grundtvig Partnership Programme meeting in Rome - presenting the results of *e-senior.eu in action* project;
April 2010	Open air meetings and verification of knowledge obtained during e-learning training; The preparation of project presentation for the national and international conferences, workshops, meetings Project evaluation; Promotion of the project (leaflets, conferences, workshops) ;

The practical effect of e-courses (ICT, English, Nordic walking) is proved by the participation in Socrates Grundtvig Partnership meetings. During the international meetings, experiences and skills gained in the "e-senior.eu in action" project are presented.

The third good practice is "MindWellness - Improving learning capacities and mental health of elder people" project [6].

Mindwellness is a 2-year international project, funded by the European Union's "Grundtvig" programme.

There are 11 project partners in 9 countries, including relevant specialists in adult education, pedagogues, medical doctors, university researchers, ICT experts and social researchers.

The project has been developing innovative training material aimed at older people (working or retired) to help them retain mental flexibility.

The outcomes of the project include:

- a national and comparative analysis on the current position of older citizens and learning in higher age;
- a collection of good examples and best practice related to mind developing;
- online training material with exercises on mind developing;
- a handbook on mind developing for older people, providing a theoretical basis for use by trainers and experts.

In LLLab project PRO-MED sp. z o.o. offers Moodle platform which is a free web application that educators can use to create effective online learning sites. The usefulness of the platform for a seniors' audience was tested under "e-senior.eu in action" project. In the period September 2009 and April 2010 several e-courses for seniors were developed and delivered: e-senior - Nordic Walking, e-seniors English Club, e-seniors Fitness Club, e-seniors Photo Club.

5 Summary

The proposed workshops are located in Moodle platform (Fig. 2). The same platform is also used for the LLLab project management. Fig. 3 shows the timetable of LLLab project regarding workshops delivery and Grundtvig Partnership meetings.

Up till now PRO-MED sp. z o.o. delivered the following workshops:

1. e-cards for Christmas
2. e-cards for Easter

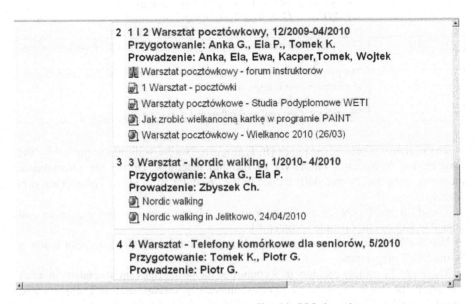

Fig. 2. Example e-workshops offered in LLLab project

2009-1-TR1-GRU06-05425 1	Dates of Workshops	Partnership meetings:
	1. 12/2009-02/2010	
	2. 03/2010-05/2010	1. Bolu
	3. 06/2010-08/2010	4-6/11/2009
	4. 9/2010-10/2010	2. Barcelona
	5. 11/2010-02/2011	26-30/05/2010
	6. 03/2011-05/2011	3. Gdańsk
		6-10/10/2010
		4. Koszyce 2011

Fig. 3. Example information about LLLab project located in Moodle

3. Nordic walking
4. Mobiles phones for seniors

The idea of establishing the online e-senior Magazine was born in 2008 during the EDEN Conference in Lisbon. The most interesting projects' events and achievements are documented there as essays [10].

References

1. European Commission Education & Training, http://ec.europa.eu/education/lifelong-learning-programme/doc86_en.htm/
2. LifeLong Learning for Active Citizenship and Capacity Building - LLLab, http://www.lilelab.com/
3. Grabowska, A.: Valorisation of European Projects Results. In: Book of Abstracts EDEN Annual Conference 2007, New Learning 2.0? Naples, p. 182 (2007)
4. A Virtual University of Third Age, UTW Online, http://www3.griffith.edu.au/03/u3a/
5. e-senior.eu in action, http://e-senior.eu/, http://utw.moodle.pl/
6. MindWellness, Improving learning capacities and mental healt of elder people, http://www.mindwellness.eu/
7. Blackboard home, http://www.blackboard.com/
8. Moodle community, http://moodle.org/
9. Creative Commons, http://creativecommons.org/
10. e-senior online magazine, http://magazinefactory.edu.fi/magazines/e_senior/

A Theoretical Framework to Foster Digital Literacy: The Case of Digital Learning Resources

Said Hadjerrouit

University of Agder, Serviceboks 422,
4604 Kristiansand, Norway
Said.Hadjerrouit@uia.no

Abstract. The New National Curriculum in Norway from 2006 recommends that teachers and students acquire a high degree of digital literacy in school education. One way to foster digital literacy is to train teachers to design and critically evaluate digital learning resources (DLRs). However, little research has been done as to which design principles and evaluation criteria are suitable for DLRs. This work proposes a theoretical framework, along with a case study, for designing and evaluating DLRs. The article draws on research in learning theory, pedagogical usability criteria, and context of use. The paper reports on the implications of the framework for the design and evaluation of DLRs.

Keywords: Digital literacy, digital learning resources, DLR, learning theory, pedagogical usability.

1 Introduction

Technical skills are obviously important elements of the digital literacy concept, but a closer look at the concept shows that it is more than the ability to use computers [1,2,3,4]. For teachers, digital literacy must include a suitable combination of pedagogical, cognitive, and evaluation skills such as knowledge of how DLRs can support pedagogical goals and knowledge of how the subject matter is transformed by the application of DLRs. Likewise, the ability to use DLRs is important to students, but not sufficient for acquiring a high-level of digital literacy skills. They also need cognitive proficiencies that help them to critically evaluate the information provided by DLRs. Clearly, digital literacy must go beyond the simple use of DLRs, and include pedagogical competencies and cognitive capabilities. However, little research has been done as to which framework is suitable to address issues that are pertinent to these dimensions under the concept of digital literacy.

The research goal of this work is to use the literature, along with a case study, to develop a framework of critical elements in DLRs design and evaluation. First, a literature review is undertaken to report on the state of research in the field of DLRs. Second, a theoretical framework is developed based on the literature review. Then, preliminary experiences with the framework are presented. Finally, some remarks on the value of the framework and elements of a future research conclude the article.

N. Reynolds and M. Turcsányi-Szabó (Eds.): KCKS 2010, IFIP AICT 324, pp. 144–154, 2010.

2   The Concept of Digital Learning Resources

A closer look at the concept of "DLR" shows that it is similar to "Web-based learning tools" found in [5], which refers to [6] to define the term as "interactive Web-based tools that support learning by enhancing, amplifying, and guiding the cognitive processes of learners". In addition, the concept of "DLRs" includes the main features of the term "Web-based learning application" defined by Liu & Johnson [7]. Accordingly, DLRs can be defined as a technology with four dimensions: (a) It is delivered through the Web; (b) It teaches content that meets specific learning objectives aligned with the curriculum; (c) It is designed on the basis of a learning theory; (d) It contains reusable elements.

From the content point of view, DLRs are computer-based implementations of a specific topic that is aligned with a given curriculum. DLRs include study material, task-based activities and exercises, and eventually assessment procedures. DLRs can also be created to support different topics of a given subject, as well as instructional material in a number of subject areas at all levels in school education.

From a pedagogical point of view, the design of DLRs is embedded within a pedagogical strategy associated with a learning theory, such as cognitivism, constructivism, and collaborative learning or a combination of them [9]. The underlying pedagogical strategy of DLRs can affect teaching and learning processes.

Finally, DLRs need to be reusable in order to suit the students' needs. Reusability is useful for teaching subjects in different classroom contexts. Hence, reusability assumes that elements of DLRs can be found to fit into a similar teaching unit [10]. It also assumes that a given teaching unit will find DLRs or elements of them from many Web-based sources or throughout a learning resource database repository.

3   Literature Review

Despite the importance of digital literacy in the curriculum, schools adapt slowly to technological and pedagogical changes. According to the research literature, schools are still confronted with a number of problems associated with the realization of digital literacy within the field of DLRs. Basically, the main research issues are the following.

First, DLRs are still the domain of technical and software experts rather than teachers, educators, and learners [11]. As a result, most DLRs basically emphasize technical usability as defined by Nielsen [12,13]. Technical usability is important to minimize the cognitive load, and helps to free more resources for the learning process itself. It enables learners to easily focus on learning materials without having to make an effort to figure how to access them. However, although technical usability is a self-evident requirement for DLRs, it is not necessarily conductive for deep learning.

Second, to support learning, research in education [14,15,16,17] suggests that developers need to design DLRs with a new dimension of usability. This dimension is called "pedagogical usability" and it is associated with aspects that are fundamental to learning. However, little attention has been paid to pedagogical usability of DLRs, which is a critical factor to the success of this technology in classroom. From the viewpoint of pedagogical usability, current DLRs lack a number of features that would make them more flexible, interactive, motivating, and collaborative. Research literature reveals that DLRs with advanced features are difficult to design, and therefore current systems are still limited in their pedagogical usability. Martinidale et al [9] stated that it is substantially more difficult to create DLRs that accommodate the demands of constructivist learning. Likewise, Liu & Johnson [7] found a lack of fit between existing DLRs and what teachers and learners need, as well as a lack of connection between DLR design and educational standards.

Third, the pedagogical value of DLRs lies in helping learners discover and explore things for themselves through interactive, flexible, differentiated, and motivating activities. Unfortunately, most DLRs provide little support to achieve a high level of activity [7,9]. This because most DLRs are developed without a previous analysis of learners' needs. Clearly, a learner-centered approach to DLRs requires a change from teacher-centered design to a model of design that emphasizes the learners' needs [18]. Indeed, a learner-centered approach offers more scope for realizing possible learning benefits than traditional instructional paradigms. However, Maddux [19] indicated that such a change demands a massive shift in values related to school culture, teaching, and learning, as well as an intensive commitment to differentiated learning.

Fourth, the integration of DLRs into classroom is strongly connected to teachers' epistemological orientations, personal theories and perceptions about teaching and learning processes. According to Jimoyiannis & Komis [20], a true integration requires that teachers consider technology, content, and pedagogy not in isolation, but rather in the complex relationships in the system defined by three key components: (a) Knowledge of the pedagogy that is applicable to the specific content; (b) Knowledge of how technology can support pedagogical goals; and (c) Knowledge of how the subject matter is transformed by the application of the technology. Clearly, teachers' technical knowledge alone is not sufficient to achieve learning outcomes using DLRs. Equally important is how DLRs can support pedagogical goals set by the teacher and how the content is transformed through the technology [18]. Clearly, teacher's epistemological orientations should not be underemphasized when it comes to design, implement, and evaluate pedagogical situations in classroom around DLRs.

Fifth, in contrast to higher education, little research has been done evaluating students' and teachers' perceptions of DLRs in school education, modalities of teaching and learning using these resources [5]. In addition, exhaustive instruments (e.g., [21]) may not be suitable to evaluate DLRs, which tend to be smaller and more numerous [16]. Furthermore, a number of evaluation frameworks that can be used to evaluate user interfaces have been proposed [13]. But, these frameworks are intended for software environments rather than DLRs in which learner-centered user interface systems should be developed to support users' activities. Another problem with evaluating DLRs is that relatively few are currently being used in schools. ITU Monitor [22] reports that the selection of DLRs is limited, and that designing, developing, and implementing DLRs, which provide added value in learning and teaching, is very demanding and time consuming. Nevertheless, some schools have made considerable progress in the use of DLRs, but many of them still have much to do to develop and use subject-specific digital DLRs.

Summarizing, the literature review reveals a lack of design and evaluation regarding DLRs in educational settings. This work sets out to address this by developing a theoretical framework for the identification of educational factors that are important to the design and evaluation of DLRs.

4 A Theoretical Framework for Design and Evaluation of DLRs

The process of designing and evaluating DLRs in school education is a many-sided field of study with a number of theoretical and practical issues. Two fields are of interest for developing a coherent theoretical framework for designing and evaluating DLRs: Pedagogical usability issues and the context of use and evaluation.

4.1 Pedagogical Usability Criteria

The concept of usability has been defined by a number of researchers, but a complete definition is difficult to achieve, outside the domain it is to be considered [23,24]. Nielsen [12,13], as one of the foremost usability researchers, proposed a definition that focuses on technical usability, which involves criteria such as the need for consistency, learner satisfaction, minimal user actions and minimal memory load, simplicity and reduction of complexity. However, the impact of Nielsen's definition is limited when it comes to DLRs, because it largely ignores the underlying processes of human learning. Clearly, DLRs are considered beneficial for the learners if they contribute to the learning process and not if they simply support technical tasks. Hence, the usability of DLRs must be re-defined and related to its learning utility [25]. In order to reformulate the concept, it must be directly related to learning theories [26]. The literature on learning theories points to the fundamental differences between them [27], but in school education, a mix of learning theories is being used. Hence, teachers must allow circumstances surrounding the learning situation to help them decide which approach to learning is the most appropriate [28]. In the case of DLRs, designers need to consider that this technology suggests more a learner-centered approach than teacher-centered methods [18] in order to realize learning benefits, since the goal is to support the learners' knowledge construction process.

Accordingly, Nokelainen [17] expanded Nielsen's definition to include pedagogical usability issues. Nokelainen defined a set of criteria that can be applied to DLRs: learner control, learning activity, collaborative learning, goal orientation, applicability, added value, motivation, previous knowledge, flexibility, and feedback. These criteria can be adapted to DLRs with slight modifications, because DLRs cannot be judged in exactly the same terms as digital material that is used in other contexts. Hence, the key criteria that influence the pedagogical usability of DLRs are:

Understandability. DLRs should provide a well-structured description of the subject information using a clear and understandable language.

Added value. The added value of DLRs means that they offer more learning potentialities than traditional resources, such as textbooks, in terms of the potential capabilities of DLRs such as interactivity, differentiation, etc.

Goal-orientation. This criterion is related to the learning utility of DLRs and meaningfulness in terms of the learning goals set by the teacher and the curriculum.

Time. DLRs must allow the student to learn the subject matter within an acceptable period of time. It should preferably take less time to learn the subject information with the DLR than with textbooks.

Interactivity. DLRs should provide support for interactivity through a user-friendly accessibility of the subject information and task-based activities. Interactivity is important because it allows students to be actively involved in problem solving.

Multiple representation of information. DLRs should provide multiple representation of information using various multimedia elements. Task-based activities can contain links to multimedia applications such as games and simulations. Students should feel that their learning is enhanced through the use of multimedia.

Motivation. The material provided by DLRs should contain intrinsically motivating tasks. It should show important aspects of the subject matter that may affect the students' learning. Motivation is goal oriented and facilitates students' higher levels of engagement with the study material.

Differentiation. This criterion implies that DLRs are adapted to the students' characteristics. Differentiation involves fitting the subject information to the students' needs, taking into account their abilities, gender, language, needs, prior knowledge, and computer skills.

Flexibility. Flexibility means that DLRs provide different levels of difficulty and contain diverse assignments and tasks that are tailored to all students, so that their individual differences are taken into account.

Autonomy. This criterion means that students are able to work on their own using DLRs, and acquire knowledge without being completely dependent on the teacher. The knowledge provided by DLRs should be potentially powerful to enable the student to become less dependent on the teacher.

Collaboration. This criterion means that students can work together to reach a common goal, giving them a sense of how good solutions can be performed in collaboration. The criterion is important because learning is considered as an inherently social activity as good solutions are developed not in isolation; instead they involve collaboration with other students.

Variation. Students are able to use different learning resources in combination with DLRs. Variation is important to learning, because of different students' learning styles and preferences, or because some students favor some particular methods of interacting with others, while others prefer other approaches.

4.2 Context of Use and Evaluation of DLRs

The second key element of the framework is the context of use and evaluation of DLRs. The most appropriate approach to carefully examine the context of DLRs is to look at the influencing factors connected to them. The context is the totality of relationships between the students and surrounding elements within a pedagogical situation. This concept of context is similar to Brousseau's term of "milieu" [29], where learning is described as emerging from exchanges between the students and a "milieu" organized with teaching intentions. Accordingly, milieu is everything in the situation the learners can act on. It can be divided into two categories: Material and non material milieu. The material milieu includes a number of elements:

- The subject matter, its content, topics and subtopics, task-based activities, assignments, exercises, and problem statements taught in the classroom.
- The curriculum and its objectives, main subject areas, basic skills, including computer skills, competence aims in the subject, and subject assessment.
- Infrastructure (technical and non-technical), software tools available, number and place of computers, student/PC-ratio in the classroom.
- Study material such as textbooks, electronic and written material.

The non material milieu consists of the stakeholders involved in school education:

- Fellow learners in the classroom and their characteristics, such as age, knowledge level, gender, interests, needs, motivations, and computer skills.
- School teachers and their profile and pedagogies, information and communication technology (ICT) qualifications and attitudes towards ICT.
- School leaders, decision makers and actors supporting ICT integration.
- Trainee teachers as designers and developers of DLRs.

The mileu forms the very basis for the process underlying the design, use, and evaluation of DLRs. The milieu may change for the learner when introducing a new element - the DLR, because the learning and teaching processes are then mediated by DLRs. According to Brousseau [29], learning occurs by means of interaction between the learner and the "milieu". Learning happens through adaptation of the learner to the "milieu". This view is consistent with Piaget's work [30] that considers learning as an adaptation process to a milieu. The DLR can be considered as an element of the "milieu", and as such, it becomes a source of learning, by means of interaction with the learner.

The nature of the interaction between learners and DLRs is depending on the instructional approach and epistemological orientation adopted by the teacher. DLRs, by their very nature, require a change from teacher-centered methods to learner-centered approaches in order to achieve learning benefits [18].

5 Preliminary Experiences with the Framework

A preliminary case study within teacher education was carried out to investigate the value of the theoretical framework. This was done in collaboration with three classes from a middle school, where trainee teachers designed and evaluated DLRs. The unit of study was the learning of school subjects using the DLRs. Data collection methods consisted of student and teacher survey questionnaires. The aim was to measure the students' and teachers' perceptions of DLRs. Data from the case study came from three cohorts of participants: Sixty-five students between 14-16 years from three different classes, three school teachers, and three teams of trainee teachers as developers of DLRs. From the case study the following implications can be drawn for two major organizing themes:

- Pedagogical usability of DLR design
- Digital literacy and integration of DLRs into classroom

5.1 Pedagogical Usability and DLR Design

Pedagogical usability defines the capability of the DLRs to support the learning of the subject matter. Looking at the different dimensions of pedagogical usability some implications can be drawn.

First, learning activities are important from the point of view of the constructivist learning theory. Both students and teachers pointed out that the degree of learning activities was satisfying, but the tasks provided by the DLRs, were not sufficient to really engage the students in constructivist learning as they do not cover the entire knowledge level of a number of students who particularly demonstrated strong motivation and interests in the topics. Advanced learning activities for those students can be achieved with increased integration of motivating and multimedia elements.

Second, teachers were not quite satisfied with the degree of collaboration between students, because they felt that the students did not work together to reach a common goal. The idea of collaboration fits well with the socially situated learning theory, which assumes that learning occurs as learners improve and reflect on their understanding of the subject matter through discussion with fellow learners [31]. Accordingly, DLRs should contribute to increase the learning by collaboration in a higher degree, and allow the students to engage in levels of activity that could not be managed alone, without collaboration with fellow students. Of course, DLRs in themselves cannot contribute to collaboration, unless teachers perceive the value of collaborative learning.

Third, differentiation is an important criterion for any DLR. It includes different ways of interacting with the DLR while giving special consideration to differentiation between students according to their ability, the different ways students learn, and the different speeds at which students learn. Since it cannot be expected to develop resources with a high degree of differentiation within a limited period of time, it implies that the students' perceptions of differentiation cannot be generalized even if most students pointed out that they were satisfied with the level of differentiation and flexibility of the learning material. Nevertheless, designers of DLRs should take into account the students' preferred learning styles and knowledge levels.

Fourth, the criterion of motivation measures the degree of engagement of the students with the subject matter when using the DLR. Accordingly, DLRs cannot be considered as highly motivating if they are not adapted to the students' age, development, and interests. Student satisfaction with a DLR is, of course, a subjective phenomenon, but one that is important in keeping students engaged with the subject matter. According to Nokelainen [17], motivation can be achieved in many ways, for example through self-regulation, performance or learning goals, as well as extrinsic or intrinsic goal orientation, such as meaningful and interesting study material provided by the DLRs.

Fifth, the criterion of autonomy measures the degree of students' independence from the teacher when using DLRs. This criterion also measures the degree of independence from textbooks and other learning resources. Hence, autonomy and independence can reveal the quality of information provided by the DLR. However, DLRs can contribute to independent learning only if the added value of this technology is taken into consideration and well-perceived by teachers.

Finally, from the viewpoint of pedagogical usability, the DLRs lack a number of features that would make them more flexible, interactive, motivating, and collaborative. Even if the research literature [7,9] reveals that DLRs with advanced features are difficult to design, and therefore current DLRs are still limited in their pedagogical usability, one may ask whether the teachers really perceived the potentialities and added value of DLRs. This issue has been addressed by the teachers from different points of view. As a result, teachers still perceive textbooks as important as DLRs in terms of learning outcomes.

5.2 Digital Literacy and Integration of DLRs into Classroom

There have been ongoing efforts for many years to bring ICT into classrooms and to integrate digital literacy into the curriculum. Despite these efforts, there is a little success achieved so far [32]. It is obvious that ICT integration is a complex and demanding issue both for schools and teachers [33,20,34]. Besides cultural barriers that are caused by the nature of the educational culture and the culture at large as well, which are very difficult to change, there exist pedagogical barriers, as this work clearly demonstrated. Given this background, there are a number of implications that result from the case study for the integration of DLRs into classroom.

First, the curriculum requires that digital literacy be integrated in all subjects, otherwise teachers and students would not be able to fulfil the requirements given by the curriculum. The case study reveals that teachers clearly see the importance of DLRs, but they still consider them as supplementary aids in addition to textbooks. This means that DLRs can be used in combination with textbooks inside and outside the classroom, but they should not drastically affect teachers' ways of instruction, or change their pedagogy. As a result, teachers still perceive DLRs as neutral elements, without added value, that can be used occasionally, in addition to textbooks. Digital literacy however requires more commitment to the potentialities of DLRs.

Second, it thus is expected that DLRs introduce an added value to the learning process in comparison to printed material such as textbooks and material produced by the teacher. The added value of DLRs is in the form of the potentialities this technology offers, for example interactivity, differentiation, and collaboration, in contrast to textbooks that are more rigid and static in their use. However, DLRs can only be useful if the tasks are adapted to the capabilities of the technology. Tasks should not be a direct translation of study materials found in textbooks. They must be interactive and flexible according to students' individual differences and provide the students with immediate feedback that stimulates the learning motivation.

Third, teachers must be aware of the fact that ICT is not a value-neutral technology [37]. On the contrary, ICT is embedded within pedagogical values that potentially affect teaching and learning processes. It follows that IT can have an effect on how teachers use technology and what students learn from it. Similarly, DLRs cannot be considered as a neutral technology that can be used in classroom without radical changes of the content and ways of teaching and learning. Consequently, the introduction of DLRs can create new pedagogical situations that affect both the students' learning and the teaching content. However, teachers are not always aware of the non-neutrality of DLRs. If DLRs can create new pedagogical situations, then textbooks can no longer play the same role as before. Clearly, the added value of DLRs cannot be compensated by any textbooks or printed material.

Fourth, there is evidence in the research literature that the integration of ICT is associated with a shift from instructivist or teacher-centred to constructivist or learner-centred methods and teaching philosophies [18]. The case study seems to confirm, to a certain degree, that constructivist learning is important, since teachers reported that interactive learning activities and collaboration should be given more consideration. A shift from instructivism to constructivism requires that the teachers' role changes from transmitter of knowledge to facilitator of learning.

Fifth, another crucial factor that may promote or hinder the integration of DLRs is time. Indeed, research reveals that IT can provide positive learning opportunities, but it takes time [35,36]. Accordingly, the overall impression of researchers is that teachers' success in integrating ICT is highly dependent upon the availability of time to think deeply about pedagogical changes. Time plays also an important role for the students in terms of learning effect compared with printed material. However, the fact that DLRs can be used at any time and place does not necessarily mean that it takes less time to learn the subject matter compared to textbooks.

Finally, according to Nokelainen [17], the integration of DLRs into classrooms must be goal-oriented. This means that the objectives of using DLRs must be clear to the students. It seems that a successful integration can be achieved only if the students' goals, curriculum considerations, learning and teaching material, and the teachers' goals are closely aligned. Goals can differ according to the learning situation. The goal may be the learning of basic knowledge with clearly specified topics. The goal may also be the involvement of students in interactive activities. In addition, the goal may be collaboratively discussing important issues of the subject matter, or evaluating the students' knowledge through graded assessment procedures.

6   Conclusions and Future Work

The main research goal of this work is to use the literature, along a case study, to develop a framework of critical elements in DLR design and evaluation to foster digital literacy. To this end the framework was used to inform a case study, and the findings of the study were mapped back onto the framework in order to identify additional features found in classroom setting. As a result of this mapping the following conclusions can be drawn.

First, the main factor that impacted the design and evaluation of DLRs was the pedagogical usability dimension. While students and teachers globally agreed in their views of pedagogical usability, they differed in their perceptions regarding some key criteria: Interactivity, autonomy/independence, collaboration, and variation. The findings highlighted the importance of constructivist learning, both individually and collaboratively, for the design and evaluation of DLRs, and the added value of this technology compared with traditional learning resources. These findings are compatible both with elements of the conceptual framework and literature review.

Second, the case study revealed the existence of cultural values connected to students' preferred choices and ways of learning. Cultural usability is to a certain degree implicitly connected both to the technical and pedagogical usability of DLRs. Although the catalogue of usability criteria does not explicitly address cultural usability [38], a number of students expressed their preferred cultural values through the comments they made by means of survey questionnaires. The case study thus reveals that DLRs cannot be considered as a value-neutral technology [37]. On the contrary, cultural values are embedded within DLRs,

Future work will focus on the refinement of the theoretical framework and associated usability concepts - both pedagogical and cultural - in order to generate a more complete picture of what constitutes digital literacy in the field of DLRs. It is also important to further investigate the factors that influence the integration of DLRs into classroom and the context of use and evaluation as well.

References

1. Bruillard, E.: From the Didactics of Computer Science towards the Didactics of Instrumental Activities with ICT. In: Second Greek Conference on Didactics of Informatics, Volos (2004)
2. Drenoyianni, H.: Designing and Implementing a Project-Based ICT Course in a Teacher Education Setting: Rewards and Pitfalls. Education & Information Technologies 9(4), 387–404 (2004)
3. Krumsvik, R.: The Digital Challenges of School and Teacher Education in Norway: Some Urgent Questions and the Search for Answers. Education and Information Technologies 3&4(11), 239–256 (2006)
4. Markauskaite, L.: Exploring the Structure of Trainee Teachers' ICT Literacy: The Main Components of and Relationships between, General Cognitive and Technical Capabilities. Education Tech. Research Dev. 55, 547–572 (2007)
5. Kay, R., Knaak, L., Petrarca, D.: Exploring Teachers Perceptions of Web-Based Learning Tools. Interdisciplinary Journal of E-Learning and Learning Objects 5, 27–50 (2009)
6. Agostinho, S., Bennett, S., Lockyer, L., Harper, B.: Developing a Learning Object Metadata Application Profile Based on LOM Suitable for the Australian Higher Education Market. Australian Journal of Educational Technology 20(2), 191–208 (2004)
7. Liu, L., Johnson, D.L.: Web-Based Resources and Applications. Computer in the Schools 21(3), 131–147 (2005)
8. Norton, P., Hathaway, D.: On Its Way to K-12 Classrooms, Web 2.0 Goes to Graduate School. Computers in Schools 25(3), 163–180 (2008)
9. Martinidale, T., Cates, W.M., Qian, Y.: Analysis of Recognized Web-Based Educational Resources. Computers in the Schools 21(3), 101–117 (2005)
10. Strijker, A., Collis, B.: The Influence of Context on the Future of Learning Objects. In: Hartman, K., Koohang, A. (eds.) Learning Objects: Theory, Praxis, Issues, and Trends, pp. 83–112. Informing Science Press, Santa Rosa (2007)
11. Nam, C.S., Tonya, L., Smith-Jackson, T.L.: Web-Based Learning Environment: A Theory-Based Design Process for Development and Evaluation. Journal of Information Technology Education 6, 23–44 (2007)
12. Nielsen, J.: Designing Web Usability: The Practice of Simplicity. New Riders Publishing, Indianapolis (2000)
13. Nielsen, J.: Usability Engineering. Academic Press, Boston (1993)
14. Kukulska-Hulme, A., Shield, L.: Usability and Pedagogical Design: Are Language Learning Web Sites Special? In: Cantoni, L., McLoughlin, C. (eds.) Proceedings of World Conference on Educational Multimedia, Hypermedia and Telecommunications 2004, Chesapeake, VA, USA, pp. 4235–4242 (2004)
15. Laurillard, D.: Rethinking University Teaching: A Conversational Framework for the Effective Use of Learning Technologies, 2nd edn. Routledge, London (2002)
16. Leacock, T.L., Nesbit, J.C.: A Framework for the Quality of Multimedia Resources. Educational Technology & Society 10(2), 44–59 (2007)
17. Nokelainen, P.: An Empirical Assessment of Pedagogical Usability Criteria for Digital Learning Material with Elementary School Students. Educational Technology & Society 9(2), 178–197 (2006)
18. John, P., Sutherland, R.: Teaching and Learning with ICT: New Technology, New Pedagogy? Education, Communication & Information 4(1), 101–107 (2009)
19. Maddux, C.D.: The Web in K-12 Education. Computers in the Schools 21(3), 149–165 (2005)

20. Jimoyiannis, A., Komis, V.: Examining Teachers' Beliefs about ICT in Education: Implications of a Teacher Preparation Programme. Teacher Development 11(2), 149–173 (2007)
21. Squires, D., Preece, J.: Predicting Quality in Educational Software: Evaluating for Learning, Usability and the Synergy between Them. Interacting with Computers 11, 467–483 (1999)
22. ITU Monitor: The Digital State of Affairs in Norwegian schools (2009),
    http://www.itu.no/ITU+Monitor.9UFRDSXH.ips
23. Simbulan, M.S.: Learning Objects' User Interface. In: Hartman, K., Koohang, A. (eds.) Learning Objects: Applications, Implications, & Future Directions, pp. 259–336. Informing Science Press, Santa Rosa (2007)
24. Peterson, D.: Usability Theory, Practice and Evaluation for Learning Objects. In: Hartman, K., Koohang, A. (eds.) Learning Objects: Applications, Implications, & Future Directions, pp. 337–370. Informing Science Press, Santa Rosa (2007)
25. Sedig, K., Klawe, M., Westrom, M.: Role of Interface Manipulation Style and Scaffolding on Cognition and Concept Learning in Learnware. ACM Transactions on Computer-Human Interaction 8(1), 34–59 (2001)
26. Elliott, G.J., Jones, E., Barker, P.: A Grounded Approach to Modeling Learnability of Hypermedia Authoring Tools. Interacting with Computers 14, 547–574 (2002)
27. Lin, B., Hsieh, C.: Web-Based Teaching and Learner Control: A Research Review. Computers & Education 37(3-4), 377–386 (2001)
28. Karagiorgi, Y., Symeou, L.: Translating Constructivism into Instructional Design: Potential and Limitations. Educational Technology & Society 8(1), 17–27 (2005)
29. Brousseau, G.: Theory of Didactical Situations. Kluwer Academic Publishers, London (1998)
30. Piaget, G.: Genetic Epistemology. Basic Books, New York (1971)
31. Vygotsky, L.S.: Thought and Language. In: Translated by Kozulin, A. (ed.) MIT Press, Cambridge (1986) (Original English translation published 1962)
32. Tondeur, J., Van Keer, H., Van Braak, H., Valcke, M.: ICT Integration in the Classroom: Challenging the Potential of a School Policy. Computers & Education 51, 212–223 (2008)
33. Guelbahar, Y.: Technology Planning: A Roadmap to Successful Technology Integration in Schools. Computers & Education 49, 943–956 (2005)
34. Hadjihoma, C., Karagiorgi, Y.: The Use of ICT in Primary Schools within Emerging Communities of Implementation. Computers & Education 52, 83–91 (2009)
35. Hayes, D.N.A.: ICT and Learning: Lessons from Australian Classrooms. Computers & Education 49, 385–395 (2007)
36. Teartle, P.: A Theoretical and Instrumental Framework for Implementing Change in ICT in Education. Cambridge Journal of Education 34(3), 331–351 (2004)
37. Gadanidis, G., Schindler, K.: Learning Objects, Type II Applications, and Embedded Pedagogical Models. Computers in the Schools 21(1), 19–32 (2006)
38. Li, H., Sun, X., Zhang, K.: Culture-Centered Design: Cultural Factors in Interface Usability and Usability Tests. In: Eighth ACIS International Conference on Software Engineering, Artificial Intelligence, Networking, and Parallel/Distributed Computing, SNPD 2007, pp. 1084–1088 (2007)

Conditions for Successful Learning
of Programming Skills

Jaana Holvikivi

Helsinki Metropolia University of Applied Sciences
jaana.holvikivi@metropolia.fi

Abstract. First programming courses often fail to motivate students to continue their software studies. Students find it hard to acquire the logic of computer programming. Especially students in multicultural, heterogeneous student groups are unable to apply logical thinking consistently or to follow instructions in a systematic fashion. Transfer of thinking skills from mathematics to programming does not take place as expected. Efforts to describe the thinking process in program authoring have failed, and process of problem solving in program design remains as evasive as heuristic processes in general. Evidently, it is based on accumulated expert knowledge that is not easily describable. Programming is an independent domain of expert knowledge that requires systematic practice and self-monitoring in construction of appropriate mental patterns.

Keywords: programming skills, computer science education, expert knowledge, mental patterns.

1 Introduction

Learning fundamental programming skills has been found to be difficult and the inherent difficulties are hard to analyze [1], [2]. Research in computer science education has attempted to find efficient ways to teach programming, thus far with limited success. Undeniably, several good programming languages for beginners, as well as software and methods to assist in classroom practice have been developed. Nevertheless, none has claimed universal acceptance and the outcome of first programming courses often remains disappointing [3], [4], [5].

A growing body of research has attempted to investigate the learning process of an individual student in programming courses in order to trace common obstacles and misconceptions. Studies on individual learners, on one hand [2], and comparisons of large student populations [6], on the other hand, have been conducted. The results are, however, inconclusive. The present study attempts to shed light on the underlying conditions in learning programming. First, the current understanding in programming education research is presented, enhanced by insights from cognitive science. Second, a study on student analytical thinking abilities and programming is described, and its findings are compared with ethnographic data on classroom practice. Finally, the results are discussed, and a comprehension of how programming thinking is learnt based on cognitive abilities and accumulation of expert knowledge is outlined.

N. Reynolds and M. Turcsányi-Szabó (Eds.): KCKS 2010, IFIP AICT 324, pp. 155–164, 2010.

2 Programming Instruction and Thinking Skills

There is a considerable agreement in the literature that students experience many difficulties in learning to program [4], [5], [6]. For instance, an ACM/ICER working group 2001 reported on beginning computing students' inability to program [7]. The authors tested first year students in several universities in the US and other countries on a common set of programming problems, and the majority of students performed more poorly than expected. The research did not reveal what the principal reasons behind failures were: whether they were caused by fragile knowledge and skills or by poor problem-solving skills. An extensive follow-up research [1] aimed at determining what strategies are likely to lead to success versus those that are likely to lead to failure in program code tracing. The findings indicate that successful and failing students do not actually employ different kinds of approaches, or higher or lower order thinking skills. Most students used multiple strategies in working on a given question, different strategies were used for different questions, and many strategies that were used successfully by certain students would be used incorrectly or unsuccessfully by other students. Success was determined not just by which strategies were employed but rather by how well the particular strategies were employed.

Computer science education can be improved by various means, including development of learning tools, pedagogical methods, and the curriculum. One of the central questions concerns the choice of the initial programming language for the first CS course, which is commonly believed to be crucial for later learning and motivation in software studies [5]. Whether to start with algorithmic or object-oriented programming, or other tools and methods is eagerly debated. Accordingly, many different languages have their supporters: Ada, Pascal, C, Java, PHP, JavaScript, and Python [3], as well as visual aids and building-block kind of tools [5], [6], to mention some. One view that is strongly supported by students favors development environments and powerful languages that are used commercially, whereas an opposing view stresses development of thinking skills, particularly algorithmic thinking. Educators agree, however, that students need to learn a programming way of thinking, which is more than just knowing the syntax and semantics of a language. Moreover, other subjects in computer science such as databases and networks are complex and conceptually demanding, and understanding them requires abstract thinking and good problem-solving skills.

Many innovative approaches have been developed to aid beginner programmers. Stein [8] has introduced a view of "computing as interaction": event-based and object-oriented thinking. Her method uses Java in the introductory course, emphasizing the user-computer interaction that is central in modern networked environments. Radenski [3] has developed a "Python first, Java second" program that according to his surveys has gained popularity among students. Python comes first because its relative simplicity and Java second to offer features that are more powerful. The program includes a considerable amount of actual practice and supporting materials. In addition, several projects have utilized visualization of program elements [5], [6].

Eckerdal & Berglund [9] concentrate in object-oriented programming thinking in their study because they found that their students had difficulties in it and in describing it when interviewed. The object-oriented paradigm is built on a set of abstract concepts. Students need to reach a certain level in their understanding in order to be able to use the concepts for analysis and design in object-oriented programming tasks. However, there are ways for educators to assist students to reach such understanding. The researchers suggest that these may include problem-solving skills and a systematic way of thinking, as well as thinking about learning, that is, metacognitive skills.

The supposition that higher level thinking skills influence programming ability is based on the idea of transfer of skills from one cognitive domain to another. However, how far this is applicable and whether transfer exists is somewhat debatable. Recent neuroscientific research has tackled the question of transference of learnt skills in the brain. The results have thus far been less promising for educators: transfer of simple cognitive skills does not seem to take place, on the contrary, each task needs a new training [10], [11], [12]. However, this result has thus far been found on simple tasks only; higher level skills are still beyond the means of cognitive science and brain scanning, in particular. The common methodology in cognitive psychology is to isolate cognitive mechanisms. In order to study them in laboratory setting and to measure the results, cognitive processes have to be split into tiny parts. In reality, however, learning complex ideas depends on recruiting multiple cognitive, as well as social and motivational mechanisms and resources [10].

Vainio & Sajaniemi [2] have noticed that novice programmers have poor program tracing skills. They describe programming as a process that includes program authoring, design, program comprehension, debugging, etc. These tasks occur often in a highly overlapping fashion, for instance, program debugging requires program comprehension and detailed tracing, specifically, mental simulation of program execution. Vainio conducted exploratory interviews that included program comprehension tasks with a group of novice students. He then analyzed comprehension protocols to identify specific difficulties affecting novices' ability to trace programs. The study found that students had four kinds of specific difficulties with program tracing: single value tracing, confusing function and structure, inability to use external representations, and inability to raise the level of abstraction.

Programmers are able to hold programs only partially in their memory because of the very limited capacity of human working memory [2]. The paradox in the functioning of the brain is the contrast between the enormous capacity of long-term memory and the narrow pipeline of executive functions. The organization of the brain is far from the organization of disk storage, or any kind of modular storage of information rather, it resembles a complex and dynamic network where many modalities collaborate [13], [14]. The brain is highly analogical and parallel in its activities. For instance, much of language processing takes place in a so-called Broca's area, which together with the premotor cortex links language processing with visual perception and motor activity [14]. Writing is in itself a complex thinking process, and the same applies to coding. The physical writing activity, which is a motor process, enhances learning results.

Conscious activity is severely limited by the executive function that controls working memory. Conscious processing has a narrow pipeline where the processing is serial, which prevents multitasking. The executive function is vulnerable to distraction, as well. Because of the limited capacity of working memory, we cannot hold long, complex ideas or code fragments in our heads as long as we understand them as separate data. As soon as we learn patterns and algorithms and create mental models of them, we can tackle tasks that are more complex. Mental models or external tools help us structure ideas [15], [16].

Moreover, humans are not able to accurately report their thinking processes [17], [18]. Many studies show that thinking process actually changes when a person tries to report her thinking. Particularly heuristic problem-solving evades awareness. The evidence of many studies strongly suggests that people frequently generate a solution without knowing it [19]. Similarly, when they learn a new strategy to solve problems, it seemingly occurs outside awareness. Insight problems are solved nonconsciously, sometimes during sleep or apparently idle moments [20].

3 Methods

The preliminary data for the present analysis was gathered through a set of surveys among information technology students at a university of applied sciences in the Helsinki area in Finland. The student population consists of over 30 nationalities; predominantly male students. The surveys included questions on study habits, experiences, and difficulties in learning computer science. 124 students participated in the surveys, out of whom 62 responded to a paper-based questionnaire in the classroom and 62 answered to an on-line questionnaire. This data was subsequently compared to course results (examinations and assignment work) of introductory computer science courses. Further explanations were sought through ethnographic observation data from six years' field work. The ethnographic data included field notes on classroom activity, particular emphasis being in unexpected incidents and difficulties. As course work was replicated yearly with new student populations, certain patterns started to emerge. Additionally, students produced learning logs and team work reports, which were analyzed as regards their own perception of their learning. The research process and data are described in detail in the doctoral thesis by Holvikivi [21].

Additionally, two specific studies were conducted to test logical thinking, which was considered an essential component in programming. The first questionnaire tested verbal logic and mathematical reasoning (135 respondents), and the second test compared logical thinking skills with knowledge of Boolean logic acquired in digital circuits courses. The findings of the first study are presented in detail in Holvikivi [22]. The second test was a short questionnaire that was given out in the classroom, and included Boolean operations, four logical syllogisms, and two other reasoning tasks. 45 students of 16 nationalities answered the questions. The results of this test are described below.

4 Findings

The transfer of learning from one course to another turned out to be extremely low in this study. Especially mathematical skills were not fully applied in other contexts. Even arithmetic calculations by students who had passed basic mathematics courses failed in the context of other testing situations (overall 50 % success rate). Failure in number system conversions was even more dramatic, with a success rate of 37 %. The connection of mathematical operations and calculation to problem-solving seemed to be lost for half of the students, which could be explained by mechanical learning and lack of deep understanding [23].

4.1 Logical Reasoning

The results of applying logical thinking in syllogisms and reasoning tasks in tests indicated that logical skills are by no means transferable between different types of reasoning [22]. For instance, training in Boolean logic did not help in solving syllogisms. In fact, the group that had not received training in binary logic performed best. The test included Boolean AND and OR operations, four logical syllogisms, and one other reasoning task. The results (Table 1) show that 69% of respondents succeeded in Boolean operations, but only 37% gave correct answers to the verbal tasks, syllogisms. Thus, about half of those who mastered basic mathematical logic failed in verbal reasoning.

Table 1. Number of correct answers in the second logic test

Total respondents 45 (Men 40, Women 5)		
Syllogisms: 4 correct	6	13%
3 correct	11	24%
0, 1 or 2 correct	28	62%
Boolean AND and OR correct	31	69%

A closer look at reasoning studies in general points to the same conclusion: a reasoning task often produces results that are task-dependent or context-dependent, and predicting the outcome from previously performed tasks seldom succeeds amongst untrained subjects [12].

4.2 Working with Instructions

Additionally, coding success is not only dependent on abstract thinking but also on systematic working patterns. Coding requires an ability to follow instructions accurately. Observations at our university indicate that when inexperienced students work with laboratory assignments they might follow instructions in somewhat random order instead of from beginning to end. Assignments, such as creating Excel sheets or typing Linux command line instructions in order to create and copy files, always proceed stepwise. A command line interface requires discipline from the student, and the task leads to chaos when the order of commands is changed, or the student skips some steps or starts from the middle of the exercise. Students who type in incorrect order, and do not follow on the screen what happens, cannot comprehend whether they get an approval (which is seldom indicated by the system) or an error message. The communication process with the computer fails in these cases because a human person is not accustomed to purely formal and very sparse communication by the computer system, and might not even feel that it is a communication situation. [21]

The surveys that we conducted among students revealed that especially immigrant students feel shortcomings in communication in general: more than half of the foreign respondents reported that they found directions unclear whereas home national students had no problems of this kind. This difficulty was particularly connected to laboratory assignments, as up to 65 % of the foreign respondents stated that they often failed to understand instructions. However, the failure to understand instructions did not directly correspond with the English proficiency of the student, even though 20% of students reported language difficulties as well. The failure to understand seems to be connected to the procedural style of the instruction, and perhaps to the unwritten assumptions of what a student is expected to understand without being told [21].

Moreover, some immigrant students come from cultures with a strong oral tradition such as the Somali culture [24]. They prefer personal communication, which can be observed in regular visits to teachers' offices. Students who find it difficult to work based on written instructions would probably benefit from an apprenticeship mode of learning. The instruction at Finnish universities relies strongly on mediating artifacts, such as written or on-line materials. Finnish and other Western students are accustomed to a textual learning environment, which could be described as a "paper-trail" way of working (discussed by Teräs [25]). It pertains to their behavioral patterns, and papers (or documents on computer) are essentially integrated in the work.

4.3 Code Tracing and Programming

Students often attempt to find a solution intuitively in code tracing tasks, in spite of being told to emulate a computer (this phenomenon was also observed in [1] and [2]). They apply knowledge of natural language that involves concluding from partial information and filling in gaps. Moreover, failure in code tracing tasks indicates a lack of student capability in monitoring one's thinking process.

Additionally, code tracing and error detecting is more difficult for students who have spelling problems. Students who did not study alphabetic languages as their first language, such as Amharic or Nepalese speakers, are particularly afflicted by this impediment [21]. They are unable to "see errors" in punctuation and spelling when proofreading their texts or codes.

In addition to programming concepts that have been discussed above, such as procedural, object-oriented and event-based thinking, we have noticed difficulties in grasping many other fundamental concepts in information technology: the organization of file systems, local and global networks, relational and hierarchical data base structures, client-server architecture, and so on.

The previous schooling experience of immigrant students may consist mainly of teacher-led lectures that require memorizing of presented material. The laboratory setting might be a completely new kind of classroom environment, and students lack a model for controlling their work in it. If the student's schoolwork schema consists only of teacher speaking and student listening, she may have adopted a recipe-type learning pattern: do as told and repeat it without reflection. However, creative thinking is needed even in simple programming, which is displayed by the variety of solutions to most trivial tasks. A short piece of programming code, a tiny database table or XML structure – whatever it is, each student brings a unique solution! The ability to create new solutions is connected to the ability to apply theory to practice. It is a skill that has to be explicitly taught, and evidently, different educational systems produce it differently. As any other skill, it is developed by constant practice.

On the other hand, the application of object-oriented thinking has proven to be less challenging than in earlier studies. We have applied it in naturally occurring settings, namely manipulating parts of CSS, HTML or XML documents. The Document Object Model that is used in these languages has proven to be intuitive and the results of applying it are immediately visible on the HTML page. Therefore, teaching JavaScript as the first programming language has certain advantages in this respect, in addition to being motivating because of its easy syntax and applicability on Web. Our course program is partially based on Snyder's textbook [26]. Flowcharts in simple program design act as thinking tools and help in code tracing practice. Alternatively, XML structures and XSLT programming are also relatively easy to learn, if they are approached step-by-step proceeding from simple to more complex structures. XSLT is such a high level language that it allows concentration on structures without a need to worry about syntax details. Unfortunately, it is too specific to be used for a general introduction to programming.

5 Discussion

The variety of difficulties in programming thinking is disturbing. Success in learning programming seems to depend on general problem-solving abilities, student cognitive capacity, and analytical intelligence. If the fact is that good students are successful, what remains to be done by educators? Obviously, it is more difficult to improve the outcome, if no particular recipe or optimal working strategy can be identified. An important research finding regarding higher-level expertise has been that an individual's ability to develop his or her content-specific knowledge and apply it in varying situations often co-evolves with the development of general thinking skills and meta-cognitive strategies [19], [27]. Thus, to have better students, we need to improve their thinking and learning skills, and self-regulation.

Self-reflection and conscious monitoring of progress are important in improving practice. The development of expertise takes place through the deepening mastery of problem-solving processes. Studies on chess masters have shown that they have mental models of a huge number of chess patterns and remember locations of pieces in them effortlessly [15]. Similarly, jazz pianists have developed a large repertoire of tunes. Programmers have a set of solutions and structures in their mind, as well [2]. The central role of practice and ability to apply theoretical knowledge has also been observed in this study. Students need time and sufficient practice in various problems to build mental patterns of software structures.

Moreover, a certain amount of functional understanding of processes, in addition to technical skills, is a prerequisite for successful software engineering work [28]. Visual aids, graphs and animations help in modeling processes and structures. Additionally, understanding abstract concepts and capability in algorithmic thinking are required. Understanding computers requires an understanding of formal systems. In formal systems, a set of phenomena is encoded as symbols, and the symbols are manipulated by reference to their form only. The meanings of symbols are not interpreted while they are being manipulated [29].

The difficulties in logical reasoning that were noticed in this study can be explained with the organization of cognitive functions in the brain. Reasoning probably consists of several skills that are located separately in the brain. Recent fMRI studies indicate that brain uses different regions and networks for mathematical functions and verbal functions, different regions for enumeration and calculation, for economical decision-making and social decision-making, and so forth [30], [31], [32]. Whether programming logic is processed in the brain predominantly as a mathematical problem-solving task, as a verbal task, or even as a visuo-spatial task, is not known, but would certainly be worth studying.

6 Conclusions

When we learn, we build on existing patterns and schemas in our minds. Learning is easier when we have relevant experience and schemas that are applicable in the particular context. Accumulation of programming expertise is a continuous process of constructing new, useful patterns in the mind to be called on demand.

The traditional knowledge of introducing an easy language first [3] has once again found support from the present research findings. Students need to be allowed to concentrate on the essential patterns, and all additional details should be kept to a minimum, as student capacity to learn is always severely constrained by limitations of the brain. With a simple syntax language, students are allowed to concentrate on the problem-solving aspect, instead of being forced to struggle with a layer of initializations and definitions. Moreover, easy languages often offer fun and enjoyment of learning that motivates students.

Students must have certain basic abilities when they start learning programming. These include mental schemas in regard to procedural thinking and action, functional understanding of processes, and a comfortable relationship to technological artifacts. Knowledge construction takes place through a self-monitoring, intelligent practice that accumulates skills in small increments. In sum, learning programming follows the same patterns as any other domain of expert knowledge. The skill is built on previous experiences and abilities, and requires substantial practice.

References

1. Fitzgerald, S., Simon, B., Thomas, L.: Strategies that Students Use to Trace Code: an Analysis Based in Grounded Theory. In: Proc. of ICER 2005, pp. 69–80. ACM Press, New York (2005)
2. Vainio, V., Sajaniemi, J.: Factors in Novice Programmers' Poor Tracing Skills. In: Proc. of ITiCSE 2007. ACM, New York (2007)
3. Radenski, A.: "Python first": a Lab-Based Digital Introduction to Computer Science. In: Proc. of 11th ITICSE (2006)
4. Webber, C.G., Possamai, R.: An Immune-based Approach to Evaluate Programming Learning. In: 9th IFIP World Conference on Computers in Education (2009)
5. Koscianski, A., Bini, E.: Tackling Barriers in the Learning of Computer Programming. In: 9th IFIP World Conference on Computers in Education (2009)

6. Lahtinen, E., Ala-Mutka, K., Järvinen, H.-M.: 2005 A Study of the Difficulties of Novice Programmers. In: Proc. of ITiCSE 2005. ACM, New York (2005)
7. McCracken, M., Almstrum, V., Diaz, D., Guzdial, M., Hagen, D., Kolikant, Y., Laxer, C., Thomas, L., Utting, I., Wilusz, T.: A Multi-National, Multi-Institutional Study of Assessment of Programming Skills of First-Year CS Students. ACM SIGCSE Bulletin 33(4), 125–140 (2001)
8. Stein, L.A.: The Rethinking CS101 Project, http://www.cs101.org/
9. Eckerdal, A., Berglund, A.: What Does it Take to Learn 'Programming Thinking'? In: Proc. of ICER 2005, pp. 135–142. ACM Press, New York (2005)
10. Schwartz, D.L., Martin, T., Nasir, N.: Designs for Knowledge Evolution: Towards a Prescriptive Theory for Integrating First- and Second-Hand Knowledge. In: Gärdenfors, P., Johansson, P. (eds.) Cognition, Education, and Communication Technology, pp. 21–54. Lawrence Erlbaum Associates, Mahwah (2005)
11. Dos Santos Sequiera, S., Specht, K., Hämäläinen, H., Hugdahl, K.: The Effects of Background Noise on Dichotic Listening to Consonant-vowel Syllables. Brain and Language 107, 11–15 (2008)
12. Stanovich, K.: The fundamental computational biases in human cognition. In: Davidson, J.E., Sternberg, R. (eds.) The Psychology of Problem Solving, pp. 291–342. Cambridge University Press, Cambridge (2003)
13. Kandel, E.: The new science of mind. Scientific American Mind 17(2), 62–69 (2006)
14. Kalat, J.W.: Biological Psychology, 8th edn. Thomson Wadsworth, Belmont (2004)
15. Ericsson, K.A.: The Acquisition of Expert Performance as Problem Solving. Construction and Modification of Mediating Mechanisms through Deliberate Practice. In: Davidson, J.E., Sternberg, R. (eds.) The Psychology of Problem Solving, pp. 31–83. Cambridge University Press, Cambridge (2003)
16. Neuroscience and Education. Issues and Opportunities. A Commentary by the Teaching and Learning Research Programme. University of London (2007)
17. Scherer, K.S.: Feelings Integrate the Central Representation of Appraisal-Driven Response Organization in Emotion. In: Manstead, A.S.R., Frijda, N., Fischer, A. (eds.) Feelings and Emotions. The Amsterdam Symposium, pp. 136–157. Cambridge University Press, Cambridge (2004)
18. Wittgenstein, L.: Philosophical Investigations: The German Text with a Revised English Translation: German Text, with a Revised English Translation, 3rd rev. edn. Blackwell (January 2002) (1953)
19. Davidson, J.E., Sternberg, R. (eds.): The Psychology of Problem Solving. Cambridge University Press, Cambridge (2003)
20. Frith, C.: Making up the Mind: How the Brain Creates our Mental World. Blackwell Publishing, Oxford (2007)
21. Holvikivi, J.: Culture and Cognition in Information Technology Education. Helsinki University of Technology. SimLab Publications. Dissertation series: 5. Espoo (2009)
22. Holvikivi, J.: Logical Reasoning Ability in Engineering Students: A Case Study. IEEE Trans. Educ. 50(4), 367–372 (2007)
23. Hannula, M.S.: Affect in Mathematical Thinking and Learning. Annales Universitatis Turkuensis B 273, Turku, Finland (2004)
24. Alitolppa-Niitamo, A.: The Icebreakers. Somali-speaking Youth in Metropolitan Helsinki with a Focus on the Context of Formal Education. The Family Federation of Finland, The Population Research Institute. D42/2004 (2004)
25. Teräs, M.: Intercultural Learning and Hybridity in the Culture Laboratory. Dissertation. University of Helsinki, Department of Education (2007)

26. Snyder, L.: Fluency with Information Technology. Skills, Concepts, Capabilities. Pearson, London (2006)
27. Kirsch, D.: Metacognition, Distributed Cognition, and Visual Design. In: Gärdenfors, P., Johansson (eds.) Cognition, Education, and Communication Technology, pp. 147–179. Lawrence Erlbaum Associates, Mahwah (2005)
28. Moss, J., Kotovsky, K., Cagan, J.: The Role of Functionality in The Mental Representations of Engineering Students: Some Differences in the Early Stages of Expertise. Cognitive Science 30, 65–93 (2006)
29. Hutchins, E.: Cognition in the Wild. MIT Press, Cambridge (1995)
30. Polk, T.A., Farah, M.J.: The Neural Development and Organization of Letter Recognition: Evidence from Functional Neuroimaging, Computational Modeling, and Behavioral Studies. Proc. Natl. Acad. Sci. USA 95(3), 847–852 (1998)
31. Masataka, N., Ohnishi, T., Imabayashi, E., Hirakata, M., Matsuda, H.: Neural Correlates for Learning to Read Roman Numerals. Brain and Language 100, 276–282 (2007)
32. Tang, Y., Zhang, W., Chen, K., Feng, S., Ji, Y., Shen, J., Reiman, E., Liu, Y.: Arithmetic Processing in the Brain Shaped by Cultures. Proc. Natl. Acad. Sci. USA 103(28), 10775–10780 (2006)

Assessment of Knowledge and Competencies in 3D Virtual Worlds: A Proposal

María Blanca Ibáñez, Raquel M. Crespo, and Carlos Delgado Kloos

Departamento de Ingeniería Telemática, Universidad Carlos III de Madrid
Av. Universidad, 30. E-28911 Leganés, Madrid, Spain
{mbibanez,rcrespo,cdk}@it.uc3m.es

Abstract. Digital natives demand a more active approach to learning. Moreover, the acquisition and assessment of competencies, rather than the mere transmission of information, is becoming more relevant in the Knowledge Society. 3D virtual worlds are a promising environment to meet both of these requirements. In a 3D virtual world, learners are immersed in a rich environment that allows them to have an active experience through their avatars and interaction devices. The learning process in traditional learning management systems has been widely studied, but there is relatively little literature about the use of 3D virtual worlds for learning, although the expectations are high and the possibilities opened immense. This paper focuses on an important part of the teaching and learning process: the assessment. Our aim is to present a set of techniques adapted to this novel 3D medium that allows assessing knowledge, skills, and competencies by using the elements inherent to 3D virtual worlds (avatars, synthetic characters, smart objects) and take advantage of the new dimension introduced.

Keywords: Assessment of knowledge, Assessment of competencies, 3D virtual learning environments.

1 Introduction

Learning is nowadays shifting from merely transmitting knowledge to an active, learner-based approach. Simultaneously, new requirements posed by the Knowledge Society and lifelong learning for professional development emphasize the need of higher level abilities beyond just memorizing facts or understanding concepts. In addition, the new generation of learners, the so-called Digital Natives [1] with different patterns of work, attention, and learning preferences [2] are demanding the introduction of new technologies in the teaching-learning process.

Despite this revolution in learning conditions and requirements, Learning Management Systems continue to be predominantly "flat": contents are mostly delivered by means of texts, assessment questions and student responses are texts, etc. Recent advances have brought multimedia content into the scene (images, video, audio), which has brought more color and animation, but has not dramatically changed in particular how assessments are carried out and what can be assessed.

N. Reynolds and M. Turcsányi-Szabó (Eds.): KCKS 2010, IFIP AICT 324, pp. 165–176, 2010.

3D virtual worlds can be a solution to the motivation problem posed by the new generation of learners, but also to the activities that can be carried out to transmit knowledge and competencies. 3D worlds have been around for a long time, but thanks to advances in hardware performance and software development it has been only recently that they have evolved from systems with costly infrastructure to applications that can run on a personal computer either as stand-alone applications or even on top of web browsers. Relevant organizations have raised public interest in 3D virtual worlds for learning and teaching. From the business world, Gartner Research Group [3], a technology-related research and consulting firm, predicted that by 2011, 80% of internet users (and Fortune 500 enterprises) will be involved in virtual worlds. From the world of education, EDUCAUSE [4], a nonprofit association whose mission is "to advance higher education by promoting the intelligent use of information technology", claims that these virtual worlds will have a large impact on teaching and learning in a near future.

The advent of 3D virtual worlds has introduced new challenges for e-learning researchers such as how to use these environments effectively to transmit knowledge and promote cooperation among students. This area of research has been identified as central to building effective virtual learning systems for education and training [5]. Platforms such as Second Life [6], Croquet [7], Wonderland [8] have been successfully used for deploying 3D virtual worlds for learning [9], [10], [11], [12]. These initial experiences focus on simulation of real world environments, collaborative activities and even some aspects of learning management. In general they however lack from assessment mechanisms suited to 3D virtual worlds.

A side-project of SLOODLE [10] called quizHUD [13] can be considered as a pioneer to assess the acquisition of knowledge using not only classical interfaces in multiple choice questions, but also mechanisms inherent to 3D virtual worlds such as immersive navigation and choice of 3D objects.

Nevertheless, a rich medium such as 3D virtual worlds is expected to be useful not only to transmit knowledge, but also to promote and evaluate higher level competencies. 3D virtual worlds have been used for promoting collaborative activities, for providing students with a rich set of resources that can be used in non-standard ways and now there is a great expectation in relation to how these 3D worlds can be used for promoting and assessing competencies. Competencies have been treated in classical e-learning environments [14], for example as part of the TEN Competence Project [15] to detect the learner's competence proficiency level and suggest a set of activities the learner had to practice in order to acquire the needed competencies. Thus, this is a promising area of research but, to our knowledge, there have been no attempts to bring this competencies-based approach to 3D learning and assessment.

This paper is organized as follows. After this introduction, the terminology for learning outcomes is discussed in Section 2, differentiating knowledge, skills and competencies. Section 3 describes the elements that distinguish 3D virtual worlds from standard environments. New ways of using 3D virtual world elements such as avatars, non-player characters (NPCs), and smart objects for assessing knowledge, skills and competencies are outlined in Sections 4, 5 and 6 respectively. An illustrative case study is presented in Section 7. Finally, conclusions and future work are discussed in Section 8.

2 What Do We Assess? Knowledge, Skills and Competencies

Two big efforts have been carried out in order to provide a formalized and homogeneous framework for describing learner's abilities. The European Commission for Education & Training (ECT) [16] has developed a reference framework with eight reference levels describing for each one the *knowledge, skills* and *competences* that a learner must have. On the other hand, the U.S. Departments of Labor and Education formed the Secretary's Commission on Achieving Necessary Skills (SCANS) to study the kinds of competencies and skills that workers must have to succeed in today's workplace [17]. The know-how identified by SCANS is made up of five competencies that effective workers can productively use: resources, interpersonal skills, information, systems and technology.

The European Qualifications Framework (henceforth EQF) [18] was born in pursue of a twofold aim: promoting citizens' mobility between countries as well as facilitating lifelong learning. The EQF is meant to provide a unified and homogeneous reference framework for relating and comparing qualifications. To accomplish this goal and assuming the distance between the different national qualifications systems implemented in Europe, it applies a learning outcome based approach, emphasizing the results of learning rather than focusing on inputs related to the learning process itself (such as length of study).

According to the EQF [18], *learning outcomes* means statements of what a learner knows, understands, and is able to do on completion of a learning process. They are defined in terms of knowledge, skills and competence, where:

- *knowledge* means the outcome of the assimilation of information through learning. Knowledge is the body of facts, principles, theories and practices that is related to a field of work or study. In the context of the European Qualifications Framework, knowledge is described as theoretical and/or factual [18];
- *skills* means the ability to apply knowledge and use know-how to complete tasks and solve problems. In the context of the European Qualifications Framework, skills are described as cognitive (involving the use of logical, intuitive and creative thinking) or practical (involving manual dexterity and the use of methods, materials, tools and instruments) [18];
- *competence* means the proven ability to use knowledge, skills and personal, social and/or methodological abilities, in work or study situations and in professional and personal development. In the context of the European Qualifications Framework, competence is described in terms of responsibility and autonomy [18].

Whereas the EQF initiative provides a generic reference framework and clarifies the terminology, SCANS focuses on identifying concrete competencies which are particularly relevant for professional activity.

At the request of the U.S. Departments of Labor and Education, the SCANS commission conducted a study to determine the competencies and skills that workers must attain to succeed in today's workplace [17]. Although the commission completed its work in 1992, its findings and recommendations continue to be a valuable source of

Table 1. Excerpted from What Work Requires of Schools: A SCANS Report for America 2000, U.S. Department of Labor, June 1991, pp. xvii-xviii

Competency	Meaning	Components
Resources	Identifies, organizes, plans, and allocates resources	Time Money Materials and facilities Human resources
Interpersonal	Works with others	Participates as a member of a team Teaches others new skills Serves clients/customers Exercises leadership Negotiates
Information	Acquires and evaluates information	Acquires and evaluates information Organizes and maintains information Interprets and communicates information Uses computers to process information
Systems	Understand complex interrelationships	Understand systems Monitors and correct performance Improves or design systems
Technology	Works with a variety of technologies	Selects technology Applies technology to task Maintains and troubleshoots equipment

information for individuals and organizations involved in education and workforce development [22]. The results of this study are summarized in **Table 1**.

The SCANS study claims that these five competencies requires basic skills (reading, writing, arithmetic and mathematics, speaking and listening), thinking skills (thinking creatively, making decisions, solving problems, seeing things in the mind's eyes, knowing how to learn, and reasoning) and personal qualities (individual responsibility, self-esteem, sociability, self-management and integrity).

Although the SCANS study deals with competencies and skills for work, the proposals can be applied to the core curriculum area: Language, Mathematics, Science, Social Studies/Geography and History [23]. The competencies and skills discussed can thus be promoted and assessed in any course. Detailed information on assignments that integrate the SCANS competencies into the core curriculum area can be found in [23].

Assessment should therefore evaluate the performance of the learner for each of these aspects (knowledge, skills, and competencies). Considering the intrinsic differences of such diverse categories of learning outcomes, distinct assessment methods would apply. Although knowledge can be properly appraised using traditional exams, assessing skills and competencies poses more difficult challenges and requires complex activities. 3D worlds can help to accomplish this objective as they allow a cost-effective simulation of real-world scenarios and situations, including not only physical objects, but interaction and collaboration with colleagues too. As will be discussed in following sections, additional advantages appear related to the technical facilities provided by virtual worlds.

In this paper, the EQF terminology is followed to distinguish the different categories of learning outcomes defined there[1]. Since the SCANS document defines the set of competencies more precisely than the ECT document, the SCANS proposals are nevertheless used as illustrative cases for presenting new ways of using 3D virtual worlds to assess these competencies.

3 3D Virtual Worlds Contributions to the Assessment Process

3D virtual worlds have a set of elements –also present in video games– that may help to seduce students into learning. The use of avatars as representations of students (and instructors) and the possibilities for customizing avatars enhance the degree of realism and permit the subject to immerse him/herself in the 3D virtual environment for learning. The 3D scenarios also help to the sense of immersion and open up options of discovering new knowledge by exploring virtual worlds. The ability of avatars to interact with virtual 3D objects in collaborative environments offers new possibilities for the use of learning theories such as experiential learning, discovery learning and constructivism [19] and opens new possibilities for assessment.

3D virtual scenarios can be filled with information through text, audio, and images and also through 3D scenarios, smart objects, and NPCs. Technical elements used in video-games such as small-map, cursor indication and NPCs playing dialogues are useful to aid in orientation, to show objects with extra information and to transmit knowledge respectively. These elements are particularly useful in the assessment stages in which information should be given to students. Besides the aforementioned, one feature that distinguishes 3D virtual environments is the possibility of synchronous or asynchronous interaction of one or more users through 3D objects; this is suitable for monitoring student responses.

Non-player characters (NPCs) can improve *immersiveness* by acting in plausible ways; its activities can be programmed using artificial intelligence (AI) methods. Deterministic AI techniques such as finite states machines, decision trees or even fuzzy logic are currently being used in video games and non-deterministic techniques such as Bayesian networks, neural networks and genetic algorithms are starting to be exploited in these games [20]. 3D virtual learning environments should find which kind of synthetic characters could be used and what AI technique can be applied for programming their behaviors. The role of NPCs in the assessment process is especially important when the question is stated; when the student requires some help to answer it and also when feedback is provided.

In summary, 3D virtual worlds constitute a novel user interface, characterized by their high potential for immersiveness. They provide the learner with new interaction mechanisms with the rest of elements in the learning process: content, peer students and instructors. Such new mechanisms can be applied not only for teaching and training but also for deploying more effective methods of learning assessment. The characteristics that raise this potential can be categorized into two key features:

---

[1] Please note that although SCANS uses the term *"competencies"* while *"competences"* is used in EQF, both terms are meant to refer the same underlying concept and can thus be considered synonymous in this context for the purpose of this paper.

- *Novel user interface*: the learner can interact with 3D objects and scenarios that allow a realistic simulation of real world objects and situations. The experience can be further improved by means of haptic interfaces which provide an even more realistic interaction. New interaction mechanisms allow new kinds of tasks and activities, facilitating the assessment of practical skills involving manual dexterity or the use of (simulated) tools and instruments.
- *Monitored environment*: all actions, interactions and events in the virtual world can be monitored and logged for future analysis or assessment[2]. This functionality provides a huge advantage compared to the physical, real world, where such information is lost and unavailable for the instructor, and a powerful assessment resource. Students themselves can base on the logged data for supporting assertions on their performance and achievements. The assessment of interpersonal competencies is an obvious application of these logs. But they will also allow the instructor to distinguish individual contributions to team work (providing a fairer evaluation). Or, beyond the analysis of peer interactions, they can provide invaluable information about the student evolution, allowing the assessment of his/her planning and organizational competencies.

Therefore, the challenge is how to use these unique features of 3D virtual worlds to develop more effective assessment techniques useful to the learning process.

4 Assessment of Knowledge

An assessment item typically consists of the following elements:

- A prompt
- A response template (which can consist of choices to choose from, some part to be filled in, etc.)
- A correct response or response model
- Feedback and grades for different response options

Now, most of these parts are typically text. Prompt, correct response and feedback can be directly text. A multiple choice test contains several possible texts, from which the student has to choose the correct one or ones, a fill-in-the-blank response template is a text with a hole.

A richer kind of assessment complements or replaces text with images. So, we can have a multiple-choice question with image hot spot rendering, where the student has to click on the right part of the image to respond the question. Analogously, the prompt or the response can be in audio or video form. These improvements provide a much richer way to assess the student's learning. But all these improvements are essentially directed towards assessing the knowledge in classical environments; 3D virtual worlds offer new possibilities that are worth being explored.

The prompt of the assessment item can be provided by an NPC stating a question orally and students can take all the opportunities they need to hear it again. Even

---

[2] Of course, privacy considerations should be taken into account and the students must be previously warned and agree to such recording.

more, the NPC might point at elements of the environment; it might interact with objects or other NPCs in the world to state questions.

A response template used to request a response can be composed by a set of places that the student should visit, or a set of 3D objects to point to, take, move or modify in order to answer the question. Thus, essentially what is necessary is to have mechanisms to highlight the areas and objects of the world which correspond to the different options given to the students.

In 3D virtual worlds, students can interact with the environment, the objects, NPCs and fellows through their avatars. Any interaction that occurs is likely to be monitored in the virtual world and thus can be used to evaluate the student. Among the interactions that can be detected by an assessment engine we can mention any mouse or keyboard event, the path followed by avatars, changes in the placement, size, color of 3D objects, and any transformation allowed by learning objects created ad hoc such as whiteboards, forums etc.

Providing feedback to individual students can enhance student learning, and in 3D virtual worlds each student can receive feedback through the mechanisms mentioned before for response template. Besides, the student might also receive information about his/her performance in the peer group, or receive recommendations from other students to improve his/her performance; all this is related with social learning aspects of these environments [21].

Therefore, the new interface and elements provided by 3D virtual worlds can be applied to change the way the assessment is carried out. More natural ways of presenting information to learners, new possibilities to test their knowledge and new techniques for monitoring their progress are now available in these 3D environments that are not present in 2D systems.

5   Assessment of Skills

As explained in Section 2, *skills* are defined, according to the EQF, as the ability to apply knowledge and use know-how to complete tasks and solve problems, and can be classified into cognitive and practical. Thus, skills cover a wide variety of learning outcomes. The assessment of cognitive skills, involving mental processes, logically requires different activities to be done by the learner than the evaluation of practical ones, which are related to physical activities.

The SCANS study reports a set of skills required to fulfill the fundamental competencies identified, ranging from basic skills (reading, writing, arithmetic and mathematics, speaking and listening) to thinking skills (thinking creatively, making decisions, solving problems, seeing things in the mind's eyes, knowing how to learn, and reasoning) and personal qualities (individual responsibility, self-esteem, sociability, self-management and integrity).

The requirements for the assessment of these skills depend on their concrete nature. For some of them, mainly basic skills, assessment methods similar to the ones applied for knowledge evaluation can be used. For example, reading comprehension is traditionally assessed by means of an exam consisting on multiple-choice questions enquiring about the meaning of the text. Analogous considerations could apply to other skills of similar kind, such as listening or arithmetic and mathematics skills. In these cases, the ideas discussed in Section 4 for knowledge assessment apply.

There however exist other kinds of skills where such assessment methods are no longer suitable. Thinking skills such as thinking creatively or personal qualities such as self-management are not easily evaluated and require complex activities and processes to be completed by the learner in order to provide indicators of his/her performance.

These types of skills are closely related to competencies (in fact, the EQF defines competencies in terms of responsibility and autonomy) and pose similar requirements for their assessment. Therefore, assessment strategies discussed in Section 6 for evaluation of competencies fit to skills assessment as well.

Additionally, practical skills involving manual dexterity and the use of methods, materials, tools and instruments can benefit from the introduction of haptic interfaces. Simulators are a solution for assessing (as well as acquiring) skills related to the use of tools and instruments that may be expensive or even dangerous (aviation or space-ships are typical examples). Frequently, these simulators are however expensive themselves. The combination of the physical interaction provided by haptic devices with the inmersiveness provided by the 3D worlds facilitate the deployment of realistic virtual simulations that allows the evaluation of this kind of skills.

6 Assessment of Competencies

A 3D virtual world typically has a scenario filled with 3D objects that can be explored, manipulated by avatars populating the world. When the world is used for deploying a learning sequence, there are physical resources on it that must be used by students following a set of constraints such as limited time to carry on the activity, amount of money to spend on it, or the quality and quantity of human resources. Time can be easily controlled by the simulation of the learning experience. Resources such as money can be introduced following video-games techniques. Other organizational aspects as how to assign people to tasks can be done through NPCs previously created to play simulation roles. Monitoring the use of these resources does not pose technical problems.

3D virtual worlds have been used extensively as places for meeting and they offer a closed laboratory where students, represented by their avatars, can be fully observed, their interactions can be traced by a monitoring system coupled to the 3D virtual world. Competencies related with interpersonal relationships are subject of study of the area Computer-Supported Collaborative Learning and there are already CSCL scripting patterns [24] and authoring systems [25] suitable for Web environments that can be adapted to 3D virtual environments.

Acquiring, evaluating, communicating and handling information in general, are basic competencies inherent to any human activity. The natural workflow establishes mechanisms to acquire and evaluate information determining the accuracy of data collected from appropriate sources, store and maintain the information, and communicate to others using oral, written, graphic or multi-media methods. In our opinion, the way to assess the quality of sources consulted and how the student interprets, organizes and presents the information in a 3D virtual environment, does not differ to the techniques used in other learning environments.

Probably, understanding of systems is the most complex mental process; it involves realizing the relationships among its components and predicting eventual consequences of any change in its constituent parts. This understanding can be materialized as a physical model that can be built by the student within the 3D virtual world using 3D objects. All building activities and the overall system performance are likely to be assessed in the environments analyzed.

No matter what curriculum area is explored, it is always necessary to know how to handle materials, technology. Probably the best way to teach the most suitable equipment or tools to use, and the best technology to apply for a given task, is by doing. A 3D virtual environment provides a cheap and safe space to deploy simulations where students can be taught to use and experiment with any kind of tools. The introduction of techniques of augmented reality to virtual worlds can facilitate the teaching process [26]. To automate the assessment task, it is necessary to couple to the simulation the logic to measure how well the tool manipulation is done.

Although the assessment of competencies suffers from the difficulties inherent of monitoring the mental process of human beings, 3D virtual environments provide a unique medium to isolate students from information or stimulus irrelevant to the subject of study. Also, they allow monitoring any possible interaction.

7 Case Study: Recreating the Industrial Revolution in England

In this section we describe a case study that illustrates how knowledge and the five SCANS competencies can be assessed.

A high school History teacher gives his students a problem: "Recreate the Industrial Revolution in England". Students work together in small groups; each group tackle a different aspect of the Industrial Revolution: agriculture, manufacturing, mining, transport. They design scenes that include elements such as housing, food, clothing, and simulation of major inventions; they also include NPCs who dramatize situations reflecting how people lived and worked. When students need more information they consult websites provided by their teacher or discovered by themselves. As result of their work, students must organize, apply, produce, and communicate knowledge accurately and creatively, taking into account constraints inherent to the historical period.

First, it is convenient that students pass an assessment of knowledge about the Industrial Revolution, before beginning the activity designed for the assessment of the five SCANS competencies. The test may include questions to detect anachronisms. For instance, ask students to identify 3D objects, NPCs or actions deployed that do not belong to the historical period studied. Another assessment activity may be to dress up NPCs as characters of the 18th or the 19th century at England or to interact with an NPC in a role playing activity.

Once students have passed their knowledge test, we can proceed to assess skills and competencies. Interpersonal competencies are the focus of this educational experience, how students organize themselves into groups to work on their topic, how they distribute the work and finally how they integrate it. These activities can be carried out through student's avatars with the help of social tools embedded in the virtual world and orchestrated by the 3D virtual learning environment via collaborative patterns. A log of avatars conversations/interactions will allow the students to reflect on their work and constitute evidences supporting their performance, facilitating a fair assessment by the teacher of their team-work competencies.

The main resource to manage is the duration of the activity. To help students with this task, the 3D virtual learning environment may establish milestones in the instructional sequence. Besides, it may also provide the students with information about the advances of peer groups. These mechanisms will not only help the teacher to assess students' progress but also help students to self-assess themselves by comparison with their peers.

Information competencies can be assessed by tracking the links accessed, observing how the information is organized in files or how 3D objects included have been tagged. Object tagging can become a social activity where a peer assessment can be done.

Students plot the events that occurred in the Industrial Revolution through the deployment of 3D objects and NPCs dramatizations, avoiding anachronisms and modeling the social forces that led to this historical period. This setting of the scenes is evaluated by the teacher by observing the scene as a whole. In order to assess the individual contribution of each student to the final product, the teacher will have a log provided by the virtual learning environment with the activities that each avatar did.

There are two different aspects tied to technology competencies, the first is students´ use of tools provided by the 3D virtual learning environment and the last is the deployment of simulation of inventions during the Industrial Revolution, which needs understanding the way these inventions worked. In this case study, students provide the simulation of a technology thus, the assessment must be based on qualitative criteria, observing the invention simulation.

8   Conclusions and Future Work

This paper is mainly focused on presenting the potential use of elements of 3D virtual worlds –avatars, 3D objects, 3D scenarios, NPCs–, besides elements such as text, audio, video, hypertext, widely used in current Learning Management Systems, for assessment in 3D virtual learning environments.

We have presented a set of techniques to assess not only knowledge, but also skills and competencies. The techniques used to assess knowledge are based on the use of 3D elements to represent the four components of any assessment item: prompt response template, response model and feedback. They intend to imitate an ideal teaching-learning-environment where students can interact with a 3D environment to prove their knowledge about a given topic.

Assessment of competencies has not been treated deeply enough even in 2D learning management systems. We have followed SCAN recommendation about what are the set of competencies and skills that are needed for workers to succeed in today´s workplace and presented a set of ways of using 3D objects to this particular case of assessment. The key aspect to achieve our goal has been two characteristics of the 3D words, first the possibility of include into the world only the elements that students need for learning, practice and test his/her skills and second the possibility that we have in these environments to monitor any action or interaction students do in the 3D world.

Finally, we have illustrated the use of the techniques presented in a case study taken from a History course to show the feasibility of our proposal. We are currently developing an assessment 3D environment in the Wonderland platform using the ideas presented in this article.

Acknowledgments. This research is supported by the following projects: The Spanish project "Learn3: Towards Learning of the Third Kind" (TIN2008-05163/TSI) within the Spanish "Plan Nacional de I+D+I", the Madrid regional project "eMadrid: Investigación y Desarrollo de tecnologías para el e-learning en la Comunidad de Madrid" (S2009/TIC-1650), the European eContent*Plus* Project "iCoper: Interoperable Content for Performance in a Competency-driven Society" (PPI-2008-A-12). We also wish to thank the Gradient Lab group members for stimulating discussions of the ideas presented herein.

References

1. Prensky, M.: Digital game-based learning. McGraw-Hill, New York (2001)
2. Vassileva, J.: Toward social learning environments. IEEE Transactions on Learning Technologies 1, 199–214 (2008)
3. Gartner, Inc. Gartner says 80 percent of active Internet users will have a "Second Life" in the virtual world by the end of 2011. In: Business Wire,
   http://www.businesswire.com/portal/site/google/index.jsp?ndm
   ViewId=news_view&newsId=20070424006287&newsLang=en (2007)
4. New Media Consortium and EDUCAUSE Learning Initiative: The horizon report,
   http://www.nmc.org/pdf/2007_Horizon_Report.pdf (2007)
5. Lombardi, J., McCahill, M.: Enabling Social Dimensions of Learning Through a Persistent, Unified, Massively Multi-User, and Self-Organizing Virtual Environment. In: Proceedings of the Second International Conference on Creating, Connecting and Collaborating through Computing (2004)
6. Linden Lab, http://lindenlab.com/
7. The Croquet Consortium,
   http://www.opencroquet.org/index.php/Main_Page
8. Sun Microsystems, Project Wonderland: Toolkit for Building 3D Virtual Worlds,
   http://www.projectwonderland.com/
9. Jarmon, L., Traphagan, T., Mayrath, M., Trivedi, A.: Virtual world teaching, experiential learning, and assessment: An interdisciplinary communication course in Second Life. Computers & Education 53(1), 169–182 (2009)
10. Livingstone, D., Kemp, J.: Integrating Web-Based and 3D Learning Environments: Second Life Meets Moodle. UPGRADE, European Journal for the Informatics Professional 9(3), 8–14 (2008)
11. Open Cobalt Edusim, 3D virtual learning worlds for the interactive whiteboard,
    http://edusim3d.com/
12. Callaghan, V., Gardner, M., Horan, B., Scott, J., Shen, L., Wang, M.: A Mixed Reality Teaching and Learning Environment. In: ICHL, pp. 54–65 (2008)
13. Bloomfield, P., Livingstone, D.: Immersive learning and assessment with quizHUD. Computing and Information System Journal 13(1) (2009)
14. Santos, P., Llobert, W., Hernández-Leo, D., Blat, J.: QTI for self-assessment and embedded-assessment in competence oriented scenarios: The Agora Case. In: International Conference on Intelligent Networking and Collaborative Systems, pp. 39–45 (2009)
15. TENCompetence, Building the European network for lifelong competence development (2009), http://www.tencompetence.org

16. European Commission for Education and Training: The European Qualifications Framework, http://ec.europa.eu/education/lifelong-learning-policy/doc44_en.htm
17. The Secretary's Commission on Achieving Necessary Skills U.S. Department of Labor: What Work Requires of Schools. A SCANS report for America 2000 (June 1991)
18. Education and Culture DG (Education and Training): The European Qualifications Framework for Lifelong Learning (EQF). Luxembourg: Office for Official Publications of the European Communities (2008)
19. Kebritchi, M., Hirumi, A.: Examining the pedagogical foundation of modern educational computer games. Computers & Education 51, 1729–1743 (2008)
20. Bourg, D.M., Seeman, G.: AI for Game Developers. O'Reilly Media, Sebastopol (2004)
21. Vassileva, J.: Toward Social Learning Environments. IEEE Transactions on Learning Technologies 1(4), 199–214 (2008)
22. United States Department of Labor. Employment and Training Administration. Secretary's Commission on Achieving Necessary Skills: Background, http://wdr.doleta.gov/SCANS/
23. United States Department of Labor. Employment and Training Administration. Secretary's Commission on Achieving Necessary Skills: Teaching the SCANS Competencies (1993), http://wdr.doleta.gov/SCANS/teaching/teaching.pdf
24. Hernández-Leo, D., Villasclaras-Fernández, E., Asensio-Pérez, J., Dimitriadis, Y., Retalis, S.: CSCL Scripting Patterns: Hierarchical Relationships and Applicability. In: Proceedings of the 6th Int. Conference on Advanced Learning Technologies, pp. 388–392 (2006)
25. Hernández-Leo, D., Villasclaras-Fernández, E., Ascensio-Pérez, J., Dimitriadis, Y., Jorrín-Abellán, I., Ruiz-Requiques, I., Rubia-Avi, B.: COLLAGE: A collaborative Learning Design editor based on patterns. Educational Technology & Society 9(1), 58–71 (2006)
26. Slocum, M.: Augmented reality and the ultimate user manual. In: The ARMAR Project Shows How Augmented Reality can Revolutionize Learning. O'Reilly Radar, http://radar.oreilly.com/2010/02/augmented-reality-and-the-ulti.html

IP3 – Progress towards a Global ICT Profession

Roger G. Johnson

Department of Computer Science and Information Systems
Birkbeck University of London
Malet Street, London WC1E 7HX, UK
r.johnson@bcs.org.uk

Abstract. The International Professional Practice Partnership (IP3) was formed by the International Federation for Information processing (IFIP) in 2007 to fulfill the objective of creating a global ICT profession. This start of this programme were first presented at WCC 2008 in Milan and since then major advances have taken place – both in the collective understanding of the endeavour and also measured by actual achievements. This paper will contextualise the progress of IP3 by examining: why an ICT profession is needed and why it should be on a global basis; and the progress made by IP3 in establishing a global ICT profession.

Keywords: International Professional Practice Partnership (IP3), International Federation for Information Processing (IFIP), ICT professionalism.

1 Introduction

In 2007 the International Federation for Information Processing (IFIP) created its International Professional Practice Partnership (IP3). This paper develops further the ideas included in earlier papers on IP3 presented at the IFIP World Computer Congress held in Milan in 2008 [1, 2, 3, 4] and provides an update on the considerable progress since then. For an external assessment of IP3, the reader is referred to a paper by Raffai, [5].

Since the autumn of 2008 the programme has grown at a considerable pace and the purpose of this paper is to provide an overview of the progress made, the major issues encountered and the plan for the immediate future.

2 Background

No other technology has advanced so far so fast as ICT. Every year new advances make possible information systems that were previously impractical to build. Constructing the vast systems that run on today's computers is an engineering activity that stands comparison with the greatest achievements of the nineteenth-century engineers who transformed that society. Modern information systems are now the most complex artefacts yet made by human beings.

N. Reynolds and M. Turcsányi-Szabó (Eds.): KCKS 2010, IFIP AICT 324, pp. 177–186, 2010.
© IFIP International Federation for Information Processing 2010

The scale of the achievement comes from the ability to integrate computer technology with communications technology which together can deliver information almost instantaneously around the globe.

The modern ICT system, unlike the batch processing systems of earlier days, allows individual citizens to initiate complex applications without any external mediation by skilled staff. Without any intermediation by a skilled ICT practitioner the user risks serious inconvenience from erroneous information delivered via the internet. Further, the continuing activities of criminal groups to disrupt the economic activity of both individuals and states remind us constantly of the importance of system security.

ICT is unique in its global reach. An internet transaction from one country can involve ICT systems in several others with goods being shipped from another. All of this potentially accounted for by a company registered in yet another. Unlike many professions which have devised schemes for safeguarding the public interest while facilitating free movement of individual professionals between countries, the impact of the activities of an individual ICT practitioner in one country can be felt directly and almost instantaneously around the globe without a single person leaving their desk.

Only a global initiative can adequately respond to the global dimension of this challenge. IP3 is the first attempt to provide a framework within which to begin to address this massive challenge. By bringing together ICT membership bodies from around the globe the IP3 members believe that they can establish a global framework for a global profession.

If the citizens worldwide are to receive the full benefits of ICT they must be able to depend on the integrity of the ICT systems they use. This, in turn, relies on those systems being built, maintained and operated by staff having appropriate technical skills and personal integrity.

These requirements closely match those of many older professions. The partner member societies in IP3 believe that the time is now right to create a global profession of ICT practitioners who are recognized individually and collectively as matching the standing of the older professions.

Information technology, like architecture, engineering and accounting, is now an integral part of every walk of life so ICT systems must be built and run by professionals who understand business as well as ICT.

The innate integrity of individual practitioners is not in itself enough today. Experience in every other profession shows that only by establishing and enforcing professional standards of behaviour on practitioners can the public interest be safeguarded. The total dependence of developed societies on ICT makes it far too important to be left to individual practitioners. Organisations and governments need to know that individuals' professionalism has been certified to globally recognised standards.

This requirement has been further accelerated by the advent of legislation around corporate governance, such as Sarbanes Oxley Act of 2002 (Section 404), which requires organisations to certify the quality and integrity of their IT systems.

IP3's ultimate aim is to ensure that throughout the world there are publicly recognized and accountable ICT professionals with the appropriate education, training and personal commitment who can be entrusted to deliver global ICT solutions of the highest quality.

3   The IP3 Approach

The International Federation for Information Processing (IFIP) is a global federation of over 50 member societies and, through its regional affiliates, linking almost 100 national IT bodies with an aggregate membership of over half million individuals. IFIP was established by a UNESCO initiative in 1960 and remains a formal UNESCO consultative body on IT matters. It is incorporated in Austria as a international, not-for-profit, non-governmental organization.

This provides IFIP with a unique position from which to invite the ICT bodies of the world to join in a collaborative endeavour which its supporters believe can make a significant contribution to the designing, implementing and operating of ICT systems of the highest quality.

In 2007 IFIP invited a group of leading ICT societies to provide representatives to form a Task Force whose objective was to create a programme which could be rolled out across the globe and whose final goal was to establish a global ICT profession based on an agreed set of standards informed by global best practice among the ICT bodies and also other professions.

From the outset it was agreed, firstly, that the programme was not seeking to create a new institution but to create a global partnership of professional bodies. This was expected to add value to the membership proposition of existing societies and where no society currently existed to support the establishment and growth of new bodies. The programme was also committed to promoting the vision of an ICT profession whose members are publicly recognized for their adherence to a set of standards for competence and conduct and who would lead the way in delivering the maximum benefits of ICT for humanity.

Secondly, IP3 is not seeking to "re-invent wheels". Wherever possible, IP3 will seek to adopt existing material giving suitable acknowledgments to the original authors for granting the right to its use.

Thirdly, IP3 is not an examining body. IP3 sets standards for member societies to apply to their members when considering applications for certification in terms of demonstrating competence with the Core Body of Knowledge and also commitment to Continuing Professional Development (CPD). However, the way in which accredited bodies determine the competence of individuals they wish to certify is a matter for them. This could include traditional tertiary qualifications covered by the Seoul Accord, [6] or a combination of other qualifications, national or regional such as European Certification of Information Professionals, (EUCIP) [7]. What IP3 accreditors will wish to ascertain is that alone or in combination they achieve the minimum standard set down by IP3. Again, IP3 believes that certification of individual practitioners can increase interest in professional and vocational qualifications to the benefit of a range of existing examining bodies.

The first significant public exposure of the IP3 programme was at IFIP World Computer Congress (WCC) in 2008 in Milan. At the close of the Congress, 15 representatives from computer societies around the globe signed the *Milan Declaration,* [8]. This declared that:

Against the background outlined in this Declaration we make the following recommendations:

1. That the international ICT profession should be founded on the essential elements of professionalism – **Competences (including knowledge), Integrity, Responsibility and Accountability** and **Public Obligation**.

2. That the assessment of competence should combine technical and non-technical competences including communication and inter-personal skills, domain or business knowledge and managerial culture

3. That the assessment of competences should take into account international ICT certificates, both vendor-neutral and as delivered by ICT Industry, and the qualifications from formal education.

4. That the purpose of the international profession is equally to recognise professionalism itself and to support both individuals and organisations to develop that professionalism.

5. That in structuring the international profession provision should be made for the recognition of an appropriate number of profiles at different levels, and that there should be clear paths of entry and career progression to accommodate individuals from the widest possible academic and experience backgrounds.

Since that declaration, IP3 members have moved rapidly forward to realize the IP3 vision for the IP3 vision for the ICT profession and to implement the procedures that are necessary. Section 4 describes in more detail the key components which have been put in place so far.

In common with usage in older professions this paper uses the term "certification" to describe the granting of public recognition to a suitably qualified practitioner as a professional and the term "accreditation" for the process of granting a professional body the right to certify individual practitioners in accordance with specific guidelines.

The basic concept underlying professionalism is the existence of a group of trained practitioners who demonstrate a continuing commitment to a set of standards governing their practice and who accept that they may be disciplined, up to losing their right to practice, if they break the standards laid down. The IP3 interpretation can be summed up in Figure 1

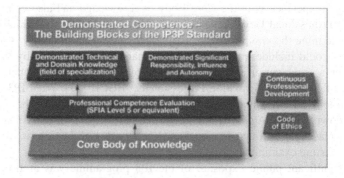

Fig. 1. The IP3 Model of ICT Professionalism

For individual practitioners, who seek public recognition as an ICT professional, IP3 asserts that, in common with members of other professions, they must:

Skills & Competences

- *have their competence to practice re-assessed on a regular basis*
- *undertake continuous professional development*

Conduct and Professional Integrity

- *conform to a published code of conduct*
- *know, and work within, the limits of their capabilities*
- *be accountable for and submit to peer review of their actions*
- *explain the implications of their work to stakeholders*
- *have regard to the public good*

Responsibility to Profession

- *support other professionals in maintaining professional standards and developing professional competence*
- *recognise obligations to the profession as well as to their employer*
- *contribute to the development of the profession,*

The role of IP3 is to accredit professional ICT bodies as meeting the IP3 standard for the certification of individual practitioners. IP3, therefore, has set down a set of threshold criteria to address each of the three groups of bullet points above. .Let us now consider briefly each of these three groups in turn.

3.1 Skills and Competences

Every profession has a Core Body of Knowledge (CBoK) which it expects all professionals to be competent with. In many professions, including ICT, this increasingly divides into two parts a Core Body of Knowledge, common to all professionals, and a Specialised Body of Knowledge of which a professional would be required to have competence in just one area. The ICT area has many CBoKs, notably the work by the ACM and IEEE-CS and similar work by the ACS and BCS, [9, 10, 11, 12]. These documents specify the basic knowledge that is required from an applicant for professional status. The simplest form of proof is successful completion of a relevant university degree programme. Ensuring that the degree held by an applicant has provided the necessary subject coverage on a case by case basis is very time consuming and consequently most professional institutions use schemes of university course accreditation. This simplifies the processing of applications and is seen by many universities as an externally awarded proof of quality in their teaching. Sometimes the accreditation is conducted by a professional institution such as the ACS or BCS or under the auspices of a national committee such as ABET in the USA, [13].

In addition to understanding the CBoK, new applicants are also expected to have undertaken successfully a period of supervised work at an appropriate level, typically for three years. This reflects the need for new entrants to the workplace to obtain experience of good practice as well as academic knowledge before being considered competent to practice unsupervised. IP3 has adopted a skills framework called the Skills Framework for the Information Age (SFIA), [14], to indicate the level of responsibility that IP3 expect a successful applicant to have demonstrated. The level adopted (SFIA level 5) represents work typically associated with a computing graduate after three years supervised employment. SFIA was originally developed in the UK, operated by a non-for-profit organization managed by its users and in use around the world.

IP3 recognises that many skills frameworks exist and is beginning a work programme of establishing mappings between some of the higher profile frameworks and SFIA. The first report has recently been received describing the mapping between SFIA and the Canadian ICTC, [15].

The CBoK used by each profession evolves as knowledge increases and in few areas as quickly as in ICT. Consequently it is surprising that ICT institutions are only latterly mandating documented Continuing Professional Development (CPD) each year as a condition for the renewal of full professional status. IP3 accreditation requires that the professional body requires an auditable record of CPD each year for each certified professional.

3.2 Conduct and Professional Integrity

The second area that IP3 requires a society to demonstrate is how it ensures that its professional membership behave in accordance with professional standard. The first essential is that all professional members sign up to a Code of Conduct, or a Code of Ethics. IP3 requires an appropriate Code of Conduct and again commends exemplars from leading societies. However, IP3 requires not only a commitment by each individual to a Code of Conduct but also that there exists an effective process to receive a complaint from a third party about a member, a capability to investigate the complaint and, if proven, to impose sanctions on that member. Numerous Codes of Conduct and/or Ethics have been published. An analysis was produced by the IFIP Special Interest Group 9.2.2 in 2008, [16].

In regulated professions, the penalty can extend to a life ban from practicing in the profession. However, ICT remains an unregulated profession worldwide so the most severe penalty that an institution can impose is expulsion from membership. Nonetheless, professionals know that criminal sanctions may be appropriate in cases involving, for example, criminal recklessness. However, such criminal prosecutions would be pursued by state prosecutors and not by professional bodies.

IP3 recognises that the powers of the professional institution vary from country to country and discipline to discipline. In some there are autonomous professional institutions with quasi-judicial powers to regulate and, when necessary, discipline members while in others there are combinations of nationally approved qualifications and statutory regulation. IP3 does not advance any particular model but is concerned only that, whatever the model in a given jurisdiction, the public interest is served whereby professionals are accountable for their actions. Indeed IP3 welcomes this diversity of practice believing that by studying practices around the globe best practice will emerge.

3.3 Responsibility to the Profession

The final area concerns the advancement of the profession and the promotion of professional values. Specifically this includes professionals accepting the need to support fellow professionals when challenged by employers or other parties in cases such as whistle blowing. It also lays on the professional a need to work with fellow professionals and others to develop the understanding of ICT, both its theory and practice, and to disseminate that knowledge for the public good.

A professional society should provide a variety of networking opportunities for members and also knowledge dissemination through events, special interest groups and publications.

4 What IP3 Has Achieved

In 2007, four societies became the founding bodies of IP3. These were:

- Australian Computer Society (ACS)
- British Computer Society (BCS)
- Canadian Information Processing Society (CIPS)
- Institute of Electrical & Electronic Engineers – Computer Society (IEEE-CS)

In 2009 three further societies joined:

- Information Processing Society of Japan (IPSJ)
- New Zealand Computer Society (NZCS)
- Computer Society of South Africa (CSSA)

A pre-requisite for membership of IP3 is to be either a Full or Affiliate member of IFIP. In addition, member societies are either accredited or planning to seek accreditation or are committed to actively promoting professionalism in ICT. Today the IP3 member bodies have an aggregate membership (in all grades) of around a quarter of a million members.

Initially these societies operated as an IFIP Task Force but as the partnership developed it became apparent that greater formality was needed and as a result the IFIP General Assembly in August 2009 approved the creation of the IP3 Board to manage the programme, operating under delegated powers from the IFIP General Assembly. The Board membership is:

- One IFIP representative
- Representatives from each founder society
- 3 members elected by the other member bodies
- Up to 3 co—opted members

As explained in Section 3 of this paper, at the heart of the IP3 Vision is the concept of a threshold set of standards to be achieved by individual practitioners before being granted public recognition as an ICT professional. Consequently IP3 has established a **Standards Committee** which is charged with maintaining the IP3 statement of its threshold standard. This committee draws on global best practice to inform its work.

The Standards Committee operates independently of the **Accreditation Committee** whose role is to organize the accreditation of each member body on a five yearly cycle. Accreditations are overseen by IP3's Chief Assessor who chairs the Assessment Committee. When accreditation visits are undertaken, a neutral visiting team is selected from the panel of trained assessors. The costs of the visit are borne by the society seeking accreditation. There are two key components to the accreditation visit. Firstly, the panel will wish to assure itself of the standards adopted to approve those to be granted professional status and secondly, the panel will wish to satisfy itself as to the society's capacity to apply those standards in a rigorous manner. This is why a process of mutual support and sharing of best practice is at the centre of the IP3 programme. Full details of the IP3 accreditation process is included in the IP3 Accreditation Guidelines, [17].

4.1 Strengthening the Professional Bodies

IP3 relies for its success on the commitment of its member societies. Part of the ethos of the IP3 programme is the sharing of best practice. This includes a process of mentoring of societies preparing to apply for accreditation. The process of setting up the internal processes within a professional body to establish that an applicant for professional status has achieved the threshold standard is a non-trivial activity. However, most of IP3's existing members have these processes already. Some of the material is already in the public domain, such as Codes of Conduct and Common Bodies of Knowledge. Other material, such as procedures for university course accreditation or complaint investigation and disciplinary process, can be made available to societies developing professional procedures in preparation for applying for accreditation. IP3 members are encouraged to make available material to other members either on a pro bono basis or under licence agreements. In this way good practice can be shared and societies have an opportunity to recoup some or possibly all of the capital cost of developing new materials.

IP3 believes that by establishing a global network of strong, mutually supportive accredited professional bodies who

- Act as voices for the global ICT profession
- Provide strong support for enhancing the skills of their members
- Set and promote technical and ethical standards of professional behaviour
- Certify ICT practitioners who meet the standard
- Act to ensure serious failures by certified individuals are investigated and, if needed, appropriate penalties imposed

this will lead to

- Enhanced standards of ICT practitioner performance
- Greater public confidence in and appreciation for the work of ICT practitioners
- Increased status for the profession
- Growth in the number and skills of new practitioners
- Stronger, more effective ICT professional bodies

Support from the ICT user and supply sectors is vital to the success of IP3. Consequently IP3 has recently begun to establish a **Global Industry Committee**, made up of leading members of the global ICT community, to offer advice and support to the IP3 Board in developing new initiatives. This is planned to inform IP3's strategy and maximize the impact of IP3's new initiatives.

4.2 Accreditation

Central to IP3 is the accreditation of member societies to grant professional status to practitioners who meet the IP3 standard. So far two societies have been successfully accredited:

- Australian Computer Society
- Canadian Information Processing Society

Between the two societies nearly 10,000 professionals are accredited as ICT professionals by IP3 accredited societies. At least two societies further are planning to seek accreditation within the next year:

- New Zealand Computer Society
- Computer Society of South Africa

Discussions are continuing with numerous other societies around the world about further expanding IP3 membership leading to more societies seeking accreditation from IP3. In this way the visibility and values associated with IP3 will be enhanced.

5 Conclusions

The member societies in IP3 are in no doubt that they have created an ambitious vision. However, working together under the IFIP umbrella, they believe that they are uniquely placed to promote the public understanding of the importance of creating a global ICT profession and also to offer a viable plan to implement their collective vision.

ICT has a unique capacity to provide benefits to humanity. However, IP3 believes it is too important and valuable for the technology to be trusted to the innate integrity of individual practitioners. Only a global profession, which enjoys the same trust and respect as older professions can be relied upon to deliver the full potential of the better world that ICT has the capacity to provide.

Acknowledgments. I would like to acknowledge the support and encouragement of colleagues in IP3 to provide this update on the programme.

References

1. Hughes, C.: The IFIP International Professional Practice Partnership: Informing and Transforming IT Professional Practice. In: Avison, D., Kasper, G., Pernici, B., Ramos, I., Roode, D. (eds.) Proceedings of the IFIP World Computer Congress Milan, Advances in Information Systems Research, Education and Practice. IFIP, vol. 274, pp. 135–138. Springer, Boston (September 2008)
2. Thompson, C.: IT Professional Role – Today and Tomorrow. In: Mazzeo, A., Bellini, R., Motta, G. (eds.) Proceedings of the IFIP World Computer Congress Milan September 2008, E-Government; ICT Professionalism and Competences. IFIP, vol. 280, pp. 69–80. Springer, Boston (2008)

3. Johnson, R.: International Professional Practice Partnership (IP3) – Role and Responsibilities of National Societies. In: Mazzeo, A., Bellini, R., Motta, G. (eds.) Proceedings of the IFIP World Computer Congress Milan September 2008, E-Government; ICT Professionalism and Competences. IFIP, vol. 280, pp. 165–171. Springer, Boston (2008)
4. Hughes, C.: International Professional Practice Partnership (IP3) – Overview. In: Mazzeo, A., Bellini, R., Motta, G. (eds.) Proceedings of the IFIP World Computer Congress Milan September 2008, E-Government; ICT Professionalism and Competences. IFIP, vol. 280, pp. 159–163. Springer, Boston (2008)
5. Raffai, M.: International Program for Standardizing Global IT Profession SEFBIS Journal. John v Neumann Computer Society, Hungary 3 (2008), HU ISSN 1788-2265
6. Seoul Accord, http://www.seoulaccord.com
7. European Certification of Information Professionals (EUCIP), http://www.eucip.org
8. WCC 2008 Declaration on ICT Professionalism and Competences, IFIP WCC 2008, Milan (2008), http://www.ifip.org/images/stories/ifip/public/Announcements/wcc08-ict-p&c-declaration.pdf
9. ACM, IEEE-CS, Curriculum Guidelines for Undergraduate Programs in Information Technology (2008), http://www.acm.org//education/curricula/IT2008%20Curriculum.pdf
10. Software Engineering Body of Knowledge, IEEE-CS (2004), http://www.swebok.org
11. ACS Professional Standards and Education – Core Body of Knowledge (October 2008) https://www.acs.org.au/attachments/ACSCBOKWorkingPaper2008.pdf
12. CITP Breadth of Knowledge Test Syllabus, BCS The Chartered Institute for IT (November 2009), http://www.bcs.org/upload/pdf/citp-bok-syllabus.pdf
13. ABET, Inc., http://www.abet.org
14. Skills Framework for the Information Age, SFIA (2008), http://www.sfia.org.uk
15. Information and Communication Technology Council, Occupational Skills Profile Model, Canada (2009), http://www.ictc-ctic.ca/en/content.aspx?id=76
16. Berleur, J., et al.: Ethics of Computing Committees: Suggestions for Function. In: Form and Structure. IFIP SIG 9.2.2, IFIP Press (2008)
17. IP3 Application and Accreditation Guidelines, IP3 (September 2008), http://www.ipthree.org/images/IP3/application%20and%20assessment%20guidelines_final.pdf

A Teacher's Perspective of Interacting with Long-Term Absent Students through Digital Communications Technologies

Anthony Jones and Karina Wilkie

Graduate School of Education, University of Melbourne, Australia
a.jones@unimelb.edu.au

Abstract. This paper uses an hypothetical scenario to report on the use of ICT to enable students with a chronic illness to partly overcome prolonged absence for school. The focus is on the responses of teachers when one of their students can no longer attend school regularly as a consequence of a serious illness, but wants to continue their education. The special education needs of students participating in the Link 'n Learn project result from a desire to continue studying while absent from school for prolonged periods. It appears that this desire for continuity is misunderstood by many adults, including teachers. Discussion is centred around a hypothetical case study of two teachers as they work with students absent for an extended period.

Keywords: Online learning, Students absent from school.

1 Introduction

To set the scene for the discussion, a brief scenario is presented and then there are some comments on teachers deciding what content to teach and how best to teach it.

Hypothetical Scenario

Parkside Secondary College is a rural/outer suburban school of some 900 students and 75 teachers. In this scenario these details, including whether Parkside is part of a government, independent or Catholic system, are not relevant. What is described here is meant to be general because Parkside could be a secondary school in any developed country.

Sam has been teaching at Parkside for three years, and overall has ten years teaching experience. Like many teachers Sam has a notebook computer that is used both at school and at home for preparation, marking, and administration.

Several weeks into Term 2 one of Sam's students is diagnosed with a chronic illness and will be absent from class for several months. A few weeks later Sam is contacted by the student's parents with a request to help the student continue studying. Sam wonders "How?", "What?", "Why?"

N. Reynolds and M. Turcsányi-Szabó (Eds.): KCKS 2010, IFIP AICT 324, pp. 187–192, 2010.

2 Reality

Interviews with teachers indicate that it is not uncommon for classroom practitioners to first consider pragmatic issues such as "How?" and "What?" when faced with a situation like Sam's. It is the latter of these two questions that causes most problems for teachers. It also appears that it is only later that they ask themselves why a student with a life threatening health condition wants to continue with their schooling.

Link 'n Learn is a research project based at the Royal Children's Hospital (RCH), a large hospital for young people 16 years of age or less. The RCH is located in Melbourne, Australia, and while the data that informs this paper comes from this hospital, children's hospitals in the UK and Europe are collecting similar data.

Hospitals such as the RCH are treating increasing numbers of primary and secondary students for illnesses that are long-term, life threatening and result in prolonged absences from school. For example in 2007 the RCH Education Institute supported 1528 students, 1146 of whom spent less than 3 weeks in hospital [1]. On the other hand there are students who have been supported for several years, as they have been unable to attend school because of ongoing cycles of treatment and recuperation. One consequence is that it is becoming more likely that a school will face Sam's dilemma as sketched above. Some responses and suggestions are offered below, structured around the three questions Sam asked, and with evidence from the *Link 'n Learn* research project. Previous discussions of findings from *Link 'n Learn* have concentrated on students and their perspectives and experiences in maintaining some degree of continuity in their education [1], [2].

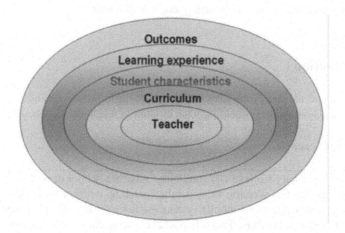

Fig. 1. Classroom teaching model

The issue of how to help these students appears to be the most readily answered of the three questions. Together with a number of other projects, Link 'n Learn has clearly demonstrated that ICT running on small computers with internet access is capable of providing adequate connections between teacher and student, either on a one-to-one basis or with the absent student digitally participating in a lesson. Digital technology has reached the stage where even inexperienced users of web-based video communications software, a group that includes many teachers, are able to quickly and easily learn to use the technology.

Figure 1 represents one model of how a classroom might work from a teacher's perspective. The teacher is at the centre because classroom teachers are not non-participating observers of what occurs in their classroom. Teachers have a curriculum that the system, the school, colleagues, parents and students expect will inform all of them about the content to be taught and learned. Classroom teachers usually collaborate with colleagues to make specific decisions about content. From a student's viewpoint the curriculum is defined by the tasks, experiences and activities used by the teacher. In this model, unless it is part of the content, ICT is usually one aspect of a multitude of learning experiences

2.1 Theory

Although this model suggests that there are distinct layers or steps, in reality many of these layers overlap. Often teachers simultaneously consider some content, the characteristics of the students in the class, and what are likely to be successful teaching strategies. This was labelled as teacher pedagogical content knowledge by Shulman [3] and is represented in Figure 2.

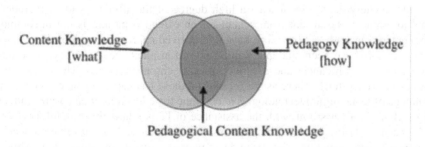

Fig. 2. Pedagogical content knowledge. (After Shulman [3]).

Teachers use their pedagogical content knowledge (PCK) to decide which learning experiences they plan to have students engage with. Teachers might have a choice that includes concrete materials (blocks, science equipment), puzzles, games, worksheets, role plays, textbook, or technology (computer hardware and software). There are many ways of presenting content, so to there are many very different learning experiences that can be provided for students.

The concept of PCK was introduced in the very early days of school and classroom use of computers. Undoubtedly this is one of the reasons why technology is not specifically mentioned. Assuming that technology is connected to content and pedagogy, it must be asked where and why technology fits into PCK. Two possible positions on this are first that technology for teaching and learning is just of the many components of PCK and shouldn't be given more prominence than other components, and second that the use of technology for teaching and learning is so important that it has to be included in a modified definition of PCK. This second position was taken by Mishra and Koehler [4] in their proposal of technological pedagogical content knowledge

(TPCK), and further modified in Thompson and Mishra's [5] technological, and content, pedagogical knowledge (TPACK). For many educators these two proposals do not reflect exemplary classroom practice because technology is named first and this implies a hierarchy. It can be argued that TPCK and TAPCK are a reversion back to the concept of technocentrism raised by Papert and others in the 1980s [6]. Papert attempted to change the idea of learners as passive receivers of knowledge by giving them "control over their learning with computers. Children were the agents of thinking and learning – not the computer ... Computers cannot produce "good" learning, but children can do "good" learning with computers" [7 p.41]

3   The Reality of the Classroom

The *Link 'n Learn* project has been operating for more than two years and over 30 students with a chronic illness have participated. While the majority of students have been in the compulsory years of schooling age range, a significant number of older students who are attempting to complete their secondary education and go on to tertiary study have been involved. Reactions of teachers who are confronted with the situation suggested in the hypothetical scenario range fro denial to a desire to assist as much as possible.

Unfortunately denial, or at least a high degree of unwillingness to help students who are going to be absent from school for an extended period, is not uncommon. Among those in *Link 'n Learn* who have not received appropriate support from teachers or schools have been students waiting on a transplant (heart, kidney, bone marrow), students with cancer and a variety of other chronic illnesses. These cases will not be considered further here as the focus is on those teachers who have accepted the challenge of using digital technologies to continue the education of an absent student.

Teaching in a classroom with the assistance of IT is relatively straightforward for most teachers. Using a single computer in a classroom usually means that the teacher is demonstrating something, for example an internet web-site or a multimedia simulation, or that a presentation is being made using a web browser or presentation software. Teaching in a computer room is more difficult for teachers to manage, control and monitor. However it is still relatively simple.

However what happens when one student from a class of 25 is not physically present in the classroom for weeks or months? In this situation the degree of control that teachers normally have over student learning is reduced significantly, partly because the student now determines when they will participate, based on how well they are and current treatment. Technically it is not difficult to set-up and implement a stable electronic video and audio communications link from one computer to another – in this case between a teachers to a student.

3.1   Discussion

In this section two short excerpts from the *Link 'n Learn* project are presented. Although pseudonyms are used to protect the privacy of students and teachers, the context and description are authentic.

Ernest was in Year 9 at a government secondary school some 200 kilometres north of the RCH, and Ms F was his English teacher. In February of the year Ernest was hospitalised with acute renal problems, Ms F offered to try connecting Ernest to English lessons with his class twice weekly. This choice of lessons was determined by times that Ernest was free from dialysis or other treatment. Although Ms F had used Skype previously for social purposes, she had neither experience nor training in teaching in this mode. In spite of these potential impediments Ernest connected to his English classes through his and Ms F's computers. The class did not see Ernest, but knew he was participating in the lesson through Skype. When the lesson finished Ernest and Ms F had a couple of minutes to discuss what should be done before the next lesson.

Mr T taught Grade 5 at a school located approximately 100 kilometres from the RCH. Jo, one of his students, was an articulate and technologically savvy student being treated for a cancer. Because of cycles of chemotherapy at the RCH followed by recuperation at home, Jo was absent from school more often than she was present. However Jo knew what was happening at school, both educationally and socially, through social networking. In an interview early in her treatment cycle Jo revealed that she connected to school friends through four different social networking sites. A few selected friends were members on all four sites, but each site was used for different purposes. One site appeared to include all the girls from Jo's class and most of the boys, while another was restricted to girls who were members of a local sporting organisation. Through these social networking sites Jo kept abreast of what happened at school and in her local community. Jo was not particularly interested in communicating with Mr T while she was in hospital, but she did connect with him electronically while recovering at home.

Jo's knowledge of what happened in class surprised Mr T, and initially he was uncertain about how and which school work could be covered online. It quickly became apparent that responding to Jo's questions about specific topics or problems was an appropriate strategy. If she didn't understand something that her friends told her, she would ask Mr T.

Eventually, after more than six months absence, Jo returned to school as a full time student and the video conferencing sessions with Mr T stopped. In this case teacher and student were able to overcome the problem of what to do in a one hour online video conferencing session that was replacing several days of school attendance, by allowing the student to take the initiative and to ask about things she had heard from others but didn't understand.

The distance between the hospital and a students' school appears to have an impact on what teachers think is the best strategy for continuing the education of a student. In theory, digital communications such as online video conferencing between teacher and student, could be used no matter where the school was located. However there were several cases where students from schools within ten kilometres of the hospital preferred to make regular visits to the hospital to talk with the student, deliver work, and collect completed work. In at least one case this appears to be a direct result of a student being disfigured by burns to the upper body, and consequently not wanting to be seen by peers and teachers. Even though the possibility of allowing the student to use online video conferencing to see the teacher and class without being seen themself was discussed, this student preferred not to.

In reflecting on the data collected for the *Link 'n Learn* project, the two most significant findings at this stage relate to the desire of students to continue their schooling, and the attitude of teachers who have successfully enabled this to occur. To the surprise of many adults, including some parents, some medical staff, and most teachers, students with a chronic illness who know they would be absent from school for an extended period wanted to continue their education. The students accepted that in some cases they might have to reduce the number of subjects being studied, but almost every student in the *Link 'n Learn* project who was at upper primary level or above expressed a desire to work around periods of medical treatment, ill health, and recuperation to maintain a level of academic continuity.

The most problematic group in the *Link 'n Learn* project have been school administrators and classroom teachers. For Ms F, Mr T, and other teachers in the *Link 'n Learn* project, a desire to assist the absent student is a much more reliable indicator of success than the technological competence of the teacher [2].

4 Conclusion

In 2010 video conferencing and other formats of electronic communication are readily available to teachers and students in hospital. When hospitalised students are loaned a netbook computer and have internet access through a wireless network, there is no technological reason for not connecting with their teachers.

In order to obtain registration to teach in Australia, applicants must have passed IT subjects in their pre-service teacher education course. However these pre-service courses are usually too short to allow candidates to gain experience with one-to-one online teaching strategies that would be appropriate for use with hospitalised students. Currently the success of educational connections between hospitalised students and their teachers is highly dependent on the personal willingness of teachers to move into pedagogical areas for which they have neither training nor experience. As more students are diagnosed with a chronic illness it is time for system administrators to ensure that schools and teachers are prepared for this eventuality.

References

1. Potas, T., Jones, A.: Ethics, Equality and Inclusion for Students with a Chronic Health Condition. In: Kendall, M., Samways, B. (eds.) Learning to Live in the Knowledge Society, pp. 71–78. Springer, New York (2008)
2. Wilkie, K.J., Jones, A.: Link and learn: Students connecting to their schools and studies using ICT despite chronic illness. In: Jeffery, P.L. (ed.) AARE 2008 Conference Papers Collection, pp. 1–13. Australian Association for Research in Education, Melbourne (2009)
3. Shulman, L.S.: Knowledge and teaching: Foundations of the new reform. Harvard Educational Review 57(1), 1–22 (1987)
4. Mishra, P., Koehla, M.: Technological pedagogical content knowledge: A framework for teacher knowledge. Teachers College Record 108(6), 1017–1054 (2006)
5. Thompson, A.D., Mishra, P.: Breaking news: TPCK becomes TPACK! Journal of Computing in Teacher Education 24(2), 38, 64 (2007)
6. Papert, S.: Computer criticism vs. technocentric thinking. Educational Researcher 16(1), 22–30 (1987)
7. Harel, I., Papert, S. (eds.): Constructionism, 2nd edn. Ablex Publishing Corp., Norwood (1993)

University as an Environment for Shaping Key Teachers' Competence for Knowledge Society

Barbara Kedzierska

European Centre for Lifelong Learning and Multimedia Education,
Pedagogical University of Krakow, Podchorazych 2,
30-084 Krakow, Poland
kedzierska@inf.up.krakow.pl

Abstract. Dynamic development of information & communication technologies determines the changes, which more and more often are taking place in all spheres of life of a contemporary human being, forcing him to lifelong learning process, which will allow him to acquire and develop social and professional competence, but first and foremost the most important ones – key competence. Synchronous and asynchronous tools of digital communication stimulate the globalization of processes and services, making people independent from time and place and Internet sources of dispersed and diversified in form information force into responsible autonomy. The following text tries to answer the questions: Does contemporary education take into consideration these determinants and needs of contemporary society? How should a didactic process look like so that university graduates can be prepared to responsible and creative social and professional activity?

Keywords: university in lifelong learning process, key competence in university education, key competence of teachers, changes in contemporary education.

1 Introduction

Technological standards, which are the consequence of a dynamic (in a continuous way) development of information & communication technologies and multiplying processes of globalization (economy, labour market, services, culture) are perceived nowadays as main factors of the changes taking place in all the areas in which societies function [1] . Constant development of particular scientific disciplines and wider and wider range of possibilities of modern ICT tools decide about the increasing pace of changes of our everyday life determinants, both in professional and social aspect. The only way to maintain professional activity on constantly changing labour market is becoming the competence, which strictly correspond with employers' expectations "here and now" [3], which means that acquiring, completing and improving competence (professional and social) has to last lifelong in a continuous way – regardless of someone's profession and age. And this creates for educational system challenges, unknown in history.

N. Reynolds and M. Turcsányi-Szabó (Eds.): KCKS 2010, IFIP AICT 324, pp. 193–199, 2010.

2 Key Competence for Lifelong Learning

Lifelong learning is becoming a key process for everyone in knowledge based society; it is becoming a strategy, which decides not only about the present, but above all about the future of particular individuals, societies and the world itself. The superior programme for cooperation in Europe is *Lifelong Learning Programme*, which aims at adjusting to the most important social needs formal education, which is and will stay priority for democracy.

The authorities of countries and continents, conscious of these determinants, define the assumptions of the concept of lifelong learning which, integrating formal, non formal and informal education into one homogenous system, forces the changes to ensure the effectiveness of shaping and developing competence; professional and social ones, but first of all key competence. The notion of *key competence* was defined in the Attachment to the Recommendation of European Parliament and the Council from 18. December 2006 – *Key Competence in Lifelong Learning – European Reference Framework* [6]. Shaping them has become one of the main aims of Operational Programme Human Capital for 2007-2013.

The competence was defined in the document as the combination of knowledge, skills and suitable in a given situation attitudes. However, *key competences* are the ones we all need (regardless of age and profession) to self-realization and personal development, to professional, social and civil activity. In the document 8 key competences were defined, which specify 8 priority areas of activity of contemporary man, however, depending on the context of discussed issues of modern system of education, within particular projects [9], programmes or institutions, various suggestions of key competences are formed [7].

Generalizing, one may assume that key competences concern:

- self-assessment, planning and effective realization of one's education,
- communication and cooperation in heterogeneous teams,
- peaceful and creative problem solving,
- effective operating (processing) of information,
- integration of information & communication technologies in the realized tasks,
- practical dimension of knowledge.

The main aim of modern educational system is to create among children and young people a conscious need and ability of effective learning, perceived as the solely efficient way of flexible adjusting to changing professional and social determinants. An exceptional role to fulfill has nowadays university education, which as the last stage of formal education for the majority of young people, should on one hand – improve key competence on the level which ensures independent and responsible learning in the next part of life, and on the other hand – prepare to satisfying entrance and activity on labour market.

Modern ways of communicating and free access to unlimited sources of diversified in form information, change the way a man functions in all his areas. In particular, are seen the changes taking place in education - the transformation is now absolutely necessary, because the first time in history children become teachers for their parents. Students have access to almost the same sources of information and knowledge as their teachers and what is more important, they make use definitely more efficiently of technological tools of acquiring, processing and presenting information [2] . In such situation, instead of transmission of information or codified knowledge, a teacher should teach young people to operate the information effectively (acquire, process, present and effectively use) in the realization of assumed aims and tasks.

Teacher's role is changing [4] and dynamical determinants of globalizing labour market force employees to current development and acquisition of new competence, which will enable the professional stability and professional/geographical mobility. In this situation a modular system of education and training, correlated with European and National Qualifications Framework seems to be inevitable. It will be able to help every single individual on each stage of life to keep up with the transformations taking place in everyday reality.

Due to global process of changes implying irreversible social and economic consequences there exists the need for constructive discussion and cooperation between universities and scientific/research centers in the field of adjusting the process of education to the needs and determinants of contemporary society.

Globalization of almost all areas of human activity and the geographical/professional mobility constitute the basis for elaborating the European Qualifications Framework, which determine a new way of interpreting qualifications in the whole Europe, becoming a fundamental European point of reference for national systems of education and local qualifications frameworks. So that according to the European Qualifications Framework and European Concept of Lifelong Learning (LLL) education could nowadays meet global challenges, redefinition of the system of education seems to be crucial; it should be thought over and it should take into consideration social and technological determinants of contemporary society, involving all levels – particularly university level.

3 Challenges for University Education

The basis for functioning in constantly changing labour market today is competence [5] – professional and also, and perhaps first of all – key competence, which determine not only professional but also social activity – regardless of age, profession or social environment. Therefore, key competence as a primary key for any activity of a man, should be shaped in a spirally increasing way from the first year of human's life in all forms of education: formal, informal and non formal [3]. University system of education has a particular role to fulfill in this respect, which – preparing directly to active entrance on labour market, should ensure a proper preparation to all its graduates.

Although key competence should be perceived as inalienable in every profession, in a particular way they determine the effectiveness of teachers' work, from whom for centuries and millennia, society has expected the preparation of young people to professional and social activity in a reality conditioned in a multicontext way. Such assumption imposes a very responsible task on universities educating teachers, the realization of which requires international cooperation[1] of institutions and people engaged in defining, directing, realization, evaluation and financing of the process of education. Globalization is gathering more and more pace [1] and it also concerns education; and the cooperation, which bases on the mobility of learners, students and scientists will be more effective if national systems of education refer to common guidelines and paradigms.

Undoubtedly, one must rank the following among the most significant international points of reference for the systems of education and improvement:

1.   European Concept of Lifelong Learning and
2.   European Qualifications Framework.

These are the documents which complement each other – the first one pays attention to the need for perceiving lifelong education of a single person as one continuous process, which lasts from birth to death. However, the second one specifies common for European countries assumptions and guidelines concerning the structure of system and the competence shaped on particular stages of education[2].

The dynamic development of information & communication technologies – particularly the Internet – has revolutionized forms of communication, offers virtual reality full of illusions/appearances and a free access to almost unlimited resources of information is assumed to be episodic and hypertext [1]. Such determinants are changing radically not only the way contemporary man functions, but also his way of learning and thinking. The competence of effective processing and using information is nowadays becoming more important than the ability of gaining indispensable information. We can no longer shape knowledge on the basis of successively built linear structure, since the fragmentary transmission of information forces hypertext structure. It is becoming more and more obvious that in such revolutionarily new conditions, forms and methods that have been used for centuries cease to be effective and the basic assumptions of the system of education require revision and redefinition. What one should do, therefore? How to define the aims? Which forms and

---

[1] Within such cooperation, in Krakow in October 2009 international scientific conference took place: *Changes in Contemporary Education; Digital Potential versus Cognitive Traps. Key Competences in the Knowledge Society for e-Inclusion,* whose *Final Document* constitutes a specific voice in international discussion concerning the direction and range of indispensable nowadays changes, which determine adjusting education to social needs and economic/technological determinants. The majority of recommendations formulated by the participants finds their reference to the determinants of academic education not only in European countries, but also on other continents; so, in order to not "reinvent the wheel" but synergistically work out common direction and a range of activities for contemporary education, which will guarantee its effectiveness and sustainability, it is worth to take into consideration already elaborated conclusions.

[2] To aforementioned definitions and recommendations refers *Final Document* of Krakow Conference, which in the form of *Memorandum* and a set of *Recommendations* suggests activities, which aim at adjusting university education to economic/technological determinants of contemporary society. International debate was organized by European Centre for Lifelong Learning and Multimedia Education at Pedagogical University in cooperation with International Foundation for Information Processing (IFIP), that is why the postulates, in a particular way concern the process of education and training of teachers, whose competence have the influence on the preparation of next generations to satisfying life in constantly changing reality.

methods of education to admit so that contemporary education will fulfill social expectations and respond to the changing economic/technological determinants?

The superior and timeless aim of education is to prepare children and youth to active, responsible and creative professional/social activity on next stages of life. Such a formulated aim makes forms and methods of education dependent on forms and methods of social/professional activity (the change of functioning in society should in an automatic way imply the change of way of educating and improving one's skills). Therefore, if contemporary forms and methods of social/professional activity differ so much from those from 20.–30. years ago, so – consistently, forms and methods which prepare to such activities should also be changed [2].

One of the most important consequences of information revolution has become the necessity for lifelong learning and improving one's skills; European Concept of Lifelong Learning perceives all the forms of education (formal, non formal, informal) as elements of one continuous lifelong process; thus, university education should be an integral – synchronized with the remaining ones, element of this process [8]. On one hand, it should take into consideration and acknowledge the competence of students acquired outside a university, and on the other, it should shape the competence helpful and indispensable in post–university activity. Ensuring the quality and effectiveness of university education requires that acknowledgement of beyond-university education and training is determined with a consistent certification of the institutions that participate in the process of lifelong learning.

It seems indispensable, therefore, to work out the procedures of recognition of qualifications acquired beyond the system of formal education (in the assessment of student's achievements effects of non formal and informal education should be taken into account). One should also sanction the recognition of foreign and national studies, accepting the alternation of the pace of studying at the same time.

Priority, it becomes modular educational offer [2], which replaced the rigid structure of the curriculum will allow for flexible and dynamic adjustment of graduate education to changing labor market conditions [5]. Shorts form of education, which base on modules, enable dynamic completion and development of competence, which employers look for "here and now". Educational offer should take into consideration applicational dimension, complexity of knowledge and the preparation of graduates to active entrance on labour market requires effective cooperation of universities with employees. The examples of good practices are: commonly defined curricula, classes at university conducted by the management of enterprises or student's practice integrated with the activity of companies. In order to ensure the effectiveness and quality of academic didactic process, inner – university systems of ensuring the quality of education are becoming indispensable, among others through current monitoring and evaluation. Single examples show that history of professional carriers of graduates constitutes an important element of the system of evaluation of the quality of university education.

A matter of priority importance for social/professional activity in knowledge-based society is key competence; although they should be shaped in a spiral way on all stages of education, university education constitutes for the majority of young people the last stage of preparation to independent and responsible life in globalizing society determined technologically so strongly [3]. Taking into consideration the fact that more important than informational & communication tools themselves are today the consequences of their presence in our life deciding about completely new standards of both social and professional functioning, universities have a very responsible task to fulfill. These are universities that should create the following abilities of:

- ➤ flexible adjusting to changing determinants of labour market,
- ➤ critical and creative thinking,
- ➤ analytical problem solving,
- ➤ both individual and team work,
- ➤ responsible conducting one's professional carrier,
- ➤ independent learning and effective use of wisely selected and effectively processed information.

Episodic and hypertext transmission of information no longer allows in the process of shaping knowledge to base on linear structures. Therefore, if technological determinants modify the cognitive process of a human, the revision and redefinition of basic assumptions of didactic process – also academic one is becoming a necessity[2].

According to cognitivistic paradigm, activating methods are becoming a basic form of didactic activities, what means that different forms of transmission of information/knowledge (lectures/classes) should be replaced by the activities which force independent work within interdisciplinary projects realized in small groups during practical or conversation classes, seminars or workshops. And the traditional methods of theoretical control of knowledge or competence of a student should be replaced with the process of systematic evaluation of assumed effects of education and competence of a student, who participates in the realization of group projects which are based on a synergic cooperation.

As comparative analysis of university education in different countries all over the world shows, adjusting academic didactic process to the needs and challenges of creating knowledge-based society, is determined with suitable priorities of a university, among which the preparation and the competence of university teachers are of significant importance. The role of a moderator or tutor, which university teacher should nowadays fulfill, requires the authority, which depends in a direct way from their pedagogical/discipline competence, updated in a continuous way in the process of lifelong learning. University teachers should be obliged to constant (cyclical) completing and broadening their knowledge and skills in a discipline, pedagogical and didactic field; lifelong development of university teachers (LLL) should take place in a planned way (coordinated by academic centres of lifelong learning).

Clear need for defining a set of key pedagogical competence for university teachers is visible. Among them what seems inalienable is full, effective and transparent integration of the potential of information & communication technologies in a didactic process [2]. It does not refer to compulsory use of multimedia during classes and basing exclusively on Internet sources of information; what is more important is the choice of proper forms and methods of education having applicational dimension, preparing students to responsible independence in the future job they are preparing themselves for. Activating methods in a university process of education should take into consideration technological determinants of everyday life, electronic forms of communication, episodic and hypertext transmission of information; they should shape the competence of flexible adjusting to the changing labour market and new forms of activity in globalizing society.

4 Conclusion

Results of international comparative studies show that the process of adjusting academic education to technological determinants and social needs should take into consideration above all the following:

> ➤ the reorganization of didactic process, which would force change of *teaching* into *learning,*
> ➤ change of teacher's role from information and codified knowledge transmitter to a guide, supervisor and moderator; a teacher should become a *lifelong learner,*
> ➤ the replacement of statistic forms of teaching with activating methods, which shape creativity, responsibility and responsible autonomit,
> ➤ transparent integrating of the potential of modern media with all elements of a didactic process.

Efficiency of such changes depends, of course, on the activity and cooperation on international (European) and country level (proper documents and regulations); however a direct efficacy is determined with the conscience and competence of teachers, who by the synergistic cooperation with students and their parents are able in a possibly shortest period of time change educational practice on all levels of education.

References

1. Bron, A., Schemmann, M. (eds.): Knowledge Society, Information Societty and Adult Education. Trends, Issues, Challenges, Munster (2003)
2. Kedzierska, B.: The Role of Audiovisual Means in Lifelong Learning. In: Audiovisual Anthropology: Theory and Practice International Conference, Moscow, pp. 269–274 (2008)
3. Kedzierska, B.: Kompetencje informacyjne w kształceniu ustawicznym. IBE Warsaw (2007)
4. Kedzierska, B., Frankowicz, M.: New Information and Communication Technology and Changing Roles of Teachers. In: Information & Communication Technology in Natural Science education – 2006 EU Sixth Framework Programme, International research Project "ARiSE" Siauliai, Lithuania, pp. 35–38 (2006)
5. Kedzierska, B.: Kompetencje informacyjne w kształceniu zawodowym. In: Kwiatkowski, S.M. (ed.) Przedsiębiorstwo w rozwoju zawodowym pracowników, pp. 131–139. IBE, Warszawa (2007)
6. E-learning in Europe, http://www.elearningeuropa.info
7. EURIDICE, http://www.euridice.org
8. Ministry of Education in Poland, http://www.menis.gov.pl
9. OECD, The Definition and Selection of Key Competencies. Executive Summary, DeSeCo (2003), http://www.oecd.org/edu/statistics/deseco

Are Wikis and Weblogs an Appropriate Approach to Foster Collaboration, Reflection and Students' Motivation?

Mathias Krebs, Christian Schmidt, Michael Henninger,
Matthias Ludwig, and Wolfgang Müller

University of Education, Kirchplatz 2,
88250 Weingarten, Germany
{krebs,schmidt,henninger,ludwig,müller}@ph-weingarten.de

Abstract. There are a few hints (e.g. PISA) that today's' German school system could be improved to prepare students for their future (professional) lives in an adequate way. To meet the requirements of today's society, education has to change to become a life-long learning process. E-Learning provides opportunities for this purpose. In this paper two studies at the University of Education Weingarten are presented, which investigate the impact of wikis and weblogs on students' learning processes. While the first one investigates the impact of weblogs on students' motivation and reflection processes, the second one concentrates on collaboration and knowledge sharing by utilizing wikis for mathematical projects.

Keywords: e-learning, social software, wikis, weblogs, motivation, reflection, collaboration.

1 Introduction

Our society is in flux. Frequently changing affordances, not only in professional life, require a life long learning process from today's students [1]. As a consequence, today's education system must be adapted to these new circumstances. Schools, as important instances of education and socialization, have the duty to qualify students for their future (professional) lives. Today, this means that they are confronted with the challenge to prepare them "for jobs that don't yet exist, using technologies that haven't yet been invented, in order to solve problems that we don't even know are problems yet" [2, p.2]. It is more and more doubtful, whether these goals can be reached by only applying traditional teaching methods that have been utilized in schools in the past. In the recent discussion the demand to focus on communicative and situated learning as well as on the fostering of learning communities are increasingly mentioned [3]. Here, the implementation of e-learning can facilitate designing adequate learning scenarios to impart the competences needed for the 21st century. High hopes are particularly pinned on the new communication and presentation technologies of the social web, also referred to as Web 2.0 [4]. "Emergent Web 2.0

N. Reynolds and M. Turcsányi-Szabó (Eds.): KCKS 2010, IFIP AICT 324, pp. 200–209, 2010.

concepts and technologies are opening new doors for more effective learning and have the potential to support life-long competence development" [5, p.72].

One of several activities set by the federal state Baden-Württemberg (Germany) in order to implement innovative teaching methods at school is the post-graduate colloquium on e-learning in schools as the basis for life-long learning to research the use of new e-learning concepts at schools systematically. Within this field, scientists from the Universities of Education in Ludwigsburg, Schwäbisch-Gmünd and Weingarten work together on different studies.

2   Studies at the University of Education Weingarten

The research group at the University of Education Weingarten focuses on the question, whether e-learning can foster collaboration, reflection, as well as students' motivation; and in which way this can be encouraged. Thereby, they highlight social software, because it can connect people with the same interests. Because learning is a social process it is recommendable to also use these tools that "have [...] been associated with collaborative activities, knowledge sharing, reflection, debate, and facilitation of communities of practice" [6, p.1] also for this purpose.

In the following the theoretical framework as well as the research design and first results of two studies are presented. While the first study examines the use of weblogs at school and its impact on students' motivation and reflection processes, the second one concentrates on collaboration and knowledge sharing by utilizing wikis for mathematical projects.

2.1   Weblogs at School – A Tool to Foster Self-determined and Motivated Learning as Well as Reflection?

Even though latest media studies [7] show that blogging as well as blog commenting has declined in popularity among teens and young adults during the last years, there still exists a gap between the use of ICT by students in their spare time and the use of such technologies at school.

First explorative studies and best practice reports – primarily in the context of higher education – came to the result that weblogs are well suited to support a self-determined learning process as well as to increase students' motivation and reflection processes [8, 9, 10]. Motivation and reflection are both key factors for a successful learning process and their impact on learning results is proofed several times in the field of learning sciences [11]. In the follow sections both constructs are specified before the research questions and the research design are presented.

2.1.1   Motivation

To be motivated in general means to be activated toward a positive valuated target. In the course of time diverse approaches and theories were developed in the field of motivation research. These can be categorized roughly by the source of activation energy. Most notably, three different energy sources can be distinguished: (1) physiological needs (e.g. instincts and drives), (2) emotions and (3) psychological needs [12].

One theory that is often mentioned regarding weblogs and motivation [13] is the self-determination theory of motivation by Deci and Ryan [14]. In that, the authors distinguish between two kinds of motivation: intrinsic and extrinsic motivation. "Intrinsic motivation is defined as the doing of an activity for its inherent satisfactions rather than for some separable consequence" [15, p.56) whereas "extrinsic motivation is construct that pertains whenever an activity is done in order to attain some separable outcome" [15, p.60]. Intrinsic motivated actions are always self-determined. This does not mean that extrinsic motivated action is invariantly non-autonomous. It can vary greatly in the degree to which it is autonomous. People can internalize and integrate external values and behavioural regulation into their own, so that they act extrinsic motivated but self-determined to reach a certain goal. For the intrinsic as well as for the extrinsic motivation the satisfaction of two psychological needs is necessary, the need to feel competent and the need to feel autonomous. For the self-determined extrinsic motivation Deci and Ryan amend that the person must feel a sense of relatedness.

In the context of learning, former research showed that students who act in a self-determined way are more willing to engage cognitively in the learning content and to assimilate the stuff more deeply [16]. Thus, one goal of instructional design should be to foster a self-determined learning process by designing learning scenarios which support the satisfaction of the three psychological needs mentioned above. Here, weblogs can help in different ways.

The chronological collection of posts reveals the gain of competence to the learner (internal perspective). Furthermore, writing a weblog affords the chance that the students' knowledge, thoughts and abilities are noticed and at best even honored, e.g. through commentaries or references, by others (external perspective). Both should have a positive impact of feeling competent.

The sense of being related to other persons can be fostered since weblogs offer the possibility to link them among each other. Thus, a decentrally organized and open community develops, which allows them to socialize and to maintain contacts.

Weblogs also can enhance the feeling of acting autonomously in two ways. Firstly, they are a way of self expression. The student decides on the individual design of his blog as well as on the topics he blogs about and by this how he will present himself to the readers. Secondly, weblogs are expected to initiate reflection processes and reflection is expected as a kind of antidote against dwindling of autonomy [17].

2.1.2 Reflection

Besides motivation, reflection is a second important psychological construct for learning. The most popular approaches to reflection are the works of Dewey [18], Vgotsky [19] and Schön [20]. Based on the findings of these authors reflection can be defined as "a process during which a person pays attention to a problem, evaluates this problem on the background of a previously set goal and of his/her past experiences, generates options for action, relates the expectable outcomes of these options to the present situation, and makes decisions for future actions with the aim of solving the problem" [21, p.56].

In the last years Web 2.0 technologies were increasingly expected as a way to foster reflection during learning processes. Regarding weblogs these assumptions are based on previous research in the field of learning journals [22]. The results suggest that writing an entry already initiates reflection processes and leads to a deeper as-similation of the learning contents. The learner has to think about his learning process, organize his thoughts and externalize them as texts or artefacts. All these processes are expected to support reflection. While the verbalization of individual thoughts is also necessary to create a blog post, weblogs furthermore provides the opportunity to integrate peers in the reflection process. They can comment the entries and participate in discussions. By this, convergent perspectives of the learning content as well as different options for further action are shown. This can also initiate a rethinking and reflection process. Thus, the possibility to leave comments supports cognitive and metacognitive strategies during the learning process and leads to a deeper learning [23]. The results of an empirical study by Du and Wagner [24] indicate that success-fully blogging can be a predictor for the success in a course or an exam. All in all, weblogs seems to have the potential to foster a more self-determined and reflected way of learning. In our study we want to figure out whether students are able to un-fold this potential.

2.1.3 Research Questions and Study Design

So far, the explanations point out that the use of weblogs at school seems to be a promising tool to foster self-determined and motivated learning as well as reflection. But at the moment there is a lack of empirical evidence for these assumptions because of the used researched methods. By using a quasi experimental research design as well as method triangulation (see figure 1), the aim of this project is to find empirical sustainable answers to the following research questions:

1. What impact has the use of weblogs at school on the parameters of the self-determination theory by Deci and Ryan and mediated by that on students' motivation?
2. Can conclusions be drawn from the use of weblogs at school to students' re-flection processes?
3. What impact has the use of weblogs at school on students' learning out-come?

The study is scheduled for the end of the current school year. It will start by collecting data about the class climate, students' interest in the subject, students' interest in Web 2.0 tools, students' media competence, teachers' behaviour and teachers' interest. Therefore a standardized questionnaire is used. These data are used as control vari-ables and based on these, matched samples are constructed. In a next step the classes are divided in a control and two experimental groups. The control group design has been chosen to research whether expected effects are really du to utilization of we-blogs or if other aspects have a greater impact on the variables. After training the teacher and students of the experimental groups in using the weblog software, they will write a weblog in addition to their lessons for four weeks. While the control group will be taught without weblogs, in the first experimental group every student will write his own weblog and in the second one a class weblog will be used. At the beginning and at the end of this phase, again data will be collected with a standard-ized questionnaire that contained items related to self-determination and motivation as well as to students' reflection. Afterwards, the teachers and a sample of students of the experimental classes will be interviewed to validate the results, especially concerning the reflection processes. Furthermore, all blog posts will be quantitatively and qualitatively analyzed.

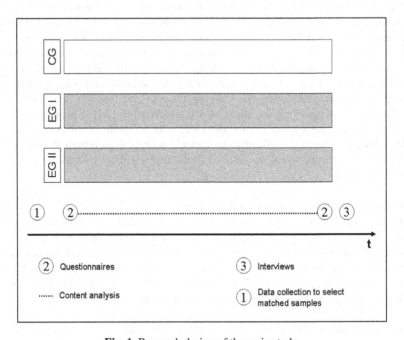

Fig. 1. Research design of the main study

On the one hand it could be doubted that meaningful results will be found after using weblogs for only four weeks. On the other hand would be problematic to do field research in classes for a longer period of time. Thus, an explorative pilot study was done at the University of Education Weingarten last year [25]. Students, studying "Media and Education Management", used weblogs in addition to their media law classes. A panel study with four measuring times at intervals of approximately four weeks revealed that the parameters of self-determination theory as well as the constructs of interest and motivation are time stable. Over all measuring times there could not be found any significant differences in the answers of the course. Thus, a four week study at school should be sufficient to answer the research questions mentioned above and it definitely facilitates to find teacher for cooperation.

On the conference first results of this project will be presented and put up for discussion.

2.2 Utilizing Wikis for Collaboration and Knowledge Sharing in Mathematical Projects

Duffy and Bruns [26] outline different uses of wikis. Among others, they mention that a wiki can be used for acting as ongoing documentation of student's work and to add summaries of their thoughts and building collaborative and annotated content as well as linked network of resources.

A considerable amount of examples on the application of wikis for learning and teaching exist [27, 28]. Most concerns how wikis can support writing [29, 30, 31]. To improve academic writing, Wheeler and Wheeler [32] used a wiki. They come to the conclusion that their "findings indicate that most students raised their skill level in writing as a result of using the Wiki space" [33, p.1]. But wikis are also used in other subjects. For example, Notari [34] used a wiki in a classroom for learning biology and highlights the importance of developing a "communication and comment culture".

Himpsl [35] provides different examples on how to apply wikis in schools. For example, he used wikis to collect information and relevant links for a specific learning objective, recording of material in brainstorming sessions, and wiki-based Web-Quests. For example a Web-Quest was done with the topic "Golden Section". Small projects were also performed with a wiki.

Although, as seen, wikis are used in education experiences for learning Mathematics, project-based fundamental surveys about unfolding their potential for collaboration, communication and discussions as well as for reflecting about content are missing.

As a consequence, we used a wiki in a seminar at University of Education Weingarten (Germany). Students in "Mathematics and Education on project-based Math learning" were given the task to use a wiki for conceptualizing and elaborate own mathematical projects beyond regular lectures [36].

Based on the wiki's page history mechanism, it was possible to trace and analyze the development process of individual pages in some detail. The analysis revealed that in fact the process of writing articles was rather cooperative than collaborative: students divided their tasks into different parts and worked rather independently and individually. Collaboration in terms of iterative editing and refining of content in the wiki by different students as well as discussions in the wiki took place only very seldom.

In a second study we developed a concept to apply wiki-based collaboration in German middle school classes [37]. Here, the idea was to foster collaboration and discussions in math classes using this technology. In this setting, students from different schools were using a wiki for a defined project work in a period of one month. Here, a project group consisted of two to four students, each from a different class from different schools (see figure 2).

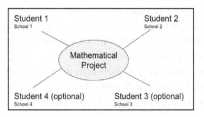

Fig. 2. Composition of a project team

A personal face-to-face meeting of participating student group members was scheduled for the project's kick-off meeting and final project presentation only. Thereby, students had to utilize the wiki during the virtual project phase to figure out strategic procedures and approaches on how to solve mathematical problems including how to do calculations. All in all, there were six project groups arranged, while students from three project groups discussed and commented mathematical procedures or calculations of group members.

The experiment revealed that collaboration in terms of that content was corrected (edited and deleted) inline took place in only a few exceptional cases. Rather, all students created and wrote their contributions linearly from top to bottom: all project groups were adding and refining content in a way that they just added content at the bottom of the wiki page (article) or discussion page.

Students used the wiki infrastructure to communicate and to place questions when contributions from other students introduced some procedures and calculations that were unclear to them.

It is interesting to mention that student groups to some extent exhibited the habit of signing new contributions to articles with signatures in terms of login name and timestamp. Apparently, information on the current state of the article, including the last contributor and last date and time of change were important for them. Most probably not being aware of the versioning feature of wikis, students invented their own strategy. So, students could see the progress of the project at once and had not to use the versioning feature of the wiki.

The way students utilized the wiki for refining content and asking questions indicates that some students reflected on the subject as well as on the content, created by group members. As one example, students of the project team with the question "How much math teachers are recommended in Germany?" tried to figure out the mathematical procedure together. There, one student asked which facts were needed for the mathematical calculation (e.g. number of students of a school, number of classes, math teaching load ...) and asked his team to eliminate unimportant facts and add facts, which were not listed by him. Further, this group apparently actively tried to understand provided material and explanations of other group members by asking questions. We think that in this situation students had to externalise their thoughts due to concretising procedures and answering questions. In another project, students discussed different ways to solve the question "Has a 21-gear bicycle really 21 different gears?" First, one student tried to do some multiplication stuff. Due to discussions with group members and the tutor, which gave strategic hints, he got the right procedure and explained it at the final presentation. However, the student had technical deficits to illustrate his result as a table in the wiki.

In this case we conclude that the student reflected on mathematical content and initiated rethinking. In fact, this is exactly one of the major goals and an important aspect of motivation in math classes today.

The project is ongoing, and we are currently investigating with larger user groups wheather our first results can be confirmed. Also, we would like to identify in some more detail how collaborative authoring of content can be promoted.

3 Summary and Outlook

In the last decades the dispersion and increasing impact of the internet and ICT on our social and professional environments has confronted education systems with new challenges. Social software, mobile devices and ubiquitous computing are just some of the newest examples for the still ongoing changes in our every day life. Thus, it is mandatory for schools to adapt their learning methods to these developments. Otherwise they run risk to loose their state as most important institutions for socialization and education.

First best practice examples suggest that weblogs and wikis are a promising way to improve students' learning and to impart their 21st century skills at the same time. But at the moment these assumptions are at the best hypotheses. Empirical research, like both studies described in this paper, is absolutely necessary. Not only to proof the potential of these tools for particular learning scenarios, but also to effectively implement them in general education. In the long run it will be inevitable to change the way we teach today students without missing the aim to prepare them for their future (professional) lives.

Acknowledgements

The presented studies are both part of the comprehensive post-graduate colloquium on e-learning in schools as the basis for life-long learning, funded by the Ministry of Science, Research and Arts of the federal state Baden-Württemberg, Germany.

References

1. Commission of the European Communities: A Memorandum on Lifelong Learning (2000), http://www.bologna-berlin2003.de/pdf/MemorandumEng.pdf (15.02.2010)
2. Fischer, K.: Did you know? (2006), http://www.lps.k12.co.us/schools/arapahoe/fisch/didyouknow/didyouknowtext.pdf (15.02.2010)
3. Weicht, W.: Manifest Schule 2.0 (2009), http://blog.schulezweipunktnull.de/2009/05/manifest-schule-20/ (13.05.2009)
4. O'Reilly, T.: What Is Web 2.0. Design Patterns and Business Models for the Next Generation of Software (2005), http://oreilly.com/web2/archive/what-is-web-20.html (21.01.2010)
5. Klamma, R., Chatti, M.A., Duval, E., Hummel, H., Hvannberg, E.H., Kravcik, M., Law, E., Naeve, A., Scott, P.: Social software for life-long learning. Journal of Educational Technology and Society 10, 72–83 (2007), http://www.ifets.info/journals/10_3/6.pdf (15.02.2010)
6. Sevelj, M.: All eLearning in the same basket? Challenging a social constructivist, fit for all'. Paper Presented at The Distance Education Association of New Zealand Biennial Conference, July 3-5. Auckland University of Technology (AUT), Auckland (2006)
7. Lenhart, A., Purcell, K., Smith, A., Zickuhr, K.: Social Media & Mobile Internet Use Among Teens and Young Adults (2010), http://pewresearch.org/pubs/1484/social-media-mobile-internet-use-teens-millennials-fewer-blog (15.02.2010)
8. Pullich, L.: Weblogs als Lernjournale. Kommunikation und Reflexion mit Weblogs im Rahmen akademischer Abschlussarbeiten. IfBM.Impuls – Schriftenreihe des Instituts für Bildungswissenschaft und Medienforschung (2007)

9. Spannagel, C.: Eine Weblog-Umgebung zur Förderung selbstbestimmt motivierten Lernens. In: Rensing, C., Rößling, G. (eds.) Procedings der Pre-Conference Workshops der 5. e-Learning Fachtagung Informeatik DeLFI 2007, Siegen, Logos, Berlin, pp. 11–18 (September 2007)

10. Christen, A., Hofmann, M., Obendrauf, M.: Portfolioarbeit mit einem eLernreisebuch und einem ePortfolio auf einem Blog mit Studierenden im 1. Semester an der Pädagogischen Hochschule Rorschach (2006), http://metablog.phrblog.kaywa.ch/files/vorstudie-eportfolio-27-08-06.pdf (14.05.2009)

11. Sawyer, R.K.: The Cambridge Handbook of the Learning Sciences. Cambridge University Press, New York (2006)

12. Rheinberg, F.: Motivation, 7th edn. Kohlhammer, Stuttgart (2008)

13. Reinmann, G.: Persönliches Wissensmanagement. Einführung und Denkanstöße (2008), http://gabi-reinmann.de//wp-content/uploads/2008/04/vortrag_ingolstadt_april_08.pdf (13.05.2009)

14. Deci, E.L., Ryan, R.M.: Die Selbstbestimmungstheorie der Motivation und ihre Bedeutung für die Pädagogik. Zeitschrift für Pädagogik 39, 223–238 (1993)

15. Ryan, R.M., Deci, E.L.: Intrinsic and Extrinsic Motivations: Classic Definitions and New Directions. Contemporary Educational Psychology 25, 54–67 (2000)

16. Pintrich, P.R., Schrauben, B.: Student's Motivational Beliefs and Their cognitive Engagement in Classroom Academic Tasks. In: Schunk, D.H., Meece, J.L. (eds.) Student Perceptions in the Classroom, pp. 149–183. Lawrence Erlbaum, Hillsdale (1992)

17. Reinmann, G., Bianco, T.: Knowledge Blogs zwischen Kompetenz, Autonomie und sozialer Eingebundenheit (2008), http://www.imb-uni-augsburg.de/files/Arbeitsbericht_17.pdf (15.02.2010)

18. Dewey, J.: How we think. In: Boydston, J.A. (ed.) John Dewey: The later works, 1925-1953, vol. 8, pp. 105–352. Southern Illinois University Press, Carbondale (1933/1986)

19. Vygotsky, L.S.: Mind in society: The development of higher psychological processes. Harvard University Press, Cambridge (1978)

20. Schön, D.A.: The reflective practitioner. Jossey-Bass, San Francisco (1983)

21. Henninger, M., Mandl, H.: Training soft skills with software. Fostering reflection in the training of speech-receptive action. In: Frey, D., von Rosenstiel, L., Mandl, H. (eds.) Knowledge and Action, pp. 53–86. Springer, New York (2006)

22. Moon, J.A.: Learning Journals: A Handbook for Academics, Students and Professional Development. Routledge Falmer, London (2004)

23. Nückles, M., Renkl, A., Fries, S.: Wechselseitiges Kommentieren und Bewerten von Lernprotokollen in einem Blended Learning Arrangement. Unterrichtswissenschaft 33, 227–243 (2005)

24. Du, H.S., Wagner, C.: Learning with Weblogs: An Empirical Investigation. In: Proceedings of the 38th Hawaii International Conference on System Sciences, vol. 7b (2005)

25. Schmidt, C., Henninger, M.: Der Einsatz von Weblogs in der Hochschullehre und seine Auswirkung auf die Paramter der Selbstbestimmungstheorie nach Deci und Ryan im zeitlichen Verlauf. Presentation at 73. Tagung der Arbeitsgruppe für Empirische Pädagogische Forschung (AEPF), Bochum, Germany (2009)

26. Duffy, P., Bruns, A.: The use of blogs, wikis and RSS in education: A conversation of possibilities. In: Proceedings of the Online Learning and Teaching Conference 2006, Brisbane (2006), http://eprints.qut.edu.au/5398/1/5398.pdf (15.02.2010)

27. Schwartz, L., Sharon, C., Cossarin, M., Rudolph, J.: Educational Wikis: Features and selection criteria. International Review of Research in Open and Distance Learning 5 (2004), http://www.irrodl.org/index.php/irrodl/article/view/163/692 (15.02.2010)

28. Honegger, B.D.: Wiki und die starken Lehrerinnnen. In: Friedrich, S. (ed.) Unterrichtskonzepte für informatische Bildung, Köllen, Bonn, pp. 173–183 (2005)
29. Rick, J., Guzdial, M., Carroll, K., Holloway-Attaway, L., Walker, B.: Collaborative learning at low cost: CoWeb use in English composition. In: Proceedings of Computer Support for Collaborative Learning Conference, Boulder, CO, USA, January 7-11, pp. 435–442 (2002)
30. Hampel, T., Selke, H., Vitt, S.: Deployment of simple user-centered collaborative technologies in educational institutions – Experiences and requirements. In: Proceedings of the 14th IEEE International Workshops on Enabling Technologies: Infrastructure for Collaborative Enterprise (WETICE 2005), Linköping, Sweden, June 13-15, pp. 207–214 (2005)
31. Bruns, A., Humphreys, S.: Wikis in teaching and assessment: The M/Cyclopedia project. In: Proceedings of the 2005 International Symposium on Wikis, San Diego, CA, USA, October 16-18, pp. 25–32 (2005)
32. Wheeler, S., Wheeler, D.: Evaluating Wiki as a tool to promote quality academic writing skills (2007), http://telearn.noe-kaleidoscope.org/warehouse/158_Final_Paper_(00168)0v1.pdf (15.02.2010)
33. Wheeler, S., Wheeler, D.: Using wikis to promote quality learning outcomes in teacher training. Learning, Media and Technolog 34, 1–10 (2009)
34. Notari, M.: How to use a wiki in education: wiki based effective constructive learning. In: Proceedings of the 2006 International Symposium on Wikis, Odense, Denmark (2006), http://www.wikisym.org/ws2006/proceedings/p131.pdf (15.02.2010)
35. Himpsl, K.: Wikis im Blended Learning: Ein Werkstattbericht. Werner Hülsbusch, Boizenburg (2007)
36. Krebs, M., Ludwig, M.: Math learning with Wikis. In: The 9. International Conference on Technology in Mathematics Teaching (ICTMT 9), Metz (2009), http://www.ictmt9.org/contribution.php?id=84&lang=en (15.02.2010)
37. Krebs, M., Ludwig, M., Müller, W.: Learning Mathematics Using a Wiki. Procedia - Social and Behavioral Sciences 2(2), 1469–1476 (2010)

Digital Literacy: A Vital Competence for 2010?

Denise Leahy and Dudley Dolan

School of Computer Science and Statistics,
Trinity College,
Dublin 2, Ireland
{denise.leahy,dudley.dolan}@cs.tcd.ie

Abstract. People are living in a fast changing world today in both their business and personal lives. With the rate of change in technology continuing at Gordon Moore's 1965 predictions [1], what competencies are needed to take full advantage of today's Knowledge Society? The EU has recognised the need for digital literacy and has included this in the definition of eInclusion [2]. This paper defines digital literacy as a competence which is vital for all citizens, examines the changing definitions of digital literacy, looks at what the certification bodies are saying and proposes the competencies which are required and which define digital literacy today.

Keywords: Digital literacy, competencies, eInclusion.

1   Introduction

In this, the second decade of the 21st century, a Knowledge Society exists from which we all should benefit. However, some people are excluded; often caused by social, economic or accessibility issues. And even if technology is available, a person will still be excluded if he or she cannot use the technology or cannot use it efficiently and safely. It is vital that these issues are addressed by governments worldwide. The European Union has recognised the need for digital literacy and has included this in their definition of eInclusion [2] - "To participate and take advantage (of the Information Society), citizens must be digitally literate - equipped with the skills to benefit from and participate in the Information Society".

Tim Berners-Lee thought of the Web as a "common information space in which we communicate by sharing information" [3]. This is already happening - the use of social networking is growing "41.7 million Europeans are regular users of social networking sites. They will be 107.4 million by the end of 2012. Europeans are using them to share personal and professional experiences, keep in contact with family and friends, and organise their social lives." [4] However, for many people the computer is not a natural tool, even causing fear of doing something wrong, of "breaking the machine", of getting lost online, etc. Such people need guidance on what is required to help them use technology, remain safe online and become confident members of the Knowledge Society. A definition of the competencies and skills is needed.

There are different levels of digital literacy competence and, with the rapid advances in technology, what is required to be digitally literate changes continually. The

N. Reynolds and M. Turcsányi-Szabó (Eds.): KCKS 2010, IFIP AICT 324, pp. 210–221, 2010.

skills required to complete a task can change with different versions of software, hardware or communications technology. What was difficult to do 20 years ago can be performed with the push of a button today. Yet, because the functionality is growing, more is expected of a digitally literate person.

This paper argues that, even with the availability of technology, without digital literacy a person cannot take full advantage of the Knowledge Society. It examines the changing definitions of digital literacy and proposes the competencies which are required and which define digital literacy today.

2 The Changing Perception of Digital Literacy

Before the 1960s, computers were mostly used in scientific laboratories or academic environments. Although there were some business machines, for example Leo, Univac, and DEC, these were not in general use in business. In 1959, IBM launched its 1400 series of business computers and a high level programming language (COBOL) was created. In 1959, a conference was held in Paris as a result of which the International Federation for Information Processing (IFIP) was founded in 1960 [5]. During the '60s there was wider use of computers in business. These computers were big machines, taking up much space and were usually operated and programmed by computer professionals. Many of these machines ran corporate systems with only cards or paper tape as input and hard copy printouts as output. The business functions running these machines and providing the services were often called Data Processing (DP) departments. At that time, to be "computer literate" meant that you were a DP professional. In the '70s the use of computers spread in business with mid-range computers such as Digital Equipment Corporation (DEC) and Data General (DG) equipment becoming common. There have been many definitions of digital literacy since these early days of computing. The term "computer literacy" appeared in writings in the 70s [6].

As computers began to be used widely in business, it was necessary for the business user to become competent in using computer systems related to their specific task or job. Business people began to use query languages and CASE tools (Computer Aided Software Engineering). However the programmer was still the professional expert and the business user had limited tools. End user tools became available during the late '70s. These tools gave the user the ability to manipulate their data and, with the advent of macros, the user could write a small amount of code. End user systems development arrived when personal computing tools allowed users to develop small systems – word processing, spreadsheets and small databases were available to all. The term "computer literacy" at this time included the use of personal computers by the non technical person. However the meaning was not entirely clear – as Van Dyke [7] stated in 1983 "if the vernacular of the term computer literacy is assured, its meaning is not". During the 90s, the term "digital literacy" began to appear.

Paul Gilster, in 1997, suggested that to be digitally literate a person should be able to find information on line and evaluate it, suggesting that the skills of such a person should include the use of email and search engines and the ability to evaluate a Web Site, other on line resources and other information resources [8]. According to Wilhelm in Digital Nation [9], to be digitally literate you should be able to "Access, manage, integrate, evaluate and create information".

The term "digital literacy" developed to include media literacy and the ability to interpret information. Eshet-Alakali et al suggest that "Having digital literacy requires more than just the ability to use software or to operate a digital device; it includes a large variety of complex skills such as cognitive, motoric, sociological, and emotional that users need to have in order to use digital environments effectively." [9]

The definitions, therefore, have included:

- Digital literacy – this term is used today, but it has different meanings. It can include all of the terms below
- Computer literacy – started off with the DP people, the technical people who were computer professionals
- Information literacy – this definition usually means digital literacy and includes the ability to verify, interpret and validate the information
- Cyber literacy – sometimes used to include competence with using the Internet, communications and the Web

The definition used by the European Union is "Digital literacy involves the confident and critical use of Information Society Technology (IST) for work, leisure and communication. It is underpinned by basic skills in ICT: the use of computers to retrieve, assess, store, produce, present and exchange information, and to communicate and participate in collaborative networks via the Internet."

3   Digital Literacy Today

Technology is becoming part of everyday life today. We talk to our distant friends using technology, sending photos, family information and chat. Businesses are using technology to communicate with customers and suppliers; governments are communicating with citizens using technology. Digital literacy is necessary take full benefit of all the Knowledge Society can offer. According to the Danish Technological Institute [10] "Digital literacy is needed by all citizens, for example in order to:

- ensure better service access and use
- ease citizens' daily life burdens (such as engaging with public administrations)
- obtain better access to education, training, work, and jobs
- improve each citizen's personal capacity (quality of life and life chances)
- enhance citizens' social networks and participation. "

The term "digital literacy" is used by the European Union in "Digital Literacy: Skills for the Information Society", saying that "Information and communications technologies (ICTs) affect our lives every day - from interacting with our governments to working from home, from keeping in touch with our friends to accessing healthcare and education".

In this paper, digital literacy is used to refer to the use of electronic equipment by all members of society, for personal and social interactions and for educational and business needs. The definition includes the ability to use technology, including a computer and mobile devices, to send e-mail, to use common household equipment, to locate and understand information on the web and to use other personal computer based tools. Microsoft defines their digital literacy curriculum as having the objective of - "The goal of Digital Literacy is to teach and assess basic computer concepts and skills so that people can use computer technology in everyday life to develop new social and economic opportunities for themselves, their families, and their communities." (http://www.microsoft.com).

4 Why Are the Competencies Required?

So much data is available on line that it is necessary to be able to discern the accuracy and integrity of such data - "IT literacy...... must also capture the notion of information literacy – the ability to assess the validity of various sources of information" [11]. We need to understand where the data comes from and which information is valid from the huge amount currently available - "If we are to be drinking from a firehose, with billions of web pages at our fingertips, then we should possess the skills to manage its flow" according to Wilhelm [12].

People need to be aware of privacy and security issues when they are using technology. Using the Internet often involves entering personal details on a web page. It is important that people know how to work safely on line. Wilhelm suggests that "we are finding ourselves at the new frontier of civil rights".

People could be socially excluded with the disappearing of local shops and services. In the United Kingdom, as in many other countries, there has been a reduction of 21% in the number of bank branches during the last decade [13]. Use of technology to provide services and communication capability will be necessary to maintain the quality of life. Knowing how to use technology can help reduce social exclusion. "Indicators of social exclusion can be income-related but also extend to areas such as social contact and support, good health and a feeling of participation and being heard" [14]. This exclusion could extend to government services and even the move to e-Democracy. Governments are increasing their on line services and their communications with their citizens – this is "eGovernment" today. Rheingold spoke of a "Citizen based democracy" [15] and people who do not have access to the Internet will be at serious disadvantage. In business, the use of technology to communicate with business partners, customers, employees and potential employees is growing, especially the use of social networking. Job advertisements are often placed on line and cvs can be uploaded.

User generated content (or user created content) is created every day. People communicate on Twitter, some news agencies get news faster through this. When something happens today, it is usually possible to find a video on "YouTube" within minutes. Shortly after Susan Boyle sang on the UK's "Britain's Got Talent", it was seen by millions of people [16]. As of January 2010, this specific video had 86,315,736 views and there are many more YouTube copies of this performance. In Dublin, during a very cold period in January 2010 a news item on the national TV station showed a man falling over on the ice – this was the most watched video on YouTube that week [17]. Video can be distributed immediately to a potential viewing audience of 100 million people [18].

Are older people excluded from this Knowledge Society? The European Commission believes they should benefit from technology. According to Frans de Bruïne,

(Director, European Commission), "By 2013, the Commission plans to invest one billion Euro in researching and piloting digital technologies that make the lives of older citizens easier" - it is possible that these initiatives could "turn the silver challenge into a golden opportunity" [19]. Research in the EU "The 2009 Ageing report" shows the number of older people in the EU will grow between 2008 and 2060, while the number of young people will decline gradually [20]. This report projects that in seven of the member states (Belgium, Ireland, France, Cyprus, Luxembourg, Sweden and the UK) the working population will grow slightly, but that this population will drop in the other 20 states. The number of elderly people will almost double, rising from 85 million in 2008 to 151 million in 2060 in the EU and the number of people over 80 years of age is projected to triple by 2060 [21]. Older people must be included.

A person with a disability can benefit from technology and will usually use assistive technology in the form of hardware or software. This involves further competence requirements for both the user and the designer. The person with the disability will need to know how to use the assistive technology and the designer of a web site will need to understand how such technology works in order to make the web site accessible [22].

Access to education can be enhanced by eLearning and digital literacy is needed to get the best from eLearning tools. According to the EU, "Digital competence" is one of the eight key competences for Life Long learning [23].

5   What Are the Certification Bodies Saying about Competencies?

There are many definitions of digital literacy. According to Wikipedia "Digital literacy is the ability to locate, organize, understand, evaluate, and create information using digital technology". There are also recognized certification bodies that have their own, similar definitions. This section looks at three of the current certifications and compares their definitions of digital literacy. These bodies are ECDL/ICDL, Microsoft and IC3. A project recently initiated by CEN to examine the requirements for an End User eSkills Framework could also contribute to the harmonization of certifications through its proposed linkage to the European Qualification Framework (EQF).

5.1   ECDL/ICDL

ECDL was set up in 1997 as an initiative of the Council of European Professional Informatics Societies (CEPIS). It is an international organization, run by the ECDL Foundation [24]. ECDL is operating in over 120 countries and, outside Europe, it is known as the International Computer Driving License (ICDL). ECDL consists of many programmes, but the core ECDL programme is accepted by many organizations as a definition of digital literacy and there were almost 10 million people registered by the end of 2009 [25].

This **core programme** consists of 7 modules as follows:

- Module 1 – Concepts of Information and Communication Technology (ICT)
- Module 2 – Using the Computer and Managing Files
- Module 3 – Word Processing

- Module 4 – Spreadsheets
- Module 5 – Using Databases
- Module 6 – Presentation
- Module 7 – Web Browsing and Communication

The core programme is recognized as a definition of digital literacy for the workplace and there are two other programmes requiring a lower level of skill. These are Equal-Skills and eCitizen. **EqualSkills** consists of Desktop Computing skills for the complete beginner and includes the basic skills necessary to use the Internet and e-mail, to turn on the computer and understand the basic component parts of a computer, to use the keyboard and the mouse and work with a modern desktop and to use a text editor to create, save and print a simple document. The **e-Citizen** is at a more advanced level and is designed to help the citizen work effectively in the e-world. It consists of three blocks - the Foundation Skills, the Information Search and The e-Participation Block

ECDL also provides advanced programmes:

- ECDL / ICDL Advanced Word Processing
- ECDL / ICDL Advanced Spreadsheets
- ECDL / ICDL Advanced Database
- ECDL / ICDL Advanced Presentation
- ECDL / ICDL CAD

And professional programmes:

- ECDL / ICDL WebStarter
- ECDL / ICDL ImageMaker
- ECDL / ICDL Health

5.2 Microsoft

The Microsoft Digital Literacy curriculum has five parts:-

- Computer Basics – consists of the fundamentals of computing, the components of a computer and the basics of operating system, and the use of a mouse and a keyboard
- The Internet and the World Wide Web – shows how to connect to the Internet, browse Web pages, navigate Web sites, use search engines, and send and receive e-mail
- Productivity Programs - explores the most common productivity software applications used in business, in education, and at home, consisting of the basics of word processing, spreadsheets, presentation software, and databases
- Computer Security and Privacy - explains the risks and threats to computer security and privacy
- Digital Lifestyles – introduction to the new digital technologies, including digital audio, digital video, and digital photography

Microsoft also provides certification at a professional level and includes the Microsoft Certified Application Specialist (MCAS) and the Microsoft Office Specialist (MOS). As specified on the Microsoft website:

"The Microsoft Certified Application Specialist (MCAS) credential validates skills in using the 2007 Microsoft Office system and the Windows Vista operating system, meeting the demand for the most up-to-date skills on the latest Microsoft technologies. Candidates who successfully complete the program by passing a certification exam show that they can meet globally recognized performance standards. Candidates must pass one certification exam in order to earn the MCAS credential.

The Microsoft Office Specialist (MOS) program offers certification tracks for Office 2003, Office XP, and Office 2000. To earn an MOS certification for Microsoft Office, you must pass one or more certification exams. MOS certification exams provide a valid and reliable measure of technical proficiency and expertise by evaluating your overall comprehension of Microsoft Office or Office Project programs, your ability to use advanced features, and your ability to integrate Office programs with other software." [26]

5.3 IC3

The Global Digital Literacy Council (GDLC) established the curriculum for Certiport Internet and Core Computing Certification. The latest standard, Global Standard 3, was signed by the council on August 1, 2008. According to the GDLC Web site, "The development of the Global Standard 3 took over 9 months of research, data collection from 400+ subject matter experts from over 30 countries and final ratification from the members of the Global Digital Literacy Council." [27]

The IC³ Global Standard 3 consists of three parts:

1. **Computing Fundamentals**
   - Computer Hardware, Peripherals and Troubleshooting – this part includes understanding the standard hardware that is used today, including input and output devices,. It also includes how to solve problems hardware problems.
   - Computer Software - examines how software and hardware work together to perform computing tasks, looks at how software is developed and upgraded including standard software such as word processing, spreadsheets, presentation software, databases, graphic and multimedia programs, etc
   - Using an Operating System – this examines how and operating systems works, its, functions and how to manage them. It looks at how to manipulate windows, folders, files and shortcuts; install, uninstall and run applications; and solve common problems

2. **Key Applications**
   - This consists of being able to start and end an application successfully and includes being able to use the functionality of word processing, spreadsheets and presentation software.

3. **Living Online**
   - This part includes the fundamentals of networking and the benefits and risks of network computing; the different types of electronic communication/collaboration and how they work, including email.

- Using the Internet and the World Wide Web, includes learning how to evaluate the quality of information found on the Web and how to browse and use websites.
- The Impact of Computing and the Internet on Society - identifies how computers are used in different areas of life, the risks of using computer hardware and software, and how to use computers and the Internet safely, ethically and legally.

5.4 What Have They in Common?

ECDL and IC3 claim to be vendor independent while Microsoft is obviously linked to Microsoft products. All three claim to have been informed by subject matter experts with a strict development process and quality assurance. Microsoft and ECDL define very basic levels of digital literacy, designed for people who want to use computing for email and simple tasks using the World Wide Web. All three programmes have a professional level of certification with are accepted by employers and some educational organizations as professional digital literacy.

At a very basic level of digital literacy they all identify that using email, searching the Web using a browser and using a text editor or word processor are the simple competence requirements. The next level includes the competence to discern the validity of information found online, the basics of computer technology ant the use of other personal productivity tools, such as spreadsheets.

5.5 A Framework

The definition of digital literacy is changing. Would a framework to identify these changing skills be of use? To address this, the European Union CEN/ISSS Workshop on ICT Skills has commissioned an End User e-Skills Framework Requirements project[1] to identify the requirements for such a framework. This project is surveying companies in industry, certifying organisations, regulatory authorities and individuals. The project plans to define what is required of end user e-Skills, to make proposals for developing such a reference framework and to outline tools that could benefit framework users.

6 What Are the Competencies Required in Today's Knowledge Society

6.1 The Core of Digital Literacy

In 1983, Spresser argued that "definitions of computer literacy abound" [28], but suggests that a knowledge of computers and how they work is a necessary part of this literacy, coupled with the ability to use the available software. More than twenty years later, Mason et al [29] believe that computer (digital) literacy consists of "awareness" and "competence". This section describes the basic competencies required for living

---

[1] http://www.ecompetences.eu/site/objects/download/
5101_EndUsereSkillsFrameworkRequirementsOverview.pdf

in and taking advantage of the opportunities offered by today's Knowledge Society. These are split into two parts – first the competencies required to be part of this society are listed, followed by a definition of what are, arguably, part of the digital literacy competencies required to exploit the technology.

Critical

- Basic knowledge of technology and basic skills
- The ability to search for and locate information
- The ability to identify the valid information
- The ability to connect to a network
- The ability to know when there is a problem
- The skill to use a computer safely, this skill involves knowledge of the basics of hardware and software
- The ability to send an email, receive an email, reply to an email and work with attachments
- Knowing how to communicate using a mobile telephone
- Knowing how to create, read and respond to texts on a mobile telephone
- The ability to use Mp3 players or iPods (and iPads)
- Vital for persons with a disability is the knowledge and skills required to use assistive technology

Other basic competencies

- Knowledge of the risks of misusing information
- Understanding security and ethics in using technology
- Having technical awareness and understanding that technology changes - e.g. current opportunities with Web 2.0, Mobile devices, etc
- Ability to access and use learning resources on computers
- Findings things using mobile telephones
- Using the computer to communicate with friends
- Using the computer to post pictures or information
- Sharing and exchanging ideas with friends and family members
- Identifying new uses for technology at home
- Accessing, copying, manipulating and playing music and videos
- Awareness of assistive technology

6.2   Digital Literacy at Work

The previous sections described the basic digital literacy competencies needed in everyday life. This section looks at digital literacy for work and education.

At work - In most cases a business person will need the basic digital literacy competencies defined above and will also need other job-specific competencies and organisational systems. Such specific work-related systems may be in manufacturing (Computer Aided Manufacturing or Computer Aided Design), finance (use of accounting systems), legal, etc For employment generally, there is a need for an understanding of the corporate or organisational "acceptable use" of technology, to have the ability to work in remote teams and to be conscious of Web 2.0 and on-going technological advances.

Teaching and Education - Jans et al [30] believe that teachers need more than just technical skills. "Teaching and learning with ICT requires specific competencies for teachers and lecturers." They identify that teachers need to be able to use a Virtual Learning Environment and understand the implications of this, including course design and education delivery using these methods. Students need to be familiar with the use of search engines to aid their research and they also need to be able to navigate Learning Management Systems (LMS) which are used in many second and third level colleges as a teaching resource.

Research – The ability to use technology as a huge source of information has changed the efforts involved in research, especially the search for previously published literature and findings. However, the ability to discern the validity of such information is vital.

Digitally literacy for the IT professional - The CEN Workshop on ICT Skills has defined a European framework for ICT Professionals[2]. This consists of a framework and a guide to implementing the framework. There are 5 high level competences with 32 competences defined at the lowest level. The framework was designed to match the requirements for IT professionals in all industry sectors.

Technical and designers - Digital literacy is necessary for the designers of web sites. While this is more difficult with user generated content, it is vital that accessibility is built into web sites to ensure eInclusion. Designers need to have the ability to design digital information and the ability to present digital information in a usable and format.

7 Conclusions

The definition of digital literacy has changed over the years, from the early days of computing when to be "computer literate" meant you were a computer professional to the new and evolving meaning of the term. This paper argues that to be digitally literate is vital in 2010. The specific competencies which make up digital literacy can vary and will change, but the basic or core competencies can be defined today. Other digital competencies can be defined for opportunities in education, business and specific jobs.

As digital literacy needs continue to evolve and new technology emerges, the challenge will be to ensure that the population at large can attain and maintain a reasonable level of competence to benefit from the Knowledge Society.

References

1. Moore, G.: Moore's Law (1965), http://www.intel.com/technology/mooreslaw/ (accessed February 1, 2010)
2. Digital Literacy: Skills for the Information Society, http://ec.europa.eu/information_society/tl/edutra/skills/index_en.htm (accessed January 31, 2010)

---

[2] http://www.ecompetences.eu/

3. Berners-Lee, T.: The World Wide Web: A Very Short Personal History (1998), http://www.w3.org/People/Berners-Lee/ShortHistory.html (accessed February 19, 2009)
4. e-Inclusion: Be Part of It! http://ec.europa.eu/information_society/activities/einclusion/bepartofit/index_en.htm (accessed January 30, 2010)
5. Computer history, http://www.computerhope.com/history/196080.htm (accessed January 25, 2010)
6. Gupta, G.K.: Computer literacy: essential in today's computer-centric world. SIGCSE Bull. 38, 115–119 (2006)
7. Van Dyke, C.: Taking "computer literacy" literally. Communications of the ACM 30, 366–374 (1987)
8. Gilster, P.: Digital literacy. John Wiley, Chichester (1997), ISBN 0471165204
9. Eshet-Alakali, Y., Amichai-Hamburger, Y.: Experiments in Digital Literacy. CyberPsychology and Behavior 7, 421–429 (2004)
10. Supporting Digital Literacy, http://www.digital-literacy.eu/ (accessed February 1, 2010)
11. Perez, J., Meg Murray, M.: Computing for the masses: extending the computer science curriculum with information technology literacy. Consortium for Computing Sciences in Colleges 24, 220–226 (2008)
12. Wilhelm, A.G.: Digital nation: toward an inclusive information society. MIT Press, Cambridge (2004)
13. Working Group on Ageing Populations and Sustainability, http://europa.eu/epc/working_groups/ageing_en.htm
14. Waterhouse, C., Angley, P.: Social exclusion among older people, a preliminary study from inner-city Melbourne (2005), http://www.bsl.org.au/pdfs/Social_exclusion_older_people.pdf (accessed February 1, 2010)
15. Rheingold: In: Hand, M. (ed.) Making digital cultures: access, interactivity, and authenticity, Aldershot, Ashgate (2008)
16. Britain's got talent, http://www.youtube.com/watch?v=9lp0IWv8QZY (accessed January 25, 2010)
17. Falling over on the ice, http://www.youtube.com/watch?v=7CT0a-Hgumo (accessed January 25, 2010)
18. YouTube Surpasses 100 Million US Viewers for the First Time, http://www.comscore.com/Press_Events/Press_Releases/2009/3/YouTube_Surpasses_100_Million_US_Viewers (accessed February 12, 2010)
19. Turning the silver challenge into a golden opportunity, http://sap.info/archive/interviews/int_Interviews_Turning_the_Silver_Challenge_into_a_Golden_Opportunity_01.08.2007.html (accessed February 2010)
20. Age Concern and Help the Aged proposals for Budget 2009 (2009), http://www.ageconcern.org.uk (accessed February 12, 2010)
21. The 2009 Ageing Report (2009), http://ec.europa.eu/economy_finance/publications/publication13782_en.pdf
22. AbilityNet: State of the eNation Reports: Social Networking Sites Lock Out Disabled Users (2008), http://www.abilitynet.org.uk/enation85 (accessed January 19, 2010)
23. Commission of the European Communities, Proposal for a recommendation of the European Parliament and of the Council on key competences for lifelong learning (2005), http://ec.europa.eu/education/policies/2010/doc/keyrec_en.pdf (accessed February 12, 2010)

24. Carpenter, D., Dolan, D., Leahy, D., Sherwood-Smith, M.: ECDL/ICDL: a global computer literacy initiative. In: 16th IFIP Congress, ICEUT200, Educational uses of Information and Communication Technologies, Beijing, China (2000)
25. ECDL, http://www.ecdl.org
26. Microsoft, http://www.microsoft.com
27. IC3, http://www.certiport.com/portal/DesktopDefault.aspx
28. Spresser, D.: A Moderate approach to Computer Literacy. Communications of the ACM (1985)
29. Mason, J., McMorrow, R.: YACLD (yet another computer literacy definition). Published by the Consortium for Computing Sciences in College (2006)
30. Jans, Sebastiaan, Awouters: Valère E-learning Competencies for Teachers in Secondary and Higher Education. International Journal of Emerging Technologies in Learning (iJET) 4(2) (2009)

Informatics Systems and Modelling – Case Studies of Expert Interviews

Leopold Lehner[1], Johannes Magenheim[1], Wolfgang Nelles[1], Thomas Rhode[1], Niclas Schaper[1], Sigrid Schubert[2], and Peer Stechert[2]

[1] University of Paderborn, Paderborn, Germany
{firstname.name}@uni-paderborn.de
[2] University of Siegen, Siegen, Germany
{firstname.name}@uni-siegen.de

Abstract. This article presents the results of two case studies undertaken within the project MoKoM funded by the German Research Foundation (DFG). In this context, expert interviews were conducted in order to identify relevant competencies empirically concerning informatics comprehension and modelling. The interviews (N = 30) were based on typical scenarios of this domain and were conducted with different expert groups (experts of informatics, experts of didactics of informatics, expert informatics teachers). The goal of the interview analyses was to exemplarily examine the competence descriptions given by the different experts with regard to the categories of a theoretically derived competence model. The competence descriptions were also compared with reference to the different expert domains. Furthermore it was tried to identify recurring response patterns in the interviews with reference to the experts' background.

Keywords: Competence Model Research, Pedagogies, Informatics System Comprehension, Informatics Modelling, Active Learning.

1 Motivation

This article describes the results of an exemplary comparison of expert interviews which have been conducted within the project MoKoM funded by the German Research Foundation (DFG). Generally, the project MoKoM pursues three goals: (1) developing a scientific and empirically proofed competence model concerning the two domains *informatics modelling* and *informatics system comprehension*, (2) developing and testing instruments which are appropriate for competence measurement and finally (3) designing and evaluating effective learning environments for competence development.

With regard to the shift towards output orientation of the German school system this competence model can be understood as a basis for the development of educational standards for these two mentioned domains of informatics secondary education.

Within the project MoKoM, the starting point for competence modelling was a competence framework which was developed on the basis of theoretical considerations involving expert papers and curricula. After that, an empirical approach to

N. Reynolds and M. Turcsányi-Szabó (Eds.): KCKS 2010, IFIP AICT 324, pp. 222–233, 2010.

identify the relevant competencies was chosen by the means of conducting expert interviews. They represent an adequate empirical method to supplement and to refine the already existing competence framework.

30 experts on informatics, with a division in three equal groups were interviewed: (1) experts of informatics, (2) experts of didactics of informatics and (3) expert informatics teachers. Each expert interview included four hypothetic scenarios (in a total of twelve), which describe typical and challenging tasks of informatics system comprehension and modelling and served as structured starting points for the competence interviews. Based on these scenarios, the interviewees were asked to describe their personal procedures and thoughts to solve the presented informatics problems in detail as well as questions referred to specific competence requirements of the framework model to solve the problem.

The main objective of this article is to compare the three expert groups (expert of informatics, expert of didactics of informatics, expert informatics teacher) concerning their specific contributions to describe competence facets for the model. In which respect do the experts differ in their competence-relevant statements and how can these different contributions be explained with reference to different expert perspectives, backgrounds and attitudes toward the topic? In order to answer these research questions, exemplary interviews of the three expert groups with reference to two complex hypothetic scenarios were content analyzed: (1) *"Merchandise Management System"* which especially treats system development requirements and (2) *"Testing of Unknown Software"* which treats system comprehension requirements in particular. The analysis was focused on three exemplary interviews concerning each scenario.

The article presents the exemplary results of these content analyses and is subdivided as follows: Section 2 gives an overview of the theoretically derived framework of the competence model whereas first refinements could be processed by content analytical results. Section 3 and 4 focus on the two hypothetical scenarios mentioned above. They analyze the experts´ described problem solving behaviour and provide information on the impact of the results on the framework. Section 5 attempts to sketch out characteristics of the different types of experts. Section 6 presents a summary and a discussion concerning the deployed research methods.

2 Theoretically Derived Framework of the Competence Model

The theoretically derived competence model comprises a total of four primary dimensions: (1) Basic Competencies, (2) Informatics Views, (3) Complexity, and (4) Non-Cognitive Skills. The first dimension includes knowledge and skill elements concerning system development, system comprehension and system application. In this context, the ability to use an informatics system (IS), the ability to comprehend the structure, processes and individual components of an IS and the capability to design and to reengineer an IS are important.

The second dimension consists of outer and inner perspectives towards an informatics system such as usability, algorithms and data structures, graphical notation techniques and so on. It is necessary for coping with complex informatics tasks and demands that learners are enabled to look at an IS from different informatics views.

K1 Basic Competencies	K2 Informatics Views
K1.1 System Application	K2.1 External View
K1.2 System Comprehension	K2.1.1 Expectations of Systems′Behavior
K.1.2.1 Requirements	K2.1.2 Informatics Literacy & Professional Practice
K.1.2.2 Test	K2.1.3 Usability
K.1.3 System Development	K2.1.4 Functional View
K1.3.1 Business Modeling	K2.2 Internal View
K1.3.2 Requirements	K2.2.1 Layered Architectures
K1.3.3 Analysis & Design	K2.2.2 Net-Centric Computing
K1.3.4 Implementation	K2.2.3 Systems of Patterns
K1.3.5 Test	K2.2.4 Algorithms & Data Structures
K1.3.6 Deployment	K2.2.5 Fundamental Ideas of Computer Science
	K2.2.6 Graphical Representations
	K2.2.7 Languages (Programming & Modeling)
	K2.2.8 Computional Thinking (imperative, functional, logical, object-orientated)
	K2.3 Change of View

Fig. 1. Competence Dimensions K1 (BASIC COMPETENCIES) and K2 (INFORMATICS VIEWS)

The third dimension deals with the demands on handling complexity of informatics systems. Requirements regarding informatics competence vary because of the complexity and intricacy of an IS. Among others, degrees of interactivity and degrees of interconnectedness are elements of this dimension.

The fourth dimension is subdivided in three categories: attitudes, social-communicative / cooperative skills and motivational / volitional skills. All of these skills are prerequisites for successful problem solving within the two focused domains.

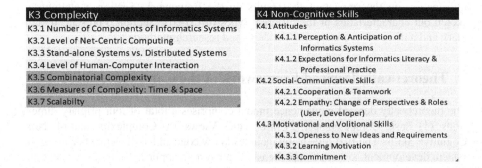

K3 Complexity	K4 Non-Cognitive Skills
K3.1 Number of Components of Informatics Systems	K4.1 Attitudes
K3.2 Level of Net-Centric Computing	K4.1.1 Perception & Anticipation of Informatics Systems
K3.3 Stand-alone Systems vs. Distributed Systems	K4.1.2 Expectations for Informatics Literacy & Professional Practice
K3.4 Level of Human-Computer Interaction	K4.2 Social-Communicative Skills
K3.5 Combinatorial Complexity	K4.2.1 Cooperation & Teamwork
K3.6 Measures of Complexity: Time & Space	K4.2.2 Empathy: Change of Perspectives & Roles (User, Developer)
K3.7 Scalabilty	K4.3 Motivational and Volitional Skills
	K4.3.1 Openess to New Ideas and Requirements
	K4.3.2 Learning Motivation
	K4.3.3 Commitment

Fig. 2. Competence Dimensions K3 (COMPLEXITY) and K4 (NON-COGNITIVE SKILLS)

These dimensions and categories were derived from curricula and expert papers covering informatics modelling and system comprehension. Thus, this step of the project MoKoM was characterized by a theoretic and deductive methodical procedure. The following step was complementary to the first one insofar as an inductive and empirical procedure was chosen to identify relevant competence facets by means of conducting expert interviews deploying the Critical Incident Technique.

During each interview, hypothetic informatics scenarios were presented and the interviewees were asked to give a detailed description of their problem solving approach. The interviews were audio-recorded, transcribed and analyzed by means of a qualitative content analysis method according to Mayring [1]. Using this method, the transcribed expert statements were summarized and structured with reference to the framework model categories in order to supplement and to refine our theoretically derived competence model.

Figures 1 and 2 show the four main dimensions, categories and facets of the competence model. The emphasized categories expose refinements of the competence model which were additionally integrated into the model on the bases of the first results of the content analysis.

3 Case Study System Comprehension

3.1 Scenario "Testing of Unknown Software"

In order to refine the theoretically derived competence model [2] we used three scenarios on system comprehension [3]: Scenario 4 "Usability Engineering", Scenario 5 "Computer configuration", and Scenario 7 "Car configuration". Our experience with the results of Scenario 4 has shown that this is not only a typical scenario of system comprehension, but it also contains aspects of system application. On the other hand, Scenario 5 and 7 are very similar if one is not focused on the issue of the concrete configuration software. Therefore, we recommend combining Scenarios 5 and 7 for evaluation, because they offer very similar results through qualitative content analysis.

In this paper the competence dimension K1.2 (SYSTEM COMPREHENSION) and its relations to other competence dimensions will be presented through concentration on the typical scenario "Testing of Unknown Software (developed by others)". This scenario and its questions were introduced to the interviewees as follows.

Scenario 5+7: *"You are asked by a colleague to test his software, which was developed to solve configuration problems, e.g., to set up a new car or a new computer."*
Question 1: *"What is your strategy of testing to solve this problem? Which aspects do you have to bear in mind?"*
Question 2: *"Which cognitive skills are required for such a software exploration?"*
Question 2.1: *"Which informatics views are important for this task?"*
Question 2.2: *"Which complexity would you assign to this task?"*
Question 3: *"Which attitudes or social-communicative and cooperative skills are necessary to accomplish this?"*
Question 4: *"Which differences of competence levels would you expect between novices and experts?"*
Question 5: *"How can you as a tester be supported by this task?"*
Question 6: *"Could you imagine a pupil's potential procedure to solve this problem?"*
Question 7: *"Which obstacles would pupils have to cope with?"*

Altogether, eight experts were interviewed with reference to such a scenario. Afterwards these interviews were analyzed with means of the above mentioned method of qualitative content analysis. We selected only one representative per expert group (one expert of informatics, one expert of didactics of informatics, one expert informatics teacher) to describe typical response and attitudinal patterns of these three expert groups.

In the following sub sections we discuss three phenomena. First, we discuss the empirical proof of the theoretically derived competence categories, second, empirical findings concerning additional competence categories, and third, flaws resp. problems of the interview method caused by the different meaning of scientific terms used in the interview questions.

3.2 Basic Competencies and Non-cognitive Skills

All three representatives of the expert groups confirmed the theoretically derived categories of K1.2 (SYSTEM COMPREHENSION) of competence dimension K1 (BASIC COMPETENCIES) with the qualitative content analysis in the following way:

Answer by an expert informatics teacher K1.2.1 (REQUIREMENTS VERSUS PERFORMANCE): *"Necessary is to check requirements and to compare them with the final system."*

Answer by an expert of informatics K1.2.2 (TEST): *"I recommend systematic testing of software. Testing is a very difficult task, especially if the tester knows only partly the semantic relations of the functionality of the system."*

Answer by an expert of didactics of informatics K1.2.3 (QUALITY OF SOFTWARE): *"Inevitable is the evaluation of the quality of the software with criteria, e.g., correctness, usability, security."*

For K4 (NON-COGNITIVE SKILLS) we observed response patterns, which were characteristic for our three expert groups of the interviews. The experts in informatics answered very briefly to K4. Experts in didactics of informatics deliver much more detailed statements to K4. But the most comprehensive version of recommendations on K4 was given by the expert informatics teachers. Some examples will illustrate this:

Answer of an expert of informatics K4.1 (ATTITUDES) and K4.3 (MOTIVATIONAL AND VOLITIONAL SKILLS): *"Such a person should be very ambitious to find errors. We should reward the finding of errors. This could be a kind of a competition in error detecting."*

Answer of an expert informatics teacher K4.2 (SOCIAL-COMMUNICATIVE SKILLS): *"In my opinion the ideal tester should have very good social-communicative skills. As a teacher I would expect to be asked in difficult situations. But I also appreciate a lot the teamwork between the learners of my groups. They should be able to act appropriately in different kinds of roles, e.g., as a customer, developer, and tester. A highlight of this learning process is the opportunity to present the results of the individual and team work in a plenum, to be open for critical comments and to feel responsible not to insult others through careless statements."*

The presented results show that we were able to confirm and refine a theoretically derived competence model of an informatics knowledge domain by means of expert interviews (especially using the Critical Incident Technique and qualitative content analysis). This demonstrates the suitability of our research methodology. In the next sub section it is shown that the methodology is also useful to identify gaps of the theoretically derived competence categories.

3.3 Complexity

We conducted the interview analysis concerning the competence dimension K3 (COM-PLEXITY) in a different way (see Fig. 3, Section 2). According to a normative analysis approach using international curricula categories this procedure would lead to a overly closed focus on informatics lessons at school [4]. In contrast to this approach it would not be helpful to use all complexity categories of theoretical informatics for our competence model [5]. So we had to find an interview and analysis method between these extremes. We will illustrate this with the following statements on K3 (COMPLEX-ITY) with our experts' groups:

Answer by an expert of informatics: *"I have to deliver a perfect specification from where the tester can recognize all possible cases which he has to evaluate. If this testing scenario should be realized, you need an authentic informatics system with a realistic functionality. This task of systematic testing leads in a combinatorial complexity."*

Answer by an expert of didactics of informatics: *"The main challenge of this test-ing task is the combination of all possible cases, which the tester has to evaluate. This means he has to cope with combinatorial complexity. The testing results are depend-ing on the resources available."*

Answer by an expert informatics teacher: *"Systematic testing means that you have to check each function with all possible parameters, which the software offers. The task is connected with a high complexity, because you have to handle all possible cases, which means combinatorial complexity."*

The method of qualitative content analysis shows clearly that our theoretically derived competence model has to be complemented. Therefore, we added the compe-tence category K3.5 (COMBINATORIAL COMPLEXITY) to the competence dimension K3 (COMPLEXITY). Combinatorial complexity means that all combinations of inputs and preconditions, e.g., of a certain system, have to be considered, even though exhaustive testing may not be feasible. Further studies delivered with the same method led to the addition of the following categories: K3.6 (COMPLEXITY MEASURES: *TIME AND SPACE*) and K3.7 (SCALABILITY). To characterize the quality of algorithms, their runtime perform-ance (including efficiency) and memory requirements are usually evaluated in infor-matics. They are referred to as complexity measures, time and space. Concerning scalability we include the following characteristic of informatics: Some standard algorithms deliver good results for a small input size, but for a large input size they deliver bad results or no solution in a given time boundary. Therefore, the criterion scalability can be used to decide, which solution (system, algorithm, process) should be applied to different problem sets.

3.4 Informatics Views

After describing the positive effects of the applied research methodology, we will now discuss the flaws resp. problems of the empirical method. In particular, these were caused by the different meanings of some scientific terms in the different expert groups we interviewed. We discovered this methodical problem when analyzing the competence dimension K2 (INFORMATICS VIEWS). The expert of informatics was not familiar with the term "informatics views" in didactics of informatics [6] and so, he did not answer adequately with reference to this competence dimension. Unfortunately, the interviewers did not recognize this misunderstanding of the expert and did not clarify it in the interview.

The informatics teacher was not familiar with the term "informatics views", either. He misinterpreted the question and described the view of an informatics system from the user´s perspective, i.e. the "graphical user interface" and gave a detailed description of menus and buttons for the interaction.

The expert of didactics of informatics had no problems with the term "informatics views". He answered this question in an adequately structured way: with reference to this competence dimension he differentiated between view of interaction, functional view, and view of system states. Consequently, he described the educational efforts of each recommended view with great detail.

Thus, we have to train the interviewers and the conductors of content analysis to be aware of these problems. The interviewers should be particularly sensitive to misinterpretations of a question and notice when the expert feels uncomfortable with some questions. In these cases, they have to be trained to efficiently clarify such misunderstandings or feelings of irritation. Additionally the questions of the interview guideline have to be revised concerning the use of informatics terms, which are accepted by all three groups of experts, not only by the small community of experts of didactics of informatics.

4 Case Study Informatics Modelling

4.1 Scenario "Merchandise Management System"

Analogous to the case study "System Comprehension", three scenarios were used to refine our theoretically derived competence model focusing the competence categories and facets of informatics modelling including non-cognitive aspects. These are *1. Merchandise Management System, 2. Chat-System* and *3. Web-based Game*. In the following the first mentioned scenario was used for our exemplary analysis.

By means of the interviewees' answers it will be discussed how to exemplarily refine our theoretically derived competence model. Analogous to the first case study, differences between the three expert groups will be illustrated. Also, potential instructional proposals how to teach the competences – stated by the experts – will be exposed.

Scenario "Merchandise Management System": *"You are asked to develop a software based merchandise management system for a small school kiosk."*
Question 1: *"What is your course of action to solve this task? Which software engineering workflows do you have to process?"*
Question 2: *"Which graphical models would you apply?"*
Question 2.1: *"Which informatics views are important for this task?"*
Question 2.2: *"Which complexity would you assign to this task?"*
Question 3: *"Which cognitive skills are required to develop such a software system?"*
Question 4: *"Could you imagine a potential pupil's procedure to solve this problem?"*
Question 5: *"Which attitudes, social communicative skills and motivational aspects are necessary to solve this problem?"*

4.2 Basic Competencies and Non-cognitive Competencies

In summary, the interviewees confirmed the competence category K1.3 (SYSTEM DE-VELOPMENT) whereas differences in managing the software development process were observable.

The expert of informatics stated that he would prefer a software development process, which runs through several iterations. This confirms our competence category of *K1.3* (SYSTEM DEVELOPMENT), which was derived from the core workflows of the *Rational Unified Process*, recommending an iterative way of proceeding [7, p. 1]. Therefore, it seems to be appropriate to add another competence category resp. facet "Sequencing Pattern" to *K1.3* (SYSTEM DEVELOPMENT). This indicates that informatics modelling covers competencies to deliberately select problem solving strategies according to the respective context (or the respective iteration) the learners are faced [8, p. 8].

In contrast, the expert informatics teacher favours a classical way of proceeding, i.e. the waterfall model. This also confirms the category of *K1.3* because the workflows of the waterfall model are in a way analogical to the core workflows of RUP. They could be interpreted as a static part of the RUP.

The expert of didactics of informatics just describes the requirements workflow, which confirms the respective category of the theoretically derived competence model *K1.3.2* (REQUIREMENTS WORKFLOW).

Concerning the relevant phases of the software engineering process the interviewees presented different ways of proceeding: the expert of informatics and the expert of didactics of informatics stick to a well established iterative course of action whereas the expert informatics teacher prefers the classic waterfall model. This circumstance might indicate that the university teachers are more involved in best practices of modern software development.

The expert of informatics recognises software development as a communicative and co-operative process. Besides social competencies like the ability to work in teams, he emphasises communication abilities as absolutely necessary for a close cooperation between developers and customers. Both groups represent different areas of expertise, which must be brought together. Avoiding domain-specific vocabulary and the use of graphical media like object-diagrams facilitate this interchanging process: *"The use of well-adapted graphical representations of object-diagrams leads to good discussions with customers and domain-experts"*.

Negotiation and communication skills seem to be also essential for a successful integration of 'non-informatics-persons' into the software-development-process; such social skills are also crucial for a successful performance within the developers' team.

The informatics expert points to another important social skill for the co-workers in the developer group: the ability of developing 'awareness'. To achieve this goal, the expert hints at the use of computer-based tools even at school.

For the expert of didactics of informatics, the ability to work together in teams is seen as a fundamental skill for the performance of software development projects at school, including the ability to adequately criticize others and to handle criticism.

The teachers' role is to act as an observer of the cooperation-processes. When some pupils are not able to work together in one team it may be necessary to initialize the reorganisation of the groups.

4.3 Complexity

Introducing different stages of the software development process the expert of informatics provides information on complexity: Starting the software-project with textual descriptions of typical use case scenarios, he raises the question, to what (depth of) detail that should be done. He assumes that it might be very difficult, especially for beginners, to find an adequate level of granularity. He is sure that the key for a successful school project is the ability to determine an adequate requirement-definition, which later on will be implementable.

Similar to the expert of informatics the expert of didactics of informatics considers complexity as difficulty to extract elements of relevance involved in a business-process: *"Crucial is the process of abstraction, the decision making about relevant and not relevant aspects."*

According to the expert informatics teacher, it is not possible to rate the complexity of this scenario. From a modelling view it is rather useful to choose an adequate structural complexity degree for this scenario. Hence, the teachers' task is to place appropriate limitations on the range of complexity of the informatics system.

5 Characteristics of Types of Experts

Beyond the analysis results considered so far, we identified some recurring characteristics of the different types of experts. In the following, we give some examples.

We assumed that informatics experts would be very sceptical towards introducing some scenarios at school. However, regarding the "Merchandise Management System", we recognized a different attitude pattern concerning the appropriateness of the scenario to be used in informatics secondary education.

Answer of the expert of informatics: *"A merchandise management system could be implemented at secondary level without a doubt."*

Answer of the expert of didactics of informatics: *"I am not able to present didactical and methodical considerations ad-hoc without any preliminary thoughts."*

Answer of the expert informatics teacher: *"This scenario might be appropriate for informatics secondary education although there may occur difficulties in some cases."*

In this case, it was the expert of informatics that expressed not a negative but a positive attitude towards the appropriateness of the scenario for informatics secondary education – in contrast to the expert of didactics and the expert teacher, which were more critical concerning the appropriateness of the scenario. So, we have to be careful to generalize that experts of informatics are more critical concerning the school-appropriateness of informatics learning contents. Such appraisals might also depend on the personal experiences or other background characteristics of an expert.

Furthermore our interview analyses showed that especially experts of informatics felt uncomfortable with scenarios, which covered parts of informatics, that were not in their research field. An expert of informatics in the field of algorithms and data structures stated: *"I want to stress that the scenario on data base systems is beyond my experience"*. However, he gave valuable hints how to cope with the scenario.

Another expert of informatics even refused to answer questions on object-oriented modelling, because he was not familiar with so called Class Responsibility Collaboration cards.

But again, this response pattern could not only be observed with reference to expert informatics. Also an expert of didactics of informatics refused to answer questions concerning the scenario "Merchandise Management System" on the fly. He stated that he has to perform a comprehensive preliminary planning before he could answer the scenarios' questions in an appropriate manner.

We also observed one expert of informatics who was very familiar with software testing who preferred to skip the scenario on software testing: *"Let us skip this scenario, the requirements specification is not accurate, so I cannot choose an adequate testing strategy"*.

These difficulties to answer the interview questions were altogether rather exceptions. In most cases the experts were willing and able to describe in detail how they would proceed in the scenario and which competence facets are relevant in the situation.

Another characteristic of experts of didactics of informatics was that they tried to describe a vision of informatics education at schools, e.g., the necessity to teach first broad knowledge in informatics followed by concrete examples: *"A necessary prerequisite to solve the problem is the understanding of fundamental mechanisms, connections and concepts"*.

Such experts of didactics of informatics have infrequently contact to pupils, so, sometimes, their answers how pupils would cope with a situation remained rather abstract and were not connected to a certain learning process: *"It just depends what the student has learnt so far"*.

The more experienced the experts were in the field of school informatics, the easier we could match their meaning units with the categories of the theoretically derived competence model. More precisely, almost every expert informatics teacher saw every scenario from a teacher's point of view even though he should explain at first, how he would cope himself with the scenario. Sometimes this dilemma was pointed out before the expert answered: *"Before I answer the question I would like to ask, whether I should answer from my own perspective or as a teacher in a concrete learning process?"*

Other experts, though, immediately switched to the teachers point of view: *"As far as I understood you, I have to realize this scenario at school. Then I would analyse the scenario and create a mind map to identify the important themes my pupils have to learn"*. Others supplement their own procedures with potential pupil's procedures to solve this problem even though they were not asked to do so.

In summary, we could identify some recurring characteristics of the different types of experts, which were illustrated here by examples. However, we have to be careful to generalize these findings based on the relative small amount of analysed data so far and concerning the mentioned counterexamples. It could also be, that the statements rather reflect the personal experiences or backgrounds of the very expert than the characteristics of the group he or she is representing.

6 Summary and Conclusions

Taken together, we can conclude that by means of these case studies we could gain some important insights into the appropriateness of the theoretically derived categories of the competence model of informatics modelling and comprehension. Especially, the competence dimension K1 (BASIC COMPETENCIES) with its categories K1.2 (SYSTEM COMPREHENSION) and K1.3 (SYSTEM DEVELOPMENT) and their sub-categories could be confirmed by the descriptions of the experts. That is of particular importance because the dimension K1 is the core dimension of the entire competence model. Furthermore, the experts´ answers on questions concerning social competence requirements provided valuable and confirming clues to the fourth dimension *Non-Cognitive Skills*. All experts generally ascribed relevance to this dimension. However, the experts´ relation to the school context has apparently an impact on the degree of description of these skills: The closer the experts´ relationship to school, the more differentiated the non-cognitive skills are described.

Furthermore, the analyses showed that the experts´ competence descriptions can also be used to derive valuable suggestions concerning the design of effective learning environments for competence development at schools. For instance, be shown for the exercising of communicative skills in system development or the limitation of the complexity of the used informatics system.

With reference to the dimension K3 (COMPLEXITY) our exemplary analysis results showed that the chosen empirical method is feasible not only to refine a theoretically derived competence model but also to adjust and complement such a model. According to this approach the sub-categories K3.5 (COMBINATORIAL COMPLEXITY), K3.6 (COMPLEXITY MEASURES): Time and Space and K 3.7 (SCALABILITY) were added to the model categories.

With regard to the competence dimension K2 (INFORMATICS VIEWS), also, methodical difficulties with the chosen empirical approach could be demonstrated. These were especially caused by misunderstandings of the term *Informatics Views* used in the interviews.

Furthermore, additional analyses with reference to response and attitude-related patterns of the specific expert groups showed that the interviewer has to be also sensitive to certain characteristics and backgrounds of the different expert groups concerning competence interviews. The presented analyses so far, display only exemplary analyses of the whole range of our interviews. So, in further steps the complete interview data have to be analyzed with the described method of content analysis. And consequently, the competence model has to be furthermore refined, adjusted and formulated.

After we have reached this point of model development we have to consider that there are further restrictions of the described empirical approach to model competencies. Firstly, this refers to the restriction of the scenario approach of the interviews. The relevant competence facets of the informatics modelling and comprehension domain might be identified only selectively by means of the scenario interviews. Secondly, the interview technique raises only verbal descriptions of how to cope with certain competence requirements. This might not cover the real requirements in every relevant aspect.

So, it is necessary to conduct additional empirical research steps to proof the content and criteria validity of the developed competence model: The evaluation of the content validity of the model can be accomplished by an expert rating. Therefore, the different informatics experts have to rate the extracted competence descriptions concerning their relevance, difficulty, representativeness and degree of differentiation.

The evaluation of the criteria validity of the competence model can be accomplished by developing instruments to measure the different facets of the competence model and the criteria behaviour. The resulting correlations between both can be interpreted as indicators for criteria validity of the competence model.

References

1. Mayring, P.: Qualitative Inhaltsanalyse. Beltz, Weinheim (2003)
2. Kollee, C., Magenheim, J., Nelles, W., Rhode, T., Schaper, N., Schubert, S., Stechert, P.: Computer science education and key competencies. In: 9th IFIP World Conference on Computers in Education – WCCE 2009, Bento Goncalves, Brazil (2009), http://www.die.informatik.uni-siegen.de/e-publikationen/Publikationen/2009/WCCE2009_pap147.pdf
3. Stechert, P.: Fachdidaktische Diskussion von Informatiksystemen und der Kompetenzentwicklung im Informatikunterricht, Development of Competencies with Informatics Systems. In: Commentarii Informaticae Didacticae, vol. 2, Universitätsverlag Potsdam (2009)
4. Tucker, A. (ed.): A Model Curriculum for K-12 Computer Science: Final Report of the ACM K-12 Task Force Curriculum Committee, 2nd edn. ACM, New York (2006), http://www.csta.acm.org
5. Cross, J., Denning, P.: Computing Curriculum 2001. The Joint Curriculum Task Force IEEE-CS/ ACM Report (2001), http://www.computer.org/education/cc2001
6. Stechert, P., Schubert, S.: A strategy to structure the learning process towards understanding of informatics systems. In: Working/Joint IFIP-Conference Informatics, Mathematics and ICT (IMICT 2007), Boston, USA (2007), http://www.die.informatik.uni-siegen.de/e-publikationen/Publikationen/2007/2007_Boston_stechert_schubert.pdf
7. Rational Software Corporation IBM. Rational unified process. best practices for software development teams, white paper (1998)
8. Magenheim, J., Nelles, W., Rhode, T., Schaper, N., Schubert, S., Stechert, P.: Competencies for Informatics Systems and Modeling. Results of Qualitative Content Analysis of Expert Interviews. In: Proceedings of the 1st Global Engineering Education Conference - Educon 2010. IEEE Computer Society, Los Alamitos (2010) (in Press)

In Search of the Affective Subject Interacting in the ROODA Virtual Learning Environment

Magalí Teresinha Longhi, Patricia Alejandra Behar, and Magda Bercht

Programa de Pós-Graduação em Informática na Educação, Federal University of Rio Grande do Sul (UFRGS), Caixa Postal 5071 – 90.041-970 – Porto Alegre – RS – Brazil
mlonghi@cesup.ufrgs.br, pbehar@terra.com.br, bercht@inf.ufrgs.br

Abstract. This paper examines elements from Piaget's and Scherer's theories that are able to offer subsidies for the specification of the affective aspects involved in Virtual Learning Environments (VLE). The affective dimension is characterized by the moods manifested during interactions in virtual space by affective portion of psychological subject. To figure moods out is a way to personalize the pedagogical activities and to understand the student's actions and competence.

Keywords: Affective subject, psychological subject, moods, virtual learning environment.

1 Introduction

Students learn through widely varying levels of competence, depending on the individual skills and structures formed but also the social environment exposure. The term competence can take on different meanings and here we use Le Bortef's definition. The author has defined competency as a result of a combination of several individual resources and of resources from the environment [1]. The individual resources are classified as the knowledge (theoretical, environmental and procedural), know-how (formalized, empirical, relational, and cognitive), skills or qualities, physiological and emotional resources.

The learning based of competence involves a variety of different dimensions. We are interested in how the affective dimension takes part in learning. The recognition of the student's affective dimension in Virtual Learning Environment (VLE) is an important resource for a teacher's practice in Distance Learning. We verify relationships between Piaget's [2] and Scherer's [3] theories regarding the definition of the affective subject and the emotional aspects involved in the VLE interactions.

VLE is understood as "*space on the Internet, which is formed by subjects and their interactions and ways of communicating that are established by means of a platform*" [4](p. 29). This platform is constituted by a technological infrastructure (graphic interface, synchronous and asynchronous communication tools and other functionalities) and by all the relationships (cognitive, affective, and symbolic) established by the subjects in this environment.

N. Reynolds and M. Turcsányi-Szabó (Eds.): KCKS 2010, IFIP AICT 324, pp. 234–245, 2010.

In Piaget's theory, cognitive development is related to three interrelated types of factors that define the psychological subject: organic, mental, and social factors. Interactions are understood according to Piaget's presuppositions [5] that knowledge is constructed from the interactions between the psychological subject and the environment. For the author, mental factors are divided in cognitive, affective and symbolic factors, which are inseparable despite the fact they are different.

The psychological subject, according to Dolle [6, 7], inspired by Piaget, is formed by: social, affective, cognitive, and biophysiological subjects. In order to explain the psychological subject in virtual space, Behar [8] presents a model of interaction between the subject and the computational environment. This suggests a resignification of the biophysiological dimension and proposes the VLE-subject. In a virtual environment, the subject acts by means of the hardware and the software and, therefore, the subject should know the technologies related to the interaction. Thus, after the evaluation of the VLE-subject, the technological subject becomes the new dimension of the psychological subject.

The affective subject is represented not only by the relationship with other subjects that form the VLE-subject, but also by all the organic components that participate in the evaluation and activation of an affective phenomenon. Scherer's theory [9] presupposes that the affective subject is formed by the organic components and the processes involved can explain the several affective phenomena experienced by the psychological subject. Scherer's theory offers subsidies in order to identify moods, which are factors associated with the way of cognitive processing and the reorganization of information in memory.

From this perspective, the studies undertaken by Dolle [6, 7] and Behar [8], regarding the affective and technological dimensions of the psychological subject, and by Scherer [3, 9], regarding the definition of the components that form the affective subject, are fundamental. Thus, this investigation intends to present the connections between the theoretical approach and the data collected in a VLE, in this case ROODA[1], with the purpose of evaluating the possibility of recognizing the affective dimension in such environment. In this study, the affective dimension is characterized based on the students' moods evidenced during interactions in virtual space.

In the next section, the interactions among psychological subjects in a virtual environment are mapped. In section 3, the Piaget's theory of affectivity is approached; whereas section 4 presents a report on the CPM model, which explains how an affective phenomenon is processed. In section 5 presents a mapping of the affective subject in the ROODA virtual environment and, in section 6, final considerations are made.

2 Understanding the VLE Interactions of the Psychological Subject

The virtual learning environment is a new setting of interaction for psychological subjects. Dolle [6] defines setting as a system formed by subjects, objects and rules (Figure 1). The subjects or people are the users of the environment (students, teachers,

---

[1] The ROODA (Cooperative Learning Net), available at http://rooda.edu.ufrgs.br, is one of the platforms made available by UFRGS for presences and distance lessons.

tutors). Artificial objects refer to the resources made available in the environments, such as, contents, forums, chats, etc. The institutional rules regulate the interindividual relationships in the environment, as well as the way the tools made available are used.

Dolle's psychological subject (Figure 1) is constituted by the biophysiological subject, or everything that is related to the body, that is, all the biological and physiological functions (genetics, neurology, neurobiology, biochemistry, etc.); by the cognitive subject, that, when he acts, acquires knowledge of himself and of the setting; by the affective subject, whose activities are reflected in the form of emotions, feelings or effects of the relationships established; and, by the social subject, who is the interiorization of the habits, rules, and the social interdicts of any type. The elements that constitute the setting and the psychological subject lead to the interactionist scheme subject ⇔ setting presented in Figure 1.

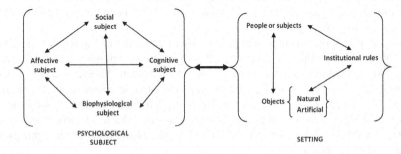

Fig. 1. Graphics of the relationship between the psychological subject and the setting [6]

Thus, the psychological subject relates to the setting VLE considering the presence of other psychological subjects, as well as the resources made available in the setting and the rules that, explicitly or not, lead or guide the relationships in this environment. Behar, based on the mental factors proposed by Piaget [5], presents a model to portray the process of interaction of a psychological subject with a computational tool [8]. This way, Behar defines the technological subject as the portion of the psychological subject that makes use of specific hardware and software to interact with the setting. According to what is illustrated in Figure 2, the psychological subject is redefined as a VLE-subject.

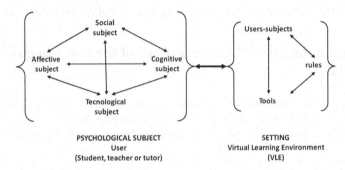

Fig. 2. Representation of the VLE-subject [10]

3 Piaget's Theory of Affectivity

Piaget [11] dedicated to investigate the process of acquisition of knowledge, and how it develops. This way, Piaget highlighted, in the activity of the subject (S), both what originates from the subject and what originates from the object of knowledge (O). That is, the relationship S ⇔ O, in which learning is "building".

Learning involves the action of S upon O and awareness of the coordination of these actions. In other words, S (for example, the student) will learn something new, or will build some new knowledge, if (1) S acts upon O (for example, study material) and (2) if S is able to assimilate O or appropriating of the *"intimate mechanisms of their actions"* [12] (p.23) upon O.

Piaget rejects the belief that S brings, in his or her genetics, ready cognitive structures (apriorism) for the acquisition of knowledge. He also rejects the idea that the social environment determines the structures of knowledge in S (empiricism). Piaget believes knowledge is built, and this happens in two complementary dimensions: as content-knowledge and as structure-knowledge (or form-knowledge) [12]. Content-knowledge refers to observable data, that is, *"objects as such or actions of the subject upon his or her material characteristics"* [13] (p. 274) and non-observable data, that is, the coordination of the actions, subjective observation (liking or not liking, being pleasurable or not, etc.); whereas structure-knowledge refers to the previous condition of knowledge, that is, how the structures are organized based on the activity of S.

Cognitive development happens at four stages: sensorimotor, preoperational, concrete operational and formal operational. In general terms, stage is a landmark of an evolution towards the balance of actions and mental operations. The duration of the subject at each stage depends on individual factors and on the setting [14]. And learning evolves from simple and concrete to complex and abstract schemes by means of two mechanisms: assimilation and accommodation. In the first, S acts, assimilating something (content-knowledge) from the environment (physical or social). In the second, the content assimilated, as it brings novelty, disturbs S who needs to reconstruct his or her assimilation tools, incorporating the new content to the former scheme, reorganizing the scheme, accommodating. During accommodation, S modifies the assimilating scheme (structure-knowledge), and, thus, modifies him or herself.

Piaget presents the theory of the reflecting abstraction, at the level of symbolic exchange, mainly at the level of language and social relations, as *"one of the motors of cognitive development and as one of the aspects of the more general processes of balance"* [13] (p. 274). Based on this, the author distinguishes empirical abstraction from reflecting abstraction (*abstraction réfléchissante*). The first one *"is based on physical objects or on material aspects of actions, such as movements, pushes, etc."* [13] (p. 5). Differently, the second one *"is based on such forms and on all cognitive activities of the subject (schemes or coordination of actions, operations, structures, etc.), in order to withdraw some characteristics from them and use them with other purposes (new adaptations, new problems, etc.)"*[13] (p. 6).

Reflecting abstraction, analyzed based on reflecting degrees, comprises two aspects: the first one, which Piaget calls *réfléchissement* is the one in which the subject, in several stages, elaborates a projection (as by a reflector) to the higher plane of what was brought from the lower plane; and the reflection (*réflexion*), or the mental act of reconstructing and reorganizing at the higher plane of what was transferred from the lower plane [13]. The formation of each plane can be represented by a spiral process, according to what is demonstrated in Figure 3[2].

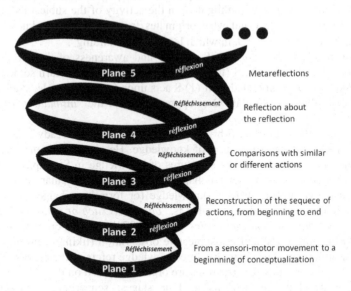

Fig. 3. Representation of the reflecting degrees

At the first plane, the most elemental *réfléchissement* leads to a sensorimotor movement to the first conceptualizations, that is, from reflexes and instinct to the first acquisitions such as habits, perceptions, and language. At the second plane, S already reconstructs a sequence of actions from beginning to end. The third plane is that of comparisons between analogue or different situations. At the fourth plane, S already makes "reflections" about the preceding reflections, continuing this process ad infinitum for the next planes reaching several degrees of metareflection or reflexive thought (*réflexive*).

Piaget warned that there is not a purely cognitive state or a purely affective state [2]. He recognized that affectivity is the motivating agent of cognitive activity, the source of energy of the structures or the motor of the action. Affectivity is not the structure, neither the action, and it does not change cognitive structures. Affectivity is characterized by positive or negative links between S and O. The first ones explain the acceleration in intellectual development when O is interesting or necessary for S. The second ones, however, explain the retardation when the affective situation related to O is an obstacle to S [2][15].

Dolle's hypothesis [7] is that the logic of affectivity is similar to that of cognitive processes, similar to that of cognitive stages. During the process of individual development, both logics operate synchronically, bur at a certain moment affectivity dominate

---

[2] The term *réfléchissement* has no equivalent in English. Therefore, in the figure, the terms used by Piaget himself are used to explain reflecting abstraction.

and at another cognition dominate. This way, the subject restructures the foundations of his or her relationship with the world [7], as intelligence is reconstituted after affectivity itself is constituted (affectivity ⇔ intelligence ⇔ affectivity ⇔ intelligence) [6]. Thus, the biophysiological subject leads to the affective subject, and this to the cognitive subject by integrations and achievements, which, in its turn, constitutes the social subject, following a spiral hierarchy, as presented in Figure 4.

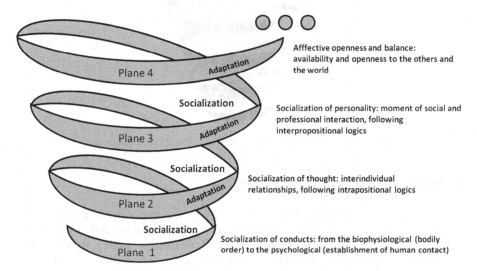

Fig. 4. Representation of the stages of the affective subject

As well as the terms *réfléchissement*-reflection, the socialization aspect refers to the plane above what is obtained from the plane below, and adaptation is the act of integrating or reorganizing affectivity. Thus, at the first plane, socialization of conducts leads to an instinctive tendency to perceptive affections (pleasure and pain, liking and disliking) and of elemental regulation (feeling of success or failure). At the second plane, the psychological subject possesses the symbolic function that enables a socialization of thoughts by means of interindividual relationships, facing the first elemental social and moral feelings. The third plane is that of normative affections, of the manifestation of autonomous moral feelings, of the socialization of personality. At the fourth plane, interindividual feelings grow with collective feelings. There is affective opening and balance that extend to the other planes.

In this study, the term cognition is understood not only as processing of information or mental functioning, but also as the capacity to react to what is perceived in the internal and external worlds. This also includes, besides the cognitive subject, the affective, the social and the biophysiological subjects. In epistemological terms, it is impossible to discuss *réfléchissement* and reflection without dealing with affective socialization and adaptation. Figure 5 illustrates the entwinement of the cognitive subject and the affective subject.

On the other hand, Scherer's theory [9][16] provides grounds in order to differentiate and understand how affective phenomena are processed in the organic subsystems.

This way, the purpose is to identify the moods and also which of them are more related to learning.

Fig. 5. Entwinement of the cognitive and the affective subjects

4 Scherer's Theory of Affectivity

The term affectivity usually refers to the ability to experience positive or negative feelings, and react to them. It is employed so as to identify psychic and physical phenomena associated with the terms emotion, mood, motivation, feeling, passion, love, personality, temperament, and many others refer to affectivity. Scherer [3] considers the terms related to affectivity to be affective phenomena. A phenomenon can be a state (disposition of the individual at a given moment) or a process (sequence of states or succession of changes that can transform the individual's disposition). However, the term emotion is commonly used to refer to the whole set of affective phenomena.

In order to define and distinguish affective phenomena, Scherer [3] established criteria to classify them as: 1) preferences (like, dislike), 2) attitudes (hate, esteem, desire), 3) moods (cheerful, glad, satisfied, willing, hopeless, upset, dissatisfied, suffering, indifferent, absent-minded, hopeful), 4) affective dispositions or personality traits (nervous, anxious, peevish, carefree, negligent, gloomy, melancholic, hostile, quarrelsome, cross, crabby, envious, jealous, curious, flexible, active, insecure, depressive, suspicious), 5) interpersonal postures or affective styles (polite, reserved, cold, warm, encouraging, disdainful, organized, sociable, kind), 6) utilitarian emotions (anger, fear, happiness, sadness, aversion, shame, guilt) and 7) aesthetic emotions (admiration, ecstasy, fascination, harmony, disagreement, solemnity, surprise, persuasion).

Leventhal & Scherer proposed a multilayered structure to explain emotional processing [17]. The sensorimotor level comprises a set of innate brain programs and activation systems stimulated automatically, without any volitive effort, comprising internal and external changes of the subject. The schematic level is automatic, and integrates the processes evaluated no level below (sensorimotor) with images stored from emotional situations that have already happened (memory or emotional experience). The conceptual level activates memory to compare two or more emotional episodes. These three levels correspond to the stages of cognitive development proposed by Piaget.

At each of these levels, processing comprises a sequential evaluation in four stages known as *appraisal process*[3]: (1) the relevance of the event; (2) the hedonic valence or the implication of the event in the well-being and immediate achievement of the objectives; (3) the coping potential or the capacity of overcoming (or facing obstacles) that the subject is able to produce; and (4) the meaning of the event, based on the subject's social rules and values.

According to Scherer's model [16], also known as Component Process Model (CPM)[4], affective phenomena are explained after the evaluation of an event that triggers an emotional episode. The psychological subject constantly scans the external and internal environment to detect, evaluate, and reevaluate changes (appraisal process). In each stage of the appraisal process, which occurs in the Central Nervous System, information are projected to the other organismic subsystems to be processed or not such as support or autonomic physiology, executive or action tendencies, communication or motor expression and monitor or subjective feeling.

As soon as the psychological subject detects an event, the subject needs a minimal attention, reorganized according to the relevance of the event, as the first selective filter of the appraisal process. Then, if the event is important for the objectives of the psychological subject, such information is passed on to the other components, which can trigger or not the kind of physiological reaction, the action to be executed, the way of expression and indication of subjective feeling. This happens, successively, for each stage of the appraisal process. The CPM model proposes that changes in the internal and external events are analyzed up to the moment the monitor subsystem signals the termination or adjustment of the resulting feeling to the emotional episode evaluated [16][18].

Sherer's model is appropriate to define and explain several affective phenomena. Among them, moods, which can trigger, inhibit or even prevent learning. They can be thought as a summary of affective responses [19], which include the various components (cognitive, physiological, expressivity, motivational and subjective) of the evaluation that the subject makes.

Considering how moods influence memory and learning, Bower [20] formulated an important theory – Bower's theory. The author considered that an event would be represented in memory in cluster of propositions. These propositions would be recorded in memory when associations between the affective episode experienced and the cognitive concepts that participated in the event are made, suggesting that there would be a congruence of the mood. For Bower, the correspondence between the affective value of a piece of information and the subject's mood during its exposition influences if it will be apprehended in memory or not. Such hypothesis has great experimental support (see [19]).

Based on Piaget's concepts assimilation and accommodation and Piaget's view on the affectivity, it is possible to relate the moods to the cognitive performance. Positive moods support the processes of assimilation, leading to new beliefs or reelaborating existing ones in learning. In the accommodation process, they modify existing mental

---

[3] The concept of appraisal was introduced by Magda B. Arnold in 1960. Initially, the subject performs an instant evaluation of the situation. The emotion constitutes the product of this evaluation. When the emotion is expressed, it is accompanied by an underlying feeling. Thus, even though the process of evaluation is unconscious, its effects are conscious.

[4] Sander and colleagues [18] elucidate and illustrate the CPM processes.

schemes more quickly. On the other hand, negative moods might make it harder to incorporate new data in the operative or action schemes or, even, encourage the learner to update beliefs in face of new knowledge. However, when related to the activation of the accommodation process, they might make things harder for the mechanisms of adaptation that structure and trigger cognitive development.

5   Mapping of the Affective Subject in ROODA VLE

In previous sections, the theoretical foundation presented offer subsidies for the analysis of the interactions in the ROODA VLE, with the aim of mapping the affective dimension starting from the cognitive and technological subjects. Piaget's theories and Scherer's theory are used to find evidence of the affective subject in the VLE-subject constructed by Behar [8] and Bassani [10]. Although in the VLE-subject Dolle's biophysiological dimension has suffered a resignification (technological subject), in this study it is applied again, as the importance of the organic components in the construction of the affective subject is verified, as presented in Scherer's theory. Thus, the VLE-subject may be represented as illustrated in Figure 6.

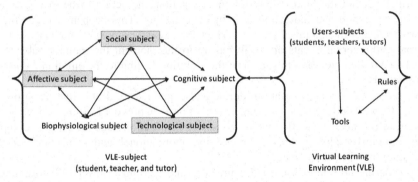

Fig. 6. Representation of the interaction VLE-subject and the study subjects

The affective dimension, which is emphasized in this study, is characterized by the externalization or not of the affective phenomena triggered during the processes that follow the other dimensions. Thus, it was decided that the moods would be approached because they are among the most representative affective phenomena in the scope of learning. With this purpose, the mood markers being cheerful, cheerless, satisfied and dissatisfied [21].

The social dimension comprises the construction of a learning virtual community by means of individual or interindividual relationships. It is characterized by the interiorization of the rules by the virtual environment, and by the interactions established with other user-subjects. The quality of the interactions may be analyzed based on the symmetry between the number of accesses and the quality of the relationships formed (social exchanges) [10].

The technological dimension determines to what point the VLE-subject is open to new technologies. It makes reference to the technological knowledge that the

VLE-subject should have to communicate and feel as participating in the virtual environment. But, it also recognizes the limitations of the VLE-subject in face of the environment. In this study, difficulties with the operationalization of the environment, technical problems and the technological knowledge necessary for the use of the environment are considered.

The biophysiological dimension of the VLE-subject can be defined based on studies about the observable behavior of the body, such as body gestures, facial expressions, muscular tension, skin conductivity, breathing, cardiac rhythm, temperature and eye movements etc., by means of visual (cameras), audio (microphones) and/or physiological sensors (seats sensitive to the pressure of the body, gloves that capture the skin conductivity, mouse sensitive to the "quality" of the pressure, EEG, ECG, ERP, thermographs, devices to measure pulsation, breathing and pupil dilation are examples of tools used to measure physiological data).

The cognitive dimension, in its turn, makes references to the processes of construction of knowledge of the object of study (content, subject, learning object, etc.), which are thoroughly discussed by Piaget and many other authors.

Figure 7, using the semantic network proposed by Bower [20], illustrates some of the studies conducted by the authors in order to evaluate the connections among the various subjects that make up the VLE-subject.

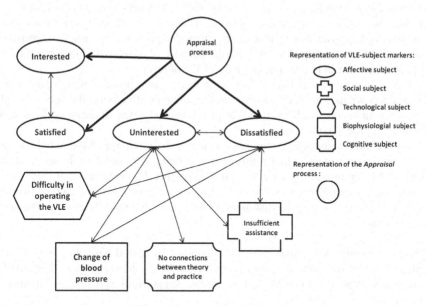

Fig. 7. Markers of the VLE-subject

The biophysiological and the cognitive dimensions will not be dealt with in this research as they are being studied by researchers at the Graduate Program in Computer Science Applied to Education at UFRGS. Studies that deal with the biophysiological dimension have just started to be conducted and several other studies focus on the cognitive dimension.

6 Final Considerations

In face of the various studies on the role of the affective dimension in human learning, affective phenomena contribute to the internal representation of the object of knowledge, and affect the way the individual learn, takes decisions, and behaves in social interactions. Affective dimensions influence the learning both positively and negatively. In the first, the sense of challenge, persistence, enthusiasm, curiosity, the satisfaction of completing a task, favor the student in consolidating the knowledge acquired, motivating the student to continue acquiring new knowledge. In the second, there is fear, uncertainty, resignation, anxiety, indifference, lack of confidence, boredom, etc. and might discourage the student to take a course or even lead him to quit a course. The affective state experienced during an activity is, mostly, determined by the characteristics and content of the task, as well as the pedagogic strategy applied.

Maehr [23], when referring that school motivation is related to the affective states of the student, suggests that the studies should be redirected: *"If they energize [the learning], how do they do so? If they undermine or confound, why and when? Again, the focus on self and self-worth reinforces the need to rediscover the role of the emotions in motivation"* (p. 184).

It can be noticed that digital technologies, mainly in a virtual context, promote changes of the relationships among learning agents: teachers, students, and tutors. In their turn, the analyses and studies that are necessary to accommodate these new paradigms need theories that validate them. With this purpose, this article emphasizes Scherer's and Piaget's contributions with the purpose of analysis and interpretation of the affective subject in interaction in VLE (VLE-Subject).

In fact, it is noticed that Piaget does not conceive of a process of *réfléchissement* and reflection without having as a premise the inherent affectivity, the subject's values. Scherer, in his turn, defines moods as processes and a way of analyzing how such processes are processed in a subject.

Therefore, this study defends the importance of the inference of the moods in virtual learning environments and, for this reason, is being developed, in the scope of the ROODA VLE, an instrument capable of providing this. It is expected that these environments soon transform from mere content repositories or means of communication to also instruments that might assist us to re(think) possible modifications in Distance Learning actions.

Acknowledgments. This study is been supported by the Brazilian agency CNPq (National Council for Scientific and Technological Development). The authors would like to thank Prof. Fernando Becker for ideas, suggestions and critical comments about the text.

References

1. Le Boterf, G.: Desenvolvendo a competência dos profissionais (Translated by Reuillard, P.C.R.), Porto Alegre, Artmed (2003)
2. Piaget, J. Inteligencia y afectividad. Aique, Buenos Aires (2005)

3. Scherer, K.: What are emotions? And how can they be measured? Social Science Information 44(4), 695–729 (2005)
4. Behar, P.A.: Modelos Pedagógicos em Educação a Distância. Artmed, Porto Alegre (2009)
5. Piaget, J.: Estudos sociológicos. Forense, Rio de Janeiro (1973)
6. Dolle, J.M.: Para além de Freud a Piaget: referenciais para novas perspectivas em psicologia. Vozes, Petrópolis (1993)
7. Dolle, J.M.: De Freud a Piaget: Elementos para um enfoque integrador de La afectividad y la inteligência. Paidos, Buenos Aires (1979)
8. Behar, P.A.: A lógica operatória e os ambientes computacionais. In: Anais do SBIE 1999 - X Simpósio Brasileiro de Informática na Educação, Curitiba, PR (November 1999)
9. Scherer, K.R.: Appraisal considered as a process of multilevel sequential checking. In: Scherer, K.R., Schorr, A., Johnstone, T. (eds.) Appraisal Processes in Emotion: Theory Methods, Research, pp. 92–129. Oxford University Press, Oxford (2001)
10. Bassani, P.B.S.: Mapeamento das interações em ambiente virtual de aprendizagem: uma possibilidade para avaliação em educação a distância. PPGIE/UFRGS, Porto Alegre (2006)
11. Piaget, J.: A epistemologia genética (Translated by Caixeiro, N.C.). Abril Cultural, São Paulo (1978)
12. Becker, F.: Educação e Construção do Conhecimento. Artmed, Porto Alegre (2001)
13. Piaget, J.: Abstração reflexionante: relações lógico-aritméticas e ordem das relações espaciais (Translated by Becker, F. & Silva, P.B.G.). Artes Médicas, Porto Alegre (1995)
14. Montangero, J., Maurice-Naville, D.: Piaget: ou a inteligência em evolução (Translated by Marques, T.B.I. & Becker, F.). Artmed, Porto Alegre (1998)
15. Piaget, J.: Problemas de Psicologia Genética. Forense, Rio de Janeiro (1973)
16. Scherer, K.R.: Toward a dynamic theory of emotion: The component process model of affective states. Geneva Studies in Emotion and Communication 1, 1–98 (1987)
17. Leventhal, H., Scherer, K.R.: The relationship of emotion and cognition: A functional approach to a semantic controversy. Cognition and Emotion 1, 3.28 (1987)
18. Sander, D., Grandjean, D., Scherer, K.R.: A systems approach to appraisal mechanisms in emotion. Neural Networks 18, 317–352 (2005)
19. Mayer, J.D., Hanson, E.: Mood-congruent judgment over time. Personality and Social Psychology Bulletin 21, 237–244 (1995)
20. Bower, G.H.: Mood and memory. American Psychologist 36, 129–148 (1981)
21. Longhi, M.T., Behar, P.A., Bercht, M.: AnimA-K: recognizing student's mood during the learning process. In: WCCE 2009 - 9th IFIP World Conference on Computers in Education, Bento Gonçalves, RS, Brazil, July 27-31 (2009)
22. Pozo, J.I.: Aquisição do Conhecimento: quando a carne se faz verbo (Translated by Antonio Feltrin). Artmed, Porto Alegre (2004)
23. Maehr, M.L.: Goal theory is not dead-not yet, anyway: A reflection on the special issue. Educational Psychology Review 13(2), 177–185 (2001)

Learning under Uncertainty: A Grounded Theory Study

Eurico Lopes

Escola Superior Tecnologia, Computer Engineering Department, Av. Empresario,
6000-767 Castelo Branco, Portugal
eurico@ipcb.pt

Abstract. This paper discusses learning under uncertainty; starting from a vision of how to support systems working within information systems, helping decision-making under uncertainty. The first results show the concept of learning under uncertainty. Then a change for a qualitative research approach was taken using Grounded Theory Methodology. The results are presented in a framework that represents a basic theory of learning under uncertainty process. This framework presents learning under uncertainty throw a tacit and operational learner capacities and a cognitive and impact on the learner. It also shows how uncertainty is sensed in order to start the learning process. Learning under uncertainty could be summarized through the use of a human approach, dialogue and interaction within social-actors in the uncertain context.

Keywords: Grounded Theory, Learning under Uncertainty, Constructivism, System Thinking, Information Systems Modelling.

1 Introduction

Initially the researcher was interested in understanding how decision support systems worked around information systems, supporting decision-making (D-M) under uncertainty. As the research continued, the researcher decided to merge other concepts found in literature such as systems thinking and complexity. At this stage, some research questions were asked and interviews were made. Then, when trying to find the answers to those questions, the researcher obtained, a commonality that unites all the related experiences; every one seemed to be embedded in a learning experience that upholds a learning concept under uncertainty. So, the necessity to discard the initial methodology was evident and a new one, Grounded Theory Methodology (GTM), was considered to suit the research purpose. Furthermore this paper will show grounded characteristics of learning under uncertainty from a qualitative research approach. Finally, a framework will be presented to explain the learning under uncertainty process.

This paper shows an introductory research inspecting how information systems and complexity guide D-M under uncertainty. The outcome is learning under uncertainty. Following an overview of learning under uncertainty in specific fields where uncertainty has been addressed in the context of learning. The choice of a qualitative approach and the use of GTM are justified. Finally the discussion of the results and a framework are presented.

N. Reynolds and M. Turcsányi-Szabó (Eds.): KCKS 2010, IFIP AICT 324, pp. 246–256, 2010.

1.1 Preliminary Research

To begin with, the researcher was inspecting how decision-makers under uncertainty and complexity build a model, an external and explicit representation of part of the reality seen by the decision-maker. By answering this question, was researched the way decision-makers comprehend the uncertain context. The researcher's hypothesis are based in the computer system engineering field [1], [2], [3] and reinforced by an initial literature review on prescriptive decision-making [4], [5], [6], [7] descriptive decision-making [8], [9], [10] systems thinking world [11], [12], [13], [14], [15] and complexity theory [16], [17], [18], [19].

The researcher was expecting answers that supported a calculated way of thinking or risk evaluation technique. At this stage, some research questions were designed and interviews were made to a set of heterogeneous participants in the business and management field, from small to global organizations. Following an open-interview format, no direct questions were asked, giving the interviewees the possibility to speak freely whilst revealing their feelings about their experience. In this way, the interviewees' accounts are subject to the reconstruction, without any preconceived questionnaire or other research strategy. After each interview, the researcher perceived that each interviewee did not relate any objectively observed natural world, he did not recount any formulated hypothesis that he had previously tested against, obtained quantified data. Each interviewee revealed how he became involved in a social interaction and what were they perceived for.

1.2 Learning Focus

The task to find answers was then a work of serendipity from the interviews, data, readings and a recurring return to the interviews.

From these experiences the researcher interpreted and constructed meanings that sustain a central concept of learning under the uncertain and complex context. This interpretation was not something that is there, waiting to be observed and measured. That reality was hidden and has to be constructed in order to have existence, it is not something that is offered as material substance or has been asked for. There now follows the first interpretations, impressions that the researcher sensed that uphold this learning concept.

1.3 Focalizing

From the first impressions and analysis of the first interview, modelling techniques from the system thinking world [14] were not used, not because they weren't asked, but because they did not keep the interviewee's D-M process going. This fact was not present, even if attempting to link with Strategic Management [17], [20], [21] or other techniques. The link does not work and the recounted experiences did not fit, sustained hypotheses were empty, and nothing made sense at this first analysis.

Furthermore, in the second analysis work over the second interview, the analysis gave the researcher a new horizon. Modelling techniques [2], [3] and risk evaluation [5], [22] were not the decision-maker support. The interviewee knew risk evaluation and game theory, however, as he argued, these techniques were not the substance that guided D-M under-uncertainty. It was not a question of risk evaluation or the use of supportive tools. At that time, the researcher perceived from the second interview that learning is indirect; it is a process that, from the interviewee's words provided meaning around the central concept of Learning.

The researcher did a third interview and the results of this interview did not give a new insight for the research. The researcher based their assumptions on suggested theories by the interviewee and he supposed that they could fit with the recounted experiences. The results were that the concept of learning stated by the interviewee guided D-M: "I think there are connections between the way people learn and the way they take decisions under uncertainty". However the idea that learning is a process under D-M under uncertainty and complexity was not clearly sustained by a common literature found in the field.

The central idea from the fourth interview was the need to learn having confidence to solve problems, to create a social relationship with professional colleagues based in daily meetings and be supported by the use of information and communications technology. A central idea of learning to decide fast and later adjust decisions if necessary also evolved.

Table 1. Analysis summary of initial research questions

Initial research questions Are decision-maker's				
Interview	using complexity theory?	making some sort of risk evaluation?	using Decision Support Systems or other tools to help?	Sensed, Interpreted and Constructed Meaning
1	No	No	Yes, but he does not understand them *"It is that I do not perceive anything of that. There are things I do not know that they had become there."*	Decisions under uncertainty are not found in this premises, in information systems
2	No, but he believes in natural evolution	Yes, but it has no impact how he decides, in his words	Yes, scenarios and game theory, but he does not feel confident with them, it his a personal position, assuming risk	Decisions under uncertainty depend on the personal confidence and risk taking behaviour and not in alternative tools
3	No, but organization history and values are important	Yes, some statistics, but in his words they do not count	Yes, managerial and statistical packages which does not account for a decision under uncertainty. *"It is not a financial model with lot of consultants, statistics and so on... it is much more about living the values"*	Decisions under uncertainty are more about the living values of the decision-maker.
4	No. *"I don't see how complexity theory helps"*	No. *"...managers don't reduce uncertainty objectively... they reduce the perception of uncertainty".*	No	Decisions under uncertainty are a question of how a personal manager reduces the perception of uncertainty
5	No	Yes, but not a way to reduce uncertainty. Decisions must be prompt in great uncertainty context, no time for reducing uncertainty	Yes, mainly to support organizational communications between bankers and the market and as a living report from successful and failed cases	Decisions under uncertainty must be prompted and not much time to reduce uncertainty

The fifth interview also offered fundamental ideas around the learning concept and a need for a social network which becomes more consistent. In the interviewee's words "opposition or disagreement is not a bad thing, it is good, it is learning", "I think too many managers spend time with computers and charts... it is much more about living the values, expressing the spirit of what should be", "I don't think I need a huge amount of statistical modelling to reach a decision, because often a decision is all about the human interaction". This is also a rejection of the initial thoughts, from where systems and modelling strategies should be important. Table 1 shows a summary analysis of how the researcher interpreted and made a construction of meaning from the interviewees' accounted experiences and table 2 presents sample phrases from each interview and it created a meaning. So, it became clear in the researcher's mind, that decisions under uncertainty depend on risk taking behaviour or are more about the living values of the decision-maker and how we learns under uncertainty.

Then another problem materialised – the literature does not make references to this learning process, and even fewer references exist of Learning under Uncertainty.

Table 2. Sample phrases from each interview and created meaning

Interview	Extracts Interview	Sensed, Interpreted and Constructed Meaning
01	"*People know that the direction is for there, but not the way! Let us say that the way become walking, experience.*" "*The reactivity of whom is in this process all has to be very great; therefore if people will not have capacity to answer to the necessities, in this case of the customers, but sometimes this can not be only customers... It can be fans, can be the proper family, it can be whatsoever, depending the type of organization, what we need is find out to react*"	Learn with experience Sense other needs, and Learn to be capable to answer them
02	"*We at SONAE assume a risk taker position and when we have much uncertainty we go to the challenge and when it arrives exactly at the dark room, where we become lost. Before this, it goes trying... and the limit is basically to never back the company.*"	Trying, going to the challenge and learning how to became out successfully
03	"*We have to look at the history institution, personal dynamics, or students want to do*" "*opposition or disagreement is not a bad thing, it is good, it is learning*"	Sense and learn the organization history and values. Learn also with disagreements
04	"*I think there are connections between the way people learn and the way they take decisions*" "*...learning value decisions ...*"	Making decisions is a Learning process
05	"*Here we have to learn to decide extraordinarily fast and always under conditions of great uncertainty. This is different from European organizations where we try first to reduce uncertainty and then take a decision*"	Learn to observe and be prompted to decide, not delaying reducing uncertainty

2 Learning Theories

Learning theories are attempts to describe how people learn. From the literature there are three main learning paradigms: Behaviourism, Cognitivism, and Constructivism [23]:

- Behaviourism is an approach to psychology where learning is a result of conditioning behaviour. This behaviour may result either in reinforcement, which increases the likelihood of that behaviour occurring again; or punishment, which decreases the likelihood of the same behaviour recurring in the future. In behaviourism, "a learner is essentially passive, responding to environmental stimuli. The learner starts off as a clean slate (i.e. tabula rasa) and behaviour is shaped through positive reinforcement or negative reinforcement" [23].

- Cognitivism expands behaviourism accepting that mental states are appropriate to analyse and subject to examination to understand mental function. Humans are assumed to act on the basis of representations of their environment that are processed in their brains [24]. Learning is a process of developing more and more accurate representations of external, pre-given reality.

> "Cognitivism uses the metaphor of the mind as computer: information comes in, is processed, and leads to certain outcomes" [23].

- Constructivism views learning as a process in which the learner constructs or builds new ideas or concepts based upon current and past knowledge. Constructivist learning involves constructing one's own knowledge from one's own experiences [25]. This should be the most appropriate learning theory for the present research, since uncertainty is not known; this should be sensed and learned with the experience, since "Learners continuously test these hypotheses through social negotiation. Each person has a different interpretation and construction of knowledge process. The learner is not a blank slate (tabula rasa), but brings past experiences and cultural factors to a situation" [23]

The following is an overview of learning under uncertainty in a specific field where uncertainty has been addressed in the context of learning.

Bligh [26] states a constructivist position in teaching to know what to teach, but also to know what students know and think. He proposes an approach using uncertainty to guide students in thinking and behaving to produce medical decisions. Bligh proposes "expressing uncertainty is the best way of learning and teaching because it allows exploration of the cognitive processes involved in clinical decision making" [26:2]. This is related with how students (doctors in training) apply the information they obtain from clinical experience and investigations, to perform a diagnosis. Bligh states "Knowing more about what students are thinking when they are presenting a case to you, or about what they are thinking after a lecture will enable teachers to help their students learn better" [26:2].

Dayan and Yu [27] in their experiments with small rats have carried out research regarding learning and uncertainty from three perspectives: statistical theories, psychological models in which attention is paid to stimuli with an effect on the speed of learning associated with those stimuli, and neurobiological data on the influence of the neuromodulators on learning and inference. Their conclusions are - the more uncertain a stimulus, the faster the animal learns about that stimulus: "It is obvious that learning should be occasioned by unfamiliarity" [27:10]. This links with the research study, - that uncertain stimuli generate learning, which is found in the current research where an uncertain and unfamiliar, or unknown context will guide learner thorough a process of dealing with that uncertainty, in order to understand it. This unfamiliar context is an uncertain context in the sense that an individual (human) will have to 'familiarise' himself with it, reconstructing it with others (assuming that reality is social-constructed), in order to know it.

In the field of Economics, Arrow states "Learning is certainly one of the most important forms of behaviour under uncertainty" [28:13]. Arrow argues that each individual achieves his satisfaction level at minimum cost. "If we assume that individuals are averse to risk, individuals and firms in planning for an uncertain future may want to make sure that their demands and outputs are mutually compatible" [28:268]. Arrow writes about consumer behaviour and so this is a very specific form of decisions and sensing markets related to consumers.

So uncertainty introduces learning like the term 'surprisal' from Hayles [29]. Bryant [30] argues that when the 'surprisal' element in the information is known, then uncertainty is reduced e.g. the first time you tell something new there may be something surprising about it, and we learn under uncertainty. Bernstein considers that the existence of surprise shows that uncertainty is more likely than probability, "prevalence of surprise in the world of business is evidence that uncertainty is more likely to prevail than mathematical probability" [22:220-1].

All the subsequent research work drew on the premise of this focus, and tried to understand how it works, what processes are involved and properties surrounding them. This changes the research strategy for a qualitative approach, which follows a justification.

3 Qualitative Approach Using GTM

There is recognition, that qualitative research is essential to capture real-world answers to the real world problems in a way that is not possible in a quantitative context [31], [32]. Glaser and Strauss [33] focus on qualitative research, which is usually the most "adequate" and "efficient" way to achieve the nature of information required, and to contend with the difficulties of an empirical situation. Regardless of these strengths, qualitative research also shows some weakness, related with qualitative samples, and there is no systemic or statistical approach, usually working with small samples of people [34]. Eldabi et al [35] claims that qualitative approaches to research take a less planned approach with more preference towards judgmental and expert knowledge rather than hard data.

The researcher decided to use GTM to investigate the phenomenon (Learning under uncertainty) within real-life contexts, especially when the boundaries between phenomenon and contexts are not clear. In addition, GTM presents a single, unified, systematic method of analysis; the previous interviews' data can be kept as well as the accounted experiences, but now the data can be analysed under a new framework. According to Charmaz [36], the major strength of GTM is that it provides tools for analyzing processes that make it easier for the researcher to follow specific steps to develop the concepts, categories, hypotheses and theory. The researcher was looking for generating data about this new topic rather than evaluating or assessing something that had already been found, as previous interviews have shown.

The study followed, using the previous interviews. However, they were now used under an assumption of qualitative data type, under GTM guidelines. A second group of interviews followed an enlargement of the professional background of the interviewees, such as a Doctor, Pilot Command, Architect, Managing Director and a Psychologist Head of School's Sixth Form. The main tool that was used for collecting the core data for this set involved again unstructured open-end interviews. Despite the fact that, in this case the concepts from the earlier were used and the aim was to enlarge the scope of the initial findings, through searching for new ideas that could generate more hypotheses in the new data.

Finally another research stage consisted of a consolidation of the previous stages, constructing a grounded theory of learning under uncertainty. For this end, a third set of interviews was directed by the emerging concepts from the previous sets, involving a selection of informants. This research stage was carried out to evaluate findings and confirm with previous interviewees the research findings. In addition, another goal was undertaken, in order to saturate categories and validate theory.

4 Discussion

Learning under uncertainty is common to all interviewees and in this interpretation the researcher looked for how individuals make meaning, i.e. how they acquire the knowledge, how they structure a network of people that can help to understand what the best under the uncertain context is. This process of learning is interpreted according to the interviewees' words as being a process of learning through experience, and sensing others' needs, and being capable to answer them. The process of learning includes learning the organization's history and values, learning through disagreements and opposition, learning to observe and be prompted to decide, not delaying the reduction of uncertainty, recognising it is a continuous practice and learning. It allows constructing a new frame, a new context, to work with constraints, to speak to others, always learning, avoiding the uncertain events. All of this process is made through the use of a human approach, dialogue and interaction with social-actors in the uncertain context. Other commonalities that have been interpreted in the interviews are the use of support systems: non-human and human, pleasure, working hard and confidence.

This is in agreement with a constructivist position where every explanation person puts forward any phenomena that is a social constructed account, and not a straightforward description of reality [37].

4.1 Framework

Using GTM, the researcher obtains a basic type of theory [38] which classifies specific dimensions of individuals, summarizing the commonalities found in discrete observations. Design a framework or diagramming offer a concrete image of the researcher ideas. The advantage of a framework is that it provides a visual representation of categories and their relationships [36:117]. So, the main goal of this framework is to give us a vision through time and place of the learning process. This framework describes the uncertainty environment and informs what an individual learner does. Figure 1 show the conceptual framework obtained. For example, a reading for this framework is: facing a context of uncertainty, from where great chances will occur, the learner will question "why" and what he "needs" to be better informed – this is a tacit position. Through these questions he will search for information from "mechanicistic" forms (newspapers, books, the internet, asking others, brainstorming with others, doing medical analysis, market analysis, etc.). He will also search for the remaining "unknown" in order to get better informed – this is an operational position. During this process the individual is learning, capturing knowledgeable information – he is reinforcing his cognitive capacities facing the uncertainty. Eventually, the learner has support help from someone (family or company). At some stage, the learner may or may not make a decision that he has enough knowledge which will have consequences and will have an impact on him as learner – impact as result from the learning under uncertainty process.

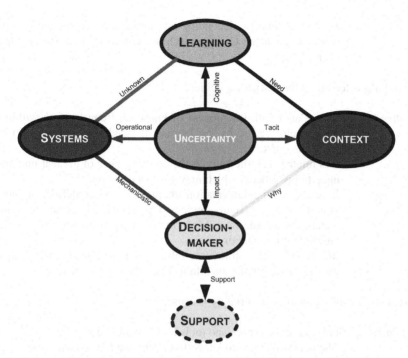

Fig. 1. Conceptual Framework derived from GTM analysis: its main goal is to give us a static vision through time and place of the learning process

The concepts shown represent:

Uncertainty   The central concept that represents the unknown context, driving two axes: The horizontal represents the *operational* and the *tacit* to deal with uncertain context. The vertical is linked with the learner's *cognitive*, communicative and social capacities, which have an *impact* on him as human being.

Context   The concept for the undefined reality, where uncertainty evolves and is reframed, resulting in a redefined context in order to achieve knowledge. It represents the learning goal.

Learning   The concept that drives the learner to understand the context, constructing a social-web in order to understand and reframe the context.

Systems   The concept that represents the set of human techniques to build on the lack of information: scenarios, brainstorming, group meetings etc.; however it also stands for computer systems and other system devices built in order to provide factual, measured information from the defined reality.

Learner   This concept represents the individual learner actor from which comes "why", the lack of information which guides the process.

Support	A volatile concept, depending on the learner's contextual uncertain world. It could be Company (Organization) or Society (People) or even Family.

Internal links referring to the learner capacities:

Cognitive	It is related with the process of knowledge construction within the social-web, created by the learner; it stands for understanding the uncertain context;
Impact	It is related with the learner, the consequences of the learning under uncertainty process which may guide a decision;
Operational	It relates to the information channel, from pre-defined computer systems and/or systems devices. Operational also refers to human techniques in order to get information from brainstorming, scenario building, group meetings, etc.
Tacit	Refers to how the strategy to reframe the uncertain context is developed, how tacitly the uncertain context is re-constructed.

External alignments show how uncertainty is sensed:

Mechanistic	Previous experiences and tools to deal with facts;
Why	The personal desire to know, to understand the context;
Unknown	Uncertain territory, no tools or anything at all to measure or obtain facts;
Need	Call for reconstruction or re-definition of the uncertain context.

Usefulness

This conceptual framework presents the results to consider learning under uncertainty. It is the GTM methodology's outcome applied in the current research study. This conceptual framework is a constructed interpretation from the interviews analysis.

5 Conclusion

This paper provides an overview of the main contributions of the research and makes the ongoing task of elucidating how learners under uncertainty gain knowledge of, developing a social-web context. The researcher at first was inspecting how decision-makers under uncertainty and complexity build a model, an external and explicit representation of part of reality as seen by the decision-maker. The results from this initial research focus in learning under uncertainty interpretation. The researcher then change for a qualitative approach, using GTM in order to study learning under uncertainty, since it is not a common subject in literature.

Furthermore, the results points of the process of learning include learning through disagreements and opposition, as well as learning to observe. It allows constructing a new frame, to work with constraints, to speak to others, always learning, avoiding the uncertain events. All of this process is made through the use of a human approach, dialogue and interaction with social-actors in the uncertain context. Other commonalities are the use of support systems: non-human and human, pleasure, working hard and confidence.

Finally it is presented a framework that provides a visual representation of categories and their relationships. The main points from it are the operational/tacit axis and the cognitive/impact axis.

This paper provides other researchers the opportunity to present a more complete picture of learning under uncertainty. In future, more research work is necessary to understand the influences from behavioural and organizational factors of learning under uncertainty.

5.1 Limitations

This research was conduced in a small set of business companies and professional activities so that the generalization of the findings to other sectors is too difficult because of different environments and context. The first limitation relates to the interviews since it is extremely demanding on research resources, therefore the researcher is obliged to rely on the experiences traces in the minds of those people who carried it out the experience of learning under uncertainty. This research proceeded on the premise that what was captured really happened, but that not all that happened was necessarily important and useful.

The second limitation is related to the results, which stands for a basic type of theory [38], although making testable predictions was not of primary concern. In addition testing is needed in order to reshape concepts and tune processes.

References

1. Checkland, P.B.: Systems Thinking, Systems Practice. Wiley, Chichester (1981)
2. Sowa, J.F., Zachman, J.A.: Extending and formalizing the framework for information systems architecture. IBM Systems Journal 31(3), 590–616 (1992)
3. Turban, E., Aronson, J.E.: Decision Support Systems and Intelligent Systems, 6th edn. Prentice Hall International, Englewood Cliffs (2001)
4. von Neumann, J., Morgenstern, O.: Theory of Games and Economic Behavior. Princeton University Press, Princeton (1944); Quoted in: Bernstein, Peter Against the gods: the remarkable story of risk. Wiley, New York, p. 269 (1996)
5. Chacko, G.K.: Decision-making under uncertainty: an applied statistics approach. Praeger (1991)
6. Biswas, T.: Decision making under uncertainty. Macmillan, Basingstoke (1997)
7. White, D.J.: Decision Theory. Aldine Transaction, New Brunswick (2006)
8. Simon, H.A.: Models of bounded rationality. MIT Press, Cambridge (1982)
9. Kahneman, D., Tversky, A.: Variants of uncertainty. In: Kahneman, Slovic, Tversky (eds.) Judgment Under Uncertainty: Heuristics and Biases, pp. 509–520. Cambridge University Press, New York (1982)
10. Thaler, R.: From Homo economicus to homo sapiens. Journal of Economics Perpectives 14, 133–141 (2000)
11. Beer, S.: The Heart of Enterprise. Wiley, Chichester (1979)
12. von Bertalanffy, L.: General System Theory: Foundations, Development, Applications. George Braziller, New York (1968) (also published 1971 by London: Allen Lane)

13. Forrester, J.: Industrial Dynamics: a major break-through for decision-making. Harvard Business Review 36(4), 37–66 (1958)
14. Pidd, M.: Tools for Thinking - Modelling in Management Science, 2nd edn. Wiley, Chichester (2003)
15. Midgley, G.: Systemic Intervention: Philosophy, Methodology and Practice. Kluwer, New York (2000)
16. Arthur, B.W.: Complexity and Economy. Science 284, 107–109 (1999)
17. Stacey, R.D.: Strategic Management and Organisational Dynamics – The Challenge of Complexity, 4th edn. Prentice Hall Financial Times, Englewood Cliffs (2003)
18. Kurtz, C.F., Snowden, D.J.: The New Dynamics of Strategy: Sense-Making in a Complex and Complicated World. IBM Systems Journal 42(3) (2003), E-Business Management
19. Mitleton-Kelly, E. (ed.): Complex Systems & Evolutionary Perspectives of Organisations: The Application of Complexity Theory to Organisations. Selected Papers on Complexity by 14 International Authors. Elsevier, Amsterdam (2003)
20. Steier, F.: Research and Reflexivity. Sage, Thousand Oaks (1991), Quoted in [18:9]
21. Levy, D.: Chaos theory and strategic: theory, application and managerial implications. Strategic Management Journal 15, 167–178 (1994)
22. Bernstein, P.: Against the gods: the remarkable story of risk. Wiley, New York (1996)
23. Learning Theories Knowledgebase. Index of Learning Theories and Models at LearningTheories.com (2008), http://www.learning-theories.com (retrieved May 26, 2008)
24. Gagne, R.M., Briggs, L.J., Wager, W.W.: Principles of instructional design. Harcourt Brace Jovanovich, Fort Worth (1992)
25. von Glasersfeld, E.: Radical constructivism: A way of knowing and learning. Falmer Press, London (1995)
26. Bligh, J.: Learning from uncertainty: a change of culture. Medical Education 35, 2 (January 2001)
27. Dayan, P., Yu, A.J.: Uncertainty and learning. IETE Journal of Research 49, 171–182 (2003)
28. Arrow, K.J.: Utilities, Attitudes and Choices: A Review Note. Econometrica, 1–23 (January 1958); Quoted in Mack, Ruth P. Planning on uncertainty: decision making in business and government administration. Wiley-Interscience, New York, p. 172 (1971)
29. Hayles, N.K.: How Became Posthuman: Virtual Bodies in Cybernetics. In: Literature and Informatics. University of Chicago Press, Chicago (1999)
30. Bryant, A.: Thinking "Informatically" A New Understanding of Informations, Communications, and Technology, p. 49. Lampeter: Edwin Mellen Press, Lewiston (2006)
31. Neuman, W.L.: Social Research Methods. Allyn and Bacon, Boston (1991)
32. Tesch, R.: Qualitative Research: Analysis Types and Software Tools. The Falmer Press, New York (1990)
33. Glaser, B.G., Strauss, A.L.: The Discovery of Grounded Theory: Strategies for Qualitative Research. Aldine Publishing Company, New York (1967)
34. Miles, M., Huberman, M.: Qualitative data analysis: A sourcebook of new methods, 2nd edn. Sage, Newbury Park (1994)
35. Eldabi, T., Irani, Z., Paul, R., Love, P.: Quantitative and Qualitative Decision Methods in Simulation Modelling. Management Decision 40(1), 64–73 (2002)
36. Charmaz, K.: Constructing Grounded Theory: A Practical Guide Through Qualitative Analysis. Sage Publications, London (2006)
37. Gergen, H.J.: The social constructionist movement in modern psychology. American Psychologist 40, 266–275 (1985)
38. Gregor, S.: The Nature of Theory in Information Systems. MIS Quarterly 30(3), 611–642 (2006)

Integration of a Video Annotation Tool into a Coactive Learning and Working Environment

Johannes Magenheim[1], Wolfgang Reinhardt[1], Alexander Roth[2]
Matthias Moi[1], and Dieter Engbring[1]

[1] University of Paderborn, Department of Computer Science, Computer Science Education
Group, Fuerstenallee 11, 33102 Paderborn, Germany
{jsm,wolle,moisun,didier}@uni-paderborn.de
[2] University of Paderborn, Faculty of Business Administration and Economics,
DS&OR-Lab, Warburger Strasse 100, 33098 Paderborn, Germany
roth@uni-paderborn.de

Abstract. In this paper we describe pedagogic scenarios where the use of a video annotation tool could be of added value to the students' overall learning process. Furthermore, we introduce ViLM, a platform-independent tool for annotating videos collaboratively or on its own and how we integrated the tool in our university's LMS. Finally, we characterise potential research opportunities and learning scenarios where the tool may successfully be applied.

Keywords: Computer Science Education, Training, Video, Learning Management Systems.

1 Introduction

The Computer Science Education Group at the University of Paderborn started the usage of multimedia and hypermedia in their student teacher training program in 1998. The aim of these efforts was to support student teachers to integrate new technologies into their teaching and learning processes and use multimedia as a very convenient tool for self-assessment of their educational practice in the classroom (see Magenheim and Schubert [1,2]). At the core of these practices is the video recording of real teaching situations and the annotation and discussion of teaching and learning strategies. The most important lessons learnt for the participating student teachers are specific strategies of pedagogies of computer science as well as the analysis and evaluation of social classroom interaction and the design and implementation of excellent lessons in computer science.

Ever since many tools were developed that aim at the individual competence development and lasting learning successes. One of these tools is ViLM (Visualization of Learning and Teaching Strategies with Multimedia) that underwent multiple upgrades; re-implementations that used advanced programming languages for the best fit to the organizational requirements. Despite these iteration cycles there were still a number inadequacies of the tool: the missing integration into the university's LMS, the separate storage of video data and additional course materials, missing streaming

N. Reynolds and M. Turcsányi-Szabó (Eds.): KCKS 2010, IFIP AICT 324, pp. 257–268, 2010.
© IFIP International Federation for Information Processing 2010

video capabilities, unavailable access to university user data stores, leading to the absence of global authentication procedures.

Based on these issues we started to reengineer the existing source code and designed a new version of the ViLM tool that makes use of our university's IT and digital learning infrastructure. The new VILM tool supports a variety of video annotation scenarios with differing permission structures and cooperative functionalities.

This paper introduces several pedagogic application scenarios for the usage of a video annotation tool, the coactive learning and working environment *koaLA* used at the University of Paderborn and the newly developed tools ViLM ControlCenter and ViLM Player. Furthermore we describe detailed application scenarios for the tools mentioned above and we discuss future research opportunities.

2 Pedagogic Application Scenarios for Video Annotation in Educational Contexts

There are many application scenarios for the use of video annotation in educational contexts using a different number of videos. In the following, selected scenarios are introduced that can make use of the meaningful and supporting application of video annotation tools in general and ViLM in particular.

2.1 Talks and Presentations (One Camera Perspective)

Each talk deals with a more or less bounded topic and it is of high importance for the audience being able to follow the talk. Therefore a sensible structuring and a golden thread are of high importance. There are certain things that can be analysed regarding a presentation including a) is the diction appropriate? b) are various media used during the talk? and c) are those media used meaningful? or d) how is the chain of reasoning constructed? and e) are mimic and gestures supporting the told? Those aspects are a selection of criteria that can be taken into account during the evaluation of presentations. Without using ViLM an observer could jot down notes during the talk or use a recording of the talk afterwards. The presentation itself and the according notes would in each case be separated from each other resulting in media disruptions [3].

In order to enhance the traceability for the presenter ViLM can be used. Therefore a recording of the talk is necessary. The camera should be oriented towards the speaker and follow his movements if applicable. For doing the analysis, the talk can be split into phases (e.g. according to the outline) with remarks to every aspect of interest during the phase. There can be different aspects of interest in different phases and it is easy to switch between them using ViLM. The speaker himself, an educational guardian or a collaborative group of students, can do the analysis of a talk.

2.2 Film Analysis (One Camera Perspective)

For doing film analysis no actual recording but instead a digital copy of the film is necessary. During a film analysis several criteria can be assessed including a) art work through the camera, b) art work after the recording, c) composition of stylistic elements, d) dubbing and e) décor of the film. During a written film analysis there is no direct connection between the notes and the described situation. Normally one would write down the time signature of a specific scene but there is no marker on the video nor can a specific time be headed to.

During a film analysis with ViLM different phases and events can be defined and directly marked in the video. A detailed analysis (by adding a description or linking to additional material) can be done for each of these annotations single-handedly or cooperatively. The markers set on the video can directly be started up making the navigation through a film analysis much easier.

2.3 Analysis of Teaching Strategies (Two Camera Perspective)

According to Blömeke et al. [3] lessons can be divided in designated phases that can be used exemplarily during the analysis of teaching strategies: a) problem, b) target agreement and significance, c) procedure agreement, d) development of foundations for problem solution, e) problem solution, f) result comparison and summary, g) application, and h) continuation and rating. Of course every student teacher is free to structure his lessons on his own.

The application of ViLM in teacher training fosters student teacher's awareness of their own behaviour in the classroom, especially regarding reactions on unforeseen situations – during group discussion at the teacher training course it can be debated whether they were appropriate. The analysis of teaching strategies involves two camera perspectives: a camera that records the (re-)actions of the teacher and another camera that records the (re-)actions of the pupils. Having two simultaneous perspectives on the same situation facilitates the direct comparison between action and reaction. Thus, discussions among students about behaviour patterns of student teachers and pupils may be activated.

2.4 Analysis of Group Work (Four Camera Perspective)

Learning co-operatively in teams is a very common method in the classroom where the number and size of groups depends on the number of pupils. In this scenario we assume four groups with one camera oriented on each of them and the simultaneous start of all four recordings. The task of the group work needs to be explained in beforehand and in order to achieve the objectives, all group members have to cooperate. To wrap up the teamwork and to present the different results a final result presentation is suggested. The recordings of the group work allow analysing a) which pupils have actively worked in their group, b) who made decisions and c) how the problem solution was worked out. ViLM facilitates the definition of different phases and the annotation of actions performed in the teams. The parallel screening of all four camera makes it easy to compare problem solution approaches and activities as well as the identification of opinion leader and passive observers. ViLM enables the teacher to gain a better insight into the single group works and a better understanding of the general scheduling of the group work task. From this analysis he or she then can optimise the group assignment, time management, and work description for future realisations. Furthermore, the teacher can show different approaches for the problem solution to his pupils by showing the recordings to them.

In this paper we present the integration of video annotation software into the coactive learning management environment *koaLA* that is used organisation-wide at the University of Paderborn. The specific functionalities that support coactive learning in groups are introduced in the following section.

3 The Coactive Learning and Working Environment *koaLA*

CSCW/L systems got great impulses from the discussion about web 2.0 or e-learning 2.0. Beside the use of already mature technologies likes RSS, web services and Asynchronous JavaScript and XML (AJAX) for implementing open environments and user-friendly interfaces, the variety of options for cooperative working and learning has steadily increased. In combination with social networks, tools like wikis, weblogs and podcasts emphasise the learner's role as content producer respectively its cooperative activities. This development leads away from completely predetermined structures and closed contexts to knowledge- and individual-centric, open environments.

In the course of a support programme of the Federal Ministry of Education and Research, the project *Locomotion* (Low Cost Multimedia Production and Organization) was executed at the University of Paderborn. This project constituted the implementation scope of the virtual learning management environment *koaLA* (Coactive learning and working, http://koala.upb.de), which focuses on individuals and individual cooperation contexts and combines this focus with conventional features of traditional course management systems. Important elements and necessities of learning, of university administration and of social networking are integrated through virtual and – depending on the context – self-organised learning and working areas. Here, the consequent alignment of individual requirements of learners is fundamentally. The implementation of *koaLA* as an open system with its focus on individually configurable learning and working contexts is well accepted by students, but also by teachers using the virtual environment to try out innovative didactic concepts and integrating a potpourri of pre-structured and self-structured scenarios into different types of courses.

In the following, we want to explain the main concepts and the functionalities, which enable the configuration and seamless combination of formal as well as informal contexts. After that, we describe the technical implementation by means of typical web 2.0 architectures and demonstrate, how differences in media formats in the university's information architecture were neutralised through integration on different levels.

The coactive learning and working environment *koaLA* was set up as an application on top of a standard architecture for web-based CSCW/L systems named *sTeam*[1], which provides the fundamental functionality for cooperative learning and working through programming interfaces. In its core, the server combines two simple but elementary concepts: On the one hand, generalization of media types, and on the other hand, the utilization of virtual knowledge spaces for implementing varieties in group structures and working contexts. In addition to a flexible rights management, the generalization of media types is an elementary precondition for a platform-wide interlinking of information, without struggling with differences in media formats.

---

[1] Structuring Information in a Team, http://www.open-steam.org

Furthermore, virtual knowledge spaces describe the semantic structuring of a knowledge area and bring together various services and communication mechanisms at a single location. The aim here is to reduce media discontinuities as introduced by Keil [4], when using different media functions for manipulating material. For instance, knowledge objects (any kind of media type) can provide the basis for a discussion (e.g. be annotated), or user groups can correspond to mail groups.

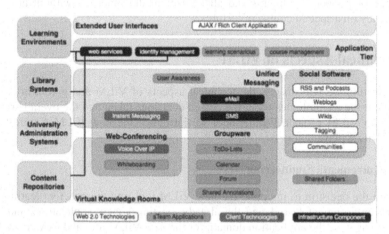

Fig. 1. The *koaLA* architecture

For the purpose of proclaiming the concept as a predominant structural characteristic for such a heterogeneous environment as a universities it-infrastructure, the server applies some common internet-protocols onto the elements of the metaphor of virtual knowledge spaces. Therefore, synchronous as well as asynchronous communication tools like instant messaging, whiteboarding, e-mail or shared annotations are natively embedded in knowledge rooms.

In the application tier, dynamic learning and working contexts are reconstructed by means of these functional components (cf. Hampel and Roth [5]). From a technical perspective, those depend often on the same functionality, but – in the end – vary in the degree of freedom in self-organization. Also, the integration of some of the universities central basic and complex services is carried out in the application tier.

The presentation layer of *koaLA* allows a unitary and easy handling in combination with a visually attractive web interface by means of AJAX-functions. This should lower user barriers and increase the users´ acceptance. As an example, the sequence of lectures can be rearranged through the drag-and-drop of a single lecture, without the necessity to reload the web page.

In the past, the *sTeam* server already provided basic services for different learning and community environments. However, new aspects in *koaLA* are a distinctive focus on social networking functionalities and the embedment of modern cooperative tools as weblogs and podcasts next to wikis and forums.

With its mass of configurable and dynamic options, different learning scenarios can be realised easily without programming skills, only through the combination and adaption of reusable functional components. As examples, the variety of scenarios includes the editing and exploitation of documents, the structuring of discourses, the rating and arrangement of media elements, and the coordination of activities, which are scattered in time and space. In particular, learners can organise themselves in small groups; they can easily jump from their own workbench to a private group to a cooperative workroom of a course and way back. This concept offers great possibilities for learners to switch between informal and formal learning contexts and collect, exchange or publish documents and all kind of media objects - without any direct dependency on a special course of lectures.

4 Technical Aspects of ViLM

In this section we will discuss the technical aspects of ViLM and give a brief overview about the technologies used, the design decisions taken and the overall architecture of the ViLM project. Furthermore we introduce the new ViLM ControlCenter and the ViLM player.

4.1 Requirements Engineering

Based on the decision to integrate the new ViLM tool into the coactive learning and working environment *koaLA* and the already existing legacy applications and code, we had to analyse the application domain for the new ViLM tool and to derivate functional and non-functional requirements for the tool. Since *koaLA* is a web-application that can run in any browser with basic JavaScript support, one requirement was to develop the new tools platform independently. Another design decision was to develop a Rich Internet Application (RIA) that offers the user a rich and engaging user experience and comes with the characteristics of desktop applications. During the design phase we evaluated the Flex[2] framework by Adobe and the JavaFX[3] framework and decided to use Flex because of its mature status and the excellent support for video display and video streaming. Furthermore, Adobe Flex guarantees high portability between the common operating systems Mac OS X, Windows and Linux. Flex not only allows developing web-based RIAs but also desktop equivalents using the AIR runtime. With the AIR runtime additional functionality like full access to the local file system and drag and drop of files into the AIR application is realised. In another project we developed an Adobe AIR based video player that allows the playback of annotated video materials and the presentation on additionally stored material. During the requirements engineering phase we decided to reuse the existing code base of the player and to evolve it to be the ViLM player, capable of streaming videos and interacting with *koaLA*.

During the design phase we decided to use streaming video instead of video playback via HTTP. The usage of a streaming server allows a more precise navigation and a smoother display of even large video files. For annotating videos and synchronisation of multiple views it is of high importance to navigate between key-frames of video files as precise as possible. To avoid costly re-encoding of video material in order to suit the capabilities of a streaming server, we were looking for a streaming

---

[2] http://www.adobe.com/products/flex/
[3] http://javafx.com/

server that was capable of dealing with H.264 encoded MP4 videos, streaming via RTMPS (Real Time Messaging Protocol over HTTPS) and easy connection to Flash-based applications, such as any Flex or AIR application. After an evaluation phase we decided for the open source Java streaming server Red5[4] because of its very good video streaming results, the easy configuration and the RTMPS support. Another influencing variable for Red5 was the possibility of extending the existing codebases to suit special needs and adaptations to fit the existing IT infrastructure. The proprietary equivalent product from Adobe (Flash Media Server[5]) was not chosen because of its pricing structure and the missing open development community that Red5 offers.

4.2 Architecture of the ViLM Project

The ViLM ControlCenter (VCC) was developed as the main interaction interface in the overall architecture. Both students and staff are using the VCC to interact with video annotation projects. The backend for the VCC is the *koaLA* learning and working environment of the University of Paderborn. All communication between the VCC and the server is event-based and uses an HTTP ActionScript API. For security reasons, all communication is secured with SSL. Using the API it is possible to authenticate and authorise against the university LDAP and to create and modify objects in the *koaLA* system. *koaLA* implements a multi-level rights management and thus supports multiple right scenarios for video annotations as well.

Whereas all project-related documents and control files are stored in a special folder of the course on *koaLA*, the respective videos are stored on the streaming server. Therefore we extended the Red5 server to handle uploads from the VCC and to authenticate any video request via the *koaLA* authentication interface. That way videos can only be viewed by legitimised individuals.

The integration of video annotations into *koaLA* was realised by the implementation of a new learning scenario (unit) that can be selected by staff members for their course in the LMS. Creating a new video annotation unit from within *koaLA* enables the VCC to create new projects within this unit. For example, a staff member could create new ViLM projects for each of the students in his course or for specific pedagogic scenarios (cf. section 2). The main control file that connects the different data sources and subsystems is an ANN-file (ANN stands as abbreviation of annotation). The file is a custom XML file), which is stored for each ViLM project within *koaLA*. The AAN-file holds information about the videos to stream, the documents used within the project and most important about marked phases and annotations in the project. The ViLM player is capable opening these ANN-files, loading the related documents and streaming the video content.

4.3 The ViLM ControlCenter

The newly developed ViLM ControlCenter (VCC) is the main application for dealing with video annotations within the University of Paderborn IT infrastructure. The VCC is an AIR application and runs on the major operating systems. The VCC enables the easy creation and administration of new or existing ViLM projects and is also the

---

[4] http://code.google.com/p/red5/
[5] http://www.adobe.com/products/flashmediaserver/

main working area for students doing their video annotations. Staff members can select from a list of different video annotation scenarios and decide on various right settings for the created projects. For newly created projects staff members can set the student owner of the project and directly upload the video recordings to the streaming server. Doing this the initial ANN-file is created and stored on *koaLA*.

When students login to the VCC, they can select video annotation projects that they have access to. Depending on the applied video annotation scenario and right settings they can annotate the available videos on their own or collaboratively. The first step in the annotation process is to synchronise the available videos, so that all recordings start at the same time. During the recording we use an audible sign to identify the synchronisation point. After the videos are synchronised, students can define different phases of interaction in the videos. Those phases can correlate to the lesson planning or simply contain noticeable events. Each phase is defined by a start- and end-time and a meaningful title. Each phase can contain multiple sub-phases for further structuring of the video. Students can add any type of additional media (such as lessons planning, intended blackboard figures, used material to prepare the lesson…) to the phases. Apart from phases, students can also define events in the videos, which are single frames within the recordings that show important scenes (a resulting blackboard figure or a special kind of interaction). The annotated phases and events are saved in the ANN-file and the references to the added documents are linked and everything is uploaded to the project store on *koaLA*.

Apart from creating new (only staff members) and annotating existing projects (mainly students), all users can view completely annotated video annotation projects using the ViLM player. The player can directly be launched from within the VCC.

Fig. 2. Screenshots of a project in the ViLM ControlCenter (left) and the ViLM player (right)

4.4   The ViLM Player

The ViLM player is responsible for the streaming of videos from the streaming server and the display of the annotated phases, events and uploaded documents. The ViLM player comes with the well-known controls (play, stop, pause) of a video player and has an additional phase menu, where all defined phases can directly be accessed. The ViLM player displays descriptions and comments to the current phase and allows direct access to the linked documents. The ViLM player uses the ANN-file to stream or download the respective files and to display the descriptions and comments. With the player it is possible to display selected phases and videos in full screen mode and to control the volume of the available videos. Doing this it becomes feasible to concentrate on a specific view of the project.

5   Detailed Inspection of Selected Application Scenarios

In this section we take a closer look on two selected application scenarios where the ViLM software is applied.

5.1   Self-reflecting Teaching Strategies in Teacher Education

In a problem-based course with the topic 'methods of teaching informatics in theory and practice' (MIU) at the University of Paderborn, student teachers should become acquainted with typical classroom situations. Therefore the course takes place at several locations. One location is the University of Paderborn where two staff members (tutors) supervise the student teachers. Furthermore up to three schools in Paderborn are involved where the student teachers observe lessons on computer science and perform own lessons. The teachers in school act as mentors for the student teachers. The MIU course is divided into three phases:

1. Learning to prepare lessons in computer science,
2. Performing lessons in computer science and learning to reflect on them,
3. Reflecting again and generalise best practices.

Phase 1: Learning to Prepare Lessons in Computer Science

In the first phase of the course the main goal is that student teachers become acquainted with typical classroom situations and learn about theoretical assumptions about teaching computer science. They should be prepared to develop their own course materials and to plan computer science lessons together with their fellow students. Materials and concepts of teaching will be delivered in form of web-based documents on the university coactive learning and working environment *koaLA* and can be accessed by all participants of the course.

During this phase of the course student teachers also visit schools to attend lessons in informatics and to analyse the teaching strategies of teachers and the pupils' concepts of learning. Theoretical assumptions about teaching informatics and practical experience of classroom situations will be discussed with their tutors in the course at university.

Phase 2: Performing Lessons in Computer Science and Learning to Reflect on Them

After having been prepared for school practice the student teachers have to teach one lesson of computer science in the classroom on their own. They will be observed by some of their fellow students and the mentors using a jointly developed observation form. The communication and collaboration in the classroom is recorded by two video cameras, one for the teacher's and one for the students' perspective (two camera perspective).

In school, the student teacher and the mentor discuss the lesson after it is over. So the teacher students may have a better chance to analyse and to reflect on their own lesson. After his own lesson the student teacher uses ViLM to watch the recordings of his teaching and annotates demonstrative phases of the videos, describes them and adds additional material if applicable. At university, one student teacher presents some annotated clips of his own lesson with the ViLM player to the other students, which have not necessarily seen this lesson and to the tutors. Referencing the real performance with the planned schedule combines theory and practice.

Another discussion of the lesson follows to learn about different possible teaching methods in the shown situations. Doing this, evaluation remains a social process, supported by video, and the result of inter-subjective social negotiations of meanings through interpersonal discourse. On the other hand, evaluation becomes a process of individual reconstruction, supported by video. The fleeting event and experiences of own teaching becomes a solid artefact, which can be used as an external memory for all teacher students involved in this course. All materials and concepts of teaching – including the annotated video – will be delivered in form of web-based documents on *koaLA* and can be accessed by all participants of the course.

Phase 3: Reflecting Again and Generalise Practices

Based on theories of constructivism, the course wants to facilitate the development of critical evaluation of learning and teaching processes by letting the students analyse their behaviour in the classroom by themselves. To foster this concept the teacher students continue to use the ViLM tool in order to reflect and annotate their own teaching strategies. Within ViLM they prepare a multimedia document containing all relevant materials from their own lesson (e.g. the video recordings, lesson designs, work sheets, results of processes, pictures of the blackboard etc.) and the respective annotations and descriptions of their work. The main objective of this process of reconstruction of classroom reality by student teachers is to establish sensibility towards effective teaching strategies and classroom interaction. In a final wrap up of the MIU course all student teachers present their final ViLM project to their fellow students and the tutors of the course.

5.2 Computer Science Tutor Training

At the computer science department of the University of Paderborn there is a student tutor training course in place where all new student tutors are prepared for their practice. According to Reinhardt and Magenheim [6], a core goal of this course is to prepare future student tutors for the needed shift in perspective from being a student to being a teacher and the different operational levels they will act in. To accomplish these goals the student tutor training is a two-part course with one part before the start of the semester and one part during semester. The first part consists of an online phase, where the future tutors learn to work with the administrative and cooperative functions of *koaLA* and an introductory workshop. Amongst others, various situations from tutorials are simulated during that workshop, recorded and discussed with the participants in order to reveal common errors, prepare for unforeseen situations, train the usage of multiple media and to allay existing fears. The recordings are viewed directly after the simulation so the usage of ViLM would not be appropriate here.

During the semester several meetings take place with the course members and common problems are discussed. Each student tutor is assigned to an observation group and gets observed by the other members two times each semester during his tutorials. Additionally, the observers have to fill out a detailed observation form where they can state special findings and hints for the student tutor. The observed tutorial gets recorded (one camera perspective) and the resulting video is provided to the tutor afterwards. Therefore, a mentor creates a new ViLM project and defines the owner of the project. For privacy reasons only the tutor himself and the mentors of the course can access the project directly. The other members of the course only see the phases of the video that are shown by the tutor in the workshops using the ViLM player.

Together with the observation form and the recording of the tutorial a student tutor then can replay his own teaching activities and annotate noticeable phases. In a mid-semester and an end-semester workshop all student tutors present noticeable phases from their tutorials using the ViLM player and link them to the remarks on the observation forms. Furthermore, the mentors define specific topics of interest (e.g. usage of media, behaviour during group work, reaction on questions from the audience) that should be presented explicitly. All presented video phases are discussed together with the tutor, respective observation group and the other members of the tutor training.

6 Conclusion and Future R&D Perspectives

In this paper we introduced ViLM, a platform-independent tool for collaborative video-annotation and its integration in the coactive web 2.0 LMS of our University, called *koaLA*. We described the advantages and the requirements of the visualised analysis of learning and teaching strategies with multimedia in different learning scenarios. Based on the requirements analysis of those scenarios, the main components of ViLM, the ViLM ControlCenter (VCC), and the ViLM player were developed. VCC enables the easy creation and administration of new or existing ViLM projects. VCC is the front-end for the students' video annotations and it is integrated in the coactive learning environment *koaLA*. The ViLM player provides students with simultaneous video streams according to the requirements of the related learning scenarios.

Up to now, mainly the analysis of two types of learning scenarios in the area of CSE were successfully put into practice, each of them supported by video streams which can be annotated by the students. Further developments of the tools will focus on the realisation of additional scenarios with multiple video-streams: movie analysis; teamwork analysis; discussion analysis, e.g. between developers and customers in the area of computer science requirements engineering. Based on our experiences and those of other projects dealing with video analysis of social interaction scenarios [7,8] the technical development of VILM should be continued: Integration of a scene graph editor in VILM, that allows students to arrange the scenes in a graph that represents intersections and a non-linear flow according to content related criteria; assembling of a video-snippet-collection (VILM-Tube) that contains relevant learning and teaching scenarios; integration of an annotation tool, that enables social tagging of snippets according to a 'learning process ontology' (LPO) and by this means facilitates information retrieval. Finally, empirical research on students' benefit from VILM is necessary in order to improve their teaching competences and to provide the developers with substantial information for further system enhancement.

References

1. Magenheim, J.: ViLM: Visualization of Learning and Teaching Strategies with Multimedia in Teacher Education. In: Proceedings of ED-MEDIA 1999, pp. 1593–1594 (1999)
2. Magenheim, J., Schubert, S.: Evaluation of teacher education in informatics. In: Benzie, D., Passey, D. (eds.) Proceedings of WCC 2000, pp. 181–184 (2000)
3. Blömeke, S., et al.: Gestaltung von Unterricht – Eine Einführung in die Didaktik (2004)
4. Keil, R.: Medienqualitäten beim eLearning: Vom Transport zur Transformation von Wissen. Bibliothek 31(1), 41–50 (2007)
5. Hampel, T., Roth, A.: Rapid Development of Non-Monolithic CSCL-Applications - About the Benefits of Using a Prescribed Terminology in Web Programming. In: Proceedings of the E-Learn 2005, pp. 2095–2102 (2005)
6. Reinhardt, W., Magenheim, J.: Modulares Konzept für die Tutorenschulung in der universitären Informatikausbildung. In: Schwill, A. (ed.) Commentarii Informaticae Didacticae, vol. 1 (2008)
7. Meixner, B., et al.: SIVA Producer – A Modular Authoring System for Interactive Videos. In: Proceedings of I-KNOW and I-SEMANTICS 2009, pp. 215–225 (2009)
8. Stephan, A., et al.: Autorentool für interaktive Videos im E-Learning. In: Breitner, M.H., et al. (eds.) E-Learning 2010, pp. 143–154. Springer, Heidelberg (2010)

Application of the Multiple Perspectives Model in an Undergraduate Course[*]

Célio Gonçalo Marques[1] and Ana Amélia A. Carvalho[2]

[1] Instituto Politécnico de Tomar, Estrada da Serra, Quinta do Contador,
2300-313 Tomar, Portugal
celiomarques@ipt.pt
[2] Universidade do Minho, Campus de Gualtar,
4710-057 Braga, Portugal
aac@ie.uminho.pt

Abstract. To meet the needs of contemporary society it is crucial that instructors strive to find and employ methodologies that enhance active learning. This paper presents a blended-learning model based on the Cognitive Flexibility Theory, called "Multiple Perspectives Model", and describes students' reactions to its application in a course module of the undergraduate programme in Human Resources Management and Organizational Behaviour offered by the Management School of the Polytechnic Institute of Tomar.

Keywords: Higher Education, Blended-Learning, Multiple Perspectives Model.

1 Introduction

Contemporary higher education faces a series of challenges that stem from lifelong learning needs, globalization and market expansion as well as the strong development of information technologies such as the learning management systems (LMS), the development of mobile technologies, the growth of Web 2.0 tools and the emergence of interactive and immersive virtual reality tools.

The Internet allows access to learning and training exempt from space and time restrictions, enabling an interactive, learner-centred learning. As Harasim [1] points out, "on-line education is more than a new delivery mode. It is a new learning domain" (p. 62). According to Siemens and Tittenberger [2], during the next decade teaching/learning practices will undergo profound changes as universities adapt to global trends at social, political, technological and educational levels. In the face of this new reality, it is of utmost importance that instructors make every effort to find and use new teaching practices where each student plays a key role in the learning process. In this context, the term blended-learning (or mixed learning) seems to have acquired a new dimension. Garrison and Vaughan [3] refer to blended-learning as "a coherent design approach that openly assesses and integrates the strengths of face-to-face and online learning to address worthwhile educational goals" (p.x). These authors believe that "when blended-learning is well understood and implemented, higher education will be transformed in a way not seen since the expansion of higher education in the

---

[*] Research in part funded by CIEd, University of Minho.

N. Reynolds and M. Turcsányi-Szabó (Eds.): KCKS 2010, IFIP AICT 324, pp. 269–280, 2010.
© IFIP International Federation for Information Processing 2010

late 1940s" (p.x). Blended learning must therefore be considered as being strategically important "in the future of universities, their students and teachers as well as in the widening community of professional education and training" (p.1) [4]. Although there are several combinations of blended-learning, there is no widely accepted model [5]. Combination is selected on a case-to-case basis [6]. Our proposal makes use of the Multiple Perspectives Model [7], which is specially suited for advanced learning.

2   The Multiple Perspectives Model

The Multiple Perspectives model is a blended-learning model which integrates a face-to-face component including an introduction to the topic and a tutorial about *Moodle*, as well as an on-line component based on learning objects structured according to the Multi-Perspectives Learning Objects model (MPLO) and the use of a forum and chat communication tools.

2.1   Learning Objects

The origins of the term *learning object* date back to Wayne Hodgins who in 1994 named the CedMA Working Group as "Learning Architectures, APIs and Learning Objects"[8], [9]. Although there is no consensual definition, it seems to us that this is a resource that can be reused in different learning contexts. Its distribution throughout the various information networks and user friendliness enables its wide dissemination and use by a large number of people, whether they are technological experts or not [10].

This approach is similar to some existing models including object-oriented programming; however, its emergence seems to be associated with the expansion of on-line teaching and learning. Its adoption is viewed as a strategic option for enterprises and educational establishments, particularly for higher education institutions. The benefits from using this approach are huge both to learners and content development managers/practitioners [11] including reduction of content development costs [11], [12], easier construction of processes and experiences to meet individual or target audience needs [11], [12] and its use across a variety of hardware and software platforms.

A learning object should be regarded as a digital, self-sufficient unit whose learning outcomes and structure are connected with a given learning theory.

2.2   The Multi-Perspectives Learning Objects Model (MPLO)

The Multiple Perspectives model focuses on the exploration of cases available in the form of learning objects structured according to the MPLO [13], [14].

The MPLO is based on our previous research regarding the Cognitive Flexibility theory [15], [16], [17], [18], [19]. Findings from those investigations evidenced the importance of knowledge deconstruction through multiple themes or perspectives.

The proposed model applies only to advanced levels of acquisition and to complex knowledge domains, which needs to be analysed from multiple perspectives, points of view or themes. It is important to study the situation (mini-case) as it occurs, allowing the learner to acquire a deep comprehension of the subject matter. This approach is context-dependent. It focuses on knowledge application rather than on theoretical aspects.

Each learning object corresponds to a case. It can be a segment of a chapter of a book, a news report, a few frames of a movie, or an event. The case has to be divided into parts (mini-cases). Each mini-case is a small unit that will later be deconstructed or analyzed according to different perspectives.

Once the case is selected, it is important to identify the perspective that will be used in the analysis (deconstruction) of the case (mini-cases). These perspectives can be concepts, theories, points of view, or themes that help the learner understand the situation (mini-case) through different insights. A comment must be written from each perspective that is applied to a mini-case, explaining how this general perspective applies to each particular situation. This is a demanding and time-consuming task for the instructor. However, all this effort is rewarded by learners' comprehension and flexibility in knowledge transfer to new situations.

Each learning object possesses three components that the learner goes through to acquire a deep comprehension of the case and develop cognitive flexibility.

The first component is the case (fig. 1). The learner has access to the full case. He/she has to be familiar with it before starting the deconstruction or analysis process. Some additional information about the case may be provided, which helps the learner to better understand it. The second component presents the perspectives that were selected to analyse the mini-cases. The learner has access to a brief description regarding each perspective to understand its boundaries. References for each perspective are also included. The third component is the deconstruction. This is the most important component. The learner is guided through each mini-case and its multiple perspectives of analysis. He/she views how a situation can be analysed or deconstructed through several perspectives. The learner has to read all comments that explain how each perspective is addressed for each mini-case.

This is a process of knowledge deconstruction and reconstruction. This way, learners develop a deeper understanding regarding the subject under study and improve cognitive flexibility, which is essential to the transfer of knowledge into new situations.

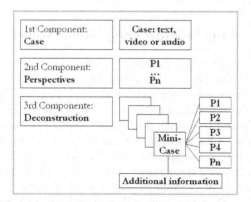

Fig. 1. MPLO model components

2.3 Activities Organized according to the Multiple Perspectives Model

In a course unit or module, several cases can be used which will be made available in the LMS. The *Moodle* platform and SCORM/AICC are used at the Polytechnic Institute of Tomar (IPT).

First, the learners should read all information regarding the case. To support students´ doubts there will be two weekly chat sessions. Using the LMS forum, the instructor will provide questions that will require association within mini-cases that, although apparently different, are approached through the same perspectives.

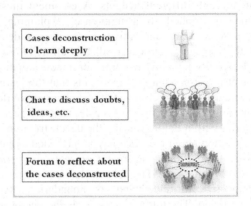

Fig. 2. Multiple Perspectives model components

This is intended to enable learners to have an insight across mini-cases [20]. Once learners have answered the questions, immediate feedback from the instructor is crucial.

This model also presupposes that the instructor guides learners in their self-directed learning, supporting students within the chat sessions and giving them feedback to their replies to the forum questions.

The instructor may combine several cases to each course module. The advantage is to reuse cases in different courses.

3 Application of the Multiple Perspectives Model

In 2009, using a research-action methodology, we applied and validated the Multiple Perspectives Model within higher education [21].

It started with a pilot study held between May and June 2009 intended to check the clarity of tools and instruments to collect data. This study included 34 students attending the Information and Communication Technologies module of the undergraduate programme in Public Administration offered by Tomar Management School. Using the pilot study as a basis, some adjustments to the model and tools have been made.

Our first research-action study started in the beginning of 2009/2010 with the application and validation of the Multiple Perspectives Model to teaching the computer architecture module. Data has been collected using questionnaires, interviews, of LMS (*Moodle*) and a knowledge test. Table 1 demonstrates the structure of first stage research-action study.

Table 1. Structure of Study

Date	Activities
Prior to Module	- Workshop on IPT LMS (*Moodle*) - Tutorials about *Moodle*
1st week: face-to-face activities	- Detailed explanation of the module and relevant work plan. - Learners complete a characterization questionnaire (*Moodle*); - Introduction to the computer architecture theme.
2nd week: on-line activities	- Definition of the weekly work plan (*Moodle*); - Provision of cases 1 and 2 (*Moodle*); - Provision of a question (1) on cases 1 and 2 in the forum (*Moodle*); - Two chat sessions (*Moodle*); - Feedback from the instructor on answers to question 1 (*Moodle*).
3rd week: on-line activities	- Definition of the weekly work plan (*Moodle*); - Provision of cases 3 and 4 (*Moodle*); - Provision of a question (2) on cases 3 and 4 in the forum (*Moodle*); - Two chat sessions (*Moodle*); - Feedback from the instructor on answers to question 2 (*Moodle*).
4th week: on-line and face-to-face activities	- Learners complete opinion survey on the module (*Moodle*); - Knowledge test; - Final commentary about the module; - Interviews.

Prior to module activities, a workshop has been provided to allow learners to familiarise themselves with LMS (*Moodle*). Three tutorials about *Moodle* have also been designed through the *Jing* tool intended for those learners who didn't have the opportunity to attend the workshop.

During the first week there were two face-to-face sessions in order to explain the structure of the module and present the work plan. In these sessions, a characterization questionnaire was completed and learners were introduced to computer architecture.

The second week was run totally on-line. On Sunday, the weekly work plan was supplied, two cases on computer architecture were provided on *Moodle* (cases 1 and 2) and one question about those two cases was launched which should be answered until Friday (question 1). Two chat sessions occurred during the week and were moderated by the instructor (in a time schedule agreed upon by learners) where they could clarify doubts on the cases and the whole computer architecture. During the weekend, the instructor gave feedback on all answers to question 1. Third week activities were identical to those of the second week with provision of cases 3 and 4 on computer architecture as well as a question related to these two cases (question 2).

During the fourth week, learners completed an opinion survey regarding the module and took a knowledge test. Finally, the instructor provided feedback on the answers. Some students were selected for an interview.

In the course module, a referendum regarding the most interesting locations of Tomar has been promoted. This promotion aims to make learners feel more comfortable on-line and allow the participants from outside of Tomar to get familiar with the cultural and natural heritage of the city. In addition to this, some performance tips have occasionally been left in the forum about *Moodle* functionalities and case reading.

3.1 The Instruments for Data Collection

Two questionnaires have been used and evaluated within this study: the sample characterization and the opinion survey on the module. Interviews have also been carried out to clarify less consensual points referred to in the opinion survey.

The characterization questionnaire inquired about age, gender, type of registration (ordinary or employed student), number of module enrolments, whether they had a computer or not, whether they had Internet access or not if so, the type and rate of usage of the Internet connection, their ability to use synchronous and asynchronous communication tools and their willingness to use the Internet to perform learning tasks. The participants were also questioned about preferred times for chat sessions.

Furthermore, the survey collected the learners' opinions about the use of the chat and forum, chat duration, its ability in clarifying doubts, and whether students had consulted the bibliographic references suggested in the cases. The learners were also asked to what extent the forum helped them to identify the gaps in their understanding of specific points of the subject matter and facilitated communication between them and the instructor.

They were also inquired as to the importance of the forum as a tool for learning and reflecting on the module, whether feedback helped them participate more in module subjects, whether it helped them recognise gaps in their understanding of specific points of the subject matter, whether they have obtained feedback from the instructor and to what extent it facilitated learning. This survey also asked whether the cases helped the learners understand the subject matter in the module and whether the cases prepared them to solve specific problems as well as whether they liked this new experience and would study further modules on-line. Finally, they were asked about preferred modes of distance learning as well as the positive and negative aspects of the experience and suggestions to improve them.

Both questionnaires were created and made available through *Moodle*.

For each learner's interview, an individual script has been prepared based on their responses to the opinion questionnaire regarding the module.

3.2 The Sample

The sample consisted of 40 students attending the Computer Applications module of the undergraduate programme in Human Resources Management and Organizational Behaviour offered by the Management School of the Polytechnic of Tomar. The vast majority (70%) of individuals inquired were female students, ranged from 18 to 59 years old. The average age is approximately 27 and the mode around 19.

Half of the individuals are employed students and 88% are enrolled for the first time in this course unit. All participants reported having a computer with Internet access, 85% reported having a laptop, 40% a desktop, 5% a PDA and 3% a netbook.

Internet access is through wireless broadband (65%), ADSL (30%), cable network (10%) and Wi-Fi access spots within the student residences.

Most participants reported connecting to the Internet every day (75%) and the remainder almost every day.

Participants also reported using different Internet tools and services such as e-mail, chat and wikis. The chat is used daily by 55% of the individuals, 30% used it two to three times a week, 13% once a week and 2% hardly used it. Forums are less used than chat: 7% reported participating in forums on a daily basis, 10% weekly, 13% occasionally, 25% hardly ever and 45% never.

When questioned whether they would study further modules through an on-line platform, 48% of the individuals answered "Yes, definitely", 50% "Yes" and 20% didn't know.

3.3 The Presentation and Analysis of Results

Results provided by *Moodle* as well as the participants regarding the use of the forum, chat and case reading are provided hereafter.

Four cases have been provided to participants. Most participants (80%) analysed four cases, 5% three cases, 5% two cases, 5% one case and 5% no cases. The suggested bibliography was consulted by 67% of the participants. Most of those who reported not having consulted it (70%) referred that they didn't have time to do so, 15% didn't consider it as being important and the other 15% consulted other bibliographies.

In the first chat session, 58% of the individuals participated, 6% in the second, 60% in the third and 75% in the fourth (Table 2). The number of interventions varied between 215 and 330. Individuals who did not participate in chat sessions invoked professional motives, *praxe* commitments, computer and Internet problems, family problems, care of his/her baby daughter and lack of doubts.

Table 2. Chat participation (n=40)

Chat session	Participation (%).	Number of Interventions (f)
1st Session	58	215
2nd Session	55	316
3rd Session	60	298
4th Session	75	330

The punctuality rate reported in the first session was low, registering 35%. In order to solve this problem, we posed a question during the opening session and advertised the name of the first student to provide the right answer in the forum as well as the names of those who participated in the forum referencing the most punctual ones from the second session onwards. In the second session there was a slight increase (46%), but it still did not reach 50% because students did not know about the implementation of this novelty. In the third session, however, the percentage of punctual students increased to 80% and in the fourth session it rose even more to 83%.

We verified that 85% answered two questions, 10% one and 5% none (Table 3). Lack of time and the fact that they found it irrelevant were invoked by the latter of students as grounds for not providing a response.

Table 3. Forum participation (n=40)

Questions	Answers	
	(f)	(%)
2 Questions	34	85
1 Question	4	10
None	2	5

3.3.1 Reactions to the Forum and Chat

Most individuals (53%) found the forum very user-friendly, 40% found it easy to use and 7% found it neither easy nor difficult to use.

The chat was described as being very user-friendly by 50% of the individuals. Furthermore, 43% found it easy to use and two individuals found it neither easy nor difficult.

Most individuals (80%) found that the ideal duration for chat sessions was 1 hour. Three individuals, however, found it to be insufficient. Some individuals (13%) had the opportunity to clarify a great number of doubts regarding the subject matter studied in chat sessions, 34% answered many questions, 40% answered some questions and 10% answered a few. One individual reported not having answered any question.

It was verified that 57% of the individuals fully agreed with the fact that chat sessions helped them realise that there were gaps in their understanding of specific aspects of the subject matter, 40% agreed partially and 3% did not know. Most individuals (80%) strongly agreed that the use of the chat facilitated student-instructor communication, 17% partially agreed and 3% did not know.

When questioned about whether detracting from focus in chat sessions was frequent, 13% of the respondents reported strongly disagreeing, 17% partially disagreeing, 7% partially agreeing and 3% strongly agreeing. The majority of individuals (60%) did not know.

Most respondents (74%) fully agreed that the forum is a very important tool in discussing module related topics, the remainder partially agree.

It was observed that 68% of the individuals fully agreed that forum questions contributed to a greater involvement in computer architecture related subjects, 29% agreed partially and 3% did not know.

Very similar figures have been obtained when questioned whether the forum helped them realise that there were gaps in their understanding of specific subject matters in the module. It was observed that 71% of individuals fully agreed with this idea, 26% partially agreed and 3% did not know.

All respondents reported having developed new skills in the forum using the instructor's feedback. It was also expressed that 82% of the respondents fully agreed that instructor's feedback within the forum has largely contributed to their learning and 18% partially agreed with this statement.

3.3.2 Reactions to the On-Line Module

We realized that 92% of the respondents consider that cases helped them understand the module subject matters; and they think this is mainly because cases promote a greater involvement within the subject matters (60%) and they allow different approaches to the problem (29%).

All respondents agreed that cases prepare them better to solve problems. Typical justifications included that cases allow the transfer of knowledge into new situations (66%) and different approaches to the same problem (24%).

It was verified that 48% of respondents liked this on-line module very much, 30% liked it much, 20% liked it and one individual did not like it. The great majority of respondents (95%) were open to study further modules on-line.

When inquired about the preferred type of learning, 88% answered blended-learning, 10% face-to-face learning and 2% fully on-line learning. These results indicate a clear preference for blended-learning and are probably related to the success of this study and therefore the model applied.

Justifications for blended-learning were that mixed learning is more effective than face-to-face or fully on-line learning (57%), it is a more suitable way of conveying knowledge (29%), it is a more comfortable method (11%) and it is a gateway into the future (3%).

When questioned about the positive aspects of the module, 33% answered that all aspects were positive, 23% mentioned the communication/collaboration among all the participants, 12% mentioned the development of useful day-to-day skills, 10% mentioned the communication between colleagues, another 10% mentioned general interaction, 7% of respondents mentioned on-line learning, and 5% learning how to use chat and forums.

As far as the negative aspects are concerned, 88% answered that there were no negative aspects, 5% indicated few chat sessions, another 5% mentioned the time schedule for chat sessions and one individual referred to the need for more intensive face-to-face pre-learning.

As far as the aspects for improvement are concerned, 83% of the respondents answered none, 10% suggested that there should be more chat sessions, 5% mentioned the time schedule as well as the amount of classes and one respondent expressed that more practical cases should be provided.

3.3.3 Results Obtained in the Knowledge Test

Once the on-line activities were completed, participants answered a knowledge test. The mean grade was 11.7 (Table 4). The highest grade was 18.9, the lowest 2.9, and the mode was established at 14.3.

When analysing the grades of the individuals who participated in two chat sessions and answered the forum questions, we find that the mean rises to 13.9 and the lowest grade to 8.6. These students' involvement seems to have a positive impact on learning outcomes.

Table 4. Test results

Descriptive statistics	Module results (0-20 grade points) n=54	Results for students who participated in the chat and the forum (0-20 grade points) n=30
Mean	11.7	13.9
Mode	14.3	14.3
Highest mark	18.9	18.9
Lowest mark	2.9	8.6

3.3.4 Interviews

The interviews allowed us to assess some less positive aspects of the module. We selected thirteen students to be interviewed but only ten showed up.

The most addressed topic was the chat room. According to some of the students interviewed, there should be more chat schedules and they should be earlier. Furthermore, some of them found chat sessions a little confusing due to the large number of participants. One of the students also reported having experienced difficulties in finding the questions and where to answer in the forum. For each question a forum was created and the question was asked in the first forum message. The students were asked to create a new message in order to answer the question but many of them answered directly to the message making it difficult to find the question, which was "lost" itself among the answers.

We have observed that the great majority of interviewed students that showed difficulties with the forum and the chat had neither attended the workshop nor watched the help videos.

Those students preferring face-to-face learning rather than mixed learning or fully on-line learning argue that it is easier to clear doubts face-to-face as opposed to on-line.

All these aspects will be taken into account in a new research-action cycle.

4 Conclusions

Blended-learning may be an answer to meet some of the challenges facing higher education. It meets several needs of contemporary students such as time and space flexibility, it provides new possibilities in project-based learning and allows one to develop cross competencies such as problem analysis and resolution.

The Multiple Perspectives model is a blended-learning model proposal for the development of advanced skills based on the Cognitive Flexibility Theory. This model focuses on the use of learning objects and communication tools of the LMS. Its use in the course Computer Applications of the Human Resources Management and Organizational Behaviour programme produced favourable results and was well accepted among students, which makes us believe that it may be a credible option for all teachers wishing to implement blended learning in their courses.

However, the opinion questionnaire and interviews showed that some adjustments still need to be made. In the next application of the model, chat sessions will be limited to 15 users and subject to prior *Moodle* registration by means of a wiki. Due to this limitation, the number of chat sessions will increase which will enable us to provide afternoon and evening sessions, thus meeting the desire of all students. A contingency plan will be created to cope with possible delays or absences in chat sessions. Most features will be maintained such as the initial chat question, advertising the name of the first student to give the right answer, the participants in that session as well, and the most punctual ones.

Case questions will start to be written in the forum title for easier tracking. In addition to this, a tutorial will be created using Jing software where students will be able to learn how to use the forum to answer the question.

The final comment will made available in podcast format, thus allowing more students to access the comment and listen to it as they wish.

The possibility of implementing *chatbots* for generic questions on how LMS works as well as the use of social bookmarking tools will also be considered. We think this sort of tools may contribute to the development of an on-line learning community stimulated by the use of chat. Ensuring that the students familiarise themselves with the LMS prior to module, either through the workshop or the videos, is also crucial.

References

1. Harasim, L.M.: On-line Education: A New Domain. In: Mason, R.D., Kaye, A.R. (eds.) Mindweave: Communication, Computers and Distance Education. Pergamon Press, Oxford (1989)
2. Siemens, G., Tittenberger, P.: Handbook of Emerging Technologies for Learning (2009), http://umanitoba.ca/learning_technologies/cetl/HETL.pdf
3. Garrison, D.R., Vaughan, N.D.: Blended Learning in Higher Education. Framework, Principles and Guidelines. Jossey-Bass, San Francisco (2008)
4. Stacey, E., Gerbic, P.: Introduction to Blended Learning Practices. In: Stacey, E., Gerbic, P. (eds.) Effective Blended Learning Practices: Evidence-Based in Perspectives in ICT-Facilitated Education, pp. 1–19. IGI Global, Hershey (2009)
5. Bersin, J.: The Blended Learning Book: Best Practises, Proven Methodologies, and Lessons Learned. Wiley, San Francisco (2004)
6. Beer, M., Mason, R.B.: Using a Blended Approach to Facilitate Postgraduate Supervision. Innovations in Education and Teaching International 46(2), 213–226 (2009)
7. Carvalho, A.A.A.: O Modelo Múltiplas Perspectivas: Uma Proposta para o Ensino Online. Lição das Provas de Agregação. Universidade do Minho, Braga (2009)
8. Wiley, D.A.: Connecting Learning Objects to Instructional Design Theory: A Definition, a Metaphor, and a Taxonomy. In: Wiley, D.A. (ed.) The Instructional Use of Learning Objects: Online Version (2000), http://reusability.org/read/chapters/wiley.doc
9. Polsani, P.R.: Use and Abuse of Reusable Learning Objects. Journal of Digital Information 3(4) (2003)
10. Marques, C.G.C., Carvalho, A.A.A.: A Pertinência dos Metadados nos Objectos de Aprendizagem. In: Dias, P., Freitas, C.V., Silva, B., Osório, A., Ramos, A. (Orgs.) Challenges 2007, pp. 432–443. Universidade do Minho, Braga (2007)
11. Shepherd, C.: Objects of Interest, TACTIX, Features, Fastrak Consulting (2000), http://www.fastrak-consulting.co.uk/tactix/features/objects/objects.htm
12. Nurmi, S., Jaakkola, T.: Problems Underlying the Learning Object Approach. E-Learning News 2(1) (2006)
13. Carvalho, A.A.A.: A Model to Structure Learning Objects: MPLO (Multiple-Perspectives Learning Objects). In: Abbott, C., Lustigova, Z. (eds.) ITET 2007 – Information Technology for Education and Training, pp. 6–15. ETIC Prague, Prague, (2007)
14. Carvalho, A.A.A.: Looking for a Model to structure Learning Objects: MPLO (Multiple-Perspectives Learning Objects). In: Bastiaens, T., Carliner, S. (eds.) Proceedings of E-Learn 2007 World Conference on E-Learning in Corporate, Government, Healthcare, & Higher Education, pp. 37–45. AACE, Chesapeake, VA (2007)

15. Carvalho, A.A.A., Dias, P.: Hypermedia Environment Using a Case-based Approach to Foster the Acquisition of Complex Knowledge. In: Muldner, T., Reeves, T.C. (eds.) ED-Media/ED-Telecom 1997, Proceedings of the Conferences on Educational Multimedia/Hypermedia and Telecommunications, pp. 142–149. AACE, Charlottesville, vol. I (1997)
16. Carvalho, A.A.A.: How to Develop Cognitive Flexibility in a Web Course. In: Crawford, M., Simonson, M. (eds.) 23rd Annual Proceedings of AECT 2000, pp. 53–60. Nova Southeastern University, North Miami Beach (2000)
17. Carvalho, A.A., Moreira, A.: Criss-crossing Cognitive Flexibility Theory based Research in Portugal: An Overview. Interactive Educational Multimedia 11, 1–26 (2005)
18. Carvalho, A.A.A., Pereira, V.: A Web-based learning platform to promote cognitive flexibility through deconstruction and reflection. In: Nall, J., Robson, R. (eds.) E-Learn 2004 – World Conference on E-Learning in Corporate, Government, Healthcare, & Higher Education, pp. 1120–1126. Association for the Advancement of Computing in Education, Norfolk (2004)
19. Marques, C.G.C., Carvalho, A.A.A.: O Fórum como Meio de Reflexão na Aprendizagem do Módulo de Arquitectura de Computadores. In: Mendes, A., Pereira, I., Costa, R. (eds.) SIIE 2005. Instituto Politécnico de Leiria, Leiria (2005)
20. Spiro, R., Jehng, J.-C.: Cognitive Flexibility and Hypertext: Theory and Technology for the Non-linear and Multidimensional Traversal of Complex Subject Matter. In: Nix, D., Spiro, R. (eds.) Cognition, Education and Multimedia: Exploring Ideas in High Technology, pp. 163–205. Lawrence Erlbaum Associates, Hillsdale (1990)
21. McNiff, J., Lomax, P., Whitehead, J.: You and Your Action Research Project. Routledge, London (1996)

Mobile Learning: Using SMS in Educational Contexts

Adelina Moura and Ana Amélia Carvalho

University of Minho
Campus de Gualtar
4710-057 Braga, Portugal
adelina8@gmail.com, aac@ie.uminho.pt

Abstract. The Short Message Service (SMS) technology is one of the most powerful mobile technologies in current usage. Most students own a mobile phone with free SMS which can be used for learning. In this paper we explain how we used SMS for teaching and learning languages (both native and foreign). The conducted experiment presented a range of opportunities for integrating text into teaching and learning strategies and for demystifying the use of SMS in educational contexts. Via SMS technology we can deliver several learning activities to students easily and immediately. The research findings showed that students had positive perceptions about the experiment and SMS use for learning improvement and the use of their own mobile phone as a learning tool. All groups showed interest in receiving educational content via SMS. Some students greatly improved their language learning performance.

Keywords: Mobile learning, SMS, mobile phones, mobile contents, language learning.

1 Introduction

Never before in the history of education, has a technology been so rapidly adopted as mobile technologies. The evolution of wireless communication has created a new educational paradigm called mobile learning (m-learning). This includes the use of mobile devices (phone, PDA, pocket PC and media players like the iPod) for educational purposes [1]. Mobile learning experiences can take many forms and have different objectives. The goal is not to challenge or replace other forms of interaction, it is a complementary methodology that can support, enrich and enhance the learning experience.

Statistics show that more than 3 billion people around the world own a mobile phone. The penetration of mobile devices into many European countries exceeds 90% and younger generations seem to be the most dependent on this device for communication [2]. However, according to Schick [3], most people with mobile phones only use their basic functions, such as voice communication and SMS.

SMS technology is a reliable communication system and popular among mobile phone users. It has become a trend as a means of communication throughout the world, even in less developed countries. It has been considered by several authors [1], [2], [4] as an appropriate tool for education.

N. Reynolds and M. Turcsányi-Szabó (Eds.): KCKS 2010, IFIP AICT 324, pp. 281–291, 2010.

Several studies, such as [5], [6], [7], [8], [9], [10], [11], [12], [13] suggest the integration of SMS by educational institutions to maintain contact with students in teaching and learning contexts. In this paper we present a learning environment supported by SMS for learning languages (Portuguese as mother tongue, and French as foreign language). We designed this study based on a few teaching and learning projects by SMS described above.

2   Mobile Learning: A New Concept in Education

The use of mobile phones and other mobile devices is having an impact on where learning takes place in many areas and contexts, including language learning [14]. Mobile technologies do not depend on a fixed location and are enable users to learn or access information. This helps maximise significant changes in teaching and learning practices.

A number of publications over the last decade [13], [14], [15], [16], [17] show that mobile learning is a growing field with interest in many areas, particularly education. Although there is no consensus on the definition of mobile learning, because it is a rapidly evolving field and due to the ambiguity of the term mobile [14], experiments and pilot studies have been conducted in this field in recent years. While the term learning is undoubted, the mobile concept can refer to the mobility of the learner as well as the mobility of content. In this sense, mobility should not only be understood in terms of spatial movement, but also in terms of processing time and without physical boundaries, thus widening the horizons of learning and information access.

Despite the fact that m-learning focuses heavily on mobility, the most important aspect is its educational effect. Through appropriate technology, learners can participate in activities directly related to their needs and contexts (just-in-time learning). This forces educators to rethink teaching and learning processes.

3   SMS: A Technology for Learning in the Digital Age

The adoption of SMS as an educational resource has become popular in recent years [18]. SMS is a technology that allows mobile phones to send and receive short text messages. The original size of the messages was 160 characters, but the latest mobile phone models support can receipt of messages with up to 612 characters.

Recently there has been much interest from academic institutions regarding the use of mobile technologies to support teaching and learning. The evolution of mobile devices, although not designed specifically for education, is increasing opportunities in education, with the potential for mobile learning contexts [12]. One example with great educational potential is sending an SMS via mobile phone that has great educational potential [2], thus meeting the needs of society in the digital age. Over the last decade, various SMS-based projects have been created to support the teaching and learning process, particularly in language learning.

3.1   SMS-Based Projects in Educational Institutions

Several studies and experiments regarding the use of SMS in different educational contexts have taken place during recent years. The following examples constitute the basis for this project.

An experiment was conducted by Naismith [8] in a university context based on sending SMS messages to students about the cancellation of classes, information, reminders, and academic pursuits. This administrative communication with students was positive and staff expected to extend this project to other institutional sectors. In another study, a tool was implemented for communication and discussion [5] based on sending SMS messages via PDA that aimed to initiate discussions and collaborative work. Results showed that the technology improved collaborative work in literature courses. A study conducted by Song [9] explored the role of SMS in learning the vocabulary of English as a foreign language. This involved ten participants and the final results showed a significant improvement in the students' performance and their attitude towards the use of SMS in learning vocabulary. Another experiment conducted by Nix et al. [10] showed the success achieved by using SMS messages to reduce early abandonment of courses by university students. It seems that sending SMS messages to students identified as being at risk was successful in helping retain students in the system.

The TXT-2-LRN system, developed by Scornavacca et al. [11], based on SMS allows the interaction between students and teachers in the classroom. Students can send questions and comments to the teacher's computer via SMS. The project PLS TXT UR Thoughts, conducted by Markett et al. [7], allowed students to send SMS in real time through their personal mobile phones during class and online after school and encouraged interactivity with the classroom.

Other authors, such as Goh & Hooper [18], explored the feasibility of using SMS in mobile phones to promote learning through the use of crossword SMS environments in the classroom, with positive participation.

3.2 SMS and m-Learning

Since mobile phones and SMS communication are so popular outside school we only need to combine these two technologies, import them, and adopt them in educational contexts. SMS is a part of m-learning (fig.1).

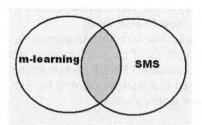

Fig. 1. SMS a part of m-learning (adapted from Lominé & Buckhingham [1])

In initial conversations with students about using SMS in an educational environment, the reaction is one of unfamiliarity, but this awkwardness will diminish following contact with activities and realising the benefits of using it. What is important is that we ensure the educational value of this resource by delivering useful content and creating teaching strategies for students. Mobile phones have become a "high tech" device because they have a camera, Internet access, and the ability to install a large number of applications. SMS is considered "low tech", when compared to the use of sound, images and videos which will make m-learning more creative and dynamic, particularly in language learning, but it should not be neglected. In addition to mobility SMS presents other advantages [1]:

i)   it forces users to express themselves concisely;
ii)   the written text uses very little memory thus keeping costs to a minimum;
iii)   using it does not require technical learning.

3.3   The Use of SMS for Learning Languages

Several authors [4], [6], [9], [19] consider SMS technology to be suitable for language learning. The possibility for students to access useful information anywhere and anytime is a potential of SMS technology [1]. Mobile devices, particularly mobile phones, are ideal for the promotion of learning by sending students SMS learning units in hours and days planned to optimize their free time.

A study was conducted based on learning Italian via SMS in an Australian university [6]. Students were sent new words, definitions and examples of words in context by SMS. Students could read these materials in between classes. The final remarks presented positive results.

Another study, conducted by Lu [20], reported the use of SMS for learning English as a foreign language in Taiwan. Messages containing vocabulary were sent to students during their lessons. They read the messages regardless of location and time. Students showed a preference for learning through the mobile phone rather than the computer because mobiles are more convenient than PCs in many situations.

In Japan, Thornton & Houser [21] conducted a study using SMS and e-mail to teach English vocabulary. Teachers introduced five words weekly as well as messages sent with mini-lessons three times a day via SMS. The lessons included learning simple terms, some explanatory words, and a review of the words learned. This provided a positive result in learning new English words.

An experiment was carried out with SMS to support the learning of technical vocabulary [22]. Spaced repetitions of the same message were sent on different days through an SMS-based system called MOLT (mobile learning tool) and developed by the authors. Results showed that students enjoyed the experiment and learned new words with the help of their mobile phones.

4   Using SMS for Language Learning: Infrastructure

In order to develop the learning-via-SMS experiment we started with ideas presented by some authors [2], [4] together with the fact that most students always have their mobile phone with them and use it mainly to communicate via SMS. Three objectives guided this project:

i)   to integrate the phone as a learning tool;
ii)   to explore a learning environment for SMS to promote language learning inside and outside the school;
iii)   to encourage students to participate spontaneously and independently in learning outside of the classroom.

This experience of learning via SMS allowed individual or group SMS messages to be sent. Student phone numbers were stored in a computer database which allowed teachers to send quick messages to each individual student or to the whole group.

The model was based on the Vodafone "SMS by Mail" system in order to provide students with curricular content units and other information via SMS. The SMS messages were written in Outlook on the teacher's computer and sent via the SMS by Mail system to student's mobile phones, to be read, stored and responded. The students in turn sent the replies to the teacher's mobile phone (fig. 2).

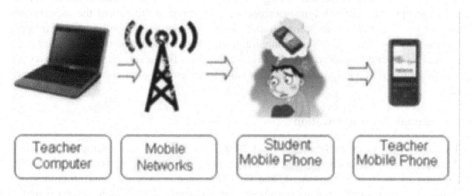

Fig. 2. SMS learning infrastructure

5 Study Description

The reported study was an exploratory one and was part of a larger study on the use of mobile phones as learning tools. We used a qualitative research methodology, with multiple cases using new educational technologies [23].

Once we had verified that all students owned a mobile phone, and that the majority had contracts with the same provider, with free SMS between SIM cards on the same network, we felt we had met the conditions for developing a learning environment by SMS in Portuguese and French classes. For about six weeks, text messages were sent daily, three-times a day, in a schedule agreed upon with students. The activities were divided into three scenarios:

i)   units of learning to read and store on mobiles not requiring student response;
ii)   activities that ask questions or demand tasks;
iii)   activities including collaborative tasks (table 1).

The activities were spread over the duration of the experiment. Approximately one hundred messages were sent and more than nine hundred received.

Table 1. Three scenarios of activities by SMS

Scenario 1 Learning unities to read and store	Scenario 2 Requesting Activities	Scenario 3 Collaborative Activities
- Thoughts - Curricular Contents - Word of the Day (Dictionary)	- Quizzes - "Who Wants to Be a Millionaire" - Read Daily - (fables) - Riddles - Proverbs	- Writing a collaborative micro story at a distance - Writing a collaborative micro story face-to-face

5.1 Data Collection

Data collection was conducted through two questionnaires, individual interviews, and focus groups. The opinion questionnaire was answered at the end of the experiment and aimed to collect information about students' perceptions regarding the activities carried out by SMS. The questionnaire used closed questions (dual or multiple-choice), open-ended questions and a Likert scale with five levels (strongly disagree to strongly agree). The individual interviews and focus groups were conducted at the end of the study.

5.2 Sample Characterization

This study took place in the school year 2008/2009, both in Escola Secundária Carlos Amarante and Escola Profissional de Braga, and was attended by four groups (table 2), aged 15 to 20 in groups A, B, and C. Those aged between 22 and 56 composed group D. A total of 68 students participated in this study, 46% female and 54% male. Participants of Group B were from a private vocational school and the other groups were from a public high school. Participants from group D were adult students who attended evening classes.

Table 2. Participant's profile

Groups	Group A (n=27)		Group B (n=18)		Group C (n=18)		Group D (n=5)	
Sex	f	%	f	%	f	%	f	%
Female	0	0	18	100	10	56	3	60
Male	27	100	0	0	8	44	2	40

5.3 Data Analysis

Data obtained from the questionnaire focused on two aspects:

i)   the educational value of learning activities by SMS;

ii)   the evaluation of learning activities by SMS. Data collected through individual interviews and focus groups helped confirm the data obtained in the questionnaire, and gave the data reliability.

Table 3. Educational value of learning activities by SMS

Items	Answer	Group A (n=27)		Group B (n=18)		Group C (n=18)		Group D (n=5)	
		f	%	f	%	f	%	f	%
Receiving stories and fables	Yes	11	4 1	10	56	14	78	5	100
motivated reading	No	16	59	8	44	4	22	0	0
Receiving word definitions	Yes	21	78	18	100	17	94	5	100
helped to enrich vocabulary	No	6	22	0	0	1	6	0	0
The set of all activities	Yes	18	67	16	89	17	94	5	100
encouraged learning	No	9	33	2	11	1	6	0	0

5.3.1 Educational Value of Learning Activities by SMS

We asked participants about the educational value of the daily "Word of the Day", reading activities and all the other learning activities by SMS such as: stories and fables which motivated the students to read (table 3).

The majority of respondents in groups B (56%) and C (78%) and all those in group D found that daily reading through stories and fables motivated reading, while most of those in group A (59%) responded negatively. Group A is composed of males; most of them (67%) did not like studying or reading. However, 41% of them found that reading through SMS motivated them to read. This strategy may have educational potential, with regards to the motivation for reading in individuals with this profile. All participants in groups B and D as well as the majority of respondents in groups A (78%) and C (94%) reported that the activity "Word of the Day" helped to enrich their vocabulary. For all the activities sent by SMS, all those in group D and the majority of other respondents (67% A, B, 89%, C 94%) said it motivated them to learn.

5.3.2 Evaluation of the SMS Learning Experience

To evaluate the participants' reactions in relation to this learning environment by SMS, we questioned students about:

i)   the satisfaction or dissatisfaction of scenario 1 learning units;
ii)   the degree of difficulty of scenario 2 learning units.

5.3.2.1   Students' Reactions to the Scenario 1 Learning Units. We questioned participants about their satisfaction or dissatisfaction in receiving learning units to read and store: "Word of the Day" for the construction of a dictionary on their mobile phone, several course contents to store on the device, and thoughts for reflection (table 4).

The majority of respondents in group A (56%), B (67%) and C (78%) and all those in group D liked the activity "Word of the day". These results are consistent with those obtained in other studies [6].

All respondents from group D and the majority of respondents from groups B (72%) and C (78%) liked to receive the curricular contents, but for the majority of respondents in group A (56%), this was irrelevant. Two students responded negatively.

Table 4. Students' reactions to the scenario 1 learning units

Items		Group A (n=27)		Group B (n=18)		Group C (n=18)		Group D (n=5)	
		f	%	f	%	f	%	f	%
Word of the Day (dictionary)	Positive	14	56	12	67	14	78	5	100
	Indifferent	11	44	6	33	4	22	0	0
	Negative	0	0	0	0	0	0	0	0
Curricular contents	Positive	10	37	13	72	14	78	5	100
	Indifferent	15	56	5	28	4	22	0	0
	Negative	2	7	0	0	0	0	0	0
Thoughts	Positive	14	52	16	89	14	78	5	100
	Indifferent	12	44	2	11	4	22	0	0
	Negative	1	4	0	0	0	0	0	0

Table 5. Degree of difficulty of the scenario 2 learning units

Items	Answers	Group A (n=27)		Group B (n=18)		Group C (n=18)		Group D (n=5)	
		f	%	f	%	f	%	f	%
Multiple Choice (curricular content)	Easy	15	55	5	25	11	61	2	40
	Moderate	11	41	13	75	7	39	3	60
	Demanding	1	4	0	0	0	0	0	0
Game: Who wants to be a millionaire?	Easy	11	41	5	28	7	39	2	40
	Moderate	14	52	11	61	11	61	3	60
	Demanding	2	7	2	11	0	0	0	0
Proverbs	Easy	8	30	8	44	6	33	1	20
	Moderate	18	66	9	50	11	61	4	80
	Demanding	1	4	1	6	1	6	0	0
Riddles	Easy	9	33	4	22	5	28	1	20
	Moderate	17	63	14	78	11	61	4	80
	Demanding	1	4	0	0	2	11	0	0
Daily reading (fables - moral of the story)	Easy	11	41	7	39	6	33	2	40
	Moderate	12	44	10	55	9	50	3	60
	Demanding	4	15	1	6	3	17	0	0

Most participants in groups A (52%), B (89%) and C (78%) and all the individuals in group D liked receiving the "Thoughts".

5.3.2.2 Degree of Difficulty of Scenario 2 Learning Units. The activities that asked students for one reply were intended to promote the reading and understanding of the different information units that were sent. In order to promote interaction between students and teachers, these activities were questions that students had to answer, so we polled students about the degree of difficulty of each activity (table 5).

The multiple choice activities with curricular content were easy for most participants in groups A (55%) and C (61%), and moderate for the majority of respondents in groups B (75%) and D (60%). The game "Who wants to be a millionaire?", Proverbs and Riddles were considered moderate by the majority of respondents from all groups. A daily reading based on fables followed by the identification of the moral of the story was considered moderate by less than half in group A (44%), half of respondents in group C, 55% in group B and 60% in group D. The fact that these activities had some degree of difficulty challenged the students to build knowledge. Many of them asked family members to look for other resources (Internet, books, etc.) to find the correct response.

5.3.2.3   Reaction to all Activities Sent by SMS. We asked students whether or not they liked all activities sent by SMS (table 6).

Table 6. Reaction to all activities sent by SMS

Did you like the activities by SMS?	Group A (n=27)		Group B (n=18)		Group C (n=18)		Group D (n=5)	
	f	%	f	%	f	%	f	%
Yes	25	93	17	94	17	94	5	100
No	2	7	1	6	1	6	0	0

All respondents in group D and the majority of participants in groups A (93%), B (94%) and C (94%) enjoyed all activities sent by SMS. The same satisfaction was confirmed by data collected through individual interviews and focus groups. All students interviewed stated that they enjoyed this type of learning. In individual interviews, students said they had improved their learning: "The SMS helped me learn the foreign language ... and I assimilated better the information that was sent", "I liked the SMS ... so much content ... it helped a lot"; "The SMS sent by the teacher ... in leisure time I copied it into my notebook and I learned better".

Students who carried out the collaborative activities by SMS to create a micro story through SMS, face-to-face and at a distance said they liked it because it was a different way of working in pairs. It helped them interact and solve problems.

6   Conclusion

In this paper we have presented a study about the development of learning languages with the support of SMS. Despite the size limitations of SMS messages, they seemed to be, in some scenarios, such as language learning, a quick and effective way of providing students with small learning units. We believe that this kind of practice can provide students and teachers with innovative learning experiences by taking advantage of the ubiquitous nature of mobile phones, the infrastructure of the SMS, and the ability to send relevant information. As noted by participants in the study, the contents were condensed and they facilitated reading and its assimilation. Receiving information broken into small units seemed to be easily understood by students [24]. In general, students liked the activities, recognised them as stimulants and felt that they promoted learning.

We must not be dazzled by technology. The teaching strategies and methods performed with technology are of utmost importance [25]. It is important that teachers promote interaction in the classroom because it has been shown that it improves learning [7], and mobile technologies enable interaction inside and outside the classroom.

The characteristics of mobile devices allow learners to construct knowledge in different contexts and to access information anywhere, anytime. One advantage of this educational concept is the possibility of interaction (teacher-student-student). The portability of these devices allows users to take notes or collect data on an ongoing basis and at any moment. Directly on the device they can write a text, capture an image, make a video or record voice. The mobile phone is a collaborative tool that allows multiple students to work together on a task even when in remote locations, and it also promotes the engagement of learners.

Mobile devices are becoming increasingly ubiquitous, enabling their use in an educational context. The ubiquity of mobile devices will make m-learning an important way of providing education and training in the future.

Acknowledgments. Thanks to Vodafone for sponsoring the SMS by Mail service used in this study, and teacher mobile devices (mobile phone and netbook).

This research is in part funded by CIEd, University of Minho.

References

1. Lominé, L.L., Buckhingham, C.: M-learning: texting (SMS) as a teaching & learning tool in higher arts education (2009), http://www.elia-artschools.org/teachers_artes/_downloads/papers/Lomine.pdf/
2. Traxler, J.: Case studies: Introduction and overview. In: Kukulska-Hulme, A., Traxler, J. (eds.) Mobile Learning: A Handbook for Educators and Trainers, pp. 70–75. Routledge, London (2005)
3. Schick, C.: The mobile lifestyle: How the fusion of the mobile and the Internet have changed the way we live, learn, and play. In: Keynote Speaker of the 6th International Conference on Mobile Learning. Melbourne, Australia (2007)
4. Kukulska-Hulme, A., Shield, L.: An Overview of Mobile Assisted Language Learning: from content delivery to supported collaboration and interaction. ReCALL 20(3), 249–252 (2008)
5. Bollen, L., Eimler, S., Hoppe, H.: SMS-based Discussions – Technology enhanced collaboration for a literature course. In: Proceedings of the 2nd IEEE International Workshop on Wireless and Mobile Technologies in Education, pp. 209–210. IEEE Computer Society, Los Alamitos (2004)
6. Levy, M., Kennedy, C.: Learning Italian via mobile SMS. In: Kukulska-Hulme, A., Traxler, J. (eds.) Mobile Learning: A Handbook for Educators and Trainers, pp. 76–83. Routledge, London (2005)
7. Markett, C., Arnedillo Sánchez, I., Weber, S., Tangney, B.: Using short message service to encourage interactivity in the classroom. Computers & Education 46, 280–293 (2006)
8. Naismith, L.: Using text messaging to support administrative communication in higher education. Active Learning in Higher Education 8, 155–171 (2007)
9. Song, Y.: SMS enhanced vocabulary learning for mobile audiences. International Journal of Mobile Learning and Organisation 2(1), 81–98 (2008)
10. Nix, J., Russel, J., Keegan, D.: Mobile learning/SMS (Short Messaging System) academic administration kit (2005), http://www.eden-online.org/contents/publications/SMS/Ericsson.Mobile.A5.pdf

11. Scornavacca, E., Huff, S., Marshall, S.: Developing a SMS-based classroom interaction system. In: Proceedings of the Conference on Mobile Learning Technologies and Applications, pp. 47–54. Massey University, Auckland (2007)
12. So, S.: The development of a SMS-based teaching and learning system. Journal of Educational Technology Development and Exchange 2(1), 113–124 (2009)
13. Moura, A., Carvalho, A.: Mobile learning: two experiments on teaching and learning with mobile phones. In: Hijón-Neira, R. (ed.) Advanced Learning, pp. 89–103. In-Teh, Vukovar (2009)
14. Kukulska-Hulme, A.: Will mobile learning change language learning? ReCALL 21(2), 157–165 (2009)
15. Kukulska-Hulme, A., Traxler, J.: Mobile Learning: A Handbook for Educators and Trainers. Routledge, London (2005)
16. Faux, F., McFarlane, A., Roche, N., Facer, K.: Handhelds: learning with handheld technologies. In: Handbook for Futurelab (2006),
    http://www.futurelab.org.uk/research/handbooks/05_01.htm/
17. Sharples, M.: Big issues in mobile learning. In: Report of a workshop by the Kaleidoscope Network of Excellence Mobile Learning Initiative. University of Nottingham, UK (2006)
18. Goh, T., Hooper, V.: To TxT or not to TxT: That's the puzzle. Journal of Information Technology Education 6, 441–453 (2007)
19. Pincas, A.: Using mobile phone support for use of Greek during the Olympic games 2004. International Journal of Instructional Technology & distance Learning 1(6) (2004),
    http://itdl.org/Journal/Jun_04/editor.htm
20. Lu, M.: Effectiveness of vocabulary learning via mobile phone. Journal of Computer Assisted Learning 24, 515–525 (2008)
21. Thornton, P., Houser, C.: Using mobile phones in English Education in Japan. Journal of Computer Assisted Learning 21, 217–228 (2005)
22. Cavus, N., Ibrahim, D.: M-Learning: An experiment in using SMS to support learning new English language words. British Journal of Educational Technology 40(1), 78–91 (2009)
23. Yin, R.K.: Case study research: Design and methods. Sage, Newbury Park (1984)
24. Habitzel, K., Märk, T.D., Stehno, B., Prock, S.: Microlearning: Emerging concepts, practices and technologies after e-learning. In: Proceedings of Microlearning 2005 Learning & Working in New Media. Conference Series, Innsbruck University Press (2006),
    http://www.microlearning.org/micropapers/microlearning2005_p
    roceedings_digitalversion.pdf/
25. Chisholm, L.A.: Micro-Learning in the Lifelong Learning Context. In: Proceedings of Microlearning 2005 Learning & Working in New Media. Conference Series, Innsbruck University Press (2006),   http://www.microlearning.org/micropapers/
    microlearning2005_proceedings_digitalversion.pdf/

Making Computer Learning Easier for Older Adults: A Community Study of Tuition Practices

Michael Nycyk and Margaret Redsell

Skylarkers 60 and Better Program, 20 Skylark Street, Brisbane, Queensland, Australia
info@skylarkers.net

Abstract. Older adults are under increasing pressure to use information technologies, yet are reluctant to learn computer software due to difficulties with ways of teaching such skills. This paper argues that examining tutoring techniques in a community computer training centre is useful to discovering why they will persist with learning. Using a Grounded Theory study design, the theory that emerged that accounted for continuance was the tutoring practices and the relationships that were built between tutor and learner. Examples from the data are presented to support the findings that link certain ways of practicing computer tutoring with repeat lesson attendance. This paper contributes to understanding the types of tutoring practices that can encourage older learners to continue the learning journey in later life. In turn, this assists with overcoming the digital divide older learners not skilled in computer use experience and allows them to participate in an increasing technologically driven society.

Keywords: computer training, older adults, digital divide.

1 Introduction to Study

As computer professionals our goal is to have our technologies used by society for the betterment of humankind. Education and training in computer technologies is a vital part of using them successfully. In order to be inclusive all age groups need to be considered as users and often older adults, for this paper defined as those over sixty years of age, are often excluded from computer training. In contemporary society the pressure for older adults to use the internet and computer software to find information and accomplish tasks is increasingly technologically dependent. How to encourage older adults to undertake and persist with computer education through community computer tuition practices is the subject of this paper. An answer to satisfying the computer training needs of this group lies in studying the types of community based tuition practices computer professionals teach older adults.

This paper's purpose is to demonstrate through a case study of a community centre's computer tuition programme how skilling older adults in computer software use is achieved economically and efficiently. This Grounded Theory study also describes the personal and societal benefits older people obtain from persistently learning computer software with empathic patient tutors. The discussion will be centred on why and what type of computer software tuition works for older adults. The community centre and its tuition practices will be described and the research study, its outcomes and

N. Reynolds and M. Turcsányi-Szabó (Eds.): KCKS 2010, IFIP AICT 324, pp. 292–300, 2010.

implications, and what was found in terms of successful tuition for older adults, is also reported. Computer and internet training is influenced by the design quality of the training which is its major success factor [1]. Tutors are chiefly responsible for that quality. This paper will explore tuition practices and what accounts for the success of the computer tuition program at Skylarkers 60 and Better Program in Brisbane.

2 Computer Training and Older Adult Populations

The risk to older adults of experiencing a digital divide, that gap between individuals and opportunities to access information technologies and the internet [2], is high if they are not trained in software use. Older adults not competent in computer software and internet skills can be at a disadvantage in participating in society and the economy. There is more information being placed on the internet, more use of email and social network sites to stay in contact with others. However, the argument that tuition makes a significant difference in addressing the digital divide problem is a growing theme in computer literature.

Early studies that suggest supportive tuition works with older adults was illustrated by Danowski and Sacks [3] whose experiments with older adults concluded that older adults repeatedly use computers if a tutor was present giving individual instruction to them. Their finding suggested supporting older learners through often complex and frustrating software applications encouraged learners to continue learning the programs. In turn, older adults' negative perceptions and attitudes towards computer software learning can change towards one of seeing benefits of learning computers. Computer experiences with tutor support can change the ease of use, remove frustrations and worries, as well as reduce the perceived complexity of navigation [4].

From a technical perspective, software trainers and researchers measure computer training success through understanding, learning performance, and motivation to use, by describing attitudes towards a system or software [5]. Much research relies on statistical methods to measure such variables as performance and motivation. However, more research over time has used qualitative methods to uncover reasons for success or failure of older adult's computer training. Some reasons include the level of caution older adults have towards computers if the tasks seem too difficult or no support is offered by anyone [6]. Other researchers suggest that the software should always be relevant and interesting [7]. The theme of the usefulness and relevance of software to older occurs in much research. This is important to note because often older adults will perceive computers as being for younger people. Finally, there is a constant call for designers to design software with older audiences in mind [8].

Computer training needs to cater to the desires and wishes of the older adult learning community. For example, Kim [9] in reviewing literature on older adults and computer learning says many pitfalls that exist on the internet, such as security and identity issues, need to be taught. More research is also called for to explore the long-term outcomes of computer training to find out the nuances and complexities of why older adults will find some software useful and others not. The importance of understanding the success or not of computer software training of older adults is argued strongly by Hollis-Sawyer and Sterns who claim computer training must always meet the individual learning and motivational needs of the older person to encourage continuation of training [10]. This paper argues that the Skylarkers Computer Tuition

Programme meets the individual needs of the student and assists in overcoming the digital divides older adults' experience.

3 The Community Centre Research Site

This research took place at Skylarkers 60 and Better Program, located in Inala, an outer suburb of Brisbane. The centre has a primary goal to enable older people at the local community level to participate in decisions and activities which affect their health and well-being [11]. The aim of healthy ageing at the centre is to organise and deliver activities that develop informal and forming community networks. It reflects The World Health Organisation's 1946 definition of health as 'a state of complete physical, mental and social well-being, rather than merely the absence of disease' [12].

The computer lessons began in 1996 and continue at the time of writing this paper. Most lessons are student and tutor only though the centre periodically runs a group workshop called Computers for the Absolutely Terrified. Volunteer tutors come from the community and employment training programs. They were of mixed ages, mostly male and either possessed some form of information technology qualification or had a very strong interest and practical experience in computers. Students' ages ranged from 55 to over 80 years of age. Lessons were run with adult educator Knowles [13] principles; students were to learn topics according to their past experiences and goals and importantly, the tutor had to be interested in the student's skill and personal development. Lessons were kept affordable at five dollars a session.

The computer topics taught were mostly software related, though tutors did assist with computer hardware issues. A problem solving approach was used with the tutor discussing the goals each student had before embarking on a course of study. The main software applications taught are Microsoft Word and Excel for letter writing and document production. Internet applications taught included information searching, email use and effectively using search engines. The tutors worked with students on complex software training applications such as using Photoshop to fix photographs, teaching database creation, website building and researching family histories. As research suggests, more adults want training in social networking sites, which tutors teach [14].

4 Research Study and Design

The study and research design was motivated by a primary observation; the centre manager observed that older adults were repeatedly attending lessons over a long period of time. Finding out the reasons for this became the centre's priority and management turned to the skills of researchers at The University of Queensland, Brisbane. The research question was what accounted for the high level of repeat computer lessons older adults learners at the centre were attending? A decision was made to design the research according to the systematic principles and methods of Strauss and Corbin's Grounded Theory methodology. This is a qualitative methodology developing theory from data by use of developing concepts and categories from interview and observational written records [15].

The primary data collection method was observations of student tutor interactions. Using Emerson et al [16] as a guide to writing field notes, the words and actions of each student tutor lesson were recorded. A total of 150 lessons were observed. This allowed the researchers to observe the types of interactions during the lessons and the reactions of the students to what the tutor's were telling them. To triangulate the data undertook fourteen semi-structured learner interviews. The age of the interviewees was from 65 to 76 and all attended lessons for a minimum of six months. These were used to gather more in-depth information and uncover views on the tutoring program and student experiences they had obtained from lessons. Interview questions focused on asking them to describe their experiences with computer technology and what computer problems of any kind they had solved by coming to lessons.

The analysis began soon after the observation data began being gathered. We consulted researchers and authors who had used Grounded Theory in their doctoral and research work specifically related to information technology issues of a broad scope. For example, Pace's [17] work on web interactions used Grounded Theory to analyse data by constant comparison methods in four stages: generating categories and their properties; integrating categories and their properties; delimiting the theory; and writing the theory. This is the direction the analysis took. Also used were procedures advocated by White and Weatherall [18] in their study of older adult computer users. Fieldnote and interview data was analysed using N6 qualitative computer software.

Grounded theory first uses open coding where a category is applied to the data text. The category is the abstract term that applies to the text. For example, all text on what software was used by the learner was grouped under the category of 'Software'. Each category is ascribed a property, which are the attributes of the property. For example, with 'Software" the attributes were 'use of', 'types of' and 'experiences with'; it is giving something a set of descriptors of what the observed thing is. Once these categories and properties have been assembled the axial coding takes place. This coding looks for links between the categories and groups them together [19]. Table 1 illustrates this process on how categories are arrived at from interview question, collected data and open and axial coding:

Table 1. Example of Grounded Theory Analysis Process

Interview Question	Transcript Text	Open Coding	Axial Coding
What is your opinion of the tutors at Skylarkers overall?	Well they're mostly pretty happy-go-lucky people and that puts you at ease straight away. they all seem to be quite with what they're doing and the vibes are passed onto you, when your learning, if they're happy with what they're doing well you certainly pick up the vibes that they're happy with what they're doing and they're happy to be there doing what they do.	Feels reassured, positive experience of learning, positive view of tutor	Tutor Learner Relationship

Once the axial categories were compared the frequency of the types of categories drew out a theory from the data. The field note data and interview samples then reached theoretical saturation. When additional data does not expand categories or add any new ideas to what is occurring with the studied data. From this systematic process a theory emerged that accounted for the high student retention rate at Skylarkers computer lessons.

5   Emerged Theory Accounting for Older Learner Continuation of Learning

The main category that emerged from the data was the category of 'Persistence' which had a consistent property for it occurring which was described as the relationships the tutors built with the learners. What theory emerged was that older learners return to lessons because of the unique tutoring techniques the tutors at the centre employed to solve individual learner's computer issues. Certain ways of teaching software and hardware topics in a particularly caring and emphatic manner caused this to occur. Interview and field note extracts are given to support these findings. In these examples the informant's name has been changed to protect their identity.

5.1   Evidence of Successful Computer Tuition Practice

The older learners attending the lessons felt overall they persisted with learning basic and advanced software because of the relationship built with the tutor over time and the tutor's teaching style. Table 2 shows the relationship between the overall category 'Persistence', its property 'Tutor Relationships' and the six dimensions of the property:

Table 2. Category, Property and Dimensions

Category	Property	Property Dimensions
Persistence	Tutor Relationships	▪ Tutor being younger was seen as a positive influence ▪ Duration of relationship did not deter participant if tutor had to leave ▪ Tutors display high amounts of patience ▪ Tutor repeats explanations until participant understands ▪ Solving meaningful problems

Each property dimension gives an example as to why the older learner returned repeatedly for lessons. Example one shows that the age of the tutors, often younger than the students, was a positive influence on their learning experience and encouraged them to explore how to use computer software:

> *I've got a microphone on my system and I talk to people in Germany, mainly Germany which is great if it's only for the fact one hears the different dialects in different parts of the country. And I was put onto that here by ... through Paltalk, you know, which gave me an insight of the possibilities and joy of it that it can bring...*

Another older learner commented that during lessons the younger tutors knew how to ease older learner's anxiety:

> *I watch and I'm very relaxed, very relaxed. I find that they don't, none of the tutors inclined to get me excited or, I find that somebody my age, I can, they see that, they seem to know how to deal with people my age and they don't push it too far. They do it slowly for your benefit and you are, when you do get older, you are a bit slower. So you need somebody that's going to be like that with you...*

An interesting dimension of the theory that kept occurring was that despite close bonds developed over time, tutors left to take up new jobs or return to study. Yet this did not deter older learners from having lessons from new tutors. The tutors that left made sure the students got acquainted with the other tutors before leaving.

The main quality an older learner computer tutor needs is high amounts of patience and willingness to repeatedly explain procedures. Each older learner valued this quality especially as they negotiated advanced features of the software they were learning as these three commented:

> *You say slow down do that again. So they slow down and do what they consider to be slow but its still not slow enough for a feeble mind like mine to catch up on.*

> *You can ask the same question again and again, come back to it at the end just to make sure that you understood what they are trying to teach you.*

> *And, no matter who it is, young or old, everyone seems to have lots of patience, is very good at explaining things. I think that's what's it all about you know.*

Constantly repeating instructions can be frustrating to some computer trainers exacerbated with the pressure to deliver training quickly and on time. Yet in a community setting, there is an opportunity to repeat complex software procedures. Older learners commented that repeating an instruction was a vital part of understanding how to perform a procedure and understanding the reasoning behind the procedure:

> *He's very informative and makes it very simple, um, you know, I can understand what he's talking about and if I don't grasp it then he repeats it for me. He's a very good tutor.*

> *That is where the one to one tuition is such a big thing in my opinion. You can ask the same question again and again, come back to it at the end just to make sure that you understood what they are trying to teach you. Sometimes I walk out of here like being on cloud in a different environment altogether because of all the new things and possibilities I am shown you know.*

An important dimension that accounted for persistence was that the tutors would solve computer problems the learner was having as this was important and meaningful to the learner. Two learners reported having serious learning issues with the software they were using. They both expressed the view that the tutors had worked with them to solve particularly difficult software issues, as these interview extracts illustrate, which assisted their learning to move forward:

> *I used to hit what I call logjams. I use the terminology logjams and I'd walk into the tutor here and say I've just had another logjam can you sort this out for me, and that meant I had problems with some of my early work of drawing up family history charts, their pretty tricky things to try and get onto a computer screen, all the lines, branches and so forth. It was a bit tricky trying to fit all that into a computer screen. That's the sort of logjams I used to have to struggle with coming here to get help with.*

> *Yes, the other day I'm, well I'm the volunteer co-ordinator of a nursing home, and, so I have to send out various flyers. And before now I've always got somebody to do it for me at the nursing home and the other day... showed me how to do one. So I went home and I did one and sent it out and that was very pleasing.*

An example from the observation data illustrated the specific interactions that reflect the tutor's systematic and patient approach was between Tom and John. The learner was elderly and had discovered that Excel would assist with his interest, share investing. However, he was continuously forgetting both how to bookmark URL's in Internet Explorer and was not aware of Boolean search engine strategies to find internet information. This exchange took place:

> *Tom explained the process of bookmarking favourites in Internet Explorer. Also showed John the History Page. Tom goes to the Google Search Engine and explains why it is a good page to keep.*

> *Tom asks John to type Chemist in Google. Tom asks John to expand the window. Tom types in ASX (Australian Stock Exchange) and the page comes up (John asked if the ASX was online). Tom advises when John gets home to bookmark the page.*

> *Tom then returns to the Chemist exercise. John types in Chemist and it results in "all the chemists in the world...that is the problem" Tom says.*

> *Tom tells John to type in CHEMIST BRISBANE into Google. Tom says that it will reduce the number of hits (sites that come up). This happens and John clicks on one of Google's hyperlinks. Tom asks John to go back to Google and*

type in CHEMIST BRISBANE INALA. This results in an accurate search where a local chemist is found on a links site. John scrolls down looking at the hyperlinks. There is a lot of text on the site. Tom comments that in the next lesson there will be more about the ways of organising URL information in favourites.

These examples illustrate that the way tutors presented information to the learner in the manner they did does suggest that older learners felt that their individual issues were solved and a positive learning relationship was built with the tutor. The current and past tutors were all reported in some way by the learners as having these skills which encouraged them to continue lessons at the centre.

6   Implications for Tutoring Older Adult Learners

The main aim of this study, finding out why older learners returned to the centre for lessons, was achieved through constant observation and asking questions of the older learner about how their computer training needs were being met. It was seen after commencing the study that the tutors' teaching strategies and behaviours were influencing the decisions to return for further lessons. In this study, there was consistency of older learners reporting the tutor's had particular skills and qualities that encouraged their confidence with computer use. Emphasis should always be placed on making the first lessons a positive initial experience to reduce anxiety and build positive attitudes [20]. Centre management ensured this was a priority skill to have when choosing new tutors for the centre's computer lesson program.

The study suggests that particular tutoring practices and qualities are responsible for persistent attendance at lessons and the willingness to continue learning computers. It is argued that our study describes and defines those tutor behaviours that can contribute to building the confidence in older adult learners. It also suggests those tutoring practices that can contribute towards encouraging the older learner to continue learning computer software.

References

1. Charness, N., Schuman, C.E., Boritz, G.M.: Training Older Adults in Word Processing: Effect of Age, Training Technique, and Computer Anxiety. Int. J. Tech. and Aging. 5, 79–106 (1992)
2. Organisation for Economic Co-Operation and Development (OECD), Understanding the Digital Divide (2001),
http://www.oecd.org/dataoecd/38/57/1888451.pdf
3. Danowski, J., Sacks, W.: Computer Communication and the Elderly. Experimental Aging Research 6(2), 125–135 (1980)
4. Adams, N., Stubbs, D., Woods, V.: Psychological Barriers to Internet usage among Older Adults in the UK. Medical Informatics & the Internet in Medicine 30(1), 3–17 (2005)
5. Bostrom, R.P., Olfman, L., Sein, M.K.: The Importance of Learning Style in End-User Training. MIS Quarterly 14(1), 101–119 (1990)
6. Ansley, J., Erber, J.T.: Computer Interaction: Effect on Attitudes and Performance in Older Adults. Educational Gerontology 14(2), 107–119 (1988)

7. McNeely, E.: Computer-Assisted Instruction and the Older-Adult Learner. Educational Gerontology 17(3), 229–237 (1991)
8. Seals, C.D., Clanton, K., Agarwal, R., Doswell, F., Thomas, C.M.: Lifelong Learning: Becoming Computer Savvy at a Later Age. Educational Gerontology 34(12), 1055–1069 (2008)
9. Young, K.S.: Reviewing and Critiquing Computer Learning and Usage Among Older Adults. Educational Gerontology 34(8), 709–735 (2008)
10. Hollis-Sawyer, L.A., Sterns, H.L.: A Novel Goal-Oriented Approach for Training Older Adult Computer Novices: Beyond the Effects of Individual-Difference Factors. Educational Gerontology 25(7), 661–684 (1999)
11. About Skylarkers, http://skylarkers.net/about.htm
12. World Health Organization Preamble to the Constitution of the World Health Organization as adopted by the International Health Conference, New York, June 19-22 (1946), http://www.who.int/about/en
13. Knowles, M.: The Adult Learner a Neglected Species, 4th edn. Gulf Publishing Company, Houston (1990)
14. Pfeil, U., Arjan, R., Zaphiris, P.: Age Differences in Online Social Networking: a Study of User Profiles and the Social Capital Divide among Teenagers and Older Users in MySpace. Computers in Human Behavior 25, 643–654 (2009)
15. Strauss, A., Corbin, J.: Basics of Qualitative Research, 2nd edn. Sage Publications, California (1998)
16. Emerson, R.M., Fretz, R.I., Shaw, L.L.: Writing Ethnographic Fieldnotes, Chicago Guides to Writing, Editing, and Publishing, 2nd edn. University of Chicago Press, Chicago (1995)
17. Pace, S.: Understanding the Flow Experiences of Web Users. PhD Thesis, The Australian National University (2003)
18. White, J., Weatherall, A.: A Grounded Theory Analysis of Older Adults and Information Technology. Educational Gerontology 26, 371–386 (2000)
19. Strauss, A., Corbin, J.: Basics of Qualitative Research, 2nd edn. Sage Publications, California (1998)
20. Mayhorn, C.B., Stronge, A.J., McLaughlin, A.C., Rogers, W.A.: Older Adults, Computer Training, and the Systems Approach: A Formula for Success. Educational Gerontology 30(3), 185–203 (2004)

The Paradox of More Flexibility in Education: Better Control of Educational Activities as a Prerequisite for More Flexibility

Henk Plessius and Pascal Ravesteyn

HU University of Applied Science, Faculty of Science and Engineering,
Nijenoord 1, 3552 AS Utrecht, The Netherlands
{henk.plessius,pascal.ravesteijn}@hu.nl
http://www.hu.nl

Abstract. The paradigm shift towards competency-based education in the Netherlands has a logical counterpart: the need for more flexibility in the curricula. After all, in competency-based education it is recognized that learning not only takes place in designated places (school, university), but may happen every time when the learner is confronted with a challenge. This observation leads to the necessity to incorporate the learning outcomes of formal and informal education in one curriculum. As a result, the educational process becomes more complex and must be better structured to control the individual learning outcomes.

In this paper we discuss this paradox: how more flexibility in the program creates the need for more control in the process. We also discuss what kind of IT-tools are helpful in controlling flexibility in curricula for higher professional education.

Keywords: competency-based education, flexibility, learning activity, higher professional education.

1 Introduction

The introduction of competency-based education in the curricula for higher professional education in the Netherlands has resulted in the need for more flexible curricula in order to comply with the individual needs of students with different backgrounds and interests. As the resulting programs become more activity-based instead of content-based, the need arises for new forms of support for the educational process. In this paper we discuss the changes brought forward by this paradigm shift and the consequences for educational tools which, in our opinion (as stated before in [1]), should incorporate the concept of flow and support learning activities, thereby transcending the current data-driven approach and become process-driven instead.

In this paper the changes that the department of Computer Science of the HU University of Applied Sciences[1] has undergone to be better equipped to support a flexible

---

[1] See http://international.hu.nl for more information on the University.

N. Reynolds and M. Turcsányi-Szabó (Eds.): KCKS 2010, IFIP AICT 324, pp. 301–309, 2010.

and practically oriented educational process, is examined. A more process-oriented approach, is supported by IT, to improve the manageability of this process is introduced.

1.1 Towards Competency-Based Education

Competency-based education in itself is not a new phenomenon, in the last decades a large amount of research has become available that defines what it is and describes what its goals are (see for example [2], [3], [4] and [5]). A competency is normally associated with a combination of knowledge, skills and attitudes appropriate in a given context. In this paper we use the definition of Dochy and Nickmans [5] who state that "a competency is a personal capability that becomes visible by showing successful behavior in a specific context". Also, a competency can change over time and can be attained by an individual. Furthermore "a competency consists of the following three elements 1) knowledge 2) skills and 3) attitude". In Dochy and Nickmans [5] the difference between domain-general competencies and profession-specific competencies is also highlighted. Universities have always been strong in teaching knowledge, skills and general competencies but in order for students to acquire profession-specific competencies, real life situations and thus involvement of external organizations is preferred.

The introduction of a competency-based curriculum implies the introduction of a new didactical approach as well: in most cases based on a constructivist learning theory (extensively described by Water [6]).

1.2 Flexibility in Competency-Based Curricula

In educational programs, flexibility has various meanings, depending on the context. In this paper we will use the definition of Schellekens [7]: flexibility is "the need to anticipate on differences between individual students in background, study method and speed, preferences etcetera".

Students enrolling a university for a bachelor or master degree have very different backgrounds. While most students come from high school or have vocational training, the number that has prior job experience is increasing. Especially for students with experience in a profession related to the degree course, it has become good practice to determine their competencies in an intake procedure and from there to decide which elements of the course are necessary and where exemptions are possible. In the Netherlands there are several centres which specialize in such procedures, for example the Dutch centre for the accreditation of prior learning (APL)[2].

For students with certified prior learning the curricula of the university should at least have flexible starting points and adaptable routes through their curricula.

A recent development in higher professional education is the introduction of studies which combine learning with work. Part of the study takes place 'on the job': students reflect on projects carried out professionally and in assessments their growth in competencies is measured. As the projects and the resulting experiences of the students vary, this asks for a high degree of flexibility in the curricula and corresponding assessments.

---

[2] See http://www.kenniscentrumevc.nl/apl-english for more information.

A form of education where flexibility is a necessity is demand-driven education (described by Everwijn [8]). In demand-driven education students compare in assessments their actual competencies with the competencies needed for graduating and from there, formulate learning goals. From these goals they choose courses and projects which may help to reach their goals. Ultimately, no fixed curriculum exists in this form of education; the university offers courses and projects (and of course supervision), while the students choose which courses they will attend to and projects they will participate in, where courses and projects may as well be found outside the university.

From the examples above it is evident that when a curriculum is more competency-based, it is less regulated and it is more difficult for the university to stay in control and decide if and when the students meet the terms of their bachelor or master degree.

In the next parts of this paper we will first provide the context for curriculum development (section 2) and outline the educational process in a competency-based setting (section 3). In section 4 we will develop an architecture for the IT-support of the educational process and finally in section 5 we will discuss the issue of flexibility in the educational program and processes.

2 Curriculum Development for Higher Professional Education

As stated above the trend in the Netherlands in professional education is towards more competency-based curricula. In the field of higher professional education in ICT a major player is the HBO-I Foundation[3]. This foundation has set a landmark for bachelor degree curricula in ICT with its publication 'Bachelor of ICT' [9] in which a reference model for ICT-competencies in higher professional education is presented.

2.1 The ICT Competencies Reference Model

The ICT competencies reference model distinguishes five profession-specific ICT-competencies based on the life cycle of ICT-systems and ten domain general competencies based on the Dublin descriptors [10]. The ICT-specific competencies are analysis, advise, design, implementation and maintenance. For the domain general competencies, see figure 1 (A more exhaustive description of all competencies involved can be found in the original publication of the HBO-I foundation, which is available in English [9]).

Recently this description of the domain of ICT has been further developed. The profession-specific competencies as described in the first publication are expanded with five so-called 'architectural layers' describing the user interaction, business processes, software, infrastructure and hardware interfacing aspects. Also three levels of command (basic, simple and complex) have been added, resulting in a 3-dimensional framework of ICT-competencies and additional domain general competencies. For the domain general competencies no levels of command have been defined up to now.

These additions are described in a second publication of the HBO-I Foundation [11] (not yet available in English) and the resulting model is outlined in figure 1.

---

[3] See http://www.hbo-i.nl/default.aspx?pageID=24 for more information.

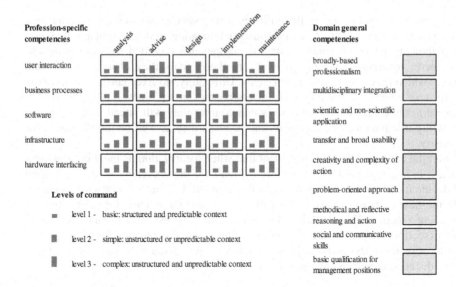

Fig. 1. Extended model for competencies for ICT educational curricula [11]

With this framework a complete curriculum can be specified by defining for each 'box' which level must be reached by students. The university may then choose in which way the students may reach the desired level: by lectures and practical work, via projects or 'on the job'.

2.2 ICT Curricula at the HU University of Applied Sciences

Last year the HU University of Applied Sciences started to update all (Bachelor) curricula in the Computer Science department so that they will be based on the competencies as described in the reference model described above. We use a constructivist approach so a central element in every curriculum is the creation by students of *professional products*; a professional product being defined as "a typical result for a professional in the line of his work and in accordance with professional standards" (see [12]).

An advice on the use of IT in a branch of the business, a software program (including design documentation), a portal for a department, the security of information during a certain period, all these are examples of professional products.

In redefining the curricula the following steps as outlined by Schmeltz [13], are taken:

1. Depending on the profession at which the curriculum is aimed, the desired level in each of the various 'boxes' of the reference model is decided upon in consultation with the ICT-industry. The resulting description defines the competency-level of the overall program.
2. For each term (in Utrecht a typical term takes three months), one or more professional products which the students are expected to create in that term, are determined together with the competencies needed to create the products, thereby using

the framework (including domain general competencies). The set of competencies per term must of course cover the competencies of the overall program.

3. Necessary knowledge elements and practical skills are added as courses to complete the terms.

In an assessment at the end of every term, students have to show that they have mastered the various competencies at the prescribed level.

The resulting curricula have quite a lot of possibilities for flexibility. Current practice is that the first professional products are made from case-descriptions, but starting in the second year these cases are replaced by real projects from real companies who in some cases also play a role in the supervision of the projects. In the third and fourth year of their study, students have the opportunity to follow their own interest and choose the subjects they prefer (restricted of course by the degree course they are enrolled in because after all, the students do have to show progress in the competencies for the jobs where the curriculum is directed at).

In a later phase when there is more experience with this model, more flexibility can easily be added (especially for students who are already working in the ICT domain); the model itself offers possibilities enough!

3 The Educational Process

In the preceding paragraphs the focus has been on the curricula and the educational programs. A program is the execution of a curriculum and is, in a traditional environment, more or less the same for all students. The educational process in such an environment consists of deciding which program a student should follow and marking the results.

Typically the educational process is supported by tools which offer the (often combined) functionality of a catalog of courses and registering marks for individual students so progress (in terms of credit points) can be measured.

In a competency-based environment the educational focus shifts as we have seen towards activities performed by students. These activities may vary quite a lot between students. To be able to follow the progress of an individual student (and not only the result of his activities), supporting tools should be able to support workflow functionality. Let us illustrate this with an example we described in an earlier paper [1]:

In a term on e-business the professional product is an e-business application where, in accordance with good software engineering practice, students are asked to model the business process, model the application, build the software and test the application. Depending on the organization, the nature of the business processes involved and the background of the various students, different approaches are possible. So students start with a plan explaining what is to be done, in which way and when. The impossibility to implement this plan in the learning environment of the course is criticized in the paper and the need for more flexible tools expressed.

In the example the support is defined in terms of an electronic learning environment. On a higher level an (individual) program can be seen as an instance of the curriculum and consists of activities and courses which both may lead to results – results being entries in the individual portfolio and/or as credit points (see figure 2).

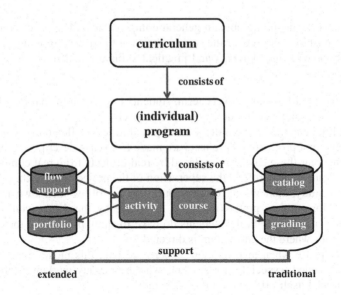

Fig. 2. Extended support for educational activities

So in a competency-based setting the need for more and different support originates from the introduction of learning activities in the educational programs.

So far we described the changing educational environment in the Netherlands which caused the need for more flexibility in the curricula. We recognized that learning no longer takes place only in designated places like a university but is spread out over many activities at many different locations both national and international. This causes the need to incorporate the learning outcomes of formal and informal education in one curriculum. As a result the educational process becomes more complex and must be better structured and supported in novel ways by information systems to enable management and control of the individual learning outcomes. While in this way the educational programs become more flexible, it also means that the supporting processes must be defined more strictly.

In the department of Computer Science of the HU University of Applied Sciences we are currently redefining our educational and supporting processes, based on the notions as described in this paper and the continuous improvement cycle (PDCA) as introduced by Deming [14].

4   IT Tools for the Educational Process

From the previous sections it becomes clear that IT-systems supporting both the educational and the supporting processes should transcend the current data driven approach. A new generation of tools should become process-driven, based upon the educational processes which are becoming less structured and contain ever more ad-hoc activities that are a natural part of a competency-based curriculum.

In a competency-based educational environment, ideally a workflow should be instantiated when a student enrolls for a degree course. This workflow can be (sparsely) populated with the milestones corresponding with the competencies that are part of a curriculum. While the students follow their programs, the university (or the students themselves) can add activities, courses and further milestones to the individual workflows. For the individual student the same tool may show itself as an electronic learning environment (ELO) in predefined courses, as a project (planning) tool while working on a professional product, as a (social) community while engaged in activities with fellow students/co-workers or as their portfolio, documenting their professional growth. Simultaneously such a system should be able to support the administrative and logistical processes that support the students' progress during their education.

4.1 A Basic Architecture for IT-Support of the Educational Process

To select, implement and align the information systems to the changing educational setting we use concepts from the domain of IT Architecture to provide a blueprint for IT projects in the university. In the Open Group Architecture Framework (TOGAF) the Open Group [15] states that it is not possible to design a good organizational structure with supporting information systems without using architecture. Lankhorst et al. [16] describe how to develop enterprise architectures in practice.

For the activity-based educational process we developed a model as shown in figure 2. By adding support for coaching, we come to a basic architecture for the support of the educational process as outlined in figure 3.

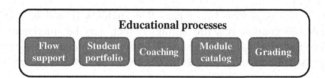

Fig. 3. Basic architecture for the support of the educational process

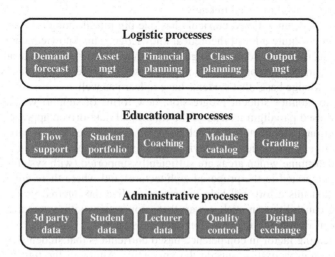

Fig. 4. Extended architecture for the support of the educational process

4.2   An Extended Architecture for IT-Support of the Educational Process

In practice a university has several more areas where IT-support is needed in support of the organizational processes, such as the logistic (planning and control) and the administrative (registration) processes. Therefore we extend our basic architecture with these processes (shown in figure 4).

The proposed architecture has three main areas of functionality: 1) logistics 2) educational and 3) administrative. Currently most universities will already have applications in place to support most of the activities and processes in these areas but typically these are not integrated. This can cause many problems ranging from a mismatch in lecturer skills compared to the competencies and modules that need to be taught to planning and production not being aligned (e.g. not enough classrooms or lecturers available when needed) or students attending classes which they are not allowed to.

5   Conclusion

As shown in the previous sections, education is changing from knowledge- to competency-based. A consequence of this change is that curricula have to become more oriented towards activities. More specific: towards real and professional activities which are related to professional products whether they are situated in a educational or real life context.

For the educational process this means that students should be given authentic questions related to genuine real life settings (which may be simulated for first year students). The best way to provide such a setting is by confronting students with genuine projects from existing companies which act as customer, thereby creating a real context.

In curricula built around competences and professional products, flexibility is a natural outcome as the individual student programs may vary as they are centered on 'need to learn' instead of 'need to know'.

Building competency-based curricula has one big pitfall though. Professionals use – often implicit – quite a lot of theoretical knowledge. This knowledge must be made explicit in a learning environment to guarantee that students reach an academic level. Therefore a curriculum consists not only of a set of professional products, but includes a 'knowledge base' that students have to learn as well.

In order to monitor student progression, new forms of support which implement the activity-based paradigm instead of the traditional data-driven approach are necessary. A functional architecture for such a system is presented in this paper. Based on this architecture, universities may review their existing applications and information systems to determine which areas are sufficiently supported (with systems that can be reused and integrated in the proposed architecture) and where there are deficiencies. We expect that this effort will help to professionalize the internal processes and organizational capabilities in such a way that cooperation with external partners will become easier, thereby giving more flexibility to students.

A complicating factor in competence-based curricula is that students are ever more taking up learning activities outside the university. Although the university encourages students to do internships and participate in external research or consultancy projects as part of their education, this increases the complexity of coordinating a student's educational process. For example examination and assessments must not only be aligned with internal courses but also to external activities. Current organizational processes and IT systems in many universities are lacking support for such a new way of working. Here we see an example of our starting hypothesis: more flexibility in the student programs creates the need for more control in the educational process.

References

1. Plessius, H., Ravesteyn, P.: E-learning Activities in Educating e-business: a Pilot with a Process-Oriented e-learning Environment. In: Education for the 21st Century — Impact of ICT and Digital Resources. Springer, Boston (2006)
2. Spady, W.G., Mitchell, D.E.: Competency-based education: Organizational Issues and Implications. Educational Researcher 6(2), 9–15 (1977)
3. Gray, I.L., Hymel, G.M.: Successful schooling for all: A primer on outcome-based education and mastery learning. Network for outcome-based schools, Johnston City, New York (1992)
4. Spady, W.G.: Outcome-based education: Critical issues and answers. American Association of School Administrators, Arlington (1994)
5. Dochy, F., Nickmans, G.: Competentiegericht opleiden en toetsen: theorie en praktijk van flexibel leren. Lemma B.V, Utrecht (2005)
6. Water, W.J.: Competentiegericht kwalificeren met onderwijslogistieke software. Master thesis. University of Utrecht (2008)
7. Schellekens, A.: Towards flexible programmes in higher professional education: an operations management approach. Maastricht, Datawyse Boekproducties (2004)
8. Everwijn, S.E.M.: Leerdoelstellingen en de ontwikkeling van competenties: een conceptueel kader. In: Schramade, P.W.J. (ed.) Handboek Effectief Opleiden, pp. 65–85. DELWEL, The Netherlands (1996)
9. Valkenburg, M. (ed.): Bachelor of ICT. A description of the competency-based profile. HBO-I Foundation, Den Haag, the Netherlands (2004)
10. Shared 'Dublin' descriptors for Short Cycle, First Cycle, Second Cycle and Third Cycle Awards (2004), http://www.jointquality.nl
11. Bordewijk, E. (ed.): Bachelor of ICT, domeinbeschrijving. HBO-I Foundation, Den Haag, The Netherlands (2009)
12. See for example, http://encyclo.nl/begrip/beroepsproduct
13. Schmeltz, J.W.: Internal publication for the department of Computer Science of the HU University of applied Sciences (2010)
14. Deming, W.E.: Out of the crisis. Massachussetts Institute of Technology (1985)
15. The Open Group. TOGAF version 8.1 (2001), http://www.togaf.com
16. Lankhorst, M., et al.: Enterprise Architecture at Work, Telematica Instituut, pp. 22–23, 229-232. Springer, Heidelberg (2005)
17. Hendriks, P., Schoonman, W.: Handboek assessment deel 1: gedragsproeven. van Gorcum, Assen (2006)
18. Oliver, R., Harper, B., Hedberg, J., Willis, S.: Information and Communication Technologies and their role in Flexible learning, AUTC project report, http://www.learningdesigns.uow.edu.au

Design and Implementation of Business Process Management Curriculum: A Case in Dutch Higher Education

Pascal Ravesteyn and Johan Versendaal

HU University of Applied Sciences Utrecht, Nijenoord 1, 3552 AS, Utrecht, NL
{pascal.ravesteijn,johan.versendaal}@hu.nl
Utrecht University, Padualaan 14, 3583 CH, Utrecht, NL
{pascalr,j.versendaal}@cs.uu.nl

Abstract. This paper describes a joint effort by two educational and scientific institutes, the HU University of Applied Sciences and Utrecht University, in designing a BPM course that not only transfers theoretical knowledge but lets students also experience real life BPM-systems and implementation issues. We also describe the implementation of the developed module with an indication of its success: it is now running for the fifth time, and although there continue to be points for improvement, over the years several scientific papers in the BPM domain resulted from the course, as well as a reasonable amount of students started their final thesis project in the BPM-domain.

Keywords: BPM, education, design, implementation.

1 Introduction

The adoption of Information Technology (IT) by organizations has grown tremendously in the last fifty years. During this period the focus of how IT is used has gradually changed from computational support to using IT as a means to realize more effective and efficient processes. One of the trends that have caused this change is the rapidly growing globalization in which organizations collaborate within and across supply chains around the world. Traditional IT support for these types of collaboration is expensive and the implementation of customized solutions does not live up to expectations [1]. Consequently one of the domains receiving increased attention is that of Business Process Management. BPM can be considered a 'holistic' management approach that enables process orientation and improvement within organizations and aims at more flexible processes and information systems, thereby making organizations more agile [2]. Based on the service-oriented architecture (SOA) paradigm BPM-systems enable analyses, modeling, execution and improvement of an organizations public and private processes thereby extending the usability of legacy systems and increasing the flexibility of processes [2, 3].

The change towards process orientation in organizations requires a cross-functional perspective on processes and customers instead of a focus on hierarchy and functions [4] and therefore emphasis has shifted from functional specialization towards

N. Reynolds and M. Turcsányi-Szabó (Eds.): KCKS 2010, IFIP AICT 324, pp. 310–321, 2010.

processes [5]. If we review the information systems curricula at Universities we notice that there is a growing attention for modules with a clear emphasis on business process analyses and automation. The importance of cross-functional integration and business process orientation has also been notified in the domain of business education; however, shortcomings in existing curricula are still there [4].

This paper addresses the topic of BPM competencies in University education and provides an example on how to set up a process oriented curriculum, based on four years of experiences by two Dutch Universities that established a joint BPM course for both fulltime and part-time undergraduate and graduate students.

In the following section we describe related work on process oriented education modules. The third section describes the course design and content. The fourth section will relate the outcomes and the experiences of the students together with the lessons learned. In the final and fifth section we present some conclusions and suggestions for further improvements to the course.

2 Related Work

As a start to this research, a study was conducted to find best-practices of other universities about the development of a BPM course [6]. However despite the amount of research available on BPM there were was little in-depth information available on curricula that specifically addressed training in skills and competencies in BPM.

Fingar [7] stated that the curricula of MBA-courses at business schools are too focused on administrative skills and hardly pay any attention to (process) innovation. He suggests a curriculum in which a core of MBA topics (such as finance and accounting, quantitative analysis, economics, marketing and organizational behaviour) is integrated with modules that teach skills in business process management, business activity monitoring, process modeling, process improvement and simulation.

In Bandare et al. [8] a study is described that determines whether there is a large demand for business process modeling skills. For this 300 online job vacancies that explicitly mentioned process modeling skills were analyzed. Subsequently she organized a focus group representing potential BPM recruiters to validate and contextualize the findings. It should be noted however, that this study was focused on business process modeling skills and not the broader set of competencies needed in business process management projects.

Zur Meuhlen [9] reveals a more detailed view on the skills that are needed in BPM efforts. He distinguishes four different groups that are involved in BPM-projects: (1) executives, (2) business analysts, (3) systems analysts, and (4) vendors or systems integrators. Each group has different responsibilities and therefore needs a differentiated set of skills. For example, executives need to ensure process performance and compliance, and hence need skills in process analysis, governance and portfolio management. In contrast systems analysts are responsible for the implementation of the process and its corresponding information systems and therefore need skills in process modeling, workflow implementation, user interface design and systems integration. In his paper Zur Meuhlen does not only provide insight in BPM skills, he also presents a preliminary list of universities that offer BPM programs.

While the papers mentioned above are interesting none of them describe how to develop a curriculum in BPM or experiences in teaching. The only paper that does focus on the development process is by Recker and Rosemann [10]. They explain in detail the setup, structure, and experiences of a course in business process modeling at the Queensland University of Technology in Australia. However the topic is on business process modeling and does not include management: the paper merely provides insights in how to develop a process oriented curriculum and which teaching techniques can be used.

Because the amount of literature on education in BPM is sparse we decided to include literature on Enterprise Resource Planning (ERP) course design. Systems for ERP as well as systems for BPM are both enterprise information systems dealing with cross-functional processes. ERP systems generally contain several sorts of workflow processes, which are made explicit in BPM systems. We found that most of the ERP education development is based on one of the following four categories of approaches [11, 12]:

1. ERP training;
2. ERP and business processes;
3. Information Systems approach;
4. Selection and implementation concepts.

The first approach is basically instruction or training in a specific ERP system. This is very similar to the training courses that the ERP and also BPM-systems developers and suppliers provide to their customers and could be done by reusing commercial training material. The second approach focuses on business processes and related concepts (e.g. financial administration or production scheduling and planning) and uses ERP to assist in the presentation and clarification of these methods and concepts. For this approach, commercial training material is not sufficient; and new material will have to be developed. The third approach uses ERP to illustrate information systems concepts. It is very similar to the second approach; only the target group or goal differs. Instead of teaching business students and business concepts, the target group will most likely be computer science / information systems students and the concepts that are taught are different. The last approach is to teach about ERP related skills, such as selection and implementation of ERP software. It is not really necessary to use a real live ERP system for this although it could give a clearer picture of the complexity of such systems. Of course, it is also possible to combine aspects of all approaches to create a more hybrid approach.

Typically in the course we aimed to develop we wanted to use a BPM-system in support and clarification to the theory. Furthermore in teaching BPM it is important to realize that not only process related knowledge and skills are essential, we also want students to have a high degree of self-awareness, be able to think critical and keep on learning continuously. In the field of BPM, particularly, it is becoming increasingly important to also understand aspects of the development, implementation and maintenance of e-business solutions due to the continuing evolution of BPM [13]. Therefore any course on BPM should in our opinion consist of three parts 1) theory and methods from a business perspective 2) theory and methods from a technical perspective and 3) a practical part that integrates the former two via lifelike exercises and confronts the student with state-of-the-art software.

3   Course Design

To teach students all three aspects of BPM as defined in section 2, five years ago the HU University of Applied Sciences together with the Utrecht University developed a course that can be followed by both Master and Bachelor students simultaneously. The course was designed with two tracks that complement each other. The first track consists of theory on BPM from both the business and technical perspectives. Each week during a three hour period we first discuss scientific theory, methods and techniques, that is then followed by a guest lecture in which practical examples are discussed in relation to the theory of the first half of the period. The second track is entirely based on a case study that we developed in which the students have to analyze, improve, implement and execute the processes in a supply chain. For this again a three hour time period is reserved. The entire course now runs for 9 weeks and is followed by presentations in week 10. Students that follow and finish the course are awarded 7.5 ECTS (European Credits) which means that the total time spent on this course should amount to 210 hours. So besides the 54 hours of classes (both theory and practical) students should spend a total of 156 hours on self study. This time should be spent for about 50% on theoretical assignments and 50% on the practical assignment. Grading of the course consists of a 50% judgment of the digestion of the theoretical part, and a 50% judgment of the practical work.

An innovative feature of the course is that we purposely combine students from bachelor level (who follow a computer science course at the HU University of Applied Sciences) with students from a masters level (from the master business informatics of the Utrecht University). This combination means that students who follow practical orientated education and tend to be very pragmatic have to work together with students that do a scientific education and have a more analytical and critical perspective. Yet, while the students have different levels of education (which in practice will be very normal during a BPM project), it does not mean that one group is better than the other. Typically the master students will take the lead in the theoretical scientific track while the bachelor students are better equipped to manage the practical track. Because we purposely combine the students into groups for their assignments they must work together. This also helps us partly to simulate the business (master business informatics) versus IT (bachelor computer science) divide which students will encounter in practice. Furthermore we let the students experience one of the most important aspects of BPM, the fact that they will need to be able to work with persons from different disciplines and with different perspectives.

An overview of the course is given in figure 1 and in the following two subsections both the theoretical and the practical track will be explained in more detail.

3.1   Theoretical Track

During the theoretical track students are presented with a wide range of topics related to BPM from both a business and IT perspective. Furthermore students (in teams of two) have to perform research and write a paper, for which the literature and state-of-the-art of BPM research and practice as presented in the lectures of the theoretical track can be used. Each year we present students with one or more topics from which

Weeks	Theory	Case study

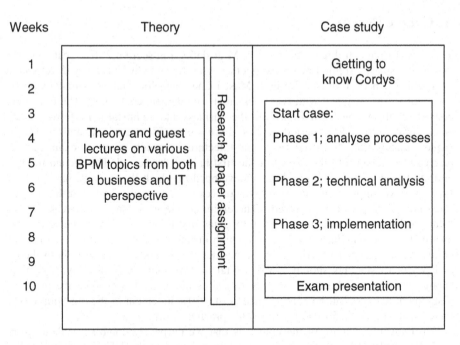

Fig. 1. Course overview

they can choose to write their paper; some of the topics in the past were: BPM-systems implementation, human interaction management, BPM-mashups, ERP and BPM, and business rules management in relation to BPM.

In the lectures, more or less the following topics are covered:

- BPM basics from a business perspective; business process management can provide organizations with the ability to save money and time. The role processes play within an enterprise, to stay competitive and remain agile in the changing global market place is highlighted.
- BPM-systems implementation; the aim of this unit is to introduce the student to the general concepts of business process management systems (BPMS). In short we cover the history of BPM-systems, its characteristics and architecture, give an overview of the providers of BPMSs etc.
- BPM standards, methods and techniques are introduced. We focus on the role of standards (modeling, information, quality, and IT). Maturity models and business and IT alignment are discussed. Also the importance of quality management methods and techniques are covered.
- Business Process Modeling. An overview of different techniques to model, analyze and improve processes is given. Furthermore the Business Process Modeling Notation and its execution language (BPEL) are taught and practiced.
- Service Oriented Architecture (SOA) in relation to BPM. The synergy and differences between BPM and SOA are presented. The SOA paradigm is

explained together with the business drivers for SOA. Important SOA concepts like loose-coupling, service granularity, service contracts, integration and enterprise service bus, governance and security. Also SOA standards and strategies for deploying SOA are discussed.

- BPM(S) Implementation. Here we take the students from process design through implementation to the management of processes and their supporting information systems. Students learn the distinction between business processes and business rules and how they can be implemented in information systems.

- Human Interaction Management / Dynamic BPM. While most current BPM efforts are focused on well structured processes there are also many ad-hoc activities and non-structured processes that need managing and control. The consequences of the fast increasing amount of knowledge workers and a changing way of working (place and time independent) are discussed together with the methods and tools to support these types of activities and processes.

- BPM and performance measurement. Here we cover the essentials of Business Intelligence (origins and drivers, major characteristics, implementation aspects, lifecycle etc.). Other important aspects that are covered are: BI strategy, business process monitoring and control, business and technical requirements for a BI architecture and the difference between BI and business activity monitoring (BAM).

Besides covering each of these topics in theoretical lectures we also invite companies to come and present their perspective and experiences. Invitations are sent to three different categories of companies a) consultancy organizations b) software developers (BPM system vendors) and c) end user organizations. In this way students obtain an overview of the different perspectives on BPM related issues. Organizations that have participated in the course are amongst others: BEA/Oracle (software developer), ASR/Fortis (end user in the financial sector), Capgemini (consultancy), Cordys (software developer), O&I (management consultancy), SNS/Reaal (end user in the financial sector), and PriceWaterhouseCoopers (consultancy). Furthermore during the last three years the chairman of the Dutch BPM-Forum (Frits Bussemaker) gave a guest lecture at the start of the course.

The grading of the theoretical part is solely based on the quality of the research paper that students need to write in teams of two. In the paper it should be easily verifiable to what degree the students were able to include and process the theory and practical lessons from the (guest) lectures.

3.2 Practical Track

The practical part of the course is developed in such a way that students are able to attain knowledge and skills in three categories of competencies related to BPM, labeled: 'business administration', 'information architecture and technology' and 'influence and alignment'.

The first group of competencies states students should be able to recognize and understand the relations between the various functions and departments in an organization and between organizations. Furthermore they should be able to identify relevant market developments for the organization and to propose process improvements and/or implementation of ICT applications as a response to these developments. Finally they should be able to identify and to model company processes and interactions within and between organizations. The second group of competencies are more technical and students that master them are 1) able to design a system architecture for collaboration in extended enterprises in which new ICT capabilities are used 2) understand the basics of SOA and BPM-systems, and 3) are able to install and configure BPM-systems and use them to integrate different information systems within an organization and across its supply chain. The final group of competencies is very much aimed at communicative skills. Within BPM projects students should 1) be able to be conversant with both the domains of business and ICT within the organization 2) be able to communicate with all organizational layers on a clear and effective way about investments, business and ICT innovations in terms of business issues and benefits 3) be able to reflect on their own choices and activities and to indicate their own skills, and 4) be able to apply the set of conversational techniques and competences in order to achieve effective communication in interviews and presentations.

To let students acquire the complete set of competencies a case study is developed in which students are challenged to improve processes across a supply chain. This chain consists of three organizations that collaborate with each other: a Retailer, a Wholesaler and a Manufacturer (see figure 2). Students are divided into teams of two and then assigned to one organization in the supply chain. Each supply chain therefore consists of at least six students. Depending on the number of students in the course more instances of supply chains are formed.

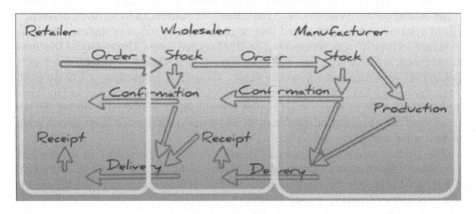

Fig. 2. An overview of the supply chain processes in the case study

The supply chain case consists of a wholesaler offering bicycles to retailers. If the retailer wants to buy from this specific wholesaler, he currently has to make a phone call or sent an email. However the students should develop a purchase application that the retailer can use to connect to the wholesalers system. This application should make use of the existing information systems and needs to be completely based on web services. To fulfill the orders of the retailer, the wholesaler has to manage stock levels in his warehouse system. When an item in stock falls below a certain threshold, the wholesaler must restock the item by ordering this at the manufacturer. In order to comply with the wholesaler's request, the manufacturer may have to execute a production run to build the finished goods. Again these processes are only automated within the boundaries of the respective organizations. It is the task of the students to analyze and improve these processes and then implement and execute them by using a particular BPM-system (in our course we use Cordys BOP 4 [14]).

During this case study students will have to go through several phases (similar to those of a real life BPM-systems implementation project) to be able to develop a good supply chain solution. During the first phase students need to create a clear picture of both the processes within the organization that they are assigned and of the interaction between the business partners in the supply chain and their own internal processes. Thereby they learn the difference between processes which will be kept internal or private to the organization and those that will be shared with partners in the supply chain, also called public processes. Together the organizations within a supply chain must agree on a process architecture for the whole supply-chain. Furthermore a set of appropriate key performance indicators for monitoring the supply chain should be determined. Performance indicators can be formulated on the activity-, business- or supply chain levels. During this phase the models are descriptive only but they should be modeled using the features available through the Cordys system. At the end of this phase (typically two to three weeks) a functional design should be handed over to the lecturer for control purposes.

In the second phase students have to identify, per organization in the supply chain, which information will be required from the other business partners and accordingly which web services have to be developed. The information that is delivered and used by the web services is deducted from the process analysis done in the first phase of the project. Next to this the students should also take into account the existing information systems (for the course we only use 3 different SQL databases). Furthermore during this phase an information architecture should be developed and integration to the systems which are going to be reused needs to be accomplished. In the case both straight through processing and human interaction activities are used to integrate the order and delivery processes, students should be aware of this.

The students are expected to at least look at the various tables in each of the partner databases (such as product-, sales-, purchase- and production-tables and various other linked tables), and develop web services or applications that are able to:

- browse through the products (productid, name, price) of the retailer, wholesaler and manufacturer
- browse through the sales and purchase orders of the wholesaler (including order details)
- browse through the sales orders of the manufacturer (including order details)
- browse through the production orders of the manufacturer
- browse through the product stock levels (aggregated)
- provide information on ordered goods
- exchange information (such as order confirmations, delivery dates, updated stock levels)
- update customer information

- update order information
- update product information (such as price, quantities)

In the final phase the proposed solution must be developed and implemented. The modeled processes should be executed by using the developed web services and applications. End-users should be able to start applications within their Internet browser and use them to start process activities. Also the identified key performance indicators should be implemented in order to monitor the operations in the supply chain. For this the students need to develop dashboards from which the performance indicators can easily be accessed by graphs, reports or performance meters.

At the end of the course each group of students that represents a supply chain are asked to present their solution. Processes are run by using the applications and several web services are checked (specifically does were the process does not seem to work correct or were students have made decisions regarding activities in a process that do not seem logical), finally the performance indicators are also checked. When the developed solution does not work properly it is often because one of the supply chain organizations has not delivered the correct web services or has an faulty integration to their backend systems. If this is the case the students that represent that specific organization are tested further on their level of knowledge and skills.

In the following section we discuss some of the outcomes and lessons learned during the five times that we have now run this course.

4 Outcomes and Lessons Learned

The course has run four complete cycles since 2006 (a fifth being taught as we write) and the amount of data for an evaluation is substantial. Over a 115 students have completed the course, of which around 34 were bachelor computer science students and 81 were graduate students business informatics. Yearly, the students evaluate the course through filling in a partly open and partly closed questionnaire. The overall conclusion is that the course is judged as being relevant (over the years scoring around 3.9 on a scale from 1 (lowest) – 5 (highest)). Each year the theoretical topics and the corresponding guest lectures are highly approved of, except for the odd guest lecture which is deemed too commercial, as e.g. a student complaints: "[…] a guest lecture in which the vendor's competitor is defined as incompetent should not be provided, and lacks an academic level […]". Furthermore, there are some topics that students find less satisfying and that return more or less every year.

First and foremost the students find that cooperation between students of the two different universities, with the different types of education and levels, is difficult and time consuming. Within a short time of typically two months they are forced to learn to know each other and work together: "[…] it is so difficult to meet with my teammate: he has a different curriculum schedule. Moreover, the difference in level is also hard to cope with: I had to do a lot of work in writing the paper […]". However, we deliberately take students out of their comfort zone and that experience is according to the evaluations not appreciated: in 2007, the students valued their collaboration with students from 'the other' university as 2.1 on a scale of 1 (lowest) – 5 (highest). As this is part of the course design and it simulates real life projects we have decided not to change this aspect, but instead to work on a better facilitation for cooperation: in 2008 we 'forced' students to create teams immediately after the kick-off (during a drink provided by the university) instead of giving them a week time. A second finding from the evaluation is that students find the BPM-system, with which they have to work in the practical track, complex and far from easy. Because most of the students haven't worked with a BPM-system before they have to get to know the user interface and functionality of the application and be able to use it to build a supply chain solution all within 9 weeks. Especially if during the theoretical track we had a guest lecture from another BPMS vendor, students often asked us to use that other system. We feel however that they do not fully realize that the effort to know and master any system is complex and any system would cause learning difficulties; moreover, demo's of vendors of systems always provide a colored reality, which is different from the real experience.

A final issue which we receive during every evaluation is the complexity that comes with collaborating between the partners within a supply chain during the practical track. Students find that they really have to communicate and come to an agreement with all organizations in the supply chain on how the processes are going to be analyzed, what methods for process improvement are used, which information needs to be exchanged, and how to develop and publish web services. This is in accordance with the final results that we observe. Each year the supply chain that provides the best solution is the one which had thought out and agreed upon a clear architecture on all levels from process to application. Furthermore such a team typically uses the architecture to communicate about the projects progress. Whereas does that do not succeed in realizing optimized and integrated supply chain processes usually paid to much attention on only optimizing and automating their own organization without communicating with the other supply chain partners (i.e. they realize stovepipe solutions).

In short we can state that the students who participate in this course value it highly even though especially in the practical track they encounter a lot of issues and problems that make it difficult to fully accomplish the assignment.

Although every year there are areas of improvement and we continue to work on those, we are confirmed in our general approach through the years as multiple published scientific papers resulted from the theoretical part, and also more and more students now perform their final thesis project on the topic of BPM, having become enthusiastic after following the course.

From a scientific viewpoint, notably, the theoretical part of the BPM-course in 2007 provided us with enough material to write an overall paper on success factors of BPMS implementations using the material in papers that students provided [15]. Based on the material from the 2008 course too an overall paper has been published, this time on method fragments in BPMS implementation, again using the input from student papers [16]. In 2009, one of the papers from students was, with changes and additions by the teachers, submitted to the International Information Management Association (IIMA) conference, and elected as best paper [17]. In 2010 we have told our current batch of students that we intend to submit the best student contributions to the IIMA 2010 Student Consortium.

5 Conclusions and Future Outlook

In conclusion, we state that the way in which the BPM course curriculum has been developed really enables students to not only acquire knowledge on BPM topics but to also attain skills that are highly valued by industry. By putting together students from different institutes and experience levels we simulate many of the 'soft' problems that people typically encounter in a real life BPM-systems implementation project.

Even though the BPM course can be considered a success there is a price we pay. Organizing the course is a major organizational effort for both universities involved. Each year, the timetables of both universities need to be synchronized for both students and lecturers, besides this arranging between 5 to 8 guest lectures takes a considerable amount of time. Also the effort needed to configure and maintain the BPM-system is substantial and finally students need a lot of energy for this course because they are taken out of their comfort zone and need to deal with a new and complex environment.

Based on the experiences of the last few years and the evaluations of the students we are continuously exploring possibilities to improve the course. One change is to make the group of students more equal. We will no longer combine groups of bachelor and master students of the two universities but we will offer this course to students who are following the bachelor business informatics. This means that there will be two different types of students in the course (more business oriented versus more technology oriented) but that they are on the same level of education. We expect that this will make the practical track of the course less complicated. Also this provides space at the master level of the business informatics education to provide a BPM advanced course that will focus completely on research in the BPM domain. Another change we are considering is the amount of involvement of business; currently this is limited to providing a number of guest lectures but we are thinking of having industry to submit small research projects that the students do as part of the course. This will further improve the practicality of the course. Finally we are continuously improving the amount of knowledge, support and information available on the BPM-system (Cordys) we use. Up till now we have used the Cordys C2 version of the application but with the currently running course we use Cordys BOP 4 and also the process factory which is a lighter version of the application that is offered as software as a service (SaaS). So while the domain of BPM is changing rapidly we aim to offer a course that is challenging and up-to-date and complies with the demands of our students, as well as science and industry.

References

1. Ravesteyn, P., Versendaal, J.M.: Constructing a Situation Sensitive Methodology for BPMS Implementation. In: 13th Pacific Asia Conference on Information Systems (2009)
2. Weske, M.: Business Process Management: Concepts, Languages, Architectures. Springer, New York (2007)
3. Hiemstra, A., Ravesteyn, P., Versendaal, J.M.: An Alignment Model for Business Process Management and Service Oriented Architecture. In: 6th International Conference on Enterprise Systems, Accounting and Logistics (2009)

4. Seethamraju, R.: Enterprise Systems Software in Business School Curriculum - Evaluation of Design and Delivery. Journal of Information Systems Education 18 (2007)
5. Malekzadeh, A.R.: Diversity, integration, globalization and critical thinking in the upper division. Journal of Management Education 22, 590–603 (1998)
6. Ravesteyn, P., Batenburg, R., De Waal, B.: In Search of Competencies Needed in BPM Projects. Communications of the IIMA 8, 23–30 (2008)
7. Fingar, P.: The MBA is Dead, Long Live the MBI (2006), http://www.bptrends.com
8. Bandare, W., Rosemann, M., Davies, I., Tan, C.: A Structured Approach to Determining Appropriate Content for Emerging Information Systems Subjects: An Example for BPM Curricula Design. In: 18th Australasian Conference on Information Systems (2007)
9. Muehlen zur, M.: Class Notes: BPM Research and Education (2008), http://www.bptrends.com
10. Recker, J., Rosemann, M.: Teaching Business Process Modeling: Experiences and Recommendations. Communications of the Association for Information Systems 25, 379–394 (2009)
11. Hawking, P., McCarthy, B., Stein, A.: Integrating ERP's Second Wave into Higher Education Curriculum. In: 9th Pacific Asia Conference on Information Systems (2005)
12. Jensen, T., Fink, J., Moller, C., Rikhardsson, P., Kraemmergaard, P.: Issues in ERP Education Development – Evaluation of the Options Using Three Different Models. In: ICESAcc Proceedings (2005)
13. McGaughey, R.E., Gunasekaran, A.: Enterprise Resource Planning (ERP): Past, Present and Future. International Journal of Enterprise Information Systems 4, 23–35 (2008)
14. Cordys, http://www.cordys.com
15. Ravesteyn, P., Versendaal, J.M.: Success Factors of Business Process Management Systems Implementation. In: 18th Australasian Conference on Information Systems (2007)
16. Ravesteyn, P., Jansen, S.: A Situational Implementation Method for Business Process Management Systems. In: 15th Americas Conference on Information Systems (2009)
17. Kristjansson, B., Mikalef, P., Versendaal, J.M., Ravesteyn, P.: Applying Human Interaction Management Concepts to E-Mailing: A Visualized Conceptual Model. Communications of the International Information Management Association 9 (2009)

All I Need to Know about Twitter in Education I Learned in Kindergarten[*]

Wolfgang Reinhardt[1], Steve Wheeler[2], and Martin Ebner[3]

[1] University of Paderborn, Institute of Computer Science,
Fuerstenallee 11, 33102 Paderborn, Germany
wolle@upb.de
[2] University of Plymouth, Faculty of Education,
Drake Circus, Plymouth, Devon PL4 8AA, UK
s.wheeler@plymouth.ac.uk
[3] Graz University of Technology, Social Learning,
Computer and Information Services,
Steyrergasse 30, 8010 Graz, Austria
martin.ebner@tugraz.at

Abstract
Share everything.
Play fair.
Don't hit people.
Put things back where you found them.
Clean up your own mess.
Don't take things that aren't yours.
Say you're sorry when you hurt somebody.
Wash your hands before you eat.
Flush.
Warm cookies and cold milk are good for you.
Live a balanced life – learn some and think some and draw and paint and sing and dance and play and work every day some.
Take a nap every afternoon.
When you go out into the world, watch out for traffic, hold hands and stick together.
Be aware of wonder.

Keywords: Twitter, Education, Microblogging.

1 Introduction

The way microblogging has changed how people are communicating, cooperating and learning online is comparable to the introduction of phones and e-mail. As McGinoney points out, Twitter[1] is the most commonly used service for microblogging and

---

[*] This paper is based on Robert Fulghum's 1988 book *All I Really Need to Know I Learned in Kindergarten*.
[1] http://twitter.com

N. Reynolds and M. Turcsányi-Szabó (Eds.): KCKS 2010, IFIP AICT 324, pp. 322–332, 2010.
© IFIP International Federation for Information Processing 2010

the *"fastest growing site in [the] Member Communities category"* [1]. In 2009 Twitter grew by nearly 2000% in terms of visitors according to a report by Nielsen[2]. These statistics indicate that microblogging in general and Twitter in particular not only added a new service to the online communication portfolio, they reshaped communication as a whole.

Templeton [2] characterizes microblogging as *a small-scale form of blogging, generally made up of short, succinct messages, used by both consumers and businesses to share news, post status updates and carry on conversations* and Owyang [3] describes the difference between blogs and microblogs as follows: *[...] long form blog posts like this seem so much slower and plodding compared to how quickly information can come and go in Twitter. [...] Information within Microblogging communities [...] encourage[s] rapid word of mouth – of both positive and negative content.*

In Twitter you share messages – so-called Tweets – of at most 140 characters with a group of people. Twitter allows for the sending of public and private messages that can be directed to one or more persons (identified by the @ sign). Everyone interested in your messages can start to follow your stream of tweets and you can decide to follow them in return. Twitter users are accomplishing a great variety of tasks on the service including sharing news, ideas and resources, asking questions and helping others, collaborating on tasks and conceiving new ways of making the service more useful for them. Through such processes, the Twitter community invented the use of the # sign for tagging their content and thus making Tweets easier to find and aggregate.

Courtesy of the open Twitter API there are countless numbers of Twitter clients that make sending and receiving tweets from any location a delight. Features such as geo-location, real-time streaming of tweets and lists of Tweeple[3] in specific domains make Twitter a serious component of today's learning and teaching landscape. In the following section we introduce successful examples of how Twitter has been applied to some diverse learning scenarios.

2 Twitter in Education: A Success Story

Twitter dominates the news with steady new features, marketing success stories and spreading news at the speed of light. In recent years open-minded teachers in primary, secondary and tertiary education have employed Twitter in their classes and found meaningful applications for the tool. The following sections describe selected use cases and their specific application of Twitter.

2.1 Twitter for Language Learning

Ullrich et al. [4] describe one of the first uses of microblogging for language learning performed at the distance University of Shanghai Jiao Tong University. The main research question of the experiment was *"how to increase the active participation of the students in oral communication courses for English as a second language"* ([4], p.710). In the eastern educational system teaching typically means the transmission of knowledge from the teacher to the students rather than the active construction of own

---

[2] http://www.nielsen.com
[3] One possible name for people who use Twitter.

knowledge through active participation [5]. Thus, the active practicing of learned tenors outside the classes often did not take place. During the lectures the students often were to shy or faced the lack of vocabulary as they were talking to their teachers.

The authors introduced Twitter to the classes and prompted the students to create their own accounts and to follow each other. With this setup each student received all the tweets from their fellow students. The students were told to post at least seven tweets per week and to read the tweets from the other students. The students did not find the time to practice English before the experiment, but they had the free choice of time for doing so with Twitter. Here they also could prepare their messages and replies sending out. The authors observed the communication of the community and ran a final questionnaire with the participants showing that the introduction of web 2.0 services indeed stimulated the active participation of students. 94% of the students stated that they had the impression their English had improved with the help of Twitter. The students encouraged each other to participate in the online activities and they even had English conversations with each other. Half of the students even felt comfortable enough to connect and converse with external Twitter users (e.g. native speakers).

2.2 Motivate Students for In-Class Discussions

In large classes the variety of teaching options is often limited to some kind of lecturing, which is not the optimum teaching method. Smith and Rankin describe an experiment with Twitter in a basic history course at the U.T. Dallas [6,7]. Thinking about ways to *"incorporate more student-centered learning techniques [... and ...] a more inte- grated classroom"* the professor came across Twitter and integrated it into the class activities so that the students would have more opportunities to participate. Two of the three weekly meetings remained as regular lectures covering basic terms and concepts of the class. The third meeting was declared as "Twitter experiment".

There was a Twitter account for the class itself and the professor asked all students to create an account themselves and to follow each other. Prior to the Twitter meeting students were required to complete a reading assignment, given some reading suggestions and questions. During the Twitter meeting the students were given an open-note quiz based on the readings and prior questions. After this they commenced their discussions using Twitter. The professor gave some defined hashtags to the students (e.g. one different hashtag per week) that the students should use and what it made easier to aggregate the weekly tweets.

The discussions on the readings were very constructive and the professor used Tweetdeck[4] to project the discussion onto a large screen. In Tweetdeck she created different columns for the different hashtags and thus made it easy to follow the ongoing discussions. During the Twitter experiment she tried various discussion strategies and came up with the finding that small group discussion was the most fruitful way to stimulate constructive discussions and to generate the most interesting ideas. During the last 5 to 10 minutes of each Twitter meeting the class came back together and worked up the discussions. During this phase the class had verbal discussions and

---

[4] http://www.tweetdeck.com/ is a Twitter client that allows creating columns for specific views on your Twitter channel.

could explain some of their ideas in more detail. The professor even marked single tweets as favourites to indicate tweets to the students, which had the potential to be helpful to them in their exams.

The Twitter experiment at the U.T. Dallas clearly demonstrates how Twitter could be used as an enhancement to traditional discussion formats and to boost student participation in otherwise pure lecture- style classes. Moreover, David Parry has highlighted some interesting points with regard to Twitter in the classroom: "*It was the single thing that changed the classroom dynamics more than anything I've ever done teaching*" [8,9].

2.3 Facilitate Process-Oriented Learning

A further research study by Ebner et al. pointed out that microblogging can also be used to enhance process-oriented learning [10]. Students of the University of Applied Sciences are required to use the open-source tool Laconica[5] to report their activities over a defined time period. The students should share, collect and discuss the given lecture tasks and provide their thoughts directly online. Instead of weekly activities reports, Microblogging affords the ability to display the learning results and outcomes just in time.

The study pointed out that students used the application very high frequently. On an average of about 4,5 posts per student every day Microblogging were used. It was shown that the tool was used mainly for communication purposes, but in new and very exciting ways. Learners wrote not only about course-related topics, but also about their feelings, thoughts and interests. As a result of the research work it is amazing that if such a tool is given completely to students for their own use within the very short lifetime of microblogging. On Twitter students talked about just about anything in addition to course related topics.

In other words, the obviously large information stream leads to a new way of managing information, a new method of communication and a new way to self-document students' learning behaviours.

Given these success stories we will next review some Twitter principles in the context of Fulghum's poem.

Share Everything

Although the question tweets should answer used to be "What are you doing?" and besides the recent change of that question to "What's happening", Twitter is all about sharing. Java et al. [11] did an analysis of Twitter users and the content they send and identified four main types of Twitter users: networker, chatter, reporter and sharer. People are sharing all kinds of data on Twitter including local or global news, links to interesting websites, new blog posts, readings, films or places they go to. Another part of the community uploads videos, pictures or audio recordings and shares them with the public. There are even Twitter clients like blURL[6] that helps users to separate tweets containing links from the rest of the data stream.

---

[5] StatusNet (formerly known as Laconica) is an open source microblogging server aiming to be an alternative to Twitter. See http://status.net for more detailed information about StatusNet.

[6] http://blurl.me

Play Fair

Don't plagiarise other people's ideas or resources. Do acknowledge your sources when you want to reuse (in the case of Twitter retweet) useful, funny or valuable tweets. See the section *Put things back where you found them* for more information on the retweet issue.

Don't Hit People

Twitter is at the speed of light. Whatever you post will be visible to all members of your community so take care what you say. There are some golden rules that prevent committing a faux pas (cf. Gordon [12]).

Whenever you receive a direct message from someone, keep the conversation private. If you want to re-tweet that message ask for permission to do so. Twitter is no instant messaging between two people, so don't post such chatter publicly and rather use the private mode. Breaching this rule is similar to including other recipients as 'copied in' to a private e-mail your respond to.

Only tweet things you would speak out loud if there would not been a Twitter channel. That means especially to be nice during presentations of others and to not abuse someone. If you have personal remarks use the private mode or displace that conversation to face-to-face.

If you rename your account name for any reason, leave a farewell note and state your new account name. Even if you take all your tweets, followers and followings with you, people can get confused if they no longer reach you in direct messages or if replies to the old account name don't reach you.

In many educational settings students will be asked to post a certain number of tweets every day/week. Tell your students to no send messages just for the sake of sending out a message. Every tweet should be relevant to the topic of the class or to tighten the class community.

Put Things Back Where You Found Them

Besides sharing links, addressing users directly with the usage of the @ sign and the tagging messages with the # sign, retweeting is another common practice on Twitter. A retweet (or RT) can be compared to the forward of an e-mail where parts of the message can be changed, exchanged or annotated. Users are using the retweet mechanism to share tweets from other users with their followers and often to add a personal note on the topic. In either case people are promoting the retweeted user to their network, often resulting in new followers for the retweeted one and thus a larger informal network. Unlike the @ mentions and the tagging, retweeting has no common convention of how to do it. Boyd, Golder, and Lotan [2] found the following syntax is used to mark Retweets: 'RT: @', 'retweeting @', 'retweet @', '(via @)', 'RT (via @)', 'thx @', 'HT @', 'r @', and '□ @'. The different syntax used shows the complexity of the retweeting task. Boyd et al. [13] even found that there exist different retweeter roles. Twitter itself incorporated a highly discussed retweet-feature to the service in late 2009.

Clean Up Your Own Mess

Hashtags are an invention of the Twitter community. As early as August 2007 Chris Messina recommended the use of the # sign for identifying groups or communities, brands and topics on Twitter [14]. Shortly after their introduction hashtags were an essential part of the Twitter world. Hashtags can order the enormous amount of data going through the channel if you use them consistently. Try to define a hashtag before the courses start and tell your students about it. The consistent use of hashtags allows various aggregation and filter methods for all communication going on in the Twitter channel.

Don't Take Things Too Seriously

Microblogging is a tool, which can be used by anyone. There is simply no guarantee who is behind an account; furthermore also robots are providing messages automatically on Twitter. With other words it must thought about how can I trust written tweets. Are tweets from an account of an avatar from anywhere of this world worth to be trusted? Is an account simply that what it stands for? Are provided information or links simply false? Especially, because of the high amount of information which is overcoming every Twitter user it becomes harder and harder to prove them, to check by using different resources.

In general this leads to the assumption that the e-literacy of the society must be improved by pointing out that every tweet can be as false as it can be true. Social networks seem to be dangerous if we begin to trust followers and friends without any doubt and without knowing them personally.

Say You're Sorry When You Hurt Somebody

As Twitter is an open forum, your words carry weight. Generally, in the heat of the moment it is easy to react to someone else's tweets emotionally. However, we must all be aware that the reduced social cues in solely text-based communication may lead to misunderstandings. The use of emoticons, or other forms of enhanced text can often reduce this misunderstanding. If – for any reason – you have offended someone, be quick to apologise, or retract your comments with good humour. This goes a long way to mending the fences. Ultimately however, if you offend someone, it is more likely they will simply 'unfollow' you rather than confront you.

Wash Your Hands of Scepticism before You Start

People new to Twitter normally are very sceptical towards the tool. Furthermore, young people know very little about Twitter before they use it during formalised education. This is no doubt due to their habituation in the use of other more closed social networking services such as Bebo[7], Myspace[8] and Facebook[9], where message exchanges are enclosed within discrete groups of 'friends'. On Twitter, the architecture is more open, and tweets are searchable using a number of popular search engines.

---

[7] http://www.bebo.com
[8] http://www.myspace.com
[9] http://www.facebook.com

Privacy is therefore less assured, which may be off-putting to some students, who report feeling 'a little exposed'. We reiterate here that any user wishing to engage with others on Twitter must be aware of the e-safety hazards that include privacy and identity issues.

Flush

One challenge of Twitter is to stow as much information as possible in a message of only 140 characters. Obviously everything that you come up with is faultless or comprehensible to your followers. Whilst there is the possibility of deleting single tweets (or even all your tweets with services like Suicidemachine[10]) your tweets are often already been consumed by other services and visible to others. The deletion of a tweet basically makes no sense other than it wont be found by non-followers later on. If you made a mistake during a tweet (e.g. posting a wrong link or forgetting to use the agreed hashtag) just repost the tweet and everything is just fine.

Warm Cookies and Cold Milk Are Good for You

There is a sense that Twitter, if used appropriately can create new friend connections, where previously there may have been no possibility to connect. The authors of this paper all enjoy conversations and friendships with colleagues from around the world. The sharing of the minutiae of life may appear to be trivial and vacuous to outsiders, but occasional humour, comedic interactions and the sharing of life's little twists and quirks often forges stronger friendships due to the effect of self-disclosure. Self-disclosure depends on people revealing some of their thoughts, feelings and emotions, which are then generally reciprocated.

Live a Balanced Life – Learn Some and Think Some and Draw and Paint and Sing and Dance and Play and Work Every Day Some

Twitter should not be seen as the only ultimate goal in life, although for some users, it can become obsessive. Teachers are advised to continue to use alternative media in the classroom and users should continue to pursue a balanced lifestyle that includes real-life interaction with friends and family. There are also means through which several social software tools can work together in concert to amplify content, combine audiences and widen the reach of the social network. These include incorporating Twitter streams into blog pages, or mashing up content using aggregation tools. Melding other content including video, audio and photographic content, through the use of Youtube[11], Audacity[12] or Flickr[13] for example, offers one's social network a rich tapestry of alternative media, which can be expressive and informative. Using Twitter to draw one's social network to visit new posts is an obvious amplification method.

Take a Nap Every Afternoon

You can't tweet 24/7 - usually people go offline while they need to concentrate on other important things like writing a report or paper or reading a book. Doing this the

---

[10] http://suicidemachine.org
[11] http://www.youtube.com
[12] http://audiacity.sourceforge.net
[13] http://flickr.com

users signalise that they won't follow what's going on and won't answer to questions. Twitter has – like many of the other social media tools – a high potential of distracting people from work and should therefore be switched of during phases of relevant and creative work where you need sereneness.

When You Go Out into the World, Watch Out for Traffic, Hold Hands and Stick together

For many Twitter users their network is an invaluable part of their personal learning network as they create new ideas and get insight in the work of other like-minded people. Ebner [15] reports how Tweeple *"have enriched my life and truly helped my professional growth"*. A scenario that is often described and seems to happen to each Twitter user is to ask a specific question to the Twitter without expecting too many responses. Often it happens that active followers start to propose links and other Twitter users, or user lists that might help solving the question. The weak social ties between the different Twitter start to become stronger through helping each other, linking to relevant data sources and chatting off-topic.

Be Aware of Wonder

Twitter is potentially a very powerful social networking tool, so approaching it with a sense of expectation is common. Users discover the serendipity of the service when they come across unexpected but extremely useful content that has been sent or retweeted by other users in their network. Students will often be challenged by the quality of the content they discover, and quickly learn to favourite (bookmark) tweets that they find useful. They also discover how to follow hashtagged streams that relate closely to the formal course content they are studying. This mix of formal and informal content has its nexus on Twitter, and further, the greater number of productive contributors the user follows, the greater will be the possibility that new and unexpected useful content will come their way.

3 Teaching with Twitter

Regarding personal communication devices (like laptops or cell phones) as a distraction is an error. Successful teachers actively try to embed them in their classes, as a means of enhancing learning opportunities. Banning such tools will not enhance a class but students may continue to use them, often surreptitiously. The same applies to a number of social networking tools, and Twitter is no exception.

There are numerous ways Twitter can be integrated into the fabric of both face to face and distance courses. For example, students in foreign language learning can be asked to translate short phrases or sentences sent to them. They may find benefit from participating in exercises where they converse in a foreign language with their tutor, or other language expert using Twitter. This kind of language tandem has been shown to be useful as a route to engaging more deeply with course content.

Twitter can be used as an instant feedback tool, as a means of quickly disseminating important announcements to an entire class, or as a simple medium for discussion during and beyond the hours of classroom learning.

Another useful application for Twitter is as a medium to promote the study of current affairs, politics or culture, through following a celebrity, politician or musician. By doing so, students will receive all tweets from that individual and can build up a dossier of thoughts and actions which over a period of time may create an informative picture of them. On a similar tack, tutors can create an account representing a figure from history or a character from literature, and tweet in the style of that person. Students following the character can enter into dialogue with them, to gain some insight into life, culture and experiences of that time period. More ideas on using Twitter in teaching and learning contexts, both formal and informal can be found on Steve Wheeler's *Learning with 'E's* blog [16].

Microblogging can bring new potential to interact and communicate with tutors and peers. If we take closer look at classroom some interesting scenarios emerge:

- In a first research study by Ebner and Schiefner, microblogging was used to connect experts over a wide distance [17]. Within a given time period the application Jaiku[14] was used to share thoughts, ideas, interests and daily work routines. Especially the exchange of hyperlinks and the possibility to read and write from a mobile device was stated as a big advantage of microblogging.

- Ebner and Maurer [18] tried to investigate if microblogs can enhance traditional essay writing as well as blogging. They introduced a so called microblogging group which have to support other groups by searching the Internet for interesting content and discuss daily opinions. These small information chunks were very useful to such groups who wrote essays about a topic and the evaluation showed that microblogging brought an exciting possibility to their learning behaviour

- A small modification was used at the Graz University of Technology to enhance mass-education [19]. When there are large numbers of students, interaction in the classroom often reduces. Teaching a group of 200 or more students constrains meaningful interactions between teacher and students. Students can feel threatened by large audiences of peers and may be anxious about making errors or being ridiculed. Lecturers often deliver their content with little or no questioning from their learners. Ebner [19] reports a first attempt to enable anonymous questioning through the use of a mobile device and a 140-character entry field. Students were encouraged to interact with the lecturer by using the sending microblogs to a specific API. It was shown that the number of questions increased, but more research on this kind of didactic scenario is required.

- A further investigation using Twitter for educational purposes was to enhance single presentation. Ebner [15] reports that a Twitterwall[15] was placed beside a usual keynote or lecture presentation. This allowed those in the auditorium to discuss, share links, thoughts, pictures and similar throughout the talk. The entire Twitter stream can be saved and subsequently offered to anyone as additional information. Clearly protracted discussions occur because whilst tweeting during presentations leads to distraction and can cause disturbance, we also need to acknowledge that additional materials, comments and questions brought by tweeting, can enhance the presented material. Also Reinhardt et al. [20] report how conference attendees use Twitter for personal sharing, discussions and learning.

---

[14] http://jaiku.com
[15] A Twitterwall is a display where all tweets for a given hashtag are aggregated automatically.

- As we pointed out in section 2.3 microblogging can also be used to allow process-oriented learning as introduced by Ebner et al. [10]. Students' daily activity reports are simply replaced by a fast just-in-time feature to send 140 characters to the Internet. The evaluation and the statistical analyses lead to the assumption that students are more engaged by the tool and this effect can lead to an increasing informal learning process.

4 Summary and Outlook

Anecdotal and empirical evidence shows that Twitter is a powerful tool that can be used in various educational settings. In this paper we have introduced some success stories where Twitter has been applied to educational contexts and surpassed the expectations of the users. Use of Twitter resulted in more active students who connected themselves with their fellow students and experts outside their own community. Twitter was also used in process-oriented learning scenarios as a motivating tool for both students and staff.

With minor adaptations, the basic principles of Fulghum's poem "*All I really need to know I learned in Kindergarten*" [21] are transferable to Twitter as a prominent part of the Social Semantic Web. If you intend to apply Twitter to your course or educational project keep those principles and mind and take into consideration that Twitter is no panacea for education. You will need to pique your student's curiosity and passion for the topic and support them with good material and a conducive learning environment to support their individual needs.

We are just beginning to explore and understand the possible fields of application of Twitter in educational settings and to develop learning scenarios that make more use of microblogging technologies. With the progression of Twitters functionalities and the inclusion of geolocation and RFID technologies in the service, Twitter will become even more interesting for learning and teaching scenarios as real location-based learning will be possible. (Personal) Learning Environments will stronger than before need to mash up data and services of different types in order to sustainably support the individual and organisational learning.

References

1. McGiboney, M.: Keep on tweet'n (March 2009),
   http://www.nielsen-online.com/blog/2009/03/20/keep-on-tweetn/
2. Templeton, M.: Microblogging defined (November 2008),
   http://microblink.com/2008/11/11/microblogging-defined/
3. Owyang, J.: Retweet: The infectious power of word of mouth (November 2008),
   http://www.web-strategist.com/blog/2008/11/23/retweet-the-infectious-power-of-the-word-of-mouth/
4. Ullrich, C., Borau, K., Luo, H., Tan, X., Shen, L., Shen, R.: Why web 2.0 is good for learning and for research: principles and prototypes. In: WWW 2008: Proceeding of the 17th International Conference on World Wide Web, pp. 705–714. ACM, New York (2008)
5. Zhang, J.: A cultural look at information and communication technologies in eastern education. Educational Technology Research and Development 55(3), 301–314 (2007)
6. Rankin, M.: Some general comments on the "twitter experiment" (2009),
   http://www.utdallas.edu/~mrankin/usweb/twitterconclusions.htm

7. Smith, K., Rankin, M.: The twitter experiment – bringing twitter to the classroom at UT Dallas (April 2009), http://kesmit3.blogspot.com/2009/04/twitter-experiment-bringing-twitter-to.html
8. Parry, D.: Twitter for academia (January 2008), http://academhack.outsidethetext.com/home/2008/twitter-for-academia/
9. Young, J.R.: A professor's tips for using twitter in the classroom (January 2008), http://chronicle.com/blogPost/A-Professor-s-Tips-for-Using/3643
10. Ebner, M., Lienhardt, C., Rohs, M., Meyer, I.: Microblogs in higher education – a chance to facilitate informal and process oriented learning? Computers & Education (2010)
11. Java, A., Song, X., Finin, T., Tseng, B.: Why we twitter: understanding microblogging usage and communities. In: Proceedings of the 9th WebKDD and 1st SNA-KDD 2007 Workshop on Web Mining and Social Network Analysis, pp. 56–65. ACM, New York (2007)
12. Gordon, J.: 100 serious twitter tips for academics (July 2009), http://www.bestcollegesonline.com/blog/2009/07/21/100-serious-twitter-tips-for-academics/
13. boyd, d., Golder, S., Lotan, G.: Tweet, tweet, retweet: Conversational aspects of retweeting on twitter. In: Proceedings of the HICSS-43 Conference (January 2010)
14. Messina, C.: Groups for twitter; or a proposal for twit- ter tag channels (August 2007), http://factoryjoe.com/blog/2007/08/25/groups-for-twitter-or-a-proposal-for-twitter-tag-channels/
15. Ebner, M.: Introducing Live Microblogging – How Single Presentations can be enhanced by the Mass. Journal of Research in Innovative Teaching (JRIT) 2(1), 91–100 (2009)
16. Wheeler, S.: Teaching with Twitter (January 2009), http://steve-wheeler.blogspot.com/2009/01/teaching-with-twitter.html
17. Ebner, M., Schiefner, M.: Microblogging – more than fun? In: Mobile Learning Conference 2008, pp. 155–159 (2008)
18. Ebner, M., Maurer, H.: Can microblogs and weblogs change traditional scientific writing? In: Proceedings of the E-Learn 2008, pp. 768–776 (2008)
19. Ebner, M.: Interactive Lecturing by Integrating Mobile Devices and Micro-blogging. Higher Education, CIT – Journal of Computing and Information Technology (accepted) (in print)
20. Reinhardt, W., Ebner, M., Beham, G., Costa, C.: How people are using twitter during conferences. In: Hornung-Prähauser, V., Luckmann, M. (eds.) Proceedings of the 5th EduMedia Conference, pp. 145–156 (2009)
21. Fulghum, R.: All I really need to know I learned in kindergarten – Uncommon thoughts on common things. Villard Books (1988)
22. Cross, J.: Informal Learning – Rediscovering the Pathways that inspire innovation and performance. Pfeiffer (2006)
23. Grosseck, G., Holotescu, C.: Can we use twitter for educational activities? In: Proceedings of the 4th International Scientific Conference eLSE "eLearning and Software for Education" (April 2008)
24. Lee, M.: How twitter changed my life (January 2009), http://www.slideshare.net/minxuan/how-twitter-changed-my-life-presentation
25. Warburton, S.: Stories of digital identity - tales from twitter (January 2010), http://warburton.typepad.com/liquidlearning/2009/01/stories-of-digital-identity-tales-from-twitter.html
26. Williams, L.A., Kessler, R.R.: All I really need to know about pair programming I learned in kindergarten. Communications of the ACM 43(5), 114 (2000)

Technology and Computers in Music and Music Education

Nicholas Reynolds

Melbourne Graduate School of Education, The University of Melbourne, Australia
nreyn@unimelb.edu.au

Abstract. The use of computers in music education is investigated from a historical perspective that draws parallels to the use of computers in education generally. Drawing upon a study into the musical compositions of primary school children working in electronic environments this paper presents approaches to the use of ICT in music education that appear at odds with approaches in other education areas. The paper provides reasons for this and offers ways in which ICT can be used differently in music education research.

Keywords: Music, children's compositions, ICT, literature.

1 Introduction

In investigating the literature into ICT in music education as part of a twelve month study into the compositional process of children aged ten to twelve years in an electronic environment, the author became aware of a representation of the use of ICT as one very much situated in an instructional approach to music teaching, rather than in the more constructivist approaches that populate the ICT in Education literature at large. This paper presents some of the literature from music education and places it against literature about the use of ICT in a broader educational context. The contrast is made within the context of the research project.

2 Background

In an investigation of the compositions and compositional processes of children working in an electronic environment the current study required the children to engage in a number of loosely structured compositional tasks over much of a school year. Meeting weekly, the children were encouraged to compose music of their own choosing. Very little was given as instruction and rarely were considerations of form or convention mandated or even discussed. This allowed the researcher to examine what the children did musically rather than what they were taught about music through the use of ICT. The seven children in the study (four boys and three girls) frequently collaborated in their compositional tasks and in the production of some 250 compositions that demonstrated approaches to music, to music perception, to musical representation, to musical preference and to musical understanding that were made accessible through the interaction with ICT.

N. Reynolds and M. Turcsányi-Szabó (Eds.): KCKS 2010, IFIP AICT 324, pp. 333–343, 2010.

3   ICT in Music Education

There still appears to be a focus in music education literature about what the technology is but little on what the technology means in terms of rich or different experiences for children. Work by Reynolds [1, 2] presents an approach that looks at the computer as something that allows the child to do something that could not be done without it. That approach draws heavily on the work of Papert [3] and McDougall [4]. Published work from the current study [5-8] presents views about how the computer allows us to investigate children's compositions and, perhaps more importantly, how it allows us to investigate and develop our own understandings about children's musical perceptions and understanding. A significant contributor to the development of our understanding is the fact that the computer allows us into the processes of composition in ways that have never before been possible. This approach is not specifically developmental, yet provides opportunities to look at musical development in different ways.

Computers and technology are viewed by Webster and Hickey [9] mainly from a perspective of computer-aided instruction (CAI). Their review of literature is one that is drawn mostly from sources that describe the uses of computers in the teaching of music. Their understanding of CAI fits with Papert's [3] less than flattering description made in the early 1980s where CAI "means making the computer teach the child" [3]. Papert's ideal is that the role of the computer is to be a "*carrier* of cultural 'germs' or 'seeds' whose intellectual products will not need technological support once they take root in an actively growing mind"[3] .

Webster and Hickey categorize software titles into music content by age group. Interestingly, they place *Audacity*, an open source, multitrack editing and recording application (and one of the programs used by the children in the aforementioned study) into their 'perception' category for 10-15 year olds, where it can be used to develop musical perception by playing teacher recorded examples of typical musical elements. In the current study the children used it not to listen to musical examples but as a compositional tool. In their 'creating' category for that age group they only list looping type titles such as *GarageBand* (a multitrack midi and audio program for Mac computers that operates through a process of dragging and dropping pre-recorded clips onto a timeline) and *Acid Studio* (another multitrack midi and audio program that is typically used by dragging pre-recorded clips onto a timeline and 'looping' them). Looping software typically constrains the user into a rigid four beats to the bar framework and relies on the piling up of short melodic phrases that align themselves tonally and rhythmically to the timeline. Webster and Hickey place programs that are equivalent to *Cakewalk*, a multitrack midi sequencer and digital audio application (the other program used in the current study) into the 'creating' category for the 16-adult age group.

From a developmental music education perspective this categorization makes sense but it doesn't fit with ideas about the use of computers as the 'knowledge machines' that Papert proposed many years ago, or with the approaches to computers in children's music making adopted as part of the current study. The developmental approach adopted by Webster and Hickey also places them at odds with Papert's ideals. In the opening sections of his book, *Mindstorms*, Papert [3] describes the book's purpose (and his beliefs about computers in education) as follows:

> This book is about how computers can be carriers of powerful ideas and of the
> seeds of cultural change, how they can help people form new relationships with
> knowledge that cut across the traditional lines separating humanities from sciences
> and knowledge of the self from both of these. It is about using computers to challenge
> current beliefs about who can understand what and at what age. It is about using
> computers to question standard assumptions in developmental psychology and in the
> psychology of aptitudes and attitudes [3].

These ideas resonate very strongly with the approach taken in the current study and
are presented here to demonstrate the significantly different approaches to and understanding of the use of computers by educators in all areas of education.

Webster and Hickey see the instant music making capacities of programs like *GarageBand, Acid Studio* and *Sooper Dooper Music Looper* (a junior and more constrained version of *Acid* that is designed specifically for primary aged children) as
being potentially beneficial in developing musical perception, but argue that their use
"needs to be tempered with expert teaching [that can] help challenge students to develop more sensitive and complex ways to think musically" [9]. They also call for
more research into how these technologies "can be done well or in a way consistent
with current theories" [9].

The notion that children don't already think in musically complex or sensitive
ways is one that needs challenging, although not necessarily here but these complex
and sensitive musical ways of thinking don't necessarily fit with developmental
approaches, with accepted musical thinking or with educational outcomes. More importantly, the call to link technology use to existing theories demonstrates a certain
cautious and traditional approach to research and to technology. While not discarding
the existing theories, and acknowledging their importance, it is important to consider
how new technologies allow for new investigations and understandings as well as the
development of *new* theories. Accordingly, it is important to embrace the potential of
computers to do much more than reinforcing musical instruction.

In a later chapter on computers and technology Webster [10] focuses on presenting
a recent historical perspective, supported by older research. Unfortunately from the
perspective of expanding the capacity of computers in music education, it offers no
new ideas about the use of computers in understanding children's engagements with
music or their own musical understandings. Despite the title including 'learning' the
chapter is really a focus on 'teaching' with technology. This reinforces that cautious
and traditional approach to the use of computers in music education.

Webster's investigation of computer technology to support composition is, as is
much of the literature, either based on young adult musicians composing or children
being given 'special' software that composes for them. Nothing could be further from
the constructivist approaches of Papert and others.

As indicated by the Webster and Hickey, and the Webster chapters much of the literature around the use of computers in music education is about the computer as
teacher. The examples of the ways children's music making is represented in the
literature, provided later in this paper, demonstrate the pervasiveness of that approach.

Folkestad, Hargreaves and Lindström, [11], Nilsson [12], and Nilsson and Folkestad [13] have provided valuable studies on the use of technology in children's and
young people's compositional approaches. Their studies focused on the role of the
computer and peripheral hardware and software in the compositional processes of

young people. The Folkestad studies investigated adolescent children, and the Nilsson studies younger children. The role of the computer in these studies was not that of teacher or instructor but one of participant in the creative and compositional processes of young people.

4 ICT and Education

A significant area of focus for the current study is the role of the computer and the electronic environment and the relationship the participants have with that environment in the compositions and compositional process. It is clear that musically the computer allows children to do things in new ways and to overcome musical technical deficiencies in order to compose or to create works of greater complexity (not the best choice of word in the context of this study) than they could without the computer [1, 12, 14]. Amongst other things children do not need to rely on other children to understand their ideas, they do not need to be able to notate a piece in order for it to be played, they do not need instrumental mastery in order to play their own works and they are presented with an almost unlimited canvas of instruments and sounds from which to create their pieces. The affordances of this environment are something that is particularly attractive to me. The following section presents an investigation of literature that is focused on research that investigates the enabling power of ICT in education.

Underpinning this study is a personal belief about the relationship that exists between children (young people) and computers. In using the term 'computers' much more is referred to than the box that sits on the desk; regardless of whether that box is a phone, a music player, a laptop (or netbook), a hand held device of any description or a standard personal computer like the ones used in this study. Papert's ideas of computers being knowledge machines are referred to earlier in this paper. These are powerful ideas (deliberate use of this term) and inform one significant part of this author's beliefs about computer use and children. Another significant part has its roots in the writings of John Perry Barlow. In the early 1990s Barlow experienced first hand a new form of interaction and communication in cyberspace and developed ideas about the nature of that 'place' and its 'inhabitants'. The idea that cyberspace affords completely different things to different groups of people is very appealing. More appealing is his description of a father's perspective of computers and cyberspace, which he refers to "as an immigrant's fear of a strange new land into which he will be forcibly moved and in which his own child is a native" [15]. This idea is expanded by Bigum and Lankshear [16], Lankshear and Bigum [17], and by Lankshear and Knobel [18] with a focus on the mindsets of the individuals using computers and interacting with cyberspace, and what that means for schools, schooling and learning. The notion of immigrants and natives is clarified by Lankshear and Bigum, who prefer the terms 'insiders' and 'newcomers'; they use Barlow to "distinguish the two broad mind sets identified; one affirms the world as the same as before, only more technologised; the other affirms the world as radically different, precisely because of the operation of new technologies" [17].

There are a number of parallels between the field of ICT in education research and the field of ICT in music education research. The first is that there has been a stream of focus that deals with tools and usage; what equipment is being used, how many schools/children are using it and attempted connections between technology and learning outcomes. Within this stream are many large projects and government reports into areas such as teacher attainment [19], pupil learning and attainment [20], student ICT literacy [21] school use [22] and, amongst other things, the impact of ICT on students [23].

A second stream, and one that has much more relevance to the current study, is that of educators working with technology as an enabler of different things. Building on the work of Papert, Resnick [24, 25] presents children's playful learning in creative and collaborative environments while working with the programming application, *Scratch*. In these environments children are encouraged to explore new and different ways of communicating ideas and of collaborating with each other on a global or local level. This focus on children making, creating, exploring, playing and communicating, and what happens when they do those things in electronic environments is closely aligned to the kinds of computing that are represented in the current study.

Narayanan [26], also working with *Scratch* and with *Pico Crickets* (programmable interactive devices) presents a view of technology enabled learning that fits with a philosophy of Slow Schooling, where time is taken, not in getting through the curriculum but in experiencing the physical and virtual environment. Her work with impoverished slum dwellers in Bangalore presents a use of technology that connects the child with their environment and allows them to interact with it and investigate it while at the same time developing language, computer and cultural skills. The technology is central to her work but it is never taught. Narayanan asks a series of questions that relates to her beliefs about "the landscapes of education and technology"

- Have the contours of this landscape been created by the tools of technology defining the nature and scope of the learning environment?
- Or have the contours of this new landscape been defined by learning needs and contexts which in turn inform the creation and sustaining of digital or virtual learning worlds?

- Are the horizons of this landscape defined by the convergence of traditional literacies integrated with conventional and new medias?
- Or do the distributed networks of new media define both the horizon and reach of the communication and literacy agendas of teachers and educators?

- Should the development goals of education with technology focus on the development of the brain, the intellect and the mind?
- Or is about developing the heart and expanding the inner self? [26]

The well known work of Sugata Mitra and his Hole in the Wall projects is another example of the use of technology in education as an enabler of powerful things. Mitra, like Narayanan does not engage in any instruction of technology, preferring to observe children playing, experimenting and teaching themselves about the electronic environments that they are beginning to experience. In a significant body of work Mitra and colleagues [27-31] present a Minimally Invasive Education (MIE) model in which the principles of play and experimentation underpin a learning environment that is non instructional and which encourages peer support. This model is applied across the curriculum and places the learning and the technology in the hands of the learner.

Throughout this body of work, running alongside the notion of MIE, is the idea of learning as "a self organizing system". Mitra puts it this way:

> Self organizing systems have low predictability, they are 'grown' and not 'made'. In a sense, they represent our transition from the industrial to the information age. 'Making it happen' was the management paradigm of the age gone by. 'Letting it happen' will be the strategy for building the systems of the new age. The real paradigm shift in education will be the conversion of the educational process into self-organizing systems. [29]

These ideas represent an approach to education and to ICT in education that has its genesis in the works of Papert and is an example of the "modern traditionalism" that McDougall [32] proposes educators who use ICT engage in; an acknowledgement of the important work done by thinkers like Papert in the Twentieth Century. It, like that of Resnick and Narayanan, and the current study, also has its roots firmly planted in the acknowledgement of the centrality of play.

Narayanan's responses are also driven by a desire to connect with and to a lost culture. The Burarra talking book project [33] is an example of the use of technologies in the recording and presentation of indigenous languages to Indigenous Australian children in order to develop literacy in what is their first language.

The Burarra project, like that of Narayanan's is an example of educational technology outside the realms of 'traditional' schooling and is an example of the learning being placed in the hands of the learner, supported by technology with minimal (visible) intervention. It takes technology out of what Narayanan calls the 'plenitude'. For her this plenitude is an example of and a result of old ways of thinking that do not see what technology can do and be. She says:

> What I also realize is that our contemporary notion of school is a place where the official curriculum is driven by ideas and attitudes that are expressed or implied in the materials, textbooks and technology that form yet another plenitude that is engulfing teachers, curriculum designers and policy makers. This is due to in large part to conventional thinking about digital technologies and learning, a way of thinking that argues that more technology, greater access and better connectivity will deliver faster learning for more learners across far distances in short periods of time [26].

There is strong resonance here with the ideas of Barlow and Lankshear discussed earlier where the mind set of the educator needs to acknowledge the mind sets of the learner when using digital technologies and the perceived affordances therein.

The work of Vincent [34, 35] in investigating the relationships between learning styles, multimedia and the crossing of semiotic boundaries is another example of the this second stream of ICT in education research that asks what happens when children can play and explore with computers, what things can they do with computers that they couldn't do without them and most importantly, what can we learn about the ways children think and learn.

The examples presented from what is termed above as the second stream are only a sample from the literature that demonstrate a way of thinking about and investigating the ways in which computers and computer technologies are used in educational settings with children. An investigation that looks at the relationship with the environment can easily accept the ideas of Barlow and his notion of mindsets and cyberspace. His ideas are in accord with those of Papert who said that when computers "enter the private worlds of children everywhere. They will do so not as mere physical objects" [3].

5   Children's Use of ICT as Represented in the Music Literature

There are an increasing number of studies that look at the use of ICT in the compositional approaches of children. The following section presents, very briefly, some of those examples and attempts to show typical use of ICT in music education research. It will be contrasted with examples from the current study to highlight the significant differences in approaches. The most significant difference is in the acknowledgement that children don't necessarily understand or work within strict conventional time structures. A problem for researchers is the graphical representation of children's compositions. In order to represent those compositions in a manner that can be understood by the reader it is necessary to convert an audio recording or a child's play into a notation system that was not applied by the child at the time of composition. In the following examples researchers have either chosen to represent children's compositions in ways that are understandable to the reader or they have manipulated the software (before the child started composing) in order to adhere to western musical convention.

Nilsson [12] presents examples of children's compositions using *Cubase Score*, a midi sequencer and notation program all examples are presented in strict four/four timing with perfectly placed notation; an indication that either the files were 'quantized' (a process in midi sequencers wherein note lengths and starting positions are moved in order to create regular beat and rhythm) or the notation representation was made at a quaver or semi quaver resolution (midi notation programs allow for notes to appear to have been 'quantized' without actually changing the played values).

Jennings [36] presented one ten year old child's work that was composed with the specially designed children's compositional software, Hyperscore. He represents the child's work as screenshots from the software. These screenshots show 'blobs' of sound that are placed along a ruler, these 'blobs' can be arranged vertically and horizontally. Interestingly, Jennings's subsequent examples are those of compositions made after teacher intervention "designed to encourage Kevin (student's name) to move beyond the superficial exploration of the interface and reframe the task in a musical context" [36]. These examples show perfectly lined up regular four bar

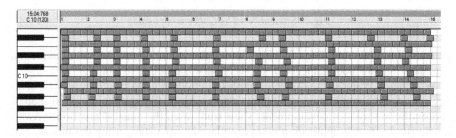

Fig. 1. Track 3 from Student Na's *Piano Roll* piece

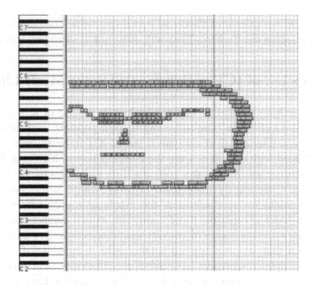

Fig. 2. Student L's *Face* composition

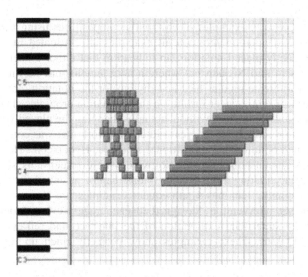

Fig. 3. Student N's *The Golfer* composition

patterns. The inference from Jennings is that the initial compositional example was somehow 'wrong' and that teacher intervention was required to 'fix it'.

Wilson and Wales [37] provide examples of children's compositions in their investigation of the complexity of children's compositions through the focus on melodic and rhythmic stages of development. Their study used the musical notation software, *Music Works*. In this application notes are placed onto a stave using the mouse. Note values are presented in a palette and notes must be selected from the palette and dropped onto the stave to represent pitch and rhythm.

It is difficult to select three examples from more than 250 but these three are representative of one approach to composition that the children engaged in. Through the use of the piano roll view in Cakewalk the children played with the notion of 'drawing' their compositions. Examples from the current study show a complete lack of understanding or consideration for conventional beat and time structures. The following examples are screenshots of children's compositions. The first example, figure 1, is not a drawing but is a visually constructed piece where layers of sound are built up and intersected. The composer's idea here was to play with those layers. The only rhythmic regularity is in the note length.

The next two examples are of musical 'pictures'. The first, figure 2, is of a face. This work, by Student L, was composed as a picture. The musical consideration (sound) was of secondary importance. The piece was, however, listened to critically by the composer.

The final example, figure 3, is an example of the layering of sound combined with a drawing. The golfer in the picture appears to be attempting to play up the 'hill' of layered notes. The composer was, however, just playing with look and sound.

6 Conclusion

The author is of the opinion that researchers of children's musical compositions work around notions of melodic and harmonic structure. Typically children's works are presented in a way that demonstrates skill, or lack of it, in melodic development, sequencing, awareness of harmony and rhythmic structure. Assumptions are either made about children's understandings of these features or the way the data was collected or analyzed did not allow for these features to be fully investigated without adult intervention. This might sound like a criticism of previous research; for the most part it is most certainly not. The work of Swanwick, Swanwick and Tillman, Folkestad, Nilsson, and Barrett, to name a few, are of significant importance; their focus and analyses are different from those of the current study, and so the way they discuss children's compositions is different. They are highlighted here in order to draw attention to the difference and because of their importance within the literature. The difference is also highlighted to demonstrate that through the use of ICT it is possible to venture into new and exciting possibilities and understanding about the way children learn and understand.

References

1. Reynolds, N.J.: Primary School Creativity and Composition in a Professional Level Music Software Environment. Faculty of Education, M ITEd. University of Melbourne, Melbourne, 110 (2001) (plus appendices)
2. Reynolds, N.J.: Computers, Creativity and Composition in the Primary School: An analysis of two compositions. Australian Journal of Music Education 1, 16–26 (2002)
3. Papert, S.: Mindstorms: Children, computers, and powerful ideas. Harvester, Brighton (1980)

4. McDougall, A.: Children, recursion and Logo programming: An investigation of Papert's conjecture about the variability of Piagetian stages in computer-rich cultures. In: McDougall, A., Dowling, C. (eds.) Computers in Education, IFIP TC 3 5th World Conference on Computers in Education - WCCE 1990. Elsevier Science, Sydney (1990)

5. Reynolds, N.J.: The Computer as Scaffold, Tool and Data Collector: Children Composing with Computers. Education and Information Technologies 10, 239–248 (2005)

6. Reynolds, N.J.: Seeking Affordances: searching for new definitions and new understandings of children's relationships with technologies in musical compositions. Australian Educational Computing 23 (2008)

7. Reynolds, N.J.: An Ecological Approach to ICT and Children. In: Benzie, D., Zammit, K. (eds.) IFIP WG 3.5 International Conference - Valuing individual and shared learning: the role of ICT. Charles University in Prague, Czech Republic (2008)

8. Reynolds, N.J.: When wrong is right: Understanding children's electronic compositions. In: ASME XVII National Conference: Musical Understanding. ASME, Launceston (2009)

9. Webster, P., Hickey, M.: Computers and Technology. In: McPherson, G. (ed.) The Child as Musician, pp. 375–395. Oxford University Press, Oxford (2006)

10. Webster, P.: Computer-Based Technology and Music Teaching and Learning: 2000-2005. In: Bresler, L. (ed.) International Handbook of Research in Arts Education; Part Two, pp. 1311–1328. Springer, Dordrecht (2007)

11. Folkestad, G., Hargreaves, D.J., Lindström, B.: Compositional Strategies in Computer-Based Music-Making. British Journal of Music Education 15, 83–97 (1998)

12. Nilsson, B.: "I can always make another one!" - Young musicians creating music with digital tools. In: Leong, S. (ed.) Musicianship in the 21st Century: Issues, Trends and Possibilities, pp. 204–218. Australian Music Centre, Sydney (2003)

13. Nilsson, B., Folkestad, G.: Children's practice of computer-based composition. Music Education Research 7, 21–37 (2005)

14. Barrett, M.: Meme Engineers: children as producers of musical culture. International Journal of Early Years Education 11, 195–212 (2003)

15. Barlow, J.P.: Crime and Puzzlement 1, vol. 2005 (1990)

16. Bigum, C., Lankshear, C.: Literacies and technologies in school settings: Findings from the field. In: Keynote address to 1998 ALEA/ATEA National Conference, Canberra, vol. 2005 (July 1998)

17. Lankshear, C., Bigum, C.: Literacies and new technologies in school settings. Pedagogy, Culture & Society 7, 445–465 (1999)

18. Lankshear, C., Knobel, M.: Mapping postmodern literacies: A preliminary chart. The Journal of Literacy and Technolgy 1 (2000)

19. Cox, M.J., Abbott, C. (eds.): ICT and Attainment: a review of the research literature. BECTA / DfES, London (2004)

20. Harrison, C., Comber, C., Fisher, T., Haw, K., Lewin, C., Lunzer, E., McFarlane, A., Mavers, D., Scrimshaw, P., Somekh, B., Watling, R.: ImpaCT2: The Impact of Information and Communication Technologies on Pupil Learning and Attainment. BECTA, London (2003)

21. Ainley, J., Fraillon, J., Freeman, C.: National Assessment Program: ICT Literacy Years 6 and 10 Report 2005. MCEETYA, Carlton South (2007)

22. Cuban, L., Kirkpatrick, H., Peck, C.: High Access and Low Use of Technologies in High School Classrooms: Explaining an Apparent Paradox. American Educational Research Journal 38, 813–834 (2001)

23. Condie, R., Munro, R.: The Impact of ICT in schools - a Landscape Review. BECTA, Coventry (2007)

24. Resnick, M.: Rethinking learning in the digital age. In: Kirkman, G. (ed.) The Global Information Technology Report: Readiness for the Networked World. Oxford University Press, New York (2002)
25. Resnick, M.: Sowing seeds for a more creative society. Learning & Leading with Technology 35, 18–22 (2008)
26. Narayanan, G.: Moving beyond the Plenitude: An Indian Fable. In: ED-MEDIA World Conference on Educational Multimedia, Hypermedia & Telecommunications. AACE, Vienna (2008)
27. Mitra, S.: Self organising systems for mass computer literacy: Findings from the 'hole in the wall' experiments. International Journal of Development Issues 4, 71–81 (2005)
28. Mitra, S., Rana, V.: Children and the Internet: Experiments with minimally invasive education in India. The British Journal of Educational Technology 32, 221–232 (2001)
29. Mitra, S.: Children and the Internet: New Paradigms for Development in the 21st Century. In: Asian Science and Technology Conference, Tokyo, Japan (2000)
30. Mitra, S., Dangwal, R., Chatterjee, S., Jha, S., Bisht, R., Kapur, P.: Acquisition of computing literacy on shared public computers: Children and the 'Hole in the Wall' Australasian. Journal of Educational Technology 21, 407–426 (2005)
31. Inamdar, P., Kulkarni, A.: 'Hole-In-The-Wall' Computer Kiosks Foster Mathematics Achievement - A comparative study. Educational Technology & Society 10, 170–179 (2007)
32. McDougall, A.: Twenty years of Australian Educational Computing: A call for modern traditionalism. Australian Educational Computing 20, 11–13 (2005)
33. Auld, G., Darcy, R.: The production and distribution of Burarra Talking Books. Australian Educational Computing 23, 19–23 (2008)
34. Vincent, J.: Writing and Coding: Assisting writers to cross the modes. Language and Education 21, 141–157 (2007)
35. Vincent, J.: Computer mediated multimodal text production: ten-year-olds crossing semiotic boundaries. Lambert Academic Publishing, Cologne (2009)
36. Jennings, K.: Hyperscore: A case study in computer mediated musical composition. Education and Information Technologies 10, 225–238 (2005)
37. Wilson, S.J., Wales, R.J.: An exploration of children's musical compositions. Journal of Research in Music Education 43, 94–111 (1995)

Collaborative Research Training Based on Virtual Spaces

Darío Rodríguez, Rodolfo Bertone, and Ramón García-Martínez

Programa de Maestría en Tecnología Informática Aplicada a la Educación,
Facultad de Informática, Universidad Nacional de La Plata, Argentina
Grupo de Investigación en Sistemas de Información. Departamento de Desarrollo
Productivo y Tecnológico, Universidad Nacional de Lanús, Argentina
Instituto de Investigaciones en Informática LIDI. Facultad de Informática,
Universidad Nacional de La Plata, Argentina
{darodriguez,rgarcia}@unla.edu.ar,
pbertone@lidi.info.unlp.edu.ar

Abstract. A possible strategy for training researchers is to provide integrated research cores with researchers-in-training under the guidance of a senior trained researcher. Information technology and communication have enabled the construction of virtual communities formed by individuals who may be far away physically but who are cognitively close, hence giving rise to collaborative research training models. In this context, this paper formulates an approach to identify the elements of the work space of a research group devoted to research training and to assess the technological feasibility of virtualization of such elements.

Keywords: Collaborative research training. Feasibility of researcher training virtualization.

1 Introduction

Several authors [1] [2] [3] [4] have noted that the research team can be made up of individuals who do not belong to the same institution or even the same country, and that the only requirement is that these individuals share the sense of belonging to a certain research group. Information technology and communication have enabled the construction of virtual communities formed by individuals who may be far away physically but cognitively close [5]. In this context, the massive use of the Internet demands a new conceptualization of notions such as research groups, research training, peer publications, socialization, and cooperation, among others. Virtualization has fostered the notion that groups are definitely not the sum of individuals but the result of a network of symbolic systems, practices, rituals and reflections. In this network of exchange of meanings among researchers regarding the object and the research project, a kind of virtual school is built where status is granted and research products are valued.

This paper introduces a possible theoretical framework (Section 2) in which the various definitions that the community has built upon research and projects (Section 2.1), training of researchers (Section 2.2) the concept of research communities

N. Reynolds and M. Turcsányi-Szabó (Eds.): KCKS 2010, IFIP AICT 324, pp. 344–353, 2010.

(Section 2.3), and the relationships between interpersonal communication, researcher training and R&D groups (Section 2.4) are presented. It also introduces a collaborative model for researcher training (Section 3) where the concept of research and research plan (Section 3.1) and the dynamics of the research group associated with the model (Section 3.2) are described in context. The technological feasibility of visualization of the model described (Section 4), identifying elements of the work space and their features, and exploring the technological feasibility of virtual work space by the construction of a web-based software artifact prototype is discussed. Finally, the conclusions and future lines of work are presented (Section 5).

2 Theoretical Framework

In this section, different aspects of the theoretical framework that the community has developed such as research, research projects, research training, research communities and their relation to the training of researchers are presented.

2.1 Research and Projects

Inciarte and Torres [6], propose that investigation is an ordering axis of research activity, having a rational basis and allowing for the integration and continuity of the efforts of one or more individuals, teams or institutions committed to the development of knowledge in a specific area. Its identification permits to establish levels of detail and specificity to address problems whose need to be solved is evident and shared. This, in turn, forms a teaching and learning scheme focused on research that has the following advantages:

[a] it promotes openness to criticize various unrestricted aspects or approaches to unique paradigmatic visions, convergence and divergence of concepts, approaches, methods and paradigms, dialogue, reflection and analysis of the deep and fruitful work of researchers-in-training. That is, openness to be observed by colleagues and strangers.

[b] it provides an excellent space to develop the research-learning process.

[c] it help to project the research allowing for an effective use of knowledge upon practice.

2.2 Research Training

Sánchez [7] argues that the training of researchers presents a pedagogical relationship in which three stages that will become the common axes of analysis may be identified:

[a] The interaction with the social environment (subjects and objects involved in the learning process).

[b] The individual appropriation or internalization on the part of the subject of knowledge generated by his/her research community.

[c] The transformation into the design of a project that is crystallized in a creation to solve a problem in one area of knowledge.

Villarreal and Guevara [8] indicate that a possible strategy for training researchers is to provide integrated research cores formed by researchers-in-training under the guidance of a trained investigator with the following objectives: to collaborate with a project a senior researcher is developing and then generate his/her own project in collaboration with the senior researcher and under his/her guidance. In agreement with this, Moreno [5] proposes that the core of scientific research today are the groups (or communities) working around specific research projects. Moreover, is based on the fact that the preparation of human resources in research is closely related to the creation of an academic community, and hence to the development of knowledge [9]. In particular, the scientific communities express and embody epistemologies that circulate through fields and disciplines and that operate as a contextual indicator of the status of research training.

2.3 Research Communities

The lonely researcher is capable of generating knowledge, but is limited by the unidimensionality in training; then, the need to comprehensively approach reality is seen, and this requires various perspectives to be gathered in order to understand the subject. Hence, groups arose that are not a number of isolated projects put together, but a structure made up of individual interests trying to get acquainted with the same thematic area or nuclear problem [10].

Sánchez and Granados [11] define a research community constituted by: senior researchers, junior researchers, PhD students, advanced master students, and near graduation students. The research seminar (or workshop) is a practice established by the research groups to review the progress of their projects, so it becomes the natural structure that integrates this revision work. One of its advantages is its horizontality because it exceeds the traditional teacher-student relationship and fosters a relationship between colleagues. The collective space dynamics allows for autonomy spaces which conjugates the different experiences of all its members. It is a space of co-construction, in which everyone learns, clarify their doubts and enrich projects with inputs from the group. The uptake of training by a researcher in a research community will benefit him because he has not yet acquired the same amount of information that trained investigators have as for instance personal collections of publications and a network of personal contacts with research expert fellows that can reduce the need for extensive information search, and therefore improve the use of information skills [12].

2.4 Interpersonal Communication, Training and R&D Group

The communication promoted within a research community is a factor that favors the development of its members who, in permanent interaction subject+subject or subject+research-object, contribute with their expertise to solve problems. This interaction is mediated by knowledge and experience from both the academic and the professional world, which are significant to those who belong to a particular research community. Communication through group sessions, open spaces for senior researcher to consolidate the progress a researcher under training has made while the latter can benefit from the comments he/she makes to his peers as well as from peer observations. Through sharing and collaborating in research groups, an inter-formative relationship among its members is developed that turns them into co-construction spaces of knowledge which acquire a pedagogical value, since those who have access to methods and experiences developed by other researchers favors with the development of skills that are necessary for professional performance.

In this context, Moreno [5] indicates that the group provides a source that makes the relationship between the apprentice (young researcher) and the researcher (principal investigator) possible. The apprentice learns by comparing his emerging knowledge with the mature knowledge of other researchers, not only in terms of management tools, which is sometimes unfortunately most important, but also from the expert judgments, which represent the most sophisticated investigative learning. That is why during this process, the guidance and advice of a senior researcher is essential to correct and encourage the progress of a researcher under training. His collaboration is crucial, his knowledge and experience devoted to guide and strengthen the performance of novice researchers allows for the development of skills that lead them to make innovative projects and generate knowledge and technology [11].

3 Collaborative Model for Research Training (MCFI)

Rodriguez, Bertone and García-Martínez [4] propose a model for the training of researchers focused on collaboration. This model defines two aspects to be considered. First, the allocation of research topics, and second, the dynamics of group-oriented research to be "per se" an institution devoted to research training.

3.1 Online Research and Research Plan

The research group focuses on a senior researcher, who defines the research topics and generates the associated research plan. He establishes the research limits and determines the area of knowledge on which to apply the research plan. All members of the Research Group work in the same domain knowledge at different levels. The Senior Researcher assigns the research subjects (PhD dissertation, Masters, Specialty or Grade) under different levels of implementation of research considering the following premises: Doctoral Thesis, which generates new knowledge within the domain established by trained investigators; Master Thesis, which establishes the manner in which the knowledge developed by PhD students can be applied to an advanced development (i.e.: Expert system); Specialty thesis, which involves a documental research project or an exploratory experimental work. This is linked to master and doctoral students. Grade Thesis, which develops a software artifact related to a master or a PhD research project. These relationships are illustrated in the diagram in Figure 1.

Within the research plan various research programs are generated, each linked in its origin to the proposal of a PhD student. For example, Figure 2 shows how the nodes marked in Figure 1 correspond to a real research program in which projects are related thesis of four different institutions.

These programs are mutually independent but are part of the domain knowledge associated with the research line defined by the senior researcher.

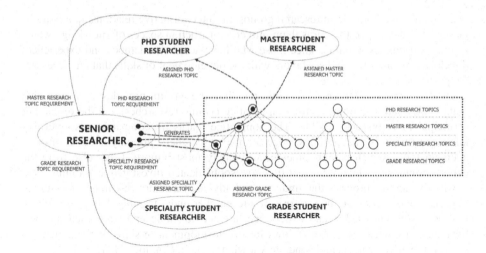

Fig. 1. Generation of research plan and allocation of research topics

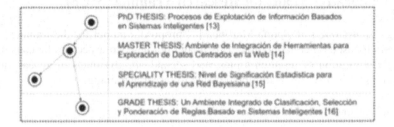

Fig. 2. Real Research Program Example

The work of the master student completes the work began by the PhD student, thus generating his own project, chained to the doctoral student. This chain is completed by other theses of specialty and grade that are incorporated in the level immediately below the feeding chain and achieve the necessary feedback to verify and validate in real and concrete fields the doctoral student proposal.

3.2 Research Group Dynamics

As we move up the research levels, a general and global overview of the research process is obtained. The role of a senior researcher in the research process is to be a counselor and facilitator to the lower levels in the context of collaborative and participative learning [17]. The same research topic is approached at different research levels (PhD, Master, others), and in a natural collaboration an integrated process is achieved. The supervision takes place among high level training researchers interacting with immediately lower level training researchers. In comparison with the senior researchers, they are peers however they achieve research management and lower level researcher's contention [18].

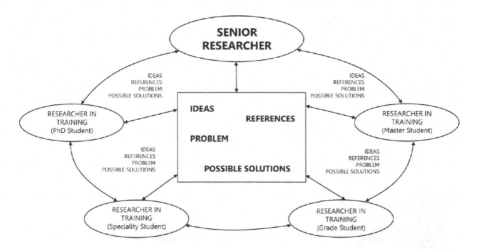

Fig. 3. Network of relationships in the researchers training collaborative model

The relationship network that guide the distribution of research tasks involves a circular collaborative network [19] that contains the senior researcher (see Figure 3) centered in ideas-problems-solutions-references associated with the various research problems, in opposition to the classical model (radial network) in which the senior researcher is in the center and researchers-in-training can only connect with him.

Under the cooperative and collaborative paradigm, the workshop or seminar of researchers-in-training coordinated by the senior researcher is the activity in which reviewing of research proposals occurs naturally and cooperation in seeking solutions for the emerging problems at each research project stage occurs naturally. In these meetings, each participant submits ideas, problems and possible solutions to the group and gets suggestions, criticisms and contributions of other members, under the supervision and guidance of a senior researcher. These tasks permits reporting the progress of each research project and receiving the corresponding feedback.

4   Technological Feasibility of Virtualization (TFV)

This section presents a developed work space which supports the collaborative model for research training in a distance teaching-learning manner. The work space has the following elements: a library of specialized publications, a repository of documents and a classroom where virtualized workshops or seminars are developed.

The classroom module is a virtual cooperation space where researchers can communicate in real time through video conferencing functionality using PC web cam and audio devices. The work space allows maintaining a channel of audio and video among multiple users simultaneously by using streaming video and voice over IP technologies. The researchers can exchange views and ideas in real time through a virtual whiteboard. Each member of the group can "draw" and make sketches, paste documents, images, and texts of any kind, while other participants see them in real time. This presents many challenges with respect to timing and transmission of data

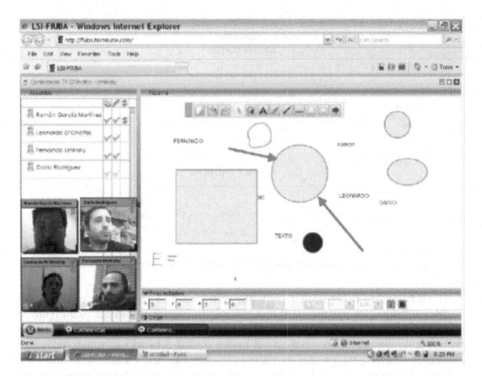

Fig. 4. Example of what a web cam based on communication and virtual whiteboard facilities looks like

among distributed programs and achieving the performance needed to ensure quality is still an open issue. Some example of free access artifacts that partially address the functionality of this module are "Skipe" [20] which enables web conference between two people and "Virtual Whiteboard" [21] which enables to share a web whiteboard among four people. Figure 4 presents what a web cam based on communication and virtual whiteboard facilities in the classroom module looks like.

The publication library module allows to managing specialized publications relevant to the domain of knowledge related to the research plan of the group in digital forms (journals, transactions and conference proceedings). Some example artifacts that are used to address this functionality are: "IEEE Computer Society Digital Library" website [22], "ACM Digital Library" website [23], and "Directory of Open Access Journals" website [24].

The document repository module allows managing two different groups of documents: the scientific production of the group (articles, communications, theses, task reports), and documents of interest from other research groups in the same domain. The documents may be stored by members of the research group in different formats and different types (i.e., text documents, spreadsheets, presentations, images, audio files, video files), be classified according to specified criteria and shared among members of the group of researchers. It also provides a search engine to facilitate the recovery of documents. Examples of some artifacts that address this functionality are:

"UBA-FI-LSI" website [25] where PhD, master and graduate theses, papers and conference communications are listed and access to them enabled, and "GRISE" website [26] which adds research reports (research documents) to previous example.

The intranet management module allows creating and managing research groups, users of the system, user profiles, permissions, parametric tables, documents, projects, scheduling conferences, and all functions necessary for the proper functioning of the platform dynamically.

5 Conclusions

The training of researchers involves interaction among persons who have different levels of professional and academic skills, on the one hand senior researchers and on the other hand various levels of trainee researchers. They constitute a community whose main activity is working on research issues within their discipline that become their focus of study.

Virtualization should allow for interaction among researchers located in different (and distant) geographical points, by creating a space to discuss research issues and exchange research documents that become the basis of virtual research groups.

We proposed a collaborative model for research training which is supported by a web-based collaborative software artifact. Besides, having a virtualized repository of scientific production of the research group constitutes the basis for two knowledge management tools, one being a record of the organizational memory and the other being a learning resource focused on a research topic. These tools ensure the flow of knowledge and work in a collaborative way inside the group.

Based on a balanced methodological model of higher education, we seek to identify technological media to virtualized training of researchers, making the needed resources that will help their learning process available to them; and making the senior researcher who guides them become a true facilitator for the acquisition of research skills.

The reality of our country (Argentina), with a few computer science research centers with capacity to train researchers at all levels, leads to the need of addressing the issue of alternative schemes for training researchers. The web communication technology for training researchers emerges as a possibility to set up research groups in which academic institutions with established research centers provide senior researchers while the rest of the university system provides the human resources to be trained in the research process.

In this context, this paper has explored the framework for research training, has introduced a scheme of collaborative training of researchers, and has presented a prototype of work space for the described virtualization scheme which runs in a single web software environment. On a following step, we expect to continue this work by defining the various related processes used by the collaborative scheme for training junior researchers, and to improve the developed software artifacts.

Acknowledgements. The Authors wish to thank Leonardo D´Onofrio and Fernando Uminsky who built the web-based software artifact (showed in Figure 4) used to prove the ideas presented in this paper.

References

1. Rivera, B., Osorio, O., Tangarife, D., Arroyave, J.: Los Semilleros de Formación de Jóvenes Investigadores: la Experiencia de ASPA. Documentos en el Programa de Maestrías. Consorcio para el Desarrollo Sostenible de la Ecorregión Andina (2000), http://www.condesan.org/memoria/COL0700.pdf (available 11/07/09)
2. Ponce Rosas, R., Landgrave Ibáñez, S., González Salinas, C., Monroy Caballero, C.: Formación de investigadores en medicina familiar: La tutorización en investigación y la relación tutor-residente (Primera parte). Archivos de Medicina Familiar 4(2), 77–81 (2002)
3. Padrón Guillen, J.: Los 7 Pecados Capitales de la Investigación Universitaria. Informe de Investigaciones Educativas 18, 69–79 (2004)
4. Rodríguez, D., Bertone, R., García-Martínez, R.: Consideraciones sobre el Uso de Espacios Virtuales en la Formación de Investigadores. Revista de Informática Educativa y Medios Audiovisuales 6, 35–42 (2009)
5. Moreno, M.: Dos Pistas para el Análisis de los Procesos de Formación de Investigadores en las Universidades Colombianas. In: Nómadas. Instituto de Estudios Sociales Contemporáneos. Facultad de Ciencias Sociales Humanidades y Artes, vol. 7, pp. 38–48. Universidad Central, Colombia (1997), http://www.ucentral.edu.co/NOMADAS/nunme-ante/610/ nomadas_07/revista_numero_7_art07_hacia_una_propuestas.pdf
6. Inciarte, A., Torres, M.: La línea y los grupos de investigación, de investigación como estrategia para la formación de investigadores. Agenda Académica 6(1), 23–28 (1999)
7. Sánchez, L.: Formación de investigadores en posgrado. Un proceso pedagógico por atender. In: XX Congreso Nacional de Posgrado, México (2006), http://www.cenidet.edu.mx/subaca/web-dda/docs/leticiacomepo06.pdf (available 11/07/09)
8. Villarreal, D., Guevara, J.: Una Experiencia en Formación de Investigadores. In: Núcleos de Investigadores en la Universidad Autónoma de Tamaulipas. Revista de la Educación Superior, Número 92. Asociación Nacional de Universidades e Instituciones de Educación Superior, vol. XXIII(4) (1994), http://www.anuies.mx/servicios/p_anuies/publicaciones/revsup /res092/txt1.htm (available 11/07/09)
9. Serrano, J.N.: se Hacen o los Hacen: Formación de Investigadores y Cultura Organizacional en las Universidades. In: Nómadas. Instituto de Estudios Sociales Contemporáneos. Facultad de Ciencias Sociales Humanidades y Artes. Universidad Central, Colombia, vol. 7, pp. 52–62 (1997), http://www.ucentral.edu.co/NOMADAS/nunme-ante/6-10/nomadas_07/revista_numero_7_art04_nacen.pdf (available 11/07/09)
10. Agudelo Cely, N.: Las Líneas de Investigación y la Formación de Investigadores: Una Mirada desde la Administración y sus Procesos Formativos. In: Revista Electrónica de la Red de Investigación Educativa, vol. 1(1) (2004) ISSN: 1794-8061, http://revista.iered.org/v1n1/pdf/ncagudelo.pdf (available 11/07/09)
11. Sánchez, L., Granados, M.: Experiencias de Autoformación y Heteroformación de Formadores de Investigadores en el Campo Tecnológico. In: IX Congreso Nacional de Investigación Educativa, México (2007), http://www.comie.org.mx/congreso/memoria/v9/ponencias/at16/P RE1178923303.pdf (available 11/07/09)
12. Barry, B.: Information skills for an electronic world: training doctoral research students. Journal of Information Science 23(3), 225–238 (1997)

13. Britos, P.: Procesos de Explotación de Información Basados en Sistemas Inteligentes. Tesis de Doctorado en Ciencias Informáticas. Facultad de Informática. Universidad Nacional de La Plata (2008)
14. Merlino, H.: Ambiente de Integración de Herramientas para Exploración de Datos Centrados en la Web. Tesis de Magister en Ingeniería de Software. Facultad de Informática. Universidad Politécnica de Madrid (2006)
15. Césari, M.: Nivel de Significación Estadística para el Aprendizaje de una Red Bayesiana. Tesis de Especialidad en Tecnologías de Explotación de Información. Insttituto Tecnológico de Buenos Aires (2006)
16. Schulz, G.: Un Ambiente Integrado de Clasificación, Selección y Ponderación de Reglas Basado en Sistemas Inteligentes. Tesis de Grado en Ingeniería Informática. Laboratorio de Sistemas Inteligentes. Facultad de Ingeniería. UBA (2008)
17. Duart, J., Sangrà, A.: Formación universitaria por medio de la web: un modelo integrador para el aprendizaje superior. In: Duart, Sangrà (eds.) Aprender en la Virtualidad, Gedisa, Barcelona (2000) ISBN: 84-8429-161-8
18. Moreno Aguilar, L., Vargas Solar, G., Sheremetov, L.: Hacia una infraestructura de componentes para la construcción de ambientes de aprendizaje colaborativo. In: XIX Simposio Internacional de Computación en la Educación. Contextos emergentes en el aprendizaje. SOMECE 2003, México (2003), http://bibliotecadigital.conevyt.org.mx/colecciones/document os/somece/59.pdf (available 11/07/09)
19. Valerio, G.: Herramientas Tecnológicas para la Administración del Conocimiento. Transferencia 57, 19–21 (2002), http://www.sistemasdeconocimiento.org/Produccion_intelectual /articulos/herramientas_km.pdf (available 11/07/09)
20. SKYPE. Sitio Oficial para Descarga de SKYPE (2009), http://www.skype.com/intl/es/ (available 11/07/09)
21. Virtual Whiteboard. Virtual Whiteboard - A Free Online Collaboration Tool (2009), http://www.virtual-whiteboard.co.uk/home.asp (available 11/07/09)
22. IEEE. IEEE Computer Society Digital Library (2009), http://www2.computer.org/portal/web/csdl/home (available 11/07/09)
23. ACM. ACM Digital Library (2009), http://portal.acm.org/dl.cfm (available 11/07/09)
24. DOAJ. Directory of Open Access Journals (2009), http://www.doaj.org/ (available 11/07/09)
25. UBA-FI-LSI. Laboratorio de Sistemas Inteligentes. Facultad de Ingeniería. UBA (2009), http://laboratorios.fi.uba.ar/lsi/z-hemerotecavirtual.htm (available 11/07/09)
26. GRISE. Grupo de Investigación en Ingeniería de Software Empírica. Facultad de Informática. UPM (2009), http://www.grise.upm.es/ (available 11/07/09)

The Human Development Process and Informatics Education in the 21st Century

Toshinori Saito

Japan Professional School of Education, Professional Program of School Education,
8-2 Niban-cho, Chiyoda-ku, Tokyo, Japan
t-saito@kyoiku-u.jp

Abstract. This paper shows a basic discussion about the human development process described under the context of the postmodern knowledge society of the 21st Century. The author presents the concept of "the cycle of human development", which is believed to offer the basis of informatics education. In accordance with that, the presumptions of the pedagogical design of informatics education and its essential contents are also proposed.

Keywords: Leaning Process, Human Development, Otherness, Knowledge Society, Lifelong Learning.

1 Introduction

The human development process in the 21st Century is thought to be described as a cycle process. In this discussion, human development is presented as a concept which stands for the positive transitions of maturity observed in various aspects of the human being such as intelligence, personality, skills, behavior, or knowledge. We argue in this paper that the human development in the 21st Century should be described as a cyclic process that includes these three steps of "encountering others", "discovering self inside others", and "reconstructing self", which the author calls "the cycle of human development".

"The cycle of human development" is an alternative to the linear and hierarchical human development model which was dominant in the 20th Century. In that era, the process of the human development was assumed to be a linear and hierarchical process which is expressed as the "start-to-goal" or the "lower-to-higher" model. These kinds of assumptions about the human development were the correspondence to the modern paradigm which was widely in common among the 20th Century societies. Under the modern paradigm, the public education system organized by the schools and its standardized curriculums was established on the basis of the linear and hierarchical structure. However, after the accomplishment of modernization, mainly around the western world, the linear and hierarchical education systems began to be insufficient to satisfy the complex demands of the society because of the change of social conditions that had justified modernization as a social objective.

In the following section, we will firstly show the theoretical background of the idea of "the cycle of human development". Secondly, the details of the idea of "the cycle

N. Reynolds and M. Turcsányi-Szabó (Eds.): KCKS 2010, IFIP AICT 324, pp. 354–360, 2010.

of human development", as a human development process of the 21st Century are discussed. Thirdly, we will argue how the pedagogical presumptions of informatics education should be described from the viewpoint of "the cycle of human development". Fourthly, we propose what we consider are the essentials of informatics education in the knowledge society of the 21st Century.

2 Theoretical Background

Psychological discussions of "self" give the basis of the idea of "the cycle of human development". Hermans and Kempen have conceptualized the conditions of polyphonic and multivoiced state of the self as "the dialogical self" [1]. The concept of the dialogical self shows a new way of understanding the relationship between the self and the others. According to the concept, the self contains plural positions and the dialogical relationship among the different positions constitutes the self. The dialogical self is thought to be a dynamic process that contains dialogical relationships between the self and the others inside of the same personality at once. This is also able to be understood as a concept that describes the state of the self kept affected by the others. If we regard the learning as a process of changing the state the self, the concept of the dialogical self will bring an insight of seeing the learning as a dialogical process that occurs inside of the human.

The idea of "the cycle of human development" is also affected by the discussions that relate to the modernized sensibility of "linear time". For example, Japanese folklore describes the concept of time held by the traditional societies as "cyclical time" that consists of the repetition of "Hare", which means the sacred time of the year, and "Ke", which means the secular time [2]. The concept of cyclical time is characterized by its own structure of involving the occasion of rebirth. Under cyclical time, the time of "Hare" functions as bringing new value from outside into the society and causing the symbolic rebirth of the society. This can be understood as a human's lifecycle of learning that consist of encountering others and bringing new value from those others.

3 The Cycle of Human Development

As mentioned above, "the cycle of human development" consists of these 3 steps.

(1) encountering others
(2) discovering self inside others
(3) reconstructing self

The meaning of each step is to be understood as explained here. The step of "Encountering others" is considered as the beginning of the cycle. This step describes any of the situations in which we come to face someone or something we don't know, or haven't experienced in our daily lives. The concept of "others" here includes the nature or the personality we find newly inside someone or something we have already known. "Discovering self inside others" comes next. It is the step in which we discover something similar to or in common with ourselves inside "others" we have

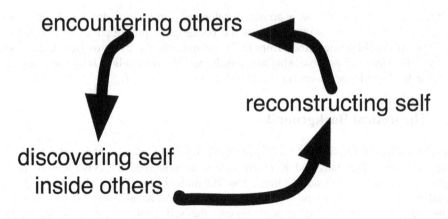

Fig. 1. The cycle of human development

encountered. This step means the beginning of building a dialogical relationship with "others". "Reconstructing self" comes last. It is the step in which we reconstruct ourselves under the influence of the dialogical relationship with "others". Reconstruction includes not only a drastic change but also a subtle change observed in our daily lives, which occurs on our sense of value or the behavior toward something we think of as "others". It would also be the essential preparation for "encountering others", which comes next.

The idea of "the cycle of human development" comes from critical considerations to the limitations of the linear development model that is applied to human learning. The linear development model sees human learning as an optimized way of achieving pre-defined goals. While the stress of learning activities is put on the goal achievement, the value of learning processes is thought to be decided depending on the extent of the goal achievement. This model is suitable for the circumstance of the modern industrial society, where they can clearly draw pedagogical goals as requirements of the society. However, it is not suitable for the circumstance of the postmodern knowledge society, where clear-cut social goals cannot be formed and the stress should be put on the learning process itself rather than the goal achievement [3].

The idea of "the cycle of human development" is also based on the observations of the nature of the human development in reality. As mentioned above, human development means positive transitions of the maturity observed in various aspects of the human being such as intelligence, personality, skills, behavior, or knowledge. The shape of the cycle is thought to be the most suitable to express the nature of these transitions, because their natures are to be understood thoroughly by using the metaphor of "the human life cycle". In this metaphor, their natures are commonly to be described as a process which contains "death and rebirth" in symbolic meanings. For maturity cannot be accomplished without an irreversible internal change of human nature, which can be compared to the symbolic "death and rebirth" upon the human life cycle.

4 The Pedagogical Presumptions of Informatics Education

From the viewpoint of building proper relationship between "the cycle of human development" and informatics education in the 21st Century, the author believes the three pedagogical presumptions listed here are required of informatics education.

(1) Informatics education should be designed to encourage the dynamism of the cycle.
(2) Informatics education should assume the human intelligence to be always under development and never to be completed.
(3) Informatics education should treat ICT as a means of bringing "otherness" to the learners.

Detail of each presumption is explained below.

Informatics education should be designed to encourage the dynamism of "the cycle of human development". As we know by the concept of "lifelong learning", the process of human development is now expected to continue throughout human life. This process is to be expressed as a recurrence of the cycle. The author believes informatics education today has the mission of encouraging the dynamism of the cycle and supporting the lifelong learning as the recurrence of the cycle through providing the basic literacy of informatics.

For the sake of giving dynamism to the cycle, informatics education should assume human intelligence, in the broadest meaning, to be always in the state of underdevelopment and never to be completed. If we consider that the growth of human intelligence could have its completion, the process of learning is going to be designed as a linear path leading toward a clear-cut goal, which brings the learners to the end of their learning. If we wish to embody informatics education that has sufficient potential of encouraging the dynamism of the cycle, every process of learning should be practiced as continuous development of human intelligence that is never to be completed.

The author also believes that informatics education should treat ICT as a means of bringing "otherness" to the learners so as to encourage the dynamism of the cycle. The otherness means the essence that makes someone or something "the others" for us. It is often experienced as the feeling of unfamiliarity or un-understandability in our daily lives. The cycle begins from "encountering others" by the learners and thus, informatics education, which considers acquiring ICT literacy as one of the most important pedagogical purposes, is expected to be the key for the learners to go into the movement of the cycle; because ICT is capable of being learned as the media to bring otherness to the learners. On the other hand, if informatics education is practiced lacking the sense of otherness, its potential of encouraging the dynamism of the cycle must be reduced.

5 Essentials of Informatics Education

The author believes that informatics education designed on the basis of the presumptions mentioned above is, at least, to have three essential contents listed below.

(1) Understanding the foundation of ICT
(2) Understanding information
(3) Producing information

5.1 Understanding the Foundation of ICT

Firstly, informatics education should provide the opportunity to understand the foundation of ICT. The foundation of ICT means the basic knowledge for learners to form the mental model of ICT that is appropriate enough to acquire ICT skills by themselves when needed. It does not necessarily mean the static and detailed knowledge obtained from the textbooks but also the working knowledge obtained from practical training.

The author believes that learning programming with small and simple tasks is the best way to obtain such knowledge [4]. In this context, programming means a series of operations that contain defining tasks to be processed by the computer, breaking defined tasks into several steps to form procedure, implementing programs by writing procedures with programming languages, and evaluating the validity of the programs as solutions to the tasks. The learners are expected to learn the principles that rule the functions of computers through the experience of programming, because it contains the opportunities to see and analyze the human tasks from the computer's viewpoint and check the validity of the analysis done. The purpose of learning programming should be put firstly on understanding the principles that enable computers to function, not on acquiring information processing skills.

5.2 Understanding Information

Secondly, understanding information should be practiced in informatics education. The concept of information stands for "the meanings or values for humans" here. Understanding information in this way is as essential for informatics education as understanding the foundation of ICT, for it is information as the meaning or the value that forms the purposes or the reasons to make use of ICT. From viewpoint of "the cycle of human development", understanding information is closely related to growing the essential capabilities of bringing dynamism to the cycle, such as the receptivity of the otherness and the appreciability of its value. This is because, according to the semiotic discussions, information as the meanings or the value is to be generated by finding the differences in the world around and articulating them with symbols. This process is never to be enabled without the sense of the otherness supported by such capabilities.

We can learn pedagogical methodologies of understanding information from the practices of the fields of media education or media literacy affected by semiotic text critique [5]. In terms of media education, the foundation of information is to be explained using the semiotic terminologies that include "text", "code", "convention", and "context". In this practice, the text that brings information is assumed to be a series of representations constructed under the influence of the codes, the conventions, and the contexts. The methodologies of recognizing and analyzing the conditions that affect the constructions of the representations have already been established as school curricula [6].

5.3 Producing Information

Thirdly, producing information should be also practiced in informatics education. It should be practiced for obtaining the capability of seeking and establishing the proper relationship with the others that the learners have found. From the viewpoint of "the cycle of human development", self-reconstruction is to be achieved through seeking the meanings of something or someone discovered as unknown others. This can be practiced through constructing the representations on ICT because the process of the construction under the media-rich environment of ICT inevitably contains the occasions of choosing the symbols available to represent the object. What are constructed here should be exactly the representations of the relationships that the composer has established with the object as the others.

Constructing the representations as producing information is to be practiced by "mission" and "target" oriented composing curriculums. "Mission" is the concept that expresses the reason or the purpose of composing, which gives the necessity and meaning of composing. On the other hand, the concept of "target" means assumed audiences of the representations. These are to be the key factors for the learners to decide on for the design of the construction. In addition to that, for the learners, they are exactly the expressions of what we call the otherness because they are to be found only if the learners try to figure out with their own imaginations. Therefore the curriculum of constructing the representations should be started from analyzing and making definitions of the mission and the target.

6 Conclusion

We discussed how the human development process should be described in the knowledge society of the 21st Century. Responding to the research question, the author presented the idea of "the cycle of human development", which contains 3 steps of "encountering others", "discovering self inside others", and "reconstructing self". Discussions on the pedagogical presumptions and the essential contents of informatics education are also shown in this paper.

The idea of "the cycle of human development" is proposed in order to establish the principle of the pedagogical practices of informatics education in the postmodern knowledge society. Its essential significance is to be found on the fact that it is expressed as a "cyclical" process. Assuming that the human development process is a cycle, the focus of the pedagogical practice would inevitably move from goal achievement to the experience of the process and its dynamism. As referred above, this comparison is a correspondence with the transition of the pedagogical requirement from that of the modern industrial society to the postmodern knowledge society. Under the idea of "the cycle of human development", one of the most important missions expected of informatics education would be to help the learners obtain basic understanding of the concept of informatics and the foundation of ICT and encourage them to bring the dynamism to the cycle by themselves making use of information and ICT environment.

At this moment, the idea and the discussions presented in this paper are at the stage of proposals that are obtained from the author's experience of studying and teaching informatics toward the undergraduate and graduate students. The author recognizes that continuous surveys and detailed descriptions of pedagogical examples are required to confirm the presented idea and establish reliable principles from it. Researches and practices on these recognized problems are now ongoing. The author strongly believes that the results would be reported on the next paper.

References

1. Hermans, H., Kempen, H.: The Dialogical Self, Elservier Inc., Amsterdam (1993); Taiwateki-Jiko, Shinyosha (2006) (in Japanese)
2. Nakazawa, S.: Kodaikara-Kita-Miraijin "Orikuchi Shinobu" (The Futurist comes from ancient time), Chikuma-syobou (2008) (in Japanese)
3. Aviram, A.: The Decline of The Modern Paradigm in Education. International Review of Education 42(5), 421–443 (1996)
4. UNESCO, Division of Higher Education, eds. Information and Communication Technology in Education. A Curriculum for Schools and Programme of Teacher Development, 121 (2002)
5. Masterman, L.: Teaching The Media. Routledge, New York (1985)
6. Ontario Ministry of Education: Media Literacy Resource Guide, Queen's Printer for Ontario (1989)

More for Less – Live Systems Learning

Andy Schaer

Fachhochschule Nordwestschweiz, Pädagogische Hochschule, Institut Weiterbildung
& Beratung, imedias - Beratungsstelle für digitale Medien in Schule und Unterricht,
Kuettigerstrasse 42, 5000 Aarau, Switzerland
andy.schaer@fhnw.ch

Abstract. The Input aims to show the implications of Cloud Computing for
learning and working and will discuss how schools' ICT concepts and media
competences might look like. But local, affordable solutions will be considered
as well. Particularly in the absence of the financial means necessary to purchase
expensive hardware and networks, local solutions could be favoured. For these
purposes the School for Teacher Education at the University of Applied Sciences Northwestern Switzerland has developed the "Lernstick".

Keywords: Cloud Computing, Learnstick, media competences, ICT concepts
for schools.

1 Introduction

The concepts of "Cloud Computing" and Saas (software as a Service) have occupied a
central position in recent discussions about their relevance in schools. To put it simply, they promise access to software directly over the Internet. Instead of being available locally on a computer, software is provided to users via Web services. In terms of
costs, this model creates advantages because the amount of money spent on the support of the individual PC and its software can be reduced significantly. In return,
reliable broadband Internet connections are necessary.

The development towards "Cloud Computing" is also taking place within educational contexts. It requires high-capacity connections to all classrooms as well as
suitable software for teaching. On a didactical level, new questions will be raised. In
particular, discussions about the possible implications of a gradual relocation of learning contents from the classroom to digital spaces will become essential.

New questions will also be asked about the consulting of schools regarding the acquisition of new infrastructure. Does it make sense to continue investing in servers
and providing classrooms with expensive hardware? Or would it, in the near future,
suffice to opt for cheaper local solutions and to invest in high-capacity networks for
every classroom and school area instead?

The input aims to show the implications of "Cloud Computing" for learning and
working and will discuss how schools' ICT concepts might look like in the future.
Local, affordable solutions will be considered and will play a central role. Particularly
in the absence of the financial means necessary to purchase expensive hardware
and networks, local solutions should be favoured. For exactly these purposes

N. Reynolds and M. Turcsányi-Szabó (Eds.): KCKS 2010, IFIP AICT 324, pp. 361–366, 2010.

"imedias" Consulting the use of digital media in class at the University of Applied Sciences Northwestern Switzerland, School for Teacher Education, Institute of Further Education (www.fhnw.ch/ph) has developed the "Lernstick" (http://www.imedias.ch/lernstick). It will be part of the presentation and available as a download to participants.

2   Global Internet Applications or Local Computer Platforms?

Schools continually renew the computer systems installed in their classrooms, corridors or computer labs. The relocation of many applications to the Internet, keyword "Cloud Computing", raises the question whether schools should continue to invest in technical infrastructure in the same scale as they do today. Against the background of limited financial resources this question becomes increasingly pressing.

Taking into consideration both the protection of resources and the simultaneous adherence to didactical promises, two different models for the didactical use of ICT will be presented. The first model makes reference to fast networks and applications on the Internet, while the second approach examines local solutions that do not require fast exchanges of data. Both models can be combined and scaled for their use in teaching.

3   Model 1: The Applications Are Available Online - How Does Cloud Computing Work?

Put simply, on the one hand, Cloud Computing facilitates the use of an IT structure at a specific location, such as a school. On the other hand, the existing IT structure obtains applications from the Internet without the need to install them on the local hard disc. The applications are purchased and used as required. However, a universal definition of the concept Cloud Computing does not exist.

From a historical point of view, the development to Cloud Computing could be compared to the industrial revolution at the end of the 19th century [1]. Electricity was originally produced with hydropower in the factory itself. Later, the production of electricity was outsourced to large, decentralised power plants. Thus, the industry switched from a self-supply model to an external supply model and had the amount of electricity required delivered directly via power lines to the factories. For that purpose, the necessary infrastructure had to be built and made available. At around the same time, it also began to supply individual households with electricity.

In a similar way to how electricity was starting to be distributed back then, broadband Internet connections now deliver applications, which do not need to be generated locally anymore. Today, Cloud Computing is a reality and applications have become a scaleable commodity.

3.1 Use of Cloud Computing

By opting out of installing permanent applications, schools can access applications over the Internet. They are either free of charge or subject to a subscription model, according to which users only pay for what they consume. Thus, it becomes conceivable for schools to upgrade their own IT infrastructure dynamically with additional resources from the "cloud" and to adjust their learning environments to the respective requirements.

3.2 Advantages of Cloud Computing

- IT infrastructure is easily scaleable, flexible and adaptable
- Data storage without server maintenance by school
- Schools do not pay for operating costs
- Schools do not need expensive system management

Braun et al. [2] distinguish between three different Cloud Computing architectures from an organisational point of view: Public Cloud, Private Cloud and Hybrid Cloud. According to them, a Public Cloud includes "the range of clouds, where the providers and the potential users do not belong to the same organisational entity"[1]. A Public Cloud bears risks that cannot be neglected in an educational context, in particular with regards to [3]:

- Data safety
- Availability of services
- Sensitivity of data stored on servers that cannot be controlled

The Private Cloud is considered to be a closed system, within which applications and user groups are clearly defined. Users obtain the necessary applications centrally. This model is interesting for educational institutions, if large schools decide to share the use of a server farm. Thus, the closed system remains manageable and facilitates the creation of e-learning environments.

However, hybrid models that incorporate both a Private and a Public Cloud seem more realistic for educational purposes. Hybrid models possess a closed area that is only available to students and teaching staff, yet they do not prevent the use of Public Clouds. This solution could have various advantages for schools. Many applications would not need to be installed on each computer. Keeping servers in each school would become superfluous. Applications could be obtained and paid for according to the actual requirements. At the same time, the use of Public Clouds, such as Google Docs, remains a possibility.

4 Model 2: The Local, Low-Cost Solution "Lernstick[2]"

The aim of the "Lernstick" is to provide schools with access to an efficient working and learning tool. The central idea of the "Lernstick" is based on the combination of the potentials inherent to Live-Systems on a USB-stick and the possibility to develop a learning environment that responds to the pedagogic needs of a school.

The "Lernstick" was designed as a portable learning space to be used flexibly in educational (as well as extracurricular) contexts. As a pedagogic and didactic learning

---

[1] My translation.
[2] USB-stick, based on Debian GNU/Linux system and software, www.imedias.ch/lernstick

and working tool it balances out its disadvantages vis-à-vis the Internet by providing students with a well-structured personal learning environment, whose content, on the one hand, is oriented towards educational objectives, yet on the other hand, it remains individually organised. Using the "Lernstick" helps developing both the students' media competencies as well as their ICT skills.

The "Lernstick" was conceived across several school levels and disciplines. Thus, it gives students access to a diverse range of contents – from language class to mathematics and IT-skills – depending on their individual interests and needs. The "Lernstick" is a tool that can be implemented flexibly and in many different ways by teachers – as a mediator during periods of instructional learning, as a learning support during periods of individualisation and as a communication medium for cooperative learning.

The "Lernstick" encourages the use of media and ICT and makes a valuable contribution to the acquisition of media competencies. Its concept is based on a technological solution that relieves schools from having to pay for elaborate and expensive support and instead allows them to focus on pedagogical questions about media education.

The concept of Live-System-Learning is an artificial expression made up of the words Live-System and e-learning. The 'e-' has been replaced by Live-System in an attempt to highlight the specific form of learning with digital media facilitated by the "Lernstick". Teachers and students have the possibility to learn from and with contents that are located directly on the data carrier. As a result, learning content is independent from spatially fixed computers, operating systems and networks. This way of supplying learning content and its use for educational purposes is called "Live-System-Learning" (LSL).

The "Lernstick" has been evaluated within the framework of a master thesis [4]. Further research projects are being carried out at the moment. A master plan [5], prepared by imedias, shows the "Lernstick's" potential for development, but also its boundaries.

5 Combining Both Models

In a client-server environment, which is being re-launched in an updated form by Cloud Computing, the "Lernstick" becomes a personal working space for students. Data that needs to be available locally can be stored on the "Lernstick" without having to use individual memory space within the school.

However, the "Lernstick" offers more than the transfer of data. It can become a space for learning environments that cannot be accessed via the Internet, either for legal reasons or because of the lack of financial resources. "To refine this view we have to consider the different levels of interaction that accompany this process. Here we find a progression from the level of individuals to the level of communities, and, finally, to the level of organisation. During the maturing process from expressing ideas to formalization we find patterns in the flow of knowledge from the individual to the organisational level." [6]

5.1 Pedagogic Concept That Combines Local and Web-Based Applications

The media are used to accomplish developmental tasks. What this means is the acquisition of skills and competencies that are necessary for a constructive and satisfactory conduct of life within a specific society [7]. This process is to be encouraged and supported. The adoption of one of the two models, or the combination of both possibilities, is based not only on economic, but also on pedagogic, cultural and education policy considerations.

Media Competence. Following the model of Dieter Baacke's [8] media competence defines the ability to use the media and their contents in a goal-oriented and needs-oriented way. Baacke distinguishes between four different dimensions: media criticism (analytical, reflexive, ethical), knowledge of the media (informative, instrumental, qualificatory), media use (use through reception, offer interactivity) and media design (innovative, creative, aesthetic). Media competence is activity based. In particular it is concerned with knowledge and skills.

Media Education. Media education expands the idea of media competency with the dimensions of reflection and behaviour. According to this concept, the media are an integral part of culture; they are a means for comprehensive education and form the background for education. In relation to lifelong learning, media education is considered to be a process "[...] in which the adolescent and the adult is building a critical distance to the media and their further developments throughout his entire life and takes a position of responsibility towards media and their handling"[3] [9]. In a context of pedagogy, Kerres et al. [10] stress that media education links the two different aspects of education towards the competent use of media on the one hand, and the competent use of media for educational purposes on the other hand. Therefore, media competence becomes part of, and at the same time prerequisite for, media education.

Media Socialisation. Socialisation describes the interaction between the subject and its environment that leads to individual development and self-discovery within a social context [11]. Children do not simply adapt to their environment but actively interact with it and participate in its creation. Hence, what is important is not the assimilation of the subject to its environment but the meaningful interrelationship between the individual and its surroundings. Media socialisation is influenced by educators, peers, the individual and the social frameworks, which create possibilities and impose restrictions on the use of media and their contents. It is a two-way process (reciprocal socialisation).

Media socialisation of children and adolescents includes all aspects, within which the media play an important role for the psychosocial development of young adults [12].

Communication media. Communication media support communication practices among students as well as between students and teachers. This stretches from educational supervision in a chat room to communication via e-mail, flipcharts used by a group of students to create a mind map, a blog (an electronic diary), or a wiki that enables the collaborative development of a text.

---

[3] My translation.

Net didactics. Moser [13/14] describes a net didactics that does not emphasise the importance of techniques but shows a new learning culture. The aim is to teach students how to learn with digital media in order to prepare them for a knowledge-based society. The requirements of Web 2.0 are the central focus of net didactics. In addition, Moser shows the didactic forms of representation and models that are available to a net didactics. He presents the didactic star as a model for the integration of media in the classroom. Moser distinguishes between mediation media, media-based learning aids and communication media.

6 Conclusion

The combination of Cloud Computing and the "Lernstick" brings into existence an interesting Personal Learning Environment (PLE). Two topics emerge for discussion: Will it be possible to meet the expectations we have for media education with the help of these tools? Which future investments will still be necessary in the area of education to ensure an up to date ICT infrastructure?

References

1. Cloud Computing. In: Elektronik-Kompendium,
   http://www.elektronik-kompendium.de/sites/com/1404051.htm
2. Braun, C., Kunze, M., Nimis, J., Tai, S.: Cloud Computing, p. 25. Springer, Heidelberg (2010)
3. Cloud Computing. In: Elektronik-Kompendium,
   http://www.elektronik-kompendium.de/sites/com/1404051.htm
4. Schwab, S.: Konzeption und Erprobung des Lernstick im schulischen und ausserschulischen Umfeld. Master Thesis. Fachhochschule Nordwestschweiz, Solothurn (2009)
5. Schwab, S., Widmer, M.: Masterplan Lernstick Live-System-Learning mit Blick auf die flächendeckende Verbreitung des Lernsticks in der Schweiz, Masterplan. Fachhochschule Nordwestschweiz, Solothurn (2009)
6. MATURE Project The MATURE project is co-funded by the European Commission, DG INFSO, Unit for Technology-Enhanced-Learning under the 7th Framework Programme, http://mature-ip.eu/maturing-scopes
7. Oerter, R., Dreher, E.: Jugendalter. In: Oerter, R., Montada, L. (eds.) Entwicklungspsychologie, 5th edn., p. 268. Beltz PVU, Weinheim (2002)
8. Baacke, D., Kornblum, S., Lauffer, J., Mikos, L., Thiele, G.A.: Handbuch Medien: Medienkompetenz. Modelle und Projekte. Bundeszentrale für politische Bildung, Bonn (1999)
9. Spahel, D.: Medienkompetenz als Schluesselbegriff der Medienpaedagogik? forum medienethik, 1/2002, Seiten 42-48. kopaed verlagsgmbh (2002)
10. Kerres, M., de Witt, C., Schweer, M.: Die Rolle von Medienpädagog/innen bei der Gestaltung der Medien- und Wissensgesellschaft. In: Neuß, N. (ed.) Beruf Medienpä- dagoge. Selbstverständnis – Aufgaben – Arbeitsfelder, kopaed, Muenchen (2003)
11. Hurrelmann, K.: Einführung in die Sozialisationstheorie, 8th edn. Beltz, Weinheim (2002)
12. Suess, D., Lampert, C., Wijnen, W.C.: Medienpaedagogik. Ein Studienbuch zur Einfuehrung. Verlag für Sozialwissenschaften, Zuerich (2009)
13. Moser, H.: Wege aus der Technikfalle. eLearning und eTeaching. Verlag Pestalozzianum, Zuerich (2005)
14. Moser, H.: Einführung in die Netzdidaktik. Lehren und Lernen in der Wissensgesellschaft. Verlag Pestalozzianum, Zuerich (2008)

ALEF: A Framework for Adaptive Web-Based Learning 2.0

Marián Šimko, Michal Barla, and Mária Bieliková

Institute of Informatics and Software Engineering,
Faculty of Informatics and Information Technologies,
Slovak University of Technology, Ilkovičova 3, 842 47 Bratislava, Slovakia
{simko,barla,bielik}@fiit.stuba.sk

Abstract. State-of-the-art learning management systems provide their stakeholders with many features coming from Web 2.0 paradigm, but often ignore the need for personalization and adaptation during the learning. More, learning activities are often fragmented – a student needs to make a decision whether he or she wants to take questions or read explanatory materials. In addition, majority of current solutions do not provide a truly interactive environment, where students are allowed to participate in content creation and maintenance. In this paper, we address these issues by proposing and developing a framework for Adaptive Web-based Learning 2.0. We describe basic requirements for such a framework and provide an overview of all its important underlying models and functionality.

Keywords: Adaptive web-based learning, framework, social learning, collaboration, personalization, 2.0.

1 Introduction

Computers and broadband Internet connection strongly influenced the way we learn and shifted the traditional in-class learning towards anytime and anywhere web-based learning. We all witnessed the emergence of complex Learning Management Systems (LMS) and e-learning standards, along with unbounded increases in available educational resources on the Web and in digital repositories. However, most of the state-of-the-art approaches just serve electronically the same "one-size-fits-all" static content, which was previously printed in student books, without actually using the benefits of computer and web-based education, namely higher degree of interaction and personalization of the learning flow.

Students, who interact with a teacher and other students in the class should be able to interact also within a virtual learning environment provided by a LMS. Such collaborative learning would not only increase the student's motivation to study (doing something in a group is mostly more fun to do than doing it alone) but also naturally brings him or her more benefits by leveraging the experience of others.

Nowadays, we are all used to the Web 2.0 concepts and are expecting web-based applications to be built and used in a similar way. In some sense, Web 2.0 represents a

N. Reynolds and M. Turcsányi-Szabó (Eds.): KCKS 2010, IFIP AICT 324, pp. 367–378, 2010.

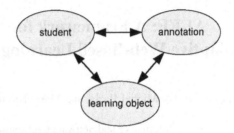

Fig. 1. The Web 2.0 core concept of annotations adapted to e-learning. By a term annotation, we mean any type of data or metadata which can be added to a learning object, e.g., a tag, comment, question.

challenge for adaptive learning systems and LMS should provide students with means for their active contribution to the presented content (in the form of tagging, commenting and other annotating mechanisms), its sharing and organization (Fig. 1).

An advantageous type of interaction, which cannot be achieved in printed books but is feasible in the virtual educational web environment, is instant feedback. All questions, quizzes and exercises can be made interactive, giving the student immediate feedback on the chosen and correct answer along with clarifications or further explanations about reasons behind the question.

An important aspect of web-based learning is personalization. With the increasing number of available learning materials it is becoming crucial to be able to support students in their way through the course, to locate, recognize and understand information, which is the most relevant, considering the given time and progress of the student. Without any support, the student can only with difficulties identify which parts of the course are relevant and which are presenting only additional, not that important information. More, if we consider that the student is not only new to the domain but also to the actual learning system, increased complexity of navigational possibilities may result in "lost-in-hyperspace" problem [1].

Looking at the educational systems from the teachers' point of view, one of the major drawbacks of adaptive course authoring, negatively affecting the spread of adaptive learning systems, is the complexity of metadata used for the personalization in both: definition of such metadata as well as their further maintenance (which is even more challenging in a collaborative environment). Some standardized domain ontologies may be used, but they only exceptionally fit to the author's needs at the desired level of granularity. The domain model has to be often created "from scratch". Unfortunately, manual construction is a demanding task even for small domains. The number of necessary metadata descriptions is counted by hundreds or even thousands.

Our contribution presented in this paper can be seen from two views. First, we propose a schema for Adaptive Web-based Learning 2.0, which new generation LMS creators should follow. This schema takes advantage of all the possibilities that the Web 2.0 currently offers and combines them with main principles of personalized access to educational resources while retaining reusability, easy maintenance and manageability of the learning content and metadata. Second, based on the proposed schema, we present ALEF (Adaptive LEarning Framework), a framework for creating adaptive and highly interactive web-based learning systems.

The framework and its underlying models are designed with respect to the course authoring that is intended to be as flexible as possible. The domain model is simple enough to allow for efficient usage of methods for automatic domain metadata extraction based on lightweight semantics acquisition.

2 Related Work

Probably the most relevant related work is a distributed architecture for adaptive e–learning, KnowledgeTree [1]. The authors identified the main drawbacks of adaptive web-based educational systems (lack of integration of multiple aspects of learning into one system, poor reuse support) and proposed a distributed architecture which allows a student to reach various interactive learning activities from one single point. However, a drawback of the whole approach is that the activities are still kept somehow separated – the system provides a student with all relevant links pointing to distinct services needs to make a decision whether he or she wants to study the explanatory materials, take some questions and quizzes or practice the acquired knowledge on several exercises. Our approach integrates all available learning and supporting activities into one single framework, which makes them easily accessible from any point of the learning flow.

Related issues were addressed also by Meccawy et al. [2]. Similarly to our work, the authors identified that adaptive educational web-based systems should follow Web 2.0 principles in order to be successful. To achieve it, the authors proposed a framework consisting of five web services integrated into the Moodle LMS, extend this LMS by personalization and adaptation features and take advantage of its Web 2.0 presentation layer, which provides collaborative parts of the course (activities, blog etc.). The weak point of the proposed solution is that student modeling process as well as whole personalization is separated from collaborative processes – the collaboration within the Moodle environment cannot directly influence any of the five web services nor their underlying models, and thus drive the behavior of the system.

When considering educational course authoring support, state-of-the-art LMS provide only a partial (and insufficient) assistance, which is related only to models derived from the domain model (e.g., adaptation model [3], goals model [4]). While the domain model forms a basis for domain knowledge representation, its automatic creation is supported very poorly, e.g. by generating course prerequisites [5]. The only relevant evidence of (semi-)automatic domain model generation we are aware of is presented by Cristea and De Mooij [6], where relationships between domain entities are acquired based on the comparison of their domain attributes (albeit these must be entered manually).

One of the reasons that only a few approaches devoted to automated domain model generation exist might be an overwhelming complexity of the used (ontological) models, which are hard to fill manually, not speaking about their automatic population. On the other hand, courses built on the top of simplified domain models with a lightweight semantics (which we are more likely to produce automatically) might give comparable learning outcomes to the students. The support for metadata authoring based rather on lightweight semantic models of the domain is even more desirable for the case of dynamic content. When a new content emerges as an effect of the collaborative effort of students, it has to be properly assigned to relevant metadata in order to use it throughout the course (e.g., for adaptation realization).

3 Principles of Adaptive Web-Based Learning 2.0

The challenge for next generation of LMS lies in the adoption of Web 2.0 concepts into the adaptive web-based learning. We identified three key principles that are required for a design of LMS:

- *Domain modeling* with respect to *(i)* possibility to automate certain domain model parts creation, *(ii)* collaborative social aspect and the need to modify or alter domain model by students themselves.
- *Extensible personalization and course adaptation* based on comprehensive user model, which allows for simultaneous employment of different adaptive techniques to enhance the student's learning experience
- *Student active participation in a learning process* with the ability to collaborate, interact and create the content by means of read-write web vision, mainly by different types of annotations allowing for rich interactions on the top of the presented content.

These three principles ensure that a learning environment is no longer seen only as a mean for educational material presentation. It is a place where students collaborate, create, edit, share and organize the educational content according to their learning needs. The notion of a learning management system is shifted towards an integrated learning environment.

Based on these principles, we designed ALEF, an adaptive learning framework for creating adaptive and highly interactive integrated learning environments. The flow of activities that take place within an adaptive Web 2.0-based learning environment and that are addressed by the framework can be seen from two perspectives (Fig. 2):

- learning flow and
- collaborating/creating flow.

The learning flow (Fig. 2, solid line) covers the entire learning process with one *presenter* module, several *personalizers* providing personalization services, respective *user* and *domain models* along with user modeling tools including *semantic logger* and *user model inferencers*. Students learn by interacting with presented materials accessed from the domain model and tailored to user needs by the personalizers taking into account students' characteristics (such as domain knowledge) present in their *user model*. All students' actions are logged and result in appropriate updates of this model.

Personalization services, which play a crucial role in an enhancement of student learning experience, can be related to any stage of the learning process – while student is reading explanatory texts, is taking quick self-assessments to get feedback about freshly acquired knowledge, is practicing on exercises etc. Our architecture allows for a composition of such personalization services by chaining and combining different personalizers.

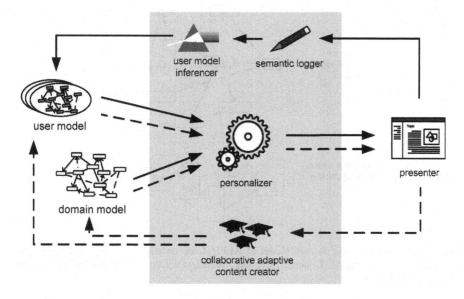

Fig. 2. Activity flows within the framework (learning – solid line, collaborating/creating – dashed line)

The collaborating/creating flow (Fig. 2, dashed line) covers activities related to learning materials enrichment by student themselves. Learning object presentation is obtained from *presenter*. Using a *collaborative adaptive content creator*, supported content type is created by a student. Content type added by the student varies depending on particular collaborative adaptive content creator used. Enrichment can be realized e.g., by assigning annotations that can have different forms: highlighted text, tags, comments or discussion threads. The content is created with respect to the student context, obtained from his or her user model. And vice versa, performing an action related to the content creation reflects into the *user model* update.

4 Models for Adaptive Web-Based Learning 2.0

Similarly to any adaptive web-based system there are two basic models in the ALEF framework: domain model and user model. However, we adapted them to address the principles of adaptive web-based learning 2.0 considering the possibility to automate their creation and collaborative aspect of learning.

4.1 Domain Model

Domain model of an adaptive educational course represents an area that is a subject of learning. In general, it consists of content entities and metadata entities (in ALEF both seen as resources) that are connected via various types of relationships (Fig. 3).

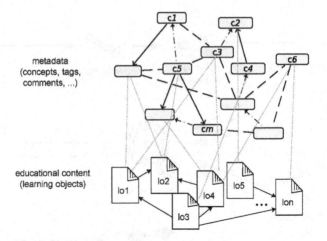

Fig. 3. An example of the domain model of ALEF. Core metadata entities – concepts – are assigned to learning objects. Concepts, like other metadata entities, are interlinked via various types of relationships.

Content

The term *content* refers mainly to a learning object as to fundamental course content representation. However, in a collaborative and read-write environment we support also other types of content entities such as blog (created by both students and teachers) or discussion thread (composed of interlinked comments added by students).

Learning objects are represented by entity `LearningObject` and are further divided into the following types (see Fig. 4):

- `Explanation`,
- `Question`,
- `Exercise`.

Different learning object types and their seamless combination is an important distinguishing feature of our approach. The student is not required to read explanations in one system and practice the acquired knowledge in another one. Different forms of interaction within one system improve student's learning experience and learning outcome.

`Explanation` represents instructional content that describes a subject domain. `Question` and `exercise` represent interactive part of a course. Questions aim to provide students with an immediate feedback on their knowledge with further explanation of respective answer choices. Exercises allow students to practice gained knowledge. Besides enriching the learning process, gathered information is also used to update student model to keep track of user's knowledge.

The domain model covers two distinct parts of every learning object:

- Actual content (text) – stored in XML files using DocBook templates. Allows for easy authoring, maintenance and supports re-usability,

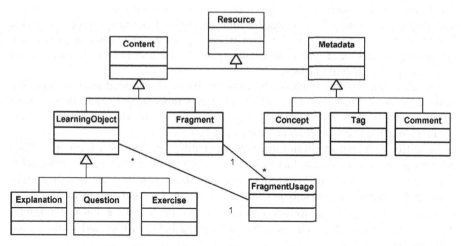

Fig. 4. Domain object model portion – *Resource* types

- Additional metadata – stored within a relational database holding learning object's identifier, type and relationships to other domain entities. Contains all information which is relevant for personalization services.

The chosen representation allows for an easy definition of other types of learning objects. The actual content goes to the textual files while its metadata comes to the model as a new subtype of LearningObject.

Learning objects are composed of reusable parts referred to as fragments. Fragments are smallest pedagogically coherent units allowing content-based adaptation Fragments are further subtyped according to a type of particular learning object. Explanation can be composed of one or many Definition fragments. Exercise can be composed of Definition, Hint, Solution and/or Clarification fragments. Similarly, question can be composed of Description and Answer fragments. Each fragment type has its pedagogical role in learning flow and "assists" a student to achieve his or her learning goals.

The order of fragments and metadata related to fragment usage within a learning object is defined by an entity FragmentUsage (see Fig. 4).

Metadata

Every content entity is associated with respective metadata. Comparing to other existing approaches, the notion of metadata in ALEF is quite simplified in order to achieve the degree of complexity, which is manageable by ordinary users (both teachers and students). This allows for automatic construction of domain model, and, on the other hand, it provides a solid basis for reasoning resulting in advanced operations such as metadata-based navigation recommendation.

We consider following metadata types:

- Concept,
- Tag,
- Comment.

The basic metadata entity is *Concept*. It is a domain knowledge element usually representing topic or subtopic contained within the content (learning object). *Tag* is a keyword or term assigned by a student when organizing their domain knowledge. *Comment* is an advanced type of metadata created by the user in order to annotate the content in a more specific fashion.

Metadata can be interconnected by different types of weighted relationships. We defined `RelatedToRelation`, which represents fundamental connection between any metadata entities. Other types of relations (e.g. prerequisite) are defined by extending `WeightedRelation` or `UnweightedRelation`.

In ALEF, both content entities and metadata entities are considered resources. This generalization is based on the fact that the boundary between content and metadata is very thin (e.g. a comment assigned to learning object can be itself assigned other comments resulting into discussion thread formation). Second reason to generalize *Content* and *Metadata* into *Resource* is the way we model interaction in the framework – relationships between user and content and between user and metadata are very similar.

4.2 User Model

Our approach to user modeling within ALEF framework is built on a well-established conception of overlay models [7] but adds several important features to it. Our user model conception is similarly to [8], separated into two layers:

- Evidence (observations) layer storing history of user's interaction with the learning environment – what actions the user has performed in relation to a certain learning object (e.g., user has seen an explanation of *lisp abstract data types* or responded wrongly a question *id42* related to concept of *recursion*).
- Inferred layer storing user characteristics derived from available observations, such as level of mastery (knowledge) or interest in certain concepts.

Moreover, the ALEF framework allows for defining and storing user's attitude (relation) to any type of object present within the learning environment:

- content – primarily learning objects such as explanations, questions, exercises,
- metadata – concepts, annotations and
- other users (students) – effectively creating social network within the system.

Relations of a user to domain objects stored in both user model layers are semantically described using typed connections to ensure the high degree of separation of further processing tools performing inference of additional knowledge or providing user model-based personalization from the particular implementation of the system and its components.

Apart from the mentioned overlay approach to user modeling, which is present in various types of user's relations to domain objects, we provide also means to represent explicit user features which are not connected to a particular object from the learning domain such as goals or backgrounds.

5 Learning Flow

The learning flow in ALEF (outlined in section 3), is based on two central concepts:

- adapting the content,
- tracking the user behavior.

It was already shown [1] that the efficient way to deliver educational content is tailoring it according to the current user knowledge level, interests and needs by employing methods and techniques for personalization and adaptation. These are based on the underlying domain model, which represents the area of learning, and a user model storing user's actual knowledge or goals. The more pedagogically complex a learning environment is, the more adaptation possibilities there exist.

The modern LMS can integrate the study of explanatory texts, quick self-assessment (in order to acquire immediate feedback), and the practice over the set of exercises during one learning session. All these forms of learning are target for personalization and adaptation. The ALEF framework addresses these requirements, as it enables to use and integrate several personalization services by means of *personalizers*. Personalizers can be either chained together to form a processing pipe or can be combined using a voting mechanism (e.g., for a combination of various content recommenders).

For our evaluation domain of learning programming, we developed four personalizers: Content Recommender, Personalized Annotator, Adaptive Test Question Selector and Sidebar Navigator (see an example of screenshot in Fig. 5).

Content Recommender. *Content Recommender* serves as a general personalizer of the content and navigation. Based on the student's knowledge it selects and recommends learning objects (in fact, any `Content` entity, see Fig. 4) tailored to the student needs. Recommendation covers the learning object instance selection and its fragments visibility preconfiguration (e.g., `Hint` fragments in the case of `Exercise` learning objects are hidden for students whose knowledge about associated concepts exceeds a certain threshold).

Personalized Annotator. *Personalized Annotator* filters actually visited learning object's annotations (tags, comments) only to those relevant for the student. It can be viewed as a general personalizer of `Metadata` (see Fig. 4). Its personalization function is similar to personalization function of the *Content Recommender*. However, different adaptation mechanisms are used.

Adaptive Test Question Selector. *Adaptive Test Question Selector* aims at selecting questions, which allow students to obtain immediate feedback about their current progress, and as a side effect it informs the system about student's knowledge, which is stored in the student model. Question selection is based on Item Response Theory (IRT) that enables an adaptive selection of questions based on the student's level of knowledge and question difficulty combined with the topic selection and prioritization following the answer history.

Sidebar Navigator. *Sidebar Navigator* focuses on tracing student's navigation within the learning object presentation page (i.e., scrolling, mouse movements). Based on

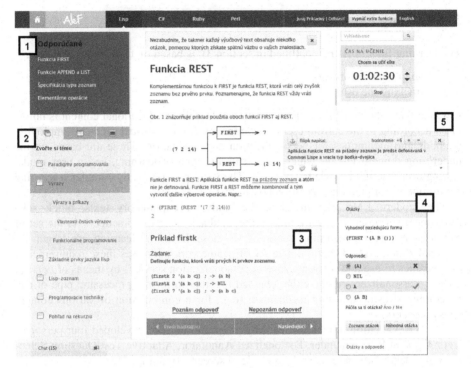

Fig. 5. Screenshot of ALEF user interface for learning Lisp programming (in Slovak). Recommendations coming from Content Recommender are presented either in a separate box (1) above the tabbed-menu or can be embedded within the main content in the form of interactive examples (3). The tabbed-menu (2) provides different navigational styles according to different learning object types and relationships. Collaboratively created questions related to current learning object are visualized on-demand in a pop-up widget (4). Displayed content can be furthermore enriched by adding different types of annotations, which are subsequently accessed by hovering the mouse over the underlined sections of text (5).

collected usage data from different users and the student's social network, it personalizes the visualization of certain learning object parts in the sidebar (e.g. by emphasizing mostly visited text).

6 Creating/Collaborating Flow

The creating/collaborating flow is the ALEF's realization of the Web 2.0 "read-write" concept. It focuses on social learning and supports students by allowing them to actively participate in the learning process. The traditional web-based learning is shifted towards integrated learning environment where students collaborate, create, edit, share and organize content. The creating/collaborating flow covers the two aspects of student participation:

– contribution to the content (metadata/annotations),
– user model update.

To support the first aspect of student participation, ALEF provides the write access to the course content with so called *collaborative adaptive content creators* entry point. There could be multiple creators, each responsible for other type of annotations. Currently we developed three collaborative adaptive content creators: Tagger, Annotation Creator and Collaborative Question Creator.

Tagger. *Tagger* is a simple form of collaborative adaptive content creator typical for any "2.0" application. It allows students to assign tags to any `Resource` entity (see Fig. 4).

Annotation Creator. *Annotation Creator* serves as a general purpose annotator of learning materials. Students can assign annotations in the form of text comments to selected *part* of any Resource entity. Comments may be assigned to other comments resulting into a discussion thread.

Collaborative Question Creator. *Collaborative Question Creator* extends the *Annotation Creator* and allows for creation of special annotations holding questions. During learning, students are encouraged to create testing questions. This way students themselves become the creators of the pedagogical content. Collaboratively created questions support learning as they are related to the content that is the most important, unclear, or controversial (from students' point of view).

The second aspect of Creating/Collaborating flow is a user model update. The ALEF captures actions related to the flow (e.g. assigning a tag, adding a comment or creating a question) and reflects these actions in the student model. For example, assigning a tag by a student is often interpreted as an increased interest in a given resource (learning object). Thus, we can define an update of user interest in concepts that are related to the given learning object.

Although ALEF allows students to participate in course enrichment, it does not support learning objects authoring. Course authoring from teacher's point of view (explanatory text creation, course sequencing, domain description with metadata, etc.) is left to the external authoring tools and pedagogical supervision of a teacher.

7 Conclusions

In this paper, we presented a schema for Adaptive Web-based Learning 2.0, which defines next generation of LMS, delivering experience of collaborative, creative and personalized learning. We defined generic-enough models used by such a system, namely *domain model* based on lightweight semantics which opens new possibilities of automated course metadata creation [9] and *student model*, which acts as a basis of personalization of the whole learning flow.

We developed an adaptive learning framework ALEF, which follows the mentioned schema and combines different learning activities (such as learning from explanatory texts, questions or exercises) along with highly interactive and social environment of the Web 2.0. The contribution of our approach is the integration of the learning and supporting activities into one single framework, making them easily accessible during learning. We already proved on our earlier educational system that such a personalized combination of texts with interactive objects like questions and exercises are improving the efficiency of learning and raise the learning outcome [10].

We proved the feasibility of the framework by using it to create a course for learning programming in Lisp language, which is used in a standard course of Functional and logic programming at our institute.

Acknowledgments. This work was partially supported by the grant KEGA 028-025STU-4/2010 and it is the partial result of the Research & Development Operational Programme for the project Support of Center of Excellence for Smart Technologies, Systems and Services, ITMS 26240120029, co-funded by the ERDF.

References

1. Brusilovsky, P.: KnowledgeTree: A Distributed Architecture for Adaptive E-Learning. In: Proc. of the 13th Int. World Wide Web Conf., WWW 2004, pp. 104–113. ACM Press, New York (2004)
2. Meccawy, M., et al.: WHURLE 2.0: Adaptive Learning Meets Web 2.0. In: Dillenbourg, P., Specht, M. (eds.) EC-TEL 2008. LNCS, vol. 5192, pp. 274–279. Springer, Heidelberg (2008)
3. De Bra, P., et al.: Authoring and Management Tools for Adaptive Educational Hypermedia Systems: The AHA! Case Study. SCI, vol. 62, pp. 285–308. Springer, Heidelberg (2007)
4. Cristea, A.I., De Mooij, A.: LAOS: Layered WWW AHS Authoring Model and their corresponding Algebraic Operators. In: Proc. of the 12th Int. World Wide Web Conf., WWW 2003, Budapest, Hungary. ACM, New York (2003)
5. Sosnovsky, S., Brusilovsky, P., Yudelson, M.: Supporting Adaptive Hypermedia Authors with Automated Content Indexing. In: 2nd Int. Workshop on Authoring of Adaptive and Adaptable Educational Hypermedia at AH 2004, pp. 23–26 (2004)
6. Cristea, A.I., De Mooij, A.: Designer Adaptation in Adaptive Hypermedia Authoring. In: Proc. of the Int. Conf. on Information Technology: Computers and Communications ITCC 2003, pp. 444–448. IEEE CS, Los Alamitos (2003)
7. Brusilovsky, P., Millán, E.: User Models for Adaptive Hypermedia and Adaptive Educational Systems. In: Brusilovsky, P., Kobsa, A., Nejdl, W. (eds.) Adaptive Web 2007. LNCS, vol. 4321, pp. 3–53. Springer, Heidelberg (2007)
8. Šimko, M., Bieliková, M.: Automated Educational Course Metadata Generation Based on Semantics Discovery. In: Cress, U., Dimitrova, V., Specht, M. (eds.) EC-TEL 2009. LNCS, vol. 5794, pp. 99–105. Springer, Heidelberg (2009)
9. Yudelson, M., et al.: A User Modeling Server for Contemporary Adaptive Hypermedia: An Evaluation of the Push Approach to Evidence Propagation. In: Conati, C., McCoy, K., Paliouras, G. (eds.) UM 2007. LNCS (LNAI), vol. 4511, pp. 27–36. Springer, Heidelberg (2007)
10. Vozár, O., Bieliková, M.: Adaptive Test Question Selection for Web-based Educational System. In: Proc. of SMAP 2008, 3rd Int. Workshop on Semantic Media Adaptation and Personalization, Prague, Czech Republic, pp. 164–169. CS IEEE Press, Los Alamitos (2008)

Design and Development of Virtual Learning Environment Using Open Source Virtual World Technology

Steven Suman[1], Ardavan Amini[1], Bruce Elson[1], and Patricia Reynolds[2]

[1] Birmingham City University, UK
[2] King's College London – UK
suman.steven@googlemail.com, ardavan.amini@tic.ac.uk,
bruce.elson@tic.ac.uk, p.a.reynolds@kcl.ac.uk

Abstract. Today's digital era, dynamic teaching and learning in higher education has moved from traditional class room, face-to face learning environments to more interactive and collaborative environments, due to a demand for online-distance learning from students, and the desire from academic institutes to promote and deliver courses across the globe. Advancement in open source virtual learning platforms technology, enables the development of flexible online learning environments to exist that can be accessed anywhere, anytime and in anyplace by students, hence enabling academics and academic institutes to teach and increase their market across the globe. Authors of this paper had the opportunity to work on the design and development of a flexible virtual learning environment within the dentistry sector part of the IVIDENT (virtual dental school) UK Higher Education Funding Council project at Kings College London. This paper will focus on the design and the development of virtual learning environment for the IVIDENT project, using advanced technological open source virtual world platforms.

Keywords: Project wonderland, architecture, 3d modelling, haptics, java technology, open source technologies.

1 Introduction

In the recent years technology has seen the development and popular use of virtual online worlds [1], early stages of online virtual world primary uses were social based, and a meeting point for end users around the world to interact with one another. As online virtual worlds have developed, many organisations and industries not just associated with information systems are turning to virtual online worlds to host virtual presentations and meeting's, with employees and partners interacting from mobile locations around the world on smart clients as well as desktop computers. The uses of virtual worlds provide many benefits, reduced costs of training staff via simulations and rich online media.

Due to the increasing demand from the educational establishment to enhance their delivery of learning material to be more flexible, accessible and available, The UK &

N. Reynolds and M. Turcsányi-Szabó (Eds.): KCKS 2010, IFIP AICT 324, pp. 379–388, 2010.

European Union is funding research projects in this particular area, for development of online virtual learning environments. The IVIDENT project based at Kings College London is a Higher Education Funding Council UK project for development of an online virtual learning platform for the training of dentists.

The research into virtual world technologies available on the market resulted in identifying a key common issue, that of virtual worlds availability and uses primarily for social networking and gaming. Recent uses of virtual worlds have resulted in an educational nature, but are yet to be dominant and mainstream as an acknowledged additional resource to aid in delivering effective learning within academic institutions.

The authors of this paper have designed and developed a prototype virtual learning environment, using the open source virtual world development kit Project Wonderland, as enhancement to the IVIDENT UK project.

2 Need for Change

Traditional methods of teaching within class rooms, lectures and face to face interaction, increases costs within the educational system, limits academic institutions from offering additional further education courses, creates unavailability of staff for teaching additional courses and limits distant learning. A paper written in 2005 by Marileena Koskela titled 'Suitability of a Virtual Learning Environment for Higher Education,' at Tampere University in Finland, conducted tests to determine how effective traditional teaching methods are compared to using e-learning resources within a virtual learning environment.

Tests included creating groups for both students and lecturers and delivered the course material to both groups, one group would interact with virtual learning environment and the other traditional education methods.

Student's performances were analysed and students using virtual learning environments preceded that of traditional methods and also found the course understanding easier to digest [2], for selected courses other tests conducted identified using virtual learning environment made little or no difference at all, also virtual learning environments proved to be a success within higher education.

The limitaitons with traditional methods is that of students embarassment of asking questions on the course material due to lack of knowledge and understanding, a key problem in both class room and lecture teaching, and many students also don't participate and fall asleep within lectures. This is a common problem across many further education academic institutions. Using a virtual learning environemt the experience becomes personal for the user, and constant interaction and engagement with the user is required. Students who are embarassed to ask questions are able to follow virtual course material at a suitable pace, and interactive applications can be developed to provide a futher detailed understanding of the material. Teaching staff are able to address a larger cohorts of students to deliver course material delivered more than once.

Students studying dental education lack the real world dentistry experience and currently work with laboratory dummies to conduct dental procedures, fillings, crowns and many more. The key element for students obtaining the real world experience is creating an immersive environment via utilising three dimensional graphics technologies to simulate realistic dental procedures and objects and with the use of haptic devices will aid in students touch and feels senses and provides a valuable resource.

3 Methodology

There are many system development life cycles, Structured Analysis and design (SSADM), Rapid Application Development (RAD) and the Spiral Model. Within the time frame feasible to develop a prototype, the Spiral Model was adopted. The Spiral model life cycle was defined by Barry Boehm in his 1988 article A Spiral Model of Software Development and Enhancement [3].

Spiral model uses iterative development cycles via obtaining the system requirements (primary research) to develop the design of the system, implement a prototype and then begin a new iteration of analyse, design and prototype based on knowledge of previous iteration cycles until system requirements are fulfilled.

Using the spiral model has the advantage of developing a system close to the customer's requirements, because consistent communication is held between the development house and customer. Changes to the system based on new requirements can be implemented on the next iteration cycle of development.

The figure 1 illustrates the prototype project life cycle mapped onto the spiral model. The first stage begins with identifying the customer requirements, which is to develop a client application to use for the virtual dental school. Once the requirements have been identified, planning the project is the next step to identify both the scope and feasibility of the project within the time frame proposed for development of prototype software, findings from the project planning stage will also aid in identifying key objectives required to complete the project.

The project risk analysis is carried out after each-iteration of the project prototype stages, risk analysis importance is of a high priority, performing a project risk analysis will identify possible risks which may occur throughout the project life cycle and countered with solutions to areas of concern. Identifying risks at an early stage will substantially assist in the project running smoothly and meeting deadlines.

Primary and secondary research is carried out to determine further understanding of the system requirements; the process involves conducting interviews with end users and stake holders of the project, and also observing the surroundings i.e. dentist practices to create realistic models reflecting real world objects and also carry out an analysis stage, using virtual world development kits to gather results of limitations and advantages of use and cross reference the results against the system requirements and project objectives.

Development of the software phase begins immediately, with basic system design principles, because this is one of the benefits of using the spiral model for system development, prototypes are developed after basic analysis and design phases and then illustrated to the end user where new requirements can be identified or existing requirements can be changed and changes to the system will be implemented within the next iteration. The end result of the software system is close to the end users requirements. Other life cycles exist which require five phases for project development Analysis, Design, Implementation, Testing and Evaluation (SSADM), each stage cannot begin without the completion of the previous stage, with this methodology communication with the end user is limited and additional requirements or changes to the system are difficult to implement once into the implementation stage of the project life cycle.

The development of the three dimensional models are developed as prototypes and illustrated to stake holders of the project, at this stage the models are evaluated and if any additional requirements and modifications are noted to be implemented over the second iteration.

Further development of the system is conducted to aid in continuing with the next iteration process and also the objective are evaluated, to determine objectives have been met or altered. This process follows into the conducting another risk analysis based on the first and following second project iterations. Another prototype is developed creating or modifying existing three dimensional models and also development of the virtual dental school client, stake holders are shown the developed prototype and evaluation of the prototype is assessed, to determine further enhancements and requirements for the next iteration of the project life cycle. The project phase then enters system testing.

The project enters third development iteration, conducting the same phases from the first and second iterations, with the additional development of a system test plan.The project life cycle ends with the development of writing a detailed project report.

The spiral model was chosen as the preferred methodology to develop the virtual learning environment for the IVIDENT project. The model along with the time scales is shown in the figure 1 below

Fig. 1. Spiral Model based upon Boehm Spiral Model [3]

4 Virtual Worlds

Virtual world's technology is enabling organisations to communicate and collaborate from remote locations around the globe. Online virtual worlds are decreasing costs within organisations, via virtual presentations and training simulations.

Integrating education with online virtual worlds exists to a degree. Many open universities Harvard, Texas, Stanford are developing virtual campuses to allow students to meet attend virtual classes and create content [4], but the used virtual world requires users to subscribe in order to use the services provided. Therefore open source technologies are used to develop a virtual world applicable to education and incorporate the common framework use of the educational system, to allow a generic virtual world to be developed and used within academic institutions.

4.1 Development Kits

Findings of open source research resulted in several virtual world development kits opensim (Microsoft), Project Wonderland (sun Microsystems) and Croquet Consortium available. Each virtual world development kit had its strengths and weaknesses based on design architecture, flexibility and ease of extending the environment further. The concept of anywhere, anytime, anyplace was not feasible with opensim because the architecture is not platform independent and additional software is required to be installed on non Microsoft window operating systems for compatibility. The scope of the croquet consortium project relies on developers developing additional functionality to the existing project, and in the long term is not applicable for IVIDENT.

As part of this project one of the main challenges was to identify an open source virtual environment that is available on the market as a software suite, which would be able to integrate with existing academic systems or academic learning tools, e.g. moodle, IVIDENT enrolment system etc. A large percentage of virtual environments researched resulted in monthly subscription payments to use the services and the host to maintain system for the end user. Other virtual worlds were hosted specifically towards virtual presentations and simulations.

4.2 Project Wonderland

Project Wonderland is Java an open source toolkit for creating collaborative 3D virtual worlds. Within those worlds, users can communicate with high-fidelity, immersive audio, share live desktop applications and documents and conduct real business. Wonderland is completely extendable; developers and graphic artists can extend its functionality to create entire new worlds and new features in existing worlds [5].

Sun Microsystems java project wonderland 0.4 versions were selected as the basis for developing the virtual world. Project wonderland provides a framework API library to develop virtual worlds, three dimensional models can be imported and rendered in the virtual environment in the format of X3D technologies, which can be developed within many three dimensional modelling packages available on the market. Open source modelling software blender was used as part of developing models for the virtual world.

4.3 3D Modelling

Three dimensional models are created from polygon meshes and are made up of triangles positioned to form the object, modelled.

Various techniques were researched into development of three dimensional modelling, and how developed models will be represented within a virtual world, without creating limitations of the hardware.

Techniques of creating low polygon meshes enable the virtual worlds to calculate and render fewer triangles which will release processing graphics information on the hardware. Increasing the polygon mesh size, results in using hardware with higher memory capacity to fulfil the graphics requests, and becomes very costly.

Back face culling is another technique used to render three dimensional models, via using graphics hardware to calculate the meshes triangle within the users view frustum.

Ian Palmer [6] explains modelling techniques for texture mapping three dimensional objects and how to preserve graphics hardware memory, which is essential to delivering high end realistic models without reaching the limitations of the hardware. The concept to texture mapping is to unwrap the mesh model into a flat blue print layout and the object vector positions are stored. The blue print layout is imported into graphics editing software packages and within the shape boundaries create or apply the images which the object will represent. The image layout of the object is then applied to the three dimensional model and from the store vectors the image is calculated and wrapped around the object mesh, creating a realistic model. The common size to use for mapping is image sizes of 256x256, as this size uses less than one megabyte of memory.

5 IVIDENT Client Architecture

Figure 2 illustrates the proposed IVIDENT client architecture and consists of a client/server relationship based on a presentation and business layer, the presentation layer consists of a client application and the business layer consists of the server components.

Creating a distributed architecture allows for the development of a thin client application where rendering of graphics and processing system information becomes more efficient due to maintain the visual elements for the user and the business logic layer maintains the system intelligence whereby controlling how the client application will behave, based on how to illustrate the visual elements and delivering effective learning capabilities.

This result in the system becoming easily maintainable and flexible breaking the system into separate components that work together to create an illusion of a single system existing, and further developments made to a layer does not affect the system within other layers and promotes the use of object orientated development.

The client application consists of five layers required to develop a virtual world, graphic engine technologies utilise the graphics card hardware to calculate the gaming physics to enable the rendering of the virtual dental school and dental objects. The client application layer relies on the graphics engine to provide data to display the virtual world, and also provides additional functionality to manipulate and customise the virtual dental school.

The game server sends the client application information regards to how the virtual dental school is to be viewed and additional information to update the state of objects present and newly created within the virtual dental school.

Extensible Mark-up Language is used for the configuration settings of the behaviour of the three dimensional models developed, and store information, pointing to where the model is stored, the orientation and scale of the model.

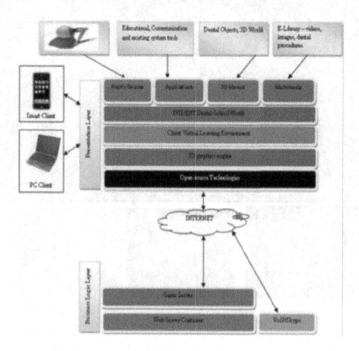

Fig. 2. Virtual Dental School Client/Server Architecture

6 The Design and Development of the Virtual Dental School

Figure 3 illustrates the design of the virtual dental school buildings based on a medieval themed virtual world developed using blender three dimensional modelling software package.

Each building represents behaviour of the system based components found within academic institutions, the Keep building defines the library of the virtual world, where end users are able to view and download a large respiratory of multimedia content ranging from e-books to videos which will be integrated into an existing library external system.

The e-commerce market will enable end users to purchase online goods from external online vendors and also trade objects with other users.

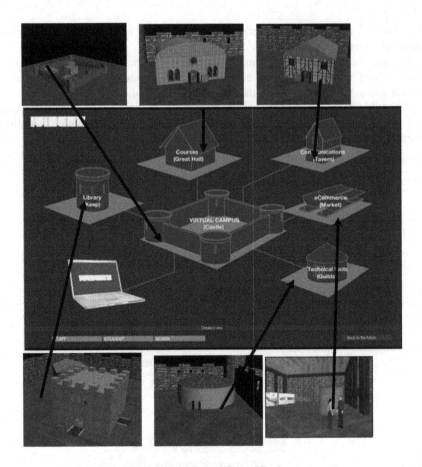

Fig. 3. Virtual Dental School Design

The tavern functionality caters for the social networking aspect of virtual worlds use, where end users are able to collaborate and interact with other end users, via project and group work collaboration, presentations and general text based and video chat tools. An additional functionality of the tavern is the student union.

The guilds building enhances the dental training, by implementing the collaborative ad productive elements of the dental school through rendering dental simulations and objects for end users to interact with and also perform dental procedures. The factor for the guilds is to create an immersive building environment, with detailed realistic dental equipment and models to aid in the engagement in student learning.

The screen shots below illustrate the progress of using Project Wonderland to prove the concepts of using open source technology to develop a flexible online virtual learning environment. The first screenshot illustrates teleportation objects, where the user is able to transport the avatar (human representation of virtual character) to the desired building object which represents an educational component.

Fig. 4. Virtual dental school development screenshots

The second screenshot illustrates three dimensional teeth models which are rendered dynamically when the end user interacts with the objects providing graphical images of the dental procedure. Using the concept of rendering three dimensional models will allow students to interact and manipulate three dimensional dental objects, to gain further understanding.

The third screenshot illustrates a market area, with the concept of e-commerce, where users of the virtual worlds will be able to purchase online goods.

7 Conclusion

Sun Microsystems has release a new version of the virtual world kit project wonderland 0.5, re-developing the virtual world architecture for flexibility to exist for development of additional project wonderland components. Further development will reside in researching and developing with web technologies and project wonderland 0.5, the current architecture for project wonderland will be extended via creating an additional data access layer to store persistence of the world in an object oriented database. The client application will also be re-developed, using the existing application as a framework to customise for the requirements of the system, because the current functionality of the client is applicable for general use of virtual worlds and many developers are improving the interface for user needs. This is one of the issues rising with use of project wonderland, the basic framework is provided, but for customisation to suit environment of use, development is inevitable.

Web technologies is also an option for development of client applications, the use of web technologies will allow the system to be accessible on various clients supporting the technology used, allowing students to access the virtual dental school via desktop and smart mobile clients.

Khronos group [7] are developing a new technology webgl which will deliver rich three dimensional content within the browser without the need to install addiotnal plug-ins. The advancement in web graphics technology will create a new interactive experience for end users, and will be researched for developing the visual graphics for IVIDENT virtual dental school.

Haptic technology is advancing, and the next stages will be to develop virtual dental instruments, for students to acquire hands on experience on the realism of performing dental procedures.

References

1. Second Life, `http://secondlife.com/?v=1.1` (retrieved January 15, 2010)
2. Marileena Koskela, P.K.: Suitability of a Virtual Learning Environment for Higher Education. Electronic Journal of e-Learning 3(1), 1–30 (2005)
3. Project Life Spans in the 1990s: The Role of the Project Life Cycle (Life Span) in project Management,
   `http://www.maxwideman.com/papers/plc-models/1990s.htm`
   (retrived November 16, 2009)
4. Virtual Environments Enable New Models of Learning (n.d.) (2009),
   `http://secondlifegrid.net/slfe/education-use-virtual-world` (retrieved November 16, 2009)
5. Project Wonderland: Toolkit for Building 3D Virtual Worlds (2007), Java.net:
   `https://lg3d-wonderland.dev.java.net/` (retrieved November 16, 2009)
6. Palmer, I.: Essential Java 3D. Great Britain: The Cromwell Press (2001)
7. Hirshon, J.: Khronos Press Releases from Khronos Group Open Standards for Media authoring and Acceleration(August 4, 2009),
   `http://www.khronos.org/news/press/releases/khronos-webgl-initiative-hardware-accelerated-3d-graphics-internet/`
   (retrieved November 16, 2009)

Educational Management Challenges for the 21st Century

Ferran Ruiz Tarragó[1] and Ann Elizabeth Wilson[2]

[1] Council for the Evaluation of the Educational System, Government of Catalonia,
Department of Education,Via Augusta 202 (annex)
08021 Barcelona, Spain
[2] PhD candidate, Autonomous University of Barcelona
Faculty of Education, Building G-5
08193 Bellaterra, Spain
{frtarrago,awilson.uab}@gmail.com

Abstract. While demands for large scale improvements in education systems increase worldwide, education system structures continuously fail to meet, or even make notable advancements, toward these demands. Inseparable from this problem is the very similar way in which education systems are managed. Educational managerial structures have become so universal, perpetual, and therefore, deeply ingrained in society, that they remain almost entirely unchallenged; this encourages the misleading, nearly unquestioned assumption that managers are not responsible for educational failures and that teachers are at fault. This paper argues that the core of most educational problems lie within current educational management structures. It calls for a complete rethinking and rebuilding of such structures in order to aid educational systems in reaching their full potential, therefore helping students within these systems fully develop 21st century skills and meet future global challenges.

Keywords: educational management, policy perspective, 21st century skills, key competencies, educational restructuring.

1 Introduction

As the world moves further into the twenty-first century, there is a seemingly universal perception that educational systems, at least in many developed countries, face serious, inextricable problems. At present, public interest and expenditure levels in education are generally higher than ever before. Nevertheless, despite the lofty aims of societies' leaders, and the innumerable efforts of committed teachers, today's educational systems are largely incapable of helping most students develop the skills, knowledge, and competencies needed to successfully confront the social and economic realities of our global times. As Victor Ordonez, former director of Unesco's Basic Education division asserts, "there is growing evidence that education structures, as they currently exist, have largely outlived the environments for which they were originally developed" [1]. Confronting this issue with the required depth and scale is not the sole responsibility of teachers, as it falls well beyond the realm and reach of

N. Reynolds and M. Turcsányi-Szabó (Eds.): KCKS 2010, IFIP AICT 324, pp. 389–400, 2010.
© IFIP International Federation for Information Processing 2010

their duties. Rather, these issues are primarily the responsibility of those who manage[1] education at all levels.

2 Educational Management Shortcomings

In order to illustrate the limitations of current educational management practices, this section considers unsettling examples of wide gaps between intended educational goals and the resulting stark realities. These vast discrepancies between goal and outcome are essentially the result of widespread leadership and management failure. Extending far beyond what can be solved by individual efforts, they point to serious flaws in the very structure of the system, and likewise, serious consequences for students.

A first example is taken from the supranational partnership of the European Union (EU). Their 2009 report, *Key competences for a changing world,* states that, "While the EU benchmark for 2010 is to reduce by 20% the percentage of low-achieving 15-year-olds in reading literacy, this share has actually increased from 21.3% in 2000 to 24.1% in 2006" [2]. Thus, instead of reducing low achievement in literacy, policies have actually led to an increase in the number of low achievers. This is a particularly serious setback for the Lisbon agenda, that is, the set of interconnected policies aiming to make Europe "the most competitive and dynamic knowledge-based economy in the world, capable of sustained economic growth with more and better jobs and greater social cohesion" [3]. Consequently, up to this point, the EU has blatantly failed to reach this very fundamental educational goal.

The underperformance of national education systems, concerning one of their key priorities, seriously hinders progress concerning the eight key competences[2], which, according the *European Framework for Key Competences for Lifelong Learning,* should already be firmly integrated into school curriculums. It is necessary to acknowledge that truly fitting these competency schemes in with the usual subject-based curriculum is not an easy task. Nevertheless, top-level school system administrators in many EU countries claim that curriculum adaptations harmonizing subject disciplines and competencies frameworks have already been carried out. Yet this "harmonizing" is not so straightforward for teachers, who face the daily realities of such changes, decided on and dictated in a far-removed, top-down manner.

Given the fact that all recent policy-making, planning, spending, and hard work has not, up to this point, been rewarded with the anticipated success, it is reasonable to

---

[1] In this paper, the terms 'management' and 'manager', and variations, such as 'managed', are used to refer to the respective activities and actual positions of the broad range of professionals whose ideas and actions influence the goals, processes, budgets, teacher education, settings and structuring of educational relationships, as well as the type, amount and deployment of resources for the functioning of both schools and education systems. According to this definition, managers range from government leaders, to top-level education system officials, to district superintendents, school inspectors, principals, school administrators and, when applicable, department heads.

[2] Those competences, necessary for personal fulfilment, active citizenship, social inclusion and employability in a knowledge society, are: 1) Communication in the mother tongue; 2) Communication in foreign languages; 3) Mathematical competence and basic competences in science and technology; 4) Digital competence; 5) Learning to learn; 6) Social and civic competences; 7) Sense of initiative and entrepreneurship; 8) Cultural awareness and expression.

suppose that this is not just a matter concerning individual teachers and specific schools alone. It is likely there is a certain level of failure on the part of those who manage these education systems.

The unintended and even counterproductive effects of massive external assessment in United States' school systems provide another, however different, large-scale example of the inability of educational managers to improve learning in a significant way. The way K-12 education is mandated through the No Child Left Behind Education Act (NCLB) results in a system in which curriculum standards and standardized tests become the dominant forces of education. Schools feel compelled to devote their best efforts to teaching to the test, given that schools, teachers, principals and even district authorities face serious professional consequences in the event that students' test results fall below the minimum established by unrealistic state-specific learning standards.

Under such circumstances, the logic of middle-management ranks (e.g. district superintendents, principals, and school department heads) is to seek short-term solutions. According to a report from the think tank *Education Sector*, "the scale of the NCLB testing requirements, competitive pressures in the testing industry, a shortage of testing experts, insufficient state resources, tight regulatory deadlines, and a lack of meaningful oversight of the sprawling NCLB testing enterprise are undermining NCLB's pursuit of higher academic standards" [4]. This seems exactly the opposite of what was originally intended. The high cost of development prevents the creation of high-quality assessment tools that could adeptly measure higher-order thinking skills. As this same report states, testing experts say that "many of the tests that states are introducing under NCLB contain many questions that require students to merely recall and restate facts rather than do more demanding tasks like applying or evaluating information, largely because it's easier and cheaper to test the simpler tasks." A great deal of the management effort devoted to external assessment is in fact hindering the development of key competencies. Not to mention that the time spent in the classroom on test preparation and administration of tests takes hours away of valuable time each week from actual teaching and learning. This somehow makes the systematic testing of students a long-term 'race to the bottom'.

These clear examples of widespread educational failures in the EU and in the U.S. are two of many that suggest that education systems are managed in ways that prevent them from delivering substantially more than they have so far. It can be argued that this, at least in part, is because education systems structure educational relationships in ways that ignore the individual, ruthlessly driving many students to a dead-end pessimistic view of their schooling. Many students drop out because they find themselves unable to take a positive role in an institutional setting that is largely incapable of responding effectively not only to the enormous diversity of students, but also to the demands of a world in constant change. This failure results in student indifference or even profound aversion for everything that is related to school, learning, and many other forms of culture.

The way in which education is commonly structured in many countries also negatively affects countless students that do not drop out; the internal workings of schools continuously impinge on the potential enthusiasm and commitment of a large percentage of the student body, which suffers from varying degrees of disinterest and apathy. Many students, even those who pass exams and receive good grades, experience a prevailing obligation to fulfil an imposed duty, far removed from their personal interests and expectations in life. They are also unable to receive adequate encouragement and support. In short, ordinary educational approaches come far from achieving what should be the ultimate goal of an educational system, which is to instil in students a desire to continue learning. Both students who reject the system by dropping out and those who accept it passively and without enthusiasm, lose the unique opportunity to enjoy their education, to use it in ways that help define personal goals and interests, to set the foundation for a broad and open vision of the world, to develop skills and competencies for life, and to feed the desire to live in an ethical, autonomous, and rational way.

All the considerations presented thus far refer to the inner workings of a system managed by a network of decision makers and administrators at a variety of levels. No educational system could function without their hard work and commitment. Nevertheless, the restrictions that the system itself imposes on its managers, as well as their all too common uncritical conformity to the imperatives of the system, makes it difficult for any deep-rooted, large-scale improvement to take place.

School systems structure educational relationships in ways that force managers to adhere to an internal logic that has remained virtually static and unchallenged in spite of significant change outside the educational sphere. Unresolved or even aggravating problems are dealt with within existing frameworks trapped dogmatically in the past. These frameworks fail to recognize and overcome the shortcomings of the system itself. As victims of tradition, routine, and high stake pressures, those who manage educational systems and schools often fail to contemplate that fundamental change is possible, much less that it is an absolute necessity in today's world. As long as the management of education continues to adhere to models, procedures, and guidelines that contribute to many of today's disappointing results and shortcomings, like those mentioned earlier, it seems likely that management jobs (and teachers' jobs as well) will be increasingly unrewarding and, moreover, that the expectation of real long-term improvement in learning and satisfaction will never be met.

3 The "More of the Same" Dynamics

Many education system authorities seem permanently trapped in a dynamic of "more of the same" principally focused on doing things better –improving current structures and processes– rather than doing better things, that is, new things that could potentially deliver more valuable outcomes. However flawed, public opinion, parents, and even teachers and other education professionals seem to share in this "more of the same" line of thinking. This is fostered by wide-ranging comparative studies of educational systems, which add a sense of competition, but skim over the real root of the problem by merely masking symptoms. It comes as no surprise that education managers are prisoners of this mentality, when one considers that their thinking and actions have forever been ascribed to this "more of the same" management paradigm.

The "more of the same" mentality is shared by many teachers and their unions. For instance, more often than not, teachers' unions place blame on high student-teacher ratios and a lack of support staff. Their solution is for more teachers to carry out their jobs in exactly the same way but with a few less students. No essentially new educational possibilities are obtainable with this line of thinking. However necessary smaller class sizes and classroom help may be, there is no seriously rethinking of existing teaching, monitoring, and evaluation methods to effectively meet students' individual needs, engaging them in learning, and developing their key competencies, thus raising the expectations of every individual student.

Although the importance of a well-trained teaching staff is widely recognized, public opinion and education stakeholders often seem to consider that increasing teacher training requirements will solve many of the existing education woes. Again by asking for "more of the same" they disregard the fact that studies show that most in-service training does little to improve classroom teaching.

Likewise, many educational managers believe that merely providing schools with more computers is a solution to their education-related woes, as these measures are often seen as a way to shore up traditional expository approaches. However, this rather simplistic view of the role of information technology in learning disregards the fact that these traditional and highly transmissive methods often are at the very root of students' rejection of education.

The "more of the same" logic is also apparent in the public call to increase schools' accountability, often by requiring more external evaluation, without any hint of consideration on how this affects teaching and learning and, in particular, the development of key competencies. The previous example of increased testing standards in the U.S. shows that schools forced to succeed on external tests do so at the expense of learning experiences crucial for knowledge society development. On the whole, too many people, including education managers, seem to believe that greater accountability can be brought about by *more* student testing, *more* external control, and *more* inspection.

In the end, more money is continually sought to revamp old structures and to further refine underperforming routines, while at the same time increasing the complexity of the system and its bureaucratic requirements. The leaders and managers of education systems and schools themselves seem to believe that without more spending, education cannot substantially improve. Their mindset is such that it compels them to build on top of existing, steadfast structures and processes, instead of rethinking them. This is done instead of investing in research and development and consequently new approaches, which could overcome the fundamental shortcomings of the system. Captives of the "more of the same" logic, educational managers tend to see increased funding through unvarying techniques as the only way to improve education, thus preventing any real change and thus thwarting the prospective shaping of the future of education.

4   The Case for Key Competencies

The biggest problem with the "more of the same" approach to education woes is that it simply cannot cope with a world in continuous change. Trapped in the past, education management is unable to bridge the widening gap between education and society. As a result, the call for a complete redesign of education in order to best serve learners fails to gather enough momentum. Such a redesign should be one in which 21st century skills and competencies are profoundly and effectively integrated in education, reaching all students throughout the entire course of their learning. This is of uppermost importance given that the requirements that societies place on individuals are ever more complex and becoming increasingly so at a rapid pace. Throughout history, "what constituted an 'ability to function competently' has evolved to reflect the changing demands and expectations of particular societies and their prevailing systems of social and economic order" [5]. Nowadays, the social and economic order is characterized by globalization and information technologies, which significantly impact the knowledge, skills, and values that people need to 'function in society', imposing a pace of change faster than ever before.

To 'function in society' today's citizens need to work with information, concepts and relationships. Such activities depend on higher-order thinking skills. They have to communicate and interact within a global technological infrastructure that requires a great deal of digital competence, creativity, and agility. They have to work in environments that are increasingly open, changing, complex and non-predictable. They no longer need to build on what was taught to them, but rather what was not taught. The organizational patterns of companies also evolve quickly. Beyond divisional structures and bureaucratic configurations, many of today's most common forms of organization are dynamic and networked, and materialize through projects, joint-ventures, and partnerships. Educated individuals are asked to be competent, creative, entrepreneurial, and responsible, open to change and willing to learn and work in teams; all while exercising influence and building leadership. In sum, the bar has been raised dramatically in recent years regarding the profile of competencies, social skills, values and expertise necessary to function in society.

In recognition of such needs, a number of proposals of desirable competencies that should be developed by students during their schooling have been proposed over the last two decades. The aforementioned EU framework of competences has counterparts in many individual countries, in international bodies such the Unesco and the World Bank, in a large number of think tanks, educational, economic, and professional organizations, and associations like P21, ISTE, of NCREL/Metiri Group in the U.S., to name just a few. These frameworks emphasize the need to apply the knowledge that students already have and stress the importance of fostering learner autonomy, their capability of collaborating in heterogeneous groups, of communicating and working effectively by means of interactive systems, and of being able to think critically and creatively.

Some scholars have their own progressive view on key competencies. Harvard professor T. Wagner makes a compelling call for the seven "survival skills for teens today" [6] which every student should develop in order to be able to enter in the labour market after high-school to continue his/her formal education.[3] Those survival skills are based on the close relationships existing between values, attitudes, and competencies.

However, building a case for key competencies often encounters serious opposition when confronted with the realities of the evaluation systems currently in place. The U.S. implementation of its "No Child Left Behind" policies is a fitting example of

---

[3] Wagner's seven survival skills are: critical thinking and problem-solving; collaboration across networks and leading by influence; agility and adaptability; initiative and entrepreneurialism; effective oral and written communication; accessing and analyzing information, and curiosity and imagination.

obstacles to such change. For conceptual, economical, and practical reasons, and as a result of tradition, evaluation systems tend to focus almost exclusively on easily measurable skills and tiny bits of factual knowledge, which fit in with the compartmentalized structure of schooling, especially in the case of secondary education.

5 Schooling's Closed Spaces

Throughout the world, educational systems are formidable social structures which resolve into a myriad of institutions moulded, more often than not, according to what Tyack and Cuban refer to as the "grammar of schooling" [7]. The rules of this 'grammar', which cause schools to be largely similar and predictable across countries, imply that the institutions established by societies to educate their youth are generally materialized in the three inherent spaces outlined in this paper: the organization space, the physical space, and the information space. These spaces are based on a divisional structure determined by disciplines or subjects. The current mindset establishes that teaching the designated subjects and grading students has by far higher relevance than the application of knowledge and competencies development.

The current way educational relationships are structured, while mandated by governments, is more a product of tradition and managerial convenience than an intrinsic requirement of educating all young people. What educational institutions suffer is similar to that which Zuboff and Maxmin discuss in their critique of industrial companies and 20th century economic organizations: "the priorities are stacked from the inside, in terms of transactional economics and also organizational narcissism. These priorities are determined through the lens of a narcissistic culture that has become so taken for granted that it's barely visible" [8]. Educationally, this narcissism means that focus is placed on getting the transaction completed (or in educational terms, imparting the lesson in the classroom). The consequence of such a narrow focus on the transaction (or the lesson) is that nobody is really responsible for student learning, even less so in the long run. Another consequence is that the individual student has to fit into the organization, adapting his or her personality, behaviour, and expectations to the what, when, and how of the organization. There is no judgment of success outside these premises.

In many societies, surrendering personal interests, inspirations, and expectations for a vague promise of benefits in a far-off future is more and more untenable for a growing number of sceptical or disenfranchised students. Many students have priorities that do not match up with what school offers. Others simply do not believe in the hypothetical benefits of schooling, often due to disappointing experiences of older peers or family members in the modern job market.

Although this problem is a concern for teachers who deal with students on a daily basis, it is primarily an issue that should be dealt with by educational management, without which no workable and general solution can be found. However, firmly installed in the comfortable mindset of the predominant grammar of schooling, educational managers are unable or unwilling to see themselves as perpetuators of the fundamental asymmetry that makes schooling, in its present form, fail. They need to promote student-centred or society-related considerations and to encourage more profound student learning, fostering the ability of these students to function in society.

5.1 Organization Space

Society generally agrees that a nation should decide what its youth should learn. Curriculum authorities define what is appropriate and relevant at every stage, set the learning pace according to age, and establish ways to control learner performance. This requires, at least initially, significant managerial effort. Many governments' emphasis on student acquisition of key competencies and 21st century skills has, up to this point, merely been superimposed on top of existing subject-based academic disciplines, since they are at the very root of school logic, organization, and power.

This subject-based division is very rarely up for discussion. Subjects or disciplines are an intimate part of the school culture and, for the most, define its organization. This is because subject-mandated divisions amalgamate knowledge and power. As M. Foucault pointed out in his critique of those divisions, power and knowledge are correlative and, "always found together in power-knowledge formations" [9]. The power of the institution over the learners is exercised mainly through this structuring device, which determines the organization of school processes, and even the very nature of what is understood by teaching and learning. School disciplines are therefore the axis on which education is organized. Such an organization blatantly disregards the possibility that the system could be based on other criteria, potentially more relevant for 21st century learners.

Academic disciplines are likely so far to be the best way to structure and organize knowledge, but this does not mean that they constitute the best way to introduce young people to knowledge while at the same time obtaining the most potentially valuable –and largely unmet– educational outcome: the joy of learning and the will to continue to do so. In this respect Howard Gardner wrote that "the understanding of the principal ideas in the various disciplines has proved much more challenging than most educators have believed....Most students prove unable to master disciplinary content sufficiently so that they can apply it appropriately in new contexts" [10]. In the same paper he argues that "few educators are willing to face the serious implication of the finding that genuine disciplinary understanding is rarely found, even among our most successful students." Some primary-level and most all secondary teachers were hired based on a certain specialization and expertise in one subject. They often tend to underestimate the difficulty for young people to understand subject matter concepts. To some extent, teachers of different subjects compete with each other for resources, teaching time, and prestige. This fosters an isolated vision and 'sanctification' of disciplines reinforced by the prominent evaluation and grading mechanisms. However, this compartmentalization of knowledge does not foster the holistic development of the student.

The inflexible organization of schools (largely characteristic of secondary education) responds to this determined and intrinsic logic, with the disastrous result that nobody ends up taking full responsibility for the overall learning, skills acquisition, personal development, and orientation of every individual student. Discussions on the development of key learning competencies do not forcefully call for a profound rethinking of today's radical subject-based school organization. It is hardly acceptable that important issues like the development of individual autonomy, communication and collaborative learning skills, application of knowledge, and even the values development associated with the intellectual comprehension of human issues and situations, are more often than not, in a no-man's-land. Subject-based schooling tends to impose an instructional focus on decontextualized content and facts which are mostly evaluated through repetition. All in all, this takes the focus away from skills and competencies and is very damaging to the dissemination of such an approach. Development of key competencies requires a global approach that is at odds with today's radical compartmentalization of knowledge in the organization space that has been inherited to a great extent from the 19th century, designed to respond to the needs and visions of that time. Overcoming the situation that has resulted from this preoccupation with the past, while at the same time, constructing fresh and sound approaches to education on a large scale, is an immense challenge for 21st century education managers.

5.2 Physical Space

Throughout the 20th century, school buildings were built with the oral transmission of knowledge and student control in mind. The classroom, the fundamental module of most any school, often built at the minimum cost possible, is by design, a closed and isolated space to impart lessons while keeping students in sight at all times. Actual classroom use normally follows an inflexible and task-unrelated timeframe marked by school bells, according to a bureaucratic arrangement of "time-period-teacher-group-subject-matter" blocks decided on by school managers. Usually frozen in its static 19th century design, the physical space of the classroom interferes with pedagogic objectives, methodologies, and resources, evaluation processes, and interactions between students and teachers.

Student learning and development is inhibited by classrooms that were not designed for student research, creative projects, cooperative work, or co-teaching. In many classrooms, there is hardly any breathing space for collaboration, development of competencies and skills, and application of knowledge. This commonly contained space prevents, or at least seriously deters, a symbiotic relationship between teachers and students, a relationship which would allow for the centrality of learners and a more supportive and individually-centred role for teachers.

Moreover, mostly for secondary school students, the physical design of classroom, and even of the whole school, represents a view of the world which is deeply ingrained in the past, a view that is static, dead, and irrelevant, inapplicable to students' out-of-classroom realities and own perceived futures. The impersonality and blandness of so many classrooms are not conducive to a positive relationship between the student and his or her learning. No profound, universal student development of 21st century skills seems feasible within traditional school designs which do not comprehend the necessary variety of individual and group working areas and that treat interaction as an unwelcomed aspect of learning.

5.3 Information Space

During the second half of the 20th century almost nobody foresaw that the information environment would transform so radically in such a short period of time. However, as

Internet use becomes ever more common, neither curriculum authorities, school managers, or examination boards have been able to grasp the full implications of this "bouleversement" for the education of today's youth. The traditional concept of 'school', premised on teachers' words and on a few books as exclusive sources of knowledge, must be completely rethought. There is no longer a need to base education around textbooks, workbooks, a few maps, and a dictionary. The Internet can provide endless student personalization and educational possibilities and has a potential that we have yet to fathom.

The stability of educational content is radically altered by the digital nature of information. Text becomes hypertext and integrates all media. Authorities are weakened and what was stable and true becomes unstable and uncertain. Administering the information space, which was an intrinsic part of teacher authority, is no longer under their control. This constitutes both a fracture of the old concept of knowledge authority and of a fundamental pillar of the school system, which requires a profound redesign beyond individual teachers' capabilities.

However, too many students are still taught to think that by obediently advancing in their textbooks and passing exams, both of which exemplify a narrowly limited information space, they will be successful after graduation. As time moves on, this results less and less true. The promise that a diploma or a transcript full of high grades guarantees a good job is no longer valid. Now what is in demand in the working world are those jobs that are more creative and cognitively demanding, jobs that require innovative thinkers, social aptitude, international perspective, initiative, and the ability to process information while thinking outside the box.

6 "A Business Reflects Its Manager"

Almost 40 years ago, in his work *The Mind of the Strategist*, the renowned business and corporate strategist Kenichi Ohmae wrote that "Management, after all, is people, and businesses are made successful by people, not by plans. Behind each success story in business are men and women who conceived the ideas, developed the strategies, and executed the planned actions." [11] Without diminishing in the least the importance of education's "line workers" (that is, teachers), this statement fundamentally applies to managers of education, who are ultimately responsible for schools, education systems, and their results.

It is time that such a crucial issue comes to the forefront of the education agenda, for there is very little that teachers can do to bring real change to institutional settings without able, forward-looking, supportive managers who act with vision, knowledge, and a commitment to profound change. As prominent management scientist W. E. Deming once wrote, "No amount of care or skill in workmanship can overcome fundamental faults of the system" [12]. This statement thoroughly applies to education, but these days seems mostly hidden behind a biased rhetoric about the uttermost importance of teacher dedication, training and accountability, which shifts the burden (and the blame) to teachers, while negating the responsibility of those on the other side of the coin, education managers. Deming also said, rightly, that "It's management's responsibility to look ahead, predict, change the product, ..." It is difficult to imagine why this principle should not apply to those who manage education, but, in fact, it is rare to find policy makers and top-level education managers who speak this language.

Innovative leadership is crucial for any sound and effective key competency strategy. Quality of education depends on the quality of its management. The opening up of organization space to genuinely make room for competencies in a subject matter-dominated context, the redesign of physical space for new types of learning, the re-thinking of information space to make room to create and apply knowledge, cannot be delegated to teachers, hoping that they, with their sacrifice and best efforts, will solve or correct planning and management deficiencies.

However, technology can help to tackle the unprecedented level of complexity. If in previous times it was not feasible to manage individual complexity, now technologies do exist to fully support the educational process of the individual learner, although many of today's education managers, having their imagination caught up in the concepts and procedures of the rigid organization space, fail to recognize such possibilities. Captives of a "more of the same" logic, many of them hope to attain better results by acting on the symptoms of problems with the conceptual, human, organizational, and financial resources with which they are familiar. Analyzing, defining and acting on the root cause of dysfunctions remains difficult and uncertain, and requires concepts and efforts of a very exceptional nature, which generally seem to go beyond managers' visions, aims, and perceived obligations.

Aside from this, the full potential of ICT in education will be liberated only when it is aligned with a new management logic devoted to fully supporting and empowering the individual learner, aiming far beyond the usual institutional imperatives. Twenty first century schooling should free itself from the limitations of earlier eras. This is not only a job for teachers; but also, and more so, it is a job for education managers.

Ohmae's insightful statement "A business reflects its manager" [13] justly summa-rizes the main thesis of this paper: responsibility for change lies at the top. Education, as generally practised today, is inseparable from the current mindset of its managers because they constitute the embodiment of dominant education norms and values. Until very recently, school and school system administrators were adept at exercising authority, derived mainly from their hierarchical position. The philosophy of 'command and control', inherent to closed spaces, likely produced adequate results in the past, but certainly reveals its limits in advanced, democratic, pluralistic, and multicul-tural societies, in which skills and knowledge are the main drivers of economic suc-cess. A much broader vision needs to inspire those at all management levels.

To meet the educational needs of the 21st century, leaders in education, Ordonez says, "must look beyond budgets, faculty unions, facility expansion and maintenance, textbook production, and so on. They must instead embark on a constant search for new ways and new paradigms to meet the learning needs of students facing uncharted futures" [14]. Or, as Ordonez put another way, the task of true educational leadership is "to look beyond improving means to re-articulating existing ends". This re-articulation of ends requires a critical view of the "more of the same" logic and of the deeply embedded asymmetry which defines schooling. This task requires establishing a solid foundation so that all students are able to develop key competencies. In order to move forward in this respect, just as crucial as excellent, innovative teachers are forward thinking, student-oriented, and fearless managers.

References

1. Ordonez, V.: The Changing Role of Leadership (or A Changing Leadership for a Changing World). In: Hershock, P.D., Mason, M., Hawkins, J.N. (eds.) Changing Education. Leadership, Innovation and Development in a Globalizing Asia Pacific. CERC Studies in Comparative Education, vol. 20, p. 272. Springer, Heidelberg (2008)
2. European Commission: Key competences for a changing world. COM, 640 final (2009)
3. Lisbon European Council 23 and 24, Presidency Conclusions (March 2000), http://www.europarl.europa.eu/summits/lis1_en.htm#b
4. Toch, T.: Margins of Error: The Education Testing Industry in the No Child Left Behind Era. Education Sector Reports (2006)
5. Skidmore, P.: Beyond Measure. Why educational measurement is failing the test. Demos (2003), http://www.demos.co.uk
6. Wagner, T.: The Global Achievement Gap. Basic Books, New York (2008)
7. Tyack, D., Cuban, L.: Tinkering Toward Utopia: A Century of Public School Reform. Harvard University Press, Cambridge (1995)
8. Zuboff, S., Maxmin, J.: The Support Economy. Viking (2002)
9. Edwards, R., Usher, R.: Globalisation and Pedagogy. Space, Place and Identity, 2nd edn., p. 54. Routledge, New York (2008)
10. Gardner, H.: How Education Changes. In: Suárez-Orozco, M.M., Baolian Qin-Hilliard, D. (eds.) Considerations of History, Science, and Values. Globalization. Culture and Education in the New Millennium, University of California Press, Berkeley (2004)
11. Ohmae, K.: The Mind of the Strategist. Penguin Books (1982)
12. Deming, W.E.: The New Economics. For Industry, Government, Education. The MIT Press, Cambridge (1994)
13. Ohmae, K.: op. cit
14. Ordonez, V.: op. cit

Supporting Productive Integration of Web 2.0-Mediated Collaboration

Mun Fie Tsoi

National Institute of Education Singapore, Nanyang Technological University,
1 Nanyang Walk, Singapore 637616
raymond.tsoi@nie.edu.sg

Abstract. This paper describes a research evidence-based practice model, TSOI Hybrid Learning Model as a viable alternative to support productive integration of Web 2.0-mediated collaboration for learning. The model is advanced from the Science learning cycle and the Kolb's experiential learning cycle. An authentic example on understanding multimedia learning pedagogy for pre-service teachers in chemistry education is illustrated. The model guides the learning design involving Web 2.0-mediated collaborative activities. Outcomes in terms of richness of collaborative learning and reflections have been positive. Implications will be discussed in the context of blended learning in science education.

Keywords: Hybrid learning model, Web 2.0, collaborative learning.

1 Introduction

This paper provides an insight into applying a research evidence-based practice model to support productive integration of Web 2.0-mediated collaboration for learning. To address the issues on the use of social software tools in education for example, quality learning, course design and delivery cited by Franklin & van Harmelen [1], Mason & Rennie [2], Minocha [3], an alternative pedagogical framework to integrate Web 2.0 such as Blogs and Wikis productively for learning is described. As such, having this in mind, the TSOI Hybrid Learning Model™ & © 2005 All rights reserved. (TSOI HLM) can serve as a useful support to integrate productively Web 2.0-mediated collaborative activities.

It is envisaged that as in previous studies on its functions and applications conducted by Tsoi [4], Tsoi [5], the learning model will contribute as an innovative approach for a productive integration of Web 2.0-mediated collaboration for learning.

2 Conceptual Framework of TSOI HLM

The TSOI HLM is advanced from the Science learning cycle model and the Kolb's experiential learning cycle. The term hybrid will mean the mixing of two different things to give a better product which in this case is a learning model that is pedagogically more innovative and comprehensive than each of the original model namely, the

N. Reynolds and M. Turcsányi-Szabó (Eds.): KCKS 2010, IFIP AICT 324, pp. 401–411, 2010.

Science learning cycle model and the Kolb's experiential learning cycle model. It is inclusive since it also encompasses the characteristics of each original model. The Science learning cycle model being inquiry-based represents an inductive application of information processing models of teaching and learning as reported by Karplus [6], Lawson [7], Renner & Marek [8]. It has three phases in a cycle: exploration, concept invention, and concept application as shown in Figure 1. The exploration phase focuses on "What did you do?" while the concept invention phase places emphasis on "What did you find out?". The concept application phase entails the application of the concept.

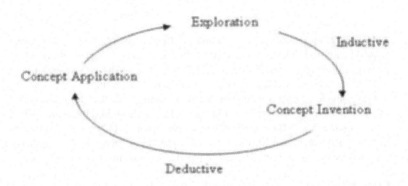

Fig. 1. The Science learning cycle model

The exploration phase (gathering of data) is often accomplished during a science activity or an experiment that is usually performed in the science laboratory. During this exploration phase, learners learn through their own actions and reactions in a new situation and have the opportunity to explore new learning materials and new ideas with minimal guidance from the teacher.

The concept invention phase gives the opportunity to the student and/ or teacher to derive the concept from the data through classroom discussion. This phase involves the introduction of a new term or terms. Ideally, learners are encouraged to discover as much of a new pattern as possible before the term is revealed to them. The third phase, concept application allows the student to explore the relevance and application. This concept application phase is essential as it allows learners to extend the range of applicability of the new concept.

The Kolb's experiential learning cycle researched by Kolb [9] as shown in Figure 2 represents learning as a process in a cycle of four stages, namely, concrete experience, reflective observation, abstract conceptualization, and active experimentation. The concrete experience stage is about "doing" while the reflective observation stage concerns the "understanding the doing". The abstract conceptualization stage focuses on the "understanding" part and the active experimentation stage is about "doing the understanding". This experiential learning cycle model has also been used by His & Agogino [10], Tsoi & Goh [11] as a framework for organizing interactive multimedia learning activities .

Kolb also created four quadrants in his model of experiential learning. He named each quadrant a learning style as diverger, converger, assimilator or accommodator (see Figure 2).

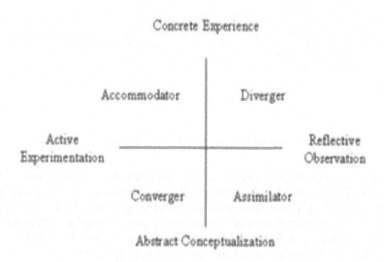

Fig. 2. Kolb's Experiential Learning Model (Smith and Kolb, 1986, p16)

For convergers, experience is grasped through abstract comprehension and transformed through action, which combines abstract conceptualization and active experimentation. For divergers, experience is grasped as opposite of convergers, that is, concretely through feelings and transformed through thought, which combines concrete experience with reflective observation. For assimilators, experience is grasped through abstract comprehension and transformed through thought, which combines abstract conceptualization and reflective observation. For the accommodators, experience is grasped concretely through feelings and transformed by action, combining the features of concrete experience and active experimentation.

The TSOI Hybrid Learning Model™ & © 2005 All rights reserved, conceptualized by Tsoi [12], Tsoi [13] represents learning as a cognitive process in a cycle of four phases: Translating, Sculpting, Operationalizing, and Integrating. One of the key features is to promote active cognitive processing in the learner for meaningful and engaged learning proceeding from inductive to deductive learning. Besides, it is inclined towards constructivism. Figure 3 shows the four phases of this learning model.

The Translating phase is similar to the exploration phase of Science learning cycle model and the concrete experience stage of Kolb's experiential learning cycle model. This is where interactive experiences are translated to beginning ideas or concepts to be further engaged in the Sculpting phase. The Sculpting phase parallels the concept invention phase of Science learning cycle model and predominantly the reflective observation stage of the Kolb's experiential learning cycle including partially the abstract conceptualization stage of the Kolb's experiential learning cycle. This is where the beginning idea or concept still in its raw form is further molded to a concrete form that is meaningful to the learner.

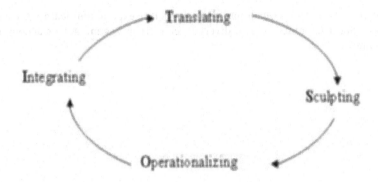

Fig. 3. TSOI Hybrid Learning Model^{TM &@} 2005 All rights reserved

The Operationalizing phase similar to predominantly the abstract conceptualization stage of the Kolb's experiential learning cycle involves increasing the understandings of the relationship between thinking and concept acquisition. The Integrating phase parallels the concept application of Science learning cycle model as well as the active experimentation stage of Kolb's experiential learning cycle. This is where the concept is applied to new domains in which the transfer of learning is practiced.

3   Integration Support for Web 2.0-Mediated Collaboration

The hybrid learning model guides the learning design implemented by the author as the researcher that involves participatory learning as well as integrates Web 2.0 such as blogs and wikis for collaboration. Face to face interactions for a preliminary experience on multimedia learning and its relation to TSOI HLM are realized in the Translating phase while a multimedia learning chemistry module designed based on the TSOI HLM as the pedagogic model is embedded in an e-learning environment for the Sculpting phase. In this phase, group collaboration for the construction of the critical attributes or features of the concept of this hybrid learning model is accomplished in the form of blogs. The Operationalizing phase focuses on interactive group activities on applications of this hybrid learning model to lesson planning of other topics. This is for internalizing purpose. Implications on the use of this hybrid learning model in teaching and learning in science education are completed individually in the form of wikis for the Integrating phase. This learning design will provide the pedagogical support needed for productive integration of Web 2.0-mediated collaborative activities. An example of a curriculum studies course on understanding multimedia learning pedagogy in chemistry education for 162 pre-service teachers of the PGDE (S) course (Postgraduate in Diploma in Education, Secondary) is used.

3.1   Integration Support: Translating Phase

During the first phase, the Translating phase, the instructional learning activity though general in nature, is designed to have an initial relationship to the principle underlying the concept which to be further engaged in the second phase, the Sculpting phase. The Translating phase emphasizes concept initial exposure for preliminary experience.

In the Translating phase, face to face interactions infused with cooperative learning strategies such as think and pair share, round table and number heads together are carried out in 2 sessions of 2 hours each in the form of group discussions. For example, responses to a question on "what do you understand by the term multimedia learning" are elicited and discussed. The idea is to give an opening experience to what does multimedia learning mean to them. The next main activity focuses on the fundamentals of TSOI HLM as the pedagogic model for multimedia learning design to prepare the trainee teachers for the Sculpting phase. As such, the beginning idea of the TSOI HLM will be further engaged in the Sculpting phase.

In chemistry education, stoichiometry, cited by Tsoi, Goh & Chia [14] as an abstract and difficult topic is used to illustrate the understanding and applications of the hybrid learning model. One of the subtopics used is solution concentration. This next section, the sculpting phase will provide insights on the application of the TSOI HLM, as an example to demonstrate its use as a pedagogic model for designing this multimedia learning module.

3.2 Integration Support: Sculpting Phase

During the second phase, the Sculpting phase, knowledge of the concept is beginning to be constructed based on the learner's facilitated multimedia experiences from the Translating phase as well as the learner's guided multimedia experiences from the Sculpting phase. The concept still in its beginning or raw form as taken from the Translating phase is logically sculpted or shaped to a more concrete form by a series of appropriate and relevant instructional learning activities that are designed meaningfully to assist the learner to identify the critical attributes of the concept. As such, the third phase, the Operationalizing phase is important as it can provide the opportunity for the learner to acquire a complete picture of all the required critical attributes of the concept for conceptual understanding and internalization. The Sculpting phase emphasizes concept construction for its critical attributes.

The development of solution concentration concept consists of four instructional learning episodes in accordance to the four phases of the TSOI HLM. The following subsections describe these four instructional learning episodes which are (a) Which is more concentrated, (b) Physical Meaning and Definition, (c) Investigating Chemical Reactions, and (d) A Simple Equation.

The translating phase is illustrated to show part of the TSOI HLM since the focus of this paper is not on designing a multimedia learning module. The first instructional learning episode," Which is more concentrated" as a Translating phase provides the learner with visual representations in which the relationship between concentration of the solution and the amount of solute particles dissolved in the solution will be formulated cognitively. In the first activity, the learner is asked to compare 2 solutions in terms of concentration which involves the amount of solute particles dissolved in the solution. Observational response is elicited. This is then extended to the second activity where the learner is posed a question as to how to make the concentration of solution A the same as solution B (see Fig 4). These visual representations act as a beginning idea or concept of solution concentration which is further molded in the next Sculpting phase of TSOI HLM, Physical Meaning and Definition.

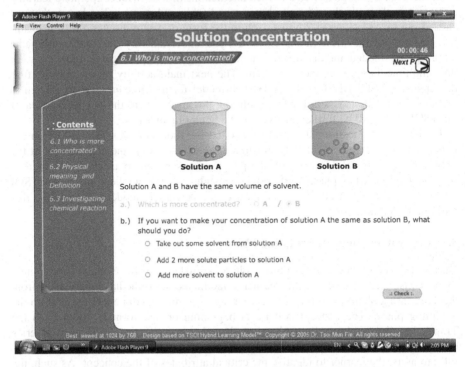

Fig. 4. Solution Concentration Multimedia Learning Module (Translating phase)

The individual learner is given a week to observe on how the multimedia learning module is developed based on the TSOI HLM as its pedagogic model and reflect on it using a journal article as a reference. After which, the group members are given a week to discuss their observations using Web 2.0 technology such as the blog tool and summarize their group discussions. The blog tool is used for its ease in providing comments and also the pre-service teachers prefer to use the blog tool than the discussion forum. Essentially, the understanding of the hybrid learning model in terms of its critical attributes or features is constructed here. A sample of a group blog is shown in Figure 5. A summary of some samples of group blog contents is shown in Figure 6.

3.3 Integration Support: Operationalizing Phase

The third phase, the Operationalizing phase is crucial as it serves as the vital bridge connecting the Sculpting phase and the Integrating phase for not only concept formation but also concept internalization in which all the critical attributes of the concept are linked together so as to prepare the learner to be operationally ready for further applications in the Integrating phase. The Operationalizing phase emphasizes concept internalization for its meaningful functionality.

In the Operationalizing phase, the group members collaborate in a 2 hour session to provide the design of a chemistry lesson for secondary school level based on the hybrid learning model. At the end of the collaborative process, the group members take turns to present their works to the class for comments in a mode of gallery walk. These classroom activities are for the internalization process.

QCY520_Tsoi(Aug09):The Teaching of Chemistry I (permalink)

Summary TG04 - Group of 4 (names removed) (permalink)

Created   on   Thursday,   10/08/2009   3:29   PM   by   **.   name   removed**
From the contributions of our group members, we conclude that the e-learning module on concentration has employed the TSOI$^©$ hybrid learning model effectively

Translating Phase

- Engage students' prior knowledge; Exploration of raw forms of concepts
- Engage students in learning, Use of visual, impactful and authentic visual aids
- Issue of assessment of prior knowledge of the students, "Correctness" of students' prior knowledge

Sculpturing Phase

- Logical sequence of content, Meaning and definition of concentration was brought across by first introducing the concept of homogenous solutions
- Developing the method to calculate the number of moles from a given volume of given concentration of solution, Facilitates learner reflection with appropriate pauses
- Students actively involved in thinking process, Crucial in determining the critical attribute of the concept
- Addressing of common misconception: What happens to the concentration of a solution when I draw out 50cm^3 from the 100cm^3 of solution? We feel that it was a good question to test if the students really understood that the concentration is not only dependent on the amount of solute but the volume of solvent as well

Operationalizing Phase

- Partially-worked problems and finally practice problems, Repeated for other problems. Connection between the symbolic representation (equations) and the microscopic level (particles shown) is illustrated.
- Facilitate students to internalize the knowledge as they are shown the links between various concepts, which they will be able use in the next phase.
- The students also start to learn more about problem solving processes. Students are slowly brought through different types of questions based on varying the 4 factors of mole, mass, concentration and volume.

Integrating Phase

- Apply what they learnt from the previous three units to novel situations and problems in this last phase of the TSOI$^©$ model
- Integrate what they have learnt so far into different contexts such as purity, titration/volumetric analysis, neutralization and dilution problems, Meaningful learning as students can apply their knowledge constructed thus far to other situations/contexts, Enhances the learning process since the students are able to use the knowledge they have learnt almost immediately

Fig. 5. A sample of a group blog

Concluding Thoughts:
In conclusion, our personal opinion is that each step of the TSOI's Learning Model is highly crucial. It is all interconnected and to go to the next stage in the construction of conceptual knowledge, there must be a systematic flow of stages. The interactive program promotes cognitive thinking on the students' part and allows them to actively participate in the activity. Applying the concepts and principles of "concentration" from simpler examples to more difficult ones also helps students to develop their knowledge on the topic in a more structured manner, hence it is easier for students to understand and integrate the knowledge. Overall, the experience has indeed been very fruitful for us.

Summary
Basically, my group has learnt that the TSOI hybrid learning model consists of 4 stages, with the first stage being one where visualizations are used, that students are able to make sense of the new concept they're being exposed to. Subsequently, the process builds up with worked examples provided at every stage, such that the new concept they are learning becomes more concretized and their knowledge of the topic is further built up. They should finally arrive at the place where they can then apply what they have learnt into situations they have not encountered before with whatever examples they have been exposed to. Incorporating both Piaget's and Kolb's learning models, the TSOI hybrid learning model makes the whole process of acquiring and processing new knowledge more complete & meaningful.

Summary
The Tsoi Hybrid Learning model is very effective in getting students to understand difficult concepts by going through the four phases in sequence; Translating, Sculpting, Operationalizing and Integrating. This gradual increase in students' thoughts is very much in line with van Hiele's model since the stages are hierarchical and students cannot skip a stage.

In the first phase Translation, students use visualization and analysis to translate their prior knowledge to what they see.

In the Sculpting Phase, students construct knowledge and when provoked with questions, followed by pauses students are allowed to generate critical ideas. And like van Hiele level 1, the students are beginning to reason inductively.

In the Operationalizing phase, the students begin to understand the relationships between the ideas and concepts generated to form an abstract idea of the processes occurring. This is also possible through problem solving processes.

In the Integrating phase, students form a network of concepts and ideas, summarizing them so as to envision the bigger picture. The learned concepts can therefore now be effectively put to practice in different context.

As such, the TSOI Hybrid Learning Model allows for systematic and logical reasoning of concepts such that learning of these concepts becomes naturally embedded to students' schemata. And in this way, learning is meaningful.

Comments
The model provides a systematic breakdown of how subjects can taught effectively, highlighting the crucial cognitive processes that take place. It is noted that the model does not only apply to chemistry, but also other subjects as well.

To conclude, the TSOI Hybrid Learning model is a useful framework for teachers to use when planning the instructional process. It is particularly useful in chemistry as many concepts are often abstract and would require a well-structured thought process for learning to be meaningful. Overall, we have learnt (1) how multimedia can be employed to provide interactive and concrete experiences for learners to build their conceptual understanding (2) how the TSOI model is a helpful guideline for teachers to plan their lessons to make learning of abstract concepts more meaningful and effective for our students.

Fig. 6. Some samples of blog contents

3.4   Integration Support: Integrating Phase

During the fourth phase, the Integrating phase emphasizes concept application for meaningful transfer of knowledge. In the Integrating phase, the Wiki tool is used within a week for personal reflections. The individual is asked to reflect and provide up to 6 points its implication on teaching and learning of chemistry as well as think & describe briefly of how you as a teacher can apply this hybrid learning model as a practice framework to guide you in your teaching of chemistry concepts. A sample of an individual wiki is shown in Figure 7.

 QCY520_Tsoi(Aug09):The Teaching of Chemistry I (permalink)

6 points of implications on teaching and learning of using Tsoi's model (permalink) last edited by . **name removed** on Sunday, 10/25/2009 12:50 PM

1) This model allows teachers to be able to teach Chemistry in a systematic way. Chemistry concepts are usually quite abstract and to enhance the learning efficiency of the students, it is important that teachers use the model to guide and reinforce the concept in a step by step manner or students can get quite lost.

2) Many teachers and students are not able to teach or learn the concepts in Chemistry in such a way that they are able to use the concept and apply in other situations. This model took that into consideration and allows teachers or students to be able to teach or learn to apply the concepts to different situations.

3) This model allows students to be active learners in the teaching process as it enables students to be able to explore and form the concepts , form linkages with other concepts and to learn on how to apply them in everyday life.

4) However it is important this process not get too guided. As in the example of the concentration, every single step is guided in the calculation and answers to questions posed can be easily obtained by clicking on the tab. Students are spoon fed instead of becoming active learners in this case.

5) The duration spent and emphasis for each phase should vary according to the ability of the students. For example, longer time and more emphasis might be place in the translating and sculpting phase for students in normal academic and technical as they are usually weaker in their concepts. However for the higher ability students, more emphasis should be on the operationalizing and internalizing phase because they are able to catch on the concepts faster and too much time spent in the beginning stages will bore them.

6) Although this is a good basic framework for teachers to build their lessons upon, it is important in real life application of this model that teachers do not become too religious with it. Lessons are dynamic and smooth flowing if teachers are too insistent on following every stage religiously, the efficiency of learning will be lost.

How can I use this in the classroom?
To me personally, I really enjoy using this framework to guide my lesson planning. It is easy to use and enables us to teach in a systematic manner. Many a times, teachers are lost in how to introduce a concept that is difficult or abstract and this framework helps them to be able to break it down different steps that they can present easily and students will be able to learn efficiently as well. However it is important that I learn to be flexible with this model. Although the model was introduced in a stage by stage manner, it need not be taught rigidly in this way. I have to vary the time and effort needed on each stage based on the ability of the students as well.

Fig. 7. A sample of an individual wiki entry

4 Discussions

The Translating phase of the TSOI HLM is a significant phase as it presents the learner an initial preliminary awareness of the concept which in this case is about a pedagogical model for teaching and learning to be learned. In other words, the experiences be it in form of an e-learning module or face-to-face mode facilitated are translated to a beginning concept by the learner. As such, it is essential to first identify the critical attributes of the concept to be learnt so that varied activities can be designed to assist the learner to identify these critical attributes and eventually leading to acquisition of concept mastery. The instructional activities experienced by the learner in the Translating phase should be familiar to the learner so that one can make connections to one's existing knowledge structures. Following the realization of the Translating phase, the learner's preliminary experience is then given more meaning in the Sculpting phase.

During the second phase, the Sculpting phase of the TSOI HLM, the beginning concept experienced still in its raw form is logically shaped to a more concrete form by a series of appropriate and relevant instructional learning activities that are "crafted" meaningfully to assist the learner to identify the critical attributes of the concept to be learned. These instructional learning activities are also designed to encourage the learner to be actively involved in the appropriate thinking processes, for example, abstracting, and observing, comparing and identifying patterns, predicting that the learner needs to accomplish to determine the critical attributes of the concept. As such, it is appropriate and productive to integrate Web 2.0 such as blogs for collaborative learning.

The Operationalizing phase is the central bridge connecting the Sculpting phase and the Integrating phase particularly in the aspect of concept internalization. There is an important need for the concept that is already constructed to be internalized for meaningful functionality. Besides, an awareness of the problem solving processes is also established. This also applies to group collaboration on the design of lessons to consolidate. During the fourth phase, the Integrating phase, the just learned concept already internalized is then applied to new situations thereby building external connections with other prior concepts as well. The concept is also integrated in different contexts in order for meaningful learning to occur. As the concept learned is a pedagogical model, it is relevant and productive to integrate Wiki, Web 2.0. in the learning process.

The outcomes of the process of integration of Web 2.0-mediated collaborative activities in terms of the richness of the contents of the blogs and wikis have been encouraging and positive to some extent. A sample of how the critical attributes of the hybrid learning model have been constructed using Blogs, Web 2.0 is shown in Figure 5 and 6. This has demonstrated richness of the blog contents in the group's efforts in their discussion and comments. Further to this use of blog tool, the Wiki tool, Web 2.0 for purpose of integrating the concept of the learning model is also well utilized by the pre-service teachers. A sample of the thought process is shown in Figure 7. Indeed, excerpts from the Web 2.0 responses lend support to the potential of the hybrid learning model for productive integration of Web 2.0-mediated collaboration. Besides, studies by Tsoi [12, 15] have found a statistically significant difference between pretest and posttest achievement means at the .05 level as they pertain to a learner's level of conceptual understanding of mole concept for each of the four groups using a multimedia learning package for learning of the mole concept, which has as its pedagogic model the TSOI hybrid learning model. It has been likely that the four phases of the hybrid learning model together as a whole entity also has a positive overall effect on the conceptual learning of mole concept.

In this preliminary study, the author recognizes limitation that lies partly in the research rigour of the process for example, empirical validation. However, this sets the groundwork for studying this alternative way of approaching the practice of integrating Web 2.0-mediated collaboration productively. In essence, the TSOI Hybrid Learning Model has the functional potential capacity to give the educator an alternative practice model for productive integration of Web 2.0-mediated collaboration. The learner will build on the concrete experience, and will learn how to create knowledge and integrate the knowledge with existing ideas and concepts in other context and more importantly, to be an active learner engaged in the various learning processes including collaborative learning.

References

1. Franklin, T., van Harmelen.: Web 2.0 for learning and teaching in higher education. Report, the Observatory of Borderless Higher Education, London (2007)
2. Mason, R., Rennie, F.: E-learning and Social Networking Handbook. Routledge, New York (2008)
3. Minocha, S.: Role of social software tools in education: a literature review. Education &Training 51, 353–369 (2009)
4. Tsoi, M.F.: Designing e-learning cognitively: TSOI Hybrid Learning Model. International Journal of Advanced Corporate Learning 1, 48–52 (2008)
5. Tsoi, M.F.: Applying TSOI hybrid learning model to enhance blended learning experience in science education. Interactive Technology and Smart Education 6, 223–233 (2009)
6. Karplus, R.: Teaching and the Development of Reasoning. University of California Press, Berkeley (1977)
7. Lawson, A.E.: Science Teaching and the Development of Thinking. Wadsworth, Belmont (1995)
8. Renner, J.W., Marek, E.A.: An educational theory base for science teaching. Journal of Research in Science Teaching 27, 241–246 (1990)
9. Kolb, D.: Experiential Learning: Experience as the Source of Learning and Development. Prentice Hall, Englewood Cliffs (1984)
10. His, S., Agogino, A.M.: The impact and instructional benefit of using multimedia case studies to teach engineering design. Journal of Educational Multimedia and Hypermedia 3, 351–376 (1994)
11. Tsoi, M.F., Goh, N.K.: Practical multimedia design for chemical education. In: Breaker, J., et al. (Series eds.) & G. Cumming et al. (Vol eds.) Advanced Research in Computers and Communications in Education: New human abilities for the networked society., vol. 1, pp. 946–949. IOS Press, The Netherlands (1999)
12. Tsoi, M.F.: Designing for Engaged e-learning: TSOI Hybrid Learning Model. The International Journal of Learning 15, 225–232 (2008)
13. Tsoi, M.F.: Designing for Engaging: Hybrid Learning Model. The International Journal of the Computer, the Internet and Management 15, 29.1–29.4 (2007)
14. Tsoi, M.F., Goh, N.K., Chia, L.S.: Some suggestions for the teaching of the Mole Concept. In: Wass, Margit (eds.) Enhancing Learning: Challenge of Integrating Thinking and Information Technology into the Curriculum, vol. 2, pp. 778–785. Educational Research Association, Singapore (1998)
15. Tsoi, M.F.: Development and effects of multimedia design on learning of mole concept. Published doctoral thesis, Nanyang Technological University, Singapore (2007)

Evaluating the Cisco Networking Academy Program's Instructional Model against Bloom's Taxonomy for the Purpose of Information Security Education for Organizational End-Users

Johan F. van Niekerk and Kerry-Lynn Thomson

Institute for ICT Advancement
Nelson Mandela Metropolitan University
{Johan.vanniekerk,Kerry-Lynn.Thomson}@nmmu.ac.za

Abstract. Organizational end-user information security end-user education is becoming increasingly more important in the current *information society*. Without the active co-operation of *knowledgeable* employees, organizations cannot effectively protect their valuable information resources. Most current information security educational programs lack a theoretical basis. This paper briefly examines the use of Bloom's learning taxonomy to help address this lack of theoretical basis. The paper further investigates the applicability of the Cisco Networking Academy Program's (CNAP) instructional model for the delivery of end-user information security instructional content, planned with the assistance of Bloom's taxonomy.

Keywords: Information Security Education, Bloom's Taxonomy, Blended Learning, E-learning.

1 Introduction

According to Carr [1] the dependency on information technology has become so great that it should no longer be viewed as conveying a competitive advantage, but rather as a basic commodity, similar to electricity. Unfortunately, the availability of one's information is often a lot more vulnerable than the availability of other commodities. Without adequate protection, information resources are extremely vulnerable. It is thus vital for organizations to be serious about the protection of information resources.

Humans, at various levels in the organization, play a vital role in the processes that secure organizational information resources. Many of the problems experienced in information security can be directly contributed to the humans involved in the process. Employees, either intentionally or through negligence, often due to a lack of knowledge, can be seen as the greatest threat to information security [2, p. 3]. It is thus imperative for organizations that are serious about the protection of its information resources to be serious about the education of its employees. The aim of corporate information security end-user education should be to ensure that each and every employee in the organization knows his/her responsibility towards information security.

N. Reynolds and M. Turcsányi-Szabó (Eds.): KCKS 2010, IFIP AICT 324, pp. 412–423, 2010.

Most current information security end-user educational programs are constructed by information security specialists who do not necessarily have a strong educational background. Puhakainen [3, pp. 33-56] reviews 59 current approaches to security awareness, most of which are not based on pedagogical theories. Puhakainen [3, p. 56] also argues that there is a need for theory-based security approaches. These approaches should also be practically effective. The nature of security educational or awareness issues are often not understood, which could lead to programs and guidelines that are ineffective in practice [4]. One possible way to introduce pedagogical theory as a basis for information security awareness programs is through the use of learning taxonomies. Arguably the most widely used of these learning taxonomies is Bloom's taxonomy of the cognitive domain.

Previous papers have shown how Bloom's taxonomy could be used in information security end-user education. Van Niekerk & Von Solms [5] argued that Bloom's taxonomy of the cognitive domain can be used as a theoretical basis to partly ensure the pedagogical integrity of information security awareness programs. Van Niekerk & Von Solms [6] showed how the use of this taxonomy could help information security specialists to answer the four so-called organizing questions when creating awareness programs. The use of Bloom's taxonomy during the creation of information security educational material could thus assist in ensuring that; the most important learning activities receive the larger share of available resources (learning question), the instructional material is planned around activities that will benefit most learners (instruction question), the chosen assessments correspond directly to what the educator intended to assess (assessment question), and that all activities align towards the intended learning outcomes (alignment question) [7, pp. 6-10].

Through the use of a learning taxonomy information security practitioners can plan what to include in information security educational programs. However, another equally important question still needs to be addressed. Namely, how the content should be delivered. Few, if any, modern organizations can afford to send each and every staff member on extensive information security educational courses. In today's organizations it is crucial to maximize return on investment. Through its very nature classroom training requires the availability of highly trained specialists to present the courses. It also requires that the learners take time off from their regular duties to attend classes. These factors make classroom training very expensive. One alternative to traditional classroom training is to provide employees with E-learning alternatives.

E-learning has been used with great effect in other information technology related fields. For example, the Cisco Networking Academy Program (CNAP) plays a widely recognized role in the education of networking professionals. This program is based on a blended learning approach, which combines E-learning, classroom instruction and hands-on practical work as part of a wide spectrum of teaching and assessment approaches. This paper will evaluate the instructional model used by CNAP against the requirements for a learning program designed according to Bloom's taxonomy. The purpose of this evaluation is to determine whether the CNAP instructional model would meet all the requirements for educating end users about information security.

The rest of this paper will firstly discuss E-learning and blended learning in general in order to demonstrate the suitability of these types of instructional programs for the specific needs of information security end-user education. Secondly, a brief outline of the CNAP instructional model will be provided and the paper will then discuss how

Bloom's taxonomy can be used in information security education. Finally a comparative analysis will be done to demonstrate how well the CNAP instructional model maps to the educational requirements of a pedagogically sound end-user information security educational program.

2 Why Blended and/or E-Learning?

In an organizational context, information security end-user education has several requirements specific to the role that such programs have to play in the overall organization's information security efforts. Van Niekerk & Von Solms [8] identified these requirements and discussed the pedagogical implications of these requirements in depth. The following is a brief summary of the identified requirements:

1. Everyone should be able to "pass" the course.
2. Employees must know *why* information security is important and why a specific policy or control is in place.
3. Learning materials should be customized to the needs of individual learners.
4. Users should be responsible for their own learning.
5. Users should be held accountable for their studies.

It can be argued that, in terms of the above requirements, e-learning solutions are ideally suited to the needs of information security end-user education. E-learning based training solutions have several benefits over more traditional approaches like classroom training. These benefits include:

- Electronic and/or web-based media is very rich. This means that educational material developed in these types of media is not restricted to simple text and static graphics, but can consist of a mixture of text, graphics, animations and even sound or video clips.
- E-learning based training solutions are inexpensive to distribute organization wide and can easily be administrated from a centralized point. This also means that it would be very easy to maintain, manage and update training materials.
- E-learning training materials can include programmatic components, which could allow virtually limitless customization.

The fact that web-based training materials can include programmatic components has several important implications for its possible use in information security end-user education. Firstly, it would make it feasible to add automated assessment modules to such training materials, which means that learners can receive continuous feedback on their progress. Automated feedback, in combination with the fact that this material would be available at all times, means that learners could be made responsible for their own learning. Automated assessment would also enable organizations to hold learners accountable for their own learning. The use of automated assessment also makes it easier to allow users multiple attempts at passing specific assessments modules. This can contribute to an environment where everyone could eventually "pass" the course.

The U.S. Department of Education published a report based on a meta-analysis of the results of more than 1000 empirical studies that were published from 1996 through July 2008 [9]. The report focused predominantly on publications after 2004 which compared the effectiveness of various forms of e-learning and blended learning to face-to-face education [9, p. xiii]. This report examined 51 identified study effects, of which 44 were drawn from research focusing on older (adult) learners. This focus on older learners is of particular importance to educators focusing on organizational information security end-user education who work exclusively with adult learners. Adults already have well-established values, beliefs, and opinions. Adults relate new information and knowledge to previously learned information, experiences, and values which might result in misunderstanding [10, p. 20]. It is therefore vital to ensure that learning approaches followed are suitable for adult learners. The fact that 44 of the 51 study effects analyzed in the meta-analysis focus on adult learners makes the results of this analysis very relevant. The following key-findings are of specific importance for the purposes of this paper [9, p. xiv-xvi]:

- "Students who took all or part of their class online performed better, on average, than those taking the same course through traditional face-to-face instruction"
- "Instruction combining online and face-to-face elements had a larger advantage relative to purely face-to-face instruction than did purely online instruction"
- "The effectiveness of online learning approaches appears quite broad across different content and learner types."

These findings make it clear that a blended or e-learning approach would not only be effective for information security end-user education, but would in fact be better than traditional face-to-face education. "A blended approach" would thus answer the question "How should educational content be delivered?". However, the question "what should be taught to organizational end-users?" still remains. The use of a learning taxonomy might assist in answering this question.

3 Bloom's Taxonomy

Bloom's taxonomy is possibly one of the best known and most widely used models of human cognitive processes. Bloom's model was originally developed in the 1950s and remained in use more or less unchanged until fairly recently [11, p. 249]. A revised version of the taxonomy was published in [7]. This revised taxonomy has become accepted as more appropriate in terms of current educational thinking [11, pp. 249-260]. The following is a brief explanation of each of the six levels of the revised taxonomy [11, pp. 250-252]:

- *Remember:* Remember refers to the rote recall and recognition of previously learned facts. This level represents the lowest level of learning in the cognitive domain because there is no presumption that the learner understands what is being recalled.
- *Understand:* This level describes the ability to "make sense" of the material. In this case the learning goes beyond rote recall. If a learner understands material it becomes available to that learner for future use in problem solving and decision making.

- *Apply:* The third level builds on the second one by adding the ability to use learned materials in new situations with a minimum of direction. This includes the application of rules, concepts, methods and theories to solve problems within the given domain. This level combines the activation of procedural memory and convergent thinking to correctly select and apply knowledge to a completely new task. Practice is essential in order to achieve this level of learning.
- *Analyze:* This is the ability to break up complex concepts into simpler component parts in order to better understand its structure. Analysis skills include the ability to recognize underlying parts of a complex system and examine the relationships between these parts and the whole. This stage is considered more complex than the previous because the learner has to be aware of the thought process in use and must understand both the content and the structure of material.
- *Evaluate:* Evaluation deals with the ability to judge the value of something based on specified criteria and standards. These criteria and/or standards might be determined by the learner or might be given to the learner. This is a high level of cognition because it requires elements from several other levels to be used in conjunction with conscious judgement based on definite criteria. To attain this level a learner needs to consolidate their thinking and should also be more receptive to alternative points of view.
- *Create:* This is the highest level in the taxonomy and refers to the ability to put various parts together in order to formulate an idea or plan that is new to the learner. This level stresses creativity and the ability to form new patterns or structures by using divergent thinking processes.

Educational taxonomies, such as Bloom's taxonomy, are useful tools in developing learning objectives and assessing learner attainment [12]. All well known educational taxonomies are generic. These taxonomies rely on the assumption that the hierarchy of learning outcomes apply to all disciplines [12]. Bloom's taxonomy would thus apply equally to a more traditional "subject", such as zoology, as to organizational information security end-user education. In addition to these levels of the cognitive domain the revised taxonomy also places major emphasis on the use of the following categorization of the knowledge dimension [7, pp. 45-62]:

- *Factual Knowledge* - The most basic elements the learner must know in order to be familiar with a discipline. I.e. Terminology or specific details and elements.
- *Conceptual Knowledge* - The interrelationships among the basic elements of larger structures that enable these elements to function together. I.e. Classification, categories, principles, theories, models, etc.
- *Procedural Knowledge* - How to do something, methods of inquiry, how to use skills, apply algorithms, techniques and methods. I.e. Subject specific skills, algorithms, techniques, and methods as well as knowledge of criteria for determining when to use appropriate procedures.
- *Meta-Cognitive Knowledge* - An awareness and knowledge of one's own cognition. I.e. Strategic knowledge, Self-knowledge, knowledge about cognitive tasks, including contextual and conditional knowledge.

The use of this taxonomy for information security end-user education will be discussed in a later section of this paper. The next section will briefly outline the instructional model used by the Cisco Networking Academy Program.

4   The Cisco Networking Academy Program Instructional Model

The Cisco Networking Academy Program (CNAP) is a global e-learning education program that teaches students to design, troubleshoot and secure communication networks. Core to CNAP is the Learning Management System. Through the Learning Management System, referred to as the Instructor Portal in CNAP, instructors are able to create online classes, enroll students and activate assessments. The progress of each student can be monitored through an online *Gradebook*. In addition, many tools and teaching guidelines are provided through the online management system to assist instructors in teaching.

Further to the Learning Management System, there are six key components that contribute to the blended learning in CNAP:

1. *Instructor-led Lessons* All CNAP instructors receive extensive training and employ traditional teaching methods to educate students, facilitate discussion, workshops and lectures.

2. *Online Learning Curricula* The CNAP curricula are available online through the Academy website or are hosted on a local server. The CNAP material is divided into Chapters by topic and when the online CNAP material is opened by the students, they are able to choose which topic to study by selecting a Chapter. The online material is extremely feature rich and includes many graphics, animations, quizzes and activities which allow students to gain immediate feedback on the knowledge acquired throughout the Chapter. Further to this, there are many web links that assist those students who would like a deeper understanding of a particular topic by guiding them to relevant websites.

3. *Self-paced Lessons* The CNAP curricula are always available online or on a local server. This allows each student to study the material at his/her own pace, which is further facilitated through e-learning techniques, as discussed in the previous sub-section.

4. *Glossary/Course Index* Each Chapter contains a Course Index, which enables easy navigation of the material, a Glossary, for referencing definitions of terms and a Search feature.

5. *Practical Lab Work* Much of the CNAP material is communicated to students through Practical Lab Work using a combination of hands-on practical activities and network simulations. Each Chapter in the Cisco curricula has related practical activities and simulations which are conducted on laboratory equipment.

6. *Assessments* For students to pass a particular class, they must pass two Final Assessments, namely; the Online Final Exam and the Practical Skills Exam. To assist students in preparation for these exams, at the end of each Chapter, students are able to test their knowledge through online Chapter exams and quizzes.

CNAP is one of the most comprehensive and widely used blended learning programs in the world. The use of its instructional model could potentially address many issues relating to the delivery and administration of information security end-user education. In order to design the learning program content in information security programs, the use of a learning taxonomy could be of assistance.

5 Using Bloom's Taxonomy

As described earlier, Bloom's taxonomy consists of six levels of the cognitive domain and is further divided into four categories of knowledge. Activities at the six levels of the cognitive domain are usually combined with one or more of the four types of knowledge in a collection of statements outlining the learning objectives of an educational program. Usually a learning objective statement will be used to create a set of learning activities. Learning activities are activities which help learners to attain the learning objectives. A learning activity consists of a verb that relates to an activity at one of the levels of the cognitive domain, and a noun providing additional insight into the relationship of the specific learning objective to a category of knowledge [7, pp. 93-109].

Learning taxonomies assist the educationalist to describe and categorize the stages in cognitive, affective and other dimensions, in which an individual operates as part of the learning process. In simpler terms one could say that learning taxonomies help us to "understand about understanding" [12]. It is this level of meta-cognition that is often missing in information security end-user education.

5.1 Bloom's Taxonomy for Information Security End-User Education

Bloom's Taxonomy for information security end-user education. According to Siponen [4] awareness and educational campaigns can be broadly described by two categories, namely framework and content [4]. The framework category contains issues that can be approached in a structural and quantitative manner. These issues constitute the more explicit knowledge. The second category, however, includes more tacit knowledge of an interdisciplinary nature. Shortcomings in this second area usually invalidate awareness frameworks [4]. *How to really motivate users to adhere to security guidelines*, for example, is an issue that would form part of this content category.

In order to ensure successful learning amongst all employees, it is extremely important to fully understand the educational needs of individual employees. Managers often attempt to address the security education needs of employees without adequately studying and understanding the underlying factors that contribute to those needs [13, pp. 27-36]. It has been argued before that educational material should ideally be tailored to the learning needs and learning styles of individual learners [8][10, p. 19]. One could also argue that awareness campaigns that have not been tailored to the specific needs of an individual, or the needs of a specific target audience, will be ineffective. It is in the understanding of these needs, that a learning taxonomy can play an important enabling role.

Information security specialists should use a taxonomy, like Bloom's taxonomy, before compiling the content category of the educational campaign. The use of such a taxonomy could help to understand the learning needs of the target audience better. It could also reduce the tendency to focus only on the framework category of these campaigns. For example, simply teaching an individual what a password is, would lie on the remember, and possibly understand level(s) of Bloom's taxonomy. However, the necessary information to understand why their own passwords are also important and should be properly constructed and guarded might lie as high as the evaluate level of the taxonomy. An information security specialist might think that teaching the users *what* a password is, would be enough, but research has shown that understanding *why* is essential to obtaining buy-in from employees. It is this level of understanding that acts as a motivating factor and thus enables behaviour change [4][8][13, pp. 78-79].

Table 1. Abbreviated example of Learning Activities based on Bloom's Taxonomy for Information Security, adapted from [7]

Level	Verb	Sample Activities
Create	design	Write a new policy item to prevent users from putting sensitive information on mobile devices. *(IS-A6)*
Evaluate	critique	Critique these two passwords and explain why you would recommend one over the other in terms of the security it provides. *(IS-A5)*
Analyze	analyze	Which of the following security incidents involving stolen passwords are more likely in our company? *(IS-A4)*
Apply	execute	Use the appropriate application to change your password for the financial sub-system. *(IS-A3)*
Understand	discuss	Why should non alpha-numeric characters be used in a password? *(IS-A2)*
Remember	define	What is the definition of *access control*? *(IS-A1)*

The use of an educational taxonomy in the construction of information security educational programs requires that both the content and the assessment criteria for this program is evaluated against the taxonomy in order to ensure that learning takes place at the correct level of the cognitive domain. The reference point for any educational program should be a set of clearly articulated "performance objectives" that have been developed based on an assessment of the target audience's needs and requirements [13, p. 96]. Correct usage of an educational taxonomy not only helps to articulate such performance objectives but, more importantly, helps the educator to correctly gauge the needs and requirements of the audience. An example of how Bloom's revised taxonomy could be used in an information security context is supplied in Table 1.

This example contains learning activities for a learning objective *(IS-LO1)* that can be briefly expressed as: "Learners should be able to understand, construct and use passwords in the correct context". This example in Table 1 is not intended to be a definitive work, but rather to serve, with the taxonomy table, shown in Table 2, towards clarifying the use of Bloom's taxonomy in an information security context, for a more detailed discussion on this topic, please refer to Van Niekerk & Von Solms [6].

Table 2. Example Taxonomy Table adapted from [7]

The Knowledge Dimension	The Cognitive Process Domain					
	Remember	Understand	Apply	Analyze	Evaluate	Create
Factual Knowledge	IS-A1 CNAP-A1				IS-A6	
Conceptual Knowledge		IS-Test1A IS-A2 CNAP-A2		IS-Test1B IS-A4	IS-A6	
Procedural Knowledge			IS-LO1 IS-A3		IS-A6	
Meta-Cognitive Knowledge				IS-A5		

5.2 Evaluating the CNAP Instructional Model against Bloom's Taxonomy

Table 3 provides an example of how learning activities in the CNAP curriculum could be categorized according to Bloom's taxonomy. This example is similar to the information security example provided in Table 1.

Table 3. Abbreviated example of Learning Activities based on Bloom's Taxonomy for the Cisco Networking Academy Program, adapted from [7]

Level	Verb	Sample Activities
Create	design	Design a converged information network to meet the needs of Company A? *(CNAP-A6)*
Evaluate	critique	Critique these two converged information network designs. Which would be best for Company A? *(CNAP-A5)*
Analyze	analyze	Analyze the given design for a converged information network and determine whether it meets Company A's requirements? *(CNAP-A4)*
Apply	execute	Implement a converged information network. *(CNAP-A3)*
Understand	discuss	How does a converged information network differ from the traditional approach of separate networks? *(CNAP-A2)*
Remember	define	What is the definition of a *converged information network*? *(CNAP-A1)*

Starting from the lowest level of the taxonomy, the first example learning activity in the above example *(CNAP-A1),* which deals with students having to remember the definition of a converged information network, is very similar to the first learning activity *(IS-A1)* in Table 1. Both of these could be further classified as being Factual

Knowledge and would thus be mapped to the same cell in Table 2. The same would be true for many different activities involving rote learning in the CNAP program. The CNAP learning model has also proven itself to be effective in both the conveying of this type of knowledge, as well as, the assessment of this kind of knowledge. CNAP learners are also able to complete self-assessment tests after completing the relevant online curriculum material. If one also considers the fact that the effectiveness of blended and e-learning was found to be "broad across different content and learner types." [9], the argument could be made that for information security related material developed to address learning needs at this level of Bloom's taxonomy, the CNAP instructional model should be equally effective.

Similarly, the second example learning activity *(CNAP-A2)*, which focuses on the understanding of a concept, can also be mapped to the same cell in Table 2 as the equivalent information security learning activity *(IS-A2)*. Once again, the CNAP learning model would also be able to cater for the teaching of the information security learning activity at the second level of the cognitive domain. CNAP currently teaches similar concepts via the online curriculum and encourages understanding by allowing learners to explore concepts, interact with simulations, and answer self-evaluative assessments. In addition, learners in a blended environment will often be able to interact with an instructor via either face-to-face communication, or via some form of electronic medium, such as conference calls, e-mail, instant messaging, etc. Giving learners control of their interactions with media and prompting learner reflection, has been shown to enhance online learning [9, p. xvi].

For the purposes of this paper, demonstrating that all learning activities in CNAP could also be categorized according to Bloom's taxonomy is not necessary. However, it is the opinion of the authors' that it would be possible to express any of the current learning activities in CNAP according to Bloom's taxonomy. As mentioned earlier, learning taxonomies are not subject specific. The preceding examples simply serve to show how similar information security learning activities, as expressed using Bloom's taxonomy, are to examples of current learning activities in the CNAP curriculum. If one accepts the preceding argument that every activity currently in the CNAP curricula could be expressed using Bloom's taxonomy it could be argued that the CNAP instructional model has sufficient content delivery mechanisms to convey information at most, if not all, of the taxonomy's levels and knowledge categories. In addition the given examples serve to demonstrate that the CNAP instructional model could also accommodate the needs of information security learning activities. These needs will not necessarily always map to the exact same cell in Table 2 as the equivalent information security activity from Table 1, nor will they always be catered for by the exact same types of learning activities that teaches the CNAP activities at the same level of the cognitive domain. It should however be clear that the requirements, in terms of learning activities, of an information security end-user education program would be very similar to the requirements of a typical learning module in the CNAP program. In fact it could be argued that the learning requirements for a typical information security end-user would mostly be at lower levels of the cognitive domain than the learning needs of an advanced networking professional.

Once again, this supports the argument that the CNAP instructional model has sufficient content delivery mechanisms to meet the requirements of an end user information security educational program specified according to Bloom's taxonomy. The CNAP instructional model, as a blended learning approach, also meets the other requirements of information security end-user education mentioned in section 2.

6 Conclusion

This paper demonstrated that a definite need for more theory based approaches exists amongst current information security end-user educational programs and that the use of a learning taxonomy could help in addressing this current lack. The use of Bloom's taxonomy of the cognitive domain as a tool to help determine the appropriate learning content for information security educational programs was briefly examined. However, knowing what to teach to a learner does not adequately address how this content should be delivered to the intended learners.

This paper presented the argument that an e-learning or a blended learning approach to delivering organizational information security end-user education would be ideally suited to the specific requirements of organizational end-user information security education. The Cisco Networking Academy Program (CNAP) was then discussed as an ideal current example of such a blended learning approach. It was argued that the CNAP instructional model would in fact meet all the requirements of an information security end-user educational program and is also capable of delivering instructional content which was planned with the help of Bloom's taxonomy. If Bloom's taxonomy is used to determine what to teach to organizational end-users in an information security end-user education program, this paper has argued that a blended learning model similar to the one used by CNAP would be an appropriate answer to the question "how should the learning content be delivered to the intended audience?".

References

1. Carr, N.G.: IT Doesn't Matter. Harvard Business Review, 41–49 (2003)
2. Mitnick, K., Simon, W.: The art of deception: Controlling the human element of security. Wiley Publishing, Chichester (2002)
3. Puhakainen, P.: A design theory for information security awareness. PhD thesis, Acta Universitatis Ouluensis A 463, The University of Oulu (2006)
4. Siponen, M.: A conceptual foundation for organizational information security awareness. Information Management & Computer Security 8(1), 31–41 (2000)
5. Van Niekerk, J., Von Solms, R.: Bloom's taxonomy for information security education. Information Security South Africa (ISSA), Johannesburg, South Africa (2008)
6. Van Niekerk, J., Von Solms, R.: Using bloom's taxonomy for information security education. Education and Technology for a Better World. In: 9th IFIP TC 3 World Conference on Computers in Education, WCCE 2009, Bento Goncalves, Brazil (July 2009)
7. Anderson, L., Krathwohl, D., Airasian, P., Cruikshank, K., Mayer, R., Pintrich, P., Raths, J., Wittrock, M.: A Taxonomy for Learning, Teaching, and Assessing: A Revision of Bloom's Taxonomy of Educational Objectives, Complete Edition. Longman (2001)

8. Van Niekerk, J., Von Solms, R.: Corporate information security education: Is outcomes based education the solution? In: 10th IFIP WG11.1 Annual Working Conference on Information Security Management, World Computer Congress (WCC), Toulouse, France (2004)
9. US Department of Education: Office of Planning, Evaluation, and Policy Development Policy and Program Studies Service.: Evaluation of Evidence-Based Practices in Online Learning: A Meta-Analysis and Review of Online Learning Studies (2009)
10. National Institute of Standards and Technology: NIST 800-16: Information Technology Security Training Requirements: A Role- and Performance-Based Model. NIST Special Publication 800-16, National Institute of Standards and Technology (1998)
11. Sousa, D.A.: How the brain learns, 3rd edn. Corwin Press (2006)
12. Fuller, U., Johnson, C.G., Ahoniemi, T., Cukierman, D., Hernán-Losada, I., Jackova, J., Lahtinen, E., Lewis, T.L., Thompson, D.M., Riedesel, C., Thompson, E.: Developing a computer science-specific learning taxonomy. SIGCSE Bull. 39(4), 152–170 (2007)
13. Roper, C., Grau, J., Fischer, L.: Security Education, Awareness and Training: From Theory to Practice. Elsevier, Butterworth (2005)

T'aint What You Do (It's the Way That You Do It): ICT and Creativity in the Primary School Classroom

Mary Welsh and Rae Condie

University of Strathclyde
76 Southbrae Drive
Glasgow G13 1PP
Scotland, UK
mary.welsh@strath.ac.uk

Abstract. This paper reports on one strand of a PhD study that examines newly qualified teachers' use of Information and Communications Technologies (ICT) to support teaching and learning in Scottish primary classrooms during the first two years of their career. Preliminary data analysis indicates that some of the new teachers are creative, innovative users of new technologies who have embedded ICT effectively into their classroom practice while others remain reluctant users. This paper looks at some of the factors that differentiate the creative from the reluctant. Three levels of influence are discussed, and the interactions between them. They are the national/authority level, the school level and the individual or personal level. Some necessary, although not in themselves sufficient, conditions for creative use of ICT are identified as well as some desirable ones.

Keywords: ICT Uptake by Teachers, Teacher Learning, Creativity.

1 Introduction

In common with counterparts in other developed countries, the teaching profession in the United Kingdom (UK) has witnessed a change in attitudes to the profession exhibited by government bodies. There has been a shift from a traditional 'functionalist' view of the profession towards a 'client-centred' model, with increased levels of public accountability. Full registration in the profession is conditional upon meeting a range of competence-based standards and, as in many parts of the world the professional development of student teachers now follows a similar approach.

1.1 The National Context

In Scotland, the Standards for Initial Teacher Education (SITE) set out the expectations for the end of pre-service training while the Standard for Full Registration (SFR) details the minimum standards expected at the end of the one year post-qualification probationary year (GTC/QAA [1], [2]). Both documents make some reference to ICT and comment on ICT knowledge, understanding and skills. For example, teacher education institutions are required to ensure that: *'Particular attention will be paid to the effective use of ICT to facilitate learning and teaching'*. (Section 4.1). However,

N. Reynolds and M. Turcsányi-Szabó (Eds.): KCKS 2010, IFIP AICT 324, pp. 424–434, 2010.

no explicit reference is made to an effective pedagogy to support learning and teaching through ICT although under 'Professional knowledge of the curriculum', it states that new teachers are expected to be able to, *'Demonstrate appropriate knowledge and understanding of ICT and its uses in education and educational settings, referring to current national guidance'*. (GTC/QAA [1], 1.1.2).

New teachers are guaranteed a one-year teaching contract maximum class commitment of 0.7 FTE, the remaining time available for professional development (SEED, [3]. They are allocated a named mentor within their school who provides in-school support and ensures that appropriate professional development is undertaken, typically school- and/or local authority-based. At the end of that time, a judgement is made as to whether they have met the expectations for full registration as a teacher, typically by the school and/or local authority. At this point, their professional knowledge and understanding should include the ability to, *'have sound knowledge and understanding of current guidance on the use of ICT in schools; use available ICT to enhance learning and teaching'* (GTC, 2006, 1.1.2).

The other theme of this paper, creativity is considered a desirable quality in the classroom but as with ICT, neither appropriate teaching approaches nor guidance on meeting the varied needs of a diverse population, in terms of fostering creativity, is offered. For example, the SITE statement states that initial teacher education should support students in acquiring *'the knowledge and understanding to fulfil their responsibilities in respect of cross curricular themes including citizenship, creativity, enterprising attitudes... and ICT, as appropriate to the sector and stage of education'*. (GTC/QAA, [1], 1.1.2).

1.2 The PGDE (P) Course

There are two main routes to qualification as a primary teacher in Scotland: a one-year postgraduate programme (Professional Graduate Diploma in Education, Primary) (PGDE (P)) or a 4-year Bachelor of Education (BEd) degree. The teachers in this study undertook the (PGDE (P)) route and participated in a course that lasted thirty-six weeks, eighteen of which were spent on teaching placement in the pre-school and primary education sectors. As part of a government-sponsored initiative the student teachers were supplied with laptop computers to support their studies.

Although students were given a basic grounding in theories of education, child psychology and development, the primary curriculum, planning, teaching and assessment, there was no designated ICT course. It was anticipated that, as graduates, the students would already have a reasonable level of ICT skill and understanding. Three demonstration lectures were provided for all students - two on the laptop software and one on how to connect to and use an interactive whiteboard.

Students were however able to choose an additional 'option' in line with their personal interests, two of which were ICT based. Thus, apart from the demonstration lectures, little consideration was given formally to the pedagogical implications of teaching with ICT or whether particular technologies were more appropriate than others in supporting specific groups of learners. In practice, a wide range of ICT-related knowledge, skills and understanding was observed among and (self-) reported by the students.

1.3 Barriers and Facilitating Factors That Influence ICT Uptake by Teachers

Research has established that a teacher's decision whether or not to embed ICT in everyday classroom practice is the result of influences operating at three levels. Policies regarding ICT implementation at the national/authority level, the school level and the individual or personal levels interact with each other in a form of symbiosis so that deficiencies/progress at one level may impact on deficiencies/progress at other levels.

A substantial body of literature about barriers and facilitating factors that affect ICT uptake at a national/authority (regional) level appears to be lacking. Most research has focused on barriers at school and individual teacher levels, the latter being concerned both with teachers' personal ICT use and their classroom practice. However, in a comparative study of ICT integration at national level in twenty-six countries, Pelgrum [4] identified 38 perceived and actual barriers to ICT uptake. Some barriers were related to material considerations such as provision and access to ICT, whereas others were related to non-material considerations such as teachers' ICT confidence, skills and abilities. Some were specific to particular countries, e.g. Internet access, and others were related to more global barriers, e.g. lack of time for teachers to explore the potential benefits of ICT in the classroom. Pelgrum's study was carried out almost ten years ago, prior to the implementation of many national initiatives designed to raise the standards of ICT provision, access and skills, it is perhaps timely to consider more recent studies.

In 2004, Becta published two companion literature reviews that examined contrasting factors – those that hindered ICT uptake by teachers and those that facilitated it. The first review, Becta, [5], identified barriers that operated at local authority, school and individual teacher level and discussed the extent to which each of these impacted on each other. Some barriers, e.g. lack of time and appropriate resources, were found to operate at school and teacher level. Others, e.g. lack of effective training, that occurred more commonly at national and local authority level. All were found to have a negative impact on teachers' confidence/competence and on their abilities to recognize the benefits of ICT in the classroom. Furthermore, this resulted in some resistance to change and in the growth of negative attitudes. Technical problems and lack of technical support hindered progress at all levels.

The second report, Becta, [6], explored factors that facilitated teachers' engagement with ICT and reported a range of enabling factors that operated at school and teacher level. At school level teachers were enabled to make effective use of ICT when the following processes were in place - participation in effective staff development programmes; access to ICT resources was timetabled in an equitable manner; on site technical support was available; the senior management team was supportive, possessed a clear vision and implemented whole-school ICT policies; and IWBs were provided in all classrooms; some other minor issues were reported also. At teacher level the following factors had a positive impact – availability of high quality resources; availability of a high level of technical support; full access to ICT resources at all times; good quality ICT training; access to an IWB and other miscellaneous factors.

Another study of the implementation of government policy on ICT in education, in the UK, identified five key factors that were *'problematic'* namely *'management, funding, technology procurement, ICT training and impact on pedagogy'* (Younie, [7], p. 385). These concerns echo those expressed previously regarding barriers operating at local authority, school and teacher levels.

Similar findings have been reported in other studies internationally. In an investigation of ICT integration and teachers' confidence in Queensland state schools Jamieson-Proctor et al. [8] found evidence of a lack of confidence and resistance to change, both of which were underpinned by the complexity of the implementation of national and state initiatives. Baskin and Williams [9] examined ICT implementation in national and state initiatives in Australia and found that, although some forms of ICT integration has been successful the question of ICT pedagogy remained largely unaddressed.

While there are significant structural barriers, less is known of the personal or situational factors at work for those who do flourish in ICT environments. Lee et al. [10] have identified some personal qualities that appear linked to achievement and satisfaction in the use of online learning environments and other factors such as gender, age, education level and learning style have also been investigated (Yukselturk and Bulut, [11]).

2 Creativity

The new Scottish curriculum, Curriculum for Excellence (CfE), identifies creativity as one of the five themes underpinning the curriculum and the support of creativity as an important dimension in teaching and learning (LTScotland, [12]. This concern with creativity reflects the wider context where, in society and the economy there is an emphasis on innovation and creative ideas in relation to economic innovation and wealth creation

The term 'creativity' is elusive and a review of the literature reveals almost as many definitions as there are researchers in the domain. Governments worldwide have highlighted the importance of promoting the development of creativity in their citizens in order to meet the demands of a 'Knowledge Society' and several reviews of the literature have attempted to reach a common understanding of the nature of creativity and of the personal attributes of creative individuals. Halliwell [13] argued that creative educators understand the need for 'inventive flexibility'. Craft [14], [15] highlighted the importance of 'no rules' and, two years later, 'possibility thinking' and asking the 'what if?' question'. The UK National Advisory Committee on Creative and Cultural Education (NACCCE) [16] identified five characteristics of creativity – using imagination, a fashioning purpose, pursuing purpose, being original and judging value. Vernon, quoted in Rhyammar and Brolin [17], talked about the production of objects valued by society and resulting from an individual's capacity to develop new ideas, etc.; Loveless [18], [19] describes creativity as 'an essential life skill'. In summary, all of these demonstrate the understanding that creativity is a personal quality that not only involves *being* creative but also *doing* creativity, i.e. being able to utilise that aspect of one's personality to enhance everyday living in some way – *'T'aint what you do it's the way that you do it'* (Oliver, and Young, [20]. In an in-depth study of creativity in the classroom Starko [21] identified seven cognitive characteristics and eleven personality characteristics of creative people.

Within education, the debate focuses on how learners can be supported in developing creativity and, in turn, the content of and contexts for an enabling curriculum and the development of pedagogy that facilitates learning (Loveless et al., [18]. 'Teaching for creativity' means designing learning experiences that allow experimentation, innovation and reflection on outcomes. Information and communication technologies (ICT) have been shown to stimulate and capture creative activity but that assumes that teachers are confident in their use, in terms of basic skills and understanding, and imaginative in their application. However, developments in ICT have gone beyond efficiency, with the development of virtual spaces for role-playing, creating digital environments and sharing knowledge and experiences HMIe, [22]; Condie and Munro, [23]. Thus the debate on ICT in education has moved on from *What can it do?* to *What can we do with it?*.

2.1 ICT and Creativity

The confidence and competence of teachers to deploy ICT in the classroom to good effect remains patchy. Evidence over recent years indicates that, broadly speaking, many teachers use ICT primarily to improve the efficiency of existing tasks. A study of the impact of new technologies on Scottish schools, indicated that both teachers and pupils used a range of technologies and software out of school but while pupils used computers to play, create and explore, teachers were much more likely to use it for work-related tasks such as preparing resources, administration and record-keeping (Condie et al., [24]. In the classroom, use extended to display and presentation using, for example, interactive whiteboards, or research using the Internet.

While pupils are more inclined to play, explore and create e.g. video, art or music, there is still a need to provide support and guidance to ensure purpose and further development. In particular, collaborative activity, where learners (and their teachers) can interact in shared spaces or virtual studios, builds on current philosophies of social constructivism and learning. In order to maximize the opportunities offered by such approaches it is essential that the teacher has some understanding of the cognitive and personality characteristics of creative people and can apply this understanding to new contexts for teaching and learning. Various approaches have been advocated.

2.2 Pre-service Teacher Education and Creativity

In order to meet the expectations of the CfE, the issue for teacher educators is that of providing the opportunities for pre-service students to both develop their own creativity and to acquire and develop skills in teaching for creativity. In terms of preparing pre-service students for the classroom to date, the emphasis has tended to on the technical aspects of the new technologies and the acquisition and development of skills in using them.

The research shows that some teachers are using ICT in more creative ways (Condie et al, [24]; HMIe, [22]) but a better understanding of the barriers and facilitating factors at work that is likely to make the task of preparing new teachers, and supporting them in post, more effective.

3 The Study

This paper reports on preliminary findings from the second and third phases of a PhD study that explores the use of ICT in the primary classroom by 17 newly qualified teachers (NQTs), from various geographical locations in Scotland, during the first two years of their career. In this paper, the focus is on 5 of this 17 who used ICT in creative ways and who aimed to support the development of ICT skills and creativity in their pupils.

Data were gathered by means of semi-structured interviews carried out at the end of each of the first two years of teaching (May to August 2008 and 2009). Each semi-structured interview lasted approximately one hour and took place at a time and location selected by the interviewees. Most interviews took place in the teacher's school during, or immediately after, the school day. The interviews aimed to ascertain teachers' perceptions of factors which impacted on their use of ICT to support teaching and learning in the primary classroom. During this period the Scottish Government was in the process of implementing "Glow", a new Scottish schools national intranet. Initial content analysis of the interviews prompted consideration of the following questions – What barriers/facilitators do these NQTs face when attempting to use ICT in the classroom? What are the personal characteristics that make these new teachers confident, creative users of ICT? In what way does the manner in which these teachers use ICT foster the development of creativity in their pupils? Are there any particular ICT tools that could be said to be more effective than others in promoting creative use of ICT by pupils and teachers?

3.1 Case Studies

In Scotland, children begin primary (elementary) school at the age of five when they enter Primary 1. They transfer to secondary school seven years later at the end of Primary 7. A composite class is the name given to a class that comprises children who would normally be in two separate primary stages.

The following case studies offer some insight into the experiences of the NQTs as they attempted to adjust to the challenge of beginning a new career in a transitional period in Scottish education. The names used are pseudonyms and the age of each teacher at the end of Year 1 is given.

Beth (Age 26) - Beth faced barriers at national/authority, school and individual levels. She voiced the opinion that national ICT guidelines were *'very outdated'* and *'hindered the children's progress'*, so she ignored them, preferring instead to select ICT activities that she believed would motivate the children and allow creative use of ICT tools. In Year 1 she taught in a Primary 4 class.

On the surface, Beth's classroom appeared fairly well equipped - there were two computers and an E-Beam projector available for her sole use. Unfortunately the projector, which had been installed by local authority staff, was poorly sited, unreliable and would not work if both computers were on. Beth stated this rendered it *'very counterproductive'* and stated that she did not use ICT *'as often as I'd like'*. She was vocal in her view that her use of ICT was restricted by the fact that although the school owned peripherals such as floor robots, many of them were not working properly and were awaiting repair by local authority staff. Despite all of the above Beth's pupils were confident users of a wide range of hardware and software and the Internet. At the time of the Year 1 interview, the pupils had just finished producing a 12-minute DVD describing the school and the surrounding area. Primary 6 pupils, acting as peer tutors, assisted them in this project and a copy of the DVD had been sent to a Dutch school where Beth had previously taught English. Beth encouraged the children to take risks and to try new things, *'I only taught a few of them certain things, the primary 6s taught a couple of them how to use the video recorder [camera] and then it spread, it multiplied'*. The response from the Dutch school was *'very positive'* and pupils there participated in a reciprocal project. The DVD produced by the Scottish pupils was later shared with other schools nationally as an example of good practice.

Beth believed that ICT helped children learn in a variety of ways and fostered in them openness to experience, 'There's a variety of ways, different learning and teaching styles, but I think ICT facilitates so much of that subconsciously ... it is that auditory sense, as well as the visual recognition and the actual doing, for the likes of the video their engagement and everything they got out of that linguistically, grammatically, socially ...'

Encouraged by the success of the project in Year 1, Beth had successfully repeated it in Year 2 with her Primary 1/2 class. On this occasion, the project had been instigated by a desire, expressed by the pupils, to create a video to teach a new pupil, who was English, some Scots language so that she would be able to understand their playground conversations, *'She got to learn the Scots words without feeling like an outsider'*. The children decided to send their DVD to the same school in Holland and the Dutch pupils sent back a DVD in which they taught the Scottish pupils how to perform the action song, *'Heads, Shoulders, Knees and Toes'* in Dutch.

Dawn (Age 24) - Dawn was the only teacher who remained in the same school in Years 1 and 2 of teaching. The head teacher of her school was a strong believer in using ICT to support teaching and learning and volunteered the school as a pilot site for a number of ICT related initiatives at local and national levels. Supported by local authority finance and parental fund-raising, the school was the first school in the authority to have an IWB in every classroom and was also a pilot site for the new national schools' intranet 'Glow'. Dawn was able to access and use a wide range of ICT tools to support active learning and stated that, ICT, in particular the IWB, helped her teach more effectively because *'it engages the children ... the enthusiasm and the motivation and they can't wait ... they see the relevance ... it makes it [learning] visual and it's more on their level'*. As a believer in *'self-directed learning'* Dawn encouraged the children to *'learn by being given responsibility'*.

In Year 2 the children in her Primary 4/5 composite class had used a 'Nintendo Wii' game, 'Endless Ocean', as a stimulus to create travel brochures for a local authority competition. The aim of the competition had been to encourage pupils to use existing resources in a new way and aimed to foster in pupils the development of a key cognitive characteristic of creative people - metaphorical thinking, i.e. the ability to use familiar tools to produce unexpected outcomes. During imaginative writing lessons the children had created animations using video cameras, video editing tools and 'Crazy

Talk' software and had demonstrated perseverance and commitment. The animations had been posted on the school website to be shared with the local community.

Emma (Age 23) - On completion of her probationary year, Emma decided to undertake an extended stay in Australia. Her comments, therefore, refer to Year 1 only. Emma taught in a Primary 5/6 composite class.

Emma believed that her ICT use in her probationary year had been hindered by her head teacher and senior colleagues who were resistant to using ICT and expressed very negative views of its importance in the curriculum. Nevertheless Emma, a confident ICT user, had seized every opportunity to enhance her ICT skills and, with the support of local authority staff, had, in her own time, completed a series of ICT-related courses, including advanced level IWB skills. Emma used ICT, particularly her classroom IWB, as much as possible to support teaching and learning, *'there's only three interactive whiteboards in my school and one of them's in my room and I've not even seen the other two switched on that often'*. Emma had been persistent and encouraged the children to explore areas of the curriculum in new ways. Despite problems with accessing ICT resources the pupils had used wide range of software, hardware and the Internet. Because of their ICT skills and as a result of Emma's local authority connections the pupils had been selected to participate in a ten-week long national pilot project to investigate whether daily use of 'Brain Training' games, using Nintendo DS hand-held machines, would enhance attainment in mental maths. The children's personal commitment to the project had resulted in improved attendance and time keeping because the 'Brain Training' sessions were the first activity each day.

Pam (Age 26) - Pam had been an enthusiastic user of ICT for some time. In the first interview, when asked if she'd been able to use ICT to support teaching she responded, *'Not as much as I would like and as I intend to next year'* - an intention realized in Year 2, *'I use the computer for everything'*.

Pam had a community arts degree and was very aware of the benefits of using digital video both for her teaching and for the children's learning. Each year, as part of an imaginative writing project she invited the children to work collaboratively in groups of 6 to create digital 'feature' films or animations, using "Flip" digital video cameras. The simplicity of these cameras contributed greatly to the children's confidence and curiosity and encouraged them to take (intellectual) risks. For these projects the authority, loaned Pam's classes a set of 6 video cameras and laptops complete with animation and digital video editing software. The children were self-directed, *'they were using the video camera, they were using the software and computers to edit and also recording sound for their film and choosing music and all the editing'*. At the end of each project, the pupils demonstrated independence in judgment by participating in peer-evaluation of the completed films. Awards were presented at an 'Oscars Ceremony' to which the local community was invited and for which everyone dressed in their finest clothes. The local authority subsequently invited Pam to share examples of the pupils' work, and her expertise, with more experienced colleagues during professional development sessions.

Tom (Age 32) - Tom worked in the same authority in Years 1 and 2 and was the other member of the group appointed to a permanent post. The authority in which he worked had a reputation as being very innovative, committed to ICT but also very controlling. Tom believed he had been supported in ICT use at authority and school levels. During Year 1, Tom and his pupils used a wide range of software, hardware and the Internet and, despite having only limited access to an IWB he had managed to use ICT to support teaching *'everyday'*. Tom trained his Primary 3 pupils to use his personal digital still camera and Dictaphone daily to record classroom events and to create records of attainment This material was made into a slide show that parents viewed on parents' night.

In Year 2, Tom once more used his own camera and Dictaphone to record attainment. He stated that he preferred to use his own equipment as that provided in the school was *'not quite as good spec'*. At the end of the school year a video of each pupil's progress was recorded onto a DVD and copies were played at parents' nights, submitted as evidence of attainment to the school management team and given to each child at the end of the school year as a souvenir. Tom was a committed, self-taught ICT user who felt that the ICT training offered within this authority did not meet his personal needs, however he accepted that as he preferred to *'muddle through, trying things out'* that was all right. He encouraged his pupils to do the same inviting them to be curious about how things worked and to investigate ICT tools for themselves.

Tom believed that ICT supported effective teaching *'if it's used properly, I think if it's used as a support rather than as a sort of ... as the main bit of what you're doing'*. He stated that ICT helped children learn, *'I think for a start 90% of children totally engage in ICT ... it doesn't scare them, they're quite happy to try something new and they are quite happy to learn from mistakes ...'*.

In Year 2, Tom's Primary 4 class had used their considerable ICT skills to support an enterprise project that a pupil in the class had devised. The children used ICT in every step of the project during which they collected materials for backpacks to be sent to the developing world to help children there to attend school. The nine year-old pupil who initiated the project was invited by the government to make a presentation about the project to stakeholders from across the educational spectrum at a national education conference, held at the national football stadium. Tom had delivered in-service ICT training to colleagues, at school and at local authority level, on a variety of topics, including how to make films with children and how to create presentations that would avoid *'death by PowerPoint'*.

4   Findings

The NQTs faced many of the same barriers to ICT use that more experienced colleagues faced. Barriers occurred at all levels, however lack of appropriate, differentiated ICT training and frequent access to ICT resources were major issues. The group highlighted one particular problem - only three of the NQTs had been given access to 'Glow', the developing national intranet. Furthermore, those who were not in permanent posts during Year 2 were unable to participate in any professional development opportunities and felt frustrated by this. Nevertheless they remained resilient, innovative and committed to fostering creativity in their pupils through effective ICT use. All responded positively to the challenges of using ICT in a period in which the pace of change was relentlessly rapid.

5   Discussion and Conclusions

ICT use in schools is affected by the interaction between policy and practice at the national/authority level, the school level and the individual level. At various times each of the NQTs faced structural barriers to ICT use at all levels .The NQTs did not complain about lack of time nor about lack of confidence. They were not resistant to change and did not have negative attitudes to ICT, rather they welcomed the challenges of working with ICT and persevered in finding solutions to problems, technical or otherwise. They were aware of the benefits of ICT and had personal access to ICT resources that they often used in the classrooms. Like more experienced teachers they welcomed differentiated ICT training, better technical support and access to IWBs. Despite some difficulties, they believed the schools were generally well resourced with respect to ICT. One word sums up their attitude to ICT use in the classroom – fearless.

These NQTs demonstrated many of the personal cognitive and personality characteristics of creative individuals. They demonstrated an ability to find parallels between ideas that appeared dissimilar; they saw things from many points of view and were able to form their own, independent judgments; they were open to new experiences, curious, flexible in their approaches and persistent. The activities these NQTs orchestrated for their pupils reflected these characteristics and aimed to foster the same in them. Pupils were encouraged to experiment with ICT to fashion new materials; to ask "What if ..?" questions; to be independent, self-directed, curious people. These NQTs and their pupils were not daunted by the pace of change in ICT developments, they were invigorated by it. Their preferred tools were digital video and IWBs.

The CfE seeks to create responsible citizens, effective contributors, successful learners and confident individuals. It is to be hoped that the Review of Initial Teacher Education, taking place in Scotland at the time of writing, will offer similar opportunities for teachers and will encourage them to develop ICT skills, knowledge and understanding in a manner that inspires them to be creative and to foster creativity in their pupils. It may be that new teachers will act as agents of change and will support more experienced colleagues in developing ICT confidence in return for support in developing their (the NQTs) confidence in other areas. The new national schools intranet, "Glow", may provide the medium for these teachers to work together to develop a deeper understanding of the pedagogy of ICT and the extent to which this may underpin creative teaching and the fostering of creative dispositions. More research in this area would be welcomed.

References

1. GTC/QAA: The Standards for Initial Teacher Education. The General Teaching Council for Scotland, Edinburgh (2006)
2. GTC/QAA: The Standards for Full Registration. The General Teaching Council for Scotland, Edinburgh (2006)

3. SEED: A Teaching Profession for the 21st Century: Agreement Reached Following Recommendations Made in the McCrone Report. Scottish Executive Education Department, Edinburgh (2001)
4. Pelgrum, W.J.: Obstacles to the Integration of ICT in Education: Results from a Worldwide Educational Assessment. Computers and Education 37, 163–178 (2001)
5. Becta: A Review of the Literature on Barriers to the Uptake of ICT by Teachers. British Educational Communications and Technology Agency, Coventry (2004)
6. Becta: Enabling Teachers to Make Successful Use of ICT. British Educational Communications and Technology Agency, Coventry (2004)
7. Younie, S.: Implementing Government Policy on ICT in Education: Lessons Learnt. Education and Information Technologies 11, 385–400 (2006)
8. Jamieson-Proctor, R., Burnett, P.C., Finger, G., Watson, G.: ICT Integration and Teachers' Confidence in Using ICT for Teaching and Learning in Queensland State Schools. Australasian Journal of Educational Technology 22, 455–473 (2006)
9. Baskin, W.: ICT Integration in Schools: Where are we now and what comes next? Australasian Journal of Educational Technology 22, 455–473 (2006)
10. Lee, I.: Gender Differences in Self-Regulated On-line Learning Strategies Within Korea's University Context. Educational Technology Research and Development, 101–111 (2002)
11. Yukselturk, E., Bulut, S.: Predictors for Student Success in an Online Course 10(2), 71–83 (2007)
12. Learning and Teaching Scotland.: A Curriculum for Excellence. Learning and Teaching Scotland/Scottish Government, Edinburgh (2004)
13. Halliwell, S. (ed.): Teacher Creativity and Teacher Education. Routledge, London (1993)
14. Craft, A.: Identity and Creativity: Educating Teachers for Postmodernism? Teacher Development 1, 83–96 (1997)
15. Craft, A.: Creative Development in the Early Years: Some Implications of Policy for Practice. The Curriculum Journal 10, 135–150 (1999)
16. NACCCE: All Our Futures: Culture, Creativity and Education. NACCCE, DfEE and DCMS, Sudbury (1999)
17. Rhyammar, L., Brolin, C.: Creativity Research: historical considerations and main lines of development. Scandinavian Journal fo Educational Research 43, 259–273 (1999)
18. Loveless, A.M.: Literature Review in Creativity, New Technologies and Learning. Futurelab, Bristol (2002)
19. Loveless, A.M.: Technology and Learning - a Review of Recent Literature. Futurelab, Bristol (2007)
20. Oliver, M., Young, J.: T'aint What You Do (It's the Way That You Do It) Recorded by Ella Fitzgerald for Decca Records, New York (1939)
21. Starko, A.J.: Creativity in the Classroom: Schools of Curious Delight, 4th edn. Routledge, London (2010)
22. HMIe: Improving Scottish Education: ICT in Learning and Teaching. HM Inspectorate of Education (HMIe)/Scottish Government, Livingston (2007)
23. Condie, R., Munro, B., Seagraves, L., Kenesson, S.: The Impact of ICT in Schools - A Landscape Review, Coventry (2007)
24. Condie, R., Munro, B., Muir, D., Collins, R.: The Impact of ICT Initiatives in Scottish Schools: Phase 3. SEED/Scottish Office, Edinburgh (2005)

Need for the Intercultural Awareness in Erasmus Mobility – Administrative Point of View

Tatjana Welzer, Marjan Družovec, Marko Hölbl, and Mirjam Bonačić

Faculty of Electrical Engineering and Computer Science, University of Maribor
Smetanova 17, Maribor, Slovenia
{welzer,marjan.druzovec,marko.holbl,mirjam.bonacic}@uni-mb.si

Abstract. In recent years, mobility has become one of the most important goals inside the European Union (EU). Different projects and programs support the mobility of students, teachers and other employed persons. From program to program and project to project, goals are different. Through employment, companies have the need for different experts or the need to work with international teams. They can also offer jobs for placements and for young experts for their first employment (like the Leonardo da Vinci program), while for students and teachers, the main goals of mobility are learning and teaching in different environments (like the Erasmus program) as well as learning languages and benefiting from cross-cultural experiences. Both students and teachers come from different cultural environments and the host organisation has to take care of intercultural awareness in all levels of activities, from administration up to teaching and passing exams.

Keywords: Lifelong learning, mobility, cultural awareness, intercultural dialogue.

1 Introduction

Since 2007 EC is running the Lifelong Learning Program, which is like an umbrella covering different programs and projects that support mobility of participants. One of those programs is also Erasmus. Erasmus students' mobility has already been running for years and different universities have collected a lot of experiences in different fields. One rarely mentioned area is administrative experience. Depending on the level of organization within the university, these administration experiences can be collected on different levels. We would like to concentrate on the faculty level. The Faculty of Electrical Engineering and Computer Science, at the University of Maribor [1], [2], does not have its own international relations office, so the administrative part is covered partly by existing staff in the students' office and primarily by the Erasmus Coordinator and International Co-operations Assistant, who are mostly responsible for administrative work (besides the student's office). Both the coordinator as well as the co-operation assistant need to have a lot of experience - not only with mobility, education programs, law conditions and such things, but also with intercultural awareness. They are involved in intercultural dialogue daily via their communication

N. Reynolds and M. Turcsányi-Szabó (Eds.): KCKS 2010, IFIP AICT 324, pp. 435–439, 2010.

with incoming students as well as outgoing students and, also importantly, with incoming and outgoing teachers and with the administration of partners' universities.

With incoming students, demands are quite natural on an administrative level. It is the most frequent communication at the beginning and end of a mobility event for each student. In this paper, we will present some experiences and suggested solutions. First, we will present the subject of intercultural awareness; experiences with some common problems will follow. Finally, in the conclusion we plan to propose some solutions.

2 Intercultural Awareness in Mobility

Intercultural awareness recognizes that people are shaped by their own cultural background, and that this influences how people interpret the world around them and how they perceive themselves and relate to other people. It means that we often view other people's behaviour and benefits through the prism of our own standards of culture. Culture itself is the sum total of ways of living, including behavioural norms, linguistic expressions, styles of communication, patterns of thinking, and beliefs [3]. Our societies are more and more multicultural because of increasing mobility and the rise of global enterprises and organizations, which are more and more multilingual as well as also multicultural [4]. Today, an important part of worldwide business and activities are carried out by international teams and working groups that are characterized by national, professional, corporate and individual cultural diversity [5]. Moreover, the mobility of students and teachers at a university play an important role in the higher-level education process.

The free circulation of people within the EU is supported by a free labour market as well as different programmes and projects have increased student and teacher mobility tremendously [6]. Students are interested in gathering experiences during their studies and placement in an academic period (a Lifelong Learning Programme - Erasmus; Programs between the EU and other non-EU countries like Canada, Japan, USA, Australia; Erasmus-Mundus, and some bilateral programs) and a professional (Leonardo da Vinci program) environment. They are also looking for work-based mobility cooperation [7].

These programmes' key objective is supporting the development of innovative action in the member states (all member states of the EU, EFTA states and EU candidate countries) by promoting mobility projects in the context of transnational partnerships, which involve different organizations with an interest in education, training and placement. Transnational partnerships promote the dissemination of expertise and mobility, including language and cultural competencies, which are oriented on promoting language and cultural competencies within the mobility context as well as within society in general [8].

3 Administrative Experiences in Erasmus Mobility

The Faculty of Electrical Engineering and Computer Science at the University of Maribor is actively involved in the Erasmus student and teacher exchange programme. We have a considerable number of incoming foreign students from different European countries. According to Table 1, the number of foreign students continues to rise from year to year. The number of students almost doubled from the 2006/2007 academic year to the 2007/2008 academic year. The large number of students strains existing problems facing with student mobility. The discussion of problems which arise from the intercultural melting pot caused by students' mobility is a topic that deserves attention. We will focus on the problems of incoming exchange students and our approach to dealing with the problem.

Table 1. Number of Incoming Erasmus Students by Country

Country	2003/2004	2004/2005	2005/2006	2006/2007	2007/2008
Austria					1
Belgium	2	1	2	1	4
Bulgaria	1				
Czech rep.	2				2
Finland	1	3	3	2	4
France	8	4	7	6	7
Greece				1	
Croatia					
Germany	1	5	1		
Netherlands		1			
Poland					1
Portugal	2	2	7	3	8
Romania		2			
Slovak rep.			1		2
Spain	7	4	10	8	16
Turkey		5	3	6	8
Summary	**24**	**27**	**34**	**27**	**53**

At the university level, the standard procedure for all Erasmus participants (incoming and outgoing) is defined. At first, students have to apply via an electronic web form, which is common for the whole university. In addition to the electronic version, they have to print out the form and send it by mail to the university. The application also includes the learning agreement with a list of lectures available at the host university (in our case the University of Maribor) which the student will take. After the application is received at the university, it is sent to the faculties that have to check the learning agreement and approve or reject the student. The first problem arises with the lectures chosen by incoming students. During the period in which the foreign student applies for the Erasmus exchange and until participating in the Erasmus mobility programme, several students have already passed a specific lecture at their university. Since a foreign student needs the written consent of the Erasmus coordinator at the host and home university when changing lectures, the procedure of choosing the lectures can be considerably protracted. In the worst case, this can lead to the situation where an exchange student can only participate in the lecture later during the semester (e.g. after a week's delay).

Most incoming students finish the lecture which they planned to perform at the beginning of their exchange, but they often face additional hurdles. The biggest problem they face is the language barrier. Although the lectures are conducted in English, many of them lack a proficient knowledge of English. Often their study obligations are left aside until the end of the semester as they first have to learn more English in order to be able to pass a specific lecture. However, this means that all their obligations regarding their study are accumulated at the end of the semester. This constitutes a problem when dealing with exchanged lectures.

Before leaving the foreign exchange, the students have to get all their documents approved by the host institution's coordinator, as required by their home university. The documents required by specific universities are very similar in content, but vary in form. The difference in application forms vary from different cultural background to the experience of a specific university. When leaving the host university, students receive a transcript of record which contains data about the work they accomplished during the exchange period (lectures passed, diploma work preparations, etc.). The whole procedure could be made easier if unified forms could be implemented for all institutions on the level of the Erasmus student mobility programme.

In order to counter some of these obstacles, different approaches were applied at our university, i.e. at the faculty. To give incoming exchange students a good starting point, web pages for incoming Erasmus students were developed at the university level and at the faculty level [1], [2]. Their aim is to ease the whole procedure for foreign students, from the filling out of application forms to the information that is offered for foreign students, while also containing culturally specific habits. In addition to the online material available, a variety of printed information and application material is offered to incoming students both at the university level and the faculty level. However, online communications cannot always replace live communication and therefore office hours for consultation and additional support for incoming exchange students are offered. Aside from the information available online, the printed and live communication, incoming exchange students are offered Slovene language courses for those who are eager to learn the language and the culture of their host country.

Another important aspect is the training and education offered to domestic students and teachers dealing with different aspect of cross-cultural problems, intercultural dialogue and the connection to the Erasmus mobility programme. The training is supported by different materials, which help complete the support for domestic teachers and students dealing with incoming students.

4   Conclusion

In the paper we discussed the cross-cultural aspects and problems arising from the Erasmus mobility programme. Intercultural problems arise from the interactions between incoming students and teachers, employees and students at the host institution. In order to try to sanitize or mitigate the problems, the following solutions were implemented by our institution: a homepage dedicated to the Erasmus mobility programme, which is supported by additional printed material (e.g. brochures), and solid communication between foreign students and domestic personnel involved in the

Erasmus mobility programme. Additionally, language courses are offered to both incoming and outgoing students. However, not only are incoming students educated, but also domestic personnel and students. This education includes training for teachers, personnel and students in topics of intercultural awareness and cross-cultural communication, which are a vital aspect in preventing cross-cultural problems with the Erasmus mobility programme.

A good example of how to deal with intercultural awareness and cross-cultural communication was made by the Valuertech programme [9]. Such research would have to be extended to a variety of areas in order to better cope with the issues and problems of our increasingly multicultural society.

References

1. University of Maribor Erasmus web pages,
   `https://help.uni-mb.si/Socrates/Enter.asp` (last visited 7.8.2009)
2. Faculty of electrical engineering and computer science Erasmus web pages,
   `http://erasmus.feri.uni-mb.si/` (last visited 7.8.2009)
3. Jandt, F.W.: An introduction to Intercultural Communication – Identities in a Global community. Sage Publication, Thousand Oaks (2004)
4. Lewis, R.D.: When Cultures Collide. Managing Successfully Across Cultures. Nicholas Brealey Publishing, London (1999)
5. Jakkola, H., Heimbürger, A.: Cross-Cultural Software Engineering, MIPRO 2009, Opatija (2009)
6. Magnan, M.: Valeurtech, a Leonardo Pilot Project: Highlighting Professional Experience Acquired in Undergraduate Technology Programmes. In: EAIE Vienna Conference September 10-13, 2003, Session 4.14 (2003)
7. Welzer, T., Brumen, B., Udir, K., Stanjko, R.: Work Based Cooperation. In: International Conference Information Society, Ljubljana (2004)
8. Welzer, T., Brumen, B., Stanjko, R., Breznik, D.: Project VALEURTECH – How to Support Young People for Professional Training in Different Countries. In: Inter Symp. 2003, Baden-Baden (2003)
9. Fleck, J., Beaumier, N., Magnan, M.: Valeurtech, working towards standards to organise and highlight student mobility. In: 3rd International Conference on New Horizons in Industry and Education, August 2003, pp. 28–29 (2003)

Home Access: Providing Computers to Families via a National Strategy

Nicola Yelland[1], Greg Neal[2], and Eva Dakich[2]

[1] Hong Kong Institute of Education, Faculty of Education Studies. 10 Lo Ping Road,
Tai Po, Hong Kong SAR
yelland@ied.edu.hk
[2] Victoria University, School of Education, Footscray Park Campus, Victoria, Australia
{Greg.neal,eva.dakich}@vu.edu.au

Abstract. In this paper we discuss the role of new technologies, and computers in particular, in lives of families in Australia. We report on part of a project that provided children families with computers and connection to the Internet. There is an increasing awareness that living in the 21st century involves using and interacting with a range of new technologies, also referred to as information and communications technologies (ICT). However, for many children and their families this is not possible because they do not have the capacity to purchase them. The Tech Packs Project (The Smith Family, 2007) grew out of the Computer for Every Child Project which was an attempt to start to bridge the 'digital divide' by providing computers so that a group of families in the targeted locations of large metropolitan cities could participate in the Information Age. The families involved were those whose personal resources did not afford them the opportunity to purchase new technologies, especially computers We surveyed the families members to determine the extent of their use of any technologies before and after receiving the computer and initiated focus groups to find out the ways in which having a computer created contexts for them to become more proficient in the use of ICT In this paper we will present the findings from both the survey and focus group data that we have collected.

Keywords: Home access, digital divide, computers for learning.

1   Introduction

The Millennials [1], that is those children born post 1985, play around in digital spaces and communicate on a daily basis with peers, family and acquaintances for a variety of purposes using many devices. A large number of homes have a variety of media options that include; TVs, mobile phones, computers, ipods, mp3 players, DVD machines, digital cameras, interactive toys and games and video game consoles and mobile devices. For many years now the Kaiser Family Foundation have conducted a surveys pertaining to the media use among children and teens in the US [2]. The latest (third) report states that since the last survey (2004) there has been a major

N. Reynolds and M. Turcsányi-Szabó (Eds.): KCKS 2010, IFIP AICT 324, pp. 440–446, 2010.

increase in use of new media that is mainly attributed to the ready access to mobile devices. For example, they report that in the past 5 years there has been a large increase in mobile phone ownership, from 39% to 66%, and the increase in ipod ownership has soared from 18% to 76%. What is also apparent is that mobile phones for example are more than for talking on. In fact more young people spend time listening to music, playing games and watching TV on their mobile phones (a total of :49 daily) than they spend talking on them (:33). The most salient finding was that "The amount of time young people spend with media has grown to where it's even more than a full-time work week" (p.1). In fact the findings reported in their documentation revealed that "Eight to eighteen year olds spend more time with media than in any other activity... an average of more than 71/2 hours a day, seven days a week" (p.1). This was an increase of one hour a day from their previous report five years prior to this survey. It represents a greater amount of time than many adults spend in full time employment, and they do it seven days a week not for five days. The report informs us that:

> In the last five years, home Internet access has expanded from 74% to 84% among young people; the proportion with a laptop has grown from just under 12% to 29%; and Internet access in the bedroom jumped from 20% to 33%. The quality of Internet access has improved as well, with high-speed access increasing from 31% to 59% (p.3).

High speed Internet access and new applications have meant that the ways in which the Internet are used by young people have changed significantly. The most popular computer activities are those of social networking and video sites like YouTube. Such sites were not widely available in 2004 – but now account for an average of :37 of their daily media time.

There is some space in the report to discuss demographic aspects of the data but this is confined to age, gender, race and parental educational levels. There is no specific consideration of socio economic status or parental income levels. Data shows that media use increases considerably in the years between 11 and 14 years of age. Girls spend more time than boys in social network contexts, listening to music and reading. Boys spend more time playing video and computer games and looking at YouTube. Black and Hispanic children spend more time with media than white children but this seems to be because they spend so much more time watching TV. They consume 13 and 12:59 hours (Black and Hispanic children respectively) while White kids consume 8:36 hours.

Yet there remain children and families who are not able to participate in the so-called 'digital revolution' for a variety of reasons that tend to be closely aligned to social and economic circumstances. Studies conducted regarding the links between social and digital engagement, especially with reference to Internet use, increasingly show that those individuals who have access to ICT, generally come from families that have more schooling, higher incomes, and high status occupations. In discussing digital and social advantage, Helsper [3] noted that "those who are most deprived socially are also least likely to have access to digital resources such as online services" (p.9). Further, Helsper reported that when those from these demographic groups do participate in digital activity, it tends to be at the basic level and involve information seeking, obtaining leisure information, making purchases on line and for individual communication with families and friends at a distance. In contrast, Helsper indicated that the advanced levels of activity characterized by social networking and civic engagement that allow participants to interact beyond their immediate networks, for example, are only conducted by 8% of the population. This then reinforces a gap since this qualitative difference in use enables those with more advanced technologies and applications to participate in activities that facilitate and extend their capabilities in cyber contexts, which are becoming increasingly important to be fluent in. In this way, simply providing access via machines is not enough. There needs to be opportunities for learning about the variety of uses beyond the basic applications which might address the important social inclusion issues that surround digital exclusion. This can often be problematic since new technologies are rapidly evolving and what constitutes digital inclusion changes accordingly. What was considered as advanced three years ago, would now be generally considered as basic to the lives of many citizens. Studies have revealed that the main factors for digital inclusion are relevance, the nature of the experience and empowerment [3]. This basically means that digital experiences have to be connected to the lives and needs of users and will only be perpetuated if they are positive and make life easier for them.

1.1 The Digital Divide

The notion of a 'digital divide' came into prominence in around 1996 when then Vice President Al Gore used it in a speech considering the role of technology in society and highlighted that their use was uneven based on income and status levels. In this way inequalities already in existence in society were being exacerbated by the new technology.

Thus, the digital divide was traditionally described in relation to physical availability of the computer and access to the Internet. Thus it was described as being the difference between the 'haves' and 'have nots'.

1.2 Digital Inclusion

The disparity or 'divide' then prompted concerns and action centered around how the divide could be minimized or indeed eliminated and in turn, prompted inquiries and discussions about equity and social justice [4]. Schemes were developed to 'deliver' machines to the disadvantaged but there was not much concern or follow up about how they were used and if the ways in which they were used was productive or not. Later as DiMaggio and Hargittai stated [5]:

> As the technology penetrates into every crevice of society, the pressing question will be *not* 'who can find a network connection at home work, or in the library or community centre from which to log on?', but instead, 'what are people doing, and what are they *able* to do, when they go on-line?'

Reconfiguration of the term "access" became the focus of literature that aimed to re-work the idea of the digital divide. According to Warschauer [6] "the simple binary notion of technology haves and have nots does not quite compute" (p.42), in his opinion the key issue is not merely access to computers but rather the unequal ways of using computers.

It was conceived that the idea of "access" needed to be redefined in social as well as technological terms. Warschauer argues that in order to achieve better outcomes for communities, technology infusion needs to be supported by relevant educational experiences and social support.

DiMaggio and Hargittai [5] highlight the role that society plays in affording all people access to the Internet by noting that the policies of public institutions shape patters of inequality and effective Internet access and use. Everyone can potentially benefit from such policies and thus it becomes increasingly important for public institutions and agencies to consider the issues around access and use of new technologies. Further, As technologies become more pervasive in our lives we also need to provide mechanisms by which assistance can be provided, both formally and informally, so that individuals and groups may participate in online experiences. Formal assistance may include backing from public organizations such as the library or private organizations such as the workplace. Personal assistance is likely to be sought from family, friends and colleagues.

2 Background

The initial focus of the Tech Packs project was to identify and distribute computers into low income communities. This took place in Victoria, NSW and Queensland in the first instance and then spread to Western Australia and Tasmania.

Data for this paper is based on most recent phase of the evaluation research from data gathered during 2009 using surveys and focus groups. The surveys consisted of a 'prepack' survey which was developed from the earlier work [7] and in discussions with the Smith Family to identify key themes about the participants. The focus groups were also developed from the pilot study and concentrated on key themes about the benefits and challenges of participating in the project.

We worked with the Smith Family community leaders to distribute surveys to willing participants at the time of initial computer training sessions. At training sessions, prepack surveys were given to willing participants. The surveys were intended to capture data about family demographics, and their perceived computers skills and knowledge prior to the collection of the Tech Packs computer. The first two communities to begin the process in the first half of 2009, they were located in rural areas of two Australian mainland States.

Once a community had completed the prepack surveys, and the Tech Packs computer had been in the home for 4-6 months, focus groups were organised with the respective Smith Family community leaders. This enabled the research to evaluate the use of the computer following its introduction into the home for a good period of time.

2.1 Children and Families

Demographic data from this particular cohort revealed that the majority of the Tech Pack participants came from English speaking countries, with most of them being born in Australia. The other most frequently spoken languages were Samoan and Vietnamese. Statistical analysis suggested that most families came from a low-socio-economic background with education levels not exceeding secondary schooling. A large proportion of survey participants reported as single parents often with children aged 18-24 still living at home.

2.2 Survey Data

A total of 272 surveys were analysed. All surveys were labelled and coded and data was collected and presented using Microsoft Excel. A descriptive statistical analysis was used to report on demographic characteristics and patterns of computer use and computers intentions from the survey participants.

While a significant number of participants said they used digital technologies in a number of different settings, including school, TAFE, work, and at a library, almost two thirds of them had never owned a computer at home. The remaining 27% of the respondents reported having access to digital hardware components including computers, computer peripherals, such as printers, digital cameras, and scanners as well as to broadband Internet connections in their family home. Current computers usage reported by participants included email and word processing, with one third of the survey sample using computers two to three times a week. Children indicated daily use of new technologies with 93% of them using computers for school purposes. Children's frequent computer use can be explained by widespread and organised access to computers in schools and public libraries.

Survey results about intended Internet usage also revealed some generational differences, with parents and grandparents wanting to use the computers for communication via email, their own research and study, and for downloading family photos and videos. Consistent with current trends in technology usage by youth, children's intended computer uses included study and research (80%) as well as the use of social networking applications such as chat rooms and Facebook. Streaming and downloading music was also a popular leisure activity.

User satisfaction when online was significantly limited by the dial-up connectivity. Participants found it difficult to navigate web pages with multimedia content and downloading applications, music or video required spending prolonged periods online. Downloads would frequently be interrupted by incoming calls. As dial-up connection often caused unnecessary frustration, many of participants indicated considering a switch to broadband connectivity.

2.3 Focus Groups

Focus groups were conducted with selected community groups from three mainland States. The groups were selected based on their availability for the community leaders to gather a suitable number of participants to a focus group session, the willingness of participants from within the community, and recognition that the community had participated in the prepack surveys.

Smith Family community leaders organised the focus group participants to ensure sufficient numbers at each focus group session. The focus groups concentrated on four major themes including:

- The benefits of having computers at home
- Important changes to daily activities/lifestyle
- Tech Pack support
- Perceived benefits/significance of the program

The focus groups were all conducted in late 2009. In addition to the participants at each of the focus groups, the Smith Family community leader also attended and participated. The conversations were audio-recorded and transcribed. Transcripts were entered into a data base and were coded and threaded for detailed analysis. This is still occurring with transcripts being finalised with some of the focus group at the time of this interim report (i.e. the Maddington communities).

Findings emerging from the focus groups highlighted that respondents believed in the importance of home computers for learning for their whole family. It became apparent from the data that benefits included making stronger connections between learning in schools and at home for children, having opportunities to engage in new learning, new patterns of intergenerational learning and knowledge transfer based on acknowledging and making use of their children's expertise with new technologies. Both survey and focus group data suggest that children and youth often took lead in installing the Tech Packs at home, helped with technical problems and taught their parents and grandparents valuable technical skills that they needed in order to use the machines. The focus group cases showed how communities indicated that having a computer at home provided children with access to online schoolwork, research, as well as extracurricular activities supported by educational software.

According to focus group participants the training sessions were successful, however, not having access to computers while attending the training appeared to have hindered the acquisition of new skills in the short term. One of the 'weakest' points of the Tech Packs support services appeared to be the under-utilisation of available helpline facilities. Participants reported to be too embarrassed to ask for help, and found it difficult to cope with being put on hold for long periods of time as well as having to explain things several times to a number of people. They stated they would rather turn to family members for help and some of them contacted local business providing technical assistance.

The data from the focus groups revealed a strong correlation between the stated intended use by families and the actual use after several months of having the computers. The most frequent applications were emailing, searching the Internet and participation in online chat sessions. In particular, setting up Facebook accounts was a popular activity for all participants regardless of age.

3 Summarizing Statements

In summary the Tech Pack project has been well-received by community members and brought a number of positive changes into their lives. The most significant benefits of the program were increased sense of belonging and social participation for adults, fun and engaging learning for children, access to online community and commercial services, and keeping in touch with family and friends by participating in social networking activities.

Recommendations for improvement to the program include:

1. The adoption of broadband connectivity for *all* participants
2. Improve the technical specifications of the Tech Packs project with the possible inclusion of a CD burner, and a printer for *all* communities. Refurbished computers may not be sufficient in terms of adequacy and longevity

3. Training sessions to be ongoing and community-based to meet the needs of the families and to provide opportunities to extend the skills and knowledge of the participants
4. Utilise existing expertise in the community (e.g. through partnerships with schools, peer-support), to provide participants with more user-friendly technical assistance.

References

1. Howe, N., Strauss, W.: Millennials rising: The next generation. Vintage, New York (2000)
2. Rideout, V.J., Foehr, U.G., Roberts, D.F.: Generation M2 Media in the lives of 8 to 18 year olds. The Henry Kaiser Family Foundation (2010) (retrieved from http://www.kff.org)
3. Helsper, E.J.: Digital inclusion: An analysis of social disadvantage and the information society. Department for Communities and Local Government (2008), http://www.communities.gov.uk/documents/.../pdf/digitalinclusionanalysis
4. Yelland, N.J.: Shift to the future: Rethinking learning with new technologies in education. Routledge, New York (2007)
5. DiMaggio, P., Hargittai, E.C., Celeste, C., Shafer, S.: From Unequal Access to Differentiated Use: A Literature Review and Agenda for Research on Digital Inequality (2001), http://www.eszter.com/research/pubs/dimaggio-etal-digitalinequality.pdf
6. Warschauer, M.: Demystifying the digital divide. Scientific American 289(2), 42–47 (2003)
7. Yelland, N.J., Beris, R., Davidson, K., Neal, G.: A computer for every child: Extending contexts for learning for disadvantaged children. International Journal of the Social Sciences 2(4), 503–515 (2007)

Working with Wikis: Collaborative Writing in the 21st Century

Katina Zammit

School of Education, University of Western Sydney,
Locked Bag 1797, Penrith South, NSW. Australia. 1797
k.zammit@uws.eu.au

Abstract. Students in primary schools have been asked to construct both written and multimodal texts for assessment purposes for many years. However these texts have been created on paper usually as individual project. This paper reports on a multiliteracies project involving students collaboratively creating a multimodal information report using the affordances of a wiki. Students found the experience very rewarding, rating the change to the process of learning, the content (Antarctica) and the use of technology as the best aspects. Working with wikis provided the opportunity for students to engage with 21st century literacy practices. It also provided a space in the classroom to trial changes to a conventional pedagogy, curriculum and assessment practices.

Keywords: creating texts, multiliteracies, multimodal texts, primary, wikis.

1 Introduction

An important problem today is how to design curricula to support students' composition of the texts of the 21st Century [1]. Teachers, parents and the general public increasingly view technology as an essential tool for initiating students into the social practices and texts of the 21st century. However, digital texts are not the same as paper-based texts [2, 3]. Print and digital texts differ according to the communication medium [4-6], highlighting both their similarities and differences. While research on reading and technology in the elementary years has acknowledged the relevance of traditional print-based literacies in the acquisition of new literacies [7, 8], the same research on written or multimedia texts and curricula design for creating multimedia digital texts in similar genres has not been as prolific.

In Australia, teachers have been trained about the organization and language features (grammar) of written texts based on their social purpose, as mandated in Australian English syllabi (see for example, [9, 10]), but they are less confident in supporting students multimedia text production using technology [11]. The medium we use to construct a text influences the choices we make, the tools we use and the modes we employ [12]. Such a shift may require teachers to 'invite participation' by bringing out of school experiences with writing into the classroom. As students create multimedia texts they will gain control over the construction of increasingly complex

N. Reynolds and M. Turcsányi-Szabó (Eds.): KCKS 2010, IFIP AICT 324, pp. 447–455, 2010.

texts. But, how do the texts and the learning about them differ from written paper-based texts? What do students think about the integration of multimodal text construction into the classroom curriculum, assessment and teacher's pedagogy?

2 Theoretical Framework

The theoretical framework that serves as a foundation for the current study is drawn from the fields of *educational linguistics*, specifically a genre-based approach to teaching writing [13, 14], *semiotics* [3, 15, 16], *multiliteracies and multimodality* [17, 18] and *technology and literacy* [19-21].

Teachers in Australian schools have been using an explicit and systematic approach to the teaching of writing for the past 10 years. This approach which was based upon the linguistically informed genre-based approach to teaching writing [22] developed as part of the Language and Social Power project to improve the educational outcomes for students from poor backgrounds. Teachers use a curriculum cycle of deconstruction, building field knowledge, joint construction and independent construction of a written text (genre) integrated into the teaching and learning about a topic in social studies or science [23]. As part of this explicit approach, teachers have developed a meta-language, a language to talk about language, of written texts that they use with students in the teaching about a written genre. This knowledge places teachers in a position to consider how this knowledge impacts on the teaching of multimedia texts and what other classroom discourse needs to be added to or modified in the curriculum. The discussion of written texts prior to the teaching a specific genre also draws upon the field of semiotics. Multimedia texts, paper or digital, convey meanings using a range of modes and together construct the meanings a reader has to comprehend [15]. Discussing the construction of multimedia texts and developing a language to talk about them can inform teachers and students about how to compose similar texts and the process that is followed.

Intersecting with the area of semiotics are the theoretical frames of multiliteracies and multimodality [17]. Combined together, these two areas provide a meta-language to use in classrooms to unpack the meanings in multimedia texts and the ways these meanings are conveyed across different modes.

The final theoretical frame that informs this study is the work on technology and literacy. While there are many aspects of this area that are relevant to the project, the one most relevant is drawing upon students out of school experiences with technology to engage them in literacy learning [24, 25]. The writing students do out of school using technology might encourage students from a language background other than English, indigenous students and students from poorer backgrounds to write. Collaborative composition of a written text occurs in a classroom and impacts on student outcomes, so collaborative composition of a digital text may also have a similar impact.

3 Methodology

The current study utilized multiple case studies employing qualitative research techniques [26]. The qualitative techniques employed in the project were a combination of co-researching participatory action methodology [27]. The action research methodology enable the teachers and researcher to collaboratively plan, construct, evaluate and discuss the teaching strategies and practices employed to support students use and creation of multimedia digital texts. As part of the project, teachers considered how the features of the information report written genre were similar or different when transformed into a digital, multimedia text using the semiotic analysis of written and visual texts [28, 29]. We also discussed ways to work within the 'new learning environments' of the electronic medium, how to scaffold students' learning of multimodal text construction and working collaboratively in an on-line environment [30].

3.1 School Context

The school is located an inner city suburb of Sydney, Australia. There were 11 classes as well as seven specialist teachers, including teacher-librarian, English as a Second Language teacher and support teacher for learning difficulties. The 260 students came from a range of different socio-cultural backgrounds. Students who first language was not English accounted for 73% of the school population, representing 29 different language groups. Of these students, 38% were Chinese speaking, and 42% of students have been learning English for three years or less. The school had 17 indigenous students.

3.2 Classroom Contexts

The project was undertaken across two primary classes: a year 5 (11 year olds) class and year 4/5 (10 and 11 year olds) class. One teacher was an experienced teacher (female) and the other was a 'new' teacher (male), having graduated the year before. Computers in class had access to the Internet either by direct connection (4 PCs in each class) or via wireless network if students were using the laptops (available from 2 trolleys with 14 laptops in each). The year 5 classroom also contained an interactive whiteboard (IWB) which was utilized frequently by the class teacher.

In collaboration with the author, the two classroom teachers, planned for the first iteration of the research. The topic was Antarctica and the genre was an information report. The multimodal information report was to be con-constructed by pairs or small groups of students using a class-based Wiki. A Wiki provides a safe environment for students to work on the information report as it is password protected and teachers can monitor students input. The wiki was set up for the students with the pages of content to be co-constructed and containing guiding questions for the content to be included on the page. Student were encouraged to assist other groups by offering suggestions for content or links, but cautioned about changing other group's page without permission especially deleting work.

3.3 Data Sources

Prior to the beginning of the project teachers assessed the students writing levels using the criteria-based standards framework from the NSW K-6 English syllabus . Base data was obtained from the multimodal paper-based texts students created in the pervious term. Students completed a background survey about their ICT knowledge and experience.

Work sample data was collected every week during the implementation of the project. An audit trail was kept electronically by the wiki, which kept a history of changes for each page, noting when, who made the change and what was changed. Student focus group interviews and student questionnaire were used to ascertain students' views about the project and their process of creating written and digital multimedia texts. At the end of the project the teachers, in consultation with the author, created a criteria-based rubric for assessment of the process and product in order to grade each group's wiki page.

Other data sources were emails between the author and classroom teachers, minutes of meetings, notes from informal discussions, teachers' and author's documentation of teaching and learning activities, teachers' reflection about the project, and author's detailed observation field notes. The team shared strategies, thoughts and issues relating to the teaching-learning of multimodal texts (what worked and what didn't; challenges and changes) and how they were supporting their students to move from written to electronic text production.

These sources were mined for recurring themes using content analysis and the grounded theory approach [31].

4 Findings

For the purposes of this paper, the student data from one class will be used to discuss the results of the project from the students' perspective. From the questionnaire data, which was triangulated with the field notes and student interview data, students found the best aspects of the wiki project were (in order): 1. the *process* undertaken (54%), 2. the *content* learnt (23%), and 3. the use of *technology* (19%). The other 4% were general comments eg fun, learn new things. NB: Total n for students: 27; Total n for comments made: 122.

Students believed the best aspect of the process was the ability to work in different locations, not just at school (Table 1). Two students worked on their wiki page while they were overseas during the term3/term 4 school holidays. They also appreciated learning how to take notes from an electronic text, so they didn't plagiarise huge chunks of information from an internet site. They became more discerning of the information to copy as notes to place on their wiki page as they drafted their multimodal text. As one student commented:

> our term 2 project we don't learn lot of skills but our term 3 we learn lots of skills. In term 2 project we didn't learn computer skills but in term 4 we can. Also learn other things we didn't know before like note taking We also do typing skills and its quite easier than just writing it. [don't get sore hand]

While students used images, audio and videos (and their link) in their wiki to create a multimodal information report, some students initially placed them on their page because they were interesting and they liked to click on the link (observation notes, teacher's comment). A lesson explicitly discussing the construction and placement of different modes of representation resulted in a change to the overall layout of the multimodal information report.

Table 1. Best aspect: Process [n=66]

	n	% Total	% Process
Location (anywhere)	13	11%	20%
To take notes	12	10%	18%
Compare work with others work	11	9%	17%
Working with others	9	7%	14%
Not carrying books etc around	5	4%	7.5%
Typing (is better/ is easier)	4	3%	6%
People help each other	2	1.6%	3%
No paper, use computer	2	1.6%	3%
Send emails to each other	2	1.6%	3%
Remember info more when type	2	1.6%	3%
Easy way to learn	2	1.6%	3%
Paragraph from notes	1	0.8%	1.5%
Putting in effort	1	0.8%	1.5%
Spelling improved	1	0.8%	1.5%

Students appreciated being able to compare their work with others and the input the teacher provided (focus group interview). The teacher's scaffolding of the content and process for each group was tailored to each group's needs. As two students commented:

> ... the term 2 project our teacher only can see it once just to mark it but on our wikispace our teacher can see it more oftenly and they can help us with spelling and grammar
> we got more help from our teacher

Students also enjoyed working with a partner or in a small group, which was different to the pedagogy employed by the teacher up until this project. Previously the teacher had students working individually and was initially hesitant about the students working collaboratively and the quality of the work that would result. One student commented:

> we worked together, we got more help from our teacher, we get to do as a whole class but our term 2 project we do by ourself we get help from our parents.

Students also enjoyed assisting others with the content of their wiki page.

> We found this website for penguins. There were images (?) of penguins. like you had to click on it, it bring to this page about penguins. So we um ...we gave the um website to penguins and penguin 2. And they were delighted.

As would be expected, students appreciated learning about Antarctica (Table 2) and the information contained within the class wikispace on different pages. They found the knowledge they were gaining was important and very interesting. What was interesting about the area of content was the comments relating to 'know more' than if they were writing and that by creating an information report collaboratively using a wiki meant they could remember the information better than if it was a paper-based information report.

Table 2. Best aspect: Content [n=28]

	n	% Total	% Content
About Antarctica	11	9%	39%
Know more - than if writing - can remember info better	7	6%	25%
About specific section of wiki	6	5%	21%
New facts	4	3%	14%

The third aspect that was considered to be the best was the use of technology (19% of total). The technical skill students learnt was rated highly (Table 3). Students were asked to write in a different font colour during the note-taking stage and then in a third (or fourth) colour for the collaborative drafting of the written text. It was apparent after the initial introduction to tools of the wiki and the different representational modes that students could include: images, audio, and video, as well as the ability to link to other internet sites, that students found the ability to include these elements on their page an exciting experience. During the development of the wiki pages, they also felt these features enhanced the information on their page, made it like an internet site and meant they didn't have to write everything on their page.

Table 3. Best aspect: Technology [n=23]

	n	% Total	% Technology
Technical - fonts, colour, - add pictures/sounds/audio, - hyperlinking	9	7%	39%
Use of tech increased/ better	4	3%	17%
Website visiting	3	2.5%	13%
Improve typing	3	2.5%	13%
About wiki	3	2.5%	13%
Learn new thing about Internet	1	0.8%	4%

However, the technology was also considered the worst aspect of the project as well. If students were working on their wiki page simultaneously at school or at home they frequently 'lost' their work when one of them saved the page. This was extremely frustrating for students as they may have spent a half an hour or more adding information or other elements to the page. Student however became very adept at returning the page to its previous iteration by using the 'history' section of the site. They also adapted when working in class together by using only one computer and collaborating face-to-face on the creation of the information report. Each student would then decide on the section they would work on out-of-school.

5   Discussion

As a result of the wiki project, the students were provided with an introduction to a range of 21st century writing skills [1]. They successfully created a multimodal information report using the affordances of a wiki to collaboratively construct the text. In addition, the pedagogy, curriculum and assessment also underwent change as the teacher adjusted to the integration of the electronic medium into her classroom program. The whole class, teachers and author learnt from the experience of working with a wiki.

The results reflect the ways in which students became aware of multimodal texts and contributed to developing students multiliteracies [17]. The wiki pages, ie the technology, provided the opportunity to manipulate and create multimodal text that 'looked' professional. The learning around using a wiki formed part of their multiliteracy skill set, which included developing their interpersonal skills. Some groups began with images or audio or video, then they focused on the written text to complement these. Others began with gathering the written information, focusing on gathering written notes. The multimodal nature of the text opened up greater possibilities for constructing a text beyond writing and pictures (drawn or printed in colour) [21][25]. This change particularly appealed to students who found print literacy a challenge and rarely completed a task if it included an extended piece of writing. These students felt confident to create meanings across modes.

Teachers also they learnt alongside the students about multimodal texts, wikis and multiliteracies. They modified their own discourse as changes occurred to the curriculum, assessment and pedagogical choices in the classroom. For example, the assessment rubric, which was developed collaboratively by the teachers and researcher included process as well as product criteria.

The pedagogy extended the teachers' understanding of explicit teaching of written texts [23] into explicit teaching of multimodal texts [30]. Students were familiar with the creation of paper-based information reports, which included written and visual texts, but not the creation of an electronic collaboratively constructed information report, which could include written, still and moving images and sound texts. The classes became sites of learning, with explicit teaching about: hyperlinks, inserting different types of texts, co-constructing a text on-line, the adaptation of the word processing tools in the wiki, and how different modes complement each other and carry meaning (layout).

After the project, the reflections of the teachers and reseacher acknowledged that more critique of the visual mode would be important for the next iteration of teaching/ learning. The possible layouts and discussion of options would have enhanced the final product. However, the wikispace was limited in relation to potential layouts and another form of on-line collaborative tool might be necessary to address this issue, such as a Internet site creation space. Another area for consideration was involving students in the assessment process, getting them to self assess using the same or similar rubric as the teachers.

6 Conclusion

If we are going to prepare students for writing in the 21st century, opportunities need to be provided in classrooms that can initiate them into the skills, affordances and processes of learning using an electronic medium. This paper reported a study involving the use of a wiki space to engage students in collaboratively creating a multimodal electronic information report. Students took responsibility for the learning, regulating their time and negotiating roles, information and the construction of their information page on the class Antarctic wiki. They came away with a different view of learning, an insight in using technology for creating a multimodal text – the highs and the problems, and a belief that they learnt more about the content area through their experience with working with wikis.

Acknowledgements. Thankyou to the students involved in the project and to their teachers, Leonie and John.

References

1. Yancey, K.: Writing in the 21st Century. National Council of Teachers of English, Urbana (2009)
2. Kress, G.: Literacy in the New Media Age. Routledge, London (2003)
3. Slatin, J.: Reading hypertext: Order and coherence in a new medium. College English 52, 870–883 (1990)
4. Burbules, N.: Rhetorics of the Web: Hyperreading and critical literacy. In: Snyder, I. (ed.) Page to Screen: Taking Literacy into the Electronic Era, pp. 102–122. Allen & Unwin, Sydney (1997)
5. Joyce, M.: New stories for new readers: contour, coherence and constructive hypertext. In: Snyder, I. (ed.) Page to Screen: Taking literacy into the Electronic Era, pp. 163–182. Allen & Unwin, Sydney (1997)
6. Kress, G.: You've just got to learn how to see: Curriculum subjects, young people and schooled engagement with the world. Linguistics and Education 11(4), 401–415 (2001)
7. Castek, J.: The changing nature of reading comprehension: Examining the acquisition of new literacies in a 7th grade science classroom. Paper presented at the National Reading Conference Los Angeles 2006 (2006)
8. Coiro, J.: Reading comprehension on the Internet: Expanding our understanding of reading comprehension to encompass new literacies. The Reading Teacher 56(5), 458–464 (2003)
9. NSW Board of Studies. English K-6 Syllabus. Board of Studies, Sydney. NSW (1998)
10. Queensland Studies Authority. Years 1-10 English Syllabus (2005), http://www.qsa.qld.edu.ay/yrs1to10/kla/english/syllabus.html(retrieved 9/ 12/ 2006)
11. Lankshear, C., Snyder, I., Green, B.: Teachers and technoliteracy: Managing literacy, technology and learning in schools. Allen & Unwin, St Leonards, NSW (2000)
12. Kress, G., Jewitt, C., Bourne, J., Franks, A., Hardcastle, J., Jones, K., et al.: English in Urban Classrooms: A Multimodal Perspective on Teaching and Learning. Routledge Falmer, Oxford (2005)
13. Derewianka, B.: Trends and issues in genre-based approaches. RELC 34(2), 133–154 (2003)
14. Kalantzis, M., Cope, B. (eds.): The Powers of Literacy: A Genre Approach to Teaching Writing. The Falmer Press, London (1993)
15. Kress, G.: Multimodality. In: Cope, B., Kalantzis, M. (eds.) Multiliteracies: Literacy Learning and the Design of Social Futures, pp. 182–202. Macmillan, Melbourne (2000)
16. Lemke, J.: Literacy and Social Semiotics (2001) (retrieved 5.12.2001)
17. Cope, B., Kalantzis, M. (eds.): Multiliteracies: Literacy Learning and the Design of Social Futures. Macmillan, Melbourne (2000)

18. Jewitt, C.: Multimodality, ``reading'' and ``writing'' for the 21st century. Discourse: Studies in the Cultural Politics of Education 26(3), 315–331 (2005)
19. Heba, G.: HyperRhetoric: Multimedia, literacy and the future of composition. Computers and Composition 14, 19–44 (1997)
20. Leu, D., Kinzer, C., Coiro, J., Cammack, D.: Toward a Theory of New Literacies Emerging from the Internet and Other Information and Communication Technologies. In: Ruddell, R., Unrau, N. (eds.) Theoretical Models and Processes of Reading, 5th edn., pp. 1568–1611. International Reading Association, Newark (2004)
21. Merchant, G.: Writing the future in the digital age. Literacy 41(3), 118–128 (2007)
22. Callaghan, M., Rothery, J.: Teaching factual writing: a genre based approach. DSP Literacy Project Metropolitan East Region, Marrickville (1988)
23. Hammond, J. (ed.): Scaffolding: Teaching and Learning in Language and Literacy Education. Primary English Teaching Association, Newtown (2001)
24. Green, H., Hannon, C.: Their space: Education for a digital generation. Demos, London (2007)
25. Lankshear, C., Knobel, M.: New literacies: Everyday practices and classroom learning, 2nd edn. Open University Press, Maidenhead (2006)
26. Barone, D.M.: Case-Study research. In: Duke, N., Mallette, M. (eds.) Literacy Research Methodologies. The Guildford Press, New York (2004)
27. Kemmis, S., McTaggart, R.: Participatory action research. In: Denzin, N., Lincoln, Y. (eds.) Handbook of Qualitative Research, 2nd edn., pp. 567–605. Sage, Beverley Hills (2000)
28. Halliday, M.A.K., Hasan, R.: Language, context, and text: Aspects of language in a social-semiotic perspective. Deakin University Press, Burwood (1985)
29. Kress, G., van Leeuwen, T.: Reading Images: The Grammar of Visual Design. Routledge Press, London (1996)
30. Zammit, K., Downes, T.: New learning environments and the mulitliterate individual: A framework for educators. Australian Journal of Language & Literacy 25, 24–36 (2002)
31. Cohen, L., Manion, L., Morrison, K.: Research Methods in Education, 6th edn. Routledge, London (2007)

Author Index